DATE DUE

DEMCO 38-296

Reconstructing the Family in Contemporary American Fiction

Studies on Themes and Motifs in Literature

Horst S. Daemmrich
General Editor

Vol. 6

PETER LANG
New York • Washington, D.C./Baltimore
Bern • Frankfurt am Main • Berlin • Vienna • Paris

Desmond F. McCarthy

Reconstructing the Family in Contemporary American Fiction

PETER LANG
New York • Washington, D.C./Baltimore
Bern • Frankfurt am Main • Berlin • Vienna • Paris

...oging-in-Publication Data

)esmond F.

Reconstructing the family ... contemporary American fiction /
Desmond F. McCarthy.
p. cm. — (Studies on themes and motifs in literature; v. 6)
Includes bibliographical references (p.   ).
1. American fiction—20th century—History and criticism. 2. Domestic
fiction, American—History and criticism. 3. Family in literature.
I. Title. II. Series.
PS374.D57M38 813'.5409355—dc20   94-38218
ISBN 0-8204-2306-8
ISSN 1056-3970

Die Deutsche Bibliothek-CIP-Einheitsaufnahme

McCarthy, Desmond F.:
Reconstructing the family in contemporary American fiction / Desmond F.
McCarthy. –New York; Washington, D.C./Baltimore; Bern; Frankfurt am
Main; Berlin; Vienna; Paris: Lang.
(Studies on themes and motifs in literature; Vol. 6)
ISBN 0-8204-2306-8
NE: GT

The paper in this book meets the guidelines for permanence and durability
of the Committee on Production Guidelines for Book Longevity
of the Council of Library Resources.

© 1997 Peter Lang Publishing, Inc., New York

Printed in the United States of America.

Acknowledgments

I am grateful for the assistance of many people who helped make this book possible. My professors at Brandeis University, Eugene Goodheart, Richard Onorato, and John Burt, were generous and judicious readers: their insightful responses were invaluable. Helen Heineman, Academic Vice President of Framingham State College, provided generous support. Heidi Burns, my editor at Peter Lang, was always patient, helpful, and encouraging: this book would not have been possible without her. I am particularly grateful to Beata Panagopoulos for her countless hours of help preparing this manuscript. Finally, I want to thank my indexer, Kelley McDaniel, and Teresa Pagliuca, who provided the author photograph.

Contents

Acknowledgments v

1   Reconstructing the Family   1
as a Utopian Project

2   The Family in Crisis   7

3   Harry Angstrom's Flights   25
from the Family

4   The Family According   57
to Garp

5   The Emergent Woman's Family   81
in *The Color Purple*

6   America as Family: 109
E. L. Doctorow's *Ragtime*

7   The Reconstructed Family   129
and Social Change

Notes   135

Bibliography   149

Index   159

1

Reconstructing the Family
as a Utopian Project

Leo Tolstoy begins his epic novel, *Anna Karenina*, with a deceptively simple observation: "Happy families are all alike; every unhappy family is unhappy in its own way."[1] While my focus is contemporary American rather than nineteenth-century Russian fiction, Tolstoy's oft-quoted maxim is an interesting point of entry into a discussion of representations of the family in fiction. Unhappy indeed are those in Tolstoy's novel who yearn for freedoms or relationships that challenge societally imposed and enforced codes of conduct. And happy are those who accede to what Tolstoy depicts as self-evident, eternal laws governing human behavior and family life.

There is little about the social organization of the American family in the late twentieth century that appears to be self-evident. We live in an era that has witnessed the decline of the traditional nuclear family (a male "provider," his wife, and their biological children). The number of American households that can be defined as traditional nuclear families declined from 60 percent in 1955 to 7 percent in 1985.[2] There is little disagreement among social historians that the accelerating loss in the last few decades of what we have idealized as a permanent and universal familial arrangement is a kind of "crisis." This widespread alarm is not surprising, given that even those who were not raised within traditional households have internalized the rigid, societally prevalent ideal of the monolithic family. We are convinced that the traditional nuclear family is a "happy" family; we suspect that deviations from or alternatives to this household arrangement are somewhat unfortunate, unhealthy, or even unnatural.

The decline of the traditional nuclear family has been accompanied by a diversification of household arrangements in the United States. The very existence of these households necessarily challenges "mainstream" attitudes concerning the proper role and place of women, the regulation of sexuality, the boundaries of families, and appropriate child-rearing environments and philosophies. But because of the ideological importance of the nuclear family, an increasingly contentious debate has been waged in recent decades about what, if anything, can or should be done to halt or reverse its decline. To the degree that this debate enshrines the traditional nuclear family as an ideal or historically permanent institution, it is as imbued with utopianism as the representations of "alternative" families in contemporary American fiction that I will discuss. Chapter 2, "The Family in Crisis," provides a brief overview of this debate.

This discussion of the disparate "readings" of the family's "crisis" offered by a number of prominent social historians is followed by an examination of the alternative families in the novels of four contemporary American writers: John Updike, John Irving, Alice Walker, and E. L. Doctorow. In a world where our closest bonds of kinship have been radically altered in a relatively brief period of time, many contemporary novelists are imagining new familial arrangements. While they are not alone in their interest in the new complexities of American domestic life, each of these writers has achieved both critical and public acclaim. Two of Updike's "Rabbit" novels received the Pulitzer prize for fiction, for example, as did Alice Walker's *The Color Purple*. The works I will discuss are also among the most widely read contemporary American novels.

The term "reconstructing" in my title is of particular importance because it underscores the utopian nature of many of these fictional families. *Webster's Third New International Dictionary* includes the following definitions of "reconstruct": "to build again: rebuild . . . reorganize, reestablish . . . rehabilitate."[3] The word connotes an imaginative act of creation that does not validate or mimic what came before. In the contemporary climate of confusion over the future of the family, some novelists are imagining compelling alternative or reconstructed families grappling with realistic and recognizable conflicts, crises, and pressures. They depict alternative families as households where some of the traditional isolation and economic and gender-based hierarchies of the nuclear family are eliminated.

In her provocative essay, "When We Dead Awaken: Writing as Re-Vision," the poet and feminist critic Adrienne Rich distinguishes between fantasy—"passive day-dreaming which need not be acted on"—and the work of the artist. The project of the artist is not simply to portray social realities in a realistic and convincing manner, but to bring a skeptical consciousness and an unfettered imagination to bear upon these conditions—to conceive of alternatives:

> For . . . a character or an action to take shape, there has to be an imaginative transformation of reality which is in no way passive. And a certain freedom of the mind is needed—freedom to press on, to enter the currents of your thought like a glider pilot, knowing that your motion can be sustained, that the buoyancy of your attention will not be suddenly snatched away. Moreover, if the imagination is to transcend and transform experience it has to question, to challenge, to conceive of alternatives, perhaps to the very life you are living at that moment.[4]

The ability of the imagination to "transform experience" is a central concern of this book: there are utopian or dystopian elements in all of the novels I will discuss. Since I will provide more detailed accounts in chapters 3-6 of the relationships between the artistic aims of Updike, Irving, Walker, and Doctorow and their representations of social realities and familial conditions in their fiction, a brief introduction will suffice for now.

John Irving's *The World According to Garp* explores the interplay between the "worlds" an artist constructs and the "reality" wherein he/she resides. In chapter 4, "The Family According to Garp," I argue that Irving's artist-protagonist, Garp, considers the generous vision of his most imaginative work of art—his first and best short story—when he seeks to reconstruct his life and his family after a terrible disaster: an accident that kills one of his children. Garp restructures his family in the wake of this devastating incident—precipitated, in part, by his overbearing paternalism—to include the transsexual Roberta Muldoon and the orphaned Ellen James. He creates an extended household that blends the best elements of the familial options in the novel. Garp's "world" is a new family.

Alice Walker is the most radical proponent of art's role in shaping alternative realities among the writers I will examine. In her collection of essays, *In Search of Our Mothers' Gardens,* she celebrates literature's capacity to offer "a kind of salvation." At its best, literature can "envision a solution, an evolution to higher consciousness on the part of society, even when society itself cannot."[5] In chapter 5, "The Emergent Woman's Family in *The Color Purple,*" I argue that Walker's novel *The Color Purple* is an explicit account of an "evolution to higher consciousness"—a process that begins when Celie, a poor black woman who has been raped by her stepfather and physically and emotionally abused by her husband, is befriended by Shug, her husband's mistress. Celie's subsequent relationship with Shug gives her the insights, resources, and self-confidence to alter her circumstances and those of the other characters in the novel. Walker's reconstruction of an institution already available in the African-American community—the extended family—is central to her utopian project of reclaiming and redeeming abusive men and abused women.

E. L. Doctorow is concerned with the effect artists and other visionaries have had on the course of history, postulating that the radical and unorthodox ideals of social "outsiders" often become the accepted norms of the next generation of our national "family." Doctorow's novel *Ragtime* is populated by dissidents and outcasts; the novel's double historical consciousness invites the reader to speculate about the construction of and relationship between "historical" and "fictional" narratives. In chapter 6, "America as Family: E. L. Doctorow's *Ragtime,*" I argue that Doctorow's novel both promotes and undermines the "melting-pot" ideal of a national "family." If America is a family, then lasting social change is possible only if the structure, composition, and operation of individual American households are altered. The composite American family that assembles at the end of his novel neither fully validates nor firmly disproves any particular ideology or model of ethnic assimilation. Doctorow's new American family—situated simultaneously in the past and the future—represents instead both the cost of ethnic strife throughout our history and the promise of a reconciliation that may yet be achieved.

John Updike serves in this book as an interesting counterpoint to these writers—both in his portrayal of the family and his conception of the role of the artist. In chapter 3, "Harry Angstrom's Flights from the Family," I argue that Updike's depiction of a dystopian alternative family in *Rabbit Redux* and his disparagement of the claim that art has a visionary purpose are connected. Although Updike proclaims himself a realist, he defends the horrific rendition of an alternative family in *Rabbit Redux* with the decidedly ideological assertion that "when you destroy one set of institutions you get something worse."[6] In Updike's four "Rabbit" novels, challenges to existing institutions and codes of conduct are invariably represented as staggeringly destructive even as his realistic depiction of the contemporary nuclear family uncovers a sobering sense of ennui and unhappiness.

Walker and Doctorow have in common an overt commitment to the efficacy of art as an instrument of or advocate for social change. While both Irving and his novelist-hero Garp claim to eschew a political or social aim in their work, the radical reordering of the world that the artist's imagination can effect is evident both in Garp's "fiction" and in the larger narrative frame of the novel itself. Irving depicts an unusual act of insemination, the identity crisis of a transsexual, and Garp's unorthodox extended family with an understanding and generosity that have unavoidable ideological implications. And while Updike cautions the artist not to engage in what Rich terms an "imaginative transformation of reality," the events depicted in *Rabbit Redux* constitute a "worst-case" scenario of the social experimentations and excesses of the late 1960s: the novel serves as a cautionary tale to those who would tamper with the institution of the family. My point here is that Updike, too, engages in the kind of imaginative reordering of the world that Rich identifies as the artist's prerogative—despite his creed of artistic realism.

The writers whose novels will be my focus also have in common some important concerns pertaining to the construction and operation of families. Each of them addresses the problem of defining individuals and groups outside the traditional familial circle. These novels grapple with the difficulty of overcoming what can be a xenophobic isolation of the traditional family unit by broadening its membership and loosening its boundaries. This project has mixed results in *Ragtime* and dire consequences in Updike's novels, in which the Biblical punishments of fire and water claim the lives of two "daughters." Walker's Celie and Irving's Garp are more successful in constructing alternative families consisting of both biological and "emotional" kin. Their families also challenge traditional gender roles and responsibilities. The novels of Updike, Irving, and Walker also depict acts of sexual violence that take place within or are linked to traditional families: Walker and Irving offer a program for recovery within alternative households. Both Updike's Rabbit and Irving's Garp wrestle with their personal culpability in the death of a child: the differences in their responses inform our readings of the familial alternatives in their worlds. Finally, there is a common difficulty in providing more than a rudimentary, sketchy glimpse of life within the alternative families in these novels. Updike provides the fullest description of an alternative family among these writers, but his aim is to discredit what he depicts as an aberrant situation. Both Garp's absence and Irving's matter-of-fact narrative style distance us from what we learn about the fate of Garp's extended family in the novel's final chapter, "Life After Garp." And Walker and Doctorow conclude with utopian visions of alternative families that serve more as prophesies of future harmony than as full accounts of life within these new households. I will return to these points of comparison among the novels of Updike, Irving, Walker, and Doctorow in chapter 7.

2

The Family in Crisis

What is a family? This question may appear to be a rhetorical one at first: most of us were born into and raised within a network of kin that supported us to varying degrees—a constellation of biological relatives whose clearly differentiated roles do not require a closer examination. Is not the family a "natural," eternal structure—a place of safety, nurturance, and love? Its value as the most important societal unit seems so undeniably obvious to so many that we refer to "the family" with a certainty that further elaboration or qualification concerning its boundaries and functions is unnecessary. In a world where an accelerating barrage of technological "advances" over the last century has transformed the economy, the workplace, our means of transportation and communication, and the very landscapes where we reside, we have clung to the comforting delusion that our most important bonds of affection and responsibility are not only unchanged, but unchangeable.

Even a cursory examination of census figures, however, indicates that the family for which we harbor such fervent emotions—whose "defense" is the cornerstone of the enormously successful neoconservative movement that came to prominence at the national level in 1980 with the election of Ronald Reagan to the presidency—no longer exists. In 1988, the U. S. Bureau of the Census reported that "a growing proportion of adults are spending a larger portion of their lives in a single status. For young men and women today, it is plausible to assume that approximately 10 percent will never marry in their lifetime. For those who do marry, approximately 50 percent will divorce."[1] A more recent Census Bureau report provided startling demographic confirmation of these predictions. "Between 1970 and 1992, the number of never-married adults nearly doubled, from 21 to 42 million.... The number of currently divorced persons has quadrupled from 4.3 million in 1970 to 16.3 million in 1992, representing 9 percent of all adults age 18 and over in 1992."[2] There has been a concurrent rise in the number of "unmarried-couple households" to "2.6 million in 1988, 1 million more than in 1980."[3] The Census Bureau also reported a dramatic rise in single-parent households: "Between 1970 and 1992, the proportion of children living with two parents declined from 85 percent to 71 percent, while the proportion living with one parent more than doubled from 12 percent to 27 percent."[4] Furthermore, "it has been estimated that about one-quarter of children today will live with a stepparent by the time they have reached 16 years of age."[5] Another radical shift in the composition of American households has been in the dramatic increase in the number of working mothers: "The proportion of all married-couple families with both partners working increased from 37 percent in 1976 to 49 percent in 1987"; 69 percent of single mothers participated in the paid labor force in 1987.[6] The significance of these numbers was emphasized in a 1987 Congressional Report: "In 1955, 60 percent of the households in the United States consisted of a working father, a housewife mother, and two or more school-age children. In 1980, that family unit was only 11 percent and in 1985 it was 7 percent."[7] In short, the traditional nuclear family is chosen by or possible for a dwindling minority of Americans.

The diversification of household arrangements in North America and in most European countries during the last three decades has contributed to a sense of uncertainty about the future of the family and has fueled an increasingly contentious debate about what a family actually is and how it should operate. Michele Barrett and Mary McIntosh address the significance of this debate in *The Anti-Social Family*:

> The definition of "family" is in itself a politically contested one and the vehemence with which academic and historical points of view are argued bears tribute to this fact. . . . In a very precise sense "the family" is an ideological construct and when we consider debates on "its place in soci-

ety," "its historical development" and "its relationship to capitalism" we have to look at the extent to which the analyses are themselves constituted in political and ideological terms.[8]

In *The Making of the Modern Family*, Edward Shorter makes the same point more straightforwardly: "The nuclear family is a state of mind rather than a particular kind of structure or set of household arrangements."[9]

Nevertheless, most of the participants in the debate over the future of the family in the United States enshrine the traditional nuclear family as a universal structure. The evidence offered by historians such as Michael Anderson who look at the multiplicity of family forms and functions over a period of centuries rather than decades is a significant rejoinder to this parochialism:

> Firstly, there is the problem of diversity—indeed, the one unambiguous fact which has emerged in the last twenty years is that there can be no simple history of *the* Western family since the sixteenth century because there is not, nor ever has there been, a single family system. The West has always been characterized by diversity of family forms, by diversity of family functions and by diversity in attitudes to family relationships not only over time but at any one point in time. There is, except at the most trivial level, no Western family type.[10]

The current decline of one familial form, the traditional nuclear family, should not, then, be viewed as a cataclysmic crisis that threatens the future well-being of western civilization. Rather, we might see some of the recent trends recorded in the demographic surveys discussed above as a natural evolution away from a structure that was situated in and more suitable for an earlier historical period and ideologically rooted in identifiable attitudes toward the role of women, the nature of the marital contract, and appropriate childrearing techniques and environments.

The "blended" or reconstructed family assembled at the dinner table hearing the latest census figures concerning the "decline of the family" on the evening news broadcast, however, is likely to respond with unself-conscious dismay. The diversification of family forms is perceived, ironically, as a "crisis" even to many of those who, whether by choice, circumstance, or necessity, do not reside within a traditional nuclear family. We have yet to discard the comforting myth of the prevalence and incontrovertible supremacy of the nuclear family despite the evidence of our own lived experiences within increasingly varied family environments:

> Confusing ideal with reality, we fail to appreciate the deep significance of what are, cross-culturally, various ideologies of intimate relationship, and at the same time we fail to reckon with the complex human bonds and experiences all too comfortably sheltered by a faith in the 'natural' source of a 'nurture' we think is found in the home.[11]

Much of the debate about the current and future status of the family is inevitably entangled in the changes in social mores and policies in recent decades. While most liberals applaud what they see as important social gains, such as greater access to civil divorce, birth control, and abortion, and wider acceptance of premarital sexual activity, both hetero- and homosexual unmarried couples, working women, and day care that may have contributed to or resulted from the decline of the traditional nuclear family, many of them share with their more conservative compatriots a disquieting sense that something of immeasurable and perhaps irretrievable importance has been lost. Conservatives have used this widespread sense of loss and the prevailing atmosphere of "crisis" to attack an array of programs, policies, and civil liberties they see as detrimental to the traditional nuclear family: "the New Right has played upon fears of family breakdown by using the term 'pro-family' to draw together opposition to the Equal Rights Amendment, abortion, and gay rights."[12] They insist that the nuclear family is more historically stable and long-lived than it really is and can foresee only apocalyptic consequences from any restructuring or loosening of its traditional components, hierarchies, or bonds. Their commitment to a patriarchal family unit in which men are "breadwinners" and women are "housewives" is rooted in culturally tenacious and societally pervasive attitudes such as a belief in male supremacy and a privileging of biological mothering over all other modes of parenting. Although their agenda is most seriously challenged by the resurgent feminist movement of the last quarter-century, historian Rochelle Gatlin's rejection of a direct cause-and-effect relationship between activism for and by women and the decline of the nuclear family is valid: "the Women's Movement did not cause the recent changes in American family life. . . . [But] because the Women's Movement furthered a new sense of women's possibilities outside marriage and motherhood, feminists have become leading scapegoats for the so-called 'breakdown' of the family."[13]

While the alleged fragility of the familial sanctuary has been used as a screen to block social progress at other junctures in our nation's history (opposition to the women's suffrage movement is perhaps the most pertinent example), the figure of "the family under siege" has never been so prominent and successful in the service of a conservative political agenda as in recent years. Antipoverty programs have been stigmatized and besieged on the grounds that they "reward" behavior and lifestyles antithetical to "traditional family values." During the 1992 presidential campaign, Vice President Dan Quayle's suggestion that a television character's decision to become a single mother set a bad example for Americans was met with derision in some quarters—but more because the spectacle of the Vice President criticizing Murphy Brown was absurd rather than because voters disagreed with his stand on single motherhood. Indeed, two years later, the Democratic victor of the 1992 campaign, Bill Clinton, allowed that Quayle's critique of single motherhood had merit—despite having spent part of his own childhood with an impoverished, widowed mother. Clinton pledged to "end welfare as we know it" during his campaign for the presidency—believing that "reforms" like forcing mothers receiving governmental assistance to work would help mitigate the public's disdain for welfare. While the leaders of the political party that designed and implemented aid programs to poor, predominantly single mother families have fretted about how or whether to reform the nation's welfare system for years, Republicans have been exploiting the reservations a growing number of Americans have about publicly funded programs that "promote" nontraditional families. Newt Gingrich and Dick Armey's "Contract With America" capitalized on the pervasive anxiety about shifts in the composition, function, stability, and self-reliance of the family: with the election in 1994 of the first Republican Congress in 40 years, reductions, rollbacks, and even wholesale elimination of programs like welfare seem inevitable. Yet, as Stephanie Coontz has documented in *The Way We Never Were: American Families and the Nostalgia Trap*, "The fact is, however, that depending on support beyond the family has been the rule rather than the exception in American history, despite recurring myths about individual achievement and family enterprise."[14] Even our colonial "forefathers," whose sacrifices and triumphs have been romanticized throughout our history, were not as self-reliant or family-centered as we've imagined: "early American families were dependent on a large network of neighbors, church institutions, courts, government officials, and legislative bodies for their sustenance. It is true that in colonial days, the poor or disabled were generally cared for in families, but not, normally, in their *own* families" (70).

Nevertheless, the notion that families operate best in a self-reliant isolation from the state is a tenacious and pervasive cultural myth. The family is "defended" by many as the last bastion of intrinsic values in the contemporary world—a "home" besieged by a burgeoning technocracy of experts whose mandates for intervention serve to reinforce their own professional interests by undermining the cohesion, hierarchy, and operation of the traditional family. While most social historians agree that the traditional nuclear family is being supplanted by an array of other familial structures and arrangements, there is a wide range of views about when this extraordinary transformation of the family began, what its causes and consequences might be, and what, if anything, can or should be done to reverse it. This dissension is amplified by changes in the field of sociology itself. As David Cheal observes in *Family and The State of Theory*, "The nostalgic feelings for family life as it existed in the 1950s that are found today among some sociologists are strengthened by an image of unity and certainty in sociological theory, which also existed at that time."[15] In other words, a proliferation of family types has taken place at the same time that sociological theory and methodologies have become more heterogeneous. Sociologists may be as confused about the current shifts in family form and function as the rest of us. Many of them are still committed to the traditional nuclear family as an object of study, whereas Cheal wonders, in fact, "whether or not the scientific study of something called 'the family' is possible" (126).

Some sociologists have become more aware that definitions of "family" and interpretations of social realities are as subjective as textual "readings." As the sociologist Richard Harvey Brown has argued in *Society as Text*, "the tradition of rhetoric suggests the metaphor of society as narrative text."[16] That contemporary readings of an institution so central to our lives can vary so dramatically is noteworthy rather than digressive in a study of representations in contemporary fiction of alternatives to the nuclear family. After all, if social theorists are in such a quandary about the history and viability of the nuclear family, then the utopianism of the reconstructed families in the contemporary novels I will examine in the chapters to follow is rooted in the confusions and conundrums of our era. While it is impossible for a work of literary criticism to represent accurately the full spectrum of sociological responses to the nuclear family's decline, a brief look at a few representative figures and their views of the relationship between the nuclear family and society is instructive. Christopher Lasch is a reference point in this discussion because he is one of the more widely read social historians of the last twenty years and because he provides a particularly cogent and compelling indictment of the forces he holds responsible for the decline of the nuclear family.

In *Haven in a Heartless World: The Family Besieged* and *The Culture of Narcissism*, Lasch applies the Marxist critique of the "socialization of production" which made the factory and the assembly line of the modern industrial age possible to what he sees as an insidious and intrusive bureaucracy of experts and social engineers who are largely responsible for the decline of the nuclear family. Following the successful usurpation of autonomy and creativity in the workplace, capitalist magnates "extended their control over the worker's private life

as well, as doctors, psychiatrists, teachers, child guidance experts, officers of the juvenile courts, and other specialists began to supervise
child-rearing, formerly the business of the family."[17] By mystifying and
problematizing sex, child-rearing, and family dynamics, argues Lasch,
this new class of experts undermined the family's confidence, independence, and cohesion while obliterating its privacy.

Health care specialists, baby experts and family therapists, and social workers, then, are cast as the proverbial serpents in the garden of
the traditional family. Lasch's vitriolic jeremiads do not differentiate
among the numerous agencies, movements, and professions that he believes have impinged upon the family (is one more influential or significant than another?); nor does he identify points of resistance within and
without the managerial elite (generational, regional, ideological)—a
deficit that contributes to the sense that Lasch is weaving a "conspiracy
theory" ("cabals of liberal bureaucrats and social reformers are plotting
to undermine the family"—a view of the world embraced by many neo-
conservatives). And while it is true that the waves of immigrant families
were primary targets of the new experts, Lasch does not fully take into
account the confluence of their mission and his own idealization of the
traditional nuclear family. The new class of social workers and health
specialists intervened, in part, to impose the structure of the nuclear
family on the extended immigrant households. Lasch is also surprisingly
cavalier about the undeniably positive effects of some governmental
regulations of the family in areas like child labor: "Convinced that poor
immigrant parents exploited their children's labor at every opportunity,
they [the 'experts'] demanded not only state prohibition of child labor
but the placement of the child under the custody of the school."[18] Surely
the record of the unsafe labor environments and excessive working
hours of children at the turn of the century is indisputable—and is man-
datory education really a form of "custody"?

Are all "interventions" by society into the familial circle invariably
detrimental? The recent strengthening of domestic violence and sexual
abuse laws, for example, can be seen as positive interventions undertaken by society at large to protect its more vulnerable citizens. Only in

the last two decades have social workers, law enforcement officials, and even relatives learned to recognize and respond to any but the most grotesque and visible incidents of domestic violence and child abuse: it seemed both implausible that such extreme violations could occur in the hallowed, safe environment of the home, and impossible for an "outsider" to intrude assertively in the private domestic sphere. Lasch simply doesn't acknowledge that life for some women and children in the traditional nuclear families more common prior to the late 1960s was frequently unbearable. "The decline of parental authority reflects the 'decline of the superego' in American society as a whole" (178), according to Lasch. Therefore, any effort to diminish the power and status that men—the traditional embodiment of parental authority—have exercised in the family has dire consequences for the future of our society, including "the decline of transcendent ideals in general"[19] It comes as no surprise, then, that Lasch reserves his most vitriolic scorn for feminists. He harbors a nostalgia for a prefeminist era when "sexual antagonism was tempered not only by chivalric, paternalistic conventions but by a more relaxed acceptance of the limitations of the other sex"[20]—an era that cannot be recovered, if it ever existed at all.

The family that Lasch extolls "attained its full flowering in the nineteenth century and now seems to be slowly decaying."[21] If we accept Lasch's premise here, then "the family" he so ardently defends in such universal terms came into being to serve as a refuge from the emerging mechanized, alienating public world of capitalism. Furthermore, this family structure existed as a recognizable, widely prevalent entity for less than a century. It is as much an ideological construct—as attuned to the economic and social imperatives of its period—as the contemporary phenomenon of the "working mother" is responsive to the real economic and social needs of the family today.

It is not hard to find evidence that the nuclear family was never as monolithic and private as Lasch suggests. Edward Shorter's *The Making of the Modern Family* is a particularly instructive source of data and case studies whose cumulative weight suggests that, regardless of what we make of the historically recent relationship between families and modern bureaucrats and "experts," the family has never been impermeable to authorities, "outsiders," or the community. According to Shorter, family members in traditional society "felt they had more in common emotionally with their various peer groups than with one another" and spent virtually all of their free time in same-sex social activities or organizations. Households—particularly in the middle class—extended beyond the nuclear family to include other relatives, apprentices, servants, and employed help: "the family's shell was pierced full of holes, permitting people from outside to flow freely through the household, observing and monitoring."[22] Acculturation and socialization took place in the community—not in the family.

In *The Policing of Families*, Jacques Donzelot argues that the transition from traditional society to the modern world entailed a substitution of one mode of social control of the family for another. According to Donzelot, the "policing" Lasch associates with the decline of the modern nuclear family might, instead, have been a fundamental force in its creation. The transition from "a government of families" (overt patriarchy) to "a government through the family"[23] was accomplished by "placing the family under an economico-moral tutelage . . . in the name of the hygienic and educative protection" of its members and "by promoting the new norms as being so many advantages favoring a more complete realization of the family's goal of increased autonomy" (91). While Donzelot, like Lasch, is disturbed by "the proliferation of political technologies that invested the body, health, modes of subsistence and lodging" under the rubric of "policing" (6), he acknowledges that developments like liberalized divorce laws are genuinely legitimate "advances" despite their "cost" as state-sanctioned trade-offs granted in return for this subtler, more insidious constitution and control of the family.

Donzelot understands that the family is a politically malleable construction whose form and function has always been adapted to serve the needs of the state. He describes the "contract" between male heads of households and the state which legitimated and enforced the patriarchal family of traditional society as follows: "You will keep your people within the rules conforming to our requirements, in return for which you can use them as you see fit, and if they go against your injunctions, we will furnish you with the support necessary to bring them back to order" (50). This is hardly a situation of familial independence from the intrusive apparatuses of the state: it is, according to Donzelot, a more overt but less effective methodology of control. He does not believe, as does Lasch, that we have strayed from a time when the family was relatively autonomous or more of a refuge from harsh political realities and reigning systems of control than it is today. Indeed, if Donzelot is correct, then the "policing" mechanisms Lasch deplores are inseparable from the modern family he is trying to save: far from undermining the nuclear family, they in fact created and shaped it to conform to the needs of the state.

Barbara Ehrenreich and Deirdre English see the decline of the nuclear family as a catalyst for deconstructing the false dichotomy of the "romantic/rationalist alternative"[24] that has bedevilled us during its reign. In *For Her Own Good: 150 Years of the Experts' Advice to Women*, Ehrenreich and English provide a history of the "privileged" bond between doctors and other specialists—whose meddling in the private world of the family is decried by Lasch, Donzelot, and others—and the mother. They find that, like other relationships between men and women, it entailed the subordination and domination of women by male authority:

> The relationship between women and the experts was not unlike conventional relationships between women and men. The experts wooed their female constituency, promising the "right" and scientific way to live, and women responded—most eagerly in the upper and middle classes, more slowly among the poor—with dependency and trust. It was never an equal relationship, for the experts' authority rested on the denial or destruction of women's autonomous sources of knowledge. (4)

The experts bridged the gap between what Ehrenreich and English term the "rationalist" and "romantic" approaches to the "Woman Question": the necessity of defining the proper place and role of women in a newly industrialized world. "The sexual rationalist program is one of *assimi-*

lation, with ancillary changes (day care, for example) as necessary to promote women's rapid integration into what has been the world of men" (21). But the "sexual romantics" recoiled from what they feared was the impending loss of the domestic hearth—the last "natural" bastion of human warmth, caring, and morality: "To dissolve the home (by removing the last domestic chores and letting women out to work) would be to remove the last refuge from the horrors of industrial society" (23). The sexual romantics' project of enforcing the hegemonic ideal of the traditional family triumphed until recent decades, according to Ehrenreich and English, because they were aided by a new class of experts—psychologists, health specialists, and "domestic scientists"—who established their legitimacy in areas that had previously been the exclusive domain of women. These specialists usurped the last remaining area of women's expertise and autonomy in the name of preserving the home—the very environment where those domestic skills were deployed.

Ehrenreich and English trace the succession of child-rearing theories in the twentieth century, approaches that had had more to do with the economy than with the legitimate needs of children. The mother has been held responsible for maintaining a family environment that has ranged—depending upon the structure and requirements of the economy—from a highly regulated sphere of discipline to one of permissiveness, where all of the child's needs are met. *For Her Own Good: 150 Years of the Experts' Advice to Women* makes a convincing case that in idealizing the perpetration of the traditional nuclear family, the sexual romantics "chose not to remake the world, but to demand that women *make-up for it*" (314). Although Lasch, Donzelot, and others are concerned that traditional male authority has been undermined and then defeated by the corporation and the state, Ehrenreich and English make clear that the new experts have actually worked to preserve the age-old subordination of women to men—in a modern domestic sphere closely monitored by predominantly male medical and health specialists. Patriarchal authority may be diffused, but it has not been obliterated.

Ehrenreich and English credit the emergence of a renewed and invigorated feminist movement in the 1960s and 1970s with the retraction of the privileged position of health and child-rearing specialists in the family. Their assertion that the reign of the "experts" is over, however, is a premature claim of victory in the name of a movement that, sadly, was already in eclipse at the end of the 1970s. The intersection of medical, legal, ethical, and maternal issues has never been more complex, as demonstrated by the renewed vigor and recent victories of the antiabortion movement, the proliferation of prenatal testing procedures— sometimes required by doctors and their insurance coverers, the advances in "test tube" baby technology, the employment of "surrogate" mothers to bear children who are not legally theirs, and the rise of "right to know" cases involving the search by adopted children for their biological parents—to cite but a few examples. Complex social conundrums are still resolved with the aim of "protecting" the family or promoting traditional motherhood: the values and aims of the "romantics" continue to reign, even as scientific and technological "advances" impose an increasing array of "rationalist" solutions. The problem, according to Michele Barrett and Mary McIntosh, is that society itself has been "familialized": "The imagery of idealized family life permeates the fabric of social existence and provides a highly significant, dominant, and unifying complex of social meaning"[25]—regardless of what the household arrangements and lived experiences of large segments of the population actually are.

Christopher Lasch concedes that we are unlikely to return to a world in which the nuclear family is the prevailing household arrangement: "It is too late, however, to call for a revival of the patriarchal family or even of the 'companionate' family that replaced it. The 'transfer of functions,' as it is known in the antiseptic jargon of the social sciences—in reality, the deterioration of child care—has been at work for a long time, and many of its consequences appear to be irreversible."[26] He nevertheless yearns for an impossible return to a society of nuclear households and dismisses all alternatives as inherently hostile to the adequate social and psychological development of children. Ehrenreich and English offer another utopian vision of the future: having claimed that the "romantic/rationalist alternative is no longer acceptable," they can offer only a sketchy prescription for a new society: "the 'womanly' values of community and caring must rise to the center as the only *human* principles."[27] But they are unable to present concrete proposals for hastening the advent of this revolution in principles, lamenting instead that for women today, "there are too many choices . . . or there are not enough" (313). Lasch's uncompromising promotion of the traditional nuclear family and Ehrenreich and English's cautious celebration of its dissolution as the predominant familial arrangement are as imbued with utopianism as the novels I will discuss—disparate though their analyses of the family might be.

This review of what selected social historians have to say about the relationship between the family and society is relevant to the novels I will discuss in the chapters to follow. The alarm so many contemporary historians and sociologists sound about the penetration of the family's boundaries by society is countered in John Irving's *The World According to Garp*, Alice Walker's *The Color Purple*, and E. L. Doctorow's *Ragtime*: these texts are concerned, in part, with the cost of maintaining the family in a state of isolation from society. Walker provides a horrific rendition of an isolated abusive family headed by a man who disposes of those under his roof as he sees fit; he is impassive to the opinions or entreaties of those—like the schoolteacher—who would intervene on Celie's behalf. Later in the novel, we are not surprised when Celie welcomes the convalescence of her husband's lover under her roof because of the respite Shug's presence provides from a life of beatings and verbal abuse. Shug's "intervention" allows Celie to escape and to forge a new, extended family. Irving's Garp deceives himself into believing that he can construct a safe environment for his family where they will be protected from the violence raging in the world—only to himself precipitate the novel's most devastating scene of carnage. The surviving members of Garp's family convalesce at his mother's "group home" for women victims; his reconstituted family will include both biological and nontraditional kin. E. L. Doctorow challenges the fear of societal incursion upon the family by constructing a family that is representative of the various class and racial strata of society. By depicting the endless permeations of a variety of family structures by society at the turn of the century, and exploring the "familialized" nature of society, Doctorow suggests that it is delusional to mourn the passing of an idealized nuclear family operating in an idyllic isolation, immune from the intrusive strictures of societal authority. This family has never existed. "Society" in these novels is rendered as one or more individuals outside the family, and not as a faceless "mass of experts"; these transgressions into the "private" world of the family are not motivated by the professional interests of a larger group.

These novelists, then, disagree with the prevailing reification of the nuclear family as a privileged space. The widening of the familial circle and the resulting decline of paternal authority has many positive outcomes. Father doesn't necessarily know best: in each of the novels I will discuss, the privileges and prerogatives accorded to men are abused in some way. Harry Angstrom's inability to reconstruct himself in Updike's "Rabbit" novels—particularly his unwillingness to examine his predatory behavior and his emotional numbness—is the chief cause of his unhappiness and the havoc he wreaks on others; Coalhouse Walker's quest for justice at any price and Mother's Younger Brother's search for meaning first in a romantic obsession and then in political fanaticism in E. L. Doctorow's *Ragtime* can be seen as signs of an inflexibility born of a masculinist ideal of autonomy and individualism. Curbing or attenuating male authority and redefining masculinity allows men like Albert and Garp, on the other hand, to become more empathetic, emotionally complex, and self-aware. Expanding the family circle has other positive outcomes in most of the novels I will discuss. The proverbial warmth of the family's hearth—so jealously guarded and husbanded in the traditional nuclear family—is neither diminished nor extinguished with the addition of "outsiders" to the familial circle; the family's security and functions are not threatened when its roster is expanded in *The World According to Garp*, *The Color Purple*, and *Ragtime*. These texts imagine a world where the rationalist/romantic dichotomy described by Ehrenreich and English has indeed collapsed.

It might be useful to review briefly the groundbreaking work of Nancy Chodorow before discussing one final feature of the alternative families constructed by Irving and Walker: the diversification of child-rearing arrangements. *The Reproduction of Mothering* provides a psychoanalytic explanation of why the inequity in gender relations is perpetrated generation after generation: our understanding of legitimate gender roles and our deepest emotional responses to them originate in and are perpetrated by the family from the earliest stages of infancy. Chodorow finds that forces and agencies external to the family have much less to do with the persistence of women's traditional roles as primary caretakers than the internal psychodynamics of the family itself. Chodorow argues that one woman—the mother—is invariably the source of a child's primary love frustration; the "anxiety, conflict, and ambivalence" generated by the formation of ego boundaries "is an infantile reaction to disruptions and discomforts in its relation with its mother."[28] We are marked by these early infantile traumas for life; they occur at a preoedipal stage of development. If Chodorow's emphasis of the importance of these primary experiences is valid, then the "invasion" of the family that so concerns Lasch and others has little effect, finally, on the most significant bond in the family: that between the infant and the woman who is its primary caretaker. Women will continue to occupy a subordinate place in the family and in society as long as men are not equally involved in the earliest care of infants. Women will continue to "reproduce" the traits of traditional "motherhood" in their own girls; boys will continue to "develop a positional [rather than personal] identification with aspects of the masculine role" (175) because of the father's emotional distance.

Chodorow's hypothesis helps to illuminate the significance of the challenges to prevailing notions of traditional parental roles in *The World According to Garp* and *The Color Purple*. Her theory is particularly provocative in the contemporary climate of familial crisis: in the words of Renate Bridenthal, our society "idealizes mother*hood* while isolating and marginalizing mother*ing*."[29] Irving and Walker imagine families in which both men and women are endowed with what Eli Zaretsky terms "the traditionally male ideal of individual independence" and "the traditionally female ideal of nurturance."[30] Children in these households are the beneficiaries, not the victims, of the struggle for an expansion of traditional gender roles and opportunities that we witness in Irving's and Walker's novels.

The nuclear family's decline may have begun between the 1870s and the 1920s, as Christopher Lasch suggests,[31] but the *effect* of that decline has been most clearly visible and keenly experienced in the last thirty years. Revolutionary demographic shifts have taken place in the last few decades that have altered both the most public and intimate aspects of our lives. Indeed, the proliferation of family theory and history in recent decades is itself, in part, a product of a growing concern for the future of the family. Although many sociologists still define the nuclear family as the "norm," some of the most astute social historians, like Judith Stacey, recognize that "contemporary family arrangements are diverse, fluid, and unresolved. . . . Americans today have crafted a multiplicity of family and household arrangements that we inhabit uneasily and reconstitute frequently in response to changing personal and occupational circumstances."[32] Some of our novelists are also responding to the decline of the family structure which has prevailed during most of the last century-and-a-half with new visions of family and community.

The ideology of the idealized family has never been more pervasive and alluring than in recent decades—particularly because "no singular family structure or ideology has arisen to supplant the modern family" (17). Now more than ever before, "the concept of family is a socially necessary illusion which simultaneously expresses and masks recruitment to relations of production, reproduction, and consumption—relations that condition different kinds of household resource bases in different class sectors."[33] The cost of that illusion will be the focus of my discussion of John Updike's "Rabbit" novels in the next chapter. Updike's understanding of the contemporary state of the family and society mirrors that of Christopher Lasch. Harry Angstrom is a Laschian "narcissist" who wreaks destruction upon everyone around him whenever he tries to break free of or restructure the boundaries of the family. But because he can neither give nor receive love, understanding, or spiritual solace within the confines of his own family, Harry Angstrom's life is marked by a self-destructive ennui and paralysis. Like Lasch, who argues that it is probably too late to revive the traditional family while at the same time decrying any alternative familial arrangement, Updike envisions a world without any attractive and viable familial options.

3

Harry Angstrom's Flights
from the Family

Harry "Rabbit" Angstrom may be the most notorious "runner" in contemporary American fiction. In the first novel of Updike's "Rabbit" series, Harry runs (flounders might be a better word) "out of a kind of
sweet panic"[1] whenever he feels entangled by the far-flung and finally
inescapable webs of social norms and customs emanating from or supporting the family. Ten years later in *Rabbit Redux*, Harry embarks on
another "trip"—an inner flight from the pain of his wife's affair and
mother's terminal illness through the enervating torpor of drugs and a
homoerotic fascination with a black messiah.

In his indispensable classic, *Love and Death in the American Novel*,
Leslie Fiedler provides us with an essential framework for discerning
what makes Rabbit run: "the typical male protagonist of our fiction has
been a man on the run, harried into the forest and out to sea, down the
river or into combat—anywhere to avoid 'civilization,' which is to say,
the confrontation of a man and woman which leads to the fall to sex,
marriage, and responsibility."[2] In the opening pages of *Rabbit, Run*,
Harry Angstrom flees the claustrophobic incubator of his family for the
paradisiacal warmth of Florida—America's playground, a place where
Rabbit imagines himself enjoying a "vacation" from the monotony of
monogamy. The names of the towns he passes through on his quest for
sexual freedom underscore his goal: "Bird in Hand, Paradise, Intercourse" (29-30). But Rabbit's experience in the wilderness is mediated
by the windshield of his car; the "Nature" he encounters as he loses his
way on this dead-end journey offers no relief, no contrast to the life he
has known: "The land refuses to change. The more he drives the more

the region resembles the country around Mt. Judge" (34). There is nowhere left to run. Panicked and lost, Rabbit "instinctively" and
"infallibly" retraces his flight like a homing pigeon: "The trip home is
easier" (37) because "he didn't know what he was going toward going
down" (39).

Near the end of the novel, Rabbit is running again—this time for the
obfuscating cover of the woods to escape the community of mourners
gathered at the graveside of his infant daughter: he cannot understand or
bear the shocked silence that follows his cavalier assignment of responsibility for the child's death to his wife, Janice. He believes that his remark has been delivered in a spirit of "forgiveness" generated by a momentary certainty of a transcendental beyond; the mourners, however,
"snap around at a voice so sudden and cruel" (296). Joyce Markle is one
Updike scholar who validates Rabbit's reading of himself and the gathered witnesses: "The shock in the faces of the mourners suddenly reveals
to him their lack of vision"; he is "freed by their hatred from further
participation."[3] But Harry Angstrom is not a "mystic" whose
"awareness of God is threatened by other people" (52), as Markle asserts: he is, rather, so narcissistic, condescending, and emotionally
stunted that he is unable to empathize with the grief of the mourners or
understand how generous and forgiving Janice and her family have been
toward him. Running through the woods, Rabbit discovers that "he is
less sheltered than he expected" (296). Once again, nature is not a pris-
tine refuge: he stumbles upon "the crumbled sandstone walls of a forgotten house" in the forest above the cemetery. "The thought that this place
was once self-conscious" fills him with a "clangorous horror"—
particularly when he imagines the domestic life of the insignificant family that has vanished, leaving few traces behind in the "deepening darkness" (299) of the ravished but resuscitating wilderness.

Rabbit Redux returns us to Harry's world a decade later. After ten
years of smoldering resentment and stupefying boredom, Rabbit is sullen, sour, and "grounded"[4] —hoping for a "new combination" to rupture
the "stale peace" (6) of his marriage. But this time it is Janice who
runs—not Harry. She moves in with Charlie Stavros, a car dealer at her

father's lot, after Rabbit learns of their affair but cannot muster the jealousy or outrage to ban his wife from seeing her lover: "No, see him if you want to. Just as long as *I* don't have to see the bastard" (78). Janice is insulted by Rabbit's unwillingness to play the part of the injured husband by fighting to win her back. But nothing can penetrate Rabbit's baffled torpor and self-destructive passivity: "I know it's happened," he confesses to his mother, "but I don't feel anything yet" (100). Later, his dying mother will make one last attempt to free her son from the constrictions of his family by begging him to "Run. Leave Brewer. I never knew why you came back." When Harry resists, she advises him to "Pray for your own rebirth."

But as Harry learned ten years earlier, "Freedom means murder. Rebirth means death" (198). Even in the heady, revolutionary days of the late 1960s, the nuclear family is a sacred institution whose violation in Updike's world leads to catastrophic violence and destruction. Rabbit responds to the collapse of his family by allowing an alternative household to take shape around him. He is coaxed into sheltering Jill, an eighteen-year-old runaway, who is in search of someone to replace her dead father. In Rabbit, she gets an insensitive lover instead. She unwittingly names the tragic tenuousness of her position in this increasingly chaotic and violent household one night while she is playing her guitar for Rabbit and his teen-aged son, Nelson: "'I've had no life,' she says, and strums. 'No man's daughter, and no man's wife'" (172). She becomes the focal point of this new community, serving inadequately as a surrogate wife and daughter to Harry and as a sister, mother, and perhaps lover to Nelson.

The tentative equilibrium these three establish is disrupted when Jill invites a crazed black revolutionary who has jumped bail on drug charges to hide out at the Angstrom house. Skeeter's boundless rage corrodes and corrupts whatever remains of the sentiment and sympathy that might have bonded this community together. Rabbit is mesmerized by the black man's almost poetic articulation of hatred and violence; he uses the drugs Skeeter provides to accelerate the flight from his emotional confusion over his mother's impending death and his wife's desertion. This inner "trip" is more successful than Rabbit's "run" was ten years earlier in obliterating the drab banality, gnawing fear, and sense of entrapment that define his life. Furthermore, since Rabbit is obsessed with the idea that blacks are closer to "Nature" than whites, Skeeter offers him the access to primitive experience that was unavailable during his earlier ill-fated flight from the family. Both men are increasingly brutal in their treatment of Jill as a sexual object. Skeeter abuses her in a perverse effort to exact retribution for America's history of racial injustice. This "alternative family" becomes a nightmare from which Rabbit abruptly awakens after one of his neighbors—appalled and incensed by the theater of interracial sex the local children have patronized at the windows of the Angstrom house—sets fire to the premises one evening. Jill is too "stoned" to escape and dies in the blaze. The rest of the novel concerns the efforts of Mim, Harry's sister, to reconcile Harry and Janice and reconstruct their nuclear family.

Fiedler's assessment of the American novel as "a gothic fiction, nonrealistic and negative, sadist and melodramatic—a literature of darkness and the grotesque in a land of light and affirmation"[5] is certainly true of *Rabbit, Run* and *Rabbit Redux*. Although Updike's uncanny and unparalleled ability to represent the sensory overload and bewildering superficiality and plasticity of American life in exquisite, scintillating prose has earned him a reputation as a realist, his "Rabbit" series is fundamentally gothic and melodramatic. Two "daughters" are sacrificed at the altar of Harry and Janice Angstrom's marriage—one by water and the other by fire.[6] Each of these ritualistic deaths resurrects this marriage at a moment of crisis and recommits its reluctant, confused, and irresponsible participants to a union that by any objective reckoning is stultifying and destructive. In *Rabbit Redux*, Updike provides what may be the most fully realized depiction of an alternative family in contemporary American fiction, but the result is a reification of the fears and prejudices of white, middle class America. He breathes life into the chimerical media creations and popular caricatures of the late 1960s: "Harry comes from the silent majority of the Nixon era, Jill is 'into' drugs and radical politics to demonstrate her rejection of the 'system' represented by her rich parents, and Skeeter has returned from Vietnam as a vengeful, drug-dealing, black militant."[7] The alternative family Updike creates is a menagerie of misfits who are engulfed by a maelstrom of violence and brutality. They are the inevitable products of Updike's revulsion toward a period he characterizes in his autobiography, *Self-Consciousness*, as "a dreamlike 'crazy' time"[8]—an apocalyptic era "of anarchy, of window-smashing and cop-bopping and drug-tripping and shouting down" (127).

Updike's creation of such a fantastical and finally implausible alternative family doesn't make sense at first blush—particularly when we consider his unsparing depictions of the unremitting boredom and joyless panorama of Rabbit's nuclear family. Why does he present an alternative to the nuclear family that is a two-dimensional, worst-case scenario? How do we reconcile Updike's cardboard counterculture figures with his dismay, in a speech accepting the 1963 National Book Award, that "*accuracy*" or "*lifelikeness*" is "a virtue seldom extolled these days?"[9]

The answer lies in Updike's conception of the social function of literature and his unabashed, delighted deference toward institutions and "realities" he takes to be more permanent and universal than they really are. He cites Cézanne's "timid reverence toward what exists" (17) as the surest state of rapture for the writer. Like Harry Angstrom, his most famous creation, Updike looks to the concrete nuances of daily life—the ingredients in a TV dinner, the sooty, bedraggled ginkgo trees that line sidewalks in communities like "Brewer," the latest pop singles or most recent news summary—for reassurance, stability, and more: the clues of a divine presence imposing order on a seemingly chaotic world. Updike seems to fear that to probe the histories, contexts or implications of the physical reality and institutions that define his world (and that of his characters) is to smudge, erase, or deny the fingerprints of the "fierce God"[10] in whom he professes to believe.

In "Why Write?" Updike rejects the conception of the writer's role "as conscience and prophet and servant of the billions not able to speak for themselves" and confesses that "the general betterment of mankind, and even the improvement of social conditions within my own violently

imperfect nation, were *not* my basic motivation as a writer."[11] Instead,
he offers a more immediate and selfish motivation: "what every writer
wants, as every aspiring writer can tell you, is to get into print. . . . it is
just this involvement in the world of commerce and industry, this imposition of one's otherwise evanescent fancies upon the machinery of
manufacture and distribution, that excites the writer's ego" (36-37).
Updike's noblest definition of the writer's task is that of faithful witness:
"We must write where we stand; wherever we do stand, there is life; and
an imitation of the life we know, however narrow, is our only ground"
(32). There is a curious defensiveness about this response: with the
apologetic qualification, "however narrow," Updike might be responding
to critics who admire his exquisite brush strokes but find the canvases he
produces are somehow lacking in depth or breadth. It is interesting to
compare Updike's most ambitious articulation of the writer's responsibility to E. L. Doctorow's idealistic call for a politically savvy fiction
"about the way power works in our society, who has it, and how it is
making history."[12] Doctorow decries "the exhaustion of the hope that
writing can change anything" among American writers—who "take on
less and less of the world" in their novels, focusing instead on "some
sort of unresounding private life" (614-15). While Updike's novels are
replete with the sensory, concrete details of "where he stands" as a
"faithful witness," he seldom addresses the implications of this position-
ing or the contexts of his place in the world and his fictional representations of it. Furthermore, in reaching beyond the scope of the world he
knows and inhabits to construct an unsympathetic, even horrific portrait
of a short-lived challenge to the nuclear family, he violates his own
conditions for a fiction of "accuracy."

Updike wants these novels to serve as a defense of the existing social order, even as his devoted renditions of life within the contemporary
American nuclear family uncovers a sobering sense of ennui and unhappiness. He reconciles this gap by "normalizing" or universalizing the
suffering of those who find that the nuclear family is failing to provide
satisfactory nurturing bonds and emotional support and by exaggerating
the costs of breaking free from the traditional familial circle. Referring

to *Rabbit, Run,* Updike acknowledges that "there is a case to be made for running away from your wife" but insists that the consequences are inevitably catastrophic: "there are all these other people who seem to get hurt."[13] Adhering to institutions is "a kind of agony"—but a necessary, inevitable, and somewhat noble agony that Updike juxtaposes to a hackneyed stereotype of humanistic theology—"an easy humanism that insists that man is an animal which feeds and sleeps and defecates and makes love and isn't that nice and natural and let's all have more of that" (509). And in one of his most direct defenses of *Rabbit Redux,* Updike confirms that he intended this novel to serve as a critique of the anti-institutional spirit of "the interminable Sixties":[14]

> There may be something also in the novelist's trade which shades you toward conservatism. Things exist because they evolved to that condition; they cannot be lightly or easily altered. It is my general sense of human institutions that they are outcroppings of human nature, that human nature is slow to change, that in general when you destroy one set of institutions you get something worse.[15]

Updike's depictions of the contemporary family and the absence of feasible alternatives in his novels is problematic. Given the hostility, resentment, and spiritual poverty that characterize the Angstrom marriage, is there really no alternative that would be healthier and more fulfilling? Why must Updike insist—as he does in the above excerpt—that the formulation of alternatives to existing institutions such as the nuclear family is a destructive enterprise? Updike's stance is at odds with the views of contemporaries like John Irving, Alice Walker, and E. L. Doctorow, whose works of fiction I will discuss in subsequent chapters. His position is analogous to that of Christopher Lasch (see chapter 2). Although Lasch admits that the family "has been slowly coming apart for more than a hundred years" and that this traditional institution is itself a political construction that met the needs of an earlier era of capitalism, he defends the nuclear family as "the last refuge of love and decency"[16] whose salvaging is instrumental for the salvation of civilization itself. Lasch's position is untenable: he defends an institution whose transformation he himself suspects is irreversible. Yet he also decries alternatives that fulfill the functions—if not the form—of the traditional nuclear family. Updike leaves us in a comparable state of frustration. We are as stymied as his unsympathetic "everyman," Harry Angstrom, whose attempts to break away from Janice in *Rabbit, Run* and operate within an alternative community in *Rabbit Redux* are so disastrous that he has no choice but to return to the more traditional environment of his unhappy family.

In *Rabbit Run*, the first volume of Updike's "Rabbit" quaternary, Harry Angstrom is chafed by the irksome irritations of his mediocre life. Because he has once known greatness as a local basketball star, he believes that his job selling "MagiPeelers" and his marriage to the sloppy, insecure, and unimaginative Janice are too constricting—a living death. Harry reminds Eccles, the ineffectual humanist minister who sees reconciling the young couple as a test of his own pastoral efficacy, why he is special: "I played first-rate basketball. I really did. And after you're first-rate at something, no matter what, it kind of takes the kick out of being second-rate. And that little thing Janice and I had going, boy, it was really second-rate" (107). One evening, "he senses he is in a trap" (15) and drives as far away from his family as he can get. His flight concludes, ironically, in the dead end of a "petting grove" off a dirt road in West Virginia. He has failed because he ignored the advice of a friendly gas station attendant: "The only way to get somewhere, you know, is to figure out where you're going before you go there" (28). But in Rabbit's world, there is no clear road map for escaping the family.

The object of Rabbit's southern crusade is a "barefoot Du Pont" (26)—an American dream girl: rich, tanned, sexually available. It is significant, therefore, that Harry must pay for the sexual experience he fantasized was so readily available outside the family, that the woman he employs to service him is ordinary and somewhat overweight, and that their encounter takes place not in Florida, but in the drab, sooty city of Brewer—only a few minutes away from the family he has deserted. Furthermore, there is nothing spontaneous or uplifting about sex with Ruth, the tough, worldly prostitute who takes him back to her apartment:

indeed, Rabbit is so unimaginative that he "makes love to her as he would to his wife" (83). Updike dwells upon the petty hagglings leading to their first night together because he wants to emphasize that, at least initially, this relationship is a cheap, squalid transaction of the flesh. After Harry pays her, we are privy to his shockingly crass calculation that she is "a dime a pound" (72). But it is also significant that their relationship begins only one night after Harry has fled from Janice. The pressure of being alone, of feeling like a "sexual suspect,"[17] is too great for Harry. One of the most striking characteristics of Rabbit's brief, live-in affair with Ruth is how quickly it becomes a "marriage": when she asks him, "Say, do you think we're married or something the way you boss me around?" during their first night together, he answers, "Yes; let's be" (77). A few minutes later, he announces, "This is our wedding night" (79). Because Rabbit insists that Ruth not use birth control, it is inevitable that he will be faced with a choice between two families at the end of the novel. Instead of escaping the family's "nets," he is more enmeshed than ever; in attempting to renounce one family, he haplessly founds another. His indecisive running from one family to the other results in the accidental drowning of his new baby with Janice and the probable abortion of the fetus he has conceived with Ruth.

Although Rabbit's flight from the nuclear family is disconcerting to the authority figures in his world, they are more titillated than angry. As Donald J. Greiner notes, "Rabbit needs advice, but no one knows what to tell him."[18] Only Janice's mother seems to retain a sense of the enormity of his actions. Harry's mother, on the other hand, is angry when her son drifts back to his wife. When Harry visits after his reconciliation with Janice, his brooding, embittered mother blurts out, "And what's going to happen to this poor girl you lived with in Brewer?" (227-28). Like the other authority figures to whom Rabbit turns for advice or a response by which to gauge his actions, she has a vicarious interest in his attempt to flee the family: her own marriage is joyless; her life is as cramped and dreary as her tiny sunless yard; she fears that if her son returns to Janice, her own prestige and influence will be diminished as he is once again assimilated into a more powerful and success-

ful family. But even if she could help her son—could offer him a concrete alternative to his life with Janice—to do so would violate the most
sacred norms of her community. Harry's father knows his son has become a social pariah, and declares Rabbit his "enemy" (164). He believes Rabbit has become a sexual deviant: "He'll just slide deeper and
deeper now until we might just as well forget him. . . . They're like
cripples only they don't limp. Human garbage, they call them" (165).
Yet Updike's novel is particularly effective because no one can offer
Harry Angstrom a compelling, selfish reason to return to his family—in
part because no one in this novel is happily married. The threat of the
law, the fear of public ostracism, and the guilt that he is not providing
for his pregnant wife and young son are the "nets" the community
throws to catch the runaway husband. He must be caught; he cannot be
persuaded.

Clearly, the dark reality of the world Updike creates is that while
sexuality outside of marriage may seem alluring and pleasurable, it is
not only socially unacceptable and morally reprehensible: it is dangerous
and perverse. Shortly after leaving Janice, Rabbit wonders whether the
two most trusted authority figures in his world—Eccles and Tothero—
have latent homosexual tendencies. Before his first golf game with Eccles, for example, Rabbit has a moment of anxiety about whether his
heterosexuality is evident to others: "The thought flits through his brain
that Eccles is known as a fag and he has become the new boy" (129).[19]
When he homes in on Tothero's room after his abortive migration south,
his old coach insists that Rabbit undress in front of him and sleep in his
"rumpled lukewarm bed" (45); Harry feels "vaguely invaded" (52) that
night when Tothero gets into his car; on their way to dinner (and a ren-
dezvous with two prostitutes), Tothero tells him, "I am a hideous person,
Harry. A person to be abhorred" (54). Tothero reveals an ugly, lecher-
ous side of himself to his young protégé, frightening Rabbit with a boisterous announcement: "You and I are two of a kind" (49). Like the protagonist in Hawthorne's "Young Goodman Brown," Harry fears that his
decision to forsake the "right way" of marriage for the "forest path" of
sin (literally, when we recall that Rabbit's flight from Brewer ends in a

West Virginia "petting grove") has initiated him into a world of debauched and sordid realities. He is anxious that he will be a target of or brother to other polymorphously perverse figures now that he is no longer safely ensconced in the cocoon of the nuclear family. In *The Hearts of Men*, Barbara Ehrenreich has undertaken a socio-historical reading of the 1950s that provides a context for Rabbit's anxiety: "The ultimate reason why a man would not just 'walk out the door' was the taint of homosexuality which was likely to follow him."[20] Ehrenreich points out that therapists believed the birth of a baby "was especially likely to precipitate infantile and/or homosexual behavior in men who had only superficially accepted their responsibilities as breadwinners" (21). One psychoanalyst, Lionel Ovesey, created the category of "pseudohomosexuality" to understand the heterosexual who "suffered from some 'adaptive failure' to meet the standards of masculine conformity, and had begun a subconscious slide toward a homosexual identity" (25).

Rabbit is not simply worried about his old coach's sexual proclivities: he decides Tothero is a "madman" (48) because of his vacillating response to Rabbit's desertion of his family. Tothero's first reaction to Harry Angstrom's news is lamenting disbelief: "I don't believe that my greatest boy would grow into such a monster" (44). But when Rabbit places his fate and marriage in his mentor's hands—"I thought maybe I could sleep a couple hours somewhere in the Sunshine [the name of the boarding house reminds us that 'fun in the sun' was the object of Rabbit's abortive trip south]. Otherwise I might as well go home" (43)— Tothero not only takes him in and sets him up with a prostitute, but he advises him not to resist the phototropic lure of pleasure: "Do what the heart commands. . . . The heart is our only guide" (53). Updike reinforces the novel's "sun" imagery with Harry's last name: an "angstrom" is a unit used in measuring the length of light waves. However, the sun of sexual freedom that beckons so alluringly outside the staid, shabby domiciles of the nuclear family can blight and destroy as well as warm: Tothero's crippling stroke ends his sojourn in the "Sunshine" and returns him—a helpless invalid—to the custody of his prim, domineering, "harried and noble" (281) wife; the death of Harry's infant daughter grounds him for good and, as we will learn in the second volume of the "Rabbit" series, eviscerates his interest in sex, but the necessity of the nuclear family has been reestablished—if for no other reason than for its role as a safe container for the volatility of libidinal energies. After the death of Harry's baby, Tothero pays a sympathy call on his former star, but instead of consolation, he offers a guilty reversal of his original advice: "When I'm dead and gone, remember how your old coach told you to avoid suffering" by adhering to human laws of "right and wrong" (280).

Although Eccles is a more consistent advocate for societal standards than Tothero, his response to Rabbit's renunciation of his familial responsibilities is also surprising and perhaps even inappropriate. He befriends Rabbit, finds him a more satisfying job, and preaches a mild and unthreatening humanist version of Christianity from the unlikely pulpit of the golf course. However, Eccles is finally unable to convince Rabbit that his flight from the family is wrong: instead, as Joyce Markle points out, "he uses the emotional susceptibility generated by crises—birth and death—to twice pull Rabbit back into the social system: when baby June is born and when she dies" (40). Like many of the other characters in this novel, he is both repelled and secretly fascinated by Rabbit's nonchalant sloughing off of his familial responsibilities. His attraction to Rabbit might be explained by his own odd marriage to Lucy, an agnostic follower of Freud. When Rabbit and the reader see them together for the first time, they are bickering about a host of issues that are undermining their marriage. Lucy accuses Eccles of "making everybody's life miserable for months" (120) because he has not had the courage to call a particularly rude parishioner; he reminds her that she had promised to keep her heart "open for *Grace*" (121) despite her lack of faith. As their argument heats up, Eccles cracks a lame joke to needle his wife and, incredibly, looks to Harry for support: "When Eccles turns to Harry to guffaw conspiratorially after this dig, bitterness cripples his laugh" (120).

Eccles and Lucy's marriage is in trouble, and Rabbit's nonchalant irresponsibility exacerbates their differences. Lucy finds Rabbit attractive, even though she is repelled when he gives her a flirtatious slap during their first encounter. She teases and mocks Rabbit following his return to Janice. After Harry attends her husband's church for the first time, she invites him to walk her home to avail herself of an opportunity to test the depth of his "reform." When Rabbit suggests that he and Eccles are "alike" in some ways, she responds, "But naturally it's the differences that I notice. . . . like the fact that you're not afraid of women" (240). She is even blunter when she tells her young daughter that "most everybody" is neurotic—"Except our friend Mr. Angstrom" (241). Their conversation comes to an abrupt, angry end after he awkwardly rejects her offer of a cup of coffee: "Was she mad because he had turned down a proposition, or because he had shown that he thought she had made one? Or was it a mixture of these opposites, that had somehow exposed her to herself?" Perhaps it is because his response—"You're a doll, but I got this wife now" (242)—shows that he is afraid of women after all. He is incapable of imagining a relationship with a woman that is not sexual, and now that he has returned to his family, Lucy's frankness and physical attractiveness are too threatening.

This incident precipitates a terrible sequence of miscues and accidents. "Whether spurned or misunderstood, Eccles' wife has jazzed him, and he reaches his apartment clever and cold with lust" (243). But Rabbit's manipulations and cajoling are in vain: Janice is not yet ready for any sexual contact with him: "She exaggerates its importance, has imagined it into something rare and precious she's entitled to half of when all he wants is to get rid of it so he can move on, on into sleep, down the straight path, for her sake" (248). Furthermore, she finds his effort to masturbate against her body to be degrading and "cheap" (248). She reminds him that nonreproductive, nonreciprocal sexuality perverts the "sanctity" of traditional marriage: "I'm not your whore, Harry" (249). Embarrassed and frustrated, Rabbit runs—again. Frightened and ashamed, Janice gets drunk the next day and accidentally drowns their baby. Updike elevates the drowning of the Angstroms' baby to the level of mythic sacrifice with the improbable and implausible assessment from Eccles that this accident is a spiritual rite of passage to a more permanent and meaningful union: "I think marriage is a sacrament, and that this tragedy, terrible as it is, has at last united you and Janice in a sacred way" (282). Harry and Janice will stay together after this death and after an equally appalling series of events in the second volume of the "Rabbit" series that will claim the life of another "daughter."

If Eccles is driven to return Rabbit to his family to justify both his ministry and his own quarrelsome marriage with Lucy, his wife senses that the failure of this mission would confirm her Freudian reading of human social and sexual behavior. This perspective is suspicious of, even antagonistic toward the institution of marriage as it is practiced and perpetuated in western cultures. In *Civilization and its Discontents*, Freud decries the restriction of sexuality in modern society to "heterosexual genital love" that is sanctified by the "legitimacy and monogamy"[21] of marriage. The suppression or repression of strong instincts is "the cause of the hostility against which all civilizations have to struggle" (44). Lucy sympathizes with Rabbit's instinct-driven flight but does not anticipate the cost of his break from "civilization." The ideological nature of the struggle between Eccles and Lucy for the "soul" of Harry Angstrom serves, then, as a critique of what Updike sees as a dangerous level of permissiveness in both humanistic theology and modern psychoanalysis. While some readers share Lucy's belief that Eccles is partly responsible for the baby's death, and others blame Lucy's Sunday morning flirtation with Rabbit, both must bear partial responsibility: neither of them has helped Rabbit understand himself; both of them have attempted to use him as a pawn or case study to validate their respective readings of the world.

Some critics overlook Rabbit's offensive behavior or accept the implausible gothic "punishments" Updike metes out in both *Rabbit, Run* and *Rabbit Redux* because they have focused too exclusively on the theological motifs that are so often woven into the fabric of Updike's novels. Wayne D. McGinnis proclaims *Rabbit, Run* "one of the most radically religious of contemporary American novels" because "salvation leads to a death" and "a state of utterly free existence."[22] Dean Doner finds the novel's central paradox to be what he perceives as Rabbit's double nature—earthly and spiritual: "There is not one good word to be said for him, yet he alone perceives the Unseen."[23] Joyce Markle agrees, depicting Rabbit as a kind of spiritual touchstone because he alone has fleeting, elated glimpses of a transcendental state of "grace." She points to Rabbit's labors in the garden of Mrs. Smith, an elderly parishioner of Eccles, as an example of his life-giving gifts. While it is true that Mrs. Smith tells Rabbit that he has the gift of life, we should note that this work is confined to the time he spends away from Janice: once he decides to return to his wife, he is unable to continue tending the garden. This is particularly significant when we consider the odd sexual overtones of their interactions, and when we remember the unexpected homoeroticism that clouds Rabbit's relationship with Tothero and Eccles after he has fled his family. The garden Harry Angstrom tends was planted by the late Harry Smith, and Rabbit's employer flatters herself by imagining the two men have more in common than their first names. The coy flirtatiousness of this decrepit woman reminds us that in Rabbit's world, virtually any encounter outside the family can be colored by polymorphous sexual energy.

"Eccles feels drawn to Rabbit in the same way that the parishioners should feel drawn to Eccles—by the force of his belief."[24] Rabbit's faith is more libidinal than theological: he is attractive, compelling, and finally dangerous because he has fled the family in search of sexual experience. Much has been made of Rabbit's response to Eccles's demand that he define the "thing that wasn't there" (133) in his marriage. The question comes during one of their golf games, and Eccles has just lectured Rabbit on the necessity of serving God. When the minister insists that this "thing" be named, Rabbit responds by sinking a golf shot: "'That's *it*!' he cries and, turning to Eccles with a smile of aggrandizement, repeats, 'That's it'" (134). Although most critics think this "it" is religious certainty or faith, an equally compelling reading of this scene might pay attention to what Rabbit is thinking about while he swings his golf clubs. He imagines that the golf clubs are the women in his life, and is mortified and angry when he cannot make them serve his will: "He's always had a touch with objects" (131). Rabbit's interior dialogue with his golf clubs is as insensitive and misogynistic as the conversations he has with Ruth and his wife. He even imagines that "Home is the hole" (132) to which his golf balls refuse to return. His motivation for hitting the perfect golf shot is "getting out of this mess"—the mess of being berated by Eccles for being "monstrously selfish" (134) as well as the mess of his poor golf performance.

Some critics have gone so far to validate the theological strands of Updike's novel that they seem to rewrite one of its most brutal moments: Rabbit's last sexual encounter with Ruth. After meeting a former teammate and learning that he used to be a client of Ruth's, Rabbit insists that she perform fellatio on him. Rabbit intends it as an act of humiliation, a rite of ownership: "I felt a wall between us and this is the one way through it. . . . Tonight you turned against me. I need to see you on your knees" (187). Joseph Waldmeir suggests that "Rabbit's humanity is affirmed" in this act of rape because "it is a woman, not a lump whom Rabbit violates."[25] Edward Vargo provides an equally insensitive reading: "The fellatio that he forces upon Ruth may be considered a ritual act of atonement which he demands of her because he felt a wall arising between them."[26] Joyce Markle is one of the few Updike scholars who recognizes the enormity of Rabbit's act: "His last sexual encounter with Ruth is cruel and disregards her reluctance for his own sexual pleasure."[27]

This scene is central to understanding the gothic contrivances of Updike's "Rabbit" novels and their ideological implications. Rabbit is not an existential hero fighting to expand the range of acceptable sexual experience in a society that Herbert Marcuse, writing a few years before the publication of *Rabbit, Run*, condemns for requiring the subjugation of instincts in order to perpetrate "specific institutions of domination" such as the "monogamic-patriarchal family."[28] In *Eros and Civilization*, Marcuse claims that sexual practices occurring outside of a monogamous relationship for purposes other than reproduction "express rebellion against the subjugation of sexuality under the order of procreation, and against the institutions which guarantee this order. Psychoanalytic theory sees in the practices that exclude or prevent procreation an opposition against continuing the chain of reproduction and thereby of paternal domination" (49). But Rabbit's "sexual practice" with Ruth is an act of violence that perpetrates rather than challenges "paternal domination." Rabbit's "run" may seem to be motivated by a desire "to change reality until it conforms to the pleasure-principle . . . to fight for instinctual liberation,"[29] as Norman O. Brown, Marcuse's philosophical ally, identifies the central project of humankind, but he is neither militating against Thanatos nor undermining patriarchal practices and institutions in any kind of significant or permanent way. The flight from the family in the world Updike depicts unleashes rather than thwarts Thanatos. Rabbit's quest for polymorphous sexuality is realized in an act of rape that ends his relationship with Ruth. On the same evening, coincidentally enough, his wife gives birth to their new daughter. This wrenching juxtaposition forces Rabbit—and the reader—to choose.

But the return to the family—the choice of the "right way" of marriage and family—will not be enough to save Rabbit. In a 1981 *Saturday Review* interview, Updike is clear about the conservative sensibility that informs his "Rabbit" novels: "There are prices to be paid for our strayings from the social net. . . . someone suffers even if it's not you."[30] Awaiting the birth of his baby at the hospital, Rabbit "is certain that as a consequence of his sin Janice or the baby will die" (196). We are not surprised when his fearful premonition is fulfilled. Similarly, in the opening pages of *Rabbit Redux*, when Harry worries that his family's irregular life style will prompt a "madman" to move in or result in the torching of his house (9), we know that both eventualities are inevitable.

At the end of *Rabbit, Run*, Updike's protagonist runs aimlessly "out of a kind of sweet panic" (309)—overwhelmed by the enormity of what has happened. But once again, he has no destination. So we are not surprised to see him, ten years later in *Rabbit Redux*, stymied and sullen, hoping for a "new combination" (6) to launch him, like the Apollo moon mission, far from the gravity of earthly fields. Instead, as he watches the television images of the rocket roaring into space, he learns from his father that it is Janice who has escaped the family's orbit. He and his father realize that "they have not been lifted, they are left here" (7)—unhappy drinkers at a bar ironically dubbed the "Phoenix"—as insignificant as a "piece of grit in the launching pad" (11). The father—a "man with no excess left to him, his face washed empty by grievances"—is the befuddled caretaker of a wife who is dying of Parkinson's disease. The son—"somehow pale and sour," with "a weakness verging on anonymity" (4)—still fantasizes about a flight that would untether him from familial bonds and responsibilities and leave him "soaring, rootless, free" (20). He is unable to muster adequate and appropriate emotional responses to his terminally ill mother, whom he avoids, his father, whom he humors with an occasional after-work drink, and his son, whom he needles mercilessly. He has ignored his wife's sexual needs since the death of their baby: even sex has become "too dark, too *serious*, too kindred to death" (36)—a burdensome obligation. When Harry confronts Janice about her affair, she accuses him of becoming increasingly inaccessible and unresponsive: "You were a beautiful brainless guy and I've had to watch that guy die day by day" (74). But Rabbit is so estranged from his emotions that he tells his wife she can continue to see her lover—a display of disinterest and apathy that prompts Janice to move out.

Donald Greiner captures Rabbit's entropy better than most: "His rebellion in the second novel has the negative factor of stagnation; it is a kind of rebellion in reverse."[31] He "feels trapped by the dying of parents, the death of babies, and the impotence in between" (71). But Updike interjects an element of permissiveness into his protagonist's resentful passivity, making Rabbit a character study of the excesses popularly associated with the late 1960s. Rabbit still shrinks from the necessity of setting boundaries and limits; he refuses to intervene in any situation that invites or demands a moral response or decision. His standard rejoinder in *Rabbit Redux* is "Why not?" (202, 212, 327)—"Chief question facing these troubled times. Why not" (163). Indeed, when Rabbit accedes to Jill's efforts to harbor a black man who has jumped bail on drug charges, he wonders, "Why has he invited this danger?" His answer? "To get Janice to rescue him" (212). Worse, he decides that "Janice has been doing some things out of the way, so I have to do things out of the way. . . . To keep up with her" (215). His sister, Mim, rightly accuses him of being responsible for the tragedies that befall him: "Everybody else has a life they try to fence in with some rules. You just do what you feel like and then when it blows up or runs down you just sit there and pout" (370).

Rabbit is adrift from the moment his wife departs. As in *Rabbit, Run,* the collapse of his family seems to marginalize him and make him vulnerable or available to people from whom he had previously been insulated. A few weeks after his wife leaves, a black co-worker startles him with the solicitous question, "Getting any tail?" (102) and an invitation to "see what develops" (103) at a local bar that evening. Although hesitant at first, Rabbit makes a last minute decision to show up; this initial, fateful step plunges him into a netherworld of drugs, prostitution, and violence.

Jimbo's Friendly Lounge—a sleazy bar catering to African Americans—is dark, "deep and more complicated than it appears on the outside" (115). Updike accentuates the exotic "otherness" of blacks through Rabbit's naive and fearful observations. For example, the bartender's head is "like one of the stone hatchets in the Brewer museum"—an image that recalls the primitive implements of a rural African tribe. This "African" motif is supported by Rabbit's discovery of stuffed gazelle heads mounted on the wall behind the bar. But Updike supplies Rabbit with sophisticated imagery and language to imagine and convey his unease with African Americans that is inappropriate for a character of Harry's limited intellectual capacity and parochial sensibilities. The gap between Updike's literary skills and the conceivable machinations of Harry Angstrom's imagination is particularly obvious when Rabbit plays with the multiple meanings of the word "soul" in the following reverie at Jimbo's Lounge:

> Soul. He used to try to picture it when a child. A parasite like a tapeworm inside. A sprig of mistletoe hung from our bones, living on air. A jellyfish

swaying between our lungs and our liver. Black men have more, bigger.
Cocks like eels. Night feeders. Their touching underbelly smell on buses,
their dread of those clean dry places Harry must be. (134)

This stream of consciousness begins as vintage Updike—theological
musings on the interrelationship of spirit and matter—and concludes
with a vivid and sophisticated sequence of images that ratify stereotypes
about the sexual mystique and prowess of black men—images that cannot credibly be attributed to Harry Angstrom's imagination. The dread
African Americans ostensibly have for "clean dry places" reminds us
that Jimbo's lounge is more like a cave than a bar; the fear and objectifi-
cation of black sexuality contained in this passage is prevalent throughout *Rabbit Redux*.

Indeed, the world that Updike creates in his novel reifies a host of
familiar racial stereotypes. Rabbit's two black co-workers at the Verity
Press drink on the job with impunity: no one can discipline them. When
Harry is laid off from his job near the end of the novel, his boss explains
why: "Buchanan, Christ, let him go we'd have every do-good outfit in
the city on our necks, it's not the way *I'd* do things. If they'd come to me
I would have told them, that man is half-soused from eleven o'clock on
every morning, they're all like that" (341). Buchanan is also a pimp, as
Harry learns when he visits Jimbo's Lounge. Babe, the prostitute who
works for Buchanan, doubles as a blues singer with enough "soul" to
resurrect "lyrics born in some distant smoke" (124). She also has a talent for palmistry, and when she examines Harry's hand, her touch is
"reptilian cool" and "slithers nice as a snake" (116)—images that recall
the "eel" simile in the passage above. Her reading of Harry's hand fo-
cuses on his "extremely plausible" thumb—an indication that Rabbit's
sexual organ can be competitive with the superior "eel-like" phallus of
the black male: "Under the right signs it would absolutely function"
(117).

Buchanan introduces a young white runaway, Jill, to Rabbit as "a
poor child" who "needs a daddy" (134); the pimp tells the teen-ager
(whose race is drawing too much attention to his operation with Babe)
that "Young Harry here lives in this fancy big house over in the fanciest

part of West Brewer, all by himself, and never gets any tail" (132). From this moment of introduction, familial and sexual roles are blurred. When Jill goes home with Harry later that evening, she tells him she is willing to sleep with him because he has a "sweet funny family side. Always worrying about who needs you" (141). Jill's first conversation with Nelson, Harry's son, concerns his good fortune in having "such a protective father" (151). Although Harry thinks of her as being "like a sister" (156) to his teenager, he is also increasingly jealous of the rapport Jill and Nelson share and suspicious of the real nature of their relationship. And he is dimly aware that his sexual relationship with Jill—a confused young woman in search of someone who will substitute for her dead father—is somehow wrong. Her reluctance to make love confuses him: instead, she "perfects ways with her fingers and mouth to bring him off. Small curdled puddles of his semen then appear on her skin, and though easily wiped away leave in his imagination a mark like an acidburn on her shoulders, her throat, the small of her back" (157). But one evening, when a frightened conversational pause makes Rabbit suspect that Jill and Nelson may not have a strictly platonic relationship, he retaliates with cruelty: "Though he doesn't pursue this guilt he has startled from her, that night he does make her take him squarely, socks it into her though she offers her mouth and her cunt is so tight it sears. She is frightened . . ." (163).

This episode is soon followed by an explosive argument that determines the hierarchy and sexual economy of this "alternative" household. Rabbit flies into a rage when he discovers that Jill and Nelson have "hustled" the money for a guitar; he accuses Jill of turning his son into a "beggar and whore" (169) like herself. This violent confrontation is a means for Rabbit to reassert his primacy in this household and his authority over Nelson: it reimposes the structure and power dynamics of the nuclear family. While Harry and Jill are fighting, Nelson is impotent, humiliated, "crying, outside the door, afraid to come in" (170). Nelson is reduced to helpless rage: "If you hurt her, I'll kill you" (169)—and it is not the last time he will utter this threat. At the end of the novel, when it becomes apparent that the torching of the Angstrom house by an unknown irate neighbor has claimed the life of Jill, Rabbit's son has to be restrained by some of the firemen who are fighting the blaze: "Nelson screams up at Harry's face: 'You fucking asshole, you've let her die. I'll kill you . . . And, though it is his son, Harry crouches and gets his hands up ready to fight" (320).

Rabbit, Jill, and Nelson "seek to reconstitute their family" (171) after this altercation, and an uneasy equilibrium is reestablished. But their implicit contracts and hierarchies arc ruptured when Jill invites a black Vietnam veteran who is "de*sire*d by the local swine" (206) for pushing drugs to stay for a few nights. When Rabbit asks Jill, "Why are you doing this to me?" (208), Skeeter answers for her: "Jesus deliver me from puking uptight honky lovers. She's doing it because I been screwing her all afternoon, right? If I go, she goes with me, hey Jill honey, right?" (209). With this sarcastic announcement, Skeeter destroys the artificial nuclear family Harry, Jill, and Nelson have constructed. Once again, Rabbit has been betrayed, and although he professes to be unconcerned by this discovery, his behavior towards Jill undergoes a marked change, ranging from callous insensitivity to blatant cruelty. The black man is now a sexual rival. So when "Skeeter unzips his fly and prepares to display" the "glory that never does fail" as a way of taunting his competitor, Rabbit is "packed . . . solid with anger and fear" (210). Oddly enough, however, the physical contact of the fight that follows leaves him somehow beholden or bonded to Skeeter. Passive and terrified, Harry agrees to let Skeeter stay.

In *Rabbit Redux*, African Americans are depicted as both "primitive" or close to nature—"loose-jointed like lions" (13)—and as a corruptive force in natural, Edenic settings. Rabbit responds to the phenomenon of "afro" hair styles by thinking, "Instead of bald-looking heads they're bushy. That's O.K., it's more Nature, Nature is what we're running out of" (12). But Harry worries that blacks have become "noisier," more numerous and visible in the late 1960s, as if the "seeds of some tropical plant sneaked in by the birds were taking over the garden. His garden. Rabbit knows it's his garden and that's why he's put a flag decal on the back window of the Falcon even though Janice says it's

corny and fascist" (13). Blacks have even "invaded" the basketball
court—a world of fame, achievement, and nostalgia for Rabbit: "The
game different now, everything the jump shot, big looping hungry blacks
lifting and floating there a second while a pink palm long as your fore-
arm launched the ball" (18). And Skeeter, the black revolutionary who
disrupts the uneasy hierarchies and routines of Harry's commune, is
clearly an insinuating serpentine presence in a new-age Eden. In the
character of Skeeter, the figures of the natural man and the serpent in the
garden come together.

    For the most part, Updike scholars are surprisingly uncritical of
Skeeter. Wayne Falke allows that Skeeter's "agony and sorrow are
somehow holy"; Rabbit realizes "that if he can participate in these he
can become a better person."[32] Joyce Markle praises Skeeter as a
"believer in a world of nonbelievers" and salutes him "as a kind of re-
deemer figure."[33] She suggests that the torching of Rabbit's house is an
example of the way Skeeter "energizes and vitalizes his surroundings."
Although Rabbit's neighbors had been "uninvolved with their society
and hardly knew each other," the threatening presence of a black man in
their midst brings them together, ironically, "for their ultimate act of
discipline and punishment" (159-60). Richard Locke asserts that the
"wide range of tones and rhythms in black speech has never been so well
reproduced in contemporary white writing"[34]; Eugene Lyons disagrees:
"Seldom, if ever has any white writer been paralyzed into sentimental
and self-contradictory blather quite so foolish in attempting to deal with
a black character."[35] Robert Alter's judgment that Updike's portrayal
"of one ordinary American's feelings towards blacks" is "generally per-
suasive" overlooks the rather considerable fact that blacks are Americans, too. Although Alter is concerned that "Updike strains the idea of
black otherness to the limits, Skeeter at times seeming more a projection
of Rabbit's fantasies than an independent personage," he backs away
from the obvious implications of his reading, concluding that "the strategy finally works through its extremeness: the conventional Angstrom is
hypnotized into a trance of passivity by the black man's sheer *outrance*,
compelled to a dazed attentiveness quite unlike his ordinary mental hab-

its by the psychological and rhetorical contortions of the utterly alien black."[36] Robert Detweiler offers an equally implausible equivocation, granting that Skeeter "is unbelievable when judged against the old patterns of reality" but insisting that "he is an embodiment of newer forms of it. He may appear to be an exaggeration, but the new patterns often partake of excess, and, seen in those terms, Skeeter is both a fitting example of the modern hyperexperience and a conceivable product of it."[37] Frederick Karl's claim that "Skeeter himself is simply words, failing to embody anything more than an idea"[38] is one of the more judicious responses to Updike's black messiah.

Updike's critics seem to have difficulty acknowledging and responding to the disturbing, threatening, and finally horrifying behavior and demeanor of one of the most important African-American characters in contemporary fiction by white Americans. To argue about the accuracy of Updike's renditions of either black colloquialisms or the psychedelic new patterns of "modern hyperexperience" is to avoid Rabbit's first and most indicative response to Skeeter: "he is poison, he is murder, he is black" (212). Skeeter is so evil, demented, and unremittingly vicious that he cannot be accepted as a plausible character. He has more in common with his literary predecessors—the shadowy, coercive Fedallah in Herman Melville's *Moby-Dick* comes to mind—than with American blacks in the late 1960s, despite the voyeuristic fascination of some readers with Updike's rather excessive rendition of "black jargon." Like Melville's Babo, the merciless mastermind of a slave ship mutiny in *Benito Cereno*, Skeeter reverses prevailing racial hierarchies, ruling the wretched inhabitants of Harry Angstrom's alternative community with an eye for exacting a grim retribution for historical wrongs. He is a "black Jesus"—a dreadful, demonic parody of a divine judge—an Antichrist with supernatural reservoirs of evil. Far from being the best representation of an African American by a white writer, Skeeter is an empty shell into which Updike pours a centuries-old brew of fear, hatred, and stereotypes.

In the weeks that follow Skeeter's arrival, all normative human bonds and relationships disintegrate within this "alternative" family—

this "refugee camp" (226). A Vietnam veteran, Skeeter claims to be a "black Jesus" who has risen from the mud of Vietnam, "where the world is redoing itself. . . where God is pushing through" (261). Each evening, Rabbit's household assembles to listen to Skeeter's revolutionary gospel of hatred and violence. Skeeter believes that if his divinity is to be manifested, it must be recognized and affirmed by Rabbit and Jill. Because Jill claims to have had a vision of God while on drugs, Skeeter reintroduces her to heroin, hoping she will see his inherent divinity and proclaim him her messiah. At first, Skeeter looks like a "chrysalis of mud. . . . a black crab" (257) to Jill when she is on heroin; however, when she becomes addicted, she tells Skeeter what he wants to hear in her desperation for another "fix."

Skeeter's strategy to win Rabbit's allegiance is more devious: he exploits Harry's fear of and fascination with blacks by offering him the experience of "being a nigger" (296). Skeeter elicits intense, dichotomous responses in Rabbit. One reaction is fathomless fear and horror: "So he is evil. Rabbit in his childhood used to lift . . . the metal waffle-patterned lid on the backyard cesspool. . . . Now this black man opens up under him in the same way: a pit of scummed stench impossible to see to the bottom of" (208). But, to his confusion, he also finds Skeeter to be physically attractive and sexually magnetic: "Physically, Skeeter fascinates Rabbit. . . . Skeeter in his house feels like a finely made electric toy; Harry wants to touch him but is afraid he will get a shock" (250-51). Because Rabbit is emotionally immobilized, lethargic, and resentful, he is particularly susceptible to Skeeter's intoxicating bouts of rage: they substitute for his own stillborn anger. So when Skeeter offers him the opportunity to "know how a Ne-gro feels" (247) by smoking marijuana, Rabbit accepts. Skeeter's increasingly insane pronouncements make sense to Harry when he is "high." Skeeter finally gets the acknowledgment of divinity he craves: Rabbit solemnly responds, "I do believe" (277) when Skeeter announces that he is "the Christ of the new Dark Age" (276).

Updike's narration becomes fragmentary and disjointed when Rabbit starts smoking marijuana—primarily to convey the disorientation of a narcotized consciousness. However, this narrative strategy also conveys Rabbit's confusion when the facade of the nuclear family he has maintained with Jill and Nelson falls away, leaving him paralyzed with uncertainty about how to behave—even toward his own son. Rabbit abdicates any pretense of paternal responsibility, letting his son fend off the taunts and insults of Skeeter at home and the blows and racial epithets of his schoolmates and neighbors. Nelson knows that his father and Jill have been narcotized by Skeeter—his father with marijuana, and Jill with heroin. But his efforts to break through his father's benumbed passivity are in vain: when Nelson pleads that "We *could*" help Jill "if you wanted to. If you cared at all," Rabbit attributes his inaction to their lack of familial alternatives: "She's too old to adopt. And you're too young to marry" (292). After Rabbit apologizes "helplessly" to his son for "the mess we all make" (293), his son's only recourse is to wish for a return to the safe, comforting confines of the nuclear family: "Gee I wish Mom would come back" (294). As Nelson is being led away by the police from the charred remains of his parents' house near the end of the novel, he "seems relieved to be at last in the arms of order, of laws and limits" (326).

Although marijuana allows Rabbit to know how it feels to be black, Skeeter has a further objective: he wants Rabbit to *be* black. He initiates a series of bizarre sexual dramas that transform Rabbit's numb response to his betrayal by Janice and Jill into the sexual disempowerment and emasculation that a fearful white society imposes upon African Americans. One evening, Skeeter complains that he is not allowed to "be a man" by whites. When Rabbit responds, "Go ahead. Be one" (250), Skeeter forces Jill to kiss him while his erstwhile competitor looks on. Although Rabbit claims not to care, his memory of Jill's "mouth defiled by Skeeter's kiss" increases his emotional distance from her. And because marijuana "severs his desires from his groin" (254), he no longer competes with Skeeter for sex with Jill. Instead, he finds himself attracted to Skeeter and fascinated by his games. Jill tells Rabbit that she is scared "Of you and him together" (251). Skeeter is increasingly violent toward Jill in his quest to "be a man," but Rabbit is too resentful of her betrayal of him with Skeeter and her upper class background to intervene. In addition, he is increasingly bound by the role Skeeter has assigned him: "As a white man, Chuck, you don't amount to much, but niggerwise you groove" (277). A few evenings after his first humiliation of Jill, Skeeter acts more aggressively, ripping her dress apart in front of Rabbit and Nelson. After Jill and Nelson escape upstairs, Skeeter demands that Harry read passages from *The Life and Times of Frederick Douglass* aloud. In one of the novel's most distasteful (and implausible) moments, Skeeter masturbates to Rabbit's reading of Douglass, interrupting the narrative with encouragements like "Oh, you do make one lovely nigger." Rabbit is both attracted and repelled:

> Lifting his eyes from the page, Rabbit sees there is no longer a patch of white on the sofa, it is solidly dark, only moving in a whispering rhythm that wants to suck him forward. His eyes do not dare follow down to the hand the live line of reflected light lying the length of Skeeter's rhythmic arm. Long as an eel, feeding. Rabbit stands and strides from the room, dropping the book as if hot. . . . He has escaped. Narrowly. (283)

Rabbit's degradation culminates in a final grotesque psychodrama enacted with Skeeter and Jill. Skeeter assigns Rabbit his role: "You is a big black man sittin' right there. You is chained to that chair. And I, I is white as snow." Skeeter is a slave owner; Jill, who looks to Rabbit for help but gets none, is forced to play an "ebony virgin torn from the valley of the river Niger" (296) in return for another heroin fix. Skeeter demands that Jill perform fellatio on him as a "de-mon-stray-shun of o-bee-deeyance" (297). Updike's horrific parody of black/white relations and the consequences of white guilt in the 1960s is complete. As Edward Vargo points out, "the fellation becomes a ritual to humiliate the white and to atone for white racism" (166). The epigraph that announces this chapter of *Rabbit Redux*—"'We've been raped, we've been raped!'—BACKGROUND NOISE ABOARD SOYUZ 5" (205)—foreshadows its climactic scene. Skeeter's drama abruptly ends when a face that may be Nelson's appears in the window. Harry wipes Jill's spittle from her chin while trying to comfort her, "and, for weeks afterward, when all is lost, will take out this handkerchief and bury his nose in it, in its imperceptible spicy smell" (299).

This handkerchief is almost all Rabbit has left when his house is firebombed by an anonymous neighbor the next evening. As dawn breaks the next day, Harry drives Skeeter out of town and drops him off at a country intersection to help him escape the police—who now want to charge him with setting fire to the Angstroms' house. When Rabbit offers his hand in farewell, Skeeter spits into the center of his palm. Although some critics see this as a baptismal offering from a black Jesus—holy water that promotes health and suggests forgiveness, Skeeter's final gesture is better understood as an act of contempt. Harry has no emotional reaction to Jill's death: when he picks through what is left of his house for any surviving valuables, he "begins to cry from the smoke and the smell" (331)—not from grief. In fact, he is almost elated by the loss of his house: "His house slips from him. He is free" (332). And the net of the law slips from him, too: when the police question him about Skeeter, Rabbit denies any knowledge of his drug dealing. Furthermore, he misrepresents his erstwhile "commune" as a typical family: "I'd come back and we'd cook supper and help the kid with his homework and sit around and talk. It was like having two more kids in the house" (328). When Jill's mother shows up at the West Brewer police station, demanding an explanation for her daughter's death, Rabbit again alters significant details of the life he has been leading: "Each time he was made to tell this story, he reduced the part Skeeter played . . . until the young black man has become in his backwards vision little more substantial than a shadow behind a chair" (344).

The anticlimactic conclusion of *Rabbit Redux* chronicles the efforts of Harry's sister Mim—a Las Vegas call girl—to reconcile Harry and Janice. Mim's intervention is ironic given her professional antipathy to the nuclear family: she seduces Janice's lover, Charlie Stavros, ending Janice's affair. His house a charred shell, Harry moves back to his parents' home and reverts to adolescence. He is "an estranged, because too much older, brother" (351) to his son, Nelson. He masturbates while imagining his sister having sex with his wife's lover. He has a schoolboy's prurient curiosity about Mim's life as a call girl: he seems more interested in her professional experiences than in her efforts to reconstitute his family. There is only one incident in these closing pages of Updike's novel that gives us reason to be sympathetic to or hopeful for Harry Angstrom. One evening, he imagines that Jill's spirit has visited him in his sleep. The palpable sense of her "very breath and presence" in his room forces him to recall the "daughterly attentiveness he had bid her hide" and "her daughterly blind grass-green looking to him for more than shelter." His spasm of grief and realization that he had "retreated to deadness" (380) are the only indications that Rabbit undergoes a moral or spiritual "redux" at the end of this novel. Yet even at this vulnerable and self-aware moment, it is clear that Harry cannot grasp why his relationship with Jill was so inappropriate and, finally, destructive. Harry remembers Skeeter's triumphant last tableau, "but in fantasy now Rabbit rises from the chair to join them, to be a father and lover to them" (381). Harry's reconstruction of this terrible scene of violation omits the power dynamics and role playing that bound him to the chair and overlooks the addiction to heroin that compelled Jill to participate. Furthermore, he is incapable of understanding why it is impossible to be both a father and a lover to them.

The Angstroms agree to discuss the future of what is left of their house and their relationship. Their house lot has appreciated significantly in value: they will realize an enormous profit from this disaster. The novel concludes with their platonic reunion at the Safe Haven Motel. In assessing this second retreat to the nuclear family, we might recall Nick Carraway's final judgment of Tom and Daisy in *The Great Gatsby*: "they smashed up things and creatures and then retreated back into their money or their vast carelessness, or whatever it was that kept them together, and let other people clean up the mess they had made."[39] Harry realizes that Janice's "trip drowns babies; his burns girls. They were made for each other" (395). In *Rabbit, Run* and *Rabbit Redux*, Updike depicts the nuclear family as a deadening, constrictive, and unattractive environment; however, given the horrors and dangers that rage beyond its hearth, it is the only "safe haven" (the name of the motel where Harry and Janice "redock")—the only structure available in contemporary society that offers the possibility of identity and a modicum of warmth and support.

While my focus here has been on the first two novels of Updike's "Rabbit" series, a brief discussion of the final volume, *Rabbit at Rest*, might shed additional light on the tension between adhering to the restrictive confines of the nuclear family and the impulse to violate its rules and norms or to break free entirely. In this fourth novel concerning the Angstrom family, Rabbit is rich and semi-retired from the Toyota business he inherited from his father-in-law; he is no more resigned to his responsibilities as a husband or a father, however, than in Updike's earlier volumes, and overeats haplessly as a means of obliterating his pain, frustration, ennui—himself, finally. He has been a passive participant in a long-term affair with Thelma, the wife of Ronnie, his high school basketball teammate and nemesis. "The whole affair was her idea, though he grew used to it over the years, and built it in."[40] Their illicit relationship is a dance of death—a transgression that the terminally ill Thelma "in her slow dying has not denied herself" (195).

Rabbit has a dream while hospitalized following his first heart attack that expresses both his yearning for a redefinition of sexual and familial boundaries and his frustration and lack of understanding when his own efforts to breach these social and institutional restrictions result in pain, destruction, and death. The dream concerns a sexual embrace of his old lover, Ruth; the physicality of their relationship is no longer taboo:

> Ruth had turned her head not, he felt, in aversion from him but in natural embarrassment at the situation, for she seemed to be living with him and Janice, all together, and Janice was somewhere near them. . . . His embrace of Ruth felt semi-permitted, like an embrace of a legal relation, and his praise of her vivid dress was meant to urge her into his own sense of well-being, of their love being at last all right. He hid his face beside her throat, in the curtain of her many-colored hair, and knew he could fuck her forever, on and on, bottomlessly spilling himself into her solid beauty. (291)

Harry associates the white polka dots on Ruth's "vivid dress" with "the confettilike bits of blossom that littered the sidewalk a month ago on that street of Bradford pear trees" (292). The dazzling, wasteful abundance of pear blossoms is an important recurring image in *Rabbit at Rest*, signifying forbidden but nevertheless irresistible sexual impulses. Harry recalls the pear blossoms before he sleeps with his daughter-in-law, Pru. Their transgression is, in part, a desperate affirmation of life following Nelson's commitment to a drug treatment center and Harry's release from the hospital after an angioplasty procedure. But it is also the last and most devastating rupture of Rabbit's familial bonds:

> The leak onto the windowsill accelerates its tapping. A brilliant close flash shocks the air everywhere and less than a second later a heart-stopping crack and splintering of thunder crushes the house from above. As if in overflow of this natural heedlessness, Pru says "*Shit*," jumps from the bed, slams shut the window, pulls down the shade, tears open her bathrobe and sheds it, and, reaching down, pulls her nightie up over her head. Her tall pale wide-hipped nakedness in the dimmed room is lovely much as those pear trees in blossom along that block in Brewer last month were lovely, all his it had seemed, a piece of paradise blundered upon, incredible. (346)

This fundamental breakdown of normative boundaries and roles can be seen, in part, as an indictment of the nuclear family: there is so little emotional nourishment available that Rabbit and Pru use sex as a means to convey reassurance and to impart or affirm life. But like the grotesque alternative family in *Rabbit Redux*, Rabbit's conduct with Pru represents a "worst case" scenario. As in the previous "Rabbit" novels, there will be devastating consequences for this blunder into the "paradise" of polymorphous sexuality—this foolhardy and destructive release of the "natural heedlessness" of Eros between illicit partners. When Janice learns of Rabbit's sexual encounter with Pru, she tells him, "This is the worst thing you've ever done, ever, ever. . . . now you've done something truly unforgivable" (433). Rabbit makes a final pathetic "run" south rather than help his family work through their shock and shame. But like his run three decades earlier, this flight doesn't take him anywhere new: he awaits with glum passivity his wife's further responses to his elemental violation of trust at the condo they now own in Florida. Given his original youthful vision of the "sunshine state" as a sexual playground in *Rabbit, Run,* it is ironic that he resides in paradise as a retiree decrepit before his time. He is drawn instead to the playground of his youth: the basketball court. Harry Angstrom's final heart attack strikes at an illusory moment of freedom as he soars for one last shot— as unmindful of the gathering coronary explosion within his chest as he is of the shattered bonds of trust and fidelity he has left behind.

4

The Family According to Garp

Midway through John Irving's enormously popular but critically under-rated novel, *The World According to Garp*, his protagonist has attained all of the goals he set for himself as a teenager: T. S. Garp is a husband, father, wrestler, and writer. These four achievements are inextricably intertwined: he "won" the hand of his first and only love, Helen Holm, the daughter of his wrestling coach, by proving to her—and himself—that he is a gifted writer, and he rejected the uncertainty of his unortho-dox upbringing by founding a traditional family. Indeed, Garp begins writing fiction at the end of his freshman year at the Steering School only because Helen has informed him that "If I marry *anybody*, I'll marry a writer."[1] Garp's wife and the "home" her last name promises are, in effect, a "reward" for having successfully completed his first and best work of fiction, "The Pension Grillparzer": "Garp, however, ex-pected more than money or transportation from 'The Pension Grill-parzer.' Very simply, he expected to get Helen Holm to live with him—even marry him" (120). T. S. Garp, a boy without a family, *imagines* a family—a rite of passage to manhood that allows him to *have* a family: "And so she married him; she did what he asked. Helen thought it was a pretty good story for a start" (129).

His domestic life has been uneventful, for the most part—interrupted only by periodic reminders that the world outside the safe, "normal" family he has constructed and striven to protect is dangerous. The random violence and senseless depravity of contemporary society marks Garp with "an urgent need to protect the few people he loved from what he imagined 'everyone else' was like" (174). But when the line between protecting and isolating his children from the world blurs, Garp becomes restless and anxious—prey to a gnawing premonition that the safety he yearns for may elude him precisely because the potential assassin of domestic sanctity and tranquillity may, in fact, be himself:

> There was so much to worry about, when worrying about children, and Garp worried so much about everything; at times, especially in these throes of insomnia, Garp thought himself to be psychologically unfit for parenthood. Then he worried about *that*, too, and felt all the more anxious for his children. What if their most dangerous enemy turned out to be *him*? (196)

This moment of self-consciousness is tragically prophetic: Garp's inability to reconstitute himself as a husband and father will have disastrous consequences. The delicate balance between love and work—between attention to family and devotion to the craft of writing—is disrupted for Garp when he moves from *imagining* a family (the project of "The Pension Grillparzer") to what can only be described as *policing* a family. As his imagination flags, Garp becomes moody, boorish, and overly intrusive in and directive of the lives of his wife and children: "he saw nothing of how his anxiety for the children made the children anxious—tense, even immature. . . . he was so protective of them that he was not allowing them to grow up" (187). As Garp becomes more preoccupied with his own family, his imagination falters; as Garp's work devolves toward second-rate, thinly disguised fictional representations of his own experience, he adopts an increasingly proprietary stance toward his family. This spiral takes on additional significance when we consider that writing, for Garp, is, in fact, a mode of parenting. He defines the writer's goal as "trying to keep everyone alive, forever. Even the ones who must die in the end. They're the most important to keep alive" (437). Even bedtime stories for his children are weighted with embedded morals and admonitions and endued with impossible hope: "the act of imagining a good story for children was a way to keep children safe forever" (187). While the wish to protect everyone forever is a utopian task, the failure of Garp's imagination in this novel *does* precipitate a series of misunderstandings and mishaps culminating in a terrible accident that disables one of his children and kills another. This "failure of imagination" is intimately linked to Garp's failure as a husband and father. When Garp is unable to "parent" with his imagination, he becomes overbearingly paternalistic with his real family. The relationship between these fields of parenting might be clarified if we consider that if Garp had been able to deploy the wisdom and empathy he discovers and promotes in his short story in his own familial relationships, he might have responded to his "crisis of confidence" (181), as Helen describes it, with more flexibility, generosity, and grace.

"The Pension Grillparzer," therefore, is not simply the accomplishment that launches Garp into adulthood: it is an interpretative touchstone that serves as a common reference point for readers and characters alike. Irving gives us the short story and—equally important—the history of its composition. It is one of only two complete works by Garp incorporated within the novel (the other, a mediocre semiautobiographical short story, "Vigilance," is written at the height of Garp's "crisis": Irving includes it as a contrast to its superior and more imaginative predecessor). "The Pension Grillparzer" is presented, as I read Irving's intention, in two parts: a "problem" and its resolution, separated by the experiences in Vienna that will provide Garp with the insight and maturity to complete his story. In an interview with Gabriel Miller, Irving discloses the metaphoric value of Vienna as the "foreign country" of adulthood: "The young Garp goes to Vienna to become a writer, but what happens to him is he goes to someplace to realize what it is he wants, that is, he wants to be married and love someone."[2] Nevertheless, Vienna is also where the fatherless Garp navigates a professional Oedipal crisis of sorts. Before he can write "The Pension Grillparzer," he takes the measure of one of Vienna's most famous writers, the nineteenth-century dramatist Franz Grillparzer, and declares himself the better artist: "Garp *knew* he could do better" (89). A pension bearing Grillparzer's name then, has psychological connotations as well: Garp has imagined a professional space for himself as a writer as well as a fictional residence for his characters.

The importance of "The Pension Grillparzer" is further emphasized by the textual assessments offered by two of the novel's characters before Irving allows Garp to continue and conclude his short story. Garp's mother, Jenny Fields, the eccentric nurse and feminist pioneer, describes it as "the sort of story she'd expect a boy without a proper family to make up." It is a work of fiction inspired, in part, by Garp's childhood experiences within a nontraditional household. Irving also gives us Helen's reading of the story at this crucial juncture in language that provides the title of his novel: "Helen would later say that it is in the conclusion of 'The Pension Grillparzer' that we can glimpse what the world according to Garp would be like" (121). This echo of the novel's title is hardly accidental; Garp's writing instructor at Steering, Mr. Tinch, describes the story as full of "lunacy and sorrow" (129)—the working title of Irving's novel and the title of Donald Whitcomb's posthumous biography of Garp. As Helen's remark indicates, when Garp reconstructs his "world" after the terrible accident that looms at the center of Irving's novel, he will draw upon the lessons and resources of his own fiction.

What, then, distinguishes "The Pension Grillparzer" as a work of art? The story concerns the adventures of a rather conventional family employed in a rather unconventional pursuit: rating hotels and pensions for the Austrian Tourist Bureau. (It is important to note in passing that public spaces like hotels, boarding schools, and orphanages— institutions that subvert or replace the traditional structure and authority of the nuclear family—abound throughout Irving's oeuvre and that of his literary progenitor, Charles Dickens.) Like Macon Leary in Anne Tyler's *The Accidental Tourist*, Garp's characters abhor the inconveniences and disruptions that travel inevitably entails: their criteria for judging temporary residences favor regularity over spontaneity, the familiar over the unknown. The first part of the story details the family's evening at the shabbiest location on their itinerary—a pension whose owners have the audacity to ask that their rating be upgraded from a "C" to a "B." The family is treated to a range of exotic encounters and intrusive experiences: a man walking on his hands in the water closet; a moody unicycling bear careening through the halls; a Hungarian dream teller with a penchant for nonchalantly revealing the most troubling and private productions of a guest's psyche in the most public of places. The family is overwhelmed by this immersion in an alternative community: the carefully calibrated system it has constructed for evaluating the world seems an inadequate if not obsolete response to the vital, vivid universe of the Pension Grillparzer. It finds itself bereft of a methodology of gauging experiences and interpreting the world. This first fragment of the story is followed by a glimpse into its author's creative processes. Garp acknowledges frankly to himself that he is stymied: "And *then* what? Garp wondered." While he doesn't know what his story means or how it might conclude, he is convinced that "everything had to connect." Garp's project is to divine the answer to this central question: "What sort of ending might make them all part of the same world?" (110). In order to resolve his "problem," he must integrate radically disparate notions of family. How does this traditional family absorb rather than recoil from a destabilizing experience and reconstitute a more flexible and forgiving system for "rating" the world?

Garp is able to finish his story after the middle-aged prostitute with whom he has had a relationship dies of cancer. Charlotte has been a friend, lover, and mother-figure to Garp, and his confusion over the relative weight of each of these personas in their relationship allows him to speculate about the occasionally arbitrary nature of familial boundaries. When Garp returns to his story, he weaves a web of familial bonds that unites the pension's odd denizens and connects the evening's seemingly autonomous occurrences. The sister of Herr Theobald, the pension manager, married first one, then another performer of the Circus Szolnok—a bizarre, unsuccessful community of troublemakers and misfits who reside at the pension because there is nowhere else for them to go. The unconventional space of a pension hosts an alternative "family" of performers in which Herr Theobald's sister (she is never given a name, a strategy that draws attention to her familial status) enjoys a fluidity of function similar to Charlotte's: "in time, I imagined, she would cease being lover and sister to them, respectively, and become a mother to them all. She was already a mother to the bear" (124).

The traveling family of inspectors implicitly recognizes the validity of this alternative community by sanctioning the Pension Grillparzer with a "B" rating. This concession seems to precipitate the death of the narrator's grandmother—the least tolerant family member; it also renders the rest of his family unfit for the profession of ranking hotels, and they soon retire. When the narrator's father accepts a job with a detective agency, he pays homage to the Pension Grillparzer's spirit of forgiveness by refusing to work "during the Christmas season—when, he said, some people ought to be allowed to steal a little" (126). The resolution of the tension between the family of inspectors and the "blended" family of Herr Theobald mirrors a dialectic that operates within each frame of Irving's novel. *The World According to Garp* is structured around pairs of traditional and nontraditional families. The most significant pairings are Garp's unconventional childhood at the Steering School infirmary and the privileged Percy family, and Garp's attempt as an adult to maintain a traditional family and the alternatives of "Mrs. Ralph" (the sloppy, hedonistic mother of one of his children's friends) and the feminist communities that Jenny Fields supports. Irving repeatedly deconstructs these tensions—often by revealing that seemingly incontrovertible polarities are actually false dichotomies. One example will suffice for now: the Percy clan—the novel's most stereotypically normative family—also produces "Pooh," its most deranged, violent extremist.

Garp's narrator is haunted by the memory of his evening of mayhem at the Pension Grillparzer, and returns years later—only to find that many of the circus performers have died in cruelly ironic ways. Herr Theobald's sister—the lone survivor—presides over the dilapidated pension with the ennui of "a storyteller who is accepting of unhappy endings, as if her life and her companions had never been exotic to *her*—as if they had always been staging a ludicrous and doomed effort at reclassification" (128). Sadly, there are echoes of this dénouement in each of the narrative frames of Irving's novel. The brother of Garp's narrator is an innocent victim of a senseless act of political terrorism. Garp's mother will be assassinated by a right-wing antifeminist deer hunter; Garp will die at the hands of a childhood acquaintance—an adherent of a fringe feminist movement befriended (if not fully condoned) by his mother. The irony of these tragic conclusions appears to belie the efforts of characters at each layer of Irving's convoluted narrative to live purposefully and to forge cohesion and community in an atomistic age.

Nevertheless, in the world according to Irving, fate's inexorable twists fail to undermine completely the project that his novel's title announces: the necessity of formulating a consistent and consoling framework for making sense of and participating in the world. Carol C. Harter and James R. Thompson provide a reading of the novel that recognizes the comedy and spirit of generosity in Garp's fiction, but overlooks the guidance for understanding and negotiating life that his best work of art offers:

> While the characters in Garp's fiction will forever be engaged in the optimistic pursuit of transcendent value and meaning, their "efforts at reclassification"—at imbuing life with structure, order, and meaning—will inevitably be doomed. But for these efforts, Garp will always find laughter and sympathy in the artistic act and will reflect those in the stuff of his art.[3]

This assessment of the power of art to promote "laughter and sympathy" is finally somewhat constricted, however. Garp *learns* from his art: he turns to his best work in an effort to fulfill the vision of what "the world according to Garp" might be. Prior to the accident that Gabriel Miller describes as "the most devastating scene in all of Irving's fiction,"[4] Garp was unable to alter his own value system—particularly his narrow definition of parenthood—to reflect the inclusiveness and generosity of the Pension Grillparzer's extended family. Although the conventional family in Garp's short story recognizes and is transformed by the dignity and cohesion displayed by the members of this eccentric circus community rendered unemployable by the arbitrary location of the iron curtain (their acts are comprehensible only to a Hungarian audience), Garp, by contrast, is conspicuously bereft of sympathy for the extended family that is drawn to his feminist pioneering mother. Robert(a) Muldoon, a transvestite (and a former professional football player), is, significantly, the first resident of the world according to Jenny Fields who can "pass" in Garp's world: ironically, their athletic competition fosters a transaction akin to male bonding. Only Roberta can breach the barrier of disdain and outright hostility that Garp erects to distance himself from what he sees as the self-pitying solipsism of the community of "victims" that evolves around his mother and the monstrous excesses of the Ellen James Society—a cadre of radical feminists who cut out their own tongues to protest the similar mutilation of a young rape victim. After the accident, Garp is thrown together with the Ellen Jamesians as a convalescent at his mother's estate: because his broken jaw has been wired shut, he is as tongueless as the Ellen Jamesians he has so despised. It is Roberta who is able to make Garp see the irony of his condition and the lesson to be learned from his new-found perspective: "'There's such sympathy for people, in what you *write*,' Roberta told him, suddenly. 'But I don't see that much sympathy in you, in your real life,' she said" (273). Roberta aptly names the personal deficiency Garp works to correct in the latter half of Irving's novel. Garp eventually learns to be more sympathetic to the fears, failings, and eccentricities of others—even when their desperate efforts to forge community seem ludicrous. He creates an extended household that blends the best elements of the familial options to which he has been exposed. Garp's world is a new family.

The opening chapter of *The World According to Garp* has little to do with the novel's central figure. Instead, Irving provides us with a parodic sketch of "the world according to the archetypical Brahmin nuclear family." The Fields are wealthy, aristocratic, and genteel—possessed of a distant sense of noblesse oblige that requires family members to sit on the "wrong side" of the train in order to view the unsavory squalor of the working class communities where the factories manufacturing and the billboards promoting the shoe wear that bears the family name are located—"the grimy source of their independence and higher life" (4). They are repressed and repressive in a myriad of quiet, determined, and dignified ways having to do with familial expectations and socially defined roles and obligations. Jenny Fields is, significantly, the only daughter in a family dominated by powerful and successful men, and this first chapter traces her efforts to escape the heavy chains of patriarchy. She drops out of college when she suspects that the real business of Wellesley was preparing her to be "eventually mated to some well-bred man" (3). She further scandalizes her family by choosing to become a nurse—both as a means to be self-supporting and as an antidote to the rarefied, prissy, and superficial environment of her childhood. But Jenny's most egregious breach of conduct, from her family's perspective, is her decision not to marry. Rather than serving as Jenny's principal source of nurturing and support, her family becomes instead the locus of the most intense and fantastical imaginings and accusations concerning her morals and sexual conduct.

The novel's first important episode provides the reader with an opportunity to assess the prejudices Jenny's family and society fall back upon to judge her violent response to a sexual assault. No one can understand why she would slash the arm of a soldier in a movie theater who ignored her demand that he stop attempting to fondle her. Despite Jenny's protestations, the police and her family presume that she had been dating the soldier or had provoked his attention in some way. Jenny's preparedness to defend herself also makes her guilty: one police officer tells her she shouldn't carry a scalpel for self-defense because "That's asking for trouble" (9). The matter is resolved only when the police discover the soldier has a wife and child: the case against Jenny is dropped in order to spare the soldier's family the humiliation of a public trial. This is the first of many sexual assaults in *The World According to Garp*, and Irving makes clear that women are vulnerable and violated at multiple levels: Jenny is defenseless in a world where the privileged sanctity of the traditional family unit is more important than respect for the safety and autonomy of individual women. She formulates the famous first paragraph and the title of what will be her autobiography, *A Sexual Suspect*, as she ponders the hard truths this experience has taught her: "In this dirty-minded world, . . . you are either somebody's wife or somebody's whore—or fast on your way to becoming one or the other. . . I wanted a job and I wanted to live alone. . . That made me a sexual suspect" (112). This prototypical episode establishes a link between narrow societal conceptions of the proper role of women within the family and the violence that threatens those who challenge these norms.

Jenny forsakes her efforts to win her family's understanding and approval, embarking instead on a project that will fulfill her desire for "a baby with no strings attached" (12). Cast out and maligned by her own traditional family, Jenny seeks to found an alternative. She subverts the nuclear family's central rite of passage, its raison d'être, in the most bizarre conception scene in contemporary American fiction. Jenny chooses to impregnate herself with the "absurdly fertile" (21) seed of a World War II ball turret gunner with a severe head wound who is dying on her ward at Boston Mercy Hospital. This is not a "benign rape" (a troubling oxymoron) as Carol C. Harter and James R. Thompson have suggested.[5] Technical Sergeant Garp consents to this sexual union: "'*Good*,' he agreed, distinctly. But it was only a word from his wrecked memory, thrown clear for a moment when he came inside her. It was the first and last true word that Jenny Fields heard him speak: good" (22). Technical Sergeant Garp is, significantly, himself an orphan: thus, the efforts of Jenny's family to retrieve, impose, or invent a traditional male lineage for their unwelcome grandchild are completely thwarted. Jenny refuses to placate them by giving her son a name honoring one of her venerable ancestors. The baby is given initials instead of a name—T. S., referring to his father's occupation: Technical Sergeant.

> Her father was furious. 'T. S. Garp!' he hollered. 'What kind of a name for a baby is *that*?'
> 'All his own,' Jenny told him, later. 'It's his *own* goddamn name, all his own.' (24)

Throughout his novel, Irving challenges the most significant obstacle to the inextricably linked goals of equality for women and a wider range of more flexible familial models: the argument that "biology is destiny."

He subverts this notion most literally by representing a number of trans-sexual characters, most notably Roberta Muldoon. But there are subtler jabs at the theory that we are imprisoned by our predetermined biological roles and functions as well. Irving mocks, for example, the privileged and mystified status we accord male progenitors. Technical Sergeant Garp undergoes a process of biological regression even as the fetus he has fathered unwittingly is developing in Jenny's womb. Jenny charts both trajectories with keen interest, particularly when father and son achieve a kind of biological parity in their respective cycles: "He was back in the womb, Jenny knew; he resumed a fetal position, tucked up small in the center of the bed. . . . One morning Jenny watched him kick with his small, weak feet; she imagined she felt a kick *inside*" (22). Garp the father dies before the birth of his son. He would have been an un-wanted appendage to the household in which the androgynous, independent, strong-willed, and opinionated Jenny Fields will raise her child.

T. S. Garp will grow up in the untraditional environs of the boarding school that employs his mother as a residential head nurse, with a kindly, befuddled dean, a stuttering writing instructor, and the wrestling coach who will eventually be his father-in-law as male role models. Irving juxtaposes the willfully eccentric, life-enhancing individuality of these men to the placid pomposity of this community's most traditional patriarch. Stewart Percy is an incompetent buffoon—little more than a stud servicing his impeccably pedigreed wife, Midge, the last descendent of the famous merchant who founded the Steering school; he is "frequently undressed at home. . . . out of necessity—for all the pro-creation he was responsible for" (44). "Fat Stew," as he is known to the boarding school's boys, teaches a single history course called "My Part of the Pacific," focusing primarily on the rather unlikely confluence of events that led to his courtship of Midge Steering while he was stationed in the navy and she was vacationing nonchalantly on Hawaii during World War II. Irving's satire aims both to undermine the sense of entitlement and privilege that surrounds the bourgeois nuclear family and to uncover its inherent xenophobia. The stark alternative experiment of Garp's childhood is defined against the stereotypically myopic "world

according to Fat Stew" (47). While Garp is "small" and "dark," Fat
Stew's seemingly innumerable offspring are "albino-like, almost trans-
lucent-skinned" (42)—possessed of mythic Aryan traits. The Steering
community reveres the "strong, protective genes" (43) of these children;
"their hair seemed to stay in place, their skin did not break out" (42). As
the last descendants of the community's founding father, the Percys are
judged by the genes of their progenitor—not by their own merits or ac-
complishments. More than anyone else at the Steering School, Fat Stew
is affronted by the presence of Jenny Fields and her illegitimate son. His
disdain is most graphically displayed after the Percy family dog bites off
part of the young Garp's ear. When the boy stumbles into the rambling
Steering mansion for medical help, Fat Stew examines not his bleeding
ear but his eyes: "peering into these apparent indices of paternity, he
pronounced Garp Japanese."[6]

This childhood trauma will trigger a series of aftershocks that will
reverberate throughout Garp's life and lead to his premature and violent
end. Garp's first sexual experience will be with Cushie Percy, Fat
Stew's promiscuous daughter. In order to sneak her out of the Steering
estate on the night of his graduation, Garp must wrestle again with
"Bonkers," the errant Newfoundland, exacting a reciprocal retribution
by biting off part of the ancient dog's ear. Garp and Cushie make love in
a hospital bed at the Steering infirmary—reminiscent of the one night
Technical Sergeant Garp spent with Jenny Fields. Cushie's hopelessly
infantilized sister, Bainbridge, (nicknamed "Pooh" because of her predilection for diapers) is emotionally scarred by the maiming of Bonkers;
she will irrationally associate Cushie and Garp's night of sex with her
sister's death, years later, in childbirth. Pooh—who will become an adherent of the Ellen Jamesian feminist movement—will assassinate Garp
(in retribution for both his opposition to her society's practices and for
the death of Cushie) in the same womb-like wrestling room where he
first has sex with Helen Holm after winning her hand in marriage with a
successful short story. (Despite Irving's professed disdain for the self-
referential quality of much of contemporary fiction,[7] *The World According to Garp* is itself a convoluted narrative: an intricate weave of threads

from Irving's earlier fiction, veiled autobiographical echoes, and recurring systems, codes, and images.)[8]

This dialectic of sex and violence—played out in the unlikely environs of hospital beds and wrestling rooms—is intertwined with another causal spiral that touches the lives of the novel's principal characters and threatens their shared project of establishing and maintaining community. Irving plots a series of incidents precipitated by Garp's inability to be empathetic—his inadequate performances in the "fields of parenting" I discussed earlier—that lead to the novel's most significant and strategically central event. This lack of empathy is most destructively displayed in uncaring, casual sexual encounters. Irving's characters grapple with what Garp's mother describes bluntly and unsympathetically as the problem of lust: "'The world is sick with lust. . . . lust gets them all, in the end,' said Jenny Fields, morosely" (131). Jenny Fields devotes a chapter of her autobiography to the subject of "lust," using her embarrassed son as her main exhibit. Despite his upbringing by a mother who has "solved" the problem of lust by permanently repressing her erotic impulses and needs, young Garp, unfortunately, sometimes sees women as little more than a potential means to sexual gratification.

The chapter describing Garp's early married life is, ironically, a sophisticated meditation upon the relationship between lust and varying degrees of sexual violence. Ominously entitled "More Lust," the chapter lends credence to Jenny's puritanical vision. Although Garp has "won" the hand of the woman he loves, he is still subject to bouts of lust. Garp employed prostitutes during his European sojourn to sate his sexual urges; in the less cosmopolitan locale of a suburban college town, he instead targets college-aged baby sitters as potential sexual conquests. Irving's depiction of one of Garp's seductions follows an incident of child sexual abuse that serves as a sobering interpretive frame. While jogging in a local park, Garp comes upon a child who has been raped. In attempting to elicit a description of the perpetrator, Garp is horrified as much by her violation as by her devastated silence: "Apparently, her words were gone; or her *tongue*, Garp thought, recalling Ellen James" (142). Garp humiliates and assaults an elderly man he mistakes for the rapist before helping to catch "the Mustache Kid," a man who shaved his mustache after each rape to elude identification and capture. A few months after this adventure, the elderly man—who understandably has confused Garp with the real criminal—is outraged when he comes upon Garp buying a package of prophylactics which he assumes will be utilized in another act of rape. Garp, typically brusque and unempathetic, does nothing to disillusion him. But when Garp encounters the Mustache Kid working as a ticket-taker at a high school basketball game, he is taunted by the brash young rapist: "'That dumb girl wouldn't even *talk*.'" Garp, too, is outraged, and experiences a rare and important moment of empathy: "He felt a sudden sympathy for the madness of the old man. . . . He felt such a terrible sense of injustice that he could even imagine some very unhappy woman despairing enough to cut off her own tongue" (147). But Garp is unable to act upon this moment of recognition or alter his behavior to allow for a more empathetic stance toward the myriad victims who populate his world.

In the representation of one of Garp's seductions that follows, Irving makes clear that it is a callous, exploitative encounter—a premeditated exercise of privilege and power that is confusing and hurtful for the young baby sitter. Cindy is nicknamed "Little Squab Bones" by Helen because she is "a tiny thing, all flutters and twitches and coos—as trusting, as constant, and as stupid as a Steering pigeon." Garp recognizes that this young woman is needy, vulnerable, and naive, but he allows his predatory instincts to harden his heart:

> Little Squab Bones, Garp thought, was puppy-brained, and as soft and as easily influenced as a banana. But he wanted her, he realized, and he saw her as simply available—like the whores on the Kärtnerstrasse, she would be there when he asked her. And she would cost him only lies. (140)

Garp "likened his guilt for the seduction of Little Squab Bones to a rapelike situation. . . . Are not the worst crimes premeditated?" (149). The aforementioned prophylactics are actually intended for a lesser crime: a night of sex with his coerced baby sitter. The "plundered Little Squab Bones" feels terribly violated: "Cindy had cried under him, her back bent against a suitcase. . . . And though Cindy still had her tongue, she'd been *unable* to speak to him when he left her" (151). Like the raped child in the park and Ellen James (and the fanatical women who emulate Ellen James's mutilation as a means of "articulating" their rage), she becomes another silent victim of "lust."

Garp confesses his predilection for baby sitters to the wife of Harrison Fletcher, a friend and faculty colleague of Helen's who is having an affair with a student, in a vain attempt to console her by conveying a sense of the universal appeal of lust. Once the news of Garp's marital infidelity is introduced as evidence in the tense standoff between the Fletchers, it is only a matter of time before Helen is informed. Helen instigates a "spouse swapping" situation as a means of reasserting control within her marriage; she exacts a peculiar revenge by reducing Garp to a state of powerlessness "as speechless as an Ellen Jamesian" when she orders him to take Alice Fletcher home for the first time. She also aims to show her colleague that his infatuation with a young student is foolish: "'You simple son of a bitch,' Helen told him. 'You fuck a student and call her special—you insult your wife, you insult me. *I'll* show you what's special'" (156). Helen's freedom from lust in this brief and implausible episode is empowering at first, but she finds the frenzied passion of her husband and the Fletchers to be increasingly distressing. Lust has been multiplied—not diminished. "But Helen, enjoying it the least of them, suffered it the most; when she finally called an end to it, she couldn't help but show her euphoria. The other three couldn't help but show their resentment" (158). Helen has gained nothing from these months of "open marriage"; Garp is still subject to bouts of lust; Harrison is soon having an affair with yet another student.

Helen's dissatisfaction is compounded when Garp chooses to make a thinly veiled account of this marital impasse the topic of a novel, *Second Wind of the Cuckold*. This unsuccessful fictional endeavor precipitates Garp's "crisis in confidence": his own life has become so odd that his lived experience dwarfs anything his imagination might produce.[9] Garp's increasingly vigilant and protective stance toward his family is a response to his experience of diminished imagination—a sense that the "reality" of the world is more powerful than the mind's ability to shape or make sense of it. His peevish and eccentric behavior is another source of frustration and resentment for Helen. Garp's "vast and naive wish" to "make the world *safe*" (199) propels him into compromising situations and precipitates a further erosion of Helen's trust and confidence.

Irving's decision to devote a chapter to one of Garp's misunderstood missions to protect a family member underlines the importance of this futile, deluded quest and its destabilizing consequences. When Garp regrets having consented to his son's wish to stay over at a friend's house, he makes an impulsive decision to jog there in the middle of the night to confirm that Duncan is safe. The mother of Duncan's friend is known as "Mrs. Ralph" to Garp—in part because he can never remember her real name, but more importantly, because he defines her by her relationship to her son, Ralph. Like the Percy family, Mrs. Ralph is a reference point against which we can judge Garp: she is as careless and carefree about her parental responsibilities as he is diligent and overbearing. But Irving intends the reader to see that Garp is in fact an equal menace to the well-being of his children. He may be "convinced he's coming to Duncan's aid, rescuing his son from the randy Mrs. Ralph" (200), but one outcome of his anxious intrusion is a renewed awareness of his own randiness—his barely contained lust for Mrs. Ralph: "Sickened with embarrassment, Garp feels he could come by just looking at her" (207). Gabriel Miller captures the futility of Garp's excursion: "Having engaged in some pointless sexual fencing with Mrs. Ralph, also having managed clumsily to arouse Helen's jealousy, he finally retreats ineffectually from the scene, dragging along with him a sleepy and confused Duncan."[10] Furthermore, Duncan is inadvertently exposed to a spectacle worse than anything he might have witnessed at Mrs. Ralph's when the police apprehend Garp—fearing he is a kidnapper and potential child molester rather than an anxious parent retrieving his child from a slumber party gone awry; father and son are escorted home by the police, to the dismay and chagrin of Helen. The chapter ends with the first salvo of yet another argument between Helen and Garp over his inexplicable behavior: "'I love you so much, and I know you so well,' Helen began" (215).

Helen rightly suspects that lust is at the heart of Garp's misadventure with Mrs. Ralph: she is given an opportunity to act on her cumulative anger shortly after this episode when a brash, cocky graduate student offers himself as her lover. He courts her as Garp once did: with fiction. Garp "saw with a typical writer's jealousy that someone else's *words*" were occupying Helen's attention: "Some instinct told him to court her again" (228). Unfortunately, the product of these curiously vexed impulses is a second-rate short story haunted by his parental anxieties and phobias and lacking in imagination—"a dull, self-indulgent exercise about a father chasing a careless man whose driving threatens children in a quiet suburban neighborhood."[11] Helen's annoyance at Garp's current inadequacies as a writer and a husband prompts her to accede to Michael Milton's proposal. Helen "rather cold-bloodedly" pursues a relationship "that has far greater meaning for Milton than for her."[12] Her sexual exploits—here and during the spouse-swapping episode with the Fletchers—are a means to asserting control or exacting revenge: she is reacting to Garp's "lust" by acting self-indulgently.

Garp's "vigilance" precipitates the very disaster he imagines: the dangerous driver of his short story will be himself. Despite his own history of marital infidelity and the tolerance and forgiveness his best fiction extolls, Garp is enraged when he discovers Helen's affair. His intemperance contributes to a bizarre automobile accident in his own driveway that will break his jaw, sexually maim Michael Milton, blind Duncan in one eye, and kill his younger son, Walt. Irving insists upon Garp's culpability by prefacing this terrible central episode with a telling dream. In his nightmare, Garp is succumbing to his lust by looking at a pornographic magazine when he should be assisting his family at a time of crisis. His wife and mother are herding children into a bomb shelter: "If they looked at Garp at all, they regarded him with vague sadness and with scorn, as if he had let them all down and was powerless to help them now." Duncan and Walt hold hands at the end of the line of children—"the natural reaction to a disaster among children" (241)—

providing each other with the sense of guidance and safety they cannot receive from their father. Garp's impotence and guilt are compounded when he is unable to intercede in a nightmare little Walt is having—a dream within a dream: "But in Garp's dream, Garp could not wake the child from *this* one. . . . it was *not* a dream . . . Walt could not be helped" (242). The full significance of Garp's prescience is realized at the moment of the accident: as Garp's darkened Volvo, "shrouded in ice" (265), speeds toward the parked car in which Helen is performing oral sex on Michael Milton, his excited but nervous children reassure each other: "'It's like a dream!' said Walt; he reached for his brother's hand" (266).

The accident ends the cycle of lust that has determined much of what has transpired in Garp's life up to this point;[13] the second half of Irving's novel chronicles how Garp overcomes the emotional trauma this tragedy precipitates. Garp's efforts to become whole can be seen as two inextricably connected projects: reconstituting himself as a man, and reimagining the contours, context and dynamics of his family. Both tasks require a degree of empathy that Garp has been remarkably bereft of until this point in the novel—an unusual deficit, given his untraditional childhood and his profession. Garp recognizes that male sexual aggression—male lust—can be a destructive force that must be controlled and contained; he acknowledges the value of the feminine personality traits he has repressed, and seeks to develop them. My reading of *The World According to Garp* is at odds with that offered by Marilyn French, who condemns the novel in part because it is populated by "charming androgynes" who are "capable of living out all parts of themselves."[14] Rather, the novel depicts a world of victims who are physically, emotionally, or sexually maimed pursuing meaning or wholeness in ways that are alternately useful or destructive. More importantly, Irving's novel charts the *transformation* of his central character.[15] Although Garp is the son of a noted feminist pioneer, he is also raised in the male world of a boarding school: he is socialized in a world of masculine privilege and power. The Steering School—resented by Jenny and Helen because of its exclusion of girls from attendance and women from positions of authority—in some ways represents in microcosm patriarchal society at large. Although Garp is superficially concerned with gender equality in the first half of Irving's novel, simply assuming most of the household and child care responsibilities and demonstrating an aversion to the most extreme act of violence and coercion against women— rape—is not enough. As we have seen, Garp is capable of engaging in insidiously coercive behavior that he himself feels is uncomfortably analogous to rape; his wild, vengeful behavior when he learns of Helen's affair with Michael Milton is amply indicative of the double standard that operates in his marriage and the inherent lack of equality that entails.

Garp and his remaining family members recuperate in a world of women: the Fields family estate—now a feminist community of "damaged girls and women" (273) healing themselves under the aegis of Jenny Fields. With his broken jaw wired shut, Garp is reduced to a state of frustrated silence that compels him to empathize with the Ellen Jamesians who are drawn to his mother. "Thus forced to become like the group he hates, Garp begins his mental and emotional journey toward the sympathy, control, and tolerance that are missing from his headstrong personality."[16] The novel Garp writes during his convalescence, *The World According to Bensenhaver*, is really an extraordinary self-exorcism: he purges himself of the lust and need for control that have crippled him by projecting these traits onto a fictional character. "*The World According to Bensenhaver* is about the impossible desire of the husband, Dorsey Standish, to protect his wife and child from the brutal world" (319). After his wife is brutally raped, Dorsey Standish hires the police detective who helped rescue her as a family bodyguard. Although Arden Bensenhaver's role eventually devolves to policing instead of protecting the family, he is ineffectual at both. One of the Standish children accidentally chokes to death; Hope Standish's ongoing affair eludes the detection of both her husband and Bensenhaver. The family is abruptly released from its state of siege after Dorsey Standish is accidentally shot to death by Bensenhaver while prowling the house trying to outwit his family, imagined rapists and child molesters, and the detective

he has hired to protect them. Hope has a child by her lover and constructs a more flexible, forgiving, and egalitarian family structure.

> The terrible anxiety of Dorsey Standish, which has been so crippling
> to all their lives, is at last lifted from them. Hope and her children live on,
> even cheerfully dealing with the wild rantings of old Bensenhaver, too
> tough to die, who goes on and on with his versions of the nightmarish world
> from his wheelchair in an old-age home for the criminally insane. (321)

Irving again offers a number of critical responses from his characters to Garp's fiction—readings that help to shape our own understanding of the significance of Garp's artistic project. The cleaning woman
who serves as a secret "test market" for Garp's editor describes the
audience of *The World According to Bensenhaver* as those who need
"to be reminded what men in this world is like" (325). Garp's mother
admires the novel for its depiction of "the stupid male anxieties that
women are asked to suffer and endure" (323). Bensenhaver's "world"
has been Garp's, but by pouring his fear of this world—this social construct—into the mold of fiction, Garp is able to free himself of its constrictions and limitations. Garp avoids responding to his family's tragedy with the "terrible anxiety of Dorsey Standish"—a dark, doomed
reworking of himself. Imagining this alternative figure allows him to eschew Dorsey's obsession and despair in favor of forgiveness and the
life-enhancing act of fathering another child with Helen. Garp's final,
unfinished work of fiction, *My Father's Illusions*, continues this didactic
use of literature as a field within which alternative selves can be tested
and explored. This novel is another manifestation of Garp's ongoing
project of weaning himself from his dangerously impossible desire to
"make the world *safe*" (199). Garp imagines a father whose life is devoted to "establishing little utopias for his kids to grow up in"; sadly, the
utopias are experienced as impoverishing and imprisoning by his children—the source of "dreadful memories" (333) rather than feelings of
idealism or security. And near the end of his life, Garp finally recognizes
the significance of his first and best work of fiction: he makes a symbolic return to the vision of "The Pension Grillparzer" by consenting to

a special printing illustrated by Duncan. This act is conclusive evidence that Garp *has* learned from his fiction, that he has reconstituted himself in the light of his best instincts and imaginings.

The assassination of Jenny Fields at a political rally for a female gubernatorial candidate in New Hampshire thrusts Garp into a series of unaccustomed roles and experiences that accelerate his metamorphosis toward an empathetic identity. When men are banned from the "first feminist funeral," Garp disguises himself as a woman to gain entry to the memorial service and bear witness to his mother's legacy and memory—albeit from a disempowered distance. Although Garp's strong, androgynous mother and his friendship with the transvestite Roberta Muldoon have helped to breach the rigidity of his societally inherited notions of gender functions and roles, the experience of *being* a woman exposes Garp to the harassment and vulnerability that are part of women's daily lives in a society where too many men—Garp included—view them as potential sexual conquests. As Garp fends off a series of unsavory advances and propositions, he feels "a peculiar kind of unfairness overwhelm him. He had not asked to have such an anatomy" (363). Dressed in a garish costume and outfitted with enormous false breasts, Garp is himself an object of "lust"; he is forced to acknowledge his complicity in a web of attitudes and behaviors that has denied women an essential element of human dignity.

The death of Jenny Fields also precipitates an auspicious encounter between Garp and the girl whose terrible rape and mutilation inspired the sympathetic emulation of the Ellen Jamesians. Recently bereft of her own parents, Ellen James had been en route to the Fields estate at Jenny's invitation: orphaned, so to speak, once again, Ellen James approaches Garp the writer as a potential mentor. Garp "knew what his mother would have done. He knew Helen wouldn't mind; and of course Roberta would always be of help. And all those women who'd been wounded and were now healed, in their fashion" (365). Garp "adopts" Ellen James—a gesture made possible, in part, by his ability to acknowledge Roberta's status as part of an extended "family" that can be relied upon in times of need. Ellen James's desire to become a writer reinforces the link between Garp's dual "fields of parenting": the empathetic spirit and inclusive family structures he imagines in his best fiction, and his efforts to realize this vision in his own life.

Not every reader agrees that Garp's reconstruction of his family is a healthy development. Susan Gilbert, for example, finds that "from this mid-point in the novel, lines to connect their family to others are not extended but reduced. All who come to the house are in retreat, from injury, injustice, misunderstanding, intolerance."[17] But Garp *chooses* his family and associates; he does not acquiesce to an assemblage of victims, as Gilbert seems to suggest. Instead, he extends a confident and generous offer of support and recognition to concentric circles of kin. Garp now sees many of the women his mother had assisted as familial resources—not victims to be shunned or distrusted. Having been "wounded" himself, he recognizes the value of learning from the healing processes of others. "It had been a proper funeral for Jenny Fields, after all; some essential message had passed from mother to son. . . . T. S. Garp decided he would try to *be* more like his mother, Jenny Fields" (367). Because Jenny's will designates her son as the new director of the Fields foundation, Garp learns to exercise his hard-won insight to help foster a nurturing environment where women with problems can enjoy a brief respite from the world.

By adopting Ellen James, Garp is able to both atone for his callous acts of seduction and expand the boundaries of his family. (Significantly, the women Garp exploited were vulnerable precisely because they had been invited within the familial circle to serve as baby sitters—surrogate parents. Garp's inability or unwillingness to recognize the familial bond he has forged with these young women makes his coercive behavior particularly reprehensible.) After his seduction of Little Squab Bones, Garp reflected upon the vulnerability of young women in a society where predatory lust is so rampant: "Garp didn't want a daughter because of *men*. Because of *bad* men, certainly; but even, he thought, because of men like *me*" (151). But Garp's willingness to assume a parental role in the life of a young woman is the surest sign of his rehabilitation: "It was perhaps his contact with Ellen James that finally cured him of ever looking at young girls in that way. . . . Enough of his life had been influenced by lust" (378). Garp's adoption of Ellen James also signifies that he has come to terms with his inordinate fear for the fragile safety of his family. He claims as kin a young woman who has already suffered the worst of the world's violence and helps her to construct an identity and find her voice as a poet.

Although Irving provides us with a lengthy and ingenious epilogue "warning us about the future" (407), the remainder of *The World According to Garp* is somewhat anticlimactic. Garp struggles to maintain his newly-won sense of community and empathy—losing his equanimity only once, in what will prove to be a fatal—albeit understandable—display of anger. When his daughter's essay, "Why I'm Not an Ellen Jamesian" triggers a furor among those who have found meaning and purpose in sharing the mutilation of a young martyr, Garp defends her in a hostile and public debate with the most fanatical fringe of the Ellen Jamesian Society. Garp lapses into an accustomed posture—defending his family from outside threats or aggression. Unfortunately for Garp, one of the most recent adherents of this movement is his demented childhood acquaintance, "Pooh," who blames him for her sister's untimely death in childbirth because Cushie and Garp had once had sex. Garp's assassination by Pooh is a telling indication that Irving's advocacy of an extended community is not akin to the failed utopianism his protagonist imagines in his novel, *My Father's Illusions*. There *is* danger in the world: Irving advises us to forge communities and live purposefully despite the myriad threats of personal or collective extinction. Our fight for cohesion and meaning can help us live in the world—not escape it.

Garp and his extended family celebrate life even though they suspect that the "undertoad" (Walt's malapropism for "undertow"—which Garp uses to personify the dangers lurking beneath the deceptively tranquil surface of the world) will visit ruin upon each of them sooner or later. Irving's "epilogue" parallels the conclusion of Garp's "The Pension Grillparzer" in its provision of an exhaustive record of the often unfortunate and untimely demises of most of his characters—a Homeric insistence that the manner and circumstances of death are worthy of the permanence of art: "in the world according to Garp, we are all terminal cases" (437).[18] John Irving's characters are heroic because they insist upon living and loving fully in the face of the arbitrary and incomprehensible power of the "undertoad" to rob them—through violence or death—of the very connectedness to others that is their most cherished and sustaining achievement.

5

The Emergent Woman's Family
in *The Color Purple*

Alice Walker's *The Color Purple* is a blueprint for fundamental social change generated within the reconstructed family. Her narrative is completely contained within and structured by the letters of two sisters who are separated for three decades—missives that serve as screens onto which their most private agonies and exultations are scribbled into consciousness and language. The privileging of the personal realm that Walker's choice of the epistolary genre allows calls attention to the private site where social change originates in this novel. In *The Color Purple*, African-American women must marshal their courage, perseverance, and resourcefulness to challenge and reform what Walker identifies as the most significant source of and container for oppression, racism, and imperialism: the patriarchal family.[1] The structures and modes of interaction that replace the traditional family in *The Color Purple* will be my primary concern in this chapter.

The personal and the political intertwine in the letters of Celie and Nettie—sisters separated by the only circumstances and options that allow them to escape their abusive father: an arranged marriage for one; missionary and domestic work for the other. Each sister draws strength from the act of writing itself and from a faith that her letters will have a salutary effect on the other. But the agents of patriarchy contrive not only to keep the sisters apart, but to keep them silent, alone, and defeated. The novel's first sentence is a command from "Pa," who is identified in the opening letters simply as "He": *"You better not never tell nobody but God. It'd kill your mammy."*[2] The double negative reinforces the power of the admonition not to reveal his incestuous acts.

Language, or "telling," can unleash harmful—even obliterating power. But Celie's silence is to no avail: her mother dies anyway. And Celie's request for that most indirect and oblique mode of acknowledgment from God—a "sign"—goes unanswered. Furthermore, Mr. _____, the man who barters with "Pa" for possession of Celie as a kind of "cut-rate" wife, withholds Nettie's letters from Celie in retribution for Nettie's withholding herself from his sexual advances (which culminate in a rape attempt). When Celie finally does gain access to her sister's letters, she is again thwarted and isolated—this time by both the war propagandists who mistakenly inform her that Nettie and her "family" have perished, and the colonial bureaucrats in Africa who cannot or will not deliver her letters to Nettie.

Nevertheless, the sisters continue to write. These letters chronicle and reinforce Celie and Nettie's parallel struggles and intuitive discoveries in the American south and the African forests, respectively: they are also diary entries recording and illuminating their journeys to selfhood. Both women struggle against the efforts of men to dominate women; both turn to other women for solidarity and emotional support and nurturance; both argue for a technology and means of subsistence that is life-enhancing rather than spiritually and ecologically debilitating; both opt for nonhierarchical extended families over the traditional patriarchal family; both reject the orthodox theological dogma of a "male" God in favor of a Upanishadic notion of the Deity as a force pervading the universe and imbuing every living being.

Walker's advocacy of a literature that transcends or transforms existing social reality is easily documented by a reading of her eclectic and often autobiographical collections of essays. In *In Search of Our Mothers' Gardens,* for example, Walker argues that literature cannot exist in a hermetical isolation from the historical contexts of authors or audiences. In an interview with Gloria Steinem, she says, "books are by-products of our lives. Deliver me from writers who say the way they live doesn't matter. I'm not sure a bad person can write a good book. If art doesn't make us better, then what on earth is it for?"[3] Private lives, then, are irrevocably connected to public and political realities. Or as she succinctly articulates this creed in another interview, "I believe in change: change personal, and change in society."[4] Writing about the most important American social protest movement of her lifetime, the civil rights movement, Walker shuns the allure of sweeping historical panoramas in favor of the invisible but ultimately more significant unlocking and unleashing of individual consciousnesses to life's possibilities. Regardless of how successful the legal and social structures that comprise the civil rights movement's most concrete achievements actually are in erasing prejudice and promoting real equality, Walker insists that a more important barrier has been breached: "If knowledge of my condition is all the freedom I get from a 'freedom movement,' it is better than unawareness, forgottenness, and hopelessness, the existence that is like the existence of a beast" (121). Alice Walker believes literature can enable us to investigate the individual and institutional forces, traditions, and structures that limit and frustrate our quest for the fullest possible "knowledge of our condition."

But literature has a further capacity less frequently employed: it can offer "a kind of salvation." The characters who inhabit the works of writers Walker admires "can always envision a solution, an evolution to higher consciousness on the part of society, even when society itself cannot" (251). In short, literature does not simply promote or enhance awareness or consciousness: it can offer new insights and unorthodox solutions. It can serve as a repository of alternatives or as a tool for altering existing social conditions. Alice Walker would undoubtedly agree with Bertolt Brecht's oft-quoted maxim, "Art is not a mirror held up to reality, but a hammer with which to shape it." She laments that "in our particular society, it is the narrowed and the narrowing view of life that often wins." While most white American writers, according to Walker, "end their books and their characters' lives as if there were no better existence for which to struggle," African-American and third world writers struggle for a "larger freedom" (5). She agrees with Flannery O'Connor that the direction of the "serious novelist" will be "away from the 'writing of explanation,' of statistics, and further into mystery, into poetry, and into prophesy" (8). The writer's role in the contemporary world, then, is to instruct and inspire—to guide others to a higher moral or spiritual awareness or existence. Writers are contemporary prophets.

The utopian direction of Walker's work has attracted the attention of many critics whose invaluable insights shed light on the significance of *The Color Purple*'s reconstructed families. Mary Helen Washington addresses Walker's visionary purpose (and the echoes of similar elements in the work of other African-American women writers) by elaborating upon Walker's identification of three "cycles" of women characters in her oeuvre. While the women Walker categorizes as "suspended" and "assimilated" are maimed by physical violence and psychical oppression, respectively, Washington is most intrigued by the "emergent" women: "The women of this third cycle are, for the most part, women of the late Sixties, although there are some older women in Walker's fiction who exhibit the qualities of the developing, emergent model."[5] (Although *The Color Purple* was written after Washington's article, this latter qualification places Celie in the company of "emergent" women.) Washington is cognizant of the revolutionary significance of emergent characters—their status as fully realized literary role models whose courage, autonomy, and intellectual, social, and spiritual freedom women can admire and emulate. These figures represent an evolutionary step that Walker's *The Color Purple* proclaims is within everyone's grasp. They are "women coming just to the edge of a new awareness and making the first tentative steps into an uncharted region" (22-23)—a region that is psychical in nature, requiring a new understanding of self and community. In examining the alternative families that evolve in *The Color Purple*, this chapter seeks to provide a map of part of this "uncharted region."

Marie H. Buncombe applauds Walker's exploratory utopian representations of men and women who have rejected or escaped the imprisonment of traditional gender roles:

> Walker uses androgyny as a metaphor for the "wholeness," the totality of the black experience as she sees it. This "wholeness" calls for a new look at traditional definitions of such terms as "masculine," "feminine," and "lesbian" since the conventional meanings have led to polarization, fear,

and hostility, resulting in the falsification of black history and literature and the destruction of many black people.[6]

The key phrase in Buncombe's assessment is "as she sees it." Walker includes "committed to survival and wholeness of entire people, male and female," among the definitions of "womanist" that serve as epigraphs to *In Search of Our Mothers' Gardens*. Her shamanistic mission to heal individual and collective divisions is reiterated in a 1973 interview that is included in this collection: "I am preoccupied with the spiritual survival, the survival *whole* of my people" (250). It is a wholeness that must be imagined because it does not yet exist. New words like "womanist" and visionary texts like *The Color Purple* can, however, contribute to its realization. Like Washington, Buncombe celebrates this pioneering project: "As Walker's characters free themselves from being typecast as 'masculine' and 'feminine' and embrace the best characteristics of both genders, they rise to a higher level of self-perception and understanding never before realized" (423).

Ruth Nadelhaft pays homage to yet another facet of Walker's prophetic literature, praising *The Color Purple* as the first literary text "to imagine the circumstances in which the beaten wife might recreate herself and the self of the man who beats."[7] It differs from earlier texts "because it does not evade but tries to solve . . . problems" (257). According to Nadelhaft, previous texts depicting domestic violence have "demanded the dissolution of a relationship or the literal destruction of the abusive husband" (254). Walker's project—envisioning solutions in literature that might have applications in the real world—sets her and other writers committed to social change apart from those she accuses of producing texts in which the "gloom of defeat is thick."[8]

The Color Purple has drawn considerable fire for its utopianism, too: a review of the reservations one of Walker's more vehement and articulate critics, Trudier Harris, has about the novel's representation of African-American life and its political implications is instructive. Like many of Walker's critics, Harris challenges the plausibility of the novel's utopian elements. She decries the novel's "political shopping list of all the IOUs Walker felt that it was time to repay" feminists, lesbians, black nationalists, and Pan Africanists, among others.[9] In addressing these political agendas, Harris argues that the novel becomes a fairy tale offering avenues to freedom and happiness that are really unavailable to African Americans:

> The fable structure thereby perpetrates a lie in holding out to blacks a non-existent or minimally existent hope for a piece of that great American pie. The clash of characters who presumably contend with and in the real world with the idealistic, suprarealistic quality and expectations of fairy-tale worlds places a burden on the novel that diffuses its message and guarantees possibilities for unintended interpretations. (160)

For Harris, then, literature that does not conform to the most commonly accepted version of reality risks misleading those who would take its most hopeful and exuberant scenarios as representations of lives they might live. The potential volatility or subversiveness of a text must be controlled by the author: a writer like Walker who fails in this essential task risks disappointing readers who find that the path offered to them in a text is blocked or unavailable to them in their current and foreseeable circumstances. While Harris's soberingly realistic awareness of the vulnerability of Walker's audience is an important cautionary note, Walker is clearly concerned with challenging as well as consoling her audience. Her assessment of the civil rights movement provides some insight into what she expects of and from her audience: if the civil rights movement accomplished nothing else, "it gave us hope for tomorrow. It called us to life."[10] And Walker—or any other writer—cannot be afraid to instill the same sense of hope in a reader—however bleak or unlikely the prospects for succor from social oppression may be.

Harris's more provocative charge is that a text like *The Color Purple* provides ammunition to critics hostile to the very communities Walker is trying to promote and "rescue" because it accentuates the most lurid realities of marginalized African Americans. She is particularly distressed by these "unintended interpretations" and possible uses of a text she protests does not represent African Americans accurately. Harris claims that no black woman would tolerate the abuse Celie endures in the novel: "I couldn't imagine a Celie existing in any black community I knew or any that I could conceive of." *The Color Purple* is a "circus of black human interactions" that "reinforces racial stereotypes" (155): it lends validity to the prevailing racist suspicions that "black people have no morality when it comes to sexuality, that black family structure is weak if existent at all," and that "black fathers and father-figures are . . . immoral" and "sexually unrestrained" (157).

Of course, the lower percentage of nuclear families among blacks is one criterion white racists employ to justify their antipathy to African Americans. But are the standards by which African-American families are evaluated and categorized actually valid or relevant? Robert Staples and Leanor Boulin Johnson argue in their study of African-American families that every evaluation of this social unit has been "developed in some kind of political context, either positive or negative. Politics enters the study of the Black family because this social unit has not been perceived as an institution, but as a social problem."[11] In *The Way We Never Were: American Families and the Nostalgia Trap,* Stephanie Coontz observes, "In almost every decade, for 200 years, someone has 'discovered' that the black family is falling apart."[12] Nevertheless, in the three decades since the Moynihan report decried the decline of the traditional nuclear family in the African-American community, a number of sociologists have argued that many blacks receive nurturance, support, and identity through extended family networks that are effective substitutes for the nuclear family. In *All Our Kin,* Carol B. Stack claims that these extended networks are an urban phenomenon; in *The Black Extended Family,* Elmer and Joanne Martin argue that these structures have actually been prevalent for generations—although the migration of blacks to urban areas has actually strained African-American kinship networks.

The Martins denounce the narrowness of earlier studies of the black family: "Too many studies of the black family have focused on what is wrong with it—the pathology-disorganization perspective—or on why it has survived—the strength-resiliency perspective."[13] Moynihan's influential report managed to do both—praising the survival and "creative vitality" of the "Negro community" while decrying the "forced . . . matriarchal structure" that is "at the center of the tangle of pathology" that besets American blacks.[14] While Moynihan allows that there is "no special reason why a society in which males are dominant in family relationships is to be preferred to a matriarchal arrangement," he believes that minority groups should conform to the presumption of "male leadership in private and public affairs" held by the dominant culture.

The Martins define the black extended family as an interdependent, multigenerational network with a dominant family figure and an extended family base. It extends across geographical boundaries and "has a built-in mutual aid system for providing material aid and moral support to family members."[15] Stack finds that the "cooperation of close adult females" is the dynamic that binds these clusters of "kin" into an extended family.[16] Both Stack and the Martins agree on the patterns of and motivations for informal adoption within these extended family systems. Stack identifies "child-keeping" as part of the flux and elasticity of residence. "The expansion and contraction of households, and the successive recombinations of kinsmen residing together, require adults to care for the children residing in their household" (62). These insights are essential to my understanding of the alternative families that evolve in *The Color Purple*, particularly the elasticity of household structures.

The alternative families Walker presents in *The Color Purple* are central to her utopian vision of the potentialities for human growth. Her "use of the family as an imaginative structure—as a way of organizing experience" is one of her "major concerns."[17] She builds upon an institution already available in the African-American community: the extended family. Walker depicts this African-American institution as not simply a valuable social structure—an asset to blacks—but as a potential model for the provision of nurturance and emotional support for all people. Her elaborately reimagined black extended family surmounts the flaws and limitations of the traditional nuclear family.

The nuclear families Walker depicts in the first half of *The Color Purple* are stifling containers of unremitting male rage. They are ruled by patriarchs who are embittered by the myriad ways their lives have been thwarted or controlled by their own fathers and (implicit in the novel) limited by the social and economic realities of African Americans in the early twentieth century. For example, Celie's real father and his brothers were lynched because their business became too successful. "Pa" inherits their store when he marries her mother and survives only by "paying off" the local whites: "you got to give 'em something. Either your money, your land, your woman, or your ass" (167). The dependent members of the nuclear family bear the brunt of this pent-up anger and frustration, this sense of impotence. And women and children have no rights or power within the nuclear families Walker depicts—no recourse for redressing wrongs. The men who exploit and oppress them are acting out what Diana E. H. Russell terms the "masculinity mystique": "To win, to be superior, to conquer, and to control demonstrate masculinity to those who subscribe to common cultural notions of masculinity."[18] Russell links this ideology to the prevalence of rape, noting that "rape is not so much a deviant act as an over-conforming one" perpetrated by "men who feel powerless in the rest of their lives and whose masculinity is threatened by this sense of powerlessness" (117-18).

Sofia, Harpo's wife, puts this threat of violence into words when she explains to Celie why she has always been a fighter: "A girl child ain't safe in a family of men" (46). Indeed, there are three victims of sexual violence in *The Color Purple*: Celie, Mary Agnes, and Nettie. The opening letter of the novel describes the attempts of "Pa" to terrorize Celie into silence and sexual submission: "He start to choke me, saying You better shut up and git used to it" (11). She must lie to her dying mother, telling her that the baby fathered by "Pa" is God's, and that "God took it" (12). But "Pa" does have the powers of a god in Celie's world: he has complete control over every member of his household and can use or abuse them as he sees fit. As Susan Brownmiller surmises in her landmark study of rape, "interfamily sexual abuse of children . . . is rooted in the same patriarchal philosophy of sexual private property that shaped and determined historic male attitudes toward rape. For if woman was man's original corporal property, then children were, and are, a wholly owned subsidiary."[19] The word "family" is derived from a term used to describe Roman households in which the male patriarch had the power of life and death over his spouse, children, and slaves alike. "Pa" wields a similar power, and so it is not surprising or particularly shocking to Celie when he takes the child away—presumably to kill it—without feeling compelled to offer either consolation or explanation: "He took it while I was sleeping. Kilt it out there in the woods. Kill this one too, if he can" (12). Celie's emotional and physical scars from bearing and then losing two children by her father at such a young age are symbolized by the end of her menstrual cycles: "I don't bleed no more" (15). The inability to "bleed" here refers as much to an inability to feel emotions as it does to the disrupted biological rhythms of menstruation. Celie tells Sofia that she can't remember what it was like to feel emotions like anger: "Then after while every time I got mad, or start to feel mad, I got sick. Felt like throwing up. Terrible feeling. Then I start to feel nothing at all" (47). Her sterility and servility become "assets" when "Pa" barters her off to a neighboring widower: "And God done fixed her. You can do everything just like you want to and she ain't gonna make you feed it or clothe it." But just in case Celie hasn't yet been beaten into a submissive state of complete silence, "Pa" adds a final word of advice for her new proprietor: "And another thing—She tells lies" (18).

Later in the novel, "Squeak," Harpo's girlfriend, is raped by her uncle, the local white sheriff, when she approaches him with a scheme to reduce Sofia's jail term for punching the mayor. He rapes her as a means of denying their blood ties: "He saw the Hodges in me, she say. And he didn't like it one bit" (94). Like "Pa," he also contrives to ruin the credibility of his victim should she muster enough courage to accuse him publicly: "He say if he was my uncle he wouldn't do it to me. That be a sin. But this just little fornication. Everybody guilty of that." But unlike Celie, "Squeak" has a supportive community that insists she not be silenced, that she give voice to her own violation. When Shug says, "if you can't tell us, who you gon tell, God?" (95), the reader is reminded that God—Celie's only recourse—was an unresponsive audience. The support of her human audience allows "Squeak" to claim both her own story—"Shut up, Harpo, say Squeak. I'm telling it" (94)—and her real name: Mary Agnes. Their continued support encourages her to give voice to her being in other ways: "6 months after Mary Agnes went to git Sofia out of prison, she begin to sing. First she sing Shug's songs, then she begin to make up songs her own self" (96). Walker presents a series of steps toward self-realization here: first, Mary Agnes learns how to acknowledge and claim her own experience; then, she imitates the efforts of another to transform experience into narratives—song lyrics— that will make them accessible and understandable to others; finally, she is able to transcribe her own life into song. Her personal growth is complete when she is able to perform this record of her experiences—her songs—to provide information, solace, support, and entertainment to others.

When Nettie's letters to Celie—intercepted and hidden for decades by Mr. _____—are recovered, they reveal yet another interfamilial sexual assault. Nettie's first letter in the novel, like Celie's, describes a rape (Mr. _____ is unable to complete the act because Nettie is able to "hurt him bad enough to make him let me alone"). Like the other perpetrators of sexual violence in the novel, Mr. _____ acts to deny his victim the possibility of telling others of his deed: "He said because of what I'd done I'd never hear from you again, and you would never hear from me" (119).

While the male heads of households in *The Color Purple* have almost unlimited sexual license, they are vigilant in monitoring the sexual ambitions of those under their dominion and are empowered to reject marriage proposals and scuttle liaisons they find to be disadvantageous to their economic or social status. When "Pa" thinks Celie is flirting with a boy, he is quick to punish her: "He beat me today cause he say I winked at a boy in church" (15). "Pa" refuses to give Nettie to Mr. _____ in marriage because she may be an economic asset to him as a future schoolteacher. Furthermore, he wants her to take Celie's place as a "surrogate wife." Finally, there is the issue of Mr. _____'s social status and reputation to consider: "What about the scandal his wife cause when somebody kill her? And what about all this stuff he hear bout Shug Avery?" (16). Instead, he offers Celie to Mr. _____ as a kind of "package deal" with special incentives like a cow and her own linen, emphasizing the further advantages of her sterility and ability to "work like a man" (18).

When Mr. _____ brings Shug Avery home to recuperate from "the nasty woman disease," his father pays him a visit to express his disapproval. He taunts his son with Shug Avery's lack of social respectability: "Nobody even sure exactly who her daddy is. . . . And her mammy take in white people dirty clothes to this day. Plus all her children got different daddys. It all just too trifling and confuse" (59). It doesn't matter that Mr. _____ vouches that all her children are his: they must be denied and ostracized because they were born outside the confines of the nuclear family to a woman of uncertain genealogy. Despite the suffering Mr. _____ endured when his father prevented him from marrying Shug, he forbids his own son, Harpo, from marrying the woman he loves. Like his father, Mr. _____ dismisses his son's claim of paternity. He tells Sofia, the woman carrying Harpo's child, that "Young womens no good these days. . . . Got they legs open to every Tom, Dick and Harry" (38). Mr. _____ accedes to their union only when he finds a way to make Harpo's marriage profitable: Harpo agrees to work as a paid field hand for his father rather than strike out on his own.

There are only two avenues of revolt available to family members oppressed by a dominant patriarch: "getting big" or the more difficult option of getting away. For a boy, "getting big" is acquiring the physical strength of a man. When Nettie runs away from home, she knows that her younger brothers, at least, are relatively safe: "The boys be alright, she say. They can stay out his way. When they git big they gon fight him" (25). For a girl, "getting big" is becoming pregnant and acquiring whatever rights or safety motherhood and the claim she can make on a man other than her father can bring. When "Harpo girl daddy say Harpo not good enough for her" (36), Sofia gets pregnant because she "can't git out the house no other way" (37). Mr. _____'s daughters make a similar escape: "Both the girls bigged and gone" (82). Obviously, given the limited power that mothers and wives have and the abuse they receive within Walker's traditional nuclear families, this "escape" is likely to be an exchange of one form of oppression for another. However, 'getting big' *is* a successful strategy for disrupting the control over genealogical descent that family patriarchs exert.

In *The Color Purple*, then, the hierarchy and operation of the nuclear family protects the privileged position of men. Although Harpo is proud of Sofia's independence and self-assertiveness during the first few years of their marriage, he is also uncomfortably aware of the watchful disapproval of his father. Mr. _____ shames his son for not beating his wife when Harpo asks him for advice on how to make Sofia "mind": "Well how you spect to make her mind? Wives is like children. You have to let 'em know who got the upper hand. Nothing can do that better than a good sound beating" (42). Because Celie is jealous of Sofia's freedom, she also advises Harpo to beat his wife, but then suffers a month of sleepless nights because she "sin against Sofia spirit" (45). However, when Sofia proves more than capable of holding her own in a fight with Harpo, he tries, unsuccessfully, to "get big" in order to get the upper hand. His efforts to "bulk up" produce not muscle but a protruding stomach that makes him look pregnant. His "pregnancy" is symbolic of the irrepressibility of his "feminine" traits—tendencies he has been taught to ignore or deride.

While Harpo is disconcerted by his wife's expertise in traditionally "male" work like shingling the house, Sofia is more accepting of nontraditional gender roles: "To tell the truth, he love that part of housekeeping a heap more 'en me. I rather be out in the fields or fooling with the animals. Even chopping wood. But he love cooking and cleaning and doing little things round the house." The problem, once again, is the acculturation that has occurred within the family and Harpo's fear of his father's disapproval: "It seem so natural to him. But Mr. _____. You know how he is" (63). Yet later in the novel, after Mr. _____'s transformation, he reveals that he, too, had wanted to explore his "feminine" side and perform tasks traditionally thought of as women's work: "When

I was growing up, he said, I use to try to sew along with mama cause that's what she was always doing. But everybody laughed at me. But you know, I liked it" (238). Gender roles, then, are formed and enforced within the family and are passed on by one generation to the next. *The Color Purple* demonstrates convincingly why it is so difficult to moderate rigid societal notions of masculinity and femininity or curtail the prevalence of domestic violence without altering the site where these values and attitudes are inculcated.

In *The Color Purple*, changes in the family's hierarchy and milieu occur only when the women who have been subject to male domination and abuse are able to fight back or leave. An abused woman must have the support of others if she is to confront or challenge her father, husband, or lover. For women, then, the first step toward the empowerment that might enable them to assert a level of control over their lives is to share accounts of their abuse, thereby finding support and forging communities that might be used to alter their circumstances and the structures and modes of operation of their families. The difficulty of taking this first step for someone like Celie who has been raped or sexually abused is addressed by Susan Griffin in *Rape: The Politics of Consciousness*: she has been taught to regard herself as "impotent, unable to act, unable even to perceive, in no way self-sufficient, and finally, as the object and not the subject of human behavior. It is in this sense that a woman is deprived of the status of a human being. She is not free to be."[20]

Even before Shug Avery enters her life, Celie is looking at and to her for strength and solace. A picture of Shug that Celie obtains from her stepmother has an almost talismanic quality: "all night long I stare at it. An now when I dream, I dream of Shug Avery. She be dress to kill, whirling and laughing" (16). Celie looks to the picture for support when she is bartered off to Mr. _____: "I take out the picture of Shug Avery. I look into her eyes. Her eyes say Yeah, it bees that way sometime" (18). She thinks about Shug Avery on her wedding night with Mr. _____: "I know what he doing to me he done to Shug Avery and maybe she like it. I put my arm around him" (21). Shug's previous sexual acquaintanceship with Mr. _____ is comforting rather than threatening to Celie; it makes the disagreeable chore of sleeping with Mr. _____ more bearable.

Romantic triangles are as often disastrous in literature as they are in life. In *The Color Purple*, however, Shug Avery's convalescence under Celie's roof and subsequent renewal of her relationship with Mr. _____ is an opportunity for Celie—not an additional humiliation. Shug's presence in their household curtails Mr. _____'s abusive behavior—enough so that Celie is able to muster the courage to confess to Shug that "He beat me when you not here" (76). Shug's promise that she will intercede on Celie's behalf to stop this abuse gives her courage and hope. And Shug's sexual relationship with Mr. _____ allows her, unexpectedly, to become increasingly intimate with Celie, too. Sharing her husband with another woman gives Celie an ally with whom she can discuss what Shug calls her "virginity" and from whom she can learn about her body and the range of sexual expression. During Shug's subsequent visits, Celie reclaims more and more of her past by narrating her history to her friend. Each confession is accompanied by an increased level of intimacy between the two women, until Celie reveals to Shug what no one except Nettie knows: the paternity of her two lost children. This confession serves as the catalyst for sexual intimacy between Celie and Shug. The poignant language Walker employs to describe this moment confirms the link between Celie's act of self-revelation—her courage in naming the pain of both sexual abuse and the loss of her children—and her ability to acknowledge and express her sexuality: "Then I feels something real soft and wet on my breast, feel like one of my little lost babies mouth. Way after while, I act like a little lost baby too" (109). Furthermore, the mother/child imagery implies that Celie and Shug will "mother" each other—that their sexual intimacy is a means to promote healing.

In "Writing *The Color Purple*," Alice Walker claims that the genesis of her novel came during a most peculiar conversation: "I was hiking through the woods with my sister, Ruth, talking about a lovers' triangle of which we both knew. She said: 'And you know, one day The Wife asked The Other Woman for a pair of her drawers.'"[21] Walker also insists that the characters "visited" her—that she served as a vehicle for their entry or re-entry into the world. Celie, Shug, and Albert "visited" (or were imagined by) Walker as a cohesive unit. In *The Color Purple*, triangles replace relationships where husbands control and dominate their wives to an inordinate degree. These triangles are usually initiated by men who are dissatisfied with their relationships or marriages and unhappy because of the perceived inadequacies of their partners—limitations that, ironically enough, are often the result of the narrow restrictions of the traditional patriarchal families they must conform to and function within. The disruption of a "patriarchal relationship" by a third person subverts and finally destroys it: a more elastic, egalitarian, and nurturing structure evolves to take its place. Only the marriage of Sofia's sister, Odessa, and Jack—founded upon love, equality, mutual respect, and shared values—is immune to penetration by a third party. Celie describes Jack as a man who "Love children. Respect his wife, Odessa, and all Odessa amazon sisters. Anything she want to take on, he right there" (191). This is the only nurturing and healthy nuclear family in the novel.[22]

The most important triangle, of course, consists of Shug, Mr. _____, and Celie. Shug is the only woman Mr. _____ ever loved. Their early relationship, as recounted by Shug, was affectionate, boisterous, uninhibited, and egalitarian. The taciturn, moody, and abusive Mr. _____ who inhabits the pages of *The Color Purple* bears no resemblance to the affable, easygoing young Albert that Shug remembers. Unfortunately for Shug and Albert, her free-wheeling, vivacious, independent lifestyle disqualifies her as a potential wife: "His daddy told him I'm trash, my mama trash before me. His brother say the same. Albert try to stand up for us, git knock down" (116). In *The Color Purple*, marriage is an economic necessity—not a romantic partnership: men acquire wives to bear and raise their children and perform most of the domestic and field labor. Women and men accede to these disparities within marriage because they have observed the unequal distribution of tasks and power within their own families as children. Walker illustrates this process of inculcation early in the novel when a visiting sister of Mr. _____'s asks Harpo to fetch a bucket of water: "Women work, he say. What? she say. Women work. I'm a man" (29). Furthermore, wives must be subordinate to their husbands and unsullied by any unseemly behavior or associations. When Shug gives her first performance at Harpo's jukejoint, for example, Mr. _____ tells Celie, "wives don't go to places like that" (74). Mr. _____ invites Shug back into his life because she represents what is missing in the narrow relationship he allows himself to have with his wife, Celie. He sees no contradiction between enjoying his lover's performance at a jukejoint and attempting to ban his wife from attending.

Like Shug, Sofia is a strong, independent, unabashedly sexual woman who eschews the traditional role of the demure wife. Although Harpo does manage to wed her, he is obsessed with forcing her to submit to the restraints and restrictions of her new social role. When Sofia leaves Harpo because his efforts to make her "mind" become tiresome and then abusive, he finds a girlfriend who will satisfy his craving for dominance. Celie describes Squeak as "like me. She do anything Harpo say" (83). Like his father, Harpo is unable either to reconcile or to abandon the conflicting, two-dimensional stereotypes of women that he inherits from his family and the larger society. Thus, when Sofia comes "home" to attend another performance by Shug, Harpo's response is identical to his father's: "It just a scandless, a woman with five children hanging out in a jukejoint at night" (82). Harpo's response is particularly ludicrous because the jukejoint in question has been established in the house he used to share with Sofia. Like his father, Harpo does not find a jukejoint to be an objectionable environment for his girlfriend. Finally, the reader has just learned that Sofia has six children—not five; Harpo's ignorance of this fact makes his indignation all the more hollow. (Later in the novel, Harpo will be told that the sixth child, Henrietta—his favorite—was fathered by Henry Broadnax, the prizefighter with whom Sofia was involved after leaving him. His subsequent diligent care for Henrietta during her debilitating illness is an indication of his maturity—his rejection of both rigidly defined roles for women and of traditional familial structures and expectations.)

While these triangular arrangements are resisted initially by the women involved, they find subsequently that the solidarity forged by their connection to the same man can be unexpectedly beneficial. The fate of Mr. _____'s first wife, Annie Julia, is an object lesson in how vulnerable and hopeless women who are bereft of the cooperation of other women become. She accedes to an affair in a desperate attempt to escape from her unbearable marriage. Before he murders her, the man she had hoped would save her tells Annie Julia, "Whore, you ain't got no place" (36). Annie Julia doesn't have a supportive network of kin or women friends: her husband beats her; her husband's mistress, Shug, hates her; her own family "forgot about her once she married." Shug Avery's sorrow for her behavior toward Annie Julia is the only regret she voices in the novel. She confesses to Celie that Mr. _____'s first wife "never had a chance" (116). Annie Julia is denied the possibility of a reconciliation or understanding with her husband's lover that is available to Celie because Shug was "wild" with rage over Mr. _____'s unexpected arranged marriage and determined to destroy it. Annie Julia is an alternative version of Celie—a dark reminder that Celie's fate might have been different.[23]

At first, Shug is cruel to Albert's second wife, too: her first words to Celie are "you sure *is* ugly . . . like she ain't believed it" (50). Sofia and Squeak's first encounter ends in a physical altercation. Neither first meeting is particularly promising. But as we have already seen, Shug is able not only to end the abuse that has paralyzed and numbed Celie, but to support Celie's efforts to reclaim her body and her life. Celie eventually replaces Albert as the main object of Shug's sexual interest. And when Sofia is jailed and then forced to work for the mayor's wife for twelve years, Squeak takes on the task of raising her children. Indeed, it is significant that by circumstance or choice, none of the major women characters in *The Color Purple* raises her own children—the most important task assigned to women within the patriarchal family. Shug's three children by Albert are raised by her mother. Celie's two children by "Pa," we will learn later in the novel, are being raised in Africa by her sister, Nettie, and Corrine and Samuel, the missionaries who have adopted them. Celie, in turn, raises Mr. _____'s children by Annie Julia. Deprived of her own children, Sofia becomes a surrogate mother to Eleanor Jane, one of the mayor's two children. Squeak raises Sofia's six children; when Sofia's term of service is over and Squeak decides to leave for Memphis with Shug and Celie in order to pursue a singing career, Sofia offers to raise Squeak's daughter by Harpo, Suzie Q. The ease with which this decision is made and the good will that accompanies it are both indicative of the cooperation and assistance women offer each other in this novel:

> Mary Agnes, darling, say Harpo, look how Suzie Q take to Sofia.
> Yeah, say Squeak, children know good when they see it. She and Sofia smile at one nother.
> Go on sing, say Sofia. I'll look after this one till you come back.
> You will? say Squeak.
> Yeah, say Sofia.
> And look after Harpo, too, say Squeak. Please ma'am. (184-85)

Shug's condemnation of the centrality of the male image in organized patriarchal religions—"You have to git man off your eyeball, before you can see anything a'tall" (179)—also describes the obstacle Squeak and Sofia must overcome before they can move from competition and confrontation over Harpo to the spirit of cooperation that allows each woman to relieve the other of domestic duties—raising children and caring for Harpo—during a period of crisis (Sofia's involuntary servitude) or self-fulfillment (Squeak's efforts to establish a singing career). By overcoming jealousy and possessiveness, they are able to see the benefit of working together to meet their mutual needs under extraordinarily difficult circumstances.

While Sofia stays behind with Harpo when Shug, Celie, and Squeak leave for Memphis, Mr. _____ is bereft of both his lover and his wife. In a climactic moment of confrontation, Celie recounts publicly the wrongs she has suffered at Mr. _____'s hands, including his most reprehensible act: "You took my sister Nettie away from me, I say. And she was the only person love me in the world" (181). Celie has recently rejected traditional patriarchal religion for the Upanishadic philosophy that Shug outlines in the letter that gives the novel its title.[24] Shug believes that all of creation is marked by divinity: God is "Everything that is or ever was or ever will be." Full existence is "being part of everything, not separate at all." This theological concept—and the emotional security and equilibrium it offers—is expressed in the Isa Upanishad: "Who sees all beings in his own Self, and his own Self in all beings, loses all fear."[25] God is a force that is both within the individual and manifest in the extraordinary diversity and awesome beauty of the world—as accessible and visible as "the color purple in a field somewhere" (178). This new-found sense of fearlessness and connectedness to the Deity empowers Celie to curse Mr. _____ before she leaves him: "Until you do right by me, everything you touch will crumble." Indeed, Celie acts as a kind of prophet—a mouthpiece for the Deity: "I give it to him straight, just like it come to me. And it seem to come to me from the trees" (187).

Mr. _____ is powerfully impressed by his wife's curse—so much so that he becomes a sickly recluse after her departure, afraid even of the sound of his own heart at night. It is Harpo who nurses his father back to health—a process that can commence only after Mr. _____ mails Celie the remaining letters from Nettie. In order to get well, Mr. _____ must become self-sufficient and develop a concern for others. When Celie returns for Sofia's mother's funeral, Mr. _____ is a changed man. Sofia informs the incredulous Celie that "He out there in the field from sunup to sundown. And clean that house just like a woman" (199). His newly-awakened compassion is evidenced by his participation in the community effort to care for Henrietta, Harpo's daughter, during her illness. It is no coincidence that in *The Color Purple*, Alice Walker gives us two "Als" who are granted an opportunity to renounce their abusive ways. "Pa" (Alphonso) is unrepentant when Mary Ellen, the child bride he brings home to replace Celie's mother, leaves him, taking their children with her. He dismisses her loss with a laugh: "Got too old for me, I reckon" (166). He finds an even younger and more supplicating girl to take her place: the fifteen-year-old daughter of people who must work for him and live on his land. He dies, ironically, while "spending a little time in bed" (215) with his new child bride. But Mr. _____ (Albert) is able to rehabilitate himself—acknowledging his wrongs and even confessing to Celie that he had been "too big a fool to let myself care" (223) when she was living with him. The tasks of self-analysis (trying to understand why he has been deserted by his children, wife, and lover) and learning to become more empathetic and caring are mutually reinforcing: "The more I wonder, he say, the more I love" (247).

Some critics are perplexed by Mr. _____'s transformation in *The Color Purple*.[26] By denigrating Mr. _____'s evolution, Walker's detractors fail to appreciate that one of the novel's key plot lines is the emergence of "Albert"—an autonomous, self-sufficient, dignified, and spiritually aware figure—from the discarded husk of Mr. _____'s violent and authoritarian persona. The resuscitation of his humanity is evidenced by his collection of sea shells—his appreciation of "some of the things God was playful enough to make." When he tells Celie near the end of the novel that "this the first time I ever lived on earth as a natural man. It feel like a new experience" (230), he is describing a rebirth of sorts: a new, joyful awareness of being alive—of being himself. Walker is suggesting that there is nothing "natural" about the abuse and oppression of women—behavior that is associated with traditional masculinity in *The Color Purple*. It is possible to overcome and discard the precepts of the "masculinity mystique." Even abusive men are redeemable—are susceptible to inner promptings and external pressures to reform and grow.

Celie, too, must become self-sufficient. Her time in Memphis is spent making pants—a hobby that develops into a small business. The symbolism of her new vocation is obvious: Celie has moved from life with Mr. _____, who forbade her from wearing pants even when she was plowing the field, to life with Shug and the freedom to wear whatever she chose, to control over the actual manufacturing of pants that others will wear. Walker is not suggesting, as some critics have argued, that Celie finally gets an opportunity to "wear the pants" (an adage referring to control within a relationship): Celie's power instead is the opportunity to promote diversity and individuality through her pants designs. Each pair of pants is sewn to meet the unique individual needs of its owner. No two pairs are alike. Both men and women are entitled to wear pants: "Anybody can wear them" (238). No pattern is superior to another.

Celie must also struggle to become less emotionally dependent upon her lover when Shug embarks upon a "last fling" (220) with a nineteen-year-old boy. Momentarily speechless with distress when Shug confesses her passion for Germaine, Celie reverts to her first mode of communication—writing—to express her hurt and confusion. After returning home from Memphis to distance herself from Shug's affair, Celie berates herself for her emotional vulnerability: "Even thought you had the trees with you. The whole earth. The stars. But look at you. When Shug left, happiness desert" (229). In *The Color Purple*, the "emergent woman" must become more emotionally autonomous than her predecessors; furthermore, she must develop and maintain a diverse and varied "family" network so that she can sustain the loss of a lover or a close friend. Celie's emotional crisis prompts a renewal of contact with her estranged husband: a platonic friendship with the reformed Albert slowly evolves. Celie underscores the necessity of inner equilibrium in her last letter to Nettie in the novel when she describes her response to the news that Shug may return home: "*I be so calm*. If she come, I be happy. If she don't, I be content. And then I figure this the lesson I was suppose to learn" (247-48).

The importance of Celie's insights is reinforced by Nettie's parallel experiences and discoveries in Africa. Walker constructs yet another triangular "household" with Samuel, Corrine, and Nettie. This arrangement fails, however, because Corrine is fearful that Samuel and Nettie's innocent friendship and professional relationship diminish her own conjugal status in the eyes of the African villagers. Sadly, Corrine finds Nettie's presence to be increasingly threatening. Her intolerance is exacerbated by the villagers' assumption that Nettie is also a wife to Samuel, and that Adam and Olivia are their biological offspring. Corrine sets limits upon Nettie's inclusion and participation in her family, insisting that the children not call her "Mama Nettie" and that Samuel not visit her alone. When Corrine becomes ill, she finally gives voice to the anxiety that has plagued her for years: like the villagers, she too suspects that Nettie and Samuel are Adam and Olivia's parents. Her recovery is impeded by her refusal to believe Nettie's revelation of her status as the children's biological aunt. Nettie writes, "She gets weaker and weaker, and unless she can believe us and start to feel something for her children, I fear we will lose her." Corrine does eventually believe Nettie, but her change of heart comes too late to alter the course of her illness. Corrine dies from "unbelief" (169): an inability—uncharacteristic in this text—to trust another woman.

Like Celie, Nettie looks to other women for solace and community. She admires the Olinka women for their ability to assist and sustain one another. She discovers that the Olinka women can "share a husband but the husband does not share their friendships"—an analogous situation to that of the women in Walker's American "triangles." The women cohabiting these polygamous households "will do anything for one another." They cooperate in appeasing their husbands, for "a grown child is a dangerous thing, especially since, among the Olinka, the husband has life and death power over the wife. If he accuses one of his wives of witchcraft or infidelity, she can be killed" (153). The circumstances of the Olinka women remind the reader of what has transpired in the "America" section of the novel—particularly Celie's treatment by "Pa" and Mr. _____ and Annie Julia's murder.

Africa is neither a lost Eden nor a recovered paradise in this novel: indeed, Walker reiterates that many African tribal leaders participated in the slave trade as a means of ridding their villages of troublesome or independent individuals. And Nettie's reports to Celie of Olinka tribal life serve as a reminder that the oppression of women within familial structures is a nearly universal phenomenon. The first and most important Olinka story she relates is the myth of the roofleaf—the source of thatch for huts. According to Olinka legend, a former chief had used his prominence to procure as much land and as many wives as possible. He destroyed most of the roofleaf supply in order to plant cash crops, and used his many wives as an agricultural labor force. When a storm swept away most of the village, there was no roofleaf available for rebuilding. The chief was exiled, the modern utensils his crops had paid for were banished, and the remaining roofleaf stands were protected. Because of its invaluable purpose, the environmentally threatened roofleaf became the "Olinka God" (142). This cautionary tale shows that the Olinka people can learn to preserve—even revere—the environment that sustains them when their very survival is threatened by the chief's greedy exploitation and careless destruction of the area's natural resources. Unfortunately, they are powerless to protect this newly discovered and delicate relationship to nature when the region where their village is situated is bought by an English rubber company and then leveled to make way for vast rubber plantations. Walker links the chief's dreams of domination and his patriarchal household—his ecological degradation of the land for short-term profit and his employment of wives as involuntary laborers—and the English rubber company's imperialistic obliteration of a region's habitat and virtual enslavement of the indigenous Olinka tribe for the purpose of tending its rubber plantations.

The impact of the tribe's patriarchal culture and the rubber company's apocalyptic termination of the villagers' isolation and independence is best understood through the character of Tashi, the African girl Olivia befriends. The highest aspiration for an Olinka girl is to become one of the chief's wives, even though they are miserable and "work like donkeys" (145). Furthermore, the Olinka do not believe that a girl should be educated, since her only path to identity is to be the mother of her husband's children. So when Olivia undertakes the task of providing her friend with a rudimentary education (a project reminiscent of Nettie's earnest efforts to continue Celie's schooling), Tashi's parents intercede. They are afraid their daughter is "becoming quiet and too thoughtful," like "one of her aunts who was sold to the trader because she no longer fit into village life" (148). The Olinka respond to the destruction of their community and way of life by enforcing practices that foster cultural identity, including facial scarification and the "female initiation ceremony," or clitoridectomy. The villagers are inscribing their "identification as a people into their children's faces." When they meet with resistance from their children, "the carving is done by force" (214). Tashi is torn between knowledge of worlds, standards, and ways of life beyond her village, and the solace and expression of defiance the practices of her own cultural tradition might provide. Because the encroachment of the western world upon her village has brought grievous ruin and virtual enslavement to her people, Tashi resigns herself to the inevitable necessity of undergoing the female initiation ceremony as a means of maintaining tribal membership and rejecting western values. However, the semiotics of physical mutilation fail to provide Tashi with an individual identity. Her scars are the sign of another form of enslavement: her status as an adult female member of her tribe—important only as a potential wife and mother. Tashi flees the village in search of another community: the mbeles, a shadowy band of rebels operating from the forest to eradicate the presence of white colonialists in Africa.

Adam, however, has fallen in love with Tashi, and follows her to the guerrilla camp in the hope that he can convince her to return to America with him. Adam and Tashi negotiate a relationship that is the novel's promise for the future—its most utopian formulation. Their marriage will represent a reconciliation of sorts between America and Africa— between the descendants of Africans who sold their brothers and sisters into slavery and the descendants of those slaves—united now by their common oppression under white imperialism. Because Tashi is fearful that her scars will set her apart as a "freak" in America, Adam acquires a matching set. His willingness to undergo the facial scarification usually demanded only of women is symbolic of his desire to share and understand the plight of women in patriarchal societies. It also serves as a manifesto of independence from the cultural imperialism enforced by the rubber planters, who deprive the Olinka of their roofleaf god.

The name Adam assumes when he marries Tashi—Adam Omatangu—is a further sign of the importance Walker places upon this relationship. Omatangu is the Olinka word for the Adam who figures in their version of the creation story. According to Olinka mythology, Omatangu was the first white baby born in their village who wasn't put to death. Omatangu and subsequent whites born, mysteriously, to black mothers were, however, exiled from "the garden," never to be heard from again. It is significant that Omatangu "wasn't even the first white man" (239). A full recovery of origins is impossible: the real or first "Adam" is unknowable. However, a full knowledge of one's present circumstances *is* possible—and self-awareness is both the end and definition of human life. Celie translates the Olinka term for "Adam" as "a un-naked man somewhere near the first one God made that knowed what he was" (241). For the Olinka, then, the first man was the first fully conscious being, aware of his potentialities and eager to seize the possibilities existence afforded him. Adam Omatangu's new name bridges the biblical and the Olinka creation myths—origin stories of the first and third worlds. But Adam is also the first man in this novel who is fully aware of the political and cultural forces that structure his world. His efforts to resist imperialistic and patriarchal practices and customs exemplify the responsibility to act that comes with full consciousness of his condition.

Because Omatangu was white, Adam's name also suggests the possibility of racial reconciliation—a possibility reinforced by two incidents recounted near the end of this novel. The first is Samuel and Nettie's introduction to Doris Baines, a wealthy white missionary, during their trip to England to appeal for Olinka autonomy. Baines has used her privileged background and substantial financial assets to assist another tribe, the Akweans, maintain their independence. She owns their village and the region that surrounds it. She builds a hospital, grammar school, and college. Most importantly, she allows the Akweans to retain and continue their cultural traditions and way of life (excepting the practice of clitoridectomy) without the interference of missionaries. (Walker does not reconcile the presence of a western grammar school and college with this alleged cultural autonomy.) Because the Akwean chief assumes that a figure of Baines's power and influence cannot be a woman (despite the visual evidence to the contrary), he presents her with two wives as a token of the tribe's appreciation. Baines "adopts" the women, sends them to England for advanced academic study, and eventually participates in the lives of their children as a "grandmother"—a role she thoroughly relishes. Like Adam and Tashi's marriage, this alternative family is an individual instance of reconciliation between the first and third worlds, with the further advantage of bridging the barrier of race.

The second gesture toward racial reconciliation is made by Eleanor Jane, the daughter of the mayor for whom Sofia was required to work. She takes it upon herself to expiate the sins of her family by caring for Henrietta while Sofia clerks at the dry goods store that Celie inherits from "Pa." Eleanor Jane's family condemns her for acquiescing to a mode of interaction with blacks that is taboo: "Whoever heard of a white woman working for niggers, they rave" (288). She works for her "salvation," as Sofia puts it, by participating in the black extended family that has evolved by the novel's conclusion. Sofia's extended network of kin and friends becomes Eleanor Jane's surrogate family and primary source of nurturing and support.

Despite its emotional appeal, the reunion of Nettie and Celie after a thirty-year separation is only *The Color Purple*'s penultimate scene. Walker concludes her novel with a vision of a new family. She assembles most of the characters who have populated her novel at an Independence Day barbecue. "White people busy celebrating they independence from England July 4th, say Harpo, so most black folks don't have to work. Us can spend the day celebrating each other" (294). Walker offers us a brief parting scene of her characters operating together within an extended alternative family, including the triangles of Celie, Shug, and Albert and Harpo, Sofia, and Mary Agnes (and the children they have raised together), along with Odessa and Jack, Nettie and Samuel and the children of Celie's they have parented, Olivia and Adam, and Adam's African wife, Tashi. They are celebrating a new relation to one another—a new family that accommodates and nurtures a diversity of "kin" without regarding the structure of their relationships or their sexual orientation as matters for censure. Men and women are truly equals. The responsibilities of childrearing are shared by the extended family—

not restricted to women within the nuclear family. Walker leaves us with a prophecy of a new mode of community: an alternative family that is a utopian reconstruction of the black extended family. She has provided the black emergent woman with a prototypical family.

6

America as Family:
E. L. Doctorow's *Ragtime*

> But in retrospect, I suppose (speaking of *Ragtime* and *The Book of Daniel*)
> there is some kind of disposition—and no more than that—to propose that
> all our radicals (and we've had an astonishing number of them) and our la-
> bor leaders and our Wobblies and our anarchists and so on, have really
> been intimate members of the family—black sheep, as it were, whom no
> one likes to talk about. And I suppose one could make a case for my dis-
> position to suggest that they are indeed related, that they are part of the
> family, and that they've had an important effect on the rest of us.[1]

E. L. Doctorow's analysis of American radicals and social agitators as
eccentric, strong-willed members of an extended national family has important connotations for my study of his novel, *Ragtime*, in which three
ethnically and economically disparate families are thrown together by
the accident of their increasingly interconnected fates—eventually con-
glomerating into a single family unit. The metaphor of the nation as
family imposes, ironically, implicit limits on the subversive efficacy of
radical discourse and activity even as it suggests that the worst intentions or excesses of the ruling elites might be mitigated through the interventions of their more ethical and visionary kin. If America's critics
are "family," then it is more difficult for them to attain the independence
of perspective and cogency of argument that would be required to precipitate or facilitate real structural change. Not only are our radicals at
least partially implicated in the national perpetration of imperialism and
injustice by means of their familial membership, but the accusation that
their "mother" country is ostracizing, silencing, or persecuting them because of unorthodox positions or unassimilated discourses becomes
more problematic: no one can ever be fully outside the family or

completely "other." Our prophets and lonely consciences are not isolated, marginalized, and scorned Jeremiahs after all, but not-so-distant
relatives who must be heeded and respected—albeit begrudgingly and
usually belatedly—because of their blood ties to our American family:
"But I think that all writers and all nations operate as children do of
families whom they love and hate and try to distinguish themselves from
and somehow reform at the same time. And I would put a nation's artists
in that category—as loving and tortured children" (57). Doctorow posits
a dynamic of history in which the ideas of America's prodigal children—while feared and vilified by their parents—are revered by the subsequent generation of our nation's family: "The radical ideas of one generation make up the orthodoxy of subsequent generations, so the radical
role is to be sacrificial."[2]

This familial paradigm is contradicted, in part, both by Doctorow's
own use of history and historical figures in his fiction and by an alternative role he proposes for the American writer. Larry McCaffery, Paul
Levine, and Barbara Foley have all noted Doctorow's use of the past as
a screen onto which the concerns and problems of the present can be
projected. McCaffery finds that Doctorow's novels use "the past to explore not only the past but certain parallel tendencies in the present"
(37). Paul Levine suggests that "Doctorow's treatment of history is deliberately anachronistic in the way it reshapes the past to parallel the
present."[3] And Barbara Foley warns that Doctorow's "commenting
upon the age of Wilson by importing a dramatic example from the age
of Nixon [the 'black nationalist' Coalhouse Walker] . . . carries the
implication that historical change is itself chimerical."[4] Foley lauds
Doctorow's strategy, finally, as a means to *promote* social change: "In
Ragtime, however, Doctorow seems to be implying that accurate representation of the past is less crucial than revelation of the haunting continuity of the past in the present" (168). Doctorow himself seems to confirm this alternative reading of his approach to history in an essay
entitled "False Documents":

> All history is contemporary history, says Croce in *History as the Story of
> Liberty*: "However remote in time events may seem to be, every historical

judgment refers to present needs and situations." That is why history has to be written and rewritten from one generation to another. The act of composition can never end.[5]

Doctorow is more concerned, then, with finding or inventing the contemporary world in the past than with tracing a genealogical and ideological dialectic. Doctorow may subscribe to a radical version of the American belief in "progress," but his fiction seems to lament that the radical *ideals* of the past were not adopted by subsequent generations and remain unfulfilled today despite the triumph of specific radical *ideas*—their adaptation by the body politic, their absorption by mainstream America. "Little has changed despite all that has occurred in *Ragtime*," argues Arthur Saltzman. "Thus, as in every Doctorow novel, the dominant American mythology remains relatively intact."[6]

Doctorow's understanding of the dynamics of history and his vision of America as a community that embraces—awkwardly, reluctantly, or even posthumously—its artists and dissidents, is at odds with another, more universally shared ideal: the figure of the cultural or political critic operating from a position of relative objectivity and isolation. Doctorow proclaims that "writers are independent witnesses and, theoretically at least, not connected to the defense of any institution, whether it be *the family* or the Pentagon or God" [emphasis mine].[7] Doctorow celebrates and defends the writer as the most articulate, potent, and subversive of the American family's "black sheep" (the cliché he employs in the interview excerpt above).[8] There is an inherent contradiction here between the writer's ideological detachment from sacrosanct institutions like the family—indeed, his/her responsibility to uncover the realities of their operations and dynamics—and the idealistic metaphor of national affiliation Doctorow employs to reassure the writer, the outsider—himself, finally—that community is possible and progress inevitable.

The tension between an ideal of community and a sobering sense of its elusiveness is prevalent throughout E. L. Doctorow's *Ragtime*, culminating in the brief, sketchy glimpse he offers us of an alternative family at the novel's conclusion. The widowed wife of the novel's central ruling class white, Anglo-Saxon Protestant family marries Tateh, a successful Jewish immigrant, and a widower: they raise their own children and the son of the martyred black ragtime performer turned revolutionary, Coalhouse Walker. While this is an extraordinarily optimistic vision of what is possible when Americans of different racial, religious, and economic backgrounds come to meet and know one another, it is accompanied by a terrible sense of the loss and victimization that brought them together. Their union is possible only after the eradication of Tateh's cultural identity and the complete annihilation of Coalhouse Walker—a "black sheep" in all senses of the term who has hardly been heeded or included in the nation's familial embrace. Denied the possibility of having a family of his own when his fiancée is mistaken for an assassin at a rally for a vice presidential candidate and mortally wounded, Coalhouse Walker founds a renegade "family" of outcasts: a terrorist group devoted to winning justice for the collective familial unit of "Coalhouse."

This cursory examination of the novel's conclusion shows us that Doctorow's struggle to reconcile an ideal of family with the real fates suffered by America's dissidents and outsiders is inextricably linked to another dichotomy: the ideal of America as a land of inclusion and the reality of the exclusion and discrimination that was often the immigrant's lot. Put another way, Doctorow leaves us with a version of the "melting pot" family idealized by J. Hector St. John de Crèvecoeur, the first observer of the American scene to recognize the future significance of a fledgling nation of immigrants: "Here individuals of all nations are melted into a new race of men, whose labours and posterity will one day cause great changes in the world."[9] But before we are granted a fleeting glimpse of America's unrealized potential for ethnic and racial harmony, Doctorow insists that we witness the real struggle that has been waged in America between those whose aim is to enforce and profit from a system of norms and laws encoding cultural hegemony, and those who have been excluded from the "family" of America on the basis of race, religion, or ethnicity.

In an important early text in the study of ethnicity, *Assimilation in American Life*, Milton M. Gordon argues that "Anglo-conformity"—the belief that "English-oriented cultural patterns" are "dominant and standard in American life"[10]—has been "the most prevalent ideology of assimilation in America throughout the nation's history" (89), and notes that this ideology "received its fullest expression in the so-called Americanization movement which gripped the nation like a fever during World War I" (98)—the period ushered in at the end of *Ragtime*. Gordon identifies a series of articles by Horace Kallen entitled "Democracy *versus* the Melting Pot" as the first serious intellectual counterpoint to the hysterical imposition of cultural hegemony that was fueled by the war. Kallen's plea for cultural pluralism—as Doctorow's novel attests—went largely unheeded by his countrymen. Kallen saw America at a "cultural crossroads": "It can attempt to impose by force an artificial, Anglo-Saxon-oriented uniformity on its peoples, or it can consciously allow and encourage its ethnic groups to develop democratically, each emphasizing its particular deep-rooted cultural heritage" (142). For the characters—both "fictional" and "historical"—who populate the world of *Ragtime,* this "cultural crossroads" becomes an impasse; Doctorow's double historical perspective forces us to recognize that we are still confounded by this choice today.

In some ways, Doctorow's reconstructed family is an exemplary model of the ideal of the "melting pot": Mother and Tateh will forge a community with a common purpose and shared values and goals—a family. But their community will neither result in "that strange mixture of blood" (43) that Crèvecoeur postulated as the future American type nor serve as a utopia of "cultural pluralism." Their children are not the product of their union but refugees from previous marriages. Coalhouse Walker III will not be in a position to claim a cultural identity until adulthood—bereft as he is of both parents. Tateh has invented an ethnic persona—the Baron Ashkenazy—that is diametrically opposed to the reality of his socialist Jewish immigrant origins. And although Mother has renounced the xenophobia of her late husband, she still profits from the flag factory which provided him with his money and social status. That this business prospers even during father's frequent absences and after his demise is a pessimistic indication that white male power and privilege is so endemic and entrenched that it will take more than the terrorist acts of a ragtime player deranged by grief or the founding of alternative families to blunt the effects of Anglo-conformity or to restructure American society. The American social landscape remains unaltered at the end of *Ragtime*. The novel's final image is of a madman marching as a respectable citizen in an Armistice Day parade—undoubtedly waving a flag and bedecked with patriotic paraphernalia manufactured by Father.

Before I provide a closer reading of Doctorow's novel, it is useful to note yet another polarity at work in *Ragtime* in light of recent developments in ethnic studies. *Ragtime* is populated by characters who are drawn to and captivated by the ideal of America—particularly the promises of equality and equal opportunity. This is a novel of disillusionment set in an age of optimism; most of its myriad and entangled plot lines concern how Doctorow's central characters reconstruct their worlds after a devastating loss of faith in the ideals enshrined in America's founding documents. Coalhouse Walker clings tenaciously to the American ideal of equality under the law, despite all evidence to the contrary. When his automobile is vandalized by a renegade fire brigade offended by a black man owning a status symbol they cannot afford to acquire, Coalhouse Walker quickly exhausts the limited avenues of recourse available to him before resorting to increasingly drastic measures to have his car restored—to enforce America's fondest ideals of justice. His success costs him his life. Tateh, on the other hand, "sells" his dreams—moving picture books with images of the peaceful and playful life denied to his immigrant daughter—to a "novelty" company. He becomes rich and successful as a film director in the nascent motion picture industry, and renounces his ideals of worker solidarity. "Thus did the artist point his life along the lines of flow of American energy."[11] Tateh is elevated from the ranks of America's immigrants not through his own efforts and ability, but by chance. The American Dream's promise of fairness, equal opportunity, and upward mobility rings hollow in *Ragtime*.

Doctorow's vision of an America—then and now—unable to fulfill the ideals of its founding documents and his depiction of the efforts of its disillusioned ethnics and minorities to both survive and to maintain their dignity and humanity is at odds with the dialectic of "consent" and "descent" that Werner Sollors, a key contemporary theorist of ethnicity, imposes upon an American social landscape that he claims has moved, as the title of one of his books suggests, "beyond ethnicity." Sollors applies the insights of post-structuralism to the study of ethnicity, discovering that ethnic groupings are "widely shared, though intensely debated, collective fictions that are continually reinvented."[12] Nevertheless, Sollors privileges the narratives of the Pilgrims and other early white settlers of the North American continent by tracing the continuing efficacy of their "fictions" in the formation of the "American character." Sollors provides a fascinating and compelling case for the resonance throughout American history of key Biblical tropes and typologies appropriated by the Pilgrims: he argues that "the sectarian symbol system of a regionally limited group of early migrants . . . form the 'core,' the mainstream, in a polyethnic culture."[13] But this reading of America's social and cultural history undermines his argument that "Yankees" are simply one ethnic group among many—that mainstream, culturally dominant white, Anglo-Saxon Protestants cannot be robbed of their "ethnic" status. "The ethnic system of Newburyport is as incomplete without Anglo-Americans as without Afro-Americans; it is also less easily comprehensible, even though some Yankees may resent being put into an ethnic category" (36). While Sollors's call for a greater awareness of larger societal contexts in ethnic studies is valuable, he provides a curiously unsympathetic analysis of efforts to recover, uncover, or validate the diverse counternarratives and "symbol systems" of ethnic and minority groups. The "symbol systems" at the core of the white, Anglo-Saxon Protestant are, for Sollors, a master narrative of American identity.[14] Indeed, he implicitly juxtaposes the eternally relevant "symbol systems" of America's founding fathers to what he sees as the inherently dishonest attempts of ethnic groups to claim an identity apart from the mainstream: "Though they [ethnic groups] may pretend to be eternal and essential, are they not of rather recent origin and eminently pliable and unstable?"[15]

Sollors is right to criticize the isolationism perpetrated by ethnics who—obsessed with the significance of "descent"—decline to enter freely and fearlessly into America's culture of "consent." But is not much of the ethnic "invention" in America produced by the descendants of those whose fictions of freedom Sollors lauds so uncritically?[16] He unduly burdens America's ethnics with most of the blame for their disproportionate exclusion from significant participation in American society. Doctorow's rendering of American history attempts to retrieve and validate the counternarratives of America's ethnics and minorities—even as he paradoxically admits that these narratives, too, are "fictions":

> Novelists know explicitly that the world in which we live is still to be formed and that reality is amenable to any construction that is placed upon it. It is a world made for liars and we are born liars. But we are to be trusted because ours is the only profession forced to admit that it lies—and that bestows upon us the mantle of honesty.[17]

Doctorow's *Ragtime* is an intricate weave of American narratives. He gives us a complicated, multidimensional rebuttal of America's master paradigms—the fictions we have inherited precisely because they were disseminated and encoded by America's economic, intellectual, and ethnic elites. The composite American family that assembles at the end of his novel neither fully validates nor firmly disproves any particular ideology or model of ethnic assimilation. Doctorow's new American family—situated simultaneously in the past and the future—is instead a testament both to the cost of ethnic strife throughout our history and the promise of a reconciliation that may yet be achieved.

In the opening paragraphs of *Ragtime*, E. L. Doctorow provides us with a sweeping panorama of American life in the early twentieth century—a paean to a simpler, more "innocent" time that we recognize as the cultural norm:

The population customarily gathered in great numbers either out of doors for parades, public concerts, fish fries, political picnics, social outings, or indoors in meeting halls, vaudeville theatres, operas, ballrooms. There seemed to be no entertainment that did not involve great swarms of people. Trains and steamers and trolleys moved them from one place to another. That was the style, that was the way people lived. Women were stouter then. They visited the fleet carrying white parasols. Everyone wore white in summer. Tennis racquets were hefty and the racquet faces elliptical. There was a lot of sexual fainting. There were no Negroes. There were no immigrants. (3-4)

The ironic distance and mock historical tone displayed in this passage and throughout the novel accomplish two ends: Doctorow subverts both our received impressions and accounts of what life was like for the white middle class and our expectation that an objective account of history can be produced. He alerts us to the possibility that there is more than one way to tell the story of America and more than one American story to tell: "Apparently there *were* Negroes. There *were* immigrants" (5). And for these Negroes and immigrants, the size and shape of tennis racquets is hardly a matter of paramount importance or even passing interest. "Thus in *Ragtime* we get a strange mixture of lyrical evocations of a supposed 'simpler era' with a bitter debunking of such illusions,"[18] according to David S. Gross; Arthur Saltzman agrees, describing Doctorow's style as "the interplay between these two conflicting visions of America, the charmingly nostalgic and the bitterly ironic."[19]

In the opening chapters of *Ragtime*, Doctorow introduces us to a white middle class family so seemingly representative of America's Anglo norms that naming its members would grant them an individuality they don't really deserve. These characters are known simply by their function within a multigenerational American family: Father, Mother, Grandfather, Younger Brother, and the little boy. They are an ideal American family, and they prosper by exploiting the ideal of America— through Father's burgeoning flag factory and the brisk sale of patriotic paraphernalia. The more we learn about this family, however, the more distrustful we are of the assumptions we formed about them based upon the narrator's "camera eye."[20] The marriage of this quintessential

American couple—who assume, as a kind of national birthright, that "all their days would be warm and fair" (3)—actually "seemed to flourish on Father's extended absences" (10) on exotic journeys with the New York Explorers Club. And Mother's Younger Brother, bereft of appropriate avenues for utilizing his abilities or his imagination and too repressed to share his thoughts and feelings with others, is obsessed with Evelyn Nesbit—a notorious beauty he knows only through newspaper accounts and silhouette drawings: "He thought about her all the time. He was desperate to have her" (5). The little boy discovers that "the world composed and recomposed itself constantly in an endless process of dissatisfaction" (99) when he recognizes his own boredom and unhappiness with his family's thoroughly predictable routines. And when the great Harry Houdini stops at the family's home by chance one hot afternoon while waiting for the radiator of his Pope-Toledo Runabout to cool, he is overwhelmed by the stifling atmosphere of bourgeois stolidity that permeates this household: "He felt trapped by the heavy square furnishings, the drapes and dark rugs, the Oriental silk curtains, the green glass lamp shades" (8). Houdini—whose "absurd" life involved "accepting all kinds of bondage and escaping" (6)—experiences this environment as yet another false imprisonment to be escaped. He feels trapped by the trappings of the middle class.

Doctorow then introduces us to a second family that is the antithesis of this Anglo "everyfamily": he mocks the possibility that there can be a single familial model by naming these family members by *their* functions, too—albeit in a foreign tongue.

> The family lived in one room and everyone worked: Mameh, Tateh and The Little Girl in the pinafore. Mameh and the little girl sewed knee pants and got seventy cents a dozen. They sewed from the time they got up to the time they went to bed. Tateh made his living in the street. (14)

This juxtaposition of familial circumstances and prospects could hardly be more striking. The new Americans "waited for life to change. They waited for their transformation" (15). But when the promise of America fails them, Mameh is forced into prostitution by her employer and is consequently renounced by her husband. Tateh flees the slums of New York—only to become embroiled in the Lawrence Bread and Roses strike. The "transformation" of his marginal existence occurs by chance when he impulsively offers his "moving picture" book for sale to a novelty company: his success lies in his ability to create marketable illusions, and can hardly be a model or source of inspiration for other immigrants.

The characteristic dynamic in *Ragtime*, then, as we have seen in Doctorow's subversion of both American nostalgia and sentimental ideals of family in these opening chapters, is to interrogate and contest seemingly incontrovertible realities—even those established by his own narrative. Doctorow challenges the comfortable assumptions we have about life for a typical American family during the first decade of the twentieth century. In his essay, "False Documents," he explains that "if we are able to recognize and name any broad consensus of sensibility we are acknowledging its rule. Anything which governs us must by necessity be self-interested and organized to continue itself."[21] Doctorow deliberately undermines his own narrative in order to avoid either perpetrating "any broad consensus" of history or establishing a reigning narrative or master paradigm in his novel: "*Ragtime*'s episodic, free-flowing structure resists simple plot summary."[22] The novel is replete with motifs and incidents which remind the reader of the ephemeral, shadowy quality of reality. Tateh ekes out a living making silhouettes—constructing paper images "with nothing but a small scissors and some glue" (37). Houdini is "a trickster, an illusionist, a mere magician" (82)—staging populist fantasies of escape from impossible situations. Businessmen of the "era of Ragtime" (270) learn how to create larger-than-life individuals "not from the accidents of news events but from the deliberate manufactures of their own medium" (71) as a means to advertise and promote their products. The greatest businessman of them all, J. P. Morgan, "catapulted . . . beyond the world's value system," feels "an awesome responsibility to maintain the illusions of other men" (117). And Grandfather entertains the little boy with "stories of transformation" from Ovid:

> Grandfather's stories proposed to him that the forms of life were volatile
> and that everything in the world could as easily be something else. The old
> man's narrative would often drift from English to Latin without his being
> aware of it, as if he were reading to one of his classes of forty years before,
> so that it appeared nothing was immune to the principle of volatility, not
> even language. (97)

Doctorow also distrusts "systems" and insists upon the arbitrary
nature of connection—including the artifice of narrative linearity that
readers anticipate or create.[23] *Ragtime* is a book of coincidences and un-
explained phenomena. Most of Doctorow's characters are profoundly
aware of the arbitrary construction of a world rapidly being transformed
by technology and the demographics of immigration. Even the little boy
is "alert . . . to unexpected events and coincidences" (96). Emma Goldman is unfazed when she sees the celebrity model Evelyn Nesbit—whom
she despises as a "clever prostitute" (48)—in her audience at a rally
sponsored jointly by socialists and anarchists, and rescues her from the
turmoil that ensues when the police disrupt her speech. Goldman explains her concern by noting that "there are correspondences" (52) between their lives: "You came because in such ways as the universe
works, your life was destined to interact with my own" (49). It may be
that in the world of Henry Ford's assembly line—which made "the men
who built the products . . . themselves interchangeable parts" (113)—the
old forms of connection and community are outmoded and irrelevant.
Even J. P. Morgan, the undisputed "monarch of the invisible, transna-
tional kingdom of capital whose sovereignty was everywhere granted"
(115), is unnerved by the transformations he himself has wrought; he
becomes obsessed with the philosophy of the ancient Egyptians,
"wherein it was taught that the universe is changeless" (118), as a means
of coping with the rapid, tangible metamorphosis of the contemporary
world and the ultimate change of his own imminent death.

Doctorow's characters, then, are fascinated by and drawn to connection,[24] despite their bewilderment at the rapid evolution of the forms,
structures, and environments that facilitate it. "The cast of characters
separates and recombines in new and exciting ways, strengthening our

faith in some complex system of contingency and interdependence. Characters and events regularly connect in ways we can only call significant."[25] In each of Doctorow's novels, connections are made within temporary or evolving "families." In *Ragtime*, the first fateful connection is made when Mother discovers a newborn brown baby hastily buried in a shallow grave in her yard. The baby is not dead, however, and his mother is soon located hiding in a neighbor's basement. When Mother learns that the young woman will have to stand trial for attempting to kill her infant, she responds with impulsive generosity: "Mother took a deep breath. I will take the responsibility, she said. Please bring her inside. And despite the best advice of the doctor and the remonstrations of the police, she would not change her mind" (59).

Mother is unable to consult Father about these additions to their household because he has accompanied Peary on his expedition to the North Pole.[26] Segregated by the advantages of class and social position from America's impoverished immigrants and scorned minorities, Father seeks contact with "the other" through the artificial conditions and temporary exhilarations of his expeditions. Peary is accompanied by a team of Esquimos and his famous Negro assistant, Mathew Henson, on the final leg of his journey; ironically, when he takes their photograph (against a backdrop of one of Father's flags) at a site chosen arbitrarily as the North Pole, their racial characteristics and distinctions are erased: "Because of the light the faces are indistinguishable, seen only as black blanks framed by caribou fur" (68). Father's customary fastidiousness and prudery are breached only after a protracted immersion in the Arctic wilderness: "Waiting for Peary to return to the *Roosevelt* he had heard the wind howl at night and had clasped with love and gratitude the foul body, like a stinking fish, of an Esquimo woman. He had put his body into the stinking fish. The old Anglo-Saxon word he had hardly dared think of."

Yet when he returns to his family, there is "nothing . . . to tell them" (92) about his voyage. He has not been fundamentally altered by his journeys, as Younger Brother will point out accusingly in their last conversation: "You have traveled everywhere and learned nothing" (250).

And so it is not surprising that he is distressed to be greeted upon his return by "his wife holding a brown baby in her arms" (91): an interracial Madonna and child. Because the boy's mother, Sarah, has withdrawn to the attic and will have nothing to do with him, Mother has been tending to the infant—a reversal of the historic division of labor between black and white women in America. Mother has also been administrating Father's business during his lengthy absence: her expertise and acumen in this most privileged of male terrains is now the equal of her husband's. She sees the business "for the dreary unimaginative thing it was" (210). He finds that she has been reading feminist literature, including a pamphlet by Emma Goldman. Father is dismayed by these "signs of his own exclusion" (91).

Father has further cause for alarm when Coalhouse Walker initiates a weekly pilgrimage from Harlem to woo the recalcitrant Sarah and to see his son. Although Father has been to the Philippines, Africa, and the North Pole, he alone in the family has no respect for people of color, agreeing with Peary that "They're children and they have to be treated like children" (62). While "Mother was exhilarated by the situation" (131), Father finds Walker's stubborn, deliberate courtship of Sarah to be unsettling, perhaps because it is conducted by a man possessed of levels of will power and passion that are superior to his own:

> Walker didn't act or talk like a colored man. He seemed to be able to transform the customary deferences practiced by his race so that they reflected to his own dignity rather than the recipient's. When he arrived at the back door he gave it a stout rap and when admitted would solemnly greet everyone and somehow convey to them the feeling that they were Sarah's family, and that his courtesies to them simply measured the regard and respect he held for her. Father recognized certain dangers in the man. Perhaps we shouldn't encourage his suit, he said to Mother. There is something reckless about him. Even Mathew Henson knew his place. (134-35)

Father's resentment of Coalhouse Walker is shared by the immigrant, working class members of one of the local volunteer fire departments. One Sunday, they prevent Walker from leaving New Rochelle

after his weekly visit to the family by blocking his Model T and demanding an exorbitant toll for the privilege of driving past the Emerald Isle
station house. When Walker returns from a futile attempt to enlist the
police in his defense, he finds that his car has been vandalized and soiled
by mud and human excrement. His request that the car be cleaned and
repaired and that an apology be issued by the fire chief, Willie Conklin,
is deemed so audacious that he is thrown in jail; the car is completely
demolished by the firemen and dumped in a nearby pond. This ludicrous
chain of events is the catalyst for most of what will subsequently take
place in *Ragtime*—including the shattering of the boundaries separating
the novel's three families. Walker's systematic efforts to receive restitution fail. Frightened by this obsessive quest for justice and worried that
the future she has finally pledged to share with Coalhouse Walker is
jeopardized, Sarah makes an impulsive and foolhardy decision to approach a visiting dignitary—a vice-presidential candidate—intending to
make a desperate appeal. She is mistaken for an assassin and brutally
subdued. After she dies from her injuries, Coalhouse Walker, denied his
rights under the law, takes the law into his own hands. Indeed, he establishes his own set of laws under a "provisional American government"
and proceeds to bomb fire stations as a symbolic act of retribution. "His
grief for Sarah and the life they might have had was hardened into a
ceremony of vengeance in the manner of the ancient warrior" (205). A
man who created himself "by an act of will" (153) embarks on the utopian project of establishing a new American government that enforces
the ideals of justice and equality for all that are enshrined in our founding documents. This is a second American Revolution—conceived by an
African-American man and implemented by an interracial "family" that
includes Mother's Younger Brother (possessed of an identity and a sense
of purpose at last): "Younger Brother was totally integrated in their
community. He was one of them. He awoke every day into a state of solemn joy" (206).

   Father moves his family to Atlantic City for the summer to avoid
further publicity and potential ridicule or retribution for their previous
association with a black man who is now a notorious criminal. A black

maid is hired to make the presence of Walker's baby with the family less extraordinary. Mother makes a charming new friend at the beach—a moving-picture director named Baron Ashkenasky whose vitality and childlike enthusiasm are a marked contrast to Father's increasingly taciturn temperament. Tateh has sold his interest in the Franklin novelty company to finance a number of successful films. He has completely transformed his identity. He "invented a baronry for himself. It got him around in a Christian world. Instead of having to erase his thick Yiddish accent he need only roll it off his tongue with a flourish. . . He was a new man" (218). Tateh—who forsook his wife when she was forced into prostitution—has, for all his charm and creative energy, become a kind of prostitute himself. His films both exploit and perpetrate American nostalgia, sentimentality, and false idealism.

Father's vacation is interrupted when Coalhouse Walker makes an ingenious and desperate last move—successfully raiding Pierpont Morgan's library and holding his art treasures hostage. Father is called upon to serve as a negotiator between the band of "Coalhouse" (including, to his horror, Mother's Younger Brother) and the District Attorney. Coalhouse Walker's conditions are finally met. Willie Conklin himself is forced to reassemble the desecrated automobile outside Morgan's library: that a man as impaired as he can assemble a whole automobile in a single evening may be the novel's most damning indictment of the loss of creativity and autonomy mandated by the assembly line age. Walker's followers are allowed to escape in the newly refurbished Model T; Walker himself is greeted with a hail of bullets when he finally exits the library.

The final chapters of *Ragtime* chronicle the events that allow a new American community to coalesce from the wreckage of the novel's three families. The shock of Coalhouse Walker's fate creates a rift between Mother and Father that cannot be healed. "Mother and Father were now on the most correct and abbreviated speaking terms, the death of Younger Brother in Mexico [while participating in a guerrilla raid by another interracial "family" of radical outlaws] having provided final impetus for their almost continuous separation" (267). In yet another playful knotting of the strands of fiction and nonfiction, Doctorow consigns Father to a final adventure on the ill-fated Lusitania. "Poor Father, I see his final exploration. . . His toe scuffs a soft storm of sand, he kneels and his arms spread in pantomimic celebration, the immigrant, as in every moment of his life, arriving eternally on the shore of his Self" (269). Father's death at sea—and the fascination with supernatural phenomenon emanating from or pertaining to an afterlife exhibited by figures as diverse as Houdini and Morgan—serve as sobering reminders of the transient, ephemeral nature of all hierarchies and realities. Father's quests for experience have failed to familiarize him with the terrain of his own being. While Father is now a spirit immigrant, Tateh has become a quintessential American. After a period of mourning, Mother agrees to marry Tateh. Their "connection" is based, in part, upon the radical precepts of Emma Goldman: they are equals who respect the myriad differences of their backgrounds, values, and temperaments. "She adored him, she loved to be with him. They each relished the traits of character in the other" (269).

This new family is made up of immigrants from three failed unions. Tateh and Mother are unencumbered by the oppressive ideology of American idealism that crushed their previous families and destroyed the lives of Coalhouse Walker and his young fiancée. Indeed, our final insight into their future concerns Tateh's somewhat cynical exploitation of his new family: he makes a series of films about an interracial community of children—"a society of ragamuffins, like all of us, a gang, getting into trouble and getting out again" (270)—a sentimental depiction of America's ideal of equality for all reduced to the level of children's games and adventures. Tateh's films are little better than the Disney theme rides Daniel condemns as condensed historical fantasies in Doctorow's *The Book of Daniel*. They are caricatures of the rich fabric of life, culture, hope and suffering we have witnessed in the course of this novel. That a family comprised of most of the major elements of American society—black and white, Jew and gentile, immigrant and Yankee—can succeed, that these historical polarities can be collapsed is an extraordinarily optimistic indication of America's potential for harmony and equality. But Doctorow's characters forge their new family on the ashes of their ideals and former loved ones; we are not led to believe that their past sacrifices and future risks will have any lasting effect upon the structures and institutions of America. Nevertheless, this new family—situated as it is in a fluid continuum of history that includes the contemporary world as well as an imagined past—can serve as a model of sorts: perhaps America's founding ideals can be partially fulfilled after all—not through legal appeals, violence, or patriotic fervor, but within the private networks and familial assimilations of its citizens.

This community of refugees, then, is the most important alternative family in *Ragtime* and serves as a significant counterpoint to the family of "Coalhouse"—another interracial community. The Coalhouse gang exemplifies Doctorow's proposition that America's radicals are "really . . . intimate members of the family." Father, an American "everyman," finds that Mother's Younger Brother, someone who has lived under his roof, is a member of the nation's most infamous band of renegades. However, it is hard to see how Mother's Younger Brother's metamorphosis has "an important effect on the rest of us," as Doctorow intimates in his interview with Paul Levine. His participation in a spectacular revolutionary act irrevocably ruptures the family he renounces but has no impact, finally, on the structure of American society. Furthermore, his identity is never revealed to the public at large—to the extended national family. The limitations of Doctorow's vision of America as family, then, are represented in his fiction. He gives us a radical drama of American democracy as Bakhtinian carnival: a pageant of colorful eccentrics mingling and mixing in the urban melting pot.[27] The climactic "festival" (the siege of Morgan's library) brings many of the novel's characters together with both society's leading figures and the likes of Willie Conklin. But these public transactions, as Arthur Saltzman suggests, do little to alter the "dominant American mythology." The novel's climactic moment is, after all, the public "execution" of an African-American man who has dared to challenge the status quo through a desperate and foolhardy quest for justice. The hierarchy and operations of the national family remain unchanged. Emma Goldman is deported; J. P.

Morgan's interrupted cruise to Egypt is resumed; Houdini continues his regimen of performances and his frantic search for ontological certainty.

If America is a family, then lasting social change is possible only if the structure, composition, and operation of individual American households are altered. Doctorow is unable to provide more than a sketchy outline of what such a family would be like. However, it is to his credit that in proposing this alternative community, he does not gloss over the cost of constructing a new, more inclusive and egalitarian family. Like the gang of Coalhouse, Tateh and Mother's new family is a fictional antecedent of contemporary social structures and phenomena. By deconstructing the polarities of history and fiction, Doctorow encourages us to look critically upon our received notions of the past, to reject the inevitability of all institutions and hierarchies, and to imagine alternative sites and structures for the provision of familial nurturing and emotional and material support. He invites us to redefine our national and familial affiliations.

7

The Reconstructed Family
and Social Change

Although the reconstructed families depicted in the novels I have discussed are not, in the strictest sense of the word, "realistic," they are in-
habited by plausible characters negotiating recognizable conflicts and
crises. The novels of John Irving, Alice Walker, and E. L. Doctorow
challenge widely held assumptions and cherished collective mythologies
about the family. In these novels, parenting is *not* the sole responsibility
of biological mothers; families are *not* limited to biological kin alone.
These writers also deconstruct traditional notions of masculinity and address societal evils such as sexual abuse, rape, and racism, which, their
novels seem to suggest, originate in rigidly paternalistic families. Social
change must begin at home; the family is a microcosm of society. The
novels of Irving, Walker, and Doctorow share a utopian theme: disparate people can come together as kin, overcoming long-standing societal
divisions based on race, ethnicity, gender, and religion. Nevertheless,
their novels offer little more than sketchy glimpses of life within these
reconstructed families. Perhaps, given the utopian nature of imagining
new family structures and modes of interaction, it is difficult for them to
be more explicit and concrete about what the everyday dynamics of
these families might be like.

Updike's "Rabbit" novels serve as a counterpoint to this optimism
that social change is desirable and that it can emanate from the family.
Updike's view that significant social change invariably corrupts or
degrades the institutions or practices being reformed pervades his
fiction. Although he is a passionate advocate of a literature of realism,

Updike depicts a dystopian commune in *Rabbit Redux*—a surrealistic interracial family perceived through the frequently drug-blurred consciousness of an irresponsible and uncaring father and held together by drug addiction and wanton sexuality. Harry Angstrom is returned to the reality of his unhappy marriage after vigilante neighbors firebomb his home, killing Jill, who has become little more than a prostitute performing sexual acts in return for heroin. No humiliation, calamity, or transgression can permanently dissolve the Angstrom marriage—no matter how unfulfilling or emotionally empty it becomes.

Both John Updike and John Irving disparage the possibility that sexual promiscuity can lead to meaningful intimacy or lasting community. Like *Rabbit, Run* and *Rabbit Redux*, *The World According to Garp* portrays the sacrifice of a child for the sexual indiscretions of a "parent." The novels differ, however, because Garp learns from and is profoundly altered by his tragedy. Garp is "cured" of lust once he embraces both a less rigid model of masculinity and a more diverse and flexible conception of family—one that widens the family circle without jeopardizing the traditional familial functions of nurturing, instruction, and emotional support. In *Rabbit, Run* and *Rabbit Redux*, however, the deaths of the Angstroms' baby and Harry's teen-aged lover result in a bedazed, thwarted retreat back to the protective confines of the traditional nuclear family. Harry Angstrom is not "cured" of his lasciviousness by returning to his family: instead, in *Rabbit at Rest*, he violates the most fundamental law governing behavior in all family structures when he sleeps with his daughter-in-law. Unlike Irving, Updike eschews the possibility of a more flexible conception of the family's form and function, even as he provides an unsparing account of why the traditional nuclear family is not always an effective or supportive social unit.

Both *The World According to Garp* and *The Color Purple* address the issues of rape and sexual abuse. In Walker's novel, the abusers are invariably "family" members. "Pa" commits incest with his stepdaughter; Mr. _____ attempts to rape Nettie, his sister-in-law; Mary Agnes is raped by a white sheriff who doesn't want to acknowledge that he is her uncle. In Irving's novel, Garp helps to capture a child molester and eventually adopts Ellen James, the orphaned rape victim whose senseless maiming spurs the formation of a radical group bearing her name despite her disapproval of their terrible initiation rite and their isolationist stance. Although Garp is repulsed by acts of rape, he also comes to understand that his coercive acts of sex with baby-sitters are akin to sexual violence—that his predatory behavior is wrong.

In both novels, victims of sexual violence struggle to overcome a silence of shame or fear. The man who rapes Ellen James cuts out her tongue in a foolish attempt to silence her. In *The Color Purple*, "Pa" warns Celie, "*You better not never tell nobody but God. It'd kill your mammy.*"[1] The power of the oppressor to impose a sentence of silence upon his victim is the most insidious barrier to the possibility of recovery. Walker's characters struggle to find the language to name their abusers and articulate their pain: only then can they "sing" (like Mary Agnes) in an affirmation of their survival and renewal. In both novels, the victim requires a supportive community that insists she not be silenced, that she give voice to her own violation. It is only when Garp can foster such an environment that Ellen James is able to "sing" in poetry. His adoption of Ellen James is a sure sign of his rehabilitation: "It was perhaps his contact with Ellen James that finally cured him of ever looking at young girls in that way. As for other women—Helen's age, and older—Garp exercised a willpower that was not especially difficult for him. Enough of his life had been influenced by lust."[2] And Mr. _____'s assistance of Mary Agnes—his implicit recognition of the emotional maiming suffered by a victim of sexual violence—is our first indication that he is capable of reconstituting himself and atoning for his own violent treatment of Celie and Nettie. Both Mr. _____ and Garp redefine masculinity—but only under duress: Garp's loss of his child and Mr. _____'s loss of his wife and lover are events that compel each man to reexamine his life. When Mr. _____ tells Celie near the end of *The Color Purple* that "this the first time I ever lived on earth as a natural man. It feel like a new experience" (220), he is defining the "new experience" of a less rigidly constructed masculinity: he no longer has to abuse or oppress women to "prove" he is a man. Garp learns to control his "lust" and to overcome the traditionally male imperative to dominate and control. The new family envisioned in these novels requires men to discard traditionally masculine responses to women, their families, and the world.

Both *The Color Purple* and *Ragtime* conclude with sketches of multiracial reconstructed families. In Walker's novel, Eleanor Jane, the white daughter of the mayor who held Sofia in virtual bondage for nearly a dozen years, opts to provide child care for her former nanny and is "adopted" by the extended African-American family that has evolved by the end of the novel. Doctorow's vision is more problematic: the multiracial household that coalesces at the end of *Ragtime* is comprised of "immigrants" from three ruptured families. The complacent, quintessentially Anglo family of Father and Mother is torn apart by its contact with the harsh reality of American race relations. The immigrant family of Tateh is the victim of old world values and new world economic hardships: he abandons his wife when he learns she was forced to have sex with her employer. He assumes a name that hides his Jewish identity and becomes successful by producing idealized images of American life for the nascent film industry. Coalhouse Walker is denied the opportunity to bring his family together. His obsessive quest for justice in a society that will not acknowledge his legitimacy as a human being leaves his son an orphan. While the newly formed household at the end of *Ragtime* consists of refugees, the very notion that Mother, Tateh, their children, and the son of Coalhouse Walker can constitute a family is cause for optimism—an indication that America's fondest ideals of ethnic and racial harmony might yet be achieved.

The possibility that our nation's most persistent and insidious social evil—racism—might be challenged or remedied by multiracial families runs counter to the pessimistic premise of *Rabbit Redux*. In Updike's novel, the advent of a black "messiah" plunges Rabbit's alternative household into a cycle of brutality and decadence. Skeeter is literally cast as the serpent in the garden—a demonic figure of unremitting evil. After the fiery dissolution of his alternative community, Rabbit delegates its central figure to an increasingly ephemeral reality—as if

Skeeter were more a force than a human being. Racial harmony has been hindered—not forwarded. A black man becomes a fantastical presence—not a plausible human being with potentially legitimate and understandable claims.

Nevertheless, of the novels I have discussed, *Rabbit Redux* provides the most detailed depiction of life within an alternative family. John Irving, Alice Walker, and E. L. Doctorow are more comfortable depicting the evolutionary development of new families in their novels than providing more than rudimentary, sketchy glimpses of life within reconstructed families. In *The World According to Garp*, the assassination of Garp is followed by a final chapter, "Life After Garp," in which Irving traces the subsequent history of this family in a cursory, factual narrative style: the chapter might even be understood as a series of obituaries. *The Color Purple* concludes with the full assembly of Celie's extended family for the first time: the gathering takes place on the Fourth of July, a day Walker's characters devote to "celebrating each other" (294). Doctorow's *Ragtime* concludes with a brief description of a new household consisting of the survivors of the novel's three families. Irving, Walker, and Doctorow recognize and represent the forces fostering the formation of alternatives to the traditional nuclear family, but they are more guarded about providing extended accounts of daily life within these households once they have formed. Nevertheless, in an era marked by concern over the decline of the traditional nuclear family, they succeed in imagining compelling and reassuring models of reconstructed families.

Notes

1. Reconstructing the Family as a Utopian Project

1 Leo Tolstoy, *Anna Karenina*, ed. Leonard J. Kent and Nina Berberova (New York: Random, 1965) 3.

2 James M. Jeffords (Rep.—Vt.), "An Updated Report on Children in America," *Cong. Rec.* (10 Feb. 1987) H654.

3 Philip Babcock Gove, editor-in-chief, *Webster's Third New International Dictionary* (Springfield, MA: Merriam Webster, 1981) 1897.

4 Adrienne Rich, "When We Dead Awaken: Writing as Re-Vision," *On Lies, Secrets, and Silence: Selected Prose 1966-1978* (New York: Norton, 1979) 43.

5 Alice Walker, *In Search of Our Mothers' Gardens* (New York: Harcourt, 1984) 251.

6 John Updike, "One Big Interview," *Picked-Up Pieces* (New York: Knopf, 1975) 508.

2. The Family in Crisis

1 United States, Bureau of the Census, *Singleness in America*, Current Population Reports; Ser. P-23 162 (Washington, D.C.: U.S. GPO, 1988) 1.

2 United States, Bureau of the Census, *Marital Status and Living Arrangements: March 1992,* Current Population Reports; Ser. P20 468 (Washington, D.C.: U. S. GPO, 1992) vii.

3 United States, Bureau of the Census, *Marital Status and Living Arrangements: March 1988,* Current Population Reports; Ser. P-20 433 (Washington, D.C.: U. S. GPO, 1989) 1.

4 United States, Bureau of the Census, *Marital Status and Living Arrangements: March 1992,* Current Population Reports; Ser. P20 468 (Washington, D. C.: U.S. GPO, 1992) xi.

5 United States, Bureau of the Census, *Married-Couple Families With Children,* Current Population Reports; Ser. P-23 162 (Washington, D.C.: U. S. GPO, 1988) 27.

6 United States, Bureau of the Census, *Changes in American Family Life,* Current Population Reports; Ser. P-23 163 (Washington, D.C.: U. S. GPO, 1989.) 18.

7 James M. Jeffords (Rep.—Vt.), "An Updated Report on Children in America," *Cong. Rec.* (10 Feb. 1987) H654.

8 Michele Barrett and Mary McIntosh, *The Anti-Social Family* (London: Verso, 1982) 85.

9 Edward Shorter, *The Making of the Modern Family* (New York: Basic, 1975) 205.

10 Michael Anderson, *Approaches to the History of the Western Family, 1500-1914* (London: Macmillan, 1980) 14.

11 Jane Collier, Michelle Z. Rosaldo, and Sylvia Yanagisako, "Is There a Family? New Anthropological Views," *Rethinking the Family: Some Feminist Questions,* ed. Barrie Thorne and Marilyn Yalom (New York: Longman, 1982) 25.

12 Barrie Thorne, "Feminist Rethinking of the Family: an Overview," Thorne and Yalom 1.

13 Rochelle Gatlin, *American Women Since 1945* (Jackson: UP of Mississippi, 1987) 145.

14 Stephanie Coontz, *The Way We Never Were: American Families and the Nostalgia Trap* (New York: Basic, 1992) 69.

15 David Cheal, *Family and The State of Theory* (Toronto: U of Toronto P, 1991) 3.

16 Richard Harvey Brown, *Society as Text* (Chicago: U of Chicago P, 1987) 3.

17 Christopher Lasch, *Haven in a Heartless World: The Family Besieged* (New York: Basic, 1977) xxi.

18 Christopher Lasch, *The Culture of Narcissism,* 2nd ed. (New York: Norton, 1980) 155.

19 Lasch, *Haven in a Heartless World* 92.

20 Lasch, *Culture of Narcissism* 195.

21 Lasch, *Haven in a Heartless World* 6.

22 Shorter 5.

23 Jacques Donzelot, *The Policing of Families,* trans. Robert Hurley (New York: Pantheon, 1979) 92.

24 Barbara Ehrenreich and Deirdre English, *For Her Own Good: 150 Years of the Experts' Advice to Women* (Garden City: Anchor, 1979) 324. F. Ivan Nye ("Values, Family, and a Changing Society." *Readings on the Changing Family.* Ed. David A. Schulz and Robert A. Wilson. Englewood Cliffs: Prentice-Hall, 1973: 272-84) offers the terms "instrumental" and "intrinsic" to contain the same categories. Most defenses of a monolithic family are grounded in an emotional attachment to what are viewed as intrinsic properties of warmth, sharing, community, and continuity despite evidence that certain family circumstances and configurations actually deprive one or more family members of these very benefits. Nye proposes that "an era is imminent in which more normative family behavior will come to be viewed by the society as instrumentally valued only" (283); society should be "freed from the dead hand of traditional practice" (284) so that families are less rigidly structured and more responsive to actual societal circumstances and individual needs.

25 Barrett and McIntosh 29.

26 Lasch, *Culture of Narcissism* 169.

27 Ehrenreich and English 324.

28 Nancy Chodorow, *The Reproduction of Mothering* (Berkeley: U of California P, 1978) 70.

29 Renate Bridenthal, "The Family: The View From a Room of Her Own," Thorne and Yalom 232.

30 Eli Zaretsky, "The Place of the Family in the Origins of the Welfare State," Thorne and Yalom 218-19.

31 "In fact, the family has been slowly coming apart for more than a hundred years. The divorce crisis, feminism, and the revolt of youth originated in the nineteenth century, and they have been the subject of controversy ever since." Lasch, *Haven in a Heartless World* xx.

32 Judith Stacey, *Brave New Families: Stories of Domestic Upheaval in Late Twentieth Century America* (New York: Basic, 1991) 17.

33 Rayna Rapp, "Family and Class in Contemporary America," Thorne and Yalom 170.

3. Harry Angstrom's Flights from the Family

1   John Updike, *Rabbit, Run* (New York: Knopf, 1970) 39.

2   Leslie Fiedler, *Love and Death in the American Novel*, rev. ed. (New York: Stein, 1966) 26.

3   Joyce Markle, *Fighters and Lovers: Theme in the Novels of John Updike* (New York: New York UP, 1973) 53.

4   John Updike, *Rabbit Redux* (New York: Knopf, 1971) 34.

5   Fiedler 29.

6   We might consider Rabbit's obsession with the young woman he correctly surmises is Ruth's daughter in *Rabbit is Rich* as a means of coping with the loss of a third "daughter": the fetus Ruth promises to abort in her last conversation with him in *Rabbit, Run*. His indulgent sexual fantasies about the girl he suspects he may have fathered are similar to the blurring of roles and boundaries with Jill in *Rabbit, Redux* and, as we will see in *Rabbit at Rest*, with his own daughter-in-law, Pru.

7 Charles Berryman, "The Education of Harry Angstrom: Rabbit and the Moon," *Literary Review* 27 (1983): 118.

8 John Updike, *Self-Consciousness* (New York: Knopf, 1989) 147.

9 John Updike, "Accuracy," *Picked-Up Pieces* (New York: Knopf, 1975) 16.

10 "A god who is not God the Creator is not very real to me, so that, yes, it certainly *is* God who throws the lightning bolt and this God is above the nice god, above the god we can worship and empathize with. I guess I'm saying there's a fierce God above the kind God . . ." John Updike, "One Big Interview," *Picked-Up Pieces* 504.

11 John Updike, "Why Write?" *Picked-Up Pieces* 31-32.

12 E. L. Doctorow, "The Beliefs of Writers," *Michigan Quarterly Review* 24.4 (1985): 619.

13 John Updike, "One Big Interview" 502.

14 John Updike, "On One's Own Oeuvre," *Hugging the Shore* (New York: Knopf, 1983) 858.

15 John Updike, "One Big Interview" 508.

16 Christopher Lasch, *Haven in a Heartless World: The Family Besieged* (New York: Basic, 1977) xvix-xx.

17 "Sexual suspect" is the term Garp's mother, Jenny Fields, coins for anyone who defies society's gender, sexual, or marital expectations (see chapter 4).

18 Donald J. Greiner, *John Updike's Novels* (Athens: Ohio UP, 1984) 55.

19 This sentence was added to the fifth printing of *Rabbit, Run.* Updike "corrected" and reset the plates for the fifth printing (1970).

20 Barbara Ehrenreich, *The Hearts of Men: American Dreams and the Flight from Commitment* (Garden City: Anchor, 1983) 24.

21 Sigmund Freud, *Civilization and Its Discontents*, Trans. James Strachey (New York: Norton, 1961) 51-52.

22 Wayne D. McGinnis, "Salvation by Death in *Rabbit, Run*," *Notes on Contemporary Literature* 8.2 (1978): 7-8.

23 Dean Doner, "Rabbit Angstrom's Unseen World," *John Updike: A Collection of Critical Essays*, ed. David Thorburn and Howard Eiland (Englewood Cliffs: Prentice-Hall, 1979) 30.

24 Markle 41.

25 Joseph Waldmeir, "It's the Going That's Important, Not the Getting There: Rabbit's Questing Non-Quest," *Modern Fiction Studies* 20.1 (1974): 20.

26 Edward P. Vargo, *Rainstorms and Fire: Ritual in the Novels of John Updike* (Port Washington: Kennikat, 1973) 61.

27 Markle 57.

28 Herbert Marcuse, *Eros and Civilization* (Boston: Beacon, 1955) 37.

29 Norman O. Brown, *Life Against Death* (New York: Vintage, 1959) 58.

30 Michiko Kakutane, "Turning Sex and Guilt into an American Epic," *Saturday Review* Oct. 1981: 15.

31 Greiner 73.

32 Wayne Falke, "*Rabbit Redux*: Time/Order/God," *Modern Fiction Studies* 20.1 (1974): 71.

33 Markle 158-59.

34 Richard Locke, "Rabbit's Progress," Thorburn and Eiland 37.

35 Eugene Lyons, "John Updike: The Beginning and the End," *Critique* 14.2 (1972): 57-58.

36 Robert Alter, "Updike, Malamud, and the Fire This Time," Thorburn and Eiland 47.

37 Robert Detweiler, *John Updike* (Boston: Twayne, 1984) 136.

38 Frederick Karl, *American Fictions: 1940-1980* (New York: Harper, 1983) 349.

39 F. Scott Fitzgerald, *The Great Gatsby, The Fitzgerald Reader*, ed. Arthur Mizener (New York: Scribner's, 1963) 237.

40 John Updike, *Rabbit at Rest* (New York: Knopf, 1990) 193.

4. The Family According to Garp

1 John Irving, *The World According to Garp* (New York: Dutton, 1978) 63.

2 Gabriel Miller, *John Irving* (New York: Ungar, 1982) 180-81.

3 Carol C. Harter and James R. Thompson, *John Irving* (Boston: Twayne, 1986) 92.

4 Miller 109.

5 Harter and Thompson 76.

6 Randolph Runyon, *Fowles/Irving/Barthes* (Miami: Miami UP, 1981) 39.

7 John Irving has gone to great lengths to distinguish his fiction from contemporary experiments "in language and in f-f-form," as Garp's stuttering writing instructor, Mr. Tinch, describes "n-n-newer fiction" (129). In an interview with Larry McCaffery, Irving decries "the elitism, the preciousness, the specialness of so much contemporary fiction. I hate what is turning the novel—once the most public of forms—into something like contemporary painting and contemporary poetry; namely, largely designed for other painters and other poets." Larry McCaffery, "An Interview With John Irving," *Contemporary Literature* 23.1 (1982): 11.

8 Randolph Runyon provides a convincing reading of the self-referential nature of Irving's oeuvre in *Fowles/ Irving/Barthes.*

9 Only Philip Roth's Nathan Zuckerman surpasses T. S. Garp as a representation of the crisis of the imagination plaguing the prototypical contemporary American writer.

10 Miller 117.

11 Harter and Thompson 93.

12 Harter and Thompson 79.

13 Even Garp's choice of occupation, as I have already noted, is a response to lust: "Garp wrote later that he first discovered he had an imagination while trying to imagine Helen Holm's body" *Garp* 63.

14 Marilyn French, "The 'Garp' Phenomenon," *Ms.* Sept. 1982: 14-15.

15 Like Rabelais's *Gargantua*, Irving's *The World According to Garp* is a detailed account of an *education*: they also have in common an insistence upon the value of tolerance, a deep commitment to a utopian humanistic project (the Abbey of Thélème in Rabelais; Garp's extended family in Irving), and a sometimes grotesque sense of comic extravagance and excess.

16 Miller 110.

17 Susan Gilbert, "Children of the Seventies: The American Family in Recent Fiction," *Soundings* 62.2 (1980): 199.

18 The world of John Irving's subsequent novel, *The Hotel New Hampshire*, is imbued with a similar sensibility: "Thus the family maxim was that an unhappy ending did not undermine a rich and energetic life. This was based on the belief that there *were* no happy endings." John Irving, *The Hotel New Hampshire*, paperback ed. (New York: Dutton, 1981) 150.

5. The Emergent Woman's Family in *The Color Purple*

1 In *The Sexual Mountain and Black Women Writers* (New York: Anchor Press, 1987), Calvin C. Hernton maintains that *The Color Purple*—concerned as it is with "Oppression and the Process of Liberation" (3)—is an emulation of another genre: the slave narrative.

2 Alice Walker, *The Color Purple* (New York: Washington Square, 1982) 11.

3 Gloria Steinem, "Do You Know This Woman? She Knows You: A Profile of Alice Walker," *Ms.* June 1982: 94.

4 Alice Walker, *In Search of Our Mothers' Gardens* (New York: Harcourt, 1984) 252.

5 Mary Helen Washington, "Teaching Black-Eyed Susans: An Approach to the Study of Black Women Writers," *Black American Literature Forum* 11.1 (1977): 22.

6 Marie H. Buncombe, "Androgyny as Metaphor in Alice Walker's Novels," *College Language Association Journal* 30.4 (1987): 420.

7 Ruth Nadelhaft, "Domestic Violence in Literature: A Preliminary Study," *Mosaic* 17.2 (1984): 254.

8 Walker, *In Search of Our Mothers' Gardens* 5.

9 Trudier Harris, "On *The Color Purple*, Stereotypes, and Silence" *Black American Literature Forum*, 18.4 (1984): 160.

10 Walker, *In Search of Our Mothers' Gardens* 129.

11 Robert Staples and Leanor Boulin Johnson, *Black Families at the Crossroads* (San Francisco: Jossey-Bass, 1993) 46.

12 Stephanie Coontz, *The Way We Never Were: American Families and the Nostalgia Trap* (New York: Basic, 1992) 235.

13 Elmer P. and Joanne Mitchell Martin, *The Black Extended Family* (Chicago: U of Chicago P, 1978) 1.

14 Daniel Patrick Moynihan, *The Negro Family: The Case For National Action,* U.S. Dept. of Labor, Office of Policy Planning and Research (Washington, D.C.: U.S. GPO, 1965) 29. Moynihan set the stage for a national debate that has raged for more than three decades with his claim that the declining number of traditional nuclear families among blacks in urban areas is "the principal source of most of the aberrant, inadequate, or antisocial behavior that did not establish, but now serves to perpetuate the cycle of poverty and deprivation" (30).

15 Elmer P. and Joanne Mitchell Martin, 9.

16 Carol B. Stack, *All Our Kin: Strategies for Survival in a Black Community* (New York: Harper, 1974) 9.

17 Peter Erikson, "Cast Out Alone/ To Heal/ And Re-Create/ Ourselves: Family-Based Identity in the Work of Alice Walker" *College Language Association Journal*, 23.1 (1979): 71.

18 Diana E. H. Russell, *Sexual Exploitation* (Beverly Hills: Sage, 1984) 118.

19 Susan Brownmiller, *Against Our Will: Men, Women and Rape* (New York: Simon, 1975) 281.

20 Susan Griffin, *Rape: The Politics of Consciousness* (San Francisco: Harper, 1986) 17.

21 Alice Walker, "Writing *The Color Purple*," *In Search of Our Mothers' Gardens* 355.

22 Jack is the antithesis of Odessa's father, whom Sofia describes as abusive toward her mother: "He hate children and he hate where they come from" (46). By acknowledging and exploiting his emotional complexity and nurturing capabilities, Jack is able to avoid the pitfalls of the "masculinity mystique" and the lust for dominance and control it entails. When Celie designs a pair of pants for Jack, they "have big pockets so he can keep a lot of children's things" and are tailored "so he can run if he need to snatch a child out the way of something" (192). They are pants for a man actively engaged in sharing both domestic work and the lives of his children.

23 Annie Julia's story is yet another indication that *The Color Purple* is not simply a fairy tale, as Trudier Harris suggests.

24 Walker's unlikely American antecedent is Ralph Waldo Emerson, the most prominent voice of the "Transcendentalist" movement. The philosophy expounded in Emerson's essay, "The Over-Soul," for example, has much in common with Shug's insistence that a direct, unmediated experience of the Divine is possible.

25 Juan Mascaró, trans., *The Upanishads* (New York: Penguin, 1965) 49.

26 George Stade, for example, derides the novel as a ludicrous fantasy entailing "the establishment of a utopian commune presided over by the heroine and her female lover, although a couple of womanish men are allowed to hang around, as long as they behave themselves" (264). George Stade, "Womanist Fiction and Male Characters" *Partisan Review*, Vol. 52, No. 3 (1985).

6. America as Family: E. L. Doctorow's *Ragtime*

1 Paul Levine, "The Writer as Independent Witness," *E. L. Doctorow: Essays and Conversations*, ed. Richard Trenner (Princeton: Ontario Review, 1983) 67-68.

2 Larry McCaffery, "A Spirit of Transgression," Trenner 44.

3 Paul Levine, *E. L. Doctorow* (New York: Methuen, 1985) 55.

4 Barbara Foley, "From *U.S.A.* to *Ragtime*: Notes on the Forms of Historical Consciousness in Modern Fiction," Trenner 167.

5 E. L. Doctorow, "False Documents," Trenner 24.

6 Arthur Saltzman, "The Stylistic Energy of E. L. Doctorow," Trenner 99.

7 Levine, "The Writer as Independent Witness" 69.

8 In "False Documents," E. L. Doctorow names the power of the writer as the ability to construct "a private or ideal world that cannot be easily corroborated or verified—let us call that *the power of freedom.*" He juxtaposes this power to what he calls the official, bureaucratic and scientific language that is *"the power of the regime."* E. L. Doctorow, "False Documents" 16-17.

9 J. Hector St. John de Crèvecoeur, *Letters From an American Farmer* (London: Dent, 1971) 43.

10 Milton M. Gordon, *Assimilation in American Life* (New York: Oxford UP, 1964) 88.

11 E. L. Doctorow, *Ragtime* (New York: Random, 1974) 111.

12 Werner Sollors, ed., *The Invention of Ethnicity* (New York: Oxford UP, 1989) xiii.

13 Werner Sollors, *Beyond Ethnicity: Consent and Descent in American Culture* (New York: Oxford UP, 1986) 54.

14 In their introduction to *Ethnicity: Theory and Experience*, (Cambridge: Harvard UP, 1975), Nathan Glazer and Daniel P. Moynihan understand the political implications of such distinctions: "In a situation of mixed ethnic groups where one group is dominant, which is to say that its norms are seen as normal not just for it, but for others also, there follows an almost automatic consignment of other groups to inferior status" (14).

15 Sollors, *Invention of Ethnicity* xiv.

16 The 1988 presidential campaign offered an unfortunate example of how easily ethnic prejudices—even toward second-generation Americans of European descent—can be incited precisely because it is so pervasive and commonplace. George Bush—by ancestry, the quintessential Yankee—painted Michael Dukakis as an opponent who wasn't *really* an American—hence his lack of a blind, unquestioning allegiance to the narrowest notions of what "the flag" symbolizes. Dukakis's veto of an unconstitutional 1977 Massachusetts bill that would have required teachers and students to recite the "Pledge of Allegiance" became, incredibly, a central issue in the campaign. Leading Republicans used this veto as a vehicle to promote a wide range of rumors denigrating the patriotism of Dukakis and his family. Bush made numerous campaign appearances at flag factories, recited the "Pledge of Allegiance" at every opportunity (including the Republican national convention), defended his running mate's lack of combat duty in Vietnam by praising Dan Quayle's respect for Old Glory (". . . and he damn sure didn't burn the American flag!"), and distributed "Americans for Bush" bumper stickers—a slogan whose subtle implication was that only unassimilated ethnics and minorities would care to vote for a national ticket headed by a son of immigrants who couldn't be trusted with the flag. This campaign history is particularly apropos to *Ragtime* for two reasons. First, the "Pledge of Allegiance" is, in effect, a "loyalty oath" first drawn up in 1892 and recited at most public schools by World War I—the historical period of Doctorow's novel. The oath served both to indoctrinate and assimilate immigrants and to assuage the anxiety of the country's increasingly outnumbered "Anglo-Americans." And one of the central motifs in *Ragtime* is the ideological significance of the American flag. Father—who personifies the bourgeois white Anglo-Saxon Protestant traits that were and are our cultural norm—literally "owns" the flag and profits from selling replicas to the newly arrived immigrants—who worship it as a talisman of the freedom and opportunity so few of them, sadly, will actually find.

17 Doctorow, "False Documents" 26.

18 David S. Gross, "Tales of Obscene Power: Money and Culture, Modernism and History in the Fiction of E. L. Doctorow," Trenner 129.

19 Saltzman 91.

20 Many readers of *Ragtime* have commented on structural and thematic similarities between Doctorow's novel and John Dos Passos's *U.S.A.*

21 Doctorow, "False Documents" 17.

22 Saltzman 93.

23 "What is most monstrous is sequence. . . . The monstrous reader who goes from on from one word to the next. The monstrous writer who places one word after another." E. L. Doctorow, *The Book of Daniel* (New York: Random, 1971) 245-46.

24 In *The Book of Daniel*, a fictional portrayal of the Rosenberg case, Daniel Isaacson conducts an obsessive quest to "connect" with his tragic family history. "We are dealing here with a failure to make connections" (226-27), he laments at one point as he reviews the range of evidence concerning his parents' trial and execution (by means of a grisly mode of connection: electrocution) offered by a number of reformers, including his adoptive father, the law professor Robert Lewin. Daniel finds their futile appeals to be a form of complicity—born in a belief that the legal system *can* work, that justice can be won.

25 Saltzman 97.

26 The location of the North Pole, like so many of the "realities" Doctorow presents to his characters and readers alike, cannot be fully and concretely ascertained: "On this watery planet the sliding sea refused to be fixed. He couldn't find the exact place to say this spot, here, is the North Pole." *Ragtime* 68.

27 Mikhail Bakhtin (1895-1975) "is gradually emerging as one of the leading thinkers of the twentieth century," according to Michael Holquist, himself the foremost critic and translator of the evolving Bakhtinian canon (a body of work that will remain, tragically, incomplete, given the loss of many of his writings: the only copy of a key manuscript was destroyed, along with the publishing house, during World War II; many other works are lost or incomplete). At the heart of Bakhtin's work in linguistics and literary theory is the notion of "a ceaseless battle between centrifugal forces that seek to keep things apart, and centripetal forces that strive to make things cohere" (M. M. Bakhtin. *The Dialogic Imagination*. Ed. Michael Holquist. Austin: U of Texas P, 1981: xviii). Bakhtin was fascinated by medieval carnivals—festivals and feast days when the

clergy and nobility mingled with peasants, and sacred or powerful individuals and institutions could be mocked or mimicked through masks, theater, profanity and song—because the egalitarian laughter of carnival leveled hierarchy and forged community. Bakhtin's discovery of this radically destabilizing energy at work in literature by figures as diverse as Rabelais and Dostoevsky is one of his most important achievements.

7. The Reconstructed Family and Social Change

1 Alice Walker, *The Color Purple* (New York: Washington Square, 1982) 11.

2 John Irving, *The World According to Garp* (New York: Dutton, 1978) 378.

Bibliography

Alter, Robert. "Updike, Malamud, and the Fire This Time." Thorburn and Eiland. 39-49.

Anderson, Michael. *Approaches to the History of the Western Family, 1500-1914.* London: Macmillan Press, 1980.

Barrett, Michele, and Mary McIntosh. *The Anti-Social Family.* London: Verso, 1982.

Berryman, Charles. "The Education of Harry Angstrom: Rabbit and the Moon." *Literary Review* 27 (1983): 117-26.

Bridenthal, Renate. "The Family: The View From a Room of Her Own." Thorne and Yalom. 225-39.

Brown, Norman O. *Life Against Death.* New York: Vintage, 1959.

Brown, Richard Harvey. *Society as Text.* Chicago: U of Chicago P, 1987.

Brownmiller, Susan. *Against Our Will: Men, Women and Rape.* New York: Simon, 1975.

Buncombe, Marie H. "Androgyny as Metaphor in Alice Walker's Novels." *College Language Association Journal* 30.4 (1987): 19-27.

Cheal, David. *Family and The State of Theory.* Toronto: U of Toronto P, 1991.

Chodorow, Nancy. *The Reproduction of Mothering.* Berkeley: U of California P, 1978.

Collier, Jane, Michelle Z. Rosaldo, and Sylvia Yanagisako. "Is There a Family? New Anthropological Views." Thorne and Yalom. 25-39.

Coontz, Stephanie. *The Way We Never Were: American Families and the Nostalgia Trap.* New York: Basic, 1992.

Crèvecoeur, J. Hector St. John de. *Letters From an American Farmer.* London: Dent, 1971.

Detweiler, Robert. *John Updike.* Boston: Twayne, 1984.

Doctorow, E. L. "The Beliefs of Writers." *Michigan Quarterly Review* 24.4 (1985): 609-19.

_____. *The Book of Daniel.* New York: Random, 1971.

_____. "False Documents." Trenner. 16-27.

_____. *Ragtime.* New York: Random, 1974.

Doner, Dean. "Rabbit Angstrom's Unseen World." Thorburn and Eiland. 17-34.

Donzelot, Jacques. *The Policing of Families.* Trans. Robert Hurley. New York: Pantheon, 1979.

Ehrenreich, Barbara. *The Hearts of Men: American Dreams and the Flight from Commitment.* Garden City: Anchor, 1983.

_____ and Deirdre English. *For Her Own Good: 150 Years of the Experts' Advice to Women.* Garden City, Anchor, 1979.

Emerson, Ralph Waldo. "The Over-Soul." *Selected Writings of Emerson.* Ed. Donald McQuade. New York: Random, 1981.

Erickson, Peter. "Cast Out Alone/ To Heal/ And Re-Create/ Ourselves: Family-Based Identity in the Work of Alice Walker." *College Language Association Journal* 23.1 (1979): 71-94.

Falke, Wayne. "*Rabbit Redux*: Time/Order/God." *Modern Fiction Studies* 20.1 (1974): 59-75.

Fiedler, Leslie. *Love and Death in the American Novel.* Rev. ed. New York: Stein, 1966.

Fitzgerald, F. Scott. *The Great Gatsby. The Fitzgerald Reader.* Ed. Arthur Mizener. New York: Scribner, 1963.

Foley, Barbara. "From *U.S.A.* to *Ragtime*: Notes on the Forms of Historical Consciousness in Modern Fiction." Trenner. 158-78.

French, Marilyn. "The 'Garp' Phenomenon." *Ms.* Sept. 1982: 14-16.

Freud, Sigmund. *Civilization and Its Discontents.* Trans. James Strachey. New York: Norton, 1961.

Gatlin, Rochelle. *American Women Since 1945.* Jackson: UP of Mississippi, 1987.

Gilbert, Susan. "Children of the Seventies: The American Family in Recent Fiction." *Soundings* 62.2 (1980): 199-213.

Glazer, Nathan and Moynihan, Daniel P. *Ethnicity: Theory and Experience.* Cambridge: Harvard UP, 1975.

Gordon, Milton M. *Assimilation in American Life*. New York: Oxford UP, 1964.

Greiner, Donald J. *John Updike's Novels*. Athens: Ohio UP, 1984.

Griffin, Susan. *Rape: The Politics of Consciousness*. San Francisco: Harper, 1986.

Gross, David S. "Tales of Obscene Power: Money and Culture, Modernism and History in the Fiction of E. L. Doctorow." Trenner. 120-50.

Harris, Trudier. "From Victimization to Free Enterprise: Alice Walker's *The Color Purple*." *Studies in American Fiction* 14.1 (1986): 1-17.

_____. "On *The Color Purple*, Stereotypes, and Silence." *Black American Literature Forum* 18.4 (1984): 155-61.

Harter, Carol C., and James R. Thompson. *John Irving*. Boston: Twayne, 1986.

Hernton, Calvin C. *The Sexual Mountain and Black Women Writers*. New York: Anchor, 1987.

Holquist, Michael. Introduction. *The Dialogic Imagination*. By Mikhail Bakhtin. Ed. Michael Holquist. Austin: U of Texas P, 1981.

Irving, John. *The Hotel New Hampshire*. Paperback ed. New York: Dutton, 1981.

_____. *The World According to Garp*. New York: Dutton, 1978.

Jeffords, James M.(Rep.—Vt.). "An Updated Report on Children in America." *Cong. Rec.* 10 Feb. 1987: H654.

Kakutane, Michiko. "Turning Sex and Guilt into an American Epic." *Saturday Review* Oct. 1981: 14-15.

Karl, Frederick. *American Fictions: 1940-1980.* New York: Harper, 1983.

Lasch, Christopher. *The Culture of Narcissism.* 2nd ed. New York: Norton, 1980.

_____. *Haven in a Heartless World: The Family Besieged.* New York: Basic, 1977.

Levine, Paul. "The Writer as Independent Witness." Trenner. 57-69.

Locke, Richard. "Rabbit's Progress." Thorburn and Eiland. 35-38.

Lyons, Eugene. "John Updike: The Beginning and the End." *Critique* 14.2 (1972): 44-59.

Marcuse, Herbert. *Eros and Civilization.* Boston: Beacon, 1955.

Markle, Joyce. *Fighters and Lovers: Theme in the Novels of John Updike.* New York: New York UP, 1973.

Martin, Elmer P. and Joanne Mitchell. *The Black Extended Family.* Chicago: U of Chicago P, 1978.

McCaffery, Larry. "An Interview With John Irving." *Contemporary Literature* 23.1 (1982): 1-18.

_____. "A Spirit of Transgression." Trenner. 31-47.

McGinnis, Wayne D. "Salvation by Death in *Rabbit, Run.*" *Notes on Contemporary Literature* 8.2 (1978): 7-8.

Miller, Gabriel. *John Irving*. New York: Frederick Ungar Publishing Co., 1982.

Moynihan, Daniel Patrick. *The Negro Family: The Case for National Action*. United States. Dept. of Labor. Office of Policy Planning and Research. Washington: GPO, 1965.

Nadelhaft, Ruth. "Domestic Violence in Literature: A Preliminary Study," *Mosaic* 17.2 (1984): 243-60.

Nye, F. Ivan. "Values, Family, and a Changing Society." Schulz and Wilson. 272-84.

Rabelais, François. *The Histories of Gargantua and Pantagruel*. Trans. J. M. Cohen. New York: Penguin, 1955.

Rapp, Rayna. "Family and Class in Contemporary America." Thorne and Yalom. 168-87.

Rich, Adrienne. "When We Dead Awaken: Writing as Re-Vision." *On Lies, Secrets, and Silence: Selected Prose 1966-1978*. New York: Norton, 1979.

Runyon, Randolph. *Fowles/Irving/Barthes*. Miami: Miami UP, 1981.

Russell, Diana E. H. *Sexual Exploitation*. Beverly Hills: Sage, 1984.

Saltzman, Arthur. "The Stylistic Energy of E. L. Doctorow." Trenner. 73-108.

Schulz, David A., and Robert A. Wilson, eds. *Readings on the Changing Family*. Englewood Cliffs: Prentice-Hall, 1973.

Shorter, Edward. *The Making of the Modern Family.* New York: Basic, 1975.

Sollors, Werner. *Beyond Ethnicity: Consent and Descent in American Culture.* New York: Oxford UP, 1986.

_____, ed. *The Invention of Ethnicity.* New York: Oxford UP, 1989.

Stacey, Judith. *Brave New Families: Stories of Domestic Upheaval in Late Twentieth Century America.* New York: Basic, 1991.

Stack, Carol B. *All Our Kin: Strategies for Survival in a Black Community.* New York: Harper, 1974.

Stade, George. "Womanist Fiction and Male Characters." *Partisan Review* 52.3 (1985): 264-70.

Staples, Robert, and Leanor Boulin Johnson. *Black Families at the Crossroads.* San Francisco: Jossey-Bass, 1993.

Steinem, Gloria. "Do You Know This Woman? She Knows You: A Profile of Alice Walker." *Ms.* June 1982: 35+.

Thorburn, David, and Howard Eiland, eds. *John Updike: A Collection of Critical Essays.* Englewood Cliffs: Prentice-Hall, 1979.

Thorne, Barrie. "Feminist Rethinking of the Family: an Overview." Thorne and Yalom. 1-24.

_____ and Marilyn Yalom, eds. *Rethinking the Family: Some Feminist Questions.* New York: Longman, Inc., 1982.

Tolstoy, Leo. *Anna Karenina.* Ed. Leonard J. Kent and Nina Berberova. New York: Random House, 1965.

Trenner, Richard, ed. *E. L. Doctorow: Essays and Conversations*. Princeton, NJ: Princeton Review, 1983.

Tyler, Anne. *The Accidental Tourist*. New York: Knopf, 1986.

United States. Bureau of the Census. *Changes in American Family Life*. Current Population Reports. Ser. P-23 163. Washington: GPO, 1989.

_____. *Marital Status and Living Arrangements: March 1988*. Current Population Reports. Ser. P-20 433. Washington: GPO, 1989.

_____. *Marital Status and Living Arrangements: March 1992*. Current Population Reports. Ser. P20 468. Washington: GPO, 1992.

_____. *Married-Couple Families With Children*. Current Population Reports. Ser. P-23 162. Washington: GPO, 1988.

_____. *Singleness in America*. Current Population Reports. Ser. P-23 162. Washington: GPO, 1988.

_____. *Single Parents and Their Children*. Current Population Reports. Ser. P-23 162. Washington: GPO, 1988.

The Upanishads. Trans. Juan Mascaró. New York: Penguin, 1965.

Updike, John. "Accuracy." *Picked-Up Pieces*. 16-17.

_____. "On One's Own Oeuvre." *Hugging the Shore*. New York: Knopf, 1983. 837-78.

_____. "One Big Interview." *Picked-Up Pieces* 491-519.

_____. *Picked-Up Pieces*. New York: Knopf, 1975.

_____. *Rabbit at Rest*. New York: Knopf, 1990.

_____. *Rabbit is Rich*. New York: Knopf, 1981.

_____. *Rabbit Redux*. New York: Knopf, 1971.

_____. *Rabbit, Run*. New York: Knopf, 1970.

_____. *Self-Consciousness*. New York: Knopf, 1989.

_____. "Why Write?" *Picked-Up Pieces*. 29-39.

Vargo, Edward P. *Rainstorms and Fire: Ritual in the Novels of John Updike*. Port Washington: Kennikat, 1973.

Waldmeir, Joseph. "It's the Going That's Important, Not the Getting There: Rabbit's Questing Non-Quest." *Modern Fiction Studies* 20.1 (1974): 13-27.

Walker, Alice. *The Color Purple*. New York: Washington Square, 1982.

_____. *In Search of Our Mothers' Gardens*. New York: Harcourt, 1984.

_____. "Writing *The Color Purple*." *In Search of Our Mothers' Gardens* 355-60.

Washington, Mary Helen. "Teaching Black-Eyed Susans: An Approach to the Study of Black Women Writers." *Black American Literature Forum* 11.1 (1977): 20-24.

Zaretsky, Eli. "The Place of the Family in the Origins of the Welfare State." Thorne and Yalom. 188-224.

Index

abortion, 10, 19, 33
Accidental Tourist, The (Tyler), 60
Adam, 103, 105–06, 107
adoption, 106, 131, 132
affairs
    Germaine and Shug, 102
    Harry and Pru, 55
    Harry and Ruth, 32–33, 40–41, 54
    Harry and Thelma, 54
    Helen and Michael, 73–75
    Janice and Charlie, 26–27, 42, 52
Africa, 83, 102–07
African-American, 43–44, 46, 50, 81, 83, 85–88, 115, 123, 126, 132
Against Our Will: Men, Women, and Rape (Brownmiller), 89–90
age-of-Wilson
    See Wilson, age-of-
Albert, 81, 82, 91–95, 96, 97, 98–99, 100–01, 107, 130–31
All Our Kin (Stack), 87, 88
Alter, Robert, 47–48
American Fictions: 1940-1980 (Karl), 48
American Women Since 1945 (Gatlin), 11
anarchism, 120
Anderson, Michael, 9
Anglo-American, 111, 115, 117
Anglo-conformity, 112–14, 117

Angstrom, Harry, 25–29, 32–56, 130, 132–33
    and Ruth, 32–33, 54
Angstrom, Janice, 26–27, 32–34, 3738, 40–43, 52–56
Angstrom, Mim, 28, 43, 52–53
Angstrom, Nelson, 27, 45–46, 50–52
Angstrom, Pru, 55
Anna Karenina (Tolstoy), 1
Annie Julia, 98–99, 103
Anti-Social Family, The (Barrett and McIntosh), 8–9, 19
Approaches to the History of the Western Family (Anderson), 9
Armey, Dick, 12
Ashkenazy, Baron, 113, 124
    See also Tateh
Assimilation in American Life (Gordon), 112–13

Babo, 48
Baines, Doris, 106–07
Bakhtin, Mikhail, 126
Barrett, Michele, 8–9, 19
Benito Cereno (Melville), 48
Bensenhaver, Arden
    See World According to Bensenhaver, The
Berryman, Charles, 28
Beyond Ethnicity (Sollors), 115
birth control, 10, 33

black extended family, 87–88, 107, 132

Black Extended Family, The (Martin), 87–88

Black Families at the Crossroads (Staples and Johnson), 87

black nationalist, 27, 29, 86, 110
   See also Pan-Africanist

Book of Daniel, The (Doctorow), 125, 147n. 24

Brave New Families (Stacey), 23

Bread and Roses strike
   See Lawrence Bread and Roses strike

breadwinner, 8, 10, 35

Bridenthal, Renate, 22

Brown, Murphy, 11

Brown, Norman O., 41

Brown, Richard Harvey, 13

Brownmiller, Susan, 89–90

Buchanan, Daisy, 53

Buncombe, Marie H., 84–85

capitalism, 15, 31

Carraway, Nick, 52

Celie, 81–82, 84, 86, 87, 88–91, 92, 93–107, 131, 133

census data, 9
   See also demographic data; U.S. Bureau of the Census

Cézanne, 29

Charlotte, 61–62

Cheal, David, 12–13

childbirth, 35, 41

child care, 132
   See also day care; parenting; motherhood

child labor, 14

child rearing, 9, 14, 18–19, 22, 98–99, 107

Chodorow, Nancy, 22

Cindy

   See Little Squab Bones

Civilization and its Discontents (Freud), 38

civil liberties, 10
   See also abortion; Civil Rights Movement; Equal Rights Amendment; gay rights; Women's Movement

Civil Rights Movement, 83, 86

Clinton, Bill, 11

Coalhouse gang, 112, 124, 126

Collier, Jane, 10

colonialism in Africa, 104–06
   See also imperialism

colonialism in U.S., 12

Color Purple, The (Walker), 2, 4, 20, 21, 81–108, 130–32, 133

Congressional Report (1987), 8

conservativism, 7, 10, 11, 31, 41

"Contract with America," 12

Coontz, Stephanie, 12, 87

Corrine, 102–03

Crèvecoeur, J. Hector St. John de, 112, 113

cultural pluralism, 113

Culture of Narcissism, The (Lasch), 13–15, 19

day care, 10, 17–18

death of a child, 6, 26, 33, 36, 37–38, 42, 90, 130

"Democracy versus the Melting Pot," 113

demographic data, 7–8, 9
   See also U.S. Bureau of the Census

Detweiler, Robert, 48

Dickens, Charles, 60

divorce, 7–8, 10, 16

Doctorow, E. L., 29–30, 109–27, 129, 132, 133

domestic violence, 14–15, 20, 85, 89–
90, 93–94
See also rape; sexual abuse
Doner, Dean, 39
Donzelot, Jacques, 16–18
Dos Passos, John, 147n. 20
drugs, 28, 42–43, 49–52
Dukakis, Michael S., 146n. 16
dystopia, 3, 5, 132

Eccles, Lucy, 36–38
Eccles, Reverend, 32, 34, 36–40
Ehrenreich, Barbara, 17–20, 21, 35
*E. L. Doctorow: Essays and
Conversations* (Trenner), 109,
110, 111, 116, 117, 119, 121
Eleanor Jane, 99, 107, 132
Ellen James Society, 64, 68, 71, 75,
77–79
See also James, Ellen; rape
Emerson, Ralph Waldo, 144n. 24
English, Deirdre, 17–20, 21
Equal Rights Amendment, 10
Erickson, Peter, 88
Eros and Civilization (Marcuse), 40–
41
Esquimo, 121
Ethnicity: Theory and Experience
(Glazer and Moynihan), 145n. 14
"everyfamily"
See Father; Grandfather; Little
Boy; Mother; Mother's Younger
Brother
"everyman"
See Angstrom, Harry; Father

Falke, Wayne, 47
"False Documents," 110–11, 118
family
blurred boundaries within, 45, 53,
55, 130
definitions of, 7, 8–9, 13

extended, 5, 6, 12, 14, 16, 63–64
See also black extended family
interracial, 123–24, 125
isolated, 3, 6, 20
nuclear, 5, 8–10, 12–14, 16–20, 21,
23, 28, 29, 30, 31, 87–88, 89, 133
Family and the State of Theory
(Cheal), 12–13
Father, 114, 117, 121–22, 123, 124–
25, 126, 132
Fedallah, 48
feminism, 3, 11, 15, 85, 122
fiction
and history, 4–5
See also Ragtime
and reality, 3–4
*See also World According to
Garp, The*
as salvation, 4
See also Color Purple, The
Fiedler, Leslie, 25, 28
Fields, Jenny, 60, 64–68, 69, 74, 75,
77
*Fighters and Lovers: Theme in the
Novels of John Updike* (Markle),
26, 36, 39, 40, 47
Fitzgerald, F. Scott, 52
Fletcher, Alice and Harrison
See marriage, open
Foley, Barbara, 110
Ford, Henry, 120
*For Her Own Good: 150 Years of the
Experts' Advice to Women*
(Ehrenreich and English), 17–20,
21
Fowles/Irving/Barthes (Runyon), 68,
69
French, Marilyn, 74
Freud, Sigmund, 36, 38

Garp, Duncan, 72–74

Garp, T. S., 57–64, 67–80, 130–31, 133
Garp, Technical Sergeant, 66–67, 68
Garp, Walt, 72–74, 79
Gatlin, Rochelle, 11
gay rights, 10
Germaine, 102
Gilbert, Susan, 78
Gingrich, Newt, 12
Glazer, Nathan, 145n. 14
Goldman, Emma, 120, 122, 125, 126
Gordon, Milton M., 112–13
Grandfather, 117, 119
Great Gatsby, The (Fitzgerald), 52
Grenier, Donald J., 33, 42
Griffin, Susan, 94
Gross, David S., 117

Harpo, 89–90, 91–92, 93, 97–98, 99–100, 107
    and Mary Agnes, 89, 97
Harris, Trudier, 85–87
Harrison, Ronnie, 54
Harrison, Thelma, 54
Harry Angstrom
    See Angstrom, Harry
Harter, Carol R., 63, 66
Haven in a Heartless World: The Family Besieged (Lasch), 13–15, 23, 31
Hawthorne, Nathaniel, 34
Hearts of Men, The (Ehrenreich), 35
Henrietta, 97
Henson, Mathew, 121, 122
Hernton, Calvin C., 142n. 1
History as the Story of Liberty (Croce), 110–12
Holm, Helen, 57, 59, 60, 68, 70, 71–73, 74–75, 76, 77
homoeroticism, 25, 39, 41
homosexuality, 10, 34

See also gay rights; homoeroticism; lesbianism
Hotel New Hampshire, The (Irving), 142n. 18
Houdini, Harry, 118, 119, 125, 126
housewives, 8, 10, 34–35
Hugging the Shore (Updike), 31
humanism, 31, 32, 36

immigrant, 14, 112–13, 114, 117–18, 119, 122, 132
imperialism, 81, 104–05
    See also capitalism; colonialism
industrialization, 17–19
infanticide, 90
    attempted, 121
In Search of Our Mothers' Gardens (Walker), 4, 82–83, 95–96
Invention of Ethnicity, The (Sollors), 115
Irving, John, 2–3, 6, 57, 59–60, 68–69, 79–80, 127, 130–31, 133
isolationism, 116

Jack, 96, 107
James, Ellen, 64, 69, 71, 77–79, 129
    See also Ellen James Society
Jewish, 111–12, 113, 125, 132
    See also Ashkenazy, Baron; immigrant; Little Girl; Mameh; Tateh
Jill, 27–28, 42, 44–46, 49–52, 130
Jimbo's Lounge, 43–44
John Irving (Harter and Thompson), 63, 66
John Irving (Miller), 59
Johnson, Leanor Boulin, 87
John Updike (Detweiler), 48
John Updike's Novels (Greiner), 33, 42

Kakutane, Michiko, 41

Kallen, Horace, 113
Karl, Frederick, 48

labor movement
    See Lawrence Bread and Roses
    strike; solidarity
Lasch, Christopher, 13–17, 18, 19–20,
    22, 23, 24, 31
Lawrence Bread and Roses strike, 119
Leary, Mason, 60
lesbianism, 85, 95
    See also triangles: Albert, Celie,
    Shug
Letters from an American Farmer
    (Crèvecoeur, J. Hector St. John
    de), 112, 113
Levine, Paul, 110, 126
liberalism, 10, 11, 13, 16
    See also radicals
Life and Times of Frederick Douglass,
    The (Douglass), 51
little boy, 117, 119–20
little girl, 118
Little Squab Bones, 70–71, 78
Locke, Richard, 47
Love and Death in the American Novel
    (Fiedler), 25
lust, 69–71, 73, 77, 78–79, 130–32
Lyons, Eugene, 47

Making of the Modern Family, The
    (Shorter), 9, 15–16
Mameh, 118–19
Marcuse, Herbert, 40–41
Markle, Joyce, 26, 36, 39, 40, 47
marriage, 8, 11, 33
    arranged, 81–82, 90, 91–92
    Adam and Tashi, 105–06
    Eccles and Lucy, 36–38
    Fat Stew and Midge, 67–68
    Garp and Helen, 57, 69, 71–72
    Harpo and Sophia, 92–93

    Harry and Janice, 26, 32, 53–54, 130
    Jack and Odessa, 96
    Mother and Tateh, 113, 125–26
    open
        See open marriage
    married status, 7, 8
Martin, Elmer and Joanne, 87–88
Marxism, 13
Mary Anges, 89–91, 97, 99, 107, 130–
    31
Mary Ellen, 100
masculinity
    redefinition of, 57–59, 75–79, 93–
    94, 100–01, 130–32
McCaffrey, Larry, 110
McGinnis, Wayne D., 38–39
McIntosh, Mary, 8–9, 19
melting pot, 112–13
Melville, Herman, 48
middle class, 117, 118
Miller, Gabriel, 59
Milton, Michael, 73, 74, 75
Moby-Dick (Melville), 48
Morgan, J. P., 119, 120, 126–27
mother
    single, 8, 11
        See also Fields, Jenny
    working, 8, 10, 15
Mother, 111, 113, 117, 121–22, 124–
    25, 127, 132
motherhood, 10–11, 22
Mother's Younger Brother, 117–18,
    121–22, 123, 124, 126
Moynihan, Daniel P., 87–88, 145n. 14
Moynihan report, 87–88
Mr. _____
    See Albert
Muldoon, Roberta, 64, 67, 77
Murphy Brown
    See Brown, Murphy
Mustache Kid, 69–70
My Father's Illusions, 76, 79

Nadelhaft, Ruth, 85
National Book Award (1963), 29
Nesbit, Evelyn, 120
Nettie, 81–82, 89, 91, 92, 99, 100,
    102–04, 107, 130–31
never-married status, 8
    See also single status
Nye, F. Ivan, 137n. 24
1950s, 8, 12, 35
1960s, 27, 28, 31, 42, 46, 84
    See also Women's Movement,
    Nixon era, Civil Rights
    Movement, Vietnam era
Nixon era, 28, 110
nuclear family
    See family, nuclear

O'Connor, Flannery, 83
Odessa, 96, 107
Olinka, 103–06
Olivia, 103, 104, 107
Omatangu, 105–06
open marriage, 71
Ovid, 119–20

Pan-Africanist, 86
    See also black nationalist
parenting, 57–59
patriarchal authority, 18
Peary, Robert, 121–22
"Pension Grillparzer, The," 57, 58,
    59–62, 63, 76, 79–80
Percy family, 62, 72
    Bainbridge
        See Pooh
    Cushie, 68, 79
    Pooh, 68, 79
    Stewart
        See Fat Stew
        See also Steering, Midge; Fat
    Stew

Picked-Up Pieces (Updike), 29, 30, 31
Policing of Families, The (Donzelot),
    16–18
polygamy, 103
    See also open marriage; specific
    triangles
pregnancy, 92–93
premarital sexual activity, 10
prenatal testing, 19
prostitution, 32, 34, 35, 61, 69, 118–
    19, 120, 130
Pulitzer Prize, 2

Quayle, Dan, 11

Rabbit
    See Angstrom, Harry
Rabbit at Rest (Updike), 54–56
Rabbit Redux (Updike), 25, 26–28, 31,
    32, 38, 41–54, 55, 130, 133
Rabbit, Run (Updike), 25–26, 28, 30–
    41, 53, 54, 130
Rabelais, 142n. 15
racial reconciliation, 106–07, 125–27,
    132
racism, 87, 129, 132–33
    See also Skeeter; stereotype,
    racial
radicals, 109–10, 111, 112, 124
    See also anarchist; Walker,
    Coalhouse
Ragtime (Doctorow), 5, 6, 20, 21, 22,
    109–27 132–33
*Rainstorms and Fire: Ritual in the
    Novels of John Updike* (Vargo),
    40, 51
Ralph, Mrs., 62, 72–73
rape, 40, 51, 69, 75, 89–90, 129, 130–
    31
    See also Ellen James Society;
    Mustache Kid; sexual assault
    of the land, 103–05

Rape: The Politics of Consciousness
(Griffin), 94
Rapp, Rayna, 23
Reagan, Ronald, 7
realism, 5, 29–30
reconstruct,
definition of, 2
Reproduction of Mothering, The
(Chodorow), 22
Republicans, 11, 12
See also conservatism, Reagan,
Ronald; Quayle, Dan; Gingrich,
Newt; Armey, Dick
Rich, Adrienne, 3, 5–6
romantic vs. rationalist, 17–19, 21
Rosaldo, Michelle, 10
Roth, Philip, 141n. 9
Runyon, Randolph, 68, 69
Russell, Diana E. H., 89
Ruth, 32–33, 40–41, 54

Saltzman, Arthur, 111, 117, 126
Samuel, 102–03, 107
Sarah, 121–23
Saturday Review (1981), 41
Second Wind of the Cuckold, 71
seduction
Cushie and Garp, 68, 79
Garp and Little Squab Bones, 70–
71
Garp and Mrs. Ralph, 72–73
Self-Consciousness (Updike), 29
sexual abuse, 14–15, 51, 81–82, 89–
91, 129, 130–31
See also domestic violence; rape;
triangles: Harry, Jill, and Skeeter
sexual assault, 6, 65, 70, 71
Sexual Exploitation (Russell), 89
sexuality
See lust; homosexuality;
transsexuality

*Sexual Mountain and Black Women
Writers, The* (Hernton), 142n. 1
Sexual Suspect, A, 65–66
See also Fields, Jenny
Shorter, Edward, 15–16
single-parent household, 8
See also mother, single
single status, 7
See also never-married status
Skeeter, 27–29, 42, 46–53, 132–33
Smith, Mrs., 39
socialism, 113, 120
See also Goldman, Emma;
Marxism; solidarity
Society as Text (Brown), 13
solidarity, 114
See also Lawrence Bread and
Roses strike
Sollors, Werner, 115–16
Sophia, 89–90, 92–93, 97–100, 107,
132
Squeak
See Mary Agnes
Stacey, Judith, 23
Stack, Carol B., 87–88
Stade, George, 144n. 26
Standish, Dorsey and Hope
*See World According to
Bensenhaver, The*
Staples, Robert, 87
Stavros, Charlie, 26–27, 52
Steering, Midge, 67
Steering School, 62, 67–68
Steinem, Gloria, 82
stepfamily, 8, 113
stereotype, racial, 28, 44, 48, 87
See also racism; Skeeter
surrogate motherhood, 19
Suzie Q., 99

Tashi, 104–07

Tateh, 111–12, 113, 114, 118–19, 124, 125, 127, 132
  See also Ashkenazy, Baron
terrorism, 112, 114
  See also Coalhouse gang
test-tube babies, 19
Theobald, Herr
  See "Pension Grillparzer, The"
Thompson, James R., 63, 66
Thorne, Barrie, 10
Tinch, Mr., 60
Tolstoy, Leo, 1
Tothero, 34–36, 39
transsexuality
  See Muldoon, Roberta
triangles
  Albert, Celie, and Shug, 95–97, 98–99, 101–102
  Corrine, Nettie, and Samuel, 99, 102–03
  Harry, Jill, and Nelson, 27, 45–46
  Harry, Jill, and Skeeter, 28, 48–52
Tyler, Anne, 60

unmarried couples, 8, 10
Upanishads, 82, 100
Updike, John, 2, 3, 5, 6, 23, 25–56, 129–30, 132–33
upper class
  Fields, 64–65
  Jill's parents, 50–51
  Percys, 62
U.S. Bureau of the Census, 7–8
utopianism, 2–3, 129, 133
  and history of the family, 2, 13, 19, 20, 129
  and literature, 2–6, 58, 76, 79, 84, 85, 88, 105, 108, 123, 129–30, 133

Vargo, Edward, 40, 51

Vienna, 59
  See also "Pension Grillparzer, The"
Vietnam era, 46, 49
Vigilance, 59

Waldmeir, Joseph, 40
Walker, Alice, 2, 4–6, 82–86, 88, 108, 129–133
Walker, Coalhouse, 110, 112, 114, 122–25.
  See also Coalhouse gang
Washington, Mary Helen, 84
Way We Never Were, The (Coontz), 12, 87
"When We Dead Awaken: Writing as Revision" (Rich), 3
white
  See Anglo-American
"Why Write?" (Updike), 29–30
widowed status, 11, 111, 112
Wilson
  age-of-, 110
women
  role in family, 9–11, 17–20, 22
Women's Movement, 11, 18–19
working class, 122
World According to Bensenhaver, The, 75–76
World According to Garp, The (Irving), 3–4, 20, 21, 22, 57–80, 130–32, 133
writer
  role of, 29–30, 83, 110, 111

xenophobia, 113

Yanagisako, Sylvia, 10
"Young Goodman Brown" (Hawthorne), 34

Zaretsky, Eli, 22–23

Studies on Themes and Motifs in Literature

The series is designed to advance the publication of research pertaining to themes and motifs in literature. The studies cover cross-cultural patterns as well as the entire range of national literatures. They trace the development and use of themes and motifs over extended periods, elucidate the significance of specific themes or motifs for the formation of period styles, and analyze the unique structural function of themes and motifs. By examining themes or motifs in the work of an author or period, the studies point to the impulses authors received from literary tradition, the choices made, and the creative transformation of the cultural heritage. The series will include publications of colloquia and theoretical studies that contribute to a greater understanding of literature.

For more information, contact:

Peter Lang Publishing, Inc.
Acquisitions Department
275 Seventh Avenue, 28th floor
New York, New York 10001

ENGLAND

UNDER

THE ANGEVIN KINGS

BY

KATE NORGATE

IN TWO VOLUMES—VOL. II.

WITH MAPS AND PLANS

BURT FRANKLIN
NEW YORK

Published by BURT FRANKLIN
235 East 44th St., New York, N.Y. 10017
Originally Published: London 1887
Reprinted: 1969
Printed in the U.S.A.

Library of Congress Card Catalog No.: 69-18611
Burt Franklin: Research and Source Works Series 351
Selected Essays in History, Economics, and Social Science 76

LIST OF MAPS

III. IRELAND, A.D. 1172 . . . . *To face page* 82

IV. MAP TO ILLUSTRATE THE REBELLION OF
    1173–1174 . . . . . . „ 149

V. FRANCE AND BURGUNDY *c.* 1180 . . „ 185

VI. EUROPE *c.* 1180 . . . . . „ 189

VII. FRANCE AND THE ANGEVIN DOMINIONS,
    1194 . . . . . . „ 359

PLANS

VII. LES ANDELYS AND CHÂTEAU-GAILLARD . *To face page* 375

VIII. CHÂTEAU-GAILLARD . . . . „ 378

ERRATA

Page 71, line 3, *for* "the two kings" *read* "they."

,, 81, ,, 3 from foot, *for* "Caen" *read* "Avranches."

,, 81, note 6, line 11, *for* "doubtless" *read* "probably."

,, 147, ,, 3, ,, 6, *for* "Châteauneuf" *read* "Neufchâtel."

,, 152, line 16, *for* "Robert." *read* "Roger."

,, 155, ,, 8, *dele* "in person."

,, 157, ,, 7, *for* "thousand" *read* "hundred."

,, 160, ,, 22, *for* "Robert" *read* "Roger."

,, 160, lines 22, 23, *dele* "had . . . now."

,, 163, line 5 from foot, *for* "Robert" *read* "Roger."

CONTENTS

CHAPTER I

PAGE

ARCHBISHOP THOMAS, 1162–1164 I
    Note A.—The Council of Woodstock 43
    Note B.—The Council of Clarendon 44

CHAPTER II

HENRY AND ROME, 1164–1172 46

CHAPTER III

THE CONQUEST OF IRELAND, 795–1172 82

CHAPTER IV

HENRY AND THE BARONS, 1166–1175 120

CHAPTER V

THE ANGEVIN EMPIRE, 1175–1183 169

CHAPTER VI

THE LAST YEARS OF HENRY II., 1183–1189 229

CHAPTER VII

RICHARD AND ENGLAND, 1189–1194 273

CHAPTER VIII

PAGE

THE LATER YEARS OF RICHARD, 1194–1199 332

CHAPTER IX

THE FALL OF THE ANGEVINS, 1199–1206 388

Note.—The Death of Arthur 429

CHAPTER X

THE NEW ENGLAND, 1170–1206 431

CHAPTER I.

ARCHBISHOP THOMAS.

1162-1164.

SOMEWHAT more than a year after the primate's death, Thomas the chancellor returned to England. He came, as we have seen, at the king's bidding, ostensibly for the purpose of securing the recognition of little Henry as heir to the crown. But this was not the sole nor even the chief object of his mission. On the eve of his departure—so the story was told by his friends in later days—Thomas had gone to take leave of the king at Falaise. Henry drew him aside: "You do not yet know to what you are going. I will have you to be archbishop of Canterbury." The chancellor took, or tried to take, the words for a jest. "A saintly figure indeed," he exclaimed with a smiling glance at his own gay attire, "you are choosing to sit in that holy seat and to head that venerable convent! No, no," he added with sudden earnestness, "I warn you that if such a thing should be, our friendship would soon turn to bitter hate. I know your plans concerning the Church; you will assert claims which I as archbishop must needs oppose ; and the breach once made, jealous hands would take care that it should never be healed again." The words were prophetic; they sum up the whole history of the pontificate of Thomas Becket. Henry, however, in his turn passed them over as a mere jest, and at once proclaimed his intention to the chancellor's fellow-envoys, one of whom was the justiciar, Richard de Lucy. " Richard," said the king, "if I lay dead

in my shroud, would you earnestly strive to secure my first-
born on my throne ? "   " Indeed I would, my lord, with all
my might."   " Then I charge you to strive no less earnestly
to place my chancellor on the metropolitan chair of Canterbury."[1]

Thomas was appalled. He could not be altogether
taken by surprise ; he knew what had been Theobald's
wishes and hopes ; he knew that from the moment of
Theobald's death all eyes had turned instinctively upon
himself with the belief that the future of the Church rested
wholly in his all-powerful hands ; he could not but suspect
the king's own intentions,[2] although the very suspiciòn would
keep him silent, and all the more so because those intentions
ran counter to his own desires. For twelve months he had
known that the primacy was within his reach ; he had
counted the cost, and he had no mind to pay it. He was
incapable of undertaking any office without throwing his
whole energies into the fulfilment of its duties ; his conception of the duties of the primate of all Britain would
involve the sacrifice not only of those secular pursuits which
he so keenly enjoyed, but also of that personal friendship
and political co-operation with the king which seemed almost
an indispensable part of the life of both ; and neither sacrifice was he disposed to make. He had said as much to an
English friend who had been the first to hint at his coming
promotion,[3] and he repeated it now with passionate earnestness to Henry himself, but all in vain. The more he resisted,
the more the king insisted—the very frankness of his warnings only strengthening Henry's confidence in him ; and
when the legate Cardinal Henry of Pisa urged his acceptance as a sacred duty, Thomas at last gave way.[4]

The council in London was no sooner ended than Richard
de Lucy and three of the bishops[5] hurried to Canterbury, by

[1] Herb. Bosh. (Robertson, *Becket*, vol. iii.), pp. 180, 182. Cf. *Thomas Saga*
(Magnusson), vol. i. pp. 63-67.

[2] Herb. Bosh. (as above), p. 180. Anon. I. (*ib.* vol. iv.), p. 14. *Thomas Saga*
(as above), p. 63.   [3] Will. Fitz-Steph. (Robertson, *Becket*, vol. iii.), pp. 25, 26.
[4] Will. Cant. (*ib.* vol. i.), pp. 7, 8. Anon. I. (*ib.* vol. iv.), p. 18. Anon. II.
(*ib.*), p. 86.

[5] E. Grim (*ib.* vol. ii.), p. 366. The bishops were Exeter, Chichester and

the king's orders, to obtain from the cathedral chapter the election of a primate in accordance with his will. The monks of Christ Church were never very easy to manage ; in the days of the elder King Henry they had firmly and successfully resisted the intrusion of a secular clerk into the monastic chair of S. Augustine ; and a strong party among them now protested that to choose for pastor of the flock of Canterbury a man who was scarcely a clerk at all, who was wholly given to hawks and hounds and the worldly ways of the court, would be no better than setting a wolf to guard a sheepfold. But their scruples were silenced by the arguments of Richard de Lucy and by their dread of the royal wrath, and in the end Thomas was elected without a dissentient voice.[1] The election was repeated in the presence of a great council[2] held at Westminster on May 23,[3] and ratified by the bishops and clergy there assembled.[4] Only one voice was raised in protest ; it was that of Gilbert Foliot,[5] who, alluding doubtless to the great scutage, declared that Thomas was utterly unfit for the primacy, because he had persecuted the Church of God.[6] The protest was answered by Henry of Winchester in words suggested by Gilbert's

Rochester ; Garnier (Hippeau), pp. 16, 17, Anon. I. (Robertson, *Becket*, vol. iv.), pp. 14-16, and Gerv. Cant. (Stubbs), vol. i. p. 169 ; this last alone names Rochester, and adds another envoy—Abbot Walter of Battle, Chichester's old adversary and the justiciar's brother.

[1] Garnier (Hippeau), p. 17. E. Grim (Robertson, *Becket*, vol. ii.), pp. 366, 367. Herb. Bosh. (*ib.* vol. iii.), pp. 183-185. Anon. I. (*ib.* vol. iv.), p. 16. *Thomas Saga* (Magnusson, vol. i. p. 73) has quite a different version of the result.

[2] Anon. I. (Robertson, *Becket*, vol. iv.), p. 17. Will. Cant. (*ib.* vol. i.), p. 9. Garnier, as above. Gerv. Cant. (Stubbs), vol. i. p. 169. R. Diceto (Stubbs), vol. i. p. 306.

[3] The Wednesday before Pentecost. R. Diceto (as above), p. 307.

[4] Garnier, Will. Cant., Anon. I., as above. R. Diceto (as above), p. 306. Gerv. Cant. (as above), p. 170. All these writers either say or imply that the council represented, or was meant to represent, the entire *clerus et populus* of all England ; except R. Diceto, who says : "clero totius provinciæ *Cantuariorum* generaliter Lundoniæ convocato" (p. 306). Cf. *Thomas Saga* (Magnusson), vol. i. pp. 73-77 ; Will. Fitz-Steph. (Robertson, *Becket*, vol. iii.), p. 36 ; and Herb. Bosh. (*ib.*), p. 184.

[5] Garnier, Will. Cant., Will. Fitz-Steph. and Anon. I. as above. E. Grim (Robertson, *Becket*, vol. ii.), p. 367. Will. Cant., E. Grim and the Anon. call him "bishop of London" by anticipation.

[6] "Destruite ad seinte Iglise." Garnier, as above.

own phrase: "My son," said the ex-legate, addressing
Thomas, "if thou hast been hitherto as Saul the persecutor,
be thou henceforth as Paul the Apostle."[1]

The election was confirmed by the great officers of state
and the boy-king in his father's name ;[2] the consecration
was fixed for the octave of Pentecost, and forthwith the
bishops began to vie with each other for the honour of performing the ceremony. Roger of York, who till now had
stood completely aloof, claimed it as a privilege due to the
dignity of his see ; but the primate-elect and the southern
bishops declined to accept his services without a profession
of canonical obedience to Canterbury, which he indignantly
refused.[3] The bishop of London, on whom as dean of the
province the duty according to ancient precedent should
have devolved, was just dead ;[4] Walter of Rochester momentarily put in a claim to supply his place,[5] but withdrew it in
deference to Henry of Winchester, who had lately returned
from Cluny, and whose royal blood, venerable character, and
unique dignity as father of the whole English episcopate,
marked him out beyond all question as the most fitting
person to undertake the office.[6] By way of compensation,
it was Walter who, on the Saturday in Whitsun-week,
raised the newly-elected primate to the dignity of priesthood.[7]

Early next morning the consecration took place. Canterbury cathedral has been rebuilt from end to end since
that day ; it is only imagination which can picture the
church of Lanfranc and Anselm and Theobald as it stood
on that June morning, the scarce-risen sun gleaming faintly
through its eastern windows upon the rich vestures of the

---

[1] Garnier (Hippeau), p. 18.

[2] *Ibid.* Anon. I. (Robertson, *Becket*, vol. iv.), p. 17.   Will. Cant. (*ib.* vol. i.),
p. 9.   E. Grim (*ib.* vol. ii.), p. 367.   Herb. Bosh. (*ib.* vol. iii.), p. 185.

[3] Gerv. Cant. (Stubbs), vol. i. p. 170.

[4] He died on May 4.   R. Diceto (Stubbs), vol. i. p. 306.

[5] Herb. Bosh. (as above), p. 188.

[6] Gerv. Cant., R. Diceto and Herb. Bosh. as above.   MS. Lansdown. II.
(Robertson, *Becket*, vol. iv.), p. 155.   Cf. Anon. I. (*ib.*), p. 19.   There was
another claimant, a Welsh bishop, who asserted priority of consecration over all
his brother-prelates ; so at least says Gerv. Cant., but one does not see who he
can have been.   [7] R. Diceto, as above.

fourteen bishops[1] and their attendant clergy and the dark robes of the monks who thronged the choir, while the nave was crowded with spectators, foremost among whom stood the group of ministers surrounding the little king.[2] From the vestry-door Thomas came forth, clad no longer in the brilliant attire at which he had been jesting a few weeks ago, but in the plain black cassock and white surplice of a clerk ; through the lines of staring, wondering faces he passed into the choir, and there threw himself prostrate upon the altar-steps. Thence he was raised to go through a formality suggested by the prudence of his consecrator. To guard, as he hoped, against all risk of future difficulties which might arise from Thomas's connexion with the court, Henry of Winchester led him down to the entrance of the choir, and in the name of the Church called upon the king's representatives to deliver over the primate-elect fully and unreservedly to her holy service, freed from all secular obligations, actual or possible. A formal quit-claim was accordingly granted to Thomas by little Henry and the justiciars, in the king's name ;[3] after which the bishop of Winchester proceeded to consecrate him at once. A shout of applause rang through the church as the new primate of all Britain was led up to his patriarchal chair ; but he mounted its steps with eyes downcast and full of tears.[4] To him the day was one of melancholy foreboding ; yet he made its memory joyful in the Church for ever. He began his archiepiscopal career by ordaining a new festival to be kept every year on that day ––the octave of Pentecost––in honour of the most Holy Trinity ;[5] and in process of time the observance thus origin-

---

[1] See the list in Gerv. Cant. (Stubbs), vol. i. p. 170.

[2] Herb. Bosh. (Robertson, *Becket*, vol. iii.), p. 188.

[3] MS. Lansdown. II. (*ib.* vol. iv.), pp. 154, 155. Cf. Anon. I. (*ib.*), pp. 17, 18 ; Will. Cant. (*ib.* vol. i.), p. 9 ; E. Grim (*ib.* vol. ii.), p. 367; Herb. Bosh. (*ib.* vol. iii.), p. 185 ; Garnier (Hippeau), p. 19 ; and *Thomas Saga* (Magnusson), vol. i. p. 81. All these place this scene in London, immediately after the consecration. The three first, however, seem to be only following Garnier ; and the words of Will. Fitz-Steph. (Robertson, *Becket*, vol. iii. p. 36), though not very explicit, seem rather to agree with the MS. Lansdown. Garnier, Grim and the Anon. I. all expressly attribute the suggestion to Henry of Winchester.

[4] Anon. I. (as above), p. 19.   [5] Gerv. Cant. as above.

ated spread from Canterbury throughout the whole of
Christendom, which thus owes to an English archbishop the
institution of Trinity Sunday.

"The king has wrought a miracle," sneered the sarcastic
bishop of Hereford, Gilbert Foliot; "out of a soldier and
man of the world he has made an archbishop."[1] The same
royal power helped to smooth the new primate's path a little
further before him.   He was not, like most of his predecessors, obliged to go in person to fetch his pallium from
Rome ; an embassy which he despatched immediately after
his consecration obtained it for him without difficulty from
Alexander III., who had just been driven by the Emperor's
hostility to seek a refuge in France, and was in no condition
to venture upon any risk of thwarting King Henry's favourite
minister.[2]   The next messenger whom Thomas sent over
sea met with a less pleasant reception.   He was charged to
deliver up the great seal into the king's hands with a request
that Henry would provide himself with another chancellor,
"as Thomas felt scarcely equal to the cares of one office,
far less to those of two."[3]

Henry was both surprised and vexed.   It was customary
for the chancellor to resign his office on promotion to a
bishopric ; but this sudden step on the part of Thomas was
quite unexpected, and upset a cherished scheme of the
king's.   He had planned to rival the Emperor by having
an archbishop for his chancellor, as the archbishops of
Mainz and Cöln were respectively arch-chancellors of Germany and Italy ;[4] he had certainly never intended, in raising
his favourite to the primacy, to deprive himself of such a
valuable assistant in secular administration ; his aim had

---

[1] Will. Fitz-Steph. (Robertson, *Becket*, vol. iii.), p. 36.

[2] Garnier (Hippeau), pp. 24, 25.   Will. Cant. (Robertson, *Becket*, vol. i.) p. 9.
Herb. Bosh. (*ib.* vol. iii.), p. 189.   Gerv. Cant. (Stubbs), vol. i. p. 172.   R.
Diceto (Stubbs), vol. i. p. 307.   *Thomas Saga* (Magnusson), vol. i. pp. 91-95.

[3] Will. Cant. (as above), p. 12.   Cf. Garnier (Hippeau), p. 29, and R. Diceto
as above.

[4] R. Diceto (as above), p. 308.   The real work of the office in the
Empire was, however, done by another chancellor, who at this time was a certain
Reginald, of whom we shall hear again later on.   "Cancellarius" plays almost
as conspicuous and quite as unclerkly a part in the Italian wars of Barbarossa as
in the French and Aquitanian wars of Henry.

rather been to secure the services of Thomas in two departments instead of one.[1] To take away all ground of scandal, he had even procured a papal dispensation to sanction the union of the two offices in a single person.[2] Thomas, however, persisted in his resignation ; and as there was no one whom Henry cared to put in his place, the chancellorship remained vacant, while the· king brooded over his friend's unexpected conduct and began to suspect that it was caused by weariness of his service.

Meanwhile Thomas had entered upon the second phase of his strangely varied career. He had " put off the deacon " for awhile ; he was resolved now to "put off the old man " wholly and for ever. No sooner was he consecrated than he flung himself, body and soul, into his new life with an ardour more passionate, more absorbing, more exclusive than he had displayed in pursuit of the worldly tasks and pleasures of the court. On the morrow of his consecration, when some jongleurs came to him for the largesse which he had never been known to refuse, he gently but firmly dismissed them ; he was no longer, he said, the chancellor whom they had known ; his whole possessions were now a sacred trust, to be spent not on actors and jesters but in the service of the Church and the poor.[3] Theobald had doubled the amount of regular alms-givings established by his predecessors ; Thomas immediately doubled those of Theobald.[4] To be diligent in providing for the sick and needy, to take care that no beggar should ever be sent empty away from his door,[5] was indeed nothing new in the son of the good dame Rohesia of Caen. The lavish hospitality of the chancellor's household, too, was naturally transferred to that of the archbishop ; but it took a different tone and colour. All and more than all the old grandeur and orderliness were there ;

[1] Garnier (Hippeau), p. 29. Cf. *Thomas Saga* (Magnusson), vol. i. pp. 69-71.
[2] Garnier, as above.
[3] MS. Lansdown. II. (Robertson, *Becket*, vol. iv.), p. 156.
[4] Anon. I. (*ibid.*), p. 20. The Anon. II. (*ibid.*), p. 90, and Joh. Salisb. (*ib.* vol. ii.), p. 307, say that to this purpose he appropriated a *tithe* of all his revenues—a statement which reflects rather strangely upon the former archbishops.
[5] Joh. Salisb. and Anon. I. as above. Anon. II. (as above), pp. 89, 90.

the palace still swarmed with men-at-arms, servants and
retainers of all kinds, every one with his own appointed
duty, whose fulfilment was still carefully watched by the
master's eyes ; the bevy of high-born children had only increased, for by an ancient custom the second son of a baron
could be claimed by the primate for his service—as the
eldest by the king—until the age of knighthood ; a claim
which Thomas was not slow to enforce, and which the barons
were delighted to admit.   The train of clerks was of course
more numerous than ever.   The tables were still laden with
delicate viands, served with the utmost perfection, and
crowded with guests of all ranks ; Thomas was still the
most courteous and gracious of hosts.   But the banquet
wore a graver aspect than in the chancellor's hall.   The
knights and other laymen occupied a table by themselves,
where they talked and laughed as they listed ; it was the
clerks and religious who now sat nearest to Thomas.   He
himself was surrounded by a select group of clerks, his
eruditi, his " learned men " as he called them : men versed
in Scriptural and theological lore, his chosen companions in
the study of Holy Writ into which he had plunged with
characteristic energy ; while instead of the minstrelsy which
had been wont to accompany and inspire the gay talk at the
chancellor's table, there was only heard, according to ecclesiastical custom, the voice of the archbishop's cross-bearer who
sat close to his side reading from some holy book : the
primate and his confidential companions meanwhile exchang-
ing comments upon what was read, and discussing matters
too deep and solemn to interest unlearned ears or to brook
unlearned interruption.[1]   Of the meal itself Thomas partook
but sparingly ;[2] its remainder was always given away;[3] and
every day twenty-six poor men were brought into the hall
and served with a dinner of the best, before Thomas would
sit down to his own midday meal.[4]

[1] Herb. Bosh. (Robertson, *Becket*, vol. iii.), pp. 225-229. On the *eruditi* see
ib. pp. 206, 207, 523-529.
[2] *Ib.* pp. 231-236. Will. Fitz-Steph. (*ibid.*), p. 37. Joh. Salisb. (*ib.* vol.
ii.), p. 308. Anon. II. (*ib.* vol. iv.), p. 89.
[3] Joh. Salisb. (as above), p. 307. Anon. I. (*ib.* vol. iv.), pp. 20, 21.
[4] Anon. II. (*ib.*), p. 89.

The amount of work which he had got through by that time must have been quite as great as in the busiest days of his chancellorship. The day's occupations ostensibly began about the hour of tierce, when the archbishop came forth from his chamber and went either to hear or to celebrate mass,[1] while a breakfast was given at his expense to a hundred persons who were called his "poor prebendaries."[2] After mass he proceeded to his audience-chamber and there chiefly remained till the hour of nones, occupied in hearing suits and administering justice.[3] Nones were followed by dinner,[4] after which the primate shut himself up in his own apartments with his *eruditi*[5] and spent the rest of the day with them in business or study, interrupted only by the religious duties of the canonical hours, and sometimes by a little needful repose,[6] for his night's rest was of the briefest. At cock-crow he rose for prime ; immediately afterwards there were brought in to him secretly, under cover of the darkness, thirteen poor persons whose feet he washed and to whom he ministered at table with the utmost devotion and humility,[7] clad only in a hair-shirt which from the day of his consecration he always wore beneath the gorgeous robes in which he appeared in public.[8] He then returned to his bed, but only for a very short time ; long before any one else was astir he was again up and doing, in company with one specially favoured disciple—the one who tells the tale, Herbert of Bosham. In the calm silent hours of dawn, while twelve other poor persons received a secret meal and had their feet washed by the primate's almoner in his stead, the two friends sat eagerly searching the Scriptures together, till the archbishop chose to be left alone[9] for meditation and confession,

---

[1] Herb. Bosh. (Robertson, *Becket*, vol. iii.), p. 208.　　　[2] *Ib.* p. 203.
[3] *Ib.* p. 219.　　　[4] *Ib.* p. 225.　　　[5] *Ib.* pp. 236, 237.　　　[6] *Ib.* p. 238.
[7] *Ib.* p. 199. Cf. Will. Fitz-Steph. (*ibid.*), p. 38, and Joh. Salisb. (*ib.* vol. ii.), p. 307.
[8] On the hair-shirt see MS. Lansdown. II. (*ib.* vol. iv.), p. 154; Anon. I. (*ibid.*), p. 20 ; Will. Cant. (*ib.* vol. i.), p. 10; Herb. Bosh. (*ib.* vol. iii.), pp. 196, 199 ; Garnier (Hippeau), p. 23. On Thomas's troubles about his dress and how he settled them see Garnier, pp. 19, 20, 23 ; Anon. I. (as above), p. 21 ; E. Grim (*ib.* vol. ii.), p. 368 ; Herb. Bosh. (*ib.* vol. iii.), p. 196. On his whole manner of life after consecration cf. *Thomas Saga* (Magnusson), vol. i. pp. 95-111.
[9] Herb. Bosh. (as above), pp. 202-205.

scourging and prayer,[1] in which he remained absorbed until the hour of tierce called him forth to his duties in the world.[2]

He was feverishly anxious to lose no opportunity of making up for his long neglect of the Scriptural and theological studies befitting his sacred calling. He openly confessed his grievous inferiority in this respect to many of his own clerks, and put himself under their teaching with childlike simplicity and earnestness. The one whom he specially chose for monitor and guide, Herbert of Bosham, was a man in whom, despite his immeasurable inferiority, one can yet see something of a temper sufficiently akin to that of Thomas himself to account for their mutual attraction, and perhaps for some of their joint errors. As they rode from London to Canterbury on the morrow of the primate's election he had drawn Herbert aside and laid upon him a special charge to watch with careful eyes over his conduct as archbishop, and tell him without stint or scruple whatever he saw amiss in it or heard criticized by others.[3] Herbert, though he worshipped his primate with a perfect hero-worship, never hesitated to fulfil this injunction to the letter as far as his lights would permit ; but unluckily his zeal was even less tempered by discretion than that of Thomas himself. He was a far less safe guide in the practical affairs of life than in the intricate paths of abstract and mystical interpretation of Holy Writ in which he and Thomas delighted to roam together. Often, when no other quiet time could be found, the archbishop would turn his horse aside as they travelled along the road, beckon to his friend, draw out a book from its hiding-place in one of his wide sleeves, and plunge into an eager discussion of its contents as they ambled slowly on.[4] When at Canterbury, his greatest pleasure was to betake himself to the cloister and sit reading like a lowly monk in one of its quiet nooks.[5]

But the *eruditi* of Thomas, like the disciples of Theobald, were the confidants and the sharers of far more than his

---

[1] Anon. II. (Robertson, *Becket*, vol. iv.), p. 88.

[2] Herb. Bosh. (*ib.* vol. iii.), p. 205.   [3] *Ib.* p. 186.

[4] *Ib.* p. 206.   [5] Will. Fitz-Steph. (*ib.*), pp. 38, 39.

literary and doctrinal studies. It was in those evening hours which he spent in their midst, secluded from all outside interruption, that the plans of Church reform and Church revival, sketched long ago by other hands in the *Curia Theobaldi*, assumed a shape which might perhaps have startled Theobald himself. As the weeks wore quickly away from Trinity to Ember-tide, the new primate set himself to grapple at once with the ecclesiastical abuses of the time in the persons of his first candidates for ordination. On his theory the remedy for these abuses lay in the hands of the bishops, and especially of the metropolitans, who fostered simony, worldliness and immorality among the clergy by the facility with which they admitted unqualified persons into high orders, thus filling the ranks of the priesthood with unworthy, ignorant and needy clerks, who either traded upon their sacred profession as a means to secular advancement, or disgraced it by the idle wanderings and unbecoming shifts to which the lack of fit employment drove them to resort for a living. He was determined that no favour or persuasion should ever induce him to ordain any man whom he did not know to be of saintly life and ample learning, and provided with a benefice sufficient to furnish him with occupation and maintenance ; and he proclaimed and acted upon his determination with the zeal of one who, as he openly avowed, felt that he was himself the most glaring example of the evils resulting from a less stringent system of discipline.[1]

His next undertaking was one which almost every new-made prelate in any degree alive to the rights and duties of his office found it needful to begin as soon as possible : the recovery of the alienated property of his see. Gilbert Foliot, the model English bishop of the day, had no sooner been consecrated than he wrote to beg the Pope's support in this important and troublesome matter.[2] It may well be that even fourteen years later the metropolitan see had not yet received full restitution for the spoliations of the anarchy. Thomas however set to work in the most sweeping fashion, boldly laying claim to every estate which he could find to

[1] Herb. Bosh. (Robertson, *Becket*, vol. iii.), pp. 238-247.
[2] Gilb. Foliot, Ep. lxxxvii. (Giles, vol. i., p. 113).

have been granted away by his predecessors on grounds which did not satisfy his exalted ideas of ecclesiastical right, or on terms which he held detrimental to the interest and dignity of his church, and enforcing his claims without respect of persons ; summarily turning out those who held the archiepiscopal manors in ferm,[1] disputing with the earl of Clare for jurisdiction over the castle and district of Tunbridge, and reclaiming, on the strength of a charter of the Conqueror, the custody of Rochester castle from the Crown itself. Such a course naturally stirred up for him a crowd of enemies, and increased the jealousy, suspicion and resentment which his new position and altered mode of life had already excited among the companions and rivals of his earlier days. The archbishop however was still, like the chancellor, protected against them by the shield of the royal favour ; they could only work against him by working upon the mind of Henry. One by one they carried over sea their complaints of the wrongs which they had suffered, or with which they were threatened, at the primate's hands ;[2] they reported all his daily doings and interpreted them in the worst sense :—his strictness of life was superstition, his zeal for justice was cruelty, his care for his church avarice, his pontifical splendour pride, his vigour rashness and self-conceit:[3] —if the king did not look to it speedily, he would find his laws and constitutions set at naught, his regal dignity trodden under foot, and himself and his heirs reduced to mere cyphers dependent on the will and pleasure of the archbishop of Canterbury.[4]

At the close of the year Henry determined to go and see for himself the truth of these strange rumours.[5] The negotiations concerning the papal question had detained him on the continent throughout the summer; in the end both

[1] E. Grim (Robertson, *Becket*, vol. ii.) pp. 371, 372. Herb. Bosh. (*ib.* vol. iii.) pp. 250, 251. *Thomas Saga* (Magnusson), vol. i. pp. 117-121.

[2] Herb. Bosh. (as above), p. 252. *Thomas Saga* (as above), p. 121.

[3] Joh. Salisb. (Robertson, *Becket*, vol. ii.) pp. 309, 310. Anon. II. (*ib.* vol. iv.) pp. 91, 92.

[4] Joh. Salisb. (as above), p. 310. E. Grim (*ibid.*) p. 372. Anon. II. (*ib.* vol. iv.), p. 92. Cf. Arn. Lisieux, Ep. 34 (Giles, pp. 148, 149).

[5] Anon. II. as above.

he and Louis gave a cordial welcome to Alexander, and a general pacification was effected in a meeting of the two kings and the Pope which took place late in the autumn at Chouzy on the Loire. Compelled by contrary winds to keep Christmas at Cherbourg instead of in England as he had hoped,[1] the king landed at Southampton on S. Paul's day.[2] Thomas, still accompanied by the little Henry, was waiting to receive him; the two friends met with demonstrations of the warmest affection, and travelled to London together in the old intimate association.[3] One subject of disagreement indeed there was ; Thomas had actually been holding for six months the archdeaconry of Canterbury together with the archbishopric, and this Henry, after several vain remonstrances, now compelled him to resign.[4] They parted however in undisturbed harmony, the archbishop again taking his little pupil with him.[5]

The first joint work of king and primate was the translation of Gilbert Foliot from Hereford to London. Some of those who saw its consequences in after-days declared that Henry had devised the scheme for the special purpose of securing Gilbert's aid against the primate ;[6] but it is abundantly clear that no such thought had yet entered his mind, and that the suggestion of Gilbert's promotion really came from Thomas himself.[7] Like every one else, he looked upon Gilbert as the greatest living light of the English Church ; he expected to find in him his own most zealous and efficient fellow-worker in the task which lay before him as metropolitan, as well as his best helper in influencing the king for good. Gilbert was in fact the man who in the natural fitness of things had seemed marked out for the primacy ;

---

[1] Rob. Torigni, a. 1162.
[2] Herb. Bosh. (Robertson, *Becket*, vol. iii.), p. 252. The date is given by R. Diceto (Stubbs), vol. i. p. 308.
[3] Herb. Bosh. (as above), pp. 252, 253. Anon. II. (*ib.* vol. iv.), p. 92. R. Diceto (as above) tells a different tale ; but Herbert is surely a better authority on these personal matters. Cf. also *Thomas Saga* (Magnusson), vol. i. pp. 121-123.	[4] R. Diceto, as above.
[5] Herb. Bosh. (as above), p. 253.
[6] Will. Fitz-Steph. (as above), p. 46.
[7] This is the statement of Anon. II. (*ib.* vol. iv. p. 98) and Gerv. Cant. (Stubbs, vol. i. p. 173), fully borne out by the letters of Thomas.

failing that, it was almost a matter of necessity that he should be placed in the see which stood next in dignity, and where both king and primate could benefit by his assistance ever at hand, instead of having to seek out their most useful adviser in the troubled depths of the Welsh marches. The chapter of London, to whom during the pecuniary troubles and long illness of their late bishop Gilbert had been an invaluable friend and protector, were only too glad to elect him ; and his world-wide reputation combined with the pleadings of Henry to obtain the Pope's consent to his translation,[1] which was completed by his enthronement in S. Paul's cathedral on April 28, 1163.[2]

The king spent the early summer in subduing South-Wales ; the primate, in attending a council held by Pope Alexander at Tours.[3] From the day of his departure to that of his return Thomas's journey was one long triumphal progress ; Pope and cardinals welcomed him with such honours as had never been given to any former archbishop of Canterbury, hardly even to S. Anselm himself ;[4] and the request which he made to the Pope for Anselm's canoniz-ation[5] may indicate the effect which they produced on his mind—confirming his resolve to stand boldly upon his right of opposition to the secular power whenever it clashed with ecclesiastical theories of liberty and justice. The first opportunity for putting his resolve in practice arose upon a question of purely temporal administration at a council held by Henry at Woodstock on July 31, after his return from Wales. The Welsh princes came to swear fealty to Henry and his heir ; Malcolm of Scotland came to confirm

---

[1] Epp. xvi.-xix. (Robertson, *Becket*, vol. v. pp. 24-30). Herb. Bosh. (*ib.* vol. iii.), pp. 255, 256. Cf. Anon. II. (*ib.* vol. iv.), p. 98.

[2] R. Diceto (Stubbs), vol. i. p. 309.

[3] According to Gerv. Cant. (Stubbs), vol. i. p. 173, and Will. Newb., l. ii. c. 14 (Howlett, vol. i. p. 135), it opened on Trinity Sunday, May 19 ; according to R. Diceto (as above), p. 310, on May 21. The *Thomas Saga* (Magnusson), vol. i. pp. 123-127, makes out that Thomas's chief object in going there was to obtain confirmation of certain privileges of his see. Cf. also the account of this council in *Draco Norm.*, l. iii. cc. 13-15, vv. 949-1224 (Howlett, *Will. Newb.*, vol. ii. pp. 742-751).

[4] Herb. Bosh. (Robertson, *Becket*, vol. iii.), pp. 253-255. *Thomas Saga* (as above), pp. 129, 131.   [5] Ep. xxiii. (Robertson, *Becket*, vol. v. p. 35).

his alliance with the English Crown by doing homage in like manner to the little king.[1] Before the council broke up, however, Henry met the sharpest constitutional defeat which had befallen any English sovereign since the Norman conquest, and that at the hands of his own familiar friend.

The king had devised a new financial project for increasing his own revenue at the expense of the sheriffs. According to current practice, a sum of two shillings annually from every hide of land in the shire was paid to those officers for their services to the community in its administration and defence. This payment, although described as customary rather than legal,[2] and called the "sheriff's aid,"[3] seems really to have been nothing else than the Danegeld, which still occasionally made its appearance in the treasury rolls, but in such small amount that it is evident the sheriffs, if they collected it in full, paid only a fixed composition to the Crown and kept the greater part as a remuneration for their own labours. Henry now, it seems, proposed to transfer the whole of these sums from the sheriff's income to his own, and have it enrolled in full among the royal dues. Whether he intended to make compensation to the sheriffs from some other source, or whether he already saw the need of curbing their influence and checking their avarice, we know not ; but the archbishop of Canterbury started up to resist the proposed change as an injustice both to the receivers and to the payers of the aid. He seems to have looked upon it as an attempt to re-establish the Danegeld with all the odiousness attaching to its shameful origin and its unfair incidence, and to have held it his constitutional duty as representative and champion of the whole people to lift up his voice against it in their behalf. "My lord king," he said, "saving your good pleasure, we will not give you this money as revenue, for it is not yours. To your officers, who receive it as a matter of grace rather than of right, we will give it willingly so long as they do their duty ; but on no other terms will

---

[1] R. Diceto (Stubbs), vol. i. p. 311.

[2] Garnier (Hippeau), p. 30. Will. Cant. (Robertson, *Becket*, vol. i.), p. 12. E. Grim (*ib.* vol. ii.), p. 373. Anon. I. (*ib.* vol. iv.), p. 23.

[3] "L'Aïde al Vescunte." Garnier, as above.

we be made to pay it at all."—" By God's Eyes !" swore the
astonished and angry king, " what right have you to contradict me ?   I am doing no wrong to any man of yours.   I
say the moneys shall be enrolled among my royal revenues."
—" Then by those same Eyes," swore Thomas in return,
" not a penny shall you have from my lands, or from any
lands of the Church !"[1]

How the debate ended we are not told ; but one thing
we know : from that time forth the hated name of " Danegeld " appeared in the Pipe Rolls no more.   It seems therefore that, for the first time in English history since the
Norman conquest, the right of the nation's representatives
to oppose the financial demands of the Crown was asserted
in the council of Woodstock, and asserted with such success
that the king was obliged not merely to abandon his project,
but to obliterate the last trace of the tradition on which it
was founded.   And it is well to remember, too, that the first
stand made by Thomas of Canterbury against the royal will
was made in behalf not of himself or his order but of his
whole flock ;—in the cause not of ecclesiastical privilege
but of constitutional right.   The king's policy may have
been really sounder and wiser than the primate's ; but the
ground taken by Thomas at Woodstock entitles him none
the less to a place in the line of patriot-archbishops of which
Dunstan stands at the head.[2]

The next few weeks were occupied with litigation over
the alienated lands of the metropolitan see.   A crowd of
claims put in by Thomas and left to await the king's return
now came up for settlement, the most important case being
that of Earl Roger of Clare, whom Thomas had summoned
to perform his homage for Tunbridge at Westminster on
July 22.   Roger answered that he held the entire fief by
knight-service, to be rendered in the shape of money-payment,[3] of the king and not of the primate.[4]   As Roger was

---

[1] Garnier (Hippeau), p. 30.   Cf. Will. Cant. (Robertson, *Becket*, vol. i.), p.
12.   E. Grim (*ib.* vol. ii.), p. 374.   Anon. I. (*ib.* vol. iv.), pp. 23, 24.

[2] On the different account of this affair given in the *Thomas Saga*, and the
view which has been founded on it, see note A at end of chapter.

[3] " Publicis pensionibus persolvendis."   R. Diceto (Stubbs), vol. i. p. 311.

[4] *Ibid.*

connected with the noblest families in England,[1] king and barons were strongly on his side.[2] To settle the question, Henry ordered a general inquisition to be made throughout England to ascertain where the service of each landholder was lawfully due. The investigation was of course made by the royal justiciars; and when they came to the archiepiscopal estates, one at least of the most important fiefs in dispute was adjudged by them to the Crown alone.[3]

Meanwhile a dispute on a question of church patronage arose between the primate and a tenant-in-chief of the Crown, named William of Eynesford. Thomas excommunicated his opponent without observing the custom which required him to give notice to the king before inflicting spiritual penalties on one of his tenants-in-chief.[4] Henry indignantly bade him withdraw the sentence; Thomas refused, saying " it was not for the king to dictate who should be bound or who loosed."[5] The answer was indisputable in itself; but it pointed directly to the fatal subject on which the inevitable quarrel must turn: the relations and limits between the two powers of the keys and the sword.

Almost from his accession Henry seems to have been in some degree contemplating and preparing for those great schemes of legal reform which were to be the lasting glory of his reign. His earliest efforts in this direction were merely tentative; the young king was at once too inexperienced and too hard pressed with urgent business of all kinds, at home and abroad, to have either capacity or opportunity for great experiments in legislation. Throughout the past nine years, however, the projects which floated before his mind's eye had been gradually taking shape; and now that he was at last freed for a while from the

---

[1] And had moreover "the fairest sister in the whole kingdom," adds Will. Fitz-Steph. (Robertson, *Becket*, vol. iii.), p. 43.   [2] *Ibid.*
[3] R. Diceto (Stubbs), vol. i. p. 311.
[4] *Ib.* pp. 311, 312. Will. Fitz-Steph. as above. The object of this rule— one of the *avitæ consuetudines*—was, as R. Diceto explains, to guard the king against the risk of unwittingly associating with excommunicates.
[5] Will. Fitz-Steph. as above.

entanglements of politics and war, the time had come when he might begin to devote himself to that branch of his kingly duties for which he probably had the strongest inclination, as he certainly had the highest natural genius. He had by this time gained enough insight into the nature and causes of existing abuses to venture upon dealing with them systematically and in detail, and he had determined to begin with a question which was allowed on all hands to be one of the utmost gravity : the repression of crime in the clergy.

The origin of this difficulty was in the separation— needful perhaps, but none the less disastrous in some of its consequences — made by William the Conqueror between the temporal and ecclesiastical courts of justice. In William's intention the two sets of tribunals were to work side by side without mutual interference save when the secular power was called in to enforce the decisions of the spiritual judge. But in practice the scheme was soon found to involve a crowd of difficulties. The two jurisdictions were constantly coming into contact, and it was a perpetual question where to draw the line between them. The struggle for the investitures, the religious revival which followed it, the vast and rapid developement of the canon law, with the increase of knowledge brought to bear upon its interpretation through the revived study of the civil law of Rome, gave the clergy a new sense of corporate importance and strength, and a new position as a distinct order in the state ; the breakdown of all secular administration under Stephen tended still further to exalt the influence of the canonical system which alone retained some vestige of legal authority, and to throw into the Church-courts a mass of business with which they had hitherto had only an indirect concern, but which they alone now seemed capable of treating. Their proceedings were conducted on the principles of the canon law, which admitted of none but spiritual penalties ; they refused to allow any lay interference with the persons over whom they claimed sole jurisdiction ; and as these comprised the whole clerical body in the widest possible sense, extending to all who had received the lowest orders of the Church or who had taken monastic vows, the result was to place a considerable part of the population altogether outside the ordinary law of the land, and beyond the reach of adequate punishment for the most heinous crimes. Such crimes were only too common, and were necessarily fostered by this system of clerical immunities ; for a man capable of staining his holy orders with theft or murder was not likely to be restrained by the fear of losing them, which a clerical criminal knew to be the worst punishment in store for him ; and moreover, it was but too easy for the doers of such deeds to shelter themselves under the protection of a privilege to which often they had no real title. The king's justiciars declared that in the nine years since Henry's accession more than a hundred murders, besides innumerable robberies and lesser offences, had gone unpunished because they were committed by clerks, or men who represented themselves to be such.[1] The scandal was acknowledged on all hands ; the spiritual party in the Church grieved over it quite as loudly and deeply as the lay reformers ; but they hoped to remedy it in their own way, by a searching reformation and a stringent enforcement of spiritual discipline within the ranks of the clergy themselves. The subject had first come under Henry's direct notice in the summer of 1158, when he received at York a complaint from a citizen of Scarborough that a certain dean had extorted money from him by unjust means. The case was tried, in the king's presence, before the archbishop of the province, two bishops, and John of Canterbury the treasurer of York. The dean failed in his defence ; and as it was proved that he had extorted the money by a libel, an offence against which Henry had made a special decree, some of the barons present were sent to see that the law had its course. John of Canterbury, however, rose and gave it as the decision of the spiritual judges that the money should be restored to the citizen and the criminal delivered over to the mercy of his metropolitan ; and despite the justiciar's remonstrances, they refused to allow the king

[1] Will. Newb., l. ii. c. 16 (Howlett, vol. i. p. 140).

any rights in the matter. Henry indignantly ordered an appeal to the archbishop of Canterbury ; but he was called over sea before it could be heard,[1] and had never returned to England until now, when another archbishop sat in Theobald's place.

That it was Thomas of London who sat there was far from being an indication that Henry had forgotten the incident. It was precisely because Henry in these last four years had thought over the question of the clerical immunities and determined how to deal with it that he had sought to place on S. Augustine's chair a man after his own heart. He aimed at reducing the position of the clergy, like all other doubtful matters, to the standard of his grandfather's time. He held that he had a right to whatever his ancestors had enjoyed ; he saw therein nothing derogatory to either the Church or the primate, whom he rather intended to exalt by making him his own inseparable colleague in temporal administration and the supreme authority within the realm in purely spiritual matters—thus avoiding the appeals to Rome which had led to so much mischief, and securing for himself a representative to whom he could safely intrust the whole work of government in England as guardian of the little king,[2] while he himself would be free to devote his whole energies to the management of his continental affairs. He seems in fact to have hoped tacitly to repeal the severance of the temporal and ecclesiastical jurisdictions, and bring back the golden age of William and Lanfranc, if not that of Eadgar and Dunstan ; and for this he, not unnaturally, counted unreservedly upon Thomas. By slow degrees he discovered his miscalculation. Thomas had given him one direct warning which had been unheeded ; he had warned him again indirectly by resigning the chancellorship ; now, when the king unfolded his plans, he did not at once contradict him ; he merely answered all his arguments and persuasions with one set phrase :—" I will render unto Cæsar the things that are Cæsar's, and unto God the things that are God's."[3]

[1] Will. Fitz-Steph. (Robertson, *Becket*), vol. iii. pp. 43-45.
[2] Anon. II. (*ib.* vol. iv.), pp. 92-94.   [3] *Ib.* pp. 94, 95.

In July occurred a typical case which brought matters to a crisis. A clerk named Philip de Broi had been tried in the bishop of Lincoln's court for murder, had cleared himself by a legal compurgation, and had been acquitted. The king, not satisfied, commanded or permitted the charge to be revived, and the accused to be summoned to take his trial at Dunstable before Simon Fitz-Peter, then acting as justice-in-eyre in Bedfordshire, where Philip dwelt. Philip indignantly refused to plead again in answer to a charge of which he had been acquitted, and overwhelmed the judge with abuse, of which Simon on his return to London made formal complaint to the king. Henry was furious, swore his wonted oath " by God's Eyes" that an insult to his minister was an insult to himself, and ordered the culprit to be brought to justice for the contempt of court and the homicide both at once. The primate insisted that the trial should take place in his own court at Canterbury, and to this Henry was compelled unwillingly to consent. The charge of homicide was quickly disposed of ; Philip had been acquitted in a Church court, and his present judges had no wish to reverse its decision. On the charge of insulting a royal officer they sentenced him to undergo a public scourging at the hands of the offended person, and to forfeit the whole of his income for the next two years, to be distributed in alms according to the king's pleasure. Henry declared the punishment insufficient, and bitterly reproached the bishops with having perverted justice out of favour to their order.[1] They denied it ; but a story which came up from the diocese of Salisbury[2] and another from that of Worcester[3] tended still further to shew the helplessness of the royal justice against the ecclesiastical courts under the protection of the primate ; and the latter's blundering attempts to satisfy the king only increased his irritation. Not only did Thomas venture beyond the

---

[1] Garnier (Hippeau), pp. 30-32. Will. Cant. (Robertson, *Becket*, vol. i.), pp. 12, 13. E. Grim (*ib.* vol. ii.), pp. 374-376. Will. Fitz-Steph. (*ib.* vol. iii.), p. 45. Herb. Bosh. (*ib.*), pp. 265, 266. Anon. I. (*ib.* vol. iv.), pp. 24, 25. R. Diceto (Stubbs), vol. i. p. 313. There is another version in *Thomas Saga* (Magnusson), vol. i. p. 145.

[2] Herb. Bosh. (as above), pp. 264, 265. *Thomas Saga* (as above), p. 143.

[3] Will. Fitz-Steph. as above.

limits of punishment prescribed by the canon law by causing a clerk who had been convicted of theft to be branded as well as degraded,[1] but he actually took upon himself to condemn another to banishment.[2] He hoped by these severe sentences to appease the king's wrath;[3] Henry, on the contrary, resented them as an interference with his rights; what he wanted was not severe punishment in isolated cases, but the power to inflict it in the regular course of his own royal justice. At last he laid the whole question before a great council which met at Westminster on October 1.[4]

The king's first proposition, that the bishops should confirm the old customs observed in his grandfather's days,[5] opened a discussion which lasted far into the night. Henry himself proceeded to explain his meaning more fully ; he required, first, that the bishops should be more strict in the pursuit of criminal clerks;[6] secondly, that all such clerks, when convicted and degraded, should be handed over to the secular arm for temporal punishment like laymen, according to the practice usual under Henry I.;[7] and finally, that the bishops should renounce their claim to inflict any temporal punishment whatever, such as exile or imprisonment in a monastery, which he declared to be an infringement of his regal rights over the territory of his whole realm and the persons of all his subjects.[8] The primate, after vainly begging for an adjournment till the morrow, retired to consult with his suffragans.[9] When he returned, it was to set forth his view of the "two swords"—the two jurisdictions, spiritual and temporal—in terms which put an end to all hope of

---

[1] Will.ı Fitz-Steph. (Robertson, *Becket*, vol. iii.), pp. 45, 46.
[2] Herb. Bosh. (*ibid.*), p. 267.   [3] Will. Fitz-Steph. (*ibid.*), p. 46.
[4] Herb. Bosh. (*ibid.*), p. 266. Anon. II. (*ib.* vol. iv.), p. 95. *Summa Causæ* (*ibid.*), p. 201 ; this last gives the date.
[5] Garnier (Hippeau), p. 32. Anon. I. (Robertson, *Becket*, vol. iv.), pp. 25, 26. E. Grim (*ib.* vol. ii.), p. 376.
[6] Anon. II. (*ib.* vol. iv.), p. 96.
[7] *Ibid.* Cf. *Summa Causæ* (*ib.*), p. 202, Herb. Bosh. (*ib.* vol. iii.), p. 266, and *Thomas Saga* (Magnusson), vol. i. pp. 148, 149.
[8] Herb. Bosh. (as above), p. 267.
[9] *Summa Causæ* (*ib.* vol. iv.), p. 202. Their discussion is given in *Thomas Saga* (as above), p. 151.

agreement with the king. He declared the ministers of the Heavenly King exempt from all subjection to the judgement of an earthly sovereign ; the utmost that he would concede was that a clerk once degraded should thenceforth be treated as a layman and punished as such if he offended again.[1] Henry, apparently too much astonished to argue further, simply repeated his first question—" Would the bishops obey the royal customs ?" " Aye, saving our order," was the answer given by the primate in the name and with the consent of all.[2] When appealed to singly they all made the same answer.[3] Henry bade them withdraw the qualifying phrase, and accept the customs unconditionally ; they, through the mouth of their primate, refused ;[4] the king raged and swore, but all in vain. At last he strode suddenly out of the hall without taking leave of the assembly ;[5] and when morning broke they found that he had quitted London.[6] Before the day was over, Thomas received a summons to surrender some honours which he had held as chancellor and still retained ;[7] and soon afterwards the little Henry was taken out of his care.[8]

The king's wrath presently cooled so far that he invited the primate to a conference at Northampton. They met on horseback in a field near the town ; high words passed between them; the king again demanded, and the archbishop again refused, unconditional acceptance of the customs ; and

---

[1] Herb. Bosh. (Robertson, *Becket*, vol. iii.), pp. 268-272. Cf. Anon. I. (*ib.* vol. iv.), p. 22. The speech in *Thomas Saga* (Magnusson), vol. i. pp. 151-153, is much more moderate in tone, but grants no more in substance.

[2] Garnier (Hippeau), p. 32. Will. Cant. (Robertson, *Becket*, vol. i.), p. 13. E. Grim (*ib.* vol. ii.), p. 376. Herb. Bosh. (*ib.* vol. iii.), p. 273. Anon. II. (*ib.* vol. iv.), p. 97. Cf. Ep. ccxxv. (*ib.* vol. v. p. 527).

[3] For Hilary of Chichester's attempt at evasion see Herb. Bosh. (as above), pp. 273, 274, and *Thomas Saga* (Magnusson), vol. i. p. 155.

[4] Garnier, E. Grim, Herb. Bosh., Anon. II., as above. For this scene the *Saga* (as above), pp. 153-155, substitutes a wrangle between king and primate, which however comes to the same result.

[5] Herb. Bosh. (as above), p. 274.

[6] *Ib.* p. 275. *Summa Causæ* (*ib.* vol. iv.), p. 205. *Thomas Saga* (as above), p. 157.

[7] Herb. Bosh. (as above), p. 275.

[8] He was with his father at the council of Clarendon in January 1164. *Summa Causæ* (*ib.* vol. iv.), p. 208.

in this determination they parted.[1] A private negotiation
with some of the other prelates—suggested, it was said, by
the diplomatist-bishop of Lisieux—was more successful ;
Roger of York and Robert of Lincoln met the king at
Gloucester and agreed to accept his customs with no other
qualification than a promise on his part to exact nothing
contrary to the rights of their order. Hilary of Chichester
not only did the same but undertook to persuade the primate
himself. In this of course he failed.[2] Some time before
Christmas, however, there came to the archbishop three
commissioners who professed to be sent by the Pope to bid
him withdraw his opposition ; Henry having, according to
their story, assured the Pope that he had no designs against
the clergy or the Church, and required nothing beyond a
verbal assent for the saving of his regal dignity.[3] On the
faith of their word Thomas met the king at Oxford,[4] and
there promised to accept the customs and obey the king
" loyally and in good faith." Henry then demanded that as
the archbishop had withstood him publicly, so his submission
should be repeated publicly too, in an assembly of barons
and clergy to be convened for that purpose.[5] This was more
than Thomas had been led to expect ; but he made no
objection, and the Christmas season passed over in peace.
Henry kept the feast at Berkhampstead,[6] one of the castles
lately taken from the archbishop ; Thomas at Canterbury,
where he had just been consecrating the great English scholar
Robert of Melun—one of the three Papal commissioners—
to succeed Gilbert Foliot as bishop of Hereford.[7]

[1] Anon. I. (Robertson, *Becket*, vol. iv.), pp. 27-29.

[2] Garnier (Hippeau), pp. 33, 34. Will. Cant. (Robertson, *Becket*, vol. i.),
pp. 14, 15. E. Grim (*ib.* vol. ii.), pp. 377, 378. Anon. I. (*ib.* vol. iv.), pp.
30-31. Cf. Herb. Bosh. (*ib.* vol. iii.), p. 276, and *Thomas Saga* (Magnusson),
vol. i. p. 159.

[3] Garnier (Hippeau), pp. 34, 35. Will. Cant. (as above), p. 15. E. Grim (*ib.*
vol. ii.), p. 378. Anon. I. (*ib.* vol. iv.), p. 31. *Thomas Saga* (as above), p. 161.
All, except the Anon., seem to doubt the genuineness of the mission.

[4] Herb. Bosh. (as above), p. 277. The Anon. I. (*ib.* vol. iv.), p. 32, and Garnier
(Hippeau), p. 35, say Woodstock.

[5] Garnier, Will. Cant., Herb. Bosh. and *Thomas Saga*, as above. E. Grim
(Robertson, *Becket*, vol. ii.), p. 379. Anon. I. (*ib.* vol. iv.), pp. 33, 34.

[6] Eyton, *Itin. Hen. II.*, p. 66, from Pipe Roll a. 1164.

[7] On December 22. Gerv. Cant. (Stubbs), vol. i. p. 176.

On S. Hilary's day the proposed council met at the royal hunting-seat of Clarendon near Salisbury.[1] Henry called upon the archbishop to fulfil the promise he had given at Oxford and publicly declare his assent to the customs. Thomas drew back. As he saw the mighty array of barons round the king—as he looked over the ranks of his own fellow-bishops—it flashed at last even upon his unsuspicious mind that all this anxiety to draw him into such a public repetition of a scene which he had thought to be final must cover something more than the supposed papal envoys had led him to expect, and that those "customs" which he had been assured were but a harmless word might yet become a terrible reality if he yielded another step. His hesitation threw the king into one of those paroxysms of Angevin fury which scared the English and Norman courtiers almost out of their senses. Thomas alone remained undaunted ; the bishops stood " like a flock of sheep ready for slaughter," and the king's own ministers implored the primate to save them from the shame of having to lay violent hands upon him at their sovereign's command. For two days he stood firm ; on the third two knights of the Temple brought him a solemn assurance, on the honour of their order and the salvation of their souls, that his fears were groundless and that a verbal submission to the king's will would end the quarrel and restore peace to the Church. He believed them ; and though he still shrank from the formality, thus emptied of meaning, as little better than a lie, yet for the Church's sake he gave way. He publicly promised to obey the king's laws and customs loyally and in good faith, and made all the other bishops do likewise.[2]

The words were no sooner out of their mouths than Thomas learned how just his suspicions had been. A question was instantly raised—what were these customs ? It was too late to discuss them that night ; next morning the

[1] On the date see note B at end of chapter.

[2] Garnier (Hippeau), pp. 20-22, 36. Will. Cant. (Robertson, *Becket*, vol. i.), pp. 16, 17. E. Grim (*ib.* vol. ii.), pp. 380-382. Herb. Bosh. (*ib.* vol. iii.), pp. 278, 279. Anon. I. (*ib.* vol. iv.), pp. 33-36. Anon. II. (*ibid.*), p. 99. Cf. *Thomas Saga* (Magnusson), vol. i. pp. 163-167, and Gerv. Cant. (Stubbs), vol. i. pp. 177, 178.

king bade the oldest and wisest of the barons go and make
a recognition of the customs observed by his grandfather
and bring up a written report of them for ratification by the
council.[1] Nine days later[2] the report was presented. It
comprised sixteen articles, known ever since as the Constitutions of Clarendon.[3] Some of them merely re-affirmed, in a
more stringent and technical manner, the rules of William
the Conqueror forbidding bishops and beneficed clerks to
quit the realm or excommunicate the king's tenants-in-chief
without his leave, and the terms on which the temporal
position of the bishops had been settled by the compromise
between Henry I. and Anselm at the close of the struggle for
the investitures. Another aimed at checking the abuse of
appeals to Rome, by providing that no appeal should be
carried further than the archbishop's court without the assent
of the king. The remainder dealt with the settlement of
disputes concerning presentations and advowsons, which were
transferred from the ecclesiastical courts to that of the king;
the treatment of excommunicate persons ; the limits of the
right of sanctuary as regarding the goods of persons who
had incurred forfeiture to the Crown ; the ordination of
villeins ; the jurisdiction over clerks accused of crime ; the
protection of laymen cited before the Church courts against
episcopal and archidiaconal injustice ; and the method of
procedure in suits concerning the tenure of Church lands.

The two articles last mentioned are especially remarkable. The former provided that if a layman was accused
before a bishop on insufficient testimony, the sheriff should
at the bishop's request summon a jury of twelve lawful men
of the neighbourhood to swear to the truth or falsehood of
the charge.[4] The other clause decreed that when an estate
was claimed by a clerk in frank-almoign and by a layman as
a secular fief the question should be settled by the chief

---

[1] Garnier (Hippeau), p. 37. Will. Cant. (Robertson, *Becket*, vol. i.), p. 18.
E. Grim (*ib.* vol. ii.), p. 382. Herb. Bosh. (*ib.* vol. iii.), p. 279. Anon. I. (*ib.*
vol. iv.), p. 37. Anon. II. (*ibid.*), p. 102. Gerv. Cant. (Stubbs), vol. i. p. 178.

[2] On the chronology see note B at end of chapter.

[3] Will. Cant. (as above), pp. 18-23; Gerv. Cant. (as above), pp. 178-180;
Stubbs, *Select Charters*, pp. 137-140.

[4] Const. Clarend. c. 6 (Stubbs, *Select Charters*, pp. 138, 139).

justiciar in like manner on the recognition of twelve jurors.[1]
The way in which these provisions are introduced implies
that the principle contained in them was already well known
in the country ; it indicates that some steps had already
been taken towards a general remodelling of legal procedure,
intended to embrace all branches of judicial administration
and bring them all into orderly and harmonious working.
In this view the Constitutions of Clarendon were only part
of a great scheme in whose complete developement they
might have held an appropriate and useful place.[2] But the
churchmen of the day, to whom they were thus suddenly
presented as an isolated fragment, could hardly be expected
to see in them anything but an engine of state tyranny for
grinding down the Church. Almost every one of them
assumed, in some way or other, the complete subordination
of ecclesiastical to temporal authority ; the right of lay jurisdiction over clerks was asserted in the most uncompromising
terms ; while the last clause of all, which forbade the ordination of villeins without the consent of their lords, stirred a
nobler feeling than jealousy for mere class-privileges. Its
real intention was probably not to hinder the enfranchisement of serfs, but simply to protect the landowners against
the loss of services which, being attached to the soil, they
had no means of replacing, and very possibly also to prevent
the number of criminal clerks being further increased by the
admission of villeins anxious to escape from the justice of
their lords. But men who for ages had been trained to
regard the Church as a divinely-appointed city of refuge for
all the poor and needy, the oppressed and the enslaved, could
only see the other side of the measure and feel their inmost
hearts rise up in the cry of a contemporary poet—" Hath
not God called us all, bond and free, to His service?"[3]

---

[1] Const. Clarend. c. 9 (Stubbs, *Select Charters*, p. 139).

[2] It should be noticed that this was clearly understood, and full justice was
done to Henry's intentions, not only by the most impartial and philosophic historian of the time—William of Newburgh (l. ii. c. 16 ; Howlett, vol. i. p. 140)—
but even by Thomas's most ardent follower, Herbert of Bosham (Robertson,
Becket, vol. iii. pp. 272, 273, 278, 280).

[3] " Et Deus à sun servise nus a tuz apelez !
         Mielz valt filz à vilain qui est preuz et senez,

The discussion occupied six days ; [1] as each clause was read out to the assembly, Thomas rose and set forth his reasons for opposing it.[2] When at last the end was reached, Henry called upon him and all the bishops to affix their seals to the constitutions. "Never," burst out the primate —" never, while there is a breath left in my body !" [3] The king was obliged to content himself with the former verbal assent, gained on false pretences as it had been ; a copy of the obnoxious document was handed to the primate, who took it, as he said, for a witness against its contrivers, and indignantly quitted the assembly.[4] In an agony of remorse for the credulity which had led him into such a trap he withdrew to Winchester and suspended himself from all priestly functions till he had received absolution from the Pope.[5]

Que ne fet gentilz hum failliz et debutez !"
Garnier (Hippeau), p. 89. This, variously expressed, was the grand argument of the clerical-democratic party, and the true source of their strength. And they were not altogether wrong in attributing the action of their opponents, in part at least, to aristocratic contempt and exclusiveness—if we may trust Gervase of Canterbury's report of a complaint said to have been uttered at a later time by the king : " Hi quoque omnes " [*i.e.* the religious orders] " tales sibi fratres associant, pelliparios scilicet et sutores, quorum nec unus deberet instante necessitate in episcopum vel abbatem salvâ conscientiâ nostrâ promoveri." Gerv. Cant. (Stubbs), vol. i. p. 540.

[1] See note B at end of chapter.

[2] Herb. Bosh. (Robertson, *Becket*, vol. iii.), pp. 280-285. The answers to the Constitutions in Garnier (Hippeau), pp. 84-89, seem to be partly Thomas's and partly his own.

[3] " L'arcevesques respunt : Fei que dei Deu le bel,
Ço n'ert, tant cum la vie me bate en cest vessel !"
Garnier (Hippeau), p. 37. Cf. E. Grim (Robertson, *Becket*, vol. ii.), p. 383, and Anon. I. (*ib.* vol. iv.), p. 37.

[4] Garnier, as above. Will. Cant. (Robertson, *Becket*, vol. i.), p. 23. E. Grim (*ib.* vol. ii.), p. 383. Anon. I. (*ib.* vol. iv.), p. 37. Cf. Joh. Salisb. (*ib.* vol. ii.), p. 311 ; Herb. Bosh. (*ib.* vol. iii.), p. 288 ; Anon. II. (*ib.* vol. iv.), p. 103, and *Thomas Saga* (Magnusson), vol. i. pp. 167-169. Will. Fitz-Steph. (Robertson, *Becket*, vol. iii.), pp. 48, 49, says that Thomas did set his seal to the constitutions ; but his statement is at variance with those of all other authorities ; and he himself afterwards recites two speeches made at Northampton, one by Thomas and one by Hilary of Chichester, both distinctly affirming that none of the bishops sealed. *Ib.* pp. 66, 67.

[5] Garnier (Hippeau), p. 38. Will. Cant. (as above), p. 24. Joh. Salisb. (*ib.* vol. ii.), p. 312. E. Grim (*ibid.*), p. 383. Will. Fitz-Steph. (*ib.* vol. iii.), p. 49. Herb. Bosh. (*ibid.*), pp. 289-292. Anon. I. (*ib.* vol. iv.), p. 37.

It was to the Pope that both parties looked for a settlement of their dispute ; but Alexander, ill acquainted both with the merits of the case and with the characters of the disputants, and beset on all sides with political difficulties, could only strive in vain to hold the balance evenly between them. Meanwhile the political quarrel of king and primate was embittered by an incident in which Henry's personal feelings were stirred. His brother William—the favourite young brother whom he had once planned to establish as sovereign in Ireland—had set his heart upon a marriage with the widowed countess of Warren ; the archbishop had forbidden the match on the ground of affinity, and his pro-, hibition had put an end to the scheme.[1] Baffled and indignant, William returned to Normandy and poured the story of his grievance into the sympathizing ears first of his mother and then, as it seems, of the brotherhood at Bec.[2] On January 29, 1164—one day before the dissolution of the council of Clarendon—he died at Rouen ;[3] and a writer who was himself at that time a monk at Bec not only implies his own belief that the young man actually died of disappointment, but declares that Henry shared that belief, and thenceforth looked upon the primate by whom the disappointment had been caused as little less than the murderer of his brother.[4] The king's exasperation was at any rate plain to

---

[1] Will. Fitz-Steph. (Robertson, *Becket*, vol. iv.) p. 142. Isabel de Warren was the widow of Stephen's son William, who of course was cousin in the third degree to William of Anjou.

[2] "Hic" [*i.e.* Thomas] " regis fratrem pertæsum semper habebat,
    Ne consul foret hic, obvius ille fuit :
    Cum nata comitis comitem Warenna tulisset,
    Nobilis hic præsul ne nocuisset ei.
    Irâ permotus, nunquam rediturus, ab Anglis
    Advenit is, matri nunciat ista piæ.
    Hinc Beccum veniens fratrum se tradit amori."
Draco Norm., l. ii. c. 8, vv. 441-447 (Howlett, *Will. Newb.*, vol. ii. p. 676).

[3] Rob. Torigni, a. 1164. *Draco Norm.*, l. ii. c. 8, vv. 448-450 (as above). The date is from the first-named writer.

[4] *Draco Norm.*, l. ii. c. 8, vv. 453-456 (as above). Considering the abundance —one might almost say superabundance—of unquestionably authentic information which we already possess as to the origin and grounds of Henry's quarrel with Thomas, I cannot attach so much importance as Mr. Howlett apparently does (*ib.* pref. pp. lxi-lxiii) to this new contribution from Stephen of Rouen. Stephen's work is quasi-romantic in character and utterly unhistoric in style ; and his view

all eyes ; and as the summer drew on Thomas found himself gradually deserted. His best friend, John of Salisbury, had already been taken from his side, and was soon driven into exile by the jealousy of the king ;[1] another friend, John of Canterbury, had been removed out of the country early in 1163 by the ingenious device of making him bishop of Poitiers.[2] The old dispute concerning the relations between Canterbury and York had broken out afresh with intensified bitterness between Roger of Pont-l'Evêque and the former comrade of whom he had long been jealous, and who had now once again been promoted over his head ; the king, hoping to turn it to account for his own purposes, was intriguing at the Papal court in Roger's behalf, and one of his confidential agents there was Thomas's own archdeacon, Geoffrey Ridel.[3] The bishops as yet were passive ; in the

of the whole Becket controversy is simply ludicrous, for he ignores the clerical immunities and the Constitutions of Clarendon altogether, and attributes the quarrel wholly to two other causes—this affair about William, and Thomas's supposed peculations while chancellor (*ib.* l. iii. c. 12, vv. 909-914, p. 741). That the domestic tragedy of which he gives such a highly-coloured account had some bearing upon the great political drama appears from the words of Richard le Breton to Thomas at his murder seven years later, "Hoc habeas pro amore domini mei Willelmi fratris regis" (Will. Fitz-Stèph., Robertson, *Becket*, vol. iii. p. 142). But in these words there is no mention either of William's death or of Henry's feelings about it. Some allusion to either or both may have been in the speaker's mind ; but what he actually said implies nothing more than that he had been in William's service, and had therefore resented the thwarting of his lord's interests, and through them, it may be, of his own. Will. Fitz-Steph., after explaining what William's grievance was, simply adds, "Unde Willelmus . . . inconsolabiliter doluit ; et omnes sui archiepiscopo inimici facti sunt." *Ibid.*

[1] From a comparison of Will. Fitz-Steph. (Robertson, *Becket*, vol. iii.), p. 46, with Ep. lv. (*ib.* vol. v. pp. 95-103), it appears that John was separated from Thomas before the council of Clarendon. After some months of wandering he found shelter at Reims, in the great abbey of S. Remigius of which his old friend Peter of Celle was now abbot, and there he chiefly dwelt during the next seven years.

[2] Will. Fitz-Steph., as above, says John was promoted for the purpose of getting him out of the way. He was consecrated by the Pope at the council of Tours ; R. Diceto (Stubbs), vol. i. p. 311. It must be remembered that Henry had already had experience of John's zeal for clerical immunities.

[3] Epp. xiii., xxvii., xxxvi., xli.-xliii., l., li., liii., liv. (Robertson, *Becket*, vol. v. pp. 21, 22, 44-46, 59, 60, 67-69, 85, 87, 88, 91, 94) ; Will. Cant. (*ib.* vol. i.), p. 24 ; E. Grim (*ib.* vol. ii.), p. 384 ; Anon. I. (*ib.* vol. iv.), pp. 38, 39 ; Garnier (Hippeau), pp. 39, 40 ; *Thomas Saga* (Magnusson), vol. i. pp. 179-181 ; Gerv. Cant. (Stubbs), vol. i. p. 181.

York controversy Gilbert Foliot strongly supported his own metropolitan ;[1] but between him and Thomas there was already a question, amicable indeed at present but ominous nevertheless, as to whether or not the profession of obedience made to Theobald by the bishop of Hereford should be repeated by the same man as bishop of London to Theobald's successor.[2]

Thomas himself fully expected to meet the fate of Anselm ; throughout the winter his friends had been endeavouring to secure him a refuge in France ;[3] and early in the summer of 1164, having been refused an interview with the king,[4] he made two attempts to escape secretly from Romney. The first time he was repelled by a contrary wind ; the second time the sailors put back ostensibly for the same reason, but really because they had recognized their passenger and dreaded the royal wrath ;[5] and a servant who went on the following night to shut the gates of the deserted palace at Canterbury found the primate, worn out with fatigue and disappointment, sitting alone in the darkness like a beggar upon his own door-step.[6] Despairing of escape, he made another effort to see the king at Woodstock. Henry dreaded nothing so much as the archbishop's flight, for he felt that it would probably be followed by a Papal interdict on his dominions,[7] and would certainly give an immense advantage against him to Louis of France, who was at that very moment threatening war in Auvergne.[8] He therefore received Thomas courteously, though with somewhat less than the usual honours,[9] and made no allusion

---

[1] Ep. xxviii. (Robertson, *Becket*, vol. v. pp. 46, 47).

[2] Epp. xxxv., lxvii. (*ib.* pp. 56, 57, 130, 131).

[3] Epp. xxxv., xxxvi., lv. (*ib.* pp. 57, 58, 97).

[4] Will. Fitz-Steph. (*ib.*), vol. iii. p. 49.

[5] Cf. Will. Fitz-Steph. as above; Herb. Bosh. (*ibid.*), p. 293 ; Anon. II. (*ib.* vol. iv.), p. 104 ; and Alan Tewkesb. (*ib.* vol. ii.), p. 325, with E. Grim (*ibid.*), pp. 389, 390 ; Will. Cant. (*ib.* vol. i.), p. 29 ; Anon. I. (*ib.* vol. iv.), p. 40 ; and Garnier (Hippeau), p. 49.

[6] Alan Tewkesb. as above.

[7] Will. Cant. (*ib.* vol. i.), p. 29. E. Grim (*ib.* vol. ii.), p. 390. Anon. I. (*ib.* vol. iv.), p. 40. Garnier (Hippeau), p. 50.

[8] Ep. lx. (Robertson, *Becket*, vol. v., p. 115).

[9] Ep. ccxxv. (*ib.* p. 530). Herb. Bosh. (*ib.* vol. iii.), p. 294.

to the past except by a playful question "whether the archbishop did not think the realm was wide enough to contain
them both ?" ⁻ Thomas saw, however, that the old cordiality
was gone ; his enemies saw it too, and, as his biographer
says, "they came about him like bees."[1] Foremost among
them was John the king's marshal, who had ‚a suit in the
archbishop's court concerning the manor of Pageham.[2] It
was provided by one of Henry's new rules of legal procedure that if a suitor saw no chance of obtaining justice in
the court of his own lord he might, by taking an oath to
that effect and bringing two witnesses to do the same,
transfer the suit to a higher court.[3] John by this method
removed his case from the court of the archbishop to that of
the king; and thither Thomas was cited to answer his claim on
the feast of the Exaltation of the Cross. When that day camé
the primate was too ill to move ; he sent essoiners to excuse
his absence in legal form, and also a written protest against
the removal of the suit, on the ground that it had been obtained by perjury—John having taken the oath not upon
the Gospel, but upon an old song-book which he had surrep-
titiously brought into court for the purpose.[4] Henry angrily
refused to believe either Thomas or his essoiners,[5] and immediately issued orders for a great council to be held at
Northampton.[6] It was customary to call the archbishops
and the greater barons by a special writ addressed to each
individually, while the lesser tenants-in-chief received a
general summons through the sheriffs of the different
counties. Roger of York was specially called in due form ;[7]
the metropolitan of all Britain, who ought to have been in-

[1] Herb. Bosh. (Robertson, *Becket*, vol. iii.), pp. 294, 295.
[2] Will. Fitz-Steph. (*ibid.*), p. 50.
[3] Garnier (Hippeau), p. 51. Will. Cant. (Robertson, *Becket*, vol. i.), p. 31.
Anon. I. (*ib.* vol. iv.), p. 41. On this proceeding see Glanville, *De Legg. et Conss.
Angl.*, l. xii. c. 7.
[4] Garnier (Hippeau), pp. 51-53. Will. Cant. (as above), p. 30. E. Grim (*ib.*
vol. ii.), p. 390. Will. Fitz-Steph. (*ib.* vol. iii.), p. 50. Anon. I. (*ib.* vol. iv.),
p. 41. Ep. ccxxv. (*ib.* vol. v.), pp. 530, 531.
[5] Will. Fitz-Steph. as above.
[6] *Ib.* p. 49. Herb. Bosh. (*ibid.*), p. 296. Anon. I. (*ib.* vol. iv.), p. 30. Ep.
ccxxv. (*ib.* vol. v.), p. 531. Garnier (Hippeau), p. 50.
[7] R. Diceto (Stubbs), vol. i. pp. 313, 314.

vited first and most honourably of all, merely received through the sheriff of Kent a peremptory citation to be ready on the first day of the council with his defence against the claim of John the marshal.[1] The council—an almost complete gathering of the tenants-in-chief, lay and spiritual, throughout the realm [2]—was summoned for Tuesday October 6.[3] The king however lingered hawking by the river-side till late at night,[4] and it was not till next morning after Mass that the archbishop could obtain an audience. He began by asking leave to go and consult the Pope on his dispute with Roger of York and divers other questions touching the interests of both Church and state; Henry angrily bade him be silent and retire to prepare his defence for his contempt of the royal summons in the matter of John the marshal.[5] The trial took place next day. John himself did not appear, being detained in the king's service at the Michaelmas session of the Exchequer

[1] Will. Fitz-Steph. (Robertson, *Becket*, vol. iii.), p. 51.

[2] Herb. Bosh. (*ibid.*) p. 296. E. Grim (*ib.* vol. ii.), p. 390. Anon. I. (*ib.* vol. iv.), p. 41. R. Diceto (Stubbs), vol. i. p. 313. Only two bishops were absent : Nigel of Ely, disabled by paralysis, and William of Norwich, who made an excuse to avoid sharing in what he knew was to come. Gerv. Cant. (Stubbs), vol. i. p. 185. From Alan Tewkesb. however (Robertson, *Becket*, vol. ii. p. 331), it seems that Norwich came after all—only, like Rochester (Will. Fitz-Steph., *ib.* vol. iii. p. 52), somewhat late.

[3] Will. Fitz-Steph. (as above), p. 50. Herb. Bosh. (*ib.* p. 296), says " hebdomadæ feria quinta, sexta ante B. Calixti . . . diem "—a self-contradiction, for in 1164 October 9, the sixth day before the feast of S. Calixtus, was not Thursday but Friday. He makes, however, a similar confusion as to the last day of the council (*ib.* pp. 301, 304, 326) ; and as this was undoubtedly Tuesday October 13—not Wednesday 14, as he seems to make it in p. 304—it is plain that his mistake lies in placing the feast of S. Calixtus a day too early, and that the day to which he really means to assign the opening of the assembly is Thursday October 8. This really agrees with Will. Fitz-Steph., for, as will be seen, the council did not formally meet till a day after that for which it was summoned, and did not get to business till a day later still. William gives the date for which it had been summoned ; Herbert, that of its practical beginning. R. Diceto (Stubbs, vol. i. p. 313) has substituted the closing day for that of opening ; the author of *Thomas Saga* (Magnusson, vol. i. p. 241), has done the same, with a further confusion as to the days of the week ; while Gerv. Cant. (Stubbs, vol. i. p. 182) has a date which agrees with nothing, and which must be altogether wrong.   [4] Will. Fitz-Steph. as above.

[5] Garnier (Hippeau), p. 52. E. Grim (Robertson, *Becket*, vol. ii.), p. 391. Cf. Anon. I. (*ib.* vol. iv.), p. 42, and Will. Fitz-Steph. (*ib.* vol. iii.), p. 51.

VOL. II.

in London ;[1] the charge of failure of justice was apparently withdrawn, but for the alleged contempt Thomas was sentenced to a fine of five hundred pounds.[2] Indignant as he was at the flagrant illegality of the trial, in which his own suffragans had been compelled to sit in judgement on their primate, Thomas was yet persuaded to submit, in the hope of avoiding further wrangling over what seemed now to have become a mere question of money.[3] But there were other questions to follow. Henry now demanded from the archbishop a sum of three hundred pounds, representing the revenue due from the honours of Eye and Berkhampstead for the time during which he had held them since his resignation of the chancellorship.[4] Thomas remarked that he had spent far more than that sum on the repair of the royal palaces, and protested against the unfairness of making such a demand without warning. Still, however, he disdained to resist for a matter of filthy lucre, and found sureties for the required amount.[5] Next morning Henry made a further demand for the repayment of a loan made to Thomas in his chancellor days.[6] In those days the two friends had virtually had but one purse as well as "one mind and one heart," and Thomas was deeply wounded by this evident proof that their friendship was at an end. Once more he submitted ; but this time it was no easy matter to

---

[1] Will. Fitz-Steph. (Robertson, *Becket*, vol. iii.), p. 51.

[2] *Ibid.* Herb. Bosh. (*ibid.*), p. 297. Will. Cant. (*ib.* vol. i.), p. 30. E. Grim (*ib.* vol. ii.), p. 391. Anon. I. (*ib.* vol. iv.), p. 42. Garnier (Hippeau), p. 52. *Thomas Saga* (Magnusson), vol. i. p. 18. Gerv. Cant. (Stubbs), vol. i. p. 183. R. Diceto (Stubbs), vol. i. p. 313. The actual sentence was forfeiture of all his moveable goods *ad misericordiam*—commuted according to custom ; cf. Herb. Bosh. and Gerv. Cant., as above, with Will. Fitz-Steph. (as above), p. 62. Garnier makes the sum three hundred pounds ; Will. Cant., fifty ; E. Grim, the Anon. I. and R. Diceto, five hundred.

[3] Garnier (Hippeau), p. 52. E. Grim (as above), p. 391. Anon. I. (*ib.* vol. iv.), p. 43.

[4] This must be the meaning of Will. Fitz-Steph. (*ib.* vol. iii.), p. 53, compared with R. Diceto (Stubbs), vol. i. pp. 313, 314.

[5] Will. Fitz-Steph. as above.

[6] The demand is stated by Will. Fitz-Steph. (*ibid.*) as " de quingentis marcis ex causâ commodati in exercitu Tolosæ, et aliis quingentis marcis ex causâ fidejussionis regis pro eo erga quendam Judæum ibidem." This would make the total amount £666 : 3 : 8. Herb. Bosh. (*ibid.*), p. 298, and the *Thomas Saga* (Magnusson), vol. i. p. 189, make it five hundred pounds.

find sureties ;[1] and then, late on the Friday evening, there was reached the last and most overwhelming count in the long indictment thus gradually unrolled before the eyes of the astonished primate. He was called upon to render a complete statement of all the revenues of vacant sees baronies and honours of which he had had the custody as chancellor—in short, of the whole accounts of the chancery during his tenure of office.[2]

At this crushing demand the archbishop's courage gave way, and he threw himself at the king's feet in despair. All the bishops did likewise, but in vain ; Henry swore " by God's Eyes " that he would have the accounts in full. He granted, however, a respite till the morrow,[3] and Thomas spent the next morning in consultation with his suffragans.[4] Gilbert of London advised unconditional surrender ;[5] Henry of Winchester, who had already withstood the king to his face the night before,[6] strongly opposed this view,[7] and suggested that the matter should be compromised by an offer of two thousand marks. This the king rejected.[8] After long deliberation [9] it was decided—again at the suggestion

[1] Herb. Bosh. (Robertson, *Becket*, vol. iii.), pp. 298, 299.
[2] Garnier (Hippeau), p. 53. Will. Cant. (Robertson, *Becket*, vol. i.), p. 31. Joh. Salisb. (*ib.* vol. ii.), p. 312. E. Grim (*ibid.*), p. 392. Will. Fitz-Steph. (*ib.* vol. iii.), p. 54. Herb. Bosh. (*ibid.*), p. 299. Anon. I. (*ib.* vol. iv.), p. 43. Anon. II. (*ibid.*), p. 104. R. Diceto (Stubbs), vol. i. p. 314. The total sum due was assessed in the end at thirty thousand pounds, according to Garnier (p. 65), Will. Cant. (p. 38), E. Grim (p. 396) and Anon. I. (p. 49). Herb. Bosh., however (as above), makes it thirty thousand marks (*i.e.* twenty thousand pounds). The *Thomas Saga* (Magnusson), vol. i. p. 191, says thirty thousand marks "of burnt silver," *i.e.* blanch ; while Gilbert Foliot, when reciting the story to the Pope's legates in 1167, is reported as stating it at forty-four thousand marks (£2933 : 6 : 8) ; Ep. cccxxxix. (Robertson, *Becket*, vol. vi. p. 271). Herb. Bosh. (as above) places this demand on the Saturday morning, and the whole history of the three days, Friday–Sunday, October 9–11, is somewhat confused by the discordant notes of time given by the various biographers. I have followed Will. Fitz-Steph., who is the most self-consistent and apparently the most trustworthy.
[3] Garnier (Hippeau), pp. 53, 54.
[4] Herb. Bosh. (Robertson, *Becket*, vol. iii.), p. 300.
[5] Alan Tewkesb. (*ib.* vol. ii.), pp. 326, 327.
[6] Garnier (Hippeau), p. 54.   [7] Alan Tewkesb. (as above), p. 327.
[8] Will. Fitz-Steph. (*ib.* vol. iii.), p. 54.
[9] The speeches of the bishops—interesting for studies of character—are given at length by Alan Tewkesb. (as above), pp. 327, 328. Cf. the account in *Thomas Saga* (Magnusson), vol. i. pp. 193-199.

of Bishop Henry—that Thomas should refuse to entertain the king's demands on the ground of the release from all secular obligations granted to him at his consecration. This answer was carried by the bishops in a body to the king. He refused to accept it, declaring that the release had been given without his authority ; and all that the bishops could wring from him was a further adjournment till the Monday morning.[1]   In the middle of Sunday night the highly-strung nervous organization of Thomas broke down under the long cruel strain ; the morning found him lying in helpless agony, and with great difficulty he obtained from the king another day's delay.[2]   Before it expired a warning reached him from the court that if he appeared there he must expect nothing short of imprisonment or death.[3]   A like rumour spread through the council, and at dawn the bishops in a body implored their primate to give up the hopeless struggle and throw himself on the mercy of the king. He refused to betray his Church by accepting a sentence which he believed to be illegal as well as unjust, forbade the bishops to take any further part in his trial, gave them notice of an appeal to Rome if they should do so, and charged them on their canonical obedience to excommunicate at once whatever laymen should dare to sit in judgement upon him.[4]   Against this last command the bishop of London instantly appealed.[5]

[1] Will. Cant. (Robertson, *Becket*, vol. i.), p. 31. E. Grim (*ib.* vol. ii.), p. 392. Herb. Bosh. (*ib.* vol. iii.), p. 300. Anon. I. (*ib.* vol. iv.), p. 43. Anon. II. (*ibid.*), pp. 104, 105. Alan Tewkesb. (*ib.* vol. ii.), pp. 328, 329, has a slightly different version ; in this, and also in *Thomas Saga* (Magnusson), vol. i. pp. 199-201, Gilbert Foliot wins the respite by a daring misrepresentation of Thomas's answer to the king. I have followed Herbert's reckoning of the days here, as it fits in with that of Will. Fitz-Steph., who seems the best guide in this matter.

[2] Garnier (Hippeau), pp. 55, 56. Will. Cant. (as above), p. 32. Alan Tewkesb. (*ib.* vol. ii.) pp. 329, 330. E. Grim (*ibid.*), pp. 392, 393. Will. Fitz-Steph. (*ib.* vol. iii.), p. 56. Herb. Bosh. (*ibid.*), pp. 300, 301. Anon. I. (*ib.* vol. iv.), p. 44. *Thomas Saga* (as above), p. 203. Here again I follow Will. Fitz-Steph. and Herbert as to the day.

[3] Garnier (Hippeau), p. 56. Will. Cant. as above. E. Grim (*ib.* vol. ii.), p. 393. Anon. I. (*ib.* vol. iv.), p. 44. *Thomas Saga* as above.

[4] Will. Fitz-Steph. (as above), p. 62. Herb. Bosh. (*ibid.*), pp. 301-303. *Thomas Saga* (as above), pp. 205-207.

[5] Herb. Bosh. (as above), p. 303. *Thomas Saga* (as above), p. 207. Some of the other biographers place this scene later in the day, but we can hardly do otherwise than follow the two eye-witnesses, William and Herbert.

All then returned to the court, except Henry of Winchester and Jocelyn of Salisbury, who lingered for a last word of pleading or of sympathy.[1] When they too were gone, Thomas went to the chapel of the monastery in which he was lodging—a small Benedictine house dedicated to S. Andrew, just outside the walls of Northampton—and with the utmost solemnity celebrated the mass of S. Stephen with its significant introit : " Princes have sat and spoken against me." The mass ended, he mounted his horse, and escorted no longer by a brilliant train of clerks and knights, but by a crowd of poor folk full of sympathy and admiration, he rode straight to the castle where the council awaited him.[2]

At the gate he took his cross from the attendant who usually bore it, and went forward alone to the hall where the bishops and barons were assembled.   They fell back in amazement at the apparition of the tall solitary figure, robed in full pontificals, and carrying the crucifix like an uplifted banner prepared at once for defence and for defiance; friends and opponents were almost equally shocked, and it was not till he had passed through their midst and seated himself in a corner of the hall that the bishops recovered sufficiently to gather round him and intreat that he would give up his unbecoming burthen.   Thomas refused ; "he would not lay down his standard, he would not part with his shield." " A fool you ever were, a fool I see you are still and will be to the end," burst out Gilbert Foliot at last, as after a long argument he turned impatiently away.[4] The others followed him, and the primate was left with only two companions,

[1] Herb. Bosh. (Robertson, *Becket*, vol. iii.), p. 303. Jocelyn's after-conduct shewed that his sympathy with the primate was not very deep.

[2] Will. Cant. (Robertson, *Becket*, vol. i.), pp. 32, 34. Alan Tewkesb. (*ib.* vol. ii.), p. 330. E. Grim (*ibid.*), p. 393. Will. Fitz-Steph. (*ib.* vol. iii.), pp. 56, 57. Herb. Bosh. (*ibid.*), p. 304. Anon. I. (*ib.* vol. iv.), p. 45. Garnier (Hippeau), pp. 56-60. *Thomas Saga* (Magnusson), vol. i. pp. 207-209.

[3] Garnier (Hippeau), p. 60. Will. Fitz-Steph. (Robertson, *Becket*, vol. iii.), p. 57. Herb. Bosh. (*ibid.*), p. 304. Alan Tewkesb. (*ib.* vol. ii.), p. 330. *Thomas Saga* (as above), p. 209.

[4] Garnier (Hippeau), pp. 60, 61. Will. Cant. (as above), p. 34. Alan Tewkesb. (*ib.* vol. ii.), p. 330. E. Grim (*ibid.*), p. 394. Will. Fitz-Steph. (*ib.* vol. iii.), p. 57. Herb. Bosh. (*ibid.*), pp. 305, 306. Anon. I. (*ib.* vol. iv.), pp. 46, 47. *Thomas Saga* (as above), pp. 211-213.

William Fitz-Stephen and his own especial friend, Herbert of Bosham.[1] The king had retired to an inner chamber and was there deliberating with his most intimate counsellors [2] when the story of the primate's entrance reached his ears. He took it as an unpardonable insult, and caused Thomas to be proclaimed a traitor. Warnings and threats ran confusedly through the hall. The archbishop bent over the disciple sitting at his feet :—" For thee I fear—yet fear not thou ; even now mayest thou share my crown." The ardent encouragement with which Herbert answered him [3] provoked one of the king's marshals to interfere and forbid that any one should speak to the " traitor." William Fitz-Stephen, who had been vainly striving to put in a gentle word, caught his primate's eyes and pointed to the crucifix, intrusting to its silent eloquence the lesson of patience and prayer which his lips were forbidden to utter. When he and Thomas, after long separation, met again in the land of exile, that speechless admonition seems to have been the first thing which recurred to the minds of both.[4]

In the chamber overhead, meanwhile, Henry had summoned the bishops to a conference.[5] On receiving from them an account of their morning's interview with Thomas, he sent down to the latter his ultimatum, requiring him to withdraw his appeal to Rome and his commands to the bishops as contrary to the customs which he had sworn to observe, and to submit to the judgement of the king's court on the chancery accounts. Seated, with eyes fixed on the cross, Thomas quietly but firmly refused. His refusal was reported to the king, who grew fiery-red with rage, caught eagerly at the barons' proposal that the archbishop should be judged for contempt of his sovereign's jurisdiction in appealing from it to another tribunal, and called upon the

---

[1] Will. Cant. (Robertson, *Becket*, vol. i.), p. 34. Herb. Bosh. (*ib.* vol. iii.), p. 307. They only mention Herbert ; William's presence appears in the sequel.

[2] Garnier (Hippeau), p. 61. Will. Cant. (as above), p. 35. E. Grim (*ib.* vol. ii.), p. 394. Herb. Bosh. (*ib.* vol. iii.), p. 305. Anon. I. (*ib.* vol. iv.), p. 47.   [3] Herb. Bosh. (*ib.* vol. iii.), pp. 306-308.

[4] Will. Fitz-Steph. (*ibid.*), p. 59.

[5] *Ib.* p. 57. Will. Cant. (*ib.* vol. i.), p. 35. Alan Tewkesb. (*ib.* vol. ii.), p. 331. Garnier (Hippeau), p. 62.

bishops to join in his condemnation.[1] York, London and
Chichester proposed that they should cite him before the
Pope instead, on the grounds of perjury at Clarendon and
unjust demands on their obedience.[2] To this Henry consented ; the appeal was uttered by Hilary of Chichester in
the name of all, and in most insulting terms ;[3] and the
bishops sat down opposite their primate to await the
sentence of the lay barons.[4]

What that sentence was no one outside the royal council-
chamber ever really knew. It was one thing to determine
it there and another to deliver it to its victim, sitting alone
and unmoved with the sign of victory in his hand. With
the utmost reluctance and hesitation the old justiciar, Earl
Robert of Leicester, came to perform his odious task. At
the word "judgement" Thomas started up, with uplifted
crucifix and flashing eyes, forbade the speaker to proceed,
and solemnly appealed to the protection of the court of
Rome. The justiciar and his companions retired in silence.[5]
" I too will go, for the hour is past," said Thomas.[6] Cross
in hand he strode past the speechless group of bishops into
the outer hall ; the courtiers followed him with a torrent of
insults, which were taken up by the squires and serving-
men outside ; as he stumbled against a pile of faggots set
ready for the fire, Ralf de Broc rushed upon him with a

---

[1] Garnier (Hippeau), pp. 65, 66. Will. Cant. (Robertson, *Becket*, vol. i.), pp.
36-38. Will. Fitz-Steph. (*ib.* vol. iii.), pp. 62-65. Cf. *Thomas Saga* (Magnusson),
vol. i. pp. 213-217.

[2] Will. Cant. (as above), p. 37. In the versions of E. Grim (*ib.* vol. ii.),
p. 396, Herb. Bosh. (*ib.* vol. iii.), p. 308, and the *Thomas Saga* (as above),
p. 217, they bluntly bargain to be let off from actually sitting in judgement on
their primate in consideration of a promise to stand by the king against him for
ever after.

[3] Will. Fitz-Steph. (Robertson, *Becket*, vol. iii.), pp. 65, 66. Alan Tewkesb.
(*ib.* vol. ii.), pp. 331, 332. According to Alan, Thomas answered but one word
—" I hear " ; according to William, he condescended to make a long speech. Cf.
Anon. I. (*ib.* vol. iv.), p. 49.   [4] Alan Tewkesb. (*ib.* vol. ii.), p. 332.

[5] Garnier (Hippeau), p. 67. Will. Cant. (as above), pp. 38, 39. Alan
Tewkesb. (*ib.* vol. ii.), pp. 332, 333. E. Grim (*ibid.*), pp. 397, 398. Will.
Fitz-Steph. (*ib.* vol. iii.), pp. 67, 68. Herb. Bosh. (*ibid.*), pp. 309, 310. Anon.
I. (*ib.* vol. iv.), pp. 50, 51. Cf. *Thomas Saga* (Magnusson), vol. i. p. 221, where
the altercation is longer, but comes to the same end.

[6] Anon. I. (as above), p. 51.

shout of "Traitor! traitor!"[1] The king's half - brother, Count Hameline, echoed the cry ;[2] but he shrank back at the primate's retort—"Were I a knight instead of a priest, this hand should prove thee a liar!"[3] Amid a storm of abuse Thomas made his way into the court-yard and sprang upon his horse, taking up his faithful Herbert behind him.[4] The outer gate was locked, but a squire of the archbishop managed to find the keys.[5] Whether there was any real intention of stopping his egress it seems impossible to determine ; the king and his counsellors were apparently too much puzzled to do anything but let matters take their course ; Henry indeed sent down a herald to quell the disturbance and forbid all violence to the primate ;[6] but the precaution came too late. Once outside the gates, Thomas had no need of such protection. From the mob of hooting enemies within he passed into the midst of a crowd of poor folk who pressed upon him with every demonstration of rapturous affection ; in every street as he rode along the people came out to throw themselves at his feet and beg his blessing.

It was with these poor folk that he supped that night, for his own household, all save a chosen few, now hastened to take leave of him.[7] Through the bishops of Rochester, Hereford and Worcester he requested of the king a safe-conduct for his journey to Canterbury ; the king declined

[1] Garnier (Hippeau), p. 68. Will. Cant. (Robertson, *Becket*, vol. i.), p. 39. E. Grim (*ib.* vol. ii.), p. 398. Anon. I. (*ib.* vol. iv.), pp. 51, 52. Cf. Will. Fitz-Steph. (*ib.* vol. iii.); p. 68.

[2] Garnier and Will. Cant. as above. Anon. I. (as above), p. 52.

[3] Anon. I. as above. Cf. Herb. Bosh. (*ib.* vol. iii.), p. 310. There is a different version in Will. Cant. (*ib.* vol. i.), pp. 39, 40.

[4] Will. Fitz-Steph. as above. Of his own escape William says nothing ; but we know from a passage later in the same page that he soon rejoined his primate.

[5] Garnier (Hippeau), p. 69. Cf. Will. Cant. (as above), p. 40 ; Alan Tewkesb. (*ib.* vol. ii.), p. 333 ; Anon. I. (*ib.* vol. iv.), p. 52 ; and *Thomas Saga* (Magnusson), vol. i. p. 222.

[6] Garnier (Hippeau), p. 70. Will. Fitz-Steph. (as above), p. 69. E. Grim (*ib.* vol. ii.), p. 399.

[7] Alan Tewkesb. (as above), p. 333. E. Grim (*ibid.*), p. 399. Herb. Bosh. (*ib.* vol. iii.), p. 310. Anon. I. (*ib.* vol. iv.), p. 52. Will. Cant. (*ib.* vol. i.), p. 40. Garnier, as above.

to answer till the morrow.[1]   The primate's suspicions were aroused. He caused his bed to be laid in the church, as if intending to spend the night in prayer.[2]   At cock-crow the monks came and sang their matins in an under-tone for fear of disturbing their weary guest;[3] but his chamberlain was watching over an empty couch. At dead of night Thomas had made his escape with two canons of Sempringham and a faithful squire of his own, named Roger of Brai. A violent storm of rain helped to cover their flight,[4] and it was not till the middle of the next day that king and council discovered that the primate was gone.

"God's blessing go with him!" murmured with a sigh of relief the aged Bishop Henry of Winchester. "We have not done with him yet!" cried the king. He at once issued orders that all the ports should be watched to prevent Thomas from leaving the country,[5] and that the temporalities of the metropolitan see should be left untouched pending an appeal to the Pope[6] which he despatched the archbishop of York and the bishops of London, Worcester, Exeter and Chichester to prosecute without delay.[7] They sailed from Dover on All Souls day;[8] that very night Thomas, after three weeks of adventurous wanderings, guarded with the most devoted vigilance by the brethren of Sempringham, embarked in a little boat from Sandwich; next day he landed in Flanders;[9] and after

[1] Alan Tewkesb. (Robertson, *Becket*, vol. ii.), p. 334. Will. Fitz-Steph. (*ib.* vol. iii.), p. 69. Herb. Bosh. (*ibid.*), p. 312.

[2] Alan Tewkesb. and Will. Fitz-Steph. as above. Will. Cant. (*ib.* vol. i.), p. 40. Anon. I. (*ib.* vol. iv.), p. 53. Garnier (Hippeau), p. 70. *Thomas Saga* (Magnusson), vol. i. p. 229.   [3] Garnier, as above.

[4] Garnier (Hippeau), p. 71. E. Grim (Robertson, *Becket*, vol. ii.), p. 399. Anon. I. (*ib.* vol. iv.), pp. 53, 54. Cf. Will. Cant. (*ib.* vol. i.), p. 40, Will. Fitz-Steph. (*ib.* vol. iii.), p. 69, and Herb. Bosh. (*ibid.*) p. 312.

[5] Anon. I. (as above), p. 55.

[6] Will. Fitz-Steph. (*ib.* vol. iii.), p. 70. Herb. Bosh. (*ibid.*), p. 322.

[7] Garnier (Hippeau), p. 79. Alan Tewkesb. (as above), p. 336. E. Grim (*ibid.*), p. 402. Will. Fitz-Steph. (*ib.* vol. iii.), p. 70. Herb. Bosh. (*ibid.*), p. 323. Anon. I. (*ib.* vol. iv.), pp. 60, 61. *Thomas Saga* (Magnusson), vol. i. p. 261.   [8] Will. Fitz-Steph. as above.

[9] Garnier (Hippeau), pp. 71-74. E. Grim (as above), pp. 399, 400. Alan Tewkesb. (*ibid.*), p. 335. Will. Fitz-Steph. (*ib.* vol. iii.), p. 70. Herb. Bosh. (*ibid.*), pp. 323-325. Anon. I. (*ib.* vol. iv.), pp. 54, 55. *Thomas*

another fortnight's hiding he made his way safe to Soissons,
where the king of France, disregarding an embassy sent by
Henry to prevent him, welcomed him with open arms. He
hurried on to Sens, where the Pope was now dwelling ; the
appellant bishops had preceded him, but Alexander was
deaf to their arguments.[1] Thomas laid at the Pope's feet
his copy of the Constitutions of Clarendon ; they were read,
discussed and solemnly condemned in full consistory.[2] The
exiled primate withdrew to a shelter which his friend Bishop
John of Poitiers had secured for him in the Cistercian abbey of
Pontigny in Burgundy.[3] On Christmas-eve, at Marlborough,
Henry's envoys reported to him the failure of their mission.
On S. Stephen's day Henry confiscated the whole possessions of the metropolitan see, of the primate himself and of
all his clerks, and ordered all his kindred and dependents,
clerical or lay, to be banished from the realm.[4]

Saga (Magnusson), vol. i. p. 245. Here again there is a confusion about the
date.

[1] Garnier (Hippeau), pp. 74-81. Will. Cant. (Robertson, *Becket*, vol. i.).
pp. 42-46. Alan Tewkesb. (*ib.* vol. ii.), pp. 335-341. E. Grim (*ibid.*), pp.
400-403. Will. Fitz-Steph. (*ib.* vol. iii.), pp. 70-74. Herb. Bosh. (*ibid.*), pp.
325-340. Anon. I. (*ib.* vol. iv.), pp. 57-61. Cf. *Thomas Saga* (Magnusson),
vol. i. pp. 265-289.

[2] Garnier (Hippeau), pp. 82-84. Will. Cant. (as above), p. 46. Alan
Tewkesb. (*ib.* vol. ii.), pp. 341, 342. E. Grim (*ibid.*), pp. 403, 404. Herb. Bosh.
(*ib.* vol. iii.), pp. 340-342. Anon. I. (*ib.* vol. iv.), pp. 61-64. The formal record
of these proceedings is the edition of the Constitutions included among the
collected letters of S. Thomas—Ep. xlv. (*ib.* vol. v. pp. 71-79), in which there
is appended to each article the Pope's verdict—" Hoc toleravit " or " Hoc
damnavit." The tolerated articles are 2, 6, 11, 13, 14 and 16. Alan of
Tewkesbury, who first collected the letters of S. Thomas, was for some years a
canon of Benevento, and probably got this annotated copy of the Constitutions
from Lombard, who had been in Thomas's suite as one of his *eruditi* during this
visit to Sens, and who was archbishop of Benevento at the time of Alan's residence
there.

[3] Garnier (Hippeau), p. 90. Will. Cant. (as above), p. 46. Joh. Salisb. (*ib.*
vol. ii.), p. 313. Alan Tewkesb. (*ibid.*), p. 345. E. Grim (*ibid.*), p. 404. Will.
Fitz-Steph. (*ib.* vol. iii.), p. 76. Herb. Bosh. (*ibid.*), p. 357. Anon. I. (*ib.* vol.
iv.), p. 64. Anon. II. (*ibid.*), p. 109. Cf. Ep. lx. (*ib.* vol. v.), p. 114.

[4] Garnier (Hippeau), p. 91. Will. Cant. (as above), pp. 46, 47. Joh. Salisb.
(*ib.* vol. ii.), pp. 313, 314. E. Grim (*ibid.*), p. 404. Will. Fitz-Steph. (*ib.* vol.
iii.), p. 75. Herb. Bosh. (*ibid.*), p. 359. Anon. I. (*ib.* vol. iv.), p. 65. The
dates are from Will. Fitz-Steph. The *Thomas Saga* (Magnusson), vol. i. pp. 347-
349, puts this banishment too late in the story.

NOTE A.

THE COUNCIL OF WOODSTOCK.

The usual view of the council of Woodstock—a view founded on contemporary accounts and endorsed by Bishop Stubbs (*Constit. Hist.*, vol. i. p. 462)—has been disputed on the authority of the Icelandic *Thomas Saga*. This Saga represents the subject of the quarrel as being, not a general levy of so much per hide throughout the country, but a special tax upon the Church lands—nothing else, in fact, than the " ungeld " which William Rufus had imposed on them to raise the money paid to Duke Robert for his temporary cession of Normandy, and which had been continued ever since. " We have read afore how King William levied a due on all churches in the land, in order to repay him all the costs at which his brother Robert did depart from the land. This money the king said he had disbursed for the freedom of Jewry, and therefore it behoved well the learned folk to repay it to their king. But because the king's court hath a mouth that holdeth fast, this due continued from year to year. At first it was called Jerusalem tax, but afterwards Warfare-due, for the king to keep up an army for the common peace of the country. But at this time matters have gone so far, that this due was exacted, as a king's tax, from every house " [" monastery," editor's note], " small and great, throughout England, under no other name than an ancient tax payable into the royal treasury without any reason being shown for it." *Thomas Saga* (Magnusson), vol. i. p. 139. Mr. Magnusson (*ib.* p. 138, note 7) thinks that this account " must be taken as representing the true history of " the tax in question. In his Preface (*ib.* vol. ii. pp. cvii-cviii) he argues that if the tax had been one upon the tax-payers in general, " evidently the primate had no right to interfere in such a matter, except so far as church lands were concerned ;" and he concludes that the version in the Saga " gives a natural clue to the archbishop's protest, which thus becomes a protest only on behalf of the Church." This argument hardly takes sufficient account of the English primate's constitutional position, which furnishes a perfectly " natural clue " to his protest, supposing that protest to have been made on behalf of the whole nation and not only of the Church :—or rather, to speak more accurately, in behalf of the Church in the true sense of that word—the sense which Theobald's disciples were always striving to give to it—as representing the whole nation viewed in a spiritual aspect, and not only the clerical order. Mr. Magnusson adds : " We have no doubt that the source of the Icelandic Saga here is Robert of

Cricklade, or . . . Benedict of Peterborough, who has had a better information on the subject than the other authorities, which, it would seem, all have Garnier for a primary source ; but he, a foreigner, might very well be supposed to have formed an erroneous view on a subject the history of which he did not know, except by hearsay evidence" (*ib.* pp. cviii, cix). It might be answered that the "hearsay evidence" on which Garnier founded his view must have been evidence which he heard in England, where he is known to have carefully collected the materials for his work (Garnier, ed. Hippeau, pp. 6, 205, 206), and that his view is entitled to just as much consideration as that of the Icelander, founded upon the evidence of Robert or Benedict ;—that of the three writers who follow Garnier, two, William of Canterbury and Edward Grim, were English (William of Canterbury may have been Irish by birth, but he was English by education and domicile) and might therefore have been able to check any errors caused by the different nationality of their guide : — and that even if the case resolved itself into a question between the authority of Garnier and that of Benedict or Robert (which can hardly be admitted), they would be of at least equal weight, and the balance of intrinsic probability would be on Garnier's side. For his story points directly to the Danegeld ; and we have the indisputable witness of the Pipe Rolls that the Danegeld, in some shape or other, was levied at intervals throughout the Norman reigns and until the year 1163, when it vanished for ever. On the other hand, the Red King's "ungeld" upon the Church lands, like all his other "ungelds," certainly died with him ; and nothing can well be more unlikely than that Henry II. in the very midst of his early reforms should have reintroduced, entirely without excuse and without necessity, one of the most obnoxious and unjust of the measures which had been expressly abolished in "the time of his grandfather King Henry."

Note B.

THE COUNCIL OF CLARENDON.

There is some difficulty as to both the date and the duration of this council. Gerv. Cant. (Stubbs, vol. i. p. 176) gives the date of meeting as January 13 ; R. Diceto (Stubbs, vol. i. p. 312) as January 25 ; while the official copy of the Constitutions (*Summa Causæ*, Robertson, *Becket*, vol. iv. p. 208 ; Stubbs, *Select Charters*, p. 140) gives the closing day as January 30 ("*quartâ die ante Purificationem S. Mariæ*"). As to the duration of the council, we learn from Herb. Bosh. (Robertson, *Becket*, vol. iii. p. 279) and Gerv. Cant.

(as above, p. 178) that there was an adjournment of at least one night; while Gilbert Foliot (Robertson, *Becket*, vol. v. Ep. ccxxv. pp. 527-529) says " Clarendonæ . . . continuato triduo id solum actum est ut observandarum regni consuetudinum et dignitatum a nobis fieret absoluta promissio ;" and that "die vero tertio," after a most extraordinary scene, Thomas "antiquas regni consuetudines antiquorum memoriâ in commune propositas et scripto commendatas, de cætero domino nostro regi se fideliter observaturum in verbo veritatis absolute promittens, in vi nobis injunxit obedientiæ sponsione simili nos obligare." This looks at first glance as if meant to describe the closing scene of the council, in which case its whole duration would be limited to three days. But it seems possible to find another interpretation which would enable us to reconcile all the discordant dates, by understanding Gilbert's words as referring to the verbal discussion at the opening of the council, before the written Constitutions were produced at all. Gilbert does indeed expressly mention "customs committed to writing"; but this may very easily be a piece of confusion either accidental or intentional. On this supposition the chronology may be arranged as follows :—The council meets on January 13 (Gerv. Cant.). That day and the two following are spent in talking over the primate ; towards evening of the third—which will be January 15—he yields, and the bishops with him (Gilb. Foliot). Then they begin to discuss what they have promised ; the debate warms and lengthens ; Thomas, worn out with his three days' struggle and seeing the rocks ahead, begs for a respite till the morrow (Herb. Bosh.). On that morrow—*i.e.* January 16 — Henry issues his commission to the "elders," and the council remains in abeyance till they are ready with their report. None of our authorities tell us how long an interval elapsed between the issue of the royal commission and its report. Herbert, indeed, seems to imply that the discussion on the constitutions began one night and the written report was brought up next day. But this is only possible on the supposition that it had been prepared secretly beforehand, of which none of the other writers shew any suspicion. If the thing was not prepared beforehand, it must have taken some time to do ; and even if it was, the king and the commissioners would surely, for the sake of appearances, make a few days' delay to give a shew of reality to their investigations. Nine days is not too much to allow for preparation of the report. On January 25, then, it is brought up, and the real business of the council begins in earnest on the day named by R. Diceto. And if Thomas fought over every one of the sixteen constitutions in the way of which Herbert gives us a specimen, six days more may very well have been spent in the discussion, which would thus end, as the *Summa Causæ* says, on January 30.

CHAPTER II.

HENRY AND ROME.

1164-1172.

WITH the archbishop's flight into France the struggle between him and the king entered upon a new phase. Its intrinsic importance was almost entirely lost, and it became simply an element in the wider questions of general European politics. In England Thomas's departure left Henry sole master of the field ; the Constitutions of Clarendon were put in force without delay and without difficulty ; a year later they were followed up by an Assize, significantly issued from the same place, which laid the foundations of the whole later English system of procedure in criminal causes ; and thenceforth the work of legal and judicial reform went on almost without a break, totally unaffected by the strife which continued to rage between king and primate for the next five years. The social condition of the country was only indirectly affected by it. The causes which had ostensibly given rise to it—the principle involved in the acceptance or rejection of the Constitutions—did not appeal strongly to the national mind, and had already become obscured and subordinated to the personal aspect which the quarrel had assumed at Northampton. As in the case of Anselm, it was on this personal aspect alone that popular feeling really fastened ; and in this point of view the advantage was strongly on the archbishop's side. Thomas, whose natural gifts had already made him a sort of popular idol, was set by the high-handed proceedings of the council in the light of a victim of regal tyranny ; and the sweeping and cruel proscriptions inflicted upon all who were in the remotest way connected with him tended still further to excite popular sympathy for his wrongs and turn it away from his persecutor. But the sympathy was for the individual, not for the cause. The principle of the clerical immunities had no hold upon the minds of the people or even of the clergy at large. Even among the archbishop's own personal friends, almost the only men who clave to it with anything like the same ardour as himself were his two old comrades of the *Curia Theobaldi*, Bishop John of Poitiers and John of Salisbury ; and even the devotion of John of Salisbury, which is one of the brightest jewels in Becket's crown, was really the devotion of friend to friend, of Churchman to primate, of a generous, chivalrous soul to what seemed the oppressed and down-trodden side, rather than the devotion of a partizan to party principle. Herbert of Bosham, the primate's shadow and second self, who clave to his side through good report and evil report and looked upon him as a hero and a martyr from first to last, was nevertheless the author of the famous verdict which all the searching criticism of later times has never yet been able to amend : " Both parties had a zeal for God ; which zeal was according to knowledge, His judgement alone can determine." [1]

Cool, dispassionate thinkers like Gilbert Foliot, on the other hand, while inclining towards the cause which Thomas had at heart, recoiled from his mode of upholding it as little less than suicidal. In Gilbert's view it was Thomas who had betrayed those " rights of his order " which he proclaimed so loudly, by forsaking the attitude of passive resistance which the bishops had adopted at Westminster and in which they were practically unassailable, and staking everything upon the king's good faith, without security, in the meeting at Oxford and the council at Clarendon :—it was Thomas who by his subsequent conduct—his rash

---

[1] Herb. Bosh. (Robertson, *Becket*, vol. iii.) p. 273. The whole passage from " O rex et o pontifex " to " judicium " (pp. 272, 273) should be compared with the admirable commentary of Will. Newb., l. ii. c. 16 (Howlett, vol. i. pp. 140-141).

attempts at flight, his rapid changes of front at Northampton
in first admitting and then denying the royal jurisdiction,
his final insult to the king in coming to the council cross in
hand, and his undignified departure from the realm—had
frustrated the efforts whereby wiser and cooler heads might
have brought the king to a better mind and induced him to
withdraw the Constitutions :—and it was not Thomas, but
his suffragans, left to bear the brunt of a storm which they
had neither deserved nor provoked, who were really in a fair
way to become confessors and martyrs for a Church brought
into jeopardy by its own primate.[1] Gilbert in fact saw
clearly that the importance of the point at issue between
king and archbishop was as nothing compared to the
disastrous consequences which must result from their protracted strife.   It threatened nothing less than ruin to the
intellectual and religious revival which Theobald had fostered
so carefully and so successfully.   The best hopes of the
movement were bound up with the alliance between Church
and state which had been cemented at Henry's accession ;
that alliance was now destroyed ; instead of the Church's
most valuable fellow-worker, the king had been made her
bitter foe ; and the work of revival was left to be carried on
—if it could be carried on at all—in the teeth of the royal
opposition and without a leader, while the man who should
have directed it was only a perpetual stumbling-block in the
path of those who had to supply as best they could the
place left deserted by his flight.   It was upon Gilbert of
London that this burthen chiefly fell ; and it is in Gilbert's
position that we may find a key to the subsequent direction
of the controversy, as far as England was concerned.

For full twenty years before Becket's rise to the primacy
Gilbert Foliot had been one of the most respected members
of the reforming party in the English Church.   While
Thomas was a worldly young subdeacon in the household of
Archbishop Theobald, while as chancellor he was outshining
the king in luxurious splendour or riding in coat of mail at
the head of his troops, Gilbert was setting the pattern of
ecclesiastical discipline and furnishing the steadiest and most

[1] Ep. ccxxv. (Robertson, *Becket*, vol. v.), pp. 526 *et seq.*

valued assistance to the primate's schemes of reform.
Trained no less than Henry of Winchester in the old
Cluniac traditions of ecclesiastical authority, his credit had
never been shaken by rashness and inconsistency such as
had marred Henry's labours ; and it would have been neither
strange nor blameworthy if he had cherished a hope of
carrying on Theobald's work as Theobald's successor.
Gilbert, however, solemnly denied that he had ever sought
after or desired the primacy;[1] and his conduct does not
seem to furnish any just ground for assuming the falsehood
of the denial. His opposition to the election of Thomas
was thoroughly consistent with his position and known
views ; equally so was the support and co-operation which
Thomas, as soon as he was fairly launched into his new
course of action, anxiously sought to obtain from him, and
which he for a while steadily gave. He had begun to find
such co-operation difficult even before the question of the
clerical immunities arose at the council of Westminster. On
that question, in itself, the primate and the bishop of London
were at one ; but they differed completely in their way of
treating it. To the impulsive, short-sighted, downright
Thomas it was the one, sole, all-absorbing question of life
and death ; to the calm, far-seeing, cautious Gilbert it was
a provoking hindrance—raised up partly by the primate's
own bad management—to the well-being of interests far
too serious and too wide-reaching to be imperilled for a
mere point of administrative detail. He took up his position
definitely at the council of Northampton. The customs
being once accepted, he held it the true Churchman's duty
to obey them, to make the best and not the worst of them,
while desiring and labouring for their abrogation, but only
by pacific means. A temporary submission was the least of
two evils. It was infinitely safer to bend to the storm and
trust to the influences of time and conciliation for turning
the mind of the king, than to run the risk of driving him
into irreconcileable hostility to the Church. For hostility to
the Church meant something far worse now than in the days
when William Rufus and Henry I. had set up their regal

[1] Ep. ccxxv. (Robertson, *Becket*, vol. v.), pp. 522, 523.

authority against primate and Pope. It meant a widening
of the schism which was rending western Christendom in
twain ; it meant the accession of the whole Angevin
dominions to the party of the Emperor and the anti-Pope,
and the severance of all the ties between the English Church
and her continental sisters which Theobald, Eugene and
Adrian had laboured so diligently to secure.

The dread of this catastrophe explains also the attitude
of the Pope. In the long dreary tale of negotiation and
intrigue which has to be traced through the maze of the
Becket correspondence, the most inconsistent and self-contradictory, the most undecided and undignified, the most
unsatisfactory and disappointing part of all is that played
by Alexander III. It is however only fair to remember
that, in this and in all like cases, the Pope's part was also
the most difficult one. No crown in Christendom pressed
so sorely on its wearer's brow as the triple tiara :—" It may
well look bright," Adrian IV. had been wont to say to his
friend John of Salisbury, " for it is a crown of fire !"
Adrian indeed, though his short reign was one of marked
vigour and prosperity, declared that if he had had any idea
of the thorns with which S. Peter's chair was filled, he would
have begged his bread in England or remained buried in
the cloisters of S. Rufus to the end of his days sooner than
thrust himself into such a thicket of troubles.[1] For it was
not only " the care of all the churches " that rested upon a
medieval Pope, but the care of all the states as well. The
court of Rome had grown into the final court of appeal for
all Christendom ; the Pope was expected to be the universal
referee, arbitrator and peacemaker of Europe, to hold the
balance between contending parties, to penetrate and dis-
entangle the intricacies of political situations which baffled
the skill of the most experienced diplomatists, to exercise a
sort of equitable jurisdiction on a vast scale over the whole
range of political as well as social life. Earlier and later
pontiffs may have voluntarily brought this burthen upon
themselves ; most of the Popes of the twelfth century, at
any rate, seem to have groaned under it as a weight too

[1] Joh. Salisb. *Polycrat.*, l. viii. c. 23 (Giles, vol. iv. p. 367).

heavy for any human strength to bear. Unprincipled as their policy often seemed, there was not a little justice in the view of John of Salisbury, that a position so exceptional could not be brought within the scope of ordinary rules of conduct, and that only those who had themselves felt its difficulties could be really competent to judge it at all.[1] Adrian's energetic spirit was worn out by it in four years ;[2] yet his position was easy compared to that of Alexander III. Alexander was a pontiff without a throne, the head of a Church in captivity and exile ; dependent on the support of the most selfish and untrustworthy of living sovereigns ; with Italy and Germany arrayed against him under the rule of a schismatic Emperor, and with the fidelity of the Angevin house hanging upon a thread which the least strain, the lightest touch, might break at any moment. Moreover Alexander was no Englishman like his predecessor. He had no inborn comprehension and no experience of the ways and tempers of the north ; he had no bosom-friend, no John of Salisbury, to stand as interpreter between him and the Angevin king or the English primate ; he understood neither of them, and he was almost equally afraid of both. His chief anxiety was to have as little as possible to do with them and their quarrel, and the fugitive archbishop was to him anything but a welcome guest.

It was of course impossible for the Pope to withhold his sympathy and his support from a prelate who came to him as a confessor for the privileges of the Church. But it was equally impossible for him to run the risk of driving Henry and his dominions into schism by espousing Thomas's cause as decisively as Thomas himself desired. Placed thus in what Adrian had once declared to be the ordinary position of a Roman pontiff—" between hammer and anvil "—Alexander drifted into a policy of shifts and contradictions, tergiversations and double-dealings, which irritated Henry and which Thomas simply failed to comprehend. If Gilbert

---

[1] Joh. Salisb., *Polycrat.*, l. viii. c. 23 (Giles, vol. iv. p. 363).

[2] *Ibid.* (pp. 366, 367). "Licet nihil aliud lædat, necesse est ut citissime vel solo labore deficiat [sc. Papa]. . . . Dum superest, ipsum interroga." This was written early in 1159, and in August Adrian died.

Foliot and Arnulf of Lisieux could have succeeded in their efforts to induce the contending parties to accept a compromise, the Pope would have been only too glad to sanction it. But it was useless to talk of compromise where Thomas Becket was concerned. To all the remoter consequences, the ultimate bearings of the quarrel, he was totally blind. For him there was but one question in the world, the one directly before him ; it could have but two sides, right and wrong, between which all adjustment was impossible, and with which considerations of present expediency or future consequences had nothing to do. All Gilbert's arguments for surrender, his solemn warnings of the peril of schism, his pleadings that it was better for the English Church to become for a while a sickly member of the ecclesiastical body than to be cut off from it altogether,[1] Thomas looked upon, at best, as proposals for doing evil that good might come. After his humiliating experience at Clarendon he seems to have felt that he was no match for Henry's subtlety ; his flight was evidently caused chiefly by dread of being again entrapped into a betrayal of what he held to be his duty ; and once, in an agony of self-reproach and self-distrust, he laid his archiepiscopal ring at the Pope's feet and prayed to be released from the burthen of an office for which he felt himself unworthy and unfit.[2] Strong as was the temptation to pacify Henry thus easily, Alexander felt that the Church could not allow such a sacrifice of her champion; and Thomas never again swerved from his determination to be satisfied with nothing short of complete surrender on the part of the king. For this one object he laboured, pleaded, argued, censured, during the next six years without ceasing ; his own suffragans, the monastic orders, Pope, cardinals, the Empress Matilda, the king of France, none of them had a moment's peace from his passionate endeavours to press them into a service which

---

[1] Ep. cviii. (Robertson, *Becket*, vol. v.), p. 207.

[2] Will. Cant. (*ib.* vol. i.), p. 46 ; Alan Tewkesb. (*ib.* vol. ii.), pp. 342, 343 ; E. Grim (*ibid.*), p. 403 ; Will. Fitz-Steph. (*ib.* vol. iii.), p. 76 ; *Thomas Saga* (Magnusson), vol. i. pp. 305-313. Will. Newb., l. ii. c. 16 (Howlett, vol. i. p. 140), gives this scene as having occurred, "ut dicitur," at the council of Tours.

he seemed to expect them all to regard as a matter of life
and death not merely for England but for all Christendom.
Doubtless it was a sad waste of energy and a sad perversion
of enthusiasm ; yet the enthusiasm contrasts pathetically,
almost heroically, with the spirit in which it was met.
There was something noble, if there was also something
exasperatingly unpractical, in a man who, absorbed in his
devotion to one mistaken idea, never even saw that he and
his cause were becoming the pretexts and the tools of half
the political intrigues of Europe, and whom the experience
of a lifetime failed to teach that all the world was not as
single-hearted as himself.   Intellectually, a mind thus constituted must needs provoke and deserve the impatient scorn
of a cool clear brain such as Gilbert Foliot's ; but its very
intellectual weakness was the source of its true strength.   It
is this dogged adherence to one fixed idea, this simplicity
of aim, which appeals to the average crowd of mankind far
more strongly than the larger and more statesmanlike
temper of men like Foliot, or like Henry himself.   Whether
or no the cause be worthy—whether or no the zeal be
according to knowledge — it is the zealot, not the philo-
sopher, who becomes the popular hero and martyr.

From the moment of Thomas's arrival in France, then,
little though he perceived it himself, the direct question at
issue between him and the king became in every point of
view save his own entirely subordinate to the indirect consequences of their quarrel ; the ecclesiastical interest became
secondary to the political, which involved matters of grave
importance to all Europe.   The one person to whom the
archbishop's flight was most thoroughly welcome was Louis
of France.   Louis and Henry were nominally at peace ; but
to Louis their alliance was simply a shield behind which he
could plan without danger his schemes for undermining
Henry's power on the continent, and no better tool for this
purpose could possibly have fallen into his hands than the
fugitive archbishop of Canterbury.   Thomas had indeed just
enough perception of the state of affairs between the two
kings—of which he must have acquired considerable experience in his chancellor days—to choose going to live on his

own resources at Pontigny rather than accept the hospitality
of his sovereign's enemy.[1]   This arrangement probably
delighted Louis, for it furnished him with a safe answer to
Henry's complaints and remonstrances about harbouring the
" traitor "—Thomas was in sanctuary in a Cistercian abbey
in Burgundy, and France was not harbouring him at all ;
while the welcome which Louis gave to the primate's exiled
friends and the sympathy which he displayed for their cause
heightened his own reputation for devotion to the Church
and served as a foil to set off more conspicuously the supposed
hostility of Henry.   To Louis in short the quarrel was something which might turn to his own advantage by helping to
bring Henry into difficulties ; and he used it accordingly
with a skill peculiar to himself, making a great shew of disinterested zeal and friendly mediation, and all the while
taking care that the breach should be kept open till its healing was required for his own interest.

With such an onlooker as this Henry knew that he must
play his game with the utmost caution.   He had been provoked by the personal opposition of his old friend into
standing upon his regal dignity more stiffly than he would
have thought it worth while to do so long as it remained
unchallenged.   On his side, too, there was a principle at
stake, and he could not give it up unconditionally ; but he
might have been induced to accept a compromise, had not
the obstinacy of Thomas forced him into a corresponding
attitude of unbending determination.   So keen was his sense
of the danger attendant upon the fugitive archbishop's
presence in France that it led him to postpone once more
the work which he had been planning in England and cross
over to Normandy again early in 1165.[2]   Lent was passed
in fruitless attempts to bring about a triple conference
between the two kings and the Pope ; Henry refused to
allow Thomas to be present ; Thomas begged the Pope not
to expose himself to Henry's wiles without him who alone
could help him to see through them ; and Alexander, now
busy with preparations for his return to Rome, was probably

---

[1] Anon. II. (Robertson, *Becket*, vol. iv.), p. 109.
[2] Rob. Torigni, a. 1165.

not sorry to escape by declaring that for a temporal prince to dictate who should or who should not form part of the Pope's suite was a claim which had never been heard of before and which he could not possibly admit.[1] Immediately after Easter he set out on his journey homewards.

The rival party saw their opportunity and seized it without delay. Their fortunes were now at a very low ebb ; the antipope Victor had died in April ; his chief supporter, Cardinal Guy of Crema, had succeeded him under the title of Paschal III. ; but Italy had cast him off, and even in Germany the tide was turning against him. The Emperor, however, clung with unwavering determination to his original policy ; and he at once saw in the English king's quarrel with the Church a means of gaining for Paschal's cause what would amply compensate for all that had been lost. Before Alexander was fairly out of the French kingdom an embassy from Germany came to Henry at Rouen, bringing proposals for an alliance to be secured by two marriages : one between the English princess Matilda, Henry's eldest daughter, and the Emperor's cousin Duke Henry of Saxony ; the other between Henry's second daughter and Frederic's own little son. The chief ambassador was Reginald, archbishop-elect of Cöln, who from the time of Frederic's accession—two years before that of Henry—had been his chancellor and confidential adviser, playing a part curiously like that of Thomas Becket, till in the very year of the English chancellor's removal to Canterbury he was appointed to the see of Cöln. There the parallel with Thomas ended ; for Reginald was the most extreme champion of the privileges not of the Church but of the Imperial Crown, and was even more closely identified with the schismatic party than Frederic himself. Henry sent him over to the queen, who had been left as regent in England, to receive from her a formal promise of her daughter's hand to the duke of Saxony, in a great council convened at Westminster for that purpose. The old justiciar Earl Robert of Leicester refused the kiss

---

[1] Alan Tewkesb. (Robertson, *Becket*, vol. ii.), pp. 346, 347 ; evidently taken from the Pope's own letter, extant only in the Icelandic version, in *Thomas Saga* (Magnusson), vol. i. p. 329.

of peace to the schismatic and caused the altars at which he had celebrated to be thrown down,[1] thereby saving Henry from the fatal blunder of committing himself publicly to the cause of the anti-pope, and England from the dangers of open schism. But he could not prevent the king from sending two clerks to a council which met at Würzburg on Whit-Sunday to abjure Pope Alexander and acknowledge Paschal ; and although the fact was strenuously denied, it seems impossible to doubt that they did take the oath at the Emperor's hands in their master's name ;[2] indeed, Reginald of Cöln boasted that Henry had promised to make all the bishops in his dominions do the same.

A crisis seemed imminent, but Henry managed to avoid it. From the Emperor's solicitations, from the Pope's remonstrances, from all the pleadings of friends and all the intrigues of foes, he suddenly made his escape by flying back to England and plunging into a Welsh war which kept him all the summer safe out of their reach,[3] and furnished him with an excuse for postponing indefinitely the completion of his alliance with the schismatic party. Such an alliance would in fact have cost far more than it was worth. Alexander was once more safely seated upon S. Peter's chair, and was urging Thomas to throw himself wholly on the protection of the king of France ; Louis was in the highest state of triumph, rejoicing over the birth of his long-desired son ; while the whole Angevin dominions, which Eleanor was governing in her husband's absence, were full of suppressed disaffection and surrounded with threatening or intriguing foes.[4] In Lent 1166 therefore Henry hurried back to Nor-

---

[1] R. Diceto (Stubbs), vol. i. p. 318. He mistakenly thinks that the *king* was at Westminster, and he also thinks the embassy came in 1167. Its true date, 1165, is shown by the letters referred to in next note.

[2] Epp. xcviii.-ci. (Robertson, *Becket*, vol. v. pp. 184-195). Will. Cant. (*ib.* vol. i.), pp. 52, 53. *Thomas Saga* (Magnusson), vol. i. p. 331.

[3] Gerv. Cant. (Stubbs, vol. i. p. 197) says Henry went into Wales in 1165, "quo facilius domini Papæ vel etiam Cantuariensis archiepiscopi...declinaret sententiam."

[4] "Movetur enim [rex] Francorum invidiâ, calumniisque Flandrensium, Wallensium improbitate, Scottorum insidiis, temeritate Britonum, Pictavorumque fœderibus, interioris Aquitaniæ sumptibus, Gasconum levitate, et (quod gravius est) simultate fere omnium quoscumque ditioni ejus constat esse subjectos." Ep. clxii. (Robertson, *Becket*, vol. v.), pp. 313, 314.

mandy to hold a conference with Louis, and, if possible, to free his own hands for the work which lay before him.

The work was in truth a vast and complex one. At the age of thirty-three Henry was already planning out an elaborate scheme for the future of his children and the distribution of his territories, in which the election of his eldest son as joint-king in England was but the first and least difficult step. Normandy and Anjou, as well as England, had to be secured for little Henry ; Aquitaine was if possible to be settled upon Richard as his mother's heir ; for Geoffrey Henry was bent upon acquiring the Breton duchy.[1] Conan IV., whom Henry had in 1158 established as duke of Britanny, had but one child, a daughter, whose hand, together with the reversion of her father's territories, the king was anxious to secure for his son. This however required the assent not only of Conan but of Louis of France, and also of the Breton barons, who bitterly resented the Norman interference which had set Conan as ruler over them, and were inclined to resist to the uttermost an arrangement which would bring them still more directly under the Norman yoke ; while Louis was but too ready to encourage them in their resistance. A campaign in the summer of 1166, however, another in August 1167, and a third in the following spring so far broke their opposition[2] that in May

---

[1] Will. Newb. l. ii. c. 18 (Howlett, vol. i. pp. 145, 146).

[2] On the Breton campaign of 1166 see R. Diceto (Stubbs), vol. i. p. 329, and Rob. Torigni *ad ann.* Henry was near Fougères on June 28 (Ep. ccix., Robertson, *Becket*, vol. v. p. 421); he was besieging Fougères itself on July 13-14 (Eyton, *Itin. Hen. II.*, p. 96). On the campaigns of 1167 and 1168 see Rob. Torigni *ad ann.*, the meagre entries in a Breton chronicle, a. 1168-1169 (Morice, *Hist. Bret., preuves*, vol. i. col. 104; *Rer. Gall. Scriptt.*, vol. xii. p. 560), and Chron. S. Albin. a. 1167 (Marchegay, *Eglises*, p. 40), which tells of Louis's share in the matter. See also the account of Henry's correspondence with King Arthur in *Draco Norm.*, l. ii. cc. 17-22, vv. 941-1282 (Howlett, *Will. Newb.*, vol. ii. pp. 695-707). According to this writer, one of the Breton leaders—" Arturi dapifer, Rollandus, consul et idem tunc Britonum " (Mr. Howlett suggests that this may be Roland of Dinan, *ib.* p. 696 note)—wrote a letter to Arthur imploring his aid for Britanny, and received a reassuring answer ; Henry also received a long epistle from the blameless king, to which, " subridens sociis, nil pavefactus," (c. 21, v. 1218, p. 705) he returned a polite and diplomatic answer. Unluckily the good monk omits to say how the letters were conveyed, and gives us no light upon the postal arrangements between Britanny and Avalon—which by the way he places among " silvas . . . Cornubiæ, proxima castra loco," whatever that may mean

1169 Geoffrey was sent into Britanny to receive their homage as heir to the dukedom ; three months later his father joined him,[1] and at Christmas they held their court together at Nantes,[2] whence they made a sort of triumphal progress through the duchy, receiving homage and fealty wherever they went.[3]

It had proved easier to subdue Britanny than to hold Aquitaine. The half independent princes of the south, so scornful of a king beyond the Loire, were at least equally scornful of a king from beyond the sea ; in November 1166 Henry was obliged to summon them to a conference at Chinon,[4] and to relieve Eleanor of her task of government by sending her to keep Christmas in England,[5] while he himself took her place at Poitiers.[6] His foes seized their opportunity to revive the vexed question of Toulouse ; a meeting with Raymond at Grandmont and an attempt to assert Henry's ducal authority over the count of Auvergne led to a fresh rupture with Louis ;[7] and in the spring of 1168 the discontented barons of Aquitaine, secure of the French king's goodwill, broke into open revolt. In the midst of a negotiation with Louis, Henry hurried away to subdue them.[8]   Scarcely had he turned northward again when Earl Patrick of Salisbury, whom he had appointed to

(c. 20, vv. 1213, 1214, p. 705). It is quite possible that some of the Breton leaders did seek to rouse the spirit of their followers by publishing an imaginary correspondence with the mythic hero-king whose existence was to most of the common people in Britanny at that time almost as much an article of faith as any in the Creed ; it is possible too that they were themselves so far carried away by the same illusion as to attempt to work upon Henry by similar means ; and in that case it is extremely probable that Henry, with his Angevin tact and sense of humour, would meet the appeal pretty much as the Bec writer represents. But the letters given in the *Draco* must be the monk's own composition. Neither Roland nor Henry can have been capable of stringing together such a quantity of pseudo-history, ancient and modern, as is therein contained.

[1] Rob. Torigni, a. 1169.
[2] R. Diceto (Stubbs), vol. i. p. 337.   *Gesta Hen.* ["Benedict of Peterborough"] (Stubbs), vol. i. p. 3.   Rog. Howden (Stubbs), vol. ii. p. 3.
[3] *Gesta Hen.* as above.   [4] Ep. ccliii. (Robertson, *Becket,* vol. vi.), p. 74.
[5] Eyton, *Itin. Hen. II.,* pp. 104, 108.
[6] Rob. Torigni, a. 1167.   Cf. Ep. cclxxvii. (Robertson, *Becket,* vol. vi.), p. 131.
[7] Rob. Torigni, a. 1167.   Cf. Chronn. S. Albin. and S. Serg. a. 1166 (Marchegay, *Eglises,* pp. 40, 149).
[8] Rob. Torigni, a. 1168.   Ep. ccccix. (Robertson, *Becket,* vol. vi.), p. 408.

assist Eleanor in the government of the duchy, was murdered
by one of the rebel leaders ;[1] and Eleanor was once more
left to stand her ground alone in Poitou, while her husband
was fighting the Bretons, staving off the ecclesiastical censures which threatened him, and vainly endeavouring to
pacify Louis, who now openly shewed himself as the
champion of all Henry's disaffected vassals, Breton, Poitevin,
Scottish and Welsh,[2] as well as of the exiled archbishop.

Henry meanwhile was endeavouring to strengthen his
political position by alliances in more remote quarters ; the
marriage of his eldest daughter with the duke of Saxony

---

[1] Gerv. Cant. (Stubbs), vol. i. p. 205. R. Diceto (Stubbs), vol. i. p. 331.
Rob. Torigni, a. 1168. Rog. Howden (Stubbs), vol. i. pp. 273, 274. This last
writer states that the slayer was Guy of Lusignan, and that Guy fled to Jerusalem
(of which he afterwards became king) to escape the punishment of this crime.
This story has been generally adopted by modern historians. But its latter half
is incompatible with the appearance of " Guy of Lusignan " among the rebels in
Aquitaine in 1173, five years after the death of Patrick (*Gesta Hen.*, Stubbs, vol. i.
p. 46) ; and the whole of it seems to rest solely on Roger's misunderstanding of
the passage in the *Gesta* which he was copying. In that passage Guy is introduced as " Guido de Lezinan, frater Gaufridi de Lezinan, qui Patricium comitem
Salesbiriensem tempore hostilitatis . . . occiderat. Erat enim prædictus Guido,"
etc. ; then comes an account of his adventures in Palestine (*Gesta Hen.*, Stubbs,
vol. i. p. 343). Roger of Howden chose to make *qui* refer to *Guido ;* but it
might just as well, or even better, refer to *Gaufridus.* Guy comes upon the historical
scene for the first time in 1173. It seems pretty clear that Geoffrey was his elder
brother, and took a leading part in southern politics and warfare long before Guy
was of an age to join in them. If Patrick was slain by either of the brothers,
therefore, it was by Geoffrey and not by Guy. Admitting this much, however,
there is still no ground for looking upon even Geoffrey as a murderer who had
committed such a crime as to be obliged to fly from justice. For " Geoffrey of
Lusignan " stood by the side of Guy among the rebels of 1173 (*Gesta Hen.*, Stubbs,
vol. i. p. 46) ; " Geoffrey of Lusignan " and his brothers claimed La Marche
against King Henry between 1178 and 1180 (Geoff. Vigeois, l. i. c. 70, Labbe,
Nova Biblioth., vol. ii. p. 324) ; " Geoffrey of Lusignan " rose against Richard in
1188 (*Gesta Hen.*, Stubbs, vol. ii. p. 34 ; Rog. Howden, Stubbs, vol. ii. p. 339 ;
R. Diceto, Stubbs, vol. ii. pp. 54, 55) ; and it was not till after he had in this
revolt slain a special friend of Richard's, that he betook himself to Palestine, where
he arrived in the summer of the same year (*Itin. Reg. Ric.*, Stubbs, p. 26), and where,
moreover, he and Richard afterwards became firm allies. Geoffrey may therefore
enjoy the benefit of the plea which Bishop Stubbs (*Itin. Reg. Ric.*, introd. p.
cxxiv, note) puts forward for Guy, that " there is nothing to show that Patrick
was not killed in fair fight." But it seems pretty clear that for the heroic king of
Jerusalem himself no such plea is needed at all.

[2] Rob. Torigni, a. 1168 ; Epp. ccccix., ccccxxxiv. (Robertson, *Becket*, vol. vi.),
pp. 408, 455, 456.

had taken place early in 1168 ;[1] two years before, the hand
of one of her sisters had been half promised to the marquis
of Montferrat for his son, in return for his good offices with
the Pope ;[2] and a project was now on foot for the marriage
of Henry's second daughter, Eleanor, with the king of
Castille—a marriage which took place in 1169 ;[3] while the
infant Jane, who was scarcely four years old, was betrothed
to the boy-king William of Sicily.[4]   For Richard his father
was now endeavouring to gain the hand of Adela of France,
the younger daughter of Louis and Constance, as a sort of
security for the investiture of Aquitaine ; while at the same
time Henry was on the one hand making interest with the
Emperor's Italian foes, the rising commonwealths of Lom-
bardy and the jurisconsults of Bologna ;[5] and on the other,
Frederic was endeavouring to regain his alliance by an
embassy headed by his own cousin, Henry's new-made son-
in-law, the duke of Saxony.[6]

    All this political, ecclesiastical and diplomatic coil Henry
had to unravel almost single-handed. Of the group of counsellors who had stood around him in his early years, Arnulf
of Lisieux on one side of the sea and Richard de Lucy on
the other were almost the sole survivors. He had lost the
services of his constable Henry of Essex under very painful
circumstances a few months before that council at Woodstock which saw the beginning of his quarrel with Thomas.
The constable was accused by Robert de Montfort of having

---

[1] Gerv. Cant. (Stubbs), vol. i. p. 205.   From the Pipe Roll of the year, with
Mr. Eyton's comment (*Itin. Hen. II.*, p. 109), it seems that Matilda and her
mother crossed the sea together in September 1167, and that Matilda went on to
Germany, where she was married early next year, while Eleanor returned to
England before Christmas.   Rob. Torigni, a. 1167.

[2] Ep. cclii. (Robertson, *Becket*, vol. vi.), p. 68.

[3] R. Diceto (Stubbs), vol. i. p. 334.   The original scheme seems to have been
for marrying both Eleanor and Jane to Spanish sovereigns, among whom, however, Castille is not named.   In a letter written in the summer of 1168 John of
Salisbury speaks of "regum, Navariensis aut Aragonensis scilicet, quibus filias
suas dare disponit [rex]."   Ep. ccccxxxiv. (Robertson, *Becket*, vol. vi.) p. 457.

[4] Ep. dxxxviii. (*ib.* vol. vii.) p. 26.   Jane was born at Angers in October
1165 ; Rob. Torigni, *ad ann.*

[5] Epp. dxxxviii., dxxxix. (Robertson, *Becket*, vol. vii.), pp. 26, 30, 31.

[6] Rob. Torigni, a. 1168.   Gerv. Cant. (Stubbs), vol. i. p. 205.   *Draco Norm.*,
l. iii. cc. 4, 5, vv. 191-360 (Howlett, *Will. Newb.*, vol. ii. pp. 718-724).

committed high treason six years before by purposely letting
fall the standard and falsely proclaiming the king's death at
the battle of Consilt.   Henry of Essex declared that he
had dropped the standard in the paralysis of despair, really
believing the king to be dead ; and it is evident from the
high commands which he held in the war of Toulouse and
elsewhere that the king continued to treat him with undiminished confidence, and to regard him as one of his most
valuable ministers and friends.   The charge once made,
however, could only be met by ordeal of battle.   The
encounter took place at Reading; Henry of Essex went
down before his accuser's lance ; and all that his sovereign
could do for him was to save his life by letting the monks
of the neighbouring abbey carry his body off the field as if
for burial, and when he proved to be still alive, suffering
him to remain as a brother of the house, while his property
was confiscated to the Crown and his services were lost to
the state.[1]   The king's mother died in the autumn of 1167;[2]
his old friend and adviser Earl Robert of Leicester passed
away in 1168.[3]   A desperate attempt was even made to
part him from his wife, in order to get rid of his rights over
Aquitaine ;[4] while the man who had once been his most
successful diplomatic agent and his unfailing helper against
the wiles of all his enemies was now the most formidable
tool in their hands.

It was for his children's sake that Henry at last bent
his pride to do what he had vowed never to do again.   At
Montmirail, on the feast of Epiphany 1169, he renewed his

---

[1] Rob. Torigni, a. 1163.   Will. Newb., l. ii. c. 5 (Howlett, vol. i. p. 108).
Joc. Brakelond (Rokewode, Camden Soc.), pp. 50-52.   For date see Palgrave,
Eng. Commonwealth, vol. ii. pp. xxii, xxiii.

[2] Rob. Torigni, a. 1167.   *Draco Norm.*, l. iii. c. 1, vv. 1-12 (Howlett, *Will.
Newb.*, vol. ii. p. 711).   Chron. S. Serg., a. 1167 (Marchegay, *Eglises*, p. 150).

[3] Rob. Torigni, a. 1168.   Ann. Waverl. a. 1168 (Luard, *Ann. Monast.*, vol.
ii. p. 239).   Chron. Mailros, a. 1168.

[4] See the *Gradus cognationis inter regem et reginam* (Robertson, *Becket*, vol.
vi. p. 266).   " Hanc computationem præsentaverunt Pictavenses cardinalibus
quando S. Thomas exsulabat, sed non sunt auditi."   The " computation " as
there stated is wrong ; but the right one really does leave Henry and Eleanor
within the forbidden degrees.   (See above, vol. i. p. 393, note 2, and p. 445, note
11).   They were cousins in the fifth degree, their common ancestress being Herleva
of Falaise.

homage to Louis, made full submission to him, and promised compensation to the Breton and Poitevin barons for their losses in the recent wars.[1] Next day young Henry did homage to the French king for the counties of Anjou and Maine,[2] and, as it seems, of Britanny, which his brother Geoffrey was to hold under him.[3] Richard did the like for Aquitaine, of which Louis granted him the investiture,[4] together with a promise of Adela's hand.[5] Three weeks later young Henry, in his new capacity of count of Anjou, officiated in Paris as seneschal to the king of France ;[6] he afterwards repeated his homage to Louis's son and heir, and received that of his own brother Geoffrey for the duchy of Britanny.[7]

One thing alone was now lacking to the completion of Henry's scheme : the crowning of his heir. There can be no doubt that when he sent Thomas and the child to England together—the one to be chosen king and the other to be made primate—he intended the coronation to take place as soon as he himself could rejoin them. Its performance, delayed by his own continued absence on the continent, had however been made impossible by his quarrel with Thomas. That the archbishop of Canterbury alone could lawfully crown a king of England was a constitutional as well as an ecclesiastical tradition so deeply rooted in the minds of Englishmen that nothing short of absolute necessity had induced Henry I. to set it aside in his own case ; and still less could Henry II. venture to risk such an innovation in the case of his son.[8] Yet the prospect of a reconciliation

---

[1] Ep. cccclxi. (Robertson, *Becket*, vol. vi.), pp. 506, 507.

[2] *Ib.* p. 507. Rob. Torigni a. 1169. Gerv. Cant. (Stubbs), vol. i. p. 208.

[3] Rob. Torigni, a. 1169, and Gerv. Cant. (as above) say that young Henry did homage to Louis for Britanny ; Normandy was not mentioned, the homage done for it by young Henry in 1160 being counted sufficient (*ibid.*). The elder king himself kept Touraine on the old terms of homage to Theobald of Blois (Ep. cccclxi. as above).

[4] Ep. cccclxi., Rob. Torigni and Gerv. Cant. as above.

[5] Gerv. Cant. as above.   [6] Rob. Torigni, a. 1169.   [7] *Ibid.*

[8] The historical arguments on this subject may be seen in Will. Fitz-Steph. (Robertson, *Becket*, vol. iii.), p. 110, and Ep. dclxxxiv. (*ib.* vol. vii.), pp. 328-330. Henry was once said to have projected getting the Pope himself to crown the child ; Ep. lv. (*ib.* vol. v.), p. 100. Against this, of course, Canterbury could have had nothing to say.

with the primate seemed at this moment further off than ever.

Thomas's first impulse on entering Pontigny had been to give himself up to a course of study, devotion and self-discipline more severe than anything which he had yet attempted. He secretly assumed the habit of the "white monks,"[1] and nearly ruined his delicate constitution by a rash endeavour to practise the rigorous abstinence enjoined by the rules of the order.[2] He grew more diligent than ever in prayer, meditation, and study of Holy Scripture.[3] But his restless, impetuous nature could not rise to the serene heights of more than worldly wisdom urged upon him by John of Salisbury, who truly insisted that such occupations alone were worthy of a true confessor.[4] In spite of John's warnings and pleadings, he still kept all his friends —John himself included—ceaselessly at work in his behalf; and while he sought out in every church and convent in Gaul every rare and valuable book that he could hear of, to be copied for his cathedral library, he was also raking together for the same collection all the privileges, old or new, that could be disinterred from the Roman archives or extorted from the favour of the Pope.[5] Until Easter 1166 Alexander restrained him from any direct measures against the king;[6] then, unable to keep silence any longer, Thomas again took the matter into his own hands and wrote to Henry himself, earnestly imploring him to consider his ways and to grant his old friend a personal interview.[7] Henry was inexorable; Thomas wrote again, this time a torrent of mingled warnings, intreaties and remonstrances,[8] and with just as little effect. Then, towards the end of May, as the

---

[1] Alan Tewkesb. (Robertson, *Becket*, vol. ii.), p. 345. Anon. I. (*ib.* vol. iv.), p. 64. *Thomas Saga* (Magnusson), vol. i. p. 315.
[2] Garnier (Hippeau), pp. 126, 127. E. Grim (Robertson, *Becket*, vol. ii.), pp. 412, 413. Herb. Bosh. (*ib.* vol. iii.), pp. 376-379. *Thomas Saga* (as above), p. 317.
[3] Will. Fjtz-Steph. (Robertson, *Becket*, vol. iii.), p. 77. Herb. Bosh. (*ibid.*), p. 379.   [4] Ep. lxxxv. (*ib.* vol. v.), pp. 163, 164.
[5] Will. Fitz-Steph. as above.
[6] Ep. xcv. (Robertson, *Becket*, vol. v.), pp. 179, 180.
[7] Ep. clii. (*ib.* pp. 266-268).
[8] Ep. cliii. (*ib.* pp. 269-278), translated by Garnier (Hippeau), pp. 100-106.

king was holding council with his barons at Chinon, a barefooted monk came to him with a third letter from the
primate.[1]   Once again Thomas expressed his longing for a
personal meeting ; once again he set forth the doctrine of
the divine rights and duties of kings, and charged Henry, by
the solemn memory of his coronation-vows, to restore to
the English Church her privileges and her chief pastor.
Only in the last sentence came a significant warning : " If
not, then know of a surety that you shall feel the severity of
Divine vengeance ! " [2]   And there was no doubt about its
meaning ; for the Empress Matilda had already transmitted
to her son a threat sent to her by Thomas in plain words,
that unless she could bring him to acknowledge his error,
" shortly, yea, very shortly " the " sword of the Spirit "
should be drawn against his dominions and even against
himself.[3]

Harassed by disaster and revolt, provoked by the
primate's former letters, Henry, upon reading this one and
hearing the messenger's comment upon it—for Thomas had
charged him to say a good deal more than he wrote[4]—
might well feel that he was standing on the brink of a
volcano.   He turned desperately upon the bishops around
him, half imploring, half commanding them to help him out
of his strait, abusing them for a pack of traitors who would
not trouble themselves to rid him of this one unmanageable
foe, and exclaiming with a burst of tears that the archbishop
was destroying him soul and body together; for he naturally
expected nothing less than an interdict on his dominions
and an anathema against himself, and both sanctioned by
the Pope.   When Henry was thus at his wits' end, the only
one among his continental advisers who was likely to have
any counsel to offer him was Arnulf of Lisieux.   Once

---

[1] Garnier (Hippeau), p. 106.   E. Grim (Robertson, *Becket*, vol. ii.), p. 419.
Cf. Herb. Bosh. (*ib.* vol. iii.), pp. 383-385.   Eyton (*Itin. Hen. II.*, p. 93) dates
this council June 1, but this cannot be reconciled with Thomas's subsequent
proceedings.

[2] Ep. cliv. (Robertson, *Becket*, vol. v. pp. 278-282), translated by Garnier
(Hippeau), pp. 109-111.

[3] Ep. clxxxiv. (Robertson, *Becket*, vol. v. p. 361).

[4] Herb. Bosh. (*ib.* vol. iii.), p. 385.

more Arnulf proved equal to the occasion ; he suggested
that the primate's intended censures should be forestalled by
an appeal to the Pope. The remedy was a desperate one,
for, as John of Salisbury triumphantly remarked when he
heard of it, the king was flying in the face of his own
Constitutions and confirming that very right of appeal
which he was so anxious to abolish, by thus having
recourse to it for his own protection. But there was no
other loophole of escape; so the appeal was made, a
messenger was despatched to give notice of it in England,
close the ports and cut off all communication with Thomas
and with the Pope ; while the bishops of Lisieux and Séez
set out for Pontigny to bid the primate stay his hand till
the octave of Easter next, which was fixed for the term
of Henry's appeal.[1]

They were too late. No sooner had the barefooted
messenger returned with his tidings of the king's irreconcileable wrath than Thomas hurried to Soissons on a pilgrimage
to its three famous shrines :—those of the Blessed Virgin,
who had been the object of his special reverence ever since
he learned the Ave Maria at his mother's knee ; of S.
Gregory the Great, the patron of the whole English Church
and more particularly of Canterbury and its archbishops ;
and of S. Drausius, who was believed to have the power of
rendering invincible any champion who spent a night in
prayer before his relics. Before each of these shrines
Thomas, like a warrior preparing for mortal combat, passed
a night in solemn vigil, the last night being that of the
festival of S. Drausius, and also of Ascension-day.[2] On the
morrow he left Soissons ;[3] on Whitsun-eve[4] he reached

---

[1] Ep. cxciv. (Robertson, *Becket*, vol. v.), pp. 381, 382. Herb. Bosh. (*ib.*
vol. iii.), p. 393, confuses this appeal with a later one.

[2] It was also the anniversary of his own ordination to the priesthood—June 2.

[3] Ep. cxciv. (Robertson, vol. v.), p. 382.

[4] Herb. Bosh. (*ib.* vol. iii.), p. 391, says " proximâ ante festum die," and he
makes the festival that of S. Mary Magdalene, the patron of the place. Tempt-
ing, however, as his version is—for it would explain at once Thomas's otherwise
rather unaccountable choice of Vézelay for the scene of his proceedings, and the
great concourse of people who evidently were assembled there—it is quite irreconcileable with the minute chronological details of John of Salisbury's letter (Ep.
cxciv. as above), written within a few weeks of the events, while Herbert's story

Vézelay, a little town distant only a day's journey from Pontigny, and made famous by its great abbey, which boasted of possessing the body of S. Mary Magdalene. Thomas found the place crowded with pilgrims assembled to keep the Whitsun feast on this venerated spot. He was invited by the abbot to celebrate High Mass and preach on the festival day ;[1] his sermon ended, he solemnly anathematized the royal customs and all their upholders, and excommunicated by name seven persons whom he denounced as special enemies to the Church ; the two first being Henry's confidential envoys John of Oxford and Richard of Ilchester, who had been the medium of his communications with the Emperor ; while a third, Jocelyn de Bailleul, was one of his chief advisers, and a fourth was no less a personage than the justiciar, Richard de Lucy.[2] Thomas had set out from Soissons in the full determination to excommunicate Henry himself at the same time ; but on his way he learned that the king was dangerously ill ; he therefore contented himself with a solemn warning publicly addressed to him by name, calling him to repentance for the last time, and in default, threatening him with immediate excommunication.[3]

The news of these proceedings reached Henry when, sick and anxious, he was trying to gather up strength and energy for a campaign against the Bretons. He instantly despatched another messenger to England, bidding Richard de Lucy call an assembly of the bishops and clergy and compel them to make a general appeal to the Pope against the authority and jurisdiction of their primate.[4] The meet-

---

was written from memory, many years after. On the other hand, R. Diceto's date (Stubbs, vol. i. p. 318), Ascension-day, is more impossible still.

[1] Herb. Bosh. (Robertson, *Becket*, vol. iii.), p. 391.

[2] The details of the sentence are in Thomas's own letters, Epp. cxcv., cxcvi., cxcviii. (Robertson, *Becket*, vol. v.), pp. 386-391, 392-397. Cf. Ep. cxciv. (*ibid.*), p. 383. The other excommunicated persons were Ralf de Broc, Hugh of S. Clare and Thomas Fitz-Bernard. Their crime was invasion of Church property. Richard of Ilchester and John of Oxford were condemned for their dealings with the schismatics ; Richard de Lucy and Jocelyn de Bailleul, as being the authors of the Constitutions.

[3] Epp. cxciv., cxcvi., cxcviii. (Robertson, *Becket*, vol. v.), pp. 382, 383, 391, 396. Herb. Bosh. (*ib.* vol. iii.), pp. 391, 392.

[4] Gerv. Cant. (Stubbs), vol. i. p. 200.

ing was held in London[1] at midsummer.[2]　The appeal was
made and sent to the Pope in the name of all the bishops
and clergy of England ; but it is tolerably clear that the
main body were merely passive followers, more or less
willing, of Gilbert of London and Jocelyn of Salisbury, the
former of whom was almost certainly the writer of the letter
which conveyed the appeal to the Pope, as well as of that
which announced it to the primate.[3]　The hand of Gilbert
Foliot was indeed so plainly visible that Thomas's reply was
addressed with equal plainness to him personally.[4]　The
long and sarcastic letter with which he retorted[5] was answered
in a yet more startling fashion at the opening of the next
year.　As Gilbert stood before the high altar of his cathedral church on the feast of its patron saint a paper was
thrust into his hand ; to his dismay it proved to be a papal
brief granting to Archbishop Thomas a commission as legate
for all England, and commanding the bishops to render
him unqualified obedience and to resign within two months
whatever confiscated church property had been placed in
their charge by the king.　In an agony of distress Gilbert,
who himself had the custody of the Canterbury estates, sent

---

[1] Gerv. Cant. (Stubbs), vol. i. p. 200.　Will. Cant. (Robertson, *Becket*, vol.
i.), p. 56.　　　　　　　　　　[2] Ep. ccix. (*ib.* vol. v.), p. 421.
[3] Epp. cciv., ccv. (*ib.* vol. v.), pp. 403-413.　Cf. Ep. ccix. (*ibid.*), p. 241,
and Will. Cant. (*ib.* vol. i.), pp. 56, 57.　The bishop of Exeter consented to
appeal, but in a fashion of his own, of which however there is no trace in the
letter actually sent to the Pope.　Two prelates were absent : Walter of Rochester,
who pleaded illness, and Henry of Winchester, who wrote in excuse : "Vocatus a
summo Pontifice, nec appello nec appellare volo."　The others thought he meant
that the Pope had cited him ; "ipse vero summum Pontificem, summum Judicem
intelligebat, ad cujus tribunal jamjam trahebatur examinandus, tanquam qui in
multis diebus processerat et vitæ metis appropinquaret."　So says Will. Cant.; but
John of Salisbury says distinctly that the letter of appeal was sealed by London,
Winchester and Hereford (Ep. cclii., Robertson, *Becket*, vol. vi. p. 65).　Can William
have founded his pretty story on the old confusion (which is perpetually breaking
out in his favourite authority, Garnier, and in other writers who have less excuse
for it) between *Wincestre* and *Wirecestre*—and was Roger of Worcester the real
absentee ?　He certainly did not share in the obloquy which this appeal brought
upon Robert of Hereford, with whom hitherto he had usually been coupled by
Thomas ; on the contrary, he and Bartholomew of Exeter are henceforth always
coupled together as fellow-sufferers for their loyalty to the primate.
[4] Epp. ccxxiii., ccxxiv. (Robertson, *Becket*, vol. v. pp. 490-520).
[5] The famous "Multiplicem nobis et diffusam."　Ep. ccxxv. (*ib.* pp. 521-544).

this news to the king, imploring him to grant permission that the Pope's mandate might be obeyed, at least till some method could be devised for escaping from a dilemma which now looked well-nigh hopeless.[1] Henry, absorbed in a struggle with the Bretons, had already been provoked into a vengeance as impolitic as it was mean. He threatened the Cistercian abbots assembled on Holy Cross day at the general chapter of their order that if Thomas were not immediately expelled from Pontigny, he would send all the White Monks in his dominions to share the primate's exile.[2] When the abbot of Pontigny carried this message home, Thomas could only bid him farewell and betake himself to the sole protection left him—that of the king of France. He left Pontigny on S. Martin's day[3] 1166, and took up his abode as the guest of Louis in the abbey of S. Columba at Sens.[4]

Henry saw his own blunder as soon as it was made, and endeavoured to neutralize its effects by despatching an embassy to the Pope, requesting that he would send a legatine commission to settle the controversy. One of his envoys was the excommunicate John of Oxford ; to the horror of Thomas and the indignation of Louis, John came

[1] Ep. ccviii. (Robertson, *Becket*, vol. v. pp. 417, 418). The Pope's brief is Ep. clxxii. (*ib.* pp. 328, 329); it is dated "Anagniæ, vii. Idus Octobris," but its true date is Easter-day, April 24 (see editor's note, p. 329)—the actual date of the letter whereby Alexander notified his act to the English bishops ; Ep. clxxiii. (Robertson, as above, pp. 229-231). The diocese (not the province) of York was exempted from Thomas's legatine jurisdiction—the reason being that Roger of York was legate for Scotland (Ep. cclxx., *ib.* vol. vi. p. 119). Thomas sent the brief over to his friends Robert of Hereford and Roger of Worcester, bidding them communicate it to their brethren, beginning with London (Ep. clxxix., *ib.* vol. v. pp. 344-346). Canon Robertson supposes this brief to have been delivered to Gilbert on the feast of the Commemoration of S. Paul, *i.e.* June 30, 1166. Gilbert himself says merely "die beati Pauli"; and his letter has no date. But it mentions "legatos qui diriguntur ad nos"; and there is no hint elsewhere of any talk about sending legates till late in the autumn, or even winter. There really seems to be no reason why we should not adopt a more obvious rendering of the date, as representing the greater and better-known festival of S. Paul's Conversion. In that case, of course, the year must be 1167.

[2] Will. Cant. (Robertson, *Becket*, vol. i.), p. 50. E. Grim (*ib.* vol. ii.), p. 414. Will. Fitz-Steph. (*ib.* vol. iii.), p. 83. Herb. Bosh (*ibid.*), p. 397. Anon. I. (*ib.* vol. iv.), p. 65. Cf. *Thomas Saga* (Magnusson), vol. i. p. 371.

[3] Gerv. Cant. (Stubbs), vol. i. pp. 201, 202.

[4] E. Grim (Robertson, *Becket*, vol. ii.), p. 415. Herb. Bosh. (*ib.* vol. iii.), pp. 403, 404 ; etc.

back in triumph, boasting not only that he had been
absolved by the Pope, but that two cardinals, William and
Otto—the former of whom was a determined opponent of
Thomas—were coming with full powers to sit in judgement
on the case between primate and king and decide it without
appeal.[1]   The first half of the boast was true, but not the
second ; the cautious Pope instructed his envoys to do
nothing more than arbitrate between the contending parties,
if they could.[2]   They did not reach Normandy till the
autumn of 1167 ; Thomas came to meet them on the
French border on November 18 ; he refused to enter upon
any negotiations till the property of the metropolitan see
was restored ;[3] the legates carried their report to the king
at Argentan, and were dismissed with an exclamation of
'disappointment and disgust—" I wish I may never set eyes
upon a cardinal again !"[4]   Five of the English bishops whom
Henry had summoned to advise him renewed their appeal,[5]
its original term having expired six months ago ; and the
legates insisting that Thomas should respect the appeal,[6]
another year's delay was gained.

At last, when the two kings made their treaty at Montmirail at Epiphany 1169, Thomas, who had come to the
spot under the protection of Louis, suddenly entered the
royal presence and fell at Henry's feet, offering to place
himself unreservedly in his hands.   All parties thought the
struggle was over, till the archbishop added once again the
words which had so exasperated Henry at Oxford and at
Clarendon : " Saving God's honour and my order."   The
king burst into a fury, and the meeting broke up in confusion.[7]   Three months later, on Palm Sunday, from the

---

[1] Epp. cclxxx., cclxxxiii., cclxxxv., ccxcii. (Robertson, *Becket*, vol. vi.), pp.
140, 146, 147, 151-153, 170, 171.

[2] Ep. cccvii. (*ibid.*), p. 201.   Cf. Will. Cant. (*ib.* vol. i.), p. 65, and Gerv.
Cant. (Stubbs), vol. i. pp. 202, 203.

[3] Epp. cccxxxi., cccxxxii. (Robertson, *Becket*, vol. vi.), pp. 247-251, 256-258.

[4] Ep. cccxxxix. (*ibid.*), pp. 269, 270.

[5] Epp. cccxxxix., cccxli.-cccxlv. (*ibid.*), pp. 270-272, 276, 277, 283-288.

[6] Ep. cccxliii. (*ibid.*), pp. 284, 285.

[7] Herb. Bosh. (*ib.* vol. iii.), pp. 418-427.   Epp. ccccli., cccclxi. (*ib.* vol. vi.),
pp. 488, 489, 507-509.   Cf. Will. Cant. (*ib.* vol. i.), pp. 73, 74, and *Thomas Saga*
(Magnusson), vol. i. pp. 427-433.

high altar of Clairvaux, Thomas excommunicated ten of his opponents, first among whom was Gilbert Foliot.[1] Gilbert, who knew that the sentence had been hanging over him for more than a year, had appealed against it before it was uttered ;[2] the king, too, was forewarned, and at every sea-port guards were set to catch and punish with the utmost rigour any messenger from the primate. It was not till Ascension-day that a young layman named Berengar made his way up to the altar of Gilbert's cathedral church in the middle of High Mass and thrust into the hand of the celebrant the archbishop's letter proclaiming the excommunication of the bishop.[3] On that very day Thomas issued another string of excommunications.[4] Gilbert, driven to extremity, renewed his appeal two days later ; and he added to it a formal refusal to acknowledge the jurisdiction of a metropolitan to whom he had made no profession, and a declaration—so at least it was reported in Gaul—of his intention to claim the metropolitical dignity for his own see, as an ancient right of which it had been unjustly defrauded by Canterbury.[5] A storm of indignant protest and vehement denunciation arose from the archbishop's party ; and the terrified Pope checked further proceedings by despatching another pair of envoys, who as usual failed to agree either with the king, with the archbishop, or even with each other, and after wasting the summer in misunderstandings and recriminations left the case just

---

[1] Ep. cccclxxxviii. (Robertson, *Becket*, vol. vi. pp. 558, 559). See also Will. Fitz-Steph. (*ib.* vol. iii.), p. 87, and for date, R. Diceto (Stubbs), vol. i. p. 333.

[2] Ep. dxiii. (Robertson, *Becket*, vol. vi.), p. 614.

[3] Compare the account given by "Magister Willelmus" in Ep. dviii. (*ibid.*), pp. 603, 604, with that of Will. Fitz-Steph. (*ib.* vol. iii.), pp. 89, 90. They are clearly from the same hand.

[4] Epp. dii., dvii. (*ib.* vol. vi.), pp. 594, 601-603. For date cf. Ep. cccclxxxviii. (*ib.* pp. 558, 559).

[5] Ep. dviii. (*ibid.*), pp. 604-606—a very circumstantial account, yet one can scarcely understand how a man so wise and so learned as Gilbert can really have made such an utterly unhistorical claim. He must have known that it had no shadow of foundation, the nearest approach to such a thing being S. Gregory's abortive scheme for fixing the two archbishoprics at London and York. Gilbert's opponents, on the other hand, declared that he derived his claim from the archpriests of Jupiter who had their seat in the Roman Londinium, and denounced him as their would-be representative and successor. Epp. dxxxv., dxlvi. (*ib.* vol. vii.), pp. 10, 41.

where they had found it.[1]   By this time king and primate were both weary of their quarrel, and still more weary of mediation.   In November the two kings had another personal interview at Montmartre, and the archbishop's unconditional restoration was all but decided.[2]   Thomas, however, rashly attempted to hasten the completion of the settlement by a threat of interdict;[3] and the threat stung Henry into an act of far greater rashness.   He had met Louis, as well as Thomas, at Montmartre, and had gained his immediate object of restraining the French king yet a little longer from direct hostilities ; the settlement of Britanny was completed at Christmas, that of Aquitaine was so far secure that its conclusion might safely be left to Eleanor's care ; in March 1170 Henry went to England[4] with the fixed determination of seeing his eldest son crowned there before he left it again.

Three years before, he had wrung from the Pope—then blockaded in Rome by the Imperial troops, and in the last extremity of peril — a brief authorizing young Henry's coronation by the archbishop of York, in default of the absent primate of all England.[5]   In face of a mass of earlier and later rescripts from Alexander's predecessors and Alexander himself, all strenuously confirming the exclusive privileges of Canterbury, Henry had never yet ventured to make use of this document ; like Adrian's bull for the conquest of Ireland, it had been kept in reserve for a future day ; and that day had now come.   In vain did Thomas proclaim his threatened interdict ;[6] in vain did the Pope

---

[1] On this legation of Gratian and Vivian see R. Diceto (Stubbs), vol. i. p. 335 ; Gerv. Cant. (Stubbs), vol. i. pp. 212, 213 ; Herb. Bosh. (Robertson, *Becket*, vol. iii.), pp. 441-445 ; Will. Cant. (*ib.* vol. i.), pp. 72, 73 ; Epp. ccccxci., ccccxcii. (*ib.* vol. vi.), pp. 563, 564, 567 ; dlx., dlxi., dlxiii.-dlxviii., dlxxxi., dlxxxiv., dci., dcii. (*ib.* vol. vii.), pp. 70-76, 78-92, 115, 116, 124, 125, 151-154, etc.

[2] Will. Fitz-Steph. (Robertson, *Becket*, vol. iii.), pp. 97, 98 ; Herb. Bosh. (*ibid.*), pp. 445-451 ; Epp. dciv.-dcvii. (*ib.* vol. vii. pp. 158-168). *Thomas Saga* (Magnusson), vol. i. p. 447.   R. Diceto as above, pp. 335-337.   Gerv. Cant. as above, p. 213.

[3] Epp. dlxxiii.-dlxxvii. (Robertson, *Becket*, vol. vii. pp. 97-109), etc.

[4] *Gesta Hen.* (Stubbs), vol. i. p. 3.   Rog. Howden (Stubbs), vol. ii. p. 3.   Gerv. Cant. as above, p. 216.

[5] Ep. cccx. (Robertson, *Becket*, vol. vi. pp. 206, 207).   See the editor's note as to the date.   [6] Epp. dclxxviii.-dclxxxiii. (*ib.* vol. vii. pp. 320-325).

ratify it ;[1] in vain did both alike issue prohibitions to all the English bishops against the act which they knew to be in contemplation.[2]   The vigilance of the justiciars, quickened by a fresh set of stringent injunctions sent over by the king in the previous autumn,[3] made the delivery of letters from either primate or Pope so difficult that Thomas at last could intrust it to no one but a nun, Idonea, whom he solemnly charged with the duty of presenting to Roger of York the papal brief in which the coronation was forbidden.[4]   The ceremony was fixed for Sunday, June 14.   A week before that date young Henry, who with his girl-bride Margaret of France had been left at Caen under the care of his mother and Richard of Hommet the constable of Normandy, was summoned to join his father in England.[5]   On S. Barnabas's day the bishops and barons assembled at Westminster in obedience to the royal summons ;[6] on Saturday, the 13th, the Pope's letter was at last forced upon the archbishop of York ;[7] but none the less did he on the following morning crown and anoint young Henry in Westminster abbey; while Gilbert of London, who had managed to extort conditional absolution in the Pope's name from Archbishop Rotrou of Rouen,[8] once more stood openly by his side in the foremost rank of the English bishops.[9]

The elder king only waited to see the tenants-in-chief, with the king of Scots at their head, swear fealty to his new-made colleague ere he hurried back to Normandy to

---

[1] Epp. dcxxviii.-dcxxx. (Robertson, *Becket*, vol. vii. pp. 210-214).

[2] Epp. dcxxxii., dcxxxiii., dcxlviii.-dcli. (*ib.* pp. 216, 217, 256-264).   Herb. Bosh. (*ib.* vol. iii.), p. 462, puts this interdict too late.

[3] The "ten ordinances"; Ep. dxcix. (*ib.* vol. vii. pp. 147-149); Will. Cant. (*ib.* vol. i.), pp. 53-55 ; Gerv. Cant. (Stubbs), vol. i. pp. 214-216 ; Rog. Howden (Stubbs), vol. i. pp. 231-236 ; on the date see Bishop Stubbs's note at last reference.

[4] Ep. dclxxii. (Robertson, *Becket*, vol. vii. pp. 307-309).   See the editor's note.

[5] Ep. dclxxiii. (*ibid.*), pp. 309, 312.

[6] *Gesta Hen.* (Stubbs), vol. i. p. 5.

[7] Will. Fitz-Steph. (Robertson, *Becket*, vol. iii.), p. 103.

[8] *Ibid.* Epp. dclviii.-dclx. (*ib.* vol. vii. pp. 275-277).

[9] Will. Fitz-Steph. (as above), p. 103 ; *Gesta Hen.* (Stubbs), vol. i. p. 5 ; Gerv. Cant. (Stubbs) vol. i. p. 219.   R. Diceto (Stubbs), vol. i. p. 338, Chron. Mailros, a. 1170, Rog. Howden (Stubbs), vol. i. p. 4, Chron. S. Serg. a. 1169 (Marchegay, *Eglises*, p. 150), all give different dates, and all wrong.

meet the fast-gathering storm.[1] Louis, incensed that his daughter's husband should have been crowned without her, was already threatening war ;[2] Thomas, seeing in the king's action nothing but the climax of Canterbury's wrongs, was overwhelming the Pope with complaints, reproaches, and intreaties for summary vengeance upon all who had taken part in the coronation ; and the majority of the cardinals strongly supported his demands.[3] Henry saw that he must make peace at any price. Two days before the feast of S. Mary Magdalene he held a conference with Louis near Fréteval, on the borders of the Vendômois and the county of Chartres ;[4] they were reconciled, and as they parted Henry said jestingly to the French king : " That rascal of yours, toò, shall have his peace to-morrow; and a right good peace shall it be."[5] At dawn on S. Mary Magalene's day[6] he met Thomas in the "Traitor's Meadow,"[7] close to Fréteval ; they rode apart together, and remained in conference so long that the patience of their followers was all but exhausted, when at last Thomas was seen to dismount and throw himself at the king's feet. Henry sprang from his horse, raised the archbishop from the ground, held his stirrup while he remounted, and rode back to tell his followers that peace was made, on terms which practically amounted to a complete mutual amnesty and a return to the state of affairs which had existed before the quarrel.[8]

---

[1] *Gesta Hen.* (Stubbs), vol. i. p. 6. Gerv. Cant. (Stubbs), vol. i. p. 220. Will. Cant. (Robertson, *Becket*, vol. i.), p. 83. Henry landed at Barfleur about Midsummer ; *Gesta Hen.* as above.   [2] *Gesta Hen.* as above.

[3] Ep. dccvii. (Robertson, *Becket*, vol. vii. pp. 373, 374).

[4] "In limitibus suis inter Firmitatem, oppidum scilicet in pago Carnotensi, et Fretivalle, castrum videlicet in territorio Turonensi." Ep. dclxxxv. (*ibid.*), p. 339. This *Firmitas* must be La Ferté-Villeneuil, and *Turonensi* should be *Vindocinensi.* Herb. Bosh., who lays the scene "in confinio Carnotusiæ et *Cenomanniæ*, inter duo castella quorum unum nominatur Viefui" [Viévy-le-Rayé] "et alterum Freteval" (*ib.* vol. iii. p. 466), is no nearer to the true geography.

[5] "Et crastinâ die habebit pacem suam latro vester ; et quidem bonam habebit." Will. Fitz-Steph. (*ibid.*), p. 108.

[6] Ep. dclxxxv. (*ib.* vol. vii.), p. 340.

[7] Herb. Bosh. (*ib.* vol. iii.), p. 466. *Thomas Saga* (Magnusson), vol. i. p. 461.

[8] Epp. dclxxxiv., dclxxxv. (Robertson, *Becket*, vol. vii.), pp. 326-334, 340-342. Will. Fitz-Steph. (*ib.* vol. iii.), pp. 108-111. Herb. Bosh. (*ibid.*), p. 466. Garnier (Hippeau), pp. 150, 151. *Thomas Saga* (as above), pp. 461-465.

Henry had no sooner returned to Normandy than he fell sick almost to death ; on his recovery he went on a pilgrimage to the shrine of our Lady at Rocamadour in the Quercy,[1] and it was not until October that Thomas again saw him at Tours, on his way to a conference with Count Theobald of Blois at Amboise.[2] A difficulty had arisen about the restitution of the confiscated Church property and the absolution of the persons whom Thomas had excommunicated, each party insisting that the other should make the first step in conciliation.[3] There was also a difficulty about the kiss of peace, which Thomas required as pledge of Henry's sincerity, but which Henry seemed desirous of postponing indefinitely.[4] Nevertheless, a letter from Henry to his son, announcing the reconciliation and bidding the young king enforce the restoration of the archiepiscopal estates, was drawn up in Thomas's presence at Amboise and sent over to England by the hands of two of his clerks,[5] who presented it at Westminster on October 5.[6] The restoration was, however, not effected until Martinmas, and then it comprised little more than empty garners and ruined houses.[7] Thomas saw the king once more, at Chaumont,[8]

[1] *Gesta Hen.* (Stubbs), vol. i. pp. 6, 7.

[2] Herb. Bosh. (Robertson, *Becket*, vol. iii.) pp. 468, 469. Will. Fitz-Steph. (*ibid.*), p. 114. Garnier (Hippeau), p. 154. *Thomas Saga* (Magnusson), vol. i. p. 469. The writer of the *Gesta Hen.* (Stubbs, vol. i. p. 8) gives the date of this meeting as Tuesday, October 12. But this must be quite ten days too late, for we shall see that a letter drawn up after the meeting was received in England on October 5.

[3] Ep. dclxxxiv. (Robertson, *Becket*, vol. vii.), pp. 333-337.

[4] Henry alleged that he had publicly sworn never to give Thomas the kiss of peace, and could not face the shame of breaking his oath. Garnier (Hippeau), p. 150 ; Herb. Bosh. (Robertson, *Becket*, vol. iii.), p. 450 ; Ep. dcxxiii. (*ib.* vol. vii.) pp. 198, 199 ; *Thomas Saga*, as above, p. 449. See in Herb. Bosh. (as above), p. 469, Will. Fitz-Steph. (*ibid.*), p. 115, and *Thomas Saga* (as above), p. 469, the contrivance by which he avoided it at Tours—or Amboise, in William's version.

[5] Garnier (Hippeau), pp. 156, 157. The letter, of which Garnier gives a translation, is Ep. dcxc. (Robertson, *Becket*, vol. vii.) pp. 346, 347 ; also in Will. Cant. (*ib.* vol. i.), p. 85 ; Will. Fitz-Steph. (*ib.* vol. iii.), p. 112 ; Gerv. Cant. (Stubbs), vol. i. p. 221 ; R. Diceto (Stubbs), vol. i. p. 339.

[6] Ep. dccxv. (Robertson, *Becket*, vol. vii.), p. 389.

[7] Ep. dccxxxiii. (*ibid.*), p. 402.

[8] Chaumont on the Loire, seemingly. Herb. Bosh. (*ib.* vol. iii.), p. 470. Cf. *Thomas Saga*, as above, pp. 471-473.

and Henry promised to meet him again at Rouen, thence to
proceed with him to England in person.[1]   Before the appointed time came, however, fresh complications had arisen
with the king of France ; Henry was obliged to give up all
thought of going not only to England but even to Normandy,
and delegated the archbishop of Rouen and the dean of
Salisbury to escort Thomas in his stead.

The duty finally devolved solely upon the dean, who
was no other than Thomas's old opponent John of Oxford.[2]
Naturally enough, the primate was deeply hurt at being thus
sent back to his see under the protection of a man who, as
he truly said, ought to have been thankful for the privilege
of travelling in his suite.[3]   Thomas, however, was in haste
to be gone, although fully persuaded that he was going to
his death.   He seems indeed to have been weary of life ;
the tone of his letters and of his parting words to the friends
whom he was leaving in France indicates not so much a
morbid presentiment of his fate as a passionate longing for it.
Yet it can hardly have been from him alone that the foreboding communicated itself to so many other minds.
Warnings came to him from all quarters ; one voice after
another, from the king of France[4] down to the very pilot of
the ship in which he took his passage, implored him not to
go ; Herbert of Bosham alone upheld his resolution to the
end.[5]

We may put aside at once all the wild talk of the archbishop's biographers about plots against his life in which the
king had a share.   Even if Henry's sudden willingness for
his return was really suggested by words said to have been
uttered by one of his counsellors—" Why keep the archbishop out of England ?   It would be far better to keep
him in it "—there is no need to assume that those words
bore even in the speaker's mind, far less in that of the king,
the horrible meaning which they were afterwards supposed
to have covered ;[6] for they were true in the most literal sense.

[1] Will. Fitz-Steph. (Robertson, *Becket*, vol. iii.), pp. 115, 116.

[2] *Ib.* p. 116.   Epp. dccxxii., dccxxiii. (*ib.* vol. vii.), pp. 400, 403.   Garnier
(Hippeau), p. 160.   [3] Will. Fitz-Steph. as above.

[4] *Ib.* p. 113.   [5] Herb. Bosh. (*ibid.*), pp. 472-476.

[6] Will. Fitz-Steph. as above, pp. 106, 107.

The quarrel of king and primate would have mattered little
had it been fought out on English ground ; it was the archbishop's exile which rendered him so dangerous.   Thomas
had dealt his most fatal blow at Henry by flying from him,
and Henry, as he now perceived, had made his worst blunder
in driving Thomas into France.   Of the infinitely greater
blunder involved in the archbishop's murder—setting the
criminal aspect of the deed altogether aside—it is enough to
say that Henry was wholly incapable.   The same may be
said of Roger of York and Gilbert of London, although, like
the king himself, they were urged by dread of the archbishop
into making common cause with men of a very different
stamp :—men who hated the primate with a far more intense
personal hatred, and who were restrained by no considerations either of policy or of morality :—men such as Ralf de
Broc, a ruffian adventurer who had served as the tool of
Henry's vengeance upon the archbishop's kinsfolk, had
resumed the custody of the archiepiscopal estates when it was
resigned by Gilbert Foliot, had been for the last four years
at once fattening upon the property of Thomas and smarting
under his excommunication, and was ready to commit any
crime rather than disgorge his ill-gotten gains.[1]   It was
known that Thomas had letters from the Pope suspending
all those bishops who had taken part in the coronation of
the young king, and replacing Gilbert of London, Jocelyn of
Salisbury, and all whom Thomas had excommunicated under
the sentences from which they had been irregularly released
by some of the Papal envoys.[2]   Gilbert, Jocelyn and Roger
of York now hurried to Canterbury, intending to proceed to

---

[1] On Ralf de Broc see Will. Fitz-Steph. (Robertson, *Becket*, vol. iii.), p. 75 ;
Herb. Bosh. (*ibid.*), p. 360 ; Anon. I. (*ib.* vol. iv.) p. 65 ; E. Grim (*ib.* vol. ii.),
p. 404 ; Epp. lxxviii. (*ib.* vol. v. p. 152), cccxli., ccccxcviii. (*ib.* vol. vi. pp. 278,
582), dccxviii., dccxxiii. (*ib.* vol. vii. pp. 394, 402).   In the last place Thomas says
that Ralf "in ecclesiam Dei . . . per septem annos licentius debacchatus est";
and the writer of the *Thomas Saga* (Magnusson), vol. i. p. 321, seems to have
understood this as meaning that Ralf had had the stewardship of the Canterbury
property throughout the archbishop's exile.   This, however, does not appear to
have been the case.   Ralf certainly had the stewardship for a short time at first ;
but it was, as we have seen, soon transferred to Gilbert Foliot, and only restored
to Ralf when Gilbert resigned it early in 1167.
[2] Epp. dccxx., dccxxii. (Robertson, *Becket*, vol. vii. pp. 397-399).

Normandy as soon as Thomas set foot in England; while Ralf de Broc, Reginald de Warren and Gervase of Cornhill the sheriff of Kent undertook to catch him at the moment of landing, ransack his baggage, search his person, and seize any Papal letters which he might bring with him. Thomas, however was warned; he sent the letters over before him, and the three prelates at Canterbury read their condemnation before their judge quitted Gaul.[1] Next day he sailed from Wissant, and on the morning of December 1 he landed at Sandwich.[2] His enemies were ready to receive him; but at the sight of John of Oxford they stopped short, and John in the king's name forbade all interference with the primate.[3] Amid the rapturous greetings of the people who thronged to welcome their chief pastor, he rode on to Canterbury; there some of the royal officials came to him in the king's name, demanding the absolution of the suspended and excommunicate bishops. Thomas at first answered that he could not annul a Papal sentence; but he afterwards offered to take the risk of doing so, if the culprits would abjure their errors in the form prescribed by the Church. Gilbert and Jocelyn were inclined to yield; but Roger refused, and they ended by despatching Geoffrey Ridel to enlist the sympathies of the young king in their behalf, while they themselves carried their protest to his father in Normandy.[4]

---

[1] Ep. dccxxiii., dccxxiv. (Robertson, *Becket*, vol. vii.), pp. 403, 410. Cf. Will. Cant. (*ib.* vol. i.), pp. 87-89; Will. Fitz-Steph. (*ib.* vol. iii.), p. 117; Herb. Bosh. (*ibid.*), pp. 471, 472; Anon. I. (*ib.* vol. iv.), p. 68; Anon. II. (*ibid.*), p. 123; Garnier (Hippeau), pp. 161, 163. The version in *Thomas Saga* (Magnusson), vol. i. p. 483, seems founded on a confusion between the delivery of these Papal letters and that which Berengar delivered in S. Paul's on the Ascension-day of the previous year.

[2] Will. Fitz-Steph. (as above), p. 118. Herb. Bosh. (*ibid.*) p. 476. Anon. I. (*ib.* vol. iv.), p. 68. Garnier (Hippeau), p. 164. R. Diceto (Stubbs), vol. i. p. 339. Gerv. Cant. (Stubbs), vol. i. p. 222. *Thomas Saga* (as above), pp. 489-491. The date is from Will. Fitz-Steph., R. Diceto and the Saga; Gervase makes it November 30, and Herbert "two or three days after the feast of S. Andrew."

[3] Will. Fitz-Steph. and Garnier, as above. Ep. dccxxiii. (Robertson, *Becket*, vol. vii.), pp. 403, 404. *Thomas Saga* (as above), p. 491.

[4] Ep. dccxxiii., dccxxiv. (Robertson, *Becket*, vol. vii.), pp. 404-406, 411, 412. Will. Cant. (*ib.* vol. i.), pp. 102-105. Will. Fitz-Steph. (*ib.* vol. iii.), pp. 120, 121. Herb. Bosh. (*ibid.*), p. 480. *Thomas Saga* (Magnusson), vol. i. pp. 497-501. Garnier (Hippeau), p. 172, erroneously thinks the censures on the bishops were not issued till Christmas-day.

The young king was preparing to hold his Christmas
court at Winchester.[1]   Thomas proposed to join it, but was
stopped in London by a peremptory command to "go back
and mind his own business at Canterbury."[2]   He obeyed
under protest, and on Christmas-day again excommunicated
the De Brocs and their fellow-robbers.[3]   The elder king was
keeping the feast at his hunting-seat of Bures near Bayeux.[4]
There the three bishops threw themselves at his feet ; Roger
of York spoke in the name of all, and presented the Papal
letters ;[5] the courtiers burst into a confused storm of indignation, but not one had any counsel to offer.   In his impatience
and disappointment Henry uttered the fatal words which he
was to rue all his life : "What a parcel of fools and dastards
have I nourished in my house, that none of them can be
found to avenge me of this one upstart clerk!"[6]

The words were hardly more than he had used at Chinon
four years before, but they fell now upon other ears.   Four
knights—Hugh de Morville, William de Tracy, Reginald
Fitz-Urse and Richard le Breton[7]—took them as a warrant
for the primate's death.   That night—it was Christmas-eve[8]
—they vowed to slay him, no matter how or where ;[9] they

---

[1] Garnier (Hippeau), p. 166.   Will. Cant. (Robertson, *Becket*, vol. i.), p. 106.
Anon. II. (*ib.* vol. iv.), p. 126.   R. Diceto (Stubbs), vol. i. p. 342, says the young
king was at Woodstock when Thomas sought for an interview ; he was, however,
certainly at Winchester at Christmas.

[2] "Fère vostre mestier à Cantorbire alez."   Garnier (Hippeau), p. 171.   Cf.
Ep. dccxxiv. (Robertson, *Becket*, vol. vii.), p. 412 ; Will. Cant. (*ib.* vol. i.) pp.
106-113|; Will. Fitz-Steph. (*ib.* vol. iii.), pp. 121-123; Herb. Bosh. (*ibid.*), pp. 482,
483 ; Rog. Howden (Stubbs), vol. ii. p. 13 ; *Thomas Saga* (Magnusson), vol. i.
pp. 505-507.

[3] Will. Cant. (as above), p. 120.   E. Grim (*ib.* vol. ii.), p. 428.   Will. Fitz-
Steph. (*ib.* vol. iii.), p. 130.   Herb. Bosh. (*ibid.*), pp. 484, 485.   R. Diceto (as
above), p. 342.   *Thomas Saga* (as above), pp. 511-513.

[4] Herb. Bosh. (as above), p. 481.   Garnier (Hippeau), p. 175.   *Gesta Hen.*
(Stubbs), vol. i. p. 11.   Rob. Torigni, a. 1171.

[5] Garnier (Hippeau), pp. 175-177.   Will. Cant. (as above), pp. 122, 123.   Cf.
Thomas Saga (as above), pp. 501-503.

[6] Garnier (Hippeau), p. 175.   Will. Cant. (as above), p. 121.   E. Grim (*ib.*
vol. ii.), p. 429.   Herb. Bosh. (*ib.* vol. iii.), p. 487.

[7] In Will. Cant. (as above), pp. 128, 129, is a "descriptio spiculatorum," in
which the only point of interest is the English speech of Hugh de Morville's
mother.   [8] Garnier (Hippeau), p. 177.   Will. Cant. (as above), p. 123.

[9] Garnier, as above.   Will. Cant. (as above), p. 124.   E. Grim (*ib.* vol. ii.),

left the court in secret, crossed to England by different routes,[1] and met again at Saltwood, a castle which the archbishop had been vainly endeavouring to recover from the clutches of Ralf de Broc, and where Ralf himself was dwelling amid a crowd of his kinsfolk and dependents. There the final plot was laid.[2] How it was executed is a tale which has been told so often that its details may well be spared here. On the evening of December 29, after a scene in his own hall scarcely less disgraceful than the last scene in the king's hall at Northampton, the primate of all England was butchered at the altar's foot in his own cathedral church.[3]

The ill news travelled fast. It fell like a thunderbolt upon the Norman court still gathered round the king at Argentan,[4] whither the assembly had adjourned after the Christmas feast at Bures. Henry stood for a moment speechless with horror, then burst into a frenzy of despair, and shut himself up in his own rooms, refusing to eat or drink or to see any one.[5] In a few days more, as he anticipated, all Christendom was ringing with execration of the murder and clamouring for vengeance upon the king who was universally regarded as its instigator. The Pope ordered an interdict upon Henry's continental dominions, excommunicated the murderers and all who had given or should henceforth give them aid, shelter or support, and was only restrained from pronouncing a like sentence upon the king himself by a promise that he would make compurgation and

p. 429. Will. Fitz-Steph. (Robertson, *Becket*, vol. iii.), p. 128. Herb. Bosh. (*ibid.*), p. 487. *Thomas Saga* (Magnusson), vol. i. p. 517.

[1] Garnier (Hippeau), p. 177. Will. Cant. (Robertson, *Becket*, vol. i.) p. 124, Will. Fitz-Steph. (*ib.* vol. iii.), p. 130. *Thomas Saga* as above.

[2] Will. Fitz-Steph. as above; cf. *ib.* p. 126. *Thomas Saga*, as above, pp. 517-519. Saltwood was mentioned, as a special subject for inquiry and restitution, in the king's letter commending Thomas to his son.

[3] Will. Cant. (as above), pp. 131-135. Joh. Salisb. (*ib.* vol. ii.), pp. 319, 320. E. Grim (*ibid.*), pp. 430-438. Will. Fitz-Steph. (*ib.* vol. iii.), pp. 132-142. Herb. Bosh. (*ibid.*), pp. 488 *et seq.* Anon. I. (*ib.* vol. iv.), pp. 70-77. Anon. II. (*ibid.*), pp. 128-132. Garnier (Hippeau), pp. 179-195. R. Diceto (Stubbs), vol. i. pp. 343, 344. Gerv. Cant. (Stubbs), vol. i. pp. 224-227. *Thomas Saga* as above, pp. 523-549.

[4] R. Diceto (as above), p. 345. *Gesta Hen.* (Stubbs), vol. i. p. 14.

[5] Ep. dccxxxviii. (Robertson, *Becket*, vol. vii.), p. 438. Cf. MS. Lansdown. (*ib.* vol. iv.), pp. 159, 160, and *Gesta Hen.* as above.

submit to penance.[1] Two cardinal-legates charged with the
enforcement of these decrees were at once despatched to
Normandy ;[2] but when they arrived there, Henry was out of
their reach. The death of Duke Conan in February had
thrown Britanny completely into his hands ; he only stayed
to secure Geoffrey's final establishment there as duke[3] before
he called a council at Argentan and announced that he was
going to Ireland.[4] He quitted Normandy just as the legates
reached it,[5] leaving strict orders that the ports should be
closed to all clerks and papal envoys, and that no one should
dare to follow him without special permission.[6] Landing at
Portsmouth in the first days of August,[7] he hurried to Winchester for a last interview with the dying Bishop Henry,[8]
closed the English ports as he had closed those of Normandy,[9]
then plunged once more into the depths of South Wales, and
on October 16 sailed from Milford Haven for Waterford.[10]

The elements favoured his escape ; for five months a
persistent contrary wind hindered all communication to

[1] Epp. dccl., dccli. (Robertson, *Becket*, vol. vii. pp. 471-478).

[2] Gerv. Cant. (Stubbs), vol. i. p. 233. R. Diceto (Stubbs), vol. i. p. 346.
Gesta Hen. (Stubbs), vol. i. p. 24.

[3] Rob. Torigni, a. 1171. Conan died February 20 ; Chron. Kemperleg. *ad
ann.* (*Rer. Gall. Scriptt.*, vol. xii. p. 563). The Chron. S. Serg. a. 1169
(Marchegay, *Eglises*, p. 150), places the event two years too early. Cf. Chron.
Britann. a. 1170, 1171 (*Rer. Gall. Scriptt.*, vol. xii. p. 560; Morice, *Hist.
Bretagne, preuves*, vol. i. col. 104).   [4] Rob. Torigni, a. 1171.

[5] MS. Lansdown. (Robertson, *Becket*, vol. iv.), p. 169. Gerv. Cant. (as
above), pp. 233, 234. The *Gesta Hen.* (as above), and Rog. Howden (Stubbs,
vol. ii. pp. 28, 29) seem to imply that they arrived just before Henry left ;
but they are rather confused about these legates. They make two pairs of them
come to Normandy this summer—first, Vivian and Gratian, who come with hostile
intent, and from whom Henry runs away (*Gesta Hen.*, Stubbs, vol. i. p. 24 ; Rog.
Howden, Stubbs, vol. ii. p. 29); and secondly, Albert and Theodwine, who
apparently supersede them later in the year, and whom Henry hurries to meet
(*Gesta Hen.* as above, p. 29 ; Rog. Howden as above, p. 34). But the MS.
Lansdown. (which is the fullest account of all), Gerv. Cant. and R. Diceto
distinctly make only one pair of legates, Albert and Theodwine. The confusion
in *Thomas Saga* (Magnusson), vol. ii. pp. 31-33, is greater still.

[6] *Gesta Hen.* (as above), p. 24. Cf. Rog. Howden (as above), p. 29.

[7] *Gesta Hen.* as above, and Gerv. Cant. (Stubbs), vol. i. p. 234, say August 3 ;
R. Diceto (Stubbs), vol. i. p. 347, says August 6.

[8] R. Diceto as above. Bishop Henry died on August 8 ; *ibid.*

[9] Gerv. Cant., *Gesta Hen.* and Rog. Howden, as above.

[10] *Gesta Hen.* (as above), p. 25.

Ireland from any part of his dominions.[1] The bishops and the ministers were left to fight their own battles and make their own peace with the legates in Normandy until May 1172, when the king suddenly reappeared [2] to claim the papal absolution and offer in return not only his own spiritual obedience and that of his English and continental realms, but also that of Ireland, which he had secured for Rome as her share in the spoils of a conquest won with Adrian's bull in his hand.[3] The bargain was soon struck. On Sunday May 21 Henry met the legates at Avranches, made his purgation for the primate's death, promised the required expiation, and abjured his obnoxious "customs," his eldest son joining in the abjuration.[4] To pacify Louis, young Henry and Margaret were sent over sea with the archbishop of Rouen and by him crowned together at Winchester on August 27 ; [5] and the Norman primate returned to join a great council of the Norman clergy assembled at Caen to witness there, two days before Michaelmas, a public repetition of their sovereign's purgation and his final absolution by the legates.[6]

[1] R. Diceto (Stubbs), vol. i. p. 350. Gir. Cambr., *Expugn. Hibern.*, l. i. c. 36 (Dimock, vol. v. p. 284). [2] R. Diceto (as above), p. 351.

[3] *Gesta Hen.* (Stubbs), vol. i. p. 28.

[4] Ep. dcclxxi.-dcclxxiv. (Robertson, *Becket*, vol. vii. pp. 513-522). MS. Lansdown. (*ib.* vol. iv.), pp. 173, 174.

[5] *Gesta Hen.* (as above), p. 31 ; Rog. Howden (Stubbs), vol. ii. p. 34 ; Gerv. Cant. (Stubbs), vol. i. p. 237. R. Diceto (as above), p. 352, makes it August 21.

[6] *Gesta Hen.* (as above), pp. 32, 33. Rog. Howden (as above), pp. 35-37. Gerv. Cant. (as above), p. 238. These three are the only writers who mention this purgation in September, and they say nothing of the one in May. That it took place is however clear from the letter of the legates themselves (Ep. dcclxxiv. Robertson, *Becket*, vol. vii. p. 521), giving its date, " *Vocem jucunditatis,*" *i.e.* Rogation-Sunday. On the other hand, the MS. Lansdown. (*ib.* vol. iv. pp. 173, 174) mentions only one purgation, and this clearly is the earlier one, for it is placed before the re-crowning of young Henry. The explanation seems to be that this was a private ceremony between the king and the legates, with a few chosen witnesses ; the legates say in their letter that Henry promised to repeat it publicly at Caen ; he doubtless did so at Avranches instead. On the other hand, Rob. Torigni (a. 1172) says : "Locutus est cum eis primo Savigneii, postea Abrincis, tercio Cadomi, ubi causa illa finita est ;" and seems to make .the Michaelmas council at Avranches a mere ordinary Church synod, where moreover "obsistente regis infirmitate parum profecerunt." To add to the confusion, Gir. Cambr. (*Expugn. Hibern.*, l. i. c. 39 ; Dimock, vol. v. p. 289) says the purgation was made at Coutances.

CHAPTER III.

THE CONQUEST OF IRELAND.

795-1172.

IT is in the history of the settlements formed on the Irish coast by the northern pirates in the ninth century that we must seek for the origin of those relations between England and Ireland which led to an English invasion of the latter country in the reign of Henry II. The earliest intercourse between the two islands had been of a wholly peaceful character; but it had come utterly to an end when Bishop Colman of Lindisfarne sailed back to his old home at Iona after the synod of Whitby in 664. From the hour when her missionary work was done, Ireland sank more and more into the isolation which was a natural consequence of her geographical position, and from which she was only roused at the opening of the ninth century by the coming of the wikings. In the early days of the northmen's attack upon the British isles it was the tradition of Ireland's material prosperity and wealth, and the fame of the treasures stored in her religious houses, that chiefly tempted the "white strangers" from the Norwegian fiords across the unknown perils of the western sea; and the settlement of Thorgils in Ulster and those of his fellow-wikings along the eastern and southern coasts of Ireland formed a chief basis for the operations of the northmen upon Britain itself. The desperat fighting of the Irish succeeded in freeing Ulster after Thorgils's death; but by the middle of the ninth century the wikings were firmly established at four points on the Irish

IRELAND

A.D. 1172.

*Ostmen's settlements marked
thus:* _Dublin_.

Aileach

ULSTER

Uladh

O'riel

Armagh

Breffny

CONNAUGHT

Kells

MEATH

Tara

Clontarf

Tuam

Clonmacnoise

Dublin

Offaly

Kildare

Thomond

Ormond

LEINSTER

Ossory

Durrow

Limerick

Fernelagh

Cashel

Hy Kinsellah

Wexford

Waterford

Begery

MUNSTER

Desmond

Cork

Wagner & Debes' Geog! Estab! Leipsic.

London, Macmillan & Co.

coast, Dublin, Waterford, Cork and Limerick.[1] Under the
leadership of Olaf the Fair, Dublin became the head of a
confederacy which served as a starting-point and furnished
a constant supply of forces for the Danish conquests in England ;[2] and for a hundred years afterwards, throughout the
struggle of the house of Ælfred for the recovery of the Danelaw, the support given by the Ostmen or wikings of Ireland
to their brethren across the channel was at once the main
strength of the Northumbrian Danes and the standing difficulty of the English kings.[3]

To Ireland itself the results of the wiking invasions were
far more disastrous than either to Britain or to Gaul. Owing
to the peculiar physical character of their country, to their
geographical remoteness from the rest of Europe, and to the
political and social isolation which was a consequence of
these, the Irish people had never advanced beyond the
primitive tribal mode of life which had once been common
to the whole Aryan race, but which every European branch
of that race, except the Irish, had long since outgrown. In
the time of Ecgberht and of Charles the Great Ireland was
still, as at the very dawn of history, peopled by a number of
separate tribes or septs whose sole bond of internal cohesion
was formed by community of blood ;—whose social and
political institutions had remained purely patriarchal in
character, unaffected by local and external influences such
as had helped to mould the life of England or of Gaul :—
who had never yet coalesced into any definite territorial
organization, far less risen into national unity under a
national sovereign. The provincial kings of Ulster, Connaught, Leinster and Munster were merely the foremost
chieftains among the various groups of tribes over whom
they exercised an ever-shifting sway ; while the supremacy
of the *Ard-Righ* or chief monarch, to whom in theory was
assigned the overlordship of the whole island, was practically
little more than a sort of honorary pre-eminence attached

---

[1] On Thorgils and the wiking settlements in Ireland see *Wars of the Gaedhil
with the Gaill* (Todd), and Green, *Conquest of England*, pp. 66, 67, 74, 76.

[2] Green, *Conquest of England*, pp. 90, 91, 107.

[3] *Ib.* pp. 213, 242, 252-254, 270-272.

to certain chosen descendants of an early hero-king, Niall "of the Nine Hostages"; it carried with it little effective authority, and no territorial power; for the monarch's traditional seat at Tara had long been a heap of ruins, and a tribal under-king had ousted him from the plain of Meath which in legal theory formed his royal domain.[1]   Neither in the monarch himself nor in the provincial chieftains of a state thus constituted could there be found, when the storm-cloud from the north burst upon Ireland, a centre of unity even such as the peoples of Gaul found in their Karolingian sovereigns, far less such as the West-Franks found in the dukes of the French, or such as the English found in their kings of the house of Ecgberht.   The stress of the northmen's attack, which elsewhere gave a fresh impulse to the upgrowth of national life, crushed out all hope of its developement in Ireland.   The learning and the civilization of ages perished when Columba's Bangor, Bridget's Kildare, Ciaran's Clonmacnoise, Patrick's own Armagh, shared the fate of Bæda's Jarrow and Hild's Streoneshealh, of Cuthbert's Melrose and Aidan's Lindisfarne; and in Ireland there was no Wessex and no Ælfred.

On the other hand, the concentration of the wiking forces upon Britain had given to the Irish an advantage which enabled them to check the spread of wiking settlements in their country; and the failure of all attempts to establish a Scandinavian dominion in Britain destroyed all chance of a Scandinavian conquest of Ireland.   The Ostmen never even gained such a footing in Ireland as the followers of Hrolf gained in Frankland: their presence never received the sanction of any Ard-Righ; they were not a compact body occupying the whole of an extensive and well-defined territory, but a number of separate groups settled here and there along the coast, and holding their ground only by sheer hard fighting against a ring of implacable foes.   The long struggle may be said to have ended in a defeat of both parties.   The Irish kings of Munster succeeded in establish-

---

[1] Maine, *Early Hist. of Institutions,* lect. i.-x.; O'Donovan, Introd. to *Book of Rights;* Lynch, *Cambrensis Eversus,* with Mr. Kelly's notes; O'Donovan, notes to Four Masters, vols. i. and ii.

ing a more or less effective overlordship over the Scandinavian communities of Limerick and Waterford ; and in 989 Malachi II., supreme monarch of Ireland, reaped his reward for nine years of desperate fighting in the submission of the Ostmen of Dublin. The city was blockaded and starved into surrender, and a yearly tribute was promised to Malachi and his successors.[1] Six years later "the ring of Tomar and the sword of Carl"—two heathen relics probably of ancient heroes, which seem to have been treasured as sacred emblems of sovereignty by the Ostmen[2]—were carried off by Malachi as trophies of another victory;[3] and in 999 or 1000 a renewal of the strife ended in a rout of the Ostmen and a great slaughter of their leaders, and Dublin was sacked and burnt by the victorious Irish.[4]

Malachi's triumph, however, was gained at the cost of a disruption of the monarchy. Malachi himself was displaced by a king of the rival house of Munster, his colleague in the sack of Dublin, the famous Brian Boroimhe ;[5] Brian's career of conquest ended in 1014 on the field of Clontarf, where he was slain in battle with the men of Leinster and the Ostmen ;[6] and when Malachi, who now resumed his place, died in 1022,[7] the downfall of the Irish monarchy was complete.[8] The tradition which had so long linked it to the house of Niall had been shattered by Brian's successes ; and

---

[1] Tighernach, a. 989 (O'Conor, *Rer. Hibern. Scriptt.*, vol. ii. pp. 264, 265).

[2] See O'Donovan's introduction to the *Book of Rights*, pp. xxxviii, xxxix.

[3] Tighernach, a. 995 (as above, p. 267).

[4] *Ib.* a. 998, 999 (p. 268). *Wars of Gaedhil with Gaill* (Todd), pp. 109-117.

[5] Tighernach, a. 1000, 1001 (as above, pp. 269, 270). *Wars of Gaedhil with Gaill* (Todd), p. 119. Brian's victory was won by the help of the Ostmen, with whom he stooped to ally himself for the sake of overcoming his rival ; but the alliance was only momentary. On Brian's reign see *Wars of Gaedhil with Gaill*, pp. 119-155.

[6] *Wars of Gaedhil with Gaill* (Todd), pp. 155-211. Four Masters, a. 1013 (O'Donovan, vol. ii. pp. 773-781). Ann. Loch Cé, a. 1014 (Hennessy, vol. i. pp. 1-13).

[7] Tighernach, a. 1022 (as above, p. 274). Four Masters, a. 1022 (as above, p. 800). Ann. Loch Cé, a. 1022 (as above, p. 23).

[8] " From the death of Maelseachlainn II. the legitimate monarchy of all Ireland departed from all families during seventy-two years, until the joint reigns of Muircheartach O'Briain and Domhnall MacLochlainn ; during that time no Feis or general assembly, so agreeable to the people, was held, because Ireland had no supreme king." Quoted by Mr. Kelly, note to *Cambrensis Eversus*, vol. ii. p. 38, rom Gilla-Modud, an Irish poet of the twelfth century.

Brian had not lived to consolidate in his own house the forces which had begun to gather around himself. Thenceforth the Scandinavian colonies simply furnished an additional element to the strife of the Irish chieftains, and to the rivalry between the O'Briens of Munster and the O'Neills of Ulster for the possession of a shadowy supremacy, claimed by the one house as descendants of Brian Boroimhe and by the other as heirs of Malachi II. and of his great ancestor Niall.

The social and political system of Ireland was powerless either to expel or to absorb the foreign element thus introduced within its borders. Not only was such an union of the two peoples as had at last been effected in England simply impossible in Ireland ; the Irish Danelaw was parted from its Celtic surroundings by barriers of race and speech, of law and custom and institutions, far more insuperable than those which parted the settlers in the "northman's land" at the mouth of Seine from their West-Frankish neighbours. Even the Irish Church, which three hundred years before had won half England—one might add half Europe—to the Faith, had as yet failed to convert these pagans seated at her door. At the close of the tenth century the Ostmen were still for the most part heathens in fact if not in name, aliens from whatever culture or civilization might still remain in the nation around them. Meanwhile their relations with England had wholly altered in character. The final submission of the English Danelaw to Eadred carried with it the alliance of the Irish Danelaw; it seems that the Ostmen in their turn endeavoured to strengthen themselves against the attacks of the Irish princes by securing a good understanding with the English king, if not actually by putting themselves under his protection ; for the fact that Eadgar coined money in Dublin[1] indicates that his authority must have been in some way or other acknowledged there. The years of the Ostmen's struggle with Malachi and Brian Boroimhe were the years of England's struggle with Swein and Cnut ; but the two strifes seem to have been wholly unconnected ; and throughout the long peace which lasted from Cnut's final triumph until the coming of the Normans,

---

[1] Green, *Conquest of England*, p. 323.

new 'ties sprang up between the Ostmen and the sister-isle. Owing to their position on the sea-coast and to the spirit of merchant enterprise which was, quite as much as the spirit of military enterprise, a part of the wiking-heritage of their inhabitants, the towns of the Irish Danelaw rose fast into importance as seats of a flourishing trade with northern Europe, and above all with England through its chief sea-ports in the west, Bristol and Chester. The traffic was chiefly in slaves, bought or kidnapped in England to be sold to the merchants of Dublin or Waterford, and by these again to their Irish neighbours or to traders from yet more distant lands.[1] Horrible as this traffic was, however, even while filling the Irish coast-towns with English slaves it helped to foster a more frequent intercourse and a closer relation between Ostmen and Englishmen ; and the shelter and aid given to Harold and Leofwine in 1151 by Dermot Mac-Mael-nambo,[2] a prince of the royal house of Leinster who had acquired the sovereignty over both Leinstermen and Danes, shews that the political alliance established in Eadgar's day had been carefully renewed by Godwine.

To these commercial and political relations was added soon afterwards an ecclesiastical tie. The conversion of the Ostmen to Christianity, completed in the early years of the eleventh century, was probably due to intercourse with their Christianized brethren in England rather than to the in-fluence of the Irish clergy, whose very speech was strange to them ; and their adoption of their neighbours' creed, instead of drawing together the hostile races, soon introduced a fresh element into their strife. About the year 1040 the Ostmen of Dublin set up a bishopric of their own. Their first bishop, Donatus, was probably Irish by consecration if not by birth.[3] But when he died, in 1074,[4] the Ostmen turned

---

[1] Green, *Conquest of England*, pp. 440, 443, 444.

[2] See Freeman, *Norm. Conq.*, vol. ii. pp. 154.

[3] That is, he was certainly not consecrated in England; Lanigan, *Eccles. Hist. Ireland*, vol. iii. pp. 433-436. But might he not have been consecrated by some of the bishops in Scotland and the Isles, with which the Ostmen were in constant intercourse and alliance ?

[4] Tighernach, a. 1074 (O'Conor, *Rer. Hibern. Scriptt.*), vol. ii. p. 309. Four Masters, a. 1074 (O'Donovan, vol. ii. p. 907).

instinctively towards the neighbouring island with which
they had long been on peaceful terms, where the fruits of
the warfare waged by generation after generation of wikings
upon the shores of Britain were being reaped at last by
Norman hands, where William of Normandy was entering
upon the inheritance alike of Ælfred and of Cnut, and where
Lanfranc was infusing a new spirit of discipline and activity
into the Church of Odo and Dunstan. The last wiking-fleet
that ever sailed from Dublin to attack the English coast—a
fleet which Dermot Màc-Maelnambo, true to his alliance with
their father, had furnished to the sons of Harold—had been
beaten back six years before.[1] Since then Dermot himself
was dead ;[2] the Ostmen were once more free, subject to no
ruler save one of their own choice and their own blood ;
with the consent of their king, Godred,[3] they chose a priest
named Patrick to fill Donatus's place, and sent him to be
consecrated in England by the archbishop of Canterbury.[4]
No scruples about infringing the rights of the Irish bishops
were likely to make Lanfranc withhold his hand. At the
very moment when the Ostmen's request reached him, he
had just been putting forth against the archbishop of York
a claim to metropolitical jurisdiction over the whole of the

---

[1] Eng. Chron. (Worc.) a. 1067, 1068; Flor. Worc. (Thorpe), vol. ii. p. 2 ;
Ord. Vit. (Duchesne, *Hist. Norm. Scriptt.*), p. 513 ; Will. Jumièges, l. vii. c. 41
(*ib.* p. 290) ; Freeman, *Norm. Conq.*, vol. iv. pp. 225-227, 243-245, 788-790.

[2] He fell in battle with the king of Meath in 1072, according to the Four
Masters *ad ann.* (O'Donovan, vol. ii. pp. 901-903), and the Ann. Loch Cé (Hennessy, vol. i. p. 67). The Chron. Scot. (Hennessy, p. 291) places his death in
1069 ; Mr. Freeman (as above, p. 245) adopts this date.

[3] At the time of Donatus's appointment in 1040, one Sihtric ruled in Dublin
(see Lanigan, *Eccles. Hist. Ireland*, vol. iii. pp. 434, 435)—doubtless under the
overlordship of Dermot. On Dermot's death the Ostmen flung off the Irish
supremacy and took for their king, first a jarl named Godred, who died in 1072,
and then another of the same name, who seems to have been already king of Man.
(Freeman, as above, p. 528 and note 5). Lanfranc addresses this Godred as
" King of Ireland " (Lanfranc, Ep. 43, Giles, vol. i. p. 61) ; and no other prince
is mentioned in connexion with Patrick's consecration. But it is plain from
Lanfranc's correspondence, if from nothing else, that Terence O'Brien was
acknowledged overlord of Dublin for some time before his death (see Lanfranc,
Ep. 44, *ib.* p. 62; and Lanigan, as above, p. 474 *et seq.*); and he died in
1086.

[4] Lanfranc, Ep. 43 (as above, p. 61). Eng. Chron. Winch., Appendix (Thorpe,
vol. i. p. 387). Cf. Lanigan, as above, pp. 457, 458.

British isles, founded on the words of S. Gregory committing
" all the bishops of the Britains " to S. Augustine's charge.[1]
He therefore gladly welcomed an opportunity of securing for
the authority of his see a footing in the neighbour-isle.   He
consecrated Patrick of Dublin and received his profession of
obedience ;[2] and for the next seventy-eight years the bishops
of Dublin were suffragans not of Armagh but of Canterbury.
When in 1096 the Ostmen of Waterford also chose for
themselves a bishop, they too sought him beyond the sea ;
an Irishman, or more probably an Ostman by birth, a monk
of Winchester by profession, Malchus by name, he was consecrated by S. Anselm and professed obedience to him as
metropolitan.[3]

Through the medium of these Irish suffragans the archbishops of Canterbury endeavoured to gain a hold upon the
Irish Church by cultivating the friendship of the different
Irish princes who from time to time succeeded in winning
from the Ostmen an acknowledgement of their overlordship.
In the struggles of the provincial kings for the supreme
monarchy of Ireland it was always the Ostmen who turned
the scale ; their submission was the real test of sovereignty.
The power which had been wielded by Dermot Mac-Mael-
nambo passed after his death first to Terence or Turlogh
O'Brien, king of Munster,[4] a grandson of Brian Boroimhe,
and then to Terence's son Murtogh.[5]   Both were in correspondence with the successive English primates, Lanfranc
and Anselm,[6] and both were recognized as protectors and
patrons, in ecclesiastical matters at least, by the Ostmen,[7]

---

[1] Lanigan, *Eccles. Hist. Ireland*, vol. iii. pp. 464-466.

[2] *Ib.* p. 458.   Eng. Chron. Winch., Appendix (Thorpe, vol. i. p. 387).

[3] Eadmer, *Hist. Nov.* (Rule), pp. 76, 77.   Cf. Lanigan, as above, vol. iv. pp.
15, 16.

[4] Four Masters, a. 1073-1086 (O'Donovan, vol. ii. pp. 905-927).

[5] *Ib.* a. 1087-1119 (pp. 929-1009).

[6] Lanfranc, Ep. 44 (Giles, vol. i. pp. 62-64); Anselm, Epp. l. iii., Epp. cxlii.,
cxlvii. (Migne, *Patrol.*, vol. clix., cols. 173, 174, 178-180); Lanigan, as above,
vol. iii. pp. 474 *et seq.*, vol. iv. pp. 15, 19, 20.

[7] Samuel of Dublin in 1095 and Malchus of Waterford in 1096 were both
elected under Murtogh's sanction and sent to England for consecration with letters
of commendation from him.   Eadmer, *Hist. Nov.* (Rule), pp. 73-76 ; Lanigan,
above, vol. iv. pp. 12-15.

whose adherence during these years enabled the O'Briens to hold their ground against the advancing power of Donnell O'Lochlainn, king of Aileach or western Ulster,[1] a representative of the old royal house of the O'Neills which had fallen with Malachi II.   On Murtogh's death in 1119[2] a new aspirant to the monarchy appeared in the person of the young king of Connaught, Terence or Turlogh O'Conor.   A year before, Terence had won the submission of the Ostmen of Dublin ;[3] in 1120 he celebrated the fair of Telltown,[4] a special prerogative of the Irish monarchs ; and from the death of Donnell O'Lochlainn next year [5] Terence was undisputed monarch till 1127, when a joint rising of Ostmen and Leinstermen enabled both to throw off his yoke.[6] Meanwhile Murtogh O'Lochlainn, a grandson of Donnell, was again building up a formidable power in Ulster ; at last, in 1150, all the provincial kings, including Terence, gave him hostages for peace ;[7] and Terence's throne seems to have been only saved by a sudden change in the policy of the Ostmen, whose independent action enabled them for a moment to hold the balance and act as arbitrators between northern and southern Ireland.[8]   Four years later, however, they accepted Murtogh as their king,[9] and two years later

---

[1] Four Masters, a. 1083-1119 (O'Donovan, vol. ii. pp. 921-1009).   Cf. Ann. Loch Cé, a. 1083-1119 (Hennessy, vol. i. pp. 73-111).

[2] Four Masters, a. 1119 (as above, p. 1009).   Ann. Loch. Cé, a. 1119 (as above, p. 111).

[3] Lanigan, *Eccles. Hist. Ireland*, vol. iv. p. 48, says : "The Annals of Innisfallen have at *A.* 1118, 'Turlogh O'Conor became king of the Danes of Dublin.'" (This passage does not occur in either of the two editions of Ann. Inisfal. printed by O'Conor.)   The Four Masters, a. 1118 (as above, p. 1007), say that Terence took hostages from the Ostmen in that year.   He was, at any rate, acknowledged as their overlord by 1121, for it was he who in that year sent Gregory, bishop-elect of Dublin, to England for consecration.   Lanigan, as above, p. 47.   [4] Four Masters *ad ann.* (as above, p. 1011).

[5] *Ib.* a. 1121 (p. 1013).   Ann. Loch Cé, a. 1121 (as above, p. 113).

[6] Ann Loch Cé, a. 1127 (p. 123).

[7] Four Masters, a. 1150 (as above, p. 1093).

[8] Something of this kind must be meant by the phrase of the Four Masters (*ib.* p. 1095): "The foreigners made a year's peace between Leath-Chuinn and Leath-Mhogha."   This is in 1150, after Murtogh's appearance as " King of Ireland" and the Ostmen's submission to Terence (II.) O'Brien, whom his namesake of Connaught had set up as king in Munster.

[9] Four Masters, a. 1154 (as above, p. 1113).

still he was left sole monarch by the death of Terence O'Conor.[1]

The anarchy of the Irish state was reflected in that of the Church. If Lanfranc, when he consecrated Patrick of Dublin, knew anything at all of the ecclesiastical condition of Ireland, he may well have thought that it stood in far greater need of his reforming care than England itself. The Irish Church had never felt the organizing hand of a Theodore ; its diocesan and parochial system was quite un-developed ; it had in fact scarcely advanced beyond the primitive missionary stage. Six centuries after S. Patrick's death, the Irish clergy were still nothing but a band of mission-priests scattered over the country or gathered to-gether in vast monastic establishments like Bangor or Dur-row or Clonmacnoise ; the bishops were for the most part merely heads of ever-shifting mission-stations, to whose number there was no limit ; destitute of political rank, they were almost equally destitute of ecclesiastical authority, and differed from the ordinary priesthood by little else than their power of ordination. At the head of the whole hierarchy stood, as successor and representative of S. Patrick, the arch-bishop of Armagh. But since the death of Archbishop Maelbrigid in 927 the see of Armagh had been in the hands of a family of local chieftains who occupied its estate, usurped its revenues, handed on its title from father to son, and were bishops only in name.[2] The inferior members of the ecclesiastical body could not escape the evil which para-lyzed their head. The bishops and priests of the Irish Church furnished a long roll of names to the catalogue of saints ; but they contributed little or nothing to the political developement of the nation, and scarcely more to its social developement. The growth of a class of lay-impropriators ousted them from the management and the revenues of their church-lands, reduced them to subsist almost wholly upon the fees which they received for the performance of their spiritual functions, stripped them of all political influence,

---

[1] Four Masters, a. 1156 (O'Donovan, vol. ii. p. 1119).
[2] S. Bernard, *Vita S. Malach.*, c. 10 (Mabillon, vol. i. col. 667). Cf. Lani-gan, *Eccles. Hist. Ireland*, vol. iii. p. 382.

and left them dependent solely upon their spiritual powers and their personal holiness for whatever share of social influence they might still contrive to retain.[1] The Irish Church, in fact, while stedfastly adhering in doctrinal matters to the rest of the Latin Church, had fallen far behind it in discipline; to the monastic reforms of the tenth century, to the struggle for clerical celibacy and for freedom of investiture in the eleventh, she had remained an utter stranger. The long-continued stress of the northern invasions had cut off the lonely island in the west from all intercourse with the world at large, so completely that even the tie which bound her to Rome had sunk into a mere vague tradition of spiritual loyalty, and Rome herself knew nothing of the actual condition of a Church which had once been her most illustrious daughter.

But it was the northmen, too, who were now to become the means of knitting up again the ties which had been severed by their fathers' swords. The state of things in Ireland, as reported to Canterbury from Dublin and Waterford, might well seem to reforming churchmen like Lanfranc and Anselm too grievous to be endured. Lanfranc had urged upon Terence O'Brien the removal of two of its worst scandals, the neglect of canonical restraints upon marriage and the existence of a crowd of titular bishops without fixed sees;[2] Anselm used all his influence with Murtogh O'Brien for the same end;[3] at last, finding his efforts unavailing, he seems to have laid his complaints before the Pope. The result was that, for the first time, a papal legate was appointed for Ireland. The person chosen was Gilbert, who some two or three years before Anselm's death became the first bishop of the Ostmen of Limerick. Gilbert seems, like the first Donatus of Dublin, to have been himself an Irish prelate; he lost no time, however, in putting himself in com-

---

[1] On these lay impropriators, "comorbas" and "erenachs," see Lanigan, *Eccles. Hist. Ireland*, vol. iv. pp. 79-86.

[2] Lanfranc, Ep. 44 (Giles, vol. i. p. 63).

[3] Anselm, Epp. l. iii., Epp. cxlii., cxlvii. (Migne, *Patrol.*, vol. clix., cols. 173, 174, 178-180).

munication with Canterbury,[1] and displayed an almost
exaggerated zeal for the Roman discipline and ritual.[2] In
1118 he presided over a synod held at Rathbreasil, where
an attempt was made to map out the dioceses of Ireland on
a definite plan.[3] Little, however, could be done till the
metropolitan see was delivered from the usurpers who
had so long held it in bondage ; and it was not until
1134 that the evil tradition was broken by the election of
S. Malachi.

Malachi was the wisest and most enlightened as well as
the most saintly Irish prelate of his time ; he had already
been labouring for nearly ten years at the reform of the
diocese of Connor ; in that of Armagh itself he had earlier
still, as vicar to Archbishop Celsus, laid the foundations of a
similar work which he now took up again as primate.[4] After
a successful pontificate of three years he again retired to the
humbler position of a diocesan bishop at Down ;[5] but he
still continued to watch over the interests of the whole Irish
Church ; and in 1139 he went to Rome specially to lay its
necessities before the Pope, and if possible to obtain from
him the gift of a pallium for the archbishop of Armagh, and
another for the bishop of Cashel as metropolitan of southern
Ireland.[6] The pallium was now generally regarded as an
indispensable note of metropolitical rank, but it had never
been possessed by the successors of S. Patrick.[7] Innocent
II. refused to grant it save at the request of the Irish
clergy and people in council assembled ; he sanctioned, however, the recognition of Cashel as metropolis of southern
Ireland, and moreover he transferred to Malachi himself the
legatine commission which Gilbert of Limerick had just
resigned.[8] Gilbert seems to have died shortly afterwards :
his successor in the see of Limerick went to Theobald of

---

[1] On Gilbert's relations with Anselm see Lanigan, *Eccles. Hist. Ireland*, vol.
iv. pp. 23-26.   [2] *Ib.* pp. 26-29.   [3] *Ib.* pp. 38, 40-43.
[4] For S. Malachi see his *Life* by S. Bernard, and Lanigan, as above, pp. 59 *et seq.*
[5] S. Bern., *Vita S. Malach.*, c. 14 (Mabillon, vol. i. cols. 671-672).
[6] *Ib.* c. 15 (col. 672).
[7] *Ibid.* Cf. Lanigan's note, *Eccles. Hist. Ireland*, vol. iv. pp. 110, 111.
[8] S. Bern., *Vita S. Malach.*, c. 16 (as above, col. 674). Lanigan, as above,
p. 112.

Canterbury for consecration ; but his profession of obedience was the last ever made by an Irish bishop to an English metropolitan.[1]   In 1148 a synod held at Inispatrick by Archbishop Gelasius of Armagh, with Malachi as papal legate, decided upon sending Malachi himself to the Pope once more, charged with a formal request for the two palls, in the name of the whole Irish Church.   Malachi died on the way, at Clairvaux ;[2] but he left his commission in safe hands.   Nine years before, when on his first journey to Rome he had passed through the "bright valley," its abbot had recognized in him a kindred spirit.[3]   From that moment S. Bernard's care of all the churches extended itself even to the far-off Church of Ireland ; and if it was not he who actually forwarded his dying friend's petition to Eugene III., there can be little doubt that Eugene's favourable reception of it was chiefly owing to his influence.   The result was the mission of John Paparo as special legate to Ireland.   Stephen's refusal to let John pass through his dominions caused another year's delay ;[4] but at the close of 1151 John made his way through Scotland safe to his destination.[5]   In March 1152 he held a synod at Kells, in which the diocesan and provincial system of the Irish Church was organized upon lines which remained unaltered till the sixteenth century.   The episcopal sees were definitely fixed, and grouped under not two but four archbishoprics.   The primacy of all Ireland, with metropolitical authority over Ulster and Meath, was assigned to Armagh ; Tuam became the metropolis of Connaught, Cashel of Munster ; while the rivalry of Armagh and Canterbury for the spiritual obedience of the Ostmen was settled by the grant of a fourth pallium, with metropolitical jurisdiction over the whole of Leinster, to Bishop Gregory of Dublin himself.[6]

---

[1] Lanigan, *Eccles. Hist. Ireland*, vol. iv. pp. 114, 115, 116.

[2] S. Bern., *Vita S. Malach.*, cc. 30, 31 (Mabillon, vol. i. cols. 687-692). Lanigan, as above, pp. 129, 130.

[3] S. Bern., *Vita S. Malach.*, c. 16 (as above, cols. 673, 674).

[4] See above, vol. i. p. 380.

[5] Four Masters, a. 1151 (O'Donovan, vol. ii. p. 1095).

[6] On the synod of Kells see Four Masters, a. 1152 (as above, p. 1101) ; Rog. Howden (Stubbs), vol. i. p. 212 ; and Lanigan, as above, pp. 139-151.

It is plain that Bernard and Eugene aimed at applying to Ireland's troubles the same remedy which they were at that very time applying to those of England. They hoped to build up an united nation and a strong national government on the basis of a free and united national Church. But the foundation-stone of their work for Ireland was scarcely laid at Kells when both the wise master-builders were called away. On the other hand, their labours for England were crowned by the accession of the young Angevin king, whose restless temper, before he had been nine months on his throne, was already seeking for another sphere of activity still further beyond the sea ; overwhelming the newly-crowned, English-born Pope with suggestions of work and offers of co-operation in every quarter of Christendom,[1] and proposing to begin at once with the reduction of Ireland to political, ecclesiastical and social order after the pattern of England and Normandy.[2] Adrian IV. would have needed a wisdom and a foresight greater than those of S. Bernard himself to enable him to resist the attractions of such an offer. The so-called " Donation of Constantine "— a donation which is now known to be forged, but whose genuineness no one in Adrian's day had ever thought of doubting—vested the ultimate sovereignty of all islands in the Papacy.[3] The best and greatest Popes, from S. Gregory down to Adrian himself, seem to have interpreted this as making them in a special way responsible for the welfare of such outlying portions of Christendom, and bound to leave no means untried for providing them with a secure and orderly Christian government.[4] The action of Alexander II.

---

[1] Pet. Blois, Ep. clxviii. (Giles, vol. ii. pp. 116-118). See above, vol. i. p. 497.

[2] " Significâsti siquidem nobis, fili in Christo carissime, te Hiberniæ insulam, ad subdendum illum populum legibus et vitiorum plantaria inde exstirpanda, velle intrare ; et de singulis domibus annuam unius denarii beato Petro velle solvere pensionem ; et jura ecclesiarum illius terræ illibata et integra conservare." Bull of Adrian IV. to Henry ("Laudabiliter "), in Gir. Cambr. *Expugn. Hibern.*, l. ii. c. 5 (Dimock, vol. v. p. 317), etc.

[3] "Nam omnes insulæ, de jure antiquo, ex donatione Constantini qui eam fundavit et dotavit, dicuntur ad Romanam ecclesiam pertinere." Joh. Salisb. *Metalog.*, l. iv. c. 42 (Giles, vol. v. p. 206).

[4] " Sane Hiberniam et omnes insulas, quibus sol justitiæ Christus illuxit, et quæ documenta fidei Christianæ ceperunt, ad jus beati Petri et sacrosanctæ Romanæ ecclesiæ, quod tua etiam nobilitas recognoscit, non est dubium pertinere.

in sanctioning the Norman conquest of England was a
logical outcome of this principle, applied, however unwisely
or unjustly, to a particular case.   But there was infinitely
greater justification for applying the same principle, in the
same manner, to the case of Ireland.   Neither the labours
of S. Malachi, nor the brief visit of John Paparo, nor the
stringent decrees passed at the synod of Kells, could suffice
to reform the inveterate evils of Ireland's ecclesiastical system,
the yet more inveterate evils of her political system, or the
intellectual and moral decay which was the unavoidable
consequence of both.   On the Pope, according to the view
of the time, lay the responsibility of bringing order out of
this chaos—a chaos of whose very existence he had but just
become fully conscious, and which no doubt looked to him
far more hopeless than it really was.   In such circumstances
Henry's proposal must have sounded to Adrian like an offer
to relieve him of a great weight of care—to cut at one stroke
a knot which he was powerless to untie—to clear a path for
him through a jungle-growth of difficulties which he himself
saw no way to penetrate or overcome.   John of Salisbury
set forth the plan at Rome, in Henry's name, in the summer
of 1155 ; he carried back a bull which satisfied all Henry's
demands.   Adrian bade the king go forth to his conquest
" for the enlargement of the Church's borders, for the restraint
of vice, the correction of morals and the planting of virtue,
the increase of the Christian religion, and whatsoever may
tend to God's glory and the well-being of that land ;"[1] and
he sent with the bull a gold ring, adorned with an emerald
of great price, as a symbol of investiture with the government
of Ireland.[2]

Unde tanto in eis libentius plantationem fidelem et germen gratum Deo inserimus
quanto id a nobis interno examine districtius prospicimus exigendum." Bull
"Laudabiliter," Gir. Cambr. *Expugn. Hibern.*, l. ii. c. 5 (Dimock, vol. v. p. 317).

[1] Bull "Laudabiliter," Gir. Cambr. *Expugn. Hibern.*, l. ii. c. 5 (Dimock, vol.
v. pp. 317, 318); R. Diceto (Stubbs), vol. i. pp. 300, 301 ; Pet. Blois, Ep.
ccxxxi. (Giles, vol. ii. pp. 201, 202) ; Rymer, *Fœdera*, vol. i. p. 19; etc.   Its
authenticity has been fiercely disputed, but is now admitted by all Irish scholars.
See proofs in Lanigan, *Eccles. Hist. Ireland*, vol. iv. pp. 165, 166, and
O'Callaghan's edition of *Macariæ Excidium* (Irish Archæol. Soc.), pp. 242, 245,
where it is reprinted from Baronius's copy, found by him in the Vatican archives.

[2] Joh. Salisb. *Metalog.*, l. iv. c. 42 (Giles, vol. v. p. 206).

This strange crusade was postponed for the moment, as we have seen, in deference to objections made by the Empress Matilda.[1]   Adrian's bull and ring were stored up in the English chancery, and there, long after Adrian was dead, they still lay,[2] unused and, as it seemed, forgotten amid an ever-increasing throng of more urgent cares and labours which even Henry found to be quite as much as he was capable of sustaining. At last, however, the course of political events in Ireland itself took a turn which led almost irresistibly to a revival of his long-forsaken project.   Two years before Henry's accession Dermot Mac-Murrough, king of Leinster, had made a raid upon the district of Breffny in Connaught, on the borders of Ulster and Meath, and carried off Dervorgil, the wife of its chieftain Tighernan O'Ruark.[3] From that hour Tighernan's vengeance never slept.   During the next fourteen years, while Murtogh O'Lochlainn was striving for the mastery first against the veteran Terence O'Conor and after Terence's death with his son Rory or Roderic, the swords of the men of Breffny were thrown alternately into either scale, as their chieftain saw a hope of securing the aid of either monarch to avenge him of his enemy.[4]

---

[1] Rob. Torigni, a. 1155.   See above, vol. i. p. 431.

[2] Joh. Salisb. *Metalog.*, l. iv. c. 42 (Giles, vol. v. p. 206).

[3] Four Masters, a. 1152 (O'Donovan, vol. ii. p. 1103).   Cf. Gir. Cambr., *Expugn. Hibern.*, l. i. c. 1 (Dimock, vol. v. pp. 225, 226), and the elaborately romantic account in the Anglo-Norman Poem on the Conquest of Ireland, edited by M. Francisque Michel, pp. 2-6.   The two last-named authorities represent this affair as the *immediate* cause of Dermot's overthrow, and of all the consequent troubles.   Chronology shews this to be mere romance ; yet, notwithstanding the criticisms of some modern writers, there still seems to be some ground for the earlier view which looked upon Dervorgil as a sort of Irish Helen.   If we follow carefully the thread of the story in the Four Masters from 1153 to 1166 we can hardly avoid the conclusion that throughout those years the most important personage in Irish politics, the man whose action turned the scale in nearly all the ups and downs of fortune between Murtogh of Ulster and the kings of Connaught, was the border-chieftain whose position made him the most dangerous of foes and the most indispensable of allies—Tighernan O'Ruark ; and we can hardly help seeing in Dermot's banishment the vengeance less of Roderic O'Conor himself than of a supporter whom Roderic could not afford to leave unsatisfied.   On the other hand, it is perfectly true that the opportunity for executing that vengeance was given by the disaffection of Dermot's own subjects—and, as usual, more especially by the rising of the Ostmen of Dublin.

[4] See Four Masters, a. 1153-1166 (as above, pp. 1107-1159).

In 1166 the crisis came. Murtogh drew upon himself
the wrath of his people by blinding the king of Uladh,
for whose safety he was pledged to the archbishop of
Armagh ; Ulster, Meath, Leinster and Dublin rose against
him all at once ; he was defeated and slain in a great
battle at the Fews ; the Ostmen of Dublin acknowledged
Roderic as their king, and all the princes of southern
Ireland followed their example. Dermot's submission, however, was in vain ; the first act of the new monarch was to
banish him from the realm.[1] The Leinstermen forsook him
at once, for their loyalty had long been alienated by his
harsh government and evil deeds.[2] Left alone to the justice
of Roderic and the vengeance of O'Ruark, he fled to Cork
and thence took ship to Bristol. Here he found shelter for
a while in the priory of S. Augustine, under the protection
of its founder Robert Fitz-Harding ;[3] at the close of the
year he made his way to Normandy, and thence, with some
difficulty, tracked Henry's restless movements into the
depths of Aquitaine,[4] where he at last laid his appeal for
succour at the feet of the English king.

At the crisis of his struggles with Thomas of Canterbury,
with Louis of France and with the rebel barons of Poitou,
all that Henry could do was to accept Dermot's offer of

---

[1] Four Masters, a. 1166 (O'Donovan, vol. ii. p. 1159-1163).

[2] Gir. Cambr. *Expugn. Hibern.*, l. i. c. 1 (Dimock, vol. v. pp. 225, 226).
For specimens of his misdeeds see Four Masters, a. 1141 (as above, p. 1065),
and Ann. Clonmacnoise, a. 1135 (*ib.* p. 1051, note *f*).

[3] Anglo-Norm. Poem (Michel), p. 12.

[4] "In remotis et transmarinis Aquitannicæ Galliæ partibus." Gir. Cambr.
as above (p. 227). Henry was in Aquitaine from December 1166 till May 1167 ;
see Eyton, *Itin. Hen. II.*, pp. 103-106. The chase which he characteristically led
the Irish king is amusingly described in the Anglo-Norm. Poem (Michel), p. 13 :
> " Bien est, seignurs, ke jo vus die
> Cum Dermod va par Normandie ;
> Li rei Henri va dunc quere,
> A munt, à val, avant, arere ;
> Tant ad mandé et enquis
> Que trové ad li rei Henris,
> A une cité l'ad trové,
> Que seignur esteit clamé."

On the last line the editor (notes, p. 168) remarks : "*Seignur* (seigñ, MS.) ? Is
it not : of which he was called lord ?" One feels tempted to suggest that it might
be meant for the name of the place ; but if so, what can it be ? Saintes ?

homage and fealty,[1] promise to send him help as soon as possible,[2] and furnish him with a letter authorizing any loyal English, Norman, Welsh, Scottish or Angevin subjects who might be so disposed to join the standard of the Irish prince, as of a faithful vassal of their sovereign.[3]   Another stay of some weeks ĩn Bristol[4] convinced Dermot that his best chance of aid lay beyond the Severn.   Wales was still in the main a Celtic land, ruled in primeval Celtic fashion by native princes under little more that nominal subjection to the king of England.   The Norman conquest of Wales, so far as Wales could be said to have been conquered at all, had been effected not by the royal power but by the daring and prowess of individual adventurers who did, indeed, seek the royal sanction for their tenure of the lands which they had won, but who were scarcely more amenable to the royal authority than their Welsh neighbours, with whom they not unfrequently made common cause against it.   It was Robert of Bellême's connexion with Wales, through his border-earldom of Shrewsbury and his brother's lordship of Pem-broke, which had made him so formidable to Henry I.; it was Robert of Gloucester's tenure of the great Welsh lord-ship of Glamorgan, even more than his English honours, which had enabled him to act as an independent potentate against Stephen.   Another border-chieftain who played some part in the civil war was Gilbert de Clare, whose father had received a grant of Cardigan from Henry I. in 1107,[5] and upon whom Stephen in 1138 conferred the title of earl of Pembroke.[6]   His son Richard appears under the same title among the witnesses to Stephen's proclamation of the treaty of Wallingford in 1153 ;[7] the writers of the time, however,

---

[1] Gir. Cambr. *Expugn. Hibern.*, l. i. c. 1 (Dimock, vol. v. p. 227).   Anglo-Norm. Poem (Michel), p. 15.   [2] Anglo-Norm. Poem, as above.

[3] Gir. Cambr. as above (pp. 227, 228).

[4] *Ib.* c. 2 (p. 228).   He was at Bristol "quinzein u un meins"; Anglo-Norm. Poem (Michel), p. 16.   [5] *Brut y Tywys.*, a. 1107 (Williams, p. 105).

[6] Ord. Vit. (Duchesne, *Hist. Norm. Scriptt.*), p. 917.

[7] Rymer, *Fœdera*, vol. i. p. 18.   Richard de Clare became known to later generations by the nickname of " Strongbow."   Its use is convenient, as helping to avoid confusion with the other Richards of the period ; but it seems to have no contemporary authority.   See Mr. Dimock's note, *Gir. Cambr.*, vol. v. p. 228, note 4.

usually describe him as earl of Striguil, a fortress which
seems to have occupied the site whence the ruins of Chepstow
castle now look down upon the Wye. His earldom of
Pembroke, indeed, as one of Stephen's fictitious creations,
must have been forfeited on Henry's accession ; but the lord
of Striguil was still a mighty man on the South-Welsh border
when in the spring of 1167 he promised to bring all the
forces which he could muster to aid in restoring Dermot,
who in return offered him his daughter's hand, together with
the succession to his kingdom.[1] A promise of the town of
Wexford and its adjoining territory won a like assurance of
aid from two half-brothers in whose veins the blood of
Norman adventurers was mingled with the ancient royal
blood of South-Wales : Maurice Fitz-Gerald, a son of Gerald
constable of Pembroke by his marriage with Nest, aunt of
the reigning prince Rees Ap-Griffith, and Robert Fitz-
Stephen, son of the same Nest by her second husband,
Stephen constable of Cardigan.[2] Another Pembrokeshire
knight, Richard Fitz-Godoberd, volunteered to accompany
Dermot at once with a little band of Norman-Welsh
followers.[3] With these Dermot returned to Ireland in
August 1167 ;[4] he was defeated in a pitched battle with
Roderic O'Conor and Tighernan O'Ruark ;[5] but in his own

---

[1] Gir. Cambr. *Expugn. Hibern.*, l. i. c. 2 (Dimock, vol. v. p. 228). Anglo-
Norm. Poem (Michel), p. 17.

[2] Gir. Cambr. as above (p. 229). The circumstances of Fitz-Stephen's enlist-
ment illustrate the condition of South-Wales at this time. He had been cast into
prison three years before by his cousin Rees, and at the moment of Dermot's
arrival had just been released on condition of joining Rees in an attack upon
England. His Norman blood, however, was loyal enough to revolt against the
fulfilment of the condition ; and Rees, who had warmly espoused Dermot's
interest, was persuaded to allow its exchange for service in Ireland. *Ibid.*; cf.
Anglo-Norm. Poem (Michel), pp. 19, 20. For pedigree of Nest's descendants see
Mr. Dimock's edition of *Gir. Cambr. Opp.*, vol. v. App. B. to pref., pp. c, ci.

[3] Anglo-Norm. Poem (Michel), p. 21.

[4] About August 1, according to Gir. Cambr. *Expugn. Hibern.*, l. i. c. 2
(Dimock, vol. v. p. 229).

[5] Four Masters, a. 1167 (O'Donovan, vol. ii. pp. 1165-1167). Among the
slain they mention "the son of the king of Britain, who was the battle-prop of the
island of Britain, who had come across the sea in the army of Mac Murchadha."
This can only mean a son or brother of Rees ; but neither Gerald nor the Welsh
chronicles make any mention of such a person in Ireland.

hereditary principality of Kinsellagh[1] he was safe; there throughout the winter he lay hid at Ferns,[2] and thence, when spring returned, he sent his bard Maurice Regan to claim from his Welsh allies the fulfilment of their promises.[3]

In the first days of May[4] Robert Fitz-Stephen landed at Bannow, between Wexford and Waterford, with thirty picked knights of his own immediate following, and a body of auxiliaries to the number of sixty men-at-arms and three hundred archers.[5] With him came three of his nephews, Meiler Fitz-Henry, Miles Fitz-David[6] and Robert de Barri ;[7] and also a ruined knight called Hervey of Mountmorris, uncle of Richard de Clare.[8] Next day an independent ad-

---

[1] The modern county of Wexford, or rather the diocese of Ferns. The Four Masters (as above, p. 1165) say that Dermot "returned from England with a force of Galls, and he took the kingdom of Ui-Ceinnsealaigh."

[2] Gir. Cambr. *Expugn. Hibern.*, l. i. c. 2 (Dimock, vol. v. p. 230).

[3] Anglo-Norm. Poem (Michel), p. 21.

[4] Gir. Cambr. *Expugn. Hibern.*, l. i. c. 3 (as above). All the later Irish historians, as well as Lord Lyttelton and Mr. Dimock (*ib.* margin) date the arrival of Fitz Stephen in May 1169. The reason apparently is that, as far as Dermot and his English auxiliaries are concerned, the year 1168 is a blank in the Four Masters, while under 1169 they say : "The fleet of the Flemings came from England in the army of Mac Murchadha, *i.e.* Diarmaid, to contest the kingdom of Leinster for him ; they were seventy heroes clad in coats of mail." But seeing that in the following year, 1170, they for the first time mention Robert Fitz-Stephen, and represent him as coming over with Richard of Striguil (O'Donovan, vol. ii. pp. 1173-1175), it is by no means evident that the foregoing entry has any reference to him. It may just as well apply to Maurice Fitz-Gerald, who certainly followed him after an interval of some months at least. Gerald (as above, c. 2, p. 229) says that Fitz-Stephen and Fitz-Gerald both promised, in the summer of 1167, to join Dermot "cum zephyris et hirundine primâ." Maurice undoubtedly made a long delay ; but there is not a word to shew that Robert did otherwise than fulfil his engagement to the letter. Nay, Gerald pointedly introduces him (*ib.* c. 3, p. 230) as "nec promissionis immemor nec fidei contemptor." He also tells us (c. 2, *ibid.*) that Dermot had *wintered* at Ferns. Why then are we to assume that by "wintered" he means "wintered, summered, and wintered again"? What could Dermot possibly have been doing there for more than twenty months?

[5] Gir. Cambr. as above, c. 3 (p. 230). For account of Fitz-Stephen himself see *ib.* c. 26 (pp. 271, 272).

[6] Anglo - Norm. Poem (Michel), p. 22. On Meiler see Gir. Cambr. as above, l. ii. c. 9 (pp. 324, 325) ; and for pedigree, Mr. Dimock's App. B. to pref. (*ib.* pp. c., ci.).

[7] Gir. Cambr. as above, l. i. c. 3 (Dimock, vol. v. p. 232). Cf. App. B. to pref., *ib.* p. c.

[8] Gir. Cambr. as above, l. i. c. 3 (p. 230). See also l. ii. c. 11 (pp. 327, 328).

venturer, Maurice de Prendergast, arrived from Milford with ten more knights and a band of archers.[1] Dermot himself came to meet them with some five hundred Irishmen. The united force marched upon Wexford, and took it in two days ;[2] they then established their head-quarters at Ferns,[3] and thence made an expedition into Ossory, whose chieftain was specially hostile to Dermot. In spite of overwhelming odds, through all the difficulties of an unknown country full of woods and marshes, and traps laid against them by their skilful foes, the Norman-Welsh knights and archers made their way into the heart of Ossory ; and a great battle ended in the rout of the Irish and the bringing of two hundred heads to Dermot's feet in his camp on the banks of the Barrow.[4] A successful raid upon Offaly was followed by one upon Glendalough, and a third upon Ossory again,[5] till in the following year the state of affairs in Leinster had become threatening enough to drive all the Irish princes and the Ostmen of Dublin into a confederacy under Roderic O'Conor for the expulsion of the intruders.[6] Dermot pledged himself to acknowledge Roderic as monarch of Ireland, and was in his turn acknowledged by Roderic as king of Leinster on condition that he should dismiss his foreign allies.[7] The agreement was however scarcely made when Maurice Fitz-Gerald landed at Wexford with some hundred and forty men ;[8] these at once joined Dermot in an expedition against Dublin, and harried the surrounding country till the citizens were reduced to promise obedience.[9] Early in the next year Dermot's son-in-law Donell

---

[1] Gir. Cambr. *Expugn. Hibern.*, l. i. c. 3 (Dimock, vol. v. p. 232).

[2] *Ibid.* (pp. 232, 233). Anglo-Norm. Poem (Michel), pp. 24, 25.

[3] Anglo-Norm. Poem (Michel), pp. 25, 26.

[4] Gir. Cambr. as above, c. 4 (p. 234). Cf. the long account in Anglo-Norm. Poem (Michel), pp. 27-38.   [5] Anglo-Norm. Poem (Michel), pp. 42-51.

[6] Roderic, in 1169, met the northern chieftains at Tara, thence marched to Dublin, and afterwards proceeded into Leinster ; and Tighernan O'Ruark, Dermot king of Meath, and the Ostmen of Dublin " went to meet the men of Munster, Leinster and Osraigh " [Ossory], "and they set nothing by the Flemings." Four Masters, a. 1169 (O'Donovan, vol. ii. p. 1173).

[7] Gir. Cambr. as above, c. 10 (p. 244).

[8] Ten knights, thirty "arcarii" or mounted archers, and about a hundred "sagittarii pedestres." *Ib.* c. 11 (pp. 244, 245).   [9] *Ibid.* (p. 245).

O'Brien, king of Limerick or Northern Munster, succeeded by the help of Robert Fitz-Stephen in throwing off the authority of Roderick O'Conor.[1] Encouraged by these successes, Dermot now began to aspire in his turn to the monarchy of all Ireland ;[2] but his auxiliaries were numerically insufficient ; and the one from whom he had expected most had as yet failed to appear at all.

The history of Richard of Striguil is far from clear. From the number of, troops which eventually accompanied him to Ireland it is evident that he had been during these two years actively preparing for his expedition ; and it may even be that the extent of his preparations had drawn upon him the suspicions of King Henry. We only know that, for some cause or other, he was now a ruined man ; his lands were forfeited to the Crown ;[3] and he seems to have lingered on, absorbed in a desperate effort to regain Henry's favour, and clinging to his lost home with a feeling that if he once turned his back upon it, he would never be allowed to see it again. A letter from Dermot, telling of the successes of his party in Leinster and renewing his former offers, forced him into action.[4] He made a last appeal to the king, intreating either for restoration of his lands or for the royal license to go and repair his fortunes elsewhere. Henry ironically bade him go, and he went.[5] On S. Bartholomew's eve, 1170, he landed at Waterford with twelve

---

[1] Gir. Cambr. *Expugn. Hibern.*, l. i. c. 11 (Dimock, vol. v. p. 245). The date, 1170, comes from the Four Masters (O'Donovan, vol. ii. p. 1175), who however do not mention Fitz-Stephen's share in the matter.

[2] Gir. Cambr. as above, c. 12 (p. 246).

[3] The cause of Richard's disgrace seems to be nowhere stated, except by William of Newburgh. He has (l. ii. c. 26 ; Howlett, vol. i. pp. 167, 168), as usual, an independent version of the whole affair. According to him, Richard's chief motive for going to Ireland was to escape from his creditors, he being deep in debt ; he went in defiance of an express prohibition from Henry, and it was on hearing of his victories—*i.e.* some time in the latter part of 1170—that Henry confiscated his estates. Dugdale (*Baronage*, vol. i. p. 208) gives 1170 as the date of the forfeiture, on the authority of a MS. in the Bodleian library. But this is irreconcileable with the very circumstantial story of Gerald. Gerv. Cant. (Stubbs), vol. i. p. 234, dates the forfeiture three years before Henry's visit to Ireland, *i.e.* 1168.

[4] Gir. Cambr. *Expugn. Hibern.*, l. i. c. 12 (as above, pp. 246, 247).

[5] *Ib.* cc. 12, 13 (pp. 247, 248). Cf. Gerv. Cant. as above.

hundred men ;[1] next day he was joined by Raymond " the Fat," a young warrior whom he had sent over three months before[2] with ten knights and seventy archers, and who with this small force had contrived to beat back an assault of three thousand Irishmen of Decies and Ostmen of Waterford upon his camp of wattle and thatch, hastily thrown up on the rocky promontory of Dundonulf.[3]   On August 25 Richard and Raymond attacked Waterford ; three assaults in one day carried both town and citadel ;[4] seven hundred citizens were slaughtered,[5] and the officers of the fortress, whose names tell of northern blood, were made prisoners.[6]   A few days later Richard was married at Waterford to Dermot's daughter Eva.[7]   He then joined his father-in-law in a circuitous march across the hills and through Glendalough,[8] whereby they avoided a great host which Roderic had gathered at Clondalkin to intercept them, and arrived in safety on S. Matthew's day beneath the walls of Dublin.[9]   Dermot sent his bard to demand

---

[1] Gir. Cambr. *Expugn. Hibern.*, l. i. c. 16 (Dimock, vol. v. p. 254).   Anglo-Norm. Poem (Michel), p. 72.   The latter gives the number of troops as fifteen hundred ; Gerald makes them two hundred knights and a thousand foot-men.

[2] So says Gerald, as above, c. 13 (p. 248) ; but Mr. Dimock (*ib.* note 2) thinks this too early.

[3] *Ibid.* (pp. 248, 249).   There is however a less heroic version of this affair in the Anglo-Norman Poem (Michel), pp. 68-70.   We are there told that Raymond and his men had provided themselves with food by "lifting" all the cattle in the neighbourhood and penning them within the camp.   At the sound of arms these creatures rushed out in a wild stampede, and it was this which put the assailants to flight.   On the site of Dundonulf see Mr. Dimock's *Glossary* to Gir. Cambr., vol. v. p. 421.

[4] Gir. Cambr. as above, c. 16 (*ib.* pp. 254; 255).

[5] Four Masters, a. 1170 (O'Donovan, vol. ii. p. 1177).

[6] Ragnald and "the two Sihtrics"; Gir. Cambr. as above (p. 255).   The Four Masters (as above) give to the commandant of the citadel—which Gerald calls " Ragnald's tower "—the name of Gillemaire.   In the Anglo-Norm. Poem (Michel), p. 72, we read that "les plus poanz de la cité" were Regenald and " Smorch."

[7] Gir. Cambr. as above.   Anglo-Norm. Poem (Michel), p. 73.   Four Masters, a. 1170 (as above).

[8] Gir. Cambr. as above, c. 17 (p. 256).

[9] Anglo - Norm. Poem (Michel), pp. 75-78.   Cf. Gir. Cambr. and Four Masters as above.   The latter say that " there was a challenge of battle between them " (*i.e.* between Roderic and the foreigners) " for three days, until lightning burned Ath-Cliath " [Dublin].

the instant surrender of the town, with thirty hostages for its fidelity. A dispute arose, probably between the Irish and Danish inhabitants, as to the selection of the hostages ;[1] Archbishop Laurence was endeavouring to compose the difficulty,[2] and Hasculf Thorgils' son, a chieftain of northern blood who commanded the citadel, had actually promised to surrender it on the morrow,[3] when a sudden attack made by Raymond the Fat on one side and by a knight called Miles Cogan on the other carried the town before the leaders of either party knew what had happened.[4] A second rush won the citadel ; Hasculf escaped by sea and took refuge in the Orkneys ;[5] Dublin was sacked,[6] and left throughout the winter under the command of Miles Cogan,[7] while Richard of Striguil was guarding Waterford against the men of Munster,[8] and Dermot, from his old head-quarters at Ferns,[9] was making raid after raid upon Meath and Breffny.[10]

In vain did the Irish clergy meet in synod at Armagh and strive to avert the wrath which seemed to have been revealed against their country by a solemn decree for the liberation of the English slaves with whom, even yet, the houses of the Irish chieftains were filled.[11] One sentence from an Irish record of the next year may serve to illustrate the condition of the country : " Seven predatory excursions

---

[1] Anglo-Norm. Poem (Michel), pp. 79, 80.

[2] Gir. Cambr. *Expugn. Hibern.*, l. i. c. 17 (Dimock, vol. v. p. 256).

[3] Anglo-Norm. Poem (Michel), p. 80. He is there called "Hesculf"; in p. 79, "Mac Turkil Esculf." In the Four Masters, a. 1170 (O'Donovan, vol. ii. p. 1177), he is "Asgall, son of Raghnall, son of Turcaill." Gir. Cambr. (as above) calls him simply "Hasculphus."

[4] Gir. Cambr. as above (pp. 256, 257). Anglo-Norm. Poem (Michel), pp. 80, 81.

[5] Four Masters, as above. Gir. Cambr. as above (p. 257).

[6] Anglo-Norm. Poem (Michel), pp. 81, 82.

[7] Gir. Cambr. as above. Anglo-Norm. Poem (Michel), p. 82.

[8] "A victory was gained by the son of Cormac, grandson of Carthach, and the people of Desmond, over the knights who were left to defend Port Lairge " [*i.e.* Waterford]. Four Masters, as above. Earl Richard returned thither early in October ; Anglo-Norm. Poem (Michel), p. 82.

[9] Anglo-Norm. Poem (Michel), p. 83.

[10] Four Masters, a. 1170 (as above, pp. 1177, 1179).

[11] Gir. Cambr. as above, c. 18 (p. 258).

were made by the Ui-Maine into Ormond from Palm Sunday till Low Sunday."[1] It made but little difference when at Whitsuntide Dermot, "by whom a trembling sod was made of all Ireland," died at Ferns " of an insufferable and unknown disease—without a will, without penance, without the Body of Christ, without unction, as his evil deeds deserved."[2] At that very moment a Viking fleet gathered from all the lands where the old sea-rovers' life still lingered —Norway, the Hebrides, Orkney, Man—appeared in Dublin bay under the command of Hasculf, the exiled leader of the Ostmen, and of a northern chief whose desperate valour won him the title of "John the Furious"—in the English speech of that day, John the Wode.[3] Something of the spirit of the old northern sagas breathes again in the story of this, the last wiking-fight ever fought upon the soil of the British isles. Bard and historian alike tell of the mighty strokes dealt by the battle - axes of John and his comrades,[4] and how they had almost hewed their way into Dublin once more, when a well-timed sally of the besieged caught them at unawares in the rear ;[5]—how an Irish chief named Gillamocholmog, whom Miles Cogan had posted on a neighbouring hill, chivalrously bidding him watch the course of the battle and join the winning side, rushed down with his followers at the critical moment and helped to complete the rout of the Ostmen ;[6]—how John the Wode fell by the hand of Miles Cogan ;[7]—how Hasculf was taken prisoner by Miles's brother Richard and brought back to be reserved for ransom, and how his hot wiking-blood spoke in words of

[1] Four Masters, a. 1171 (O'Donovan, vol. ii. p. 1185). The Ui-Maine were a tribe in south-eastern Connaught.

[2] *Ibid.* (p. 1183). Cf. Ann. Loch Cé, a. 1171 (Hennessy, vol. i. p. 145). The date, " circa Kalendas Maiæ," is given by Gir. Cambr. *Expugn. Hibern.*, l. i. c. 20 (Dimock, vol. v. p. 263).

[3] " Duce Johanne agnomine the Wode," Gir. Cambr. as above, c. 21 (p. 264). "Johan le Devé," Anglo-Norm. Poem (Michel), p. 108. It is there added that, " solum les Yrreis," he was a nephew of the king of ": Norwiche," *i.e.* Norway. The Four Masters, a. 1171 (as above, p. 1185) describe him as "Eoan, a Dane from the Orkney Islands."

[4] Anglo-Norm. Poem (Michel), p. 116. Gir. Cambr. as above.

[5] Anglo-Norm. Poem (Michel), pp. 111-114. Gir. Cambr. as above.

[6] Anglo-Norm. Poem (Michel), pp. 109-111, 115.   [7] *Ib.* p. 117.

defiance which goaded his captors to strike off his head.[1]
Fifteen hundred northmen fell upon the field ; five hundred
more were drowned in trying to regain their ships.[2] From
the shores of Ireland, as from those of England, the last
northern fleet was driven away by Norman swords.

The garrison of Dublin fought in truth even more desperately than their assailants ; for they were fighting for
their all. A remonstrance addressed by some of the Irish
princes to the king of England against the aggressions of
his subjects [3] can hardly have been needed to open Henry's
eyes to the danger gathering for him and his realm beyond
the western sea. This little band of adventurers, almost all
bound together by the closest ties of kindred,[4] were conquering Leinster neither for its native sovereign nor for their
own, but were setting up a new feudal state independent of
all royal control, under the leadership of a disgraced English
baron. Such a state, if suffered to grow unhindered, would
soon be far more dangerous to England than to Ireland, for
it would be certain to play in every struggle of the feudal
principle against the royal authority in England the part
which the Ostmen had played of old in the struggles of the
Danelaw. At the beginning of the year 1171 therefore
Henry issued an edict prohibiting all further intermeddling

---

[1] Anglo-Norm. Poem (Michel), pp. 117, 118. (On his captor cf. *ib*. p. 111).
Gir. Cambr. *Expugn. Hibern.*, l. i. c. 21 (Dimock, vol. v. pp. 264, 265).

[2] Anglo-Norm. Poem (Michel), pp. 116, 118. The date of this siege is given
by Gir. Cambr. (as above, p. 263) as "eâdem fere tempestate " (*i.e.* about the
time of Dermot's death), "circa Pentecosten." This would be at the beginning
of May. In the Poem it comes much later in the year. There seems however
no reason to upset Gerald's arrangement of events. See Mr. Dimock's remarks,
Gir. Cambr. as above, note 2.

[3] Gerv. Cant. (Stubbs), vol. i. pp. 234, 235.

[4] The close kindred of these Norman-Welsh settlers in Ireland is a very
remarkable feature of their settlement. Robert Fitz-Stephen and Maurice
Fitz-Gerald were half-brothers (Gir. Cambr. as above, c. 2, p. 229); the
two Fitz-Henrys, Raymond the Fat, Miles Fitz-David and Robert de Barri
were their nephews (*ib*. cc. 4, 13, and l. ii. c. 10, pp. 234, 248, 335); Richard
of Striguil was nephew to Hervey of Mountmorris (*ib*. l. i. c. 3, p. 230), who
afterwards married a daughter of Maurice Fitz-Gerald, while Maurice's eldest son
married Richard's daughter Alina (*ib*. l. ii. c. 4, p. 314) ; another daughter of
Richard married his constable Robert de Quincy (Anglo-Norm. Poem, Michel,
p. 130) ; and his sister Basilea became the wife of Raymond the Fat (*ib*. p. 145,
and Gir. Cambr. as above, l. ii. c. 3, pp. 312, 313).

of his subjects in Ireland, and bidding those who were already there either return before Easter or consider themselves banished for life.[1]   Not a man went back; Richard of Striguil sent Raymond over to Normandy with a written protest to the king, pleading that his conquests had been undertaken with the royal sanction and that he was ready to place them at the king's disposal ;[2] but the "Geraldines," as the kindred of Maurice Fitz-Gerald called themselves, seem to have at once accepted their sentence of exile and resolved to hold by their swords alone the lands which those swords had won.[3]

The hostility of the Ostmen had apparently ended with Hasculf's defeat ; thenceforth they seem to have made common cause with the new-comers in whom they were perhaps already beginning to recognize the stirrings of kindred blood.   But, on the other hand, the position of Earl Richard and his comrades had been seriously weakened by Dermot's death.   The king of Leinster's devise of his kingdom to his son-in-law was, like the grants which he had made to the Geraldines and like his own homage to King Henry, void in Irish law.   In Irish eyes his death removed the last shadow of excuse for the presence of the strangers on Irish soil ; their allies rapidly fell away ;[4] and by midsummer the whole country rose against them as one man. Roderic O'Conor mustered the forces of the north ; Archbishop Laurence of Dublin, whose family occupied an influential position in Leinster, called up the tribes of the south ; while a squadron of thirty ships was hired from Jarl Godred of Man.[5]   The aim of the expedition was to

---

[1] Gir. Cambr. *Expugn. Hibern.*, l. i. c. 19 (Dimock, vol. v. p. 259).

[2] *Ibid.* Cf. Gerv. Cant. (Stubbs), vol. i. p. 235.   Raymond was back again in time to share in the defence of Dublin against Roderic O'Conor—*i.e.* by the end of May or beginning of June.   Gerald says he had to seek the king in "Aquitanic Gaul," but this time the phrase cannot be taken literally.   Eyton's *Itinerary* shews plainly that throughout 1171 Henry never was further south than the Norman, or, at the utmost, the Breton border.

[3] This seems to be the key-note of a speech which Gerald puts into Maurice's mouth ; *Expugn. Hibern.*, l. i. c. 23 (as above, pp. 266, 267).

[4] Anglo-Norm. Poem (Michel), p. 83.

[5] Gir. Cambr. as above, cc. 22, 24 (pp. 265, 266, 269).   This is the archbishop afterwards canonized as S. Laurence O'Toole.

blockade Dublin, whither Earl Richard had now returned,
and where almost all the leaders of the invasion, except
Robert Fitz-Stephen and Hervey of Mountmorris, were now
gathered together.   The whole Irish land-force amounted to
sixty thousand men; half of these were under the immediate
command of Roderic, encamped at Castle-Knock ;[1] Mac-Dun-
levy, the chieftain of Uladh, planted his banner on the old
battle-field of Clontarf ;[2] Donell O'Brien, the king of North
Munster, posted himself at Kilmainham ; and Murtogh Mac-
Murrough, a brother of Dermot, whom Roderic had set up as
king of Leinster in 1167, took up his position at Dalkey.[3]
To these were added, for the northern division, the men of
Breffny and of East Meath under Tighernan O'Ruark, those
of Oiriel or southern Ulster under Murtogh O'Carroll,[4] and
those of West Meath under Murtogh O'Melaghlin; while the
archbishop's call had brought up the whole strength of
Leinster except the men of Wexford and Kinsellagh ;[5] and
even these, as the sequel proved, were preparing to fight the
same battle on other ground.

For nearly two months[6] the English knights were thus
blockaded in Dublin.   Their sole hope of relief was in
Robert Fitz-Stephen, who had been left in command at
Wexford.   They were all but starving when Donell
Kavanagh, a half-brother of Eva Mac-Murrough and a
devoted adherent of her husband, slipped into the city with
tidings that Wexford had risen ; Robert Fitz-Stephen was
blockaded in the little fort of Carrick by the townsfolk and
the men of Kinsellagh, to the number of three thousand ;
unless he could be succoured within three days, all would be
over with him and his men.[7]   Earl Richard at once called

---

[1] Cf. Anglo - Norm. Poem (Michel), p. 84, with Gerald's reckoning of
Roderic's own forces at thirty thousand. *Expugn. Hibern.*, l. i. c. 24 (Dimock,
vol. v. p. 268).

[2] " A Clontarf ficha sa banere." Anglo-Norm. Poem, as above.   [3] *Ibid.*

[4] Four Masters, a. 1171 (O'Donovan, vol. ii. p. 1185).   Gir. Cambr. *Expugn.
Hibern.*, l. i. c. 24 (Dimock, vol. v. p. 269).   [5] Gir. Cambr. as above.

[6] *Ib.* c. 22 (p. 266).   This would bring the beginning of the siege to Midsummer at latest, for it was certainly over by the middle of August.   The Four
Masters (as above) make it last only a fortnight.

[7] Gir. Cambr. as above.   The Anglo-Norm. Poem (Michel), pp. 85, 86, gives
a very hasty and confused sketch of this Wexford affair.

a council of war.   It comprised nearly all the leaders of the
English and Welsh forces in Ireland :—Richard of Striguil
himself; Maurice Fitz - Gerald with three of his gallant
nephews, Meiler Fitz-Henry, Miles Fitz-David and Raymond
the Fat ; Miles Cogan, the captor of Dublin and its chief
defender in the recent siege ; Maurice de Prendergast,[1] who
two years before had thrown up the adventure and gone
home in disgust at the faithlessness of his allies,[2] but had
returned, it seems, in Earl Richard's train, and was yet
to leave, alone of all the invading band, an honoured memory
among the Irish people ;[3] and some fourteen others.[4]   They
decided upon sending Maurice de Prendergast and Archbishop
Laurence to Roderic with an offer of surrender on condition
that Richard of Striguil should hold the kingdom of
Leinster under Roderic as overlord.   Roderic rejected the
proposal with scorn ; the knights might hold what the
earlier pirates had held—Dublin, Waterford and Wexford ;
not another rood of Irish land should be granted to the earl
and his company ; and if they refused these terms, Dublin
should be stormed on the morrow.[5]   That afternoon the
little garrison—scarce six hundred in all [6]—sallied forth and
surprized Roderic's camp while he and his men were bathing ;
Roderic himself escaped with great difficulty; fifteen hundred
Irishmen were slain, many of them perishing in the water ;

---

[1] Earl Richard, Meiler, the two Mileses and Maurice Prendergast are mentioned in the Anglo-Norm. Poem (Michel), pp. 86, 87.   Raymond is named by
Gerald, *Expugn. Hibern.*, l. i. c. 22 (Dimock, vol. v. p. 266), as "a curiâ jam
reversus " ; his presence also appears later in the Poem.   Gerald alone mentions
the presence of Maurice Fitz-Gerald, whom the Poem never names throughout the
siege ; while Gerald never names Maurice de Prendergast.   Is it possible that he
has transferred to his own uncle the exploits of his namesake?   But if so, where
can Fitz-Gerald have been ?

[2] Anglo-Norm. Poem (Michel), pp. 51-67.   [3] *Ib.* pp. 97-103.

[4] The Poem (as above), p. 87, reckons them at twenty in all, and names four
besides those already mentioned, viz., Robert de Quincy, Walter de Riddlesford,
Richard de Marreis and Walter Bluet.

[5] Anglo-Norm. Poem (Michel), pp. 87-90.

[6] The Anglo-Norm. Poem (Michel), pp. 90, 91, describes the force as composed of three divisions, each consisting of forty knights, sixty archers and a
hundred "serjanz."   Gir. Cambr. as above, c. 24 (p. 268), makes the three bands
of knights contain respectively twenty, thirty and forty, each accompanied by as
many archers and citizens as could be spared from guarding the walls.

while at sunset the victors returned, after a long pursuit, with scarcely a man missing, and laden with provisions enough to supply all Dublin for a year.[1] The rest of the besieging army dispersed at once, and the very next morning Earl Richard was free to set out for the relief of Robert Fitz-Stephen.[2]

He was however already too late. Three thousand men of Wexford and Kinsellagh, finding that they could make no impression by fair means upon Robert Fitz-Stephen shut up in the fort of Carrick with five knights and a handful of archers, at length had recourse to fraud. Two bishops and some monks were made to stand under the walls of the fort and swear upon relics brought for the purpose that Dublin was taken, the earl and his comrades slain, and Roderic on the march to Wexford at the head of his victorious host. On a promise of liberty to escape to Wales[3] Robert in his despair surrendered, only to see his little band of humbler followers slaughtered to a man, and himself and his five knights cast into chains. The men of Wexford then fired their town and took refuge with their captives on the neighbouring island of Beg-Erin,[4] whence they sent word to Richard of Striguil that if he dared to approach them he should immediately receive the heads of his six friends.[5] Notwithstanding this disaster at Wexford, and the failure of a plot to entrap the chief of Ossory—a well-deserved failure, due to the loyalty of Maurice de Prendergast[6]—the invaders were rapidly gaining ground. The king of North Munster, who was married to Eva's sister, again forsook Roderic and made alliance with his English brother-in-law;[7] an attempt made by Tighernan O'Ruark to renew the siege of Dublin ended in failure;[8] and at last Murtogh of Kinsellagh

---

[1] Gir. Cambr. *Expugn. Hibern.*, l. i. c. 24 (Dimock, vol. v. pp. 268, 269).
Anglo-Norm. Poem (Michel), pp. 90-94. Cf. the brief account in Four Masters,
a. 1171 (O'Donovan, vol. ii. p. 1185).

[2] Gir. Cambr. as above (pp. 269, 270). Anglo-Norm. Poem (Michel), p. 95.

[3] Gir. Cambr. as above, c. 25 (pp. 270, 271).

[4] *Ibid.* (p. 271). Anglo-Norm. Poem (Michel), pp. 85, 97.

[5] Gir. Cambr. as above, c. 28 (p. 273).

[6] See the story in Anglo-Norm. Poem (Michel), pp. 97-103.

[7] *Ib.* pp. 97, 98.

[8] Four Masters, a. 1171 (as above, pp. 1185-1187). Gir. Cambr. as above,
c. 29 (p. 274).

was reduced to make a surrender of his principality into
Richard's hands and accept a re-grant of it from him as
overlord, while Donell Kavanagh was invested on like
terms with the remaining portion of Leinster.[1]

The earl's triumphs, however, met with an abrupt check
from over sea. His uncle Hervey of Mountmorris, who had
gone to plead his cause with the king after the failure of
Raymond's mission, returned to Waterford[2] with tidings that
Henry himself was on his way to Ireland and required the
self-styled earl of Leinster to go and speak with him without
delay. Richard hurried over to Wales,[3] met Henry on the
border,[4] and was forgiven on condition that he should surrender Dublin and the other coast towns absolutely into the
king's hands and do him homage and fealty for the rest of
Leinster;[5] he then accompanied Henry into Pembrokeshire;[6]
where the royal fleet was assembling in Milford Haven. It
consisted of four hundred ships,[7] carrying a force of about
four thousand men, of whom some five hundred were knights
and the rest archers, mounted and unmounted.[8] The king

---

[1] Anglo-Norm. Poem (Michel), p. 103.

[2] Gir. Cambr. *Expugn. Hibern.*, l. i. c. 28 (Dimock, vol. v. p. 273). Hervey
must have gone before Midsummer ; he was clearly not in Dublin during the
second siege, and returned shortly after its conclusion.

[3] *Ibid.* Anglo-Norm. Poem (Michel), pp. 105, 106.

[4] At Newnham in Gloucestershire, according to Gerald (as above). The
Anglo-Norm. Poem (p. 106), however, says they met at Pembroke. This would
make a difference of at least ten days in the date. From the account of Henry's
movements in the *Brut y Tywys.*, a. 1171 (William, pp. 211-213), it seems that he
crossed the border about September 8 and reached Pembroke on September 20.

[5] Gir. Cambr. as above. Cf. Will. Newb., l. ii. c. 26 (Howlett, vol. i. pp.
168, 169).

[6] *Brut y Tywys.*, a. 1171 (Williams, p. 215).

[7] *Gesta Hen.* (Stubbs), vol. i. p. 25 ; Rog. Howden (Stubbs), vol. ii. p. 29 ;
Gerv. Cant. (Stubbs), vol. i. p. 235. The Four Masters, a. 1171 (O'Donovan,
vol. ii. p. 1187), and Ann. Loch. Cé, a. 1171 (Hennessy, vol. i. p. 145), give the
number as two hundred and forty.

[8] Gerald (*Expugn. Hibern.*, l. i. c. 30, Dimock, vol. v. p. 275) reckons five
hundred knights, with "arcariis [*var.* satellitibus equestribus] quoque et sagittariis
multis." The Anglo-Norm. Poem (Michel), p. 123, makes the knights four
hundred, and a few lines later sums up the whole force as "quatre mil Engleis."
Mr. W. Lynch (*View of Legal Inst. in Ireland under Hen. II.*, p. 2) argues from
the payments for arms, provisions, shipping, etc. recorded in the Pipe-Rolls for
1171, that the army must have numerically "far exceeded the force described in
our printed historians." He gives a few details of these payments, extracted from

embarked on the evening of Saturday, October 16, and landed next day at Croch, eight miles from Waterford.[1] On the morrow, S. Luke's day, he entered the town of Waterford;[2] there he was met by his seneschal William Fitz-Aldhelm, his constable Humfrey de Bohun, Hugh de Lacy, Robert Fitz-Bernard, and some other officers of his household whom he had sent over to prepare for his coming.[3] The Irish of the district and the Ostmen of the town, in the person of their chieftain Ragnald, made submission to him as their sovereign;[4] while Richard of Striguil formally surrendered the place into the king's hands and did homage to him for the earldom of Leinster.[5] The men of Wexford now, according to an agreement which they had made with Henry while he was waiting for a wind at Pembroke,[6] brought their captive Robert Fitz-Stephen to his sovereign's feet, to be by him dealt with as a rebel and a traitor. Henry loaded him with reproaches and imprisoned him afresh, but his anger was more assumed than real, and the captive was

the Pipe-Roll in question (17 Hen. II., a. 1171); some more, from this and the next year's roll, may be seen in Eyton, *Itin. Hen. II.*, pp. 161, 163. The host was no doubt composed almost wholly of English tenants-in-chivalry; but whatever may have been its numbers, there was a large proportion of these tenants who had nothing to do with it except by paying its expenses next year with a great scutage. See in Madox, *Hist. Exch.*, vol. i. pp. 629-632, the extracts from Pipe Roll 18 Hen. II. "de scutagio militum qui nec abierunt in Hyberniam nec denarios" (in some cases "nec milites nec denarios") "illuc miserunt."

[1] *Gesta Hen.* (Stubbs), vol. i. p. 25; Rog. Howden (Stubbs), vol. ii. p. 29. R. Diceto (Stubbs), vol. i. p. 348, makes October 16 the day of Henry's arrival in Ireland; Gerv. Cant. (Stubbs), vol. i. p. 235, makes it "about S. Calixtus's day" (October 16 would be two days after). Gerald, *Expugn. Hibern.*, l. i. c. 30 (Dimock, vol. v. p. 275) makes him reach Waterford "circa kalendas Novembris, die videlicet S. Lucæ." The Anglo-Norm. Poem (Michel, p. 123) turns this into "à la Tusseinz"; the Four Masters, a. 1171 (O'Donovan, vol. ii. p. 1187) record his coming without any date at all; and the *Brut y Tywys.* a. 1171 (Williams, p. 217), absurdly says he sailed on Sunday, November 16. The Anglo-Norman poet seems to have taken Croch—"à la Croiz" as he calls it—for the place of embarkation.

[2] *Gesta. Hen.*, Rog. Howden and Gir. Cambr. as above.

[3] *Gesta Hen.* and Rog. Howden, as above. Anglo-Norm. Poem (Michel), p. 124.

[4] *Gesta Hen.* as above. Rog. Howden (Stubbs), vol. ii. p. 30.

[5] Anglo-Norm. Poem (Michel), p. 124.

[6] See the curious story of their envoy's arrival and reception at Pembroke, *ib.* pp. 119-123.

VOL. II.

soon released.[1]   The submission of the English adventurers
was followed by that of the Irish princes.   Dermot Mac-
Carthy, king of Cork or South Munster, was the first of
them who came to Henry's feet at Waterford, swore him
fealty, gave hostages and promised tribute.[2]   On November
1[3] Henry advanced to Lismore, and thence, two days later,
to Cashel, where at the passage of the Suir he was met by
the king of Limerick or of Northern Munster, Donell O'Brien,
with offers of tribute and obedience.   The lesser chieftains
of southern Ireland followed the example of the two kings ;
in three weeks from his arrival all Munster was at his feet,
and its coast-towns, Wexford, Waterford, Limerick and Cork,
were all in the custody of his own officers.[4]   At Martinmas
he reached Dublin ;[5] before Christmas he received hostages
from all the princes of Leinster and Meath, from Tighernan
O'Ruark of Breffny, from O'Carroll of Oiriel, and from the
king of Uladh or eastern Ulster ;[6] his new vassals built him

---

[1] Gir. Cambr. *Expugn. Hibern.*, l. i. cc. 31, 32 (Dimock, vol. v. pp. 276, 277,
278).   Anglo-Norm. Poem (Michel), pp. 125, 126.

[2] Gir. Cambr. as above, c. 31 (p. 277).

[3] Rog. Howden (Stubbs), vol. ii. p. 30, says he stayed at Waterford fifteen
days.

[4] Gir. Cambr. as above, cc. 31, 32 (pp. 277, 278).   He adds that Henry returned
to Waterford, where he released Robert Fitz-Stephen, and thence proceeded to
Dublin.   The Anglo-Norm. Poem (Michel), pp. 126, 127, places this progress
through Cashel and Lismore in inverse order, after Henry's first visit to Dublin,
and says nothing of a second visit to Waterford.   Its account is however much less
circumstantial than Gerald's.   The *Gesta Hen.* and Rog. Howden only name two
places where Henry stayed—Waterford and Dublin ; and as they both say he
reached the latter at Martinmas, while Roger says he left Waterford when he had
been there a fortnight (*i.e.* on November 1), Gerald's story fills up the interval
very well.

[5] *Gesta Hen.* (Stubbs), vol. i. p. 28.   Rog. Howden (as above), p. 32.

[6] Gerald (as above, c. 33, p. 278) enumerates the princes who submitted
at Dublin as follows : " Machelanus Ophelan [O'Phelan], Machtalewi,
Otuetheli [O'Toole], Gillemoholmoch [Gillamocholmog of Fingal by Dublin
— see above, p. 106], Ocathesi [O'Casey], Ocaruel Urielensis [O'Carroll of
Oiriel], et Ororicius Medensis " [O'Ruark].   He then relates the half-submission
of Roderic of Connaught (of which more later), and adds : "sic itaque, præter
solos Ultonienses, subditi per se singuli." (*Ib.* p. 279.)   He need not however
have excepted the Ulstermen ; for the Ann. Loch Cé, a. 1171 (Hennessy, vol. i.
p. 145)—copying, it seems, the old Annals of Ulster (see Four Masters, O'Donovan,
vol. ii. p. 1187, note *c*, and O'Kelly's note to Lynch's *Cambr. Evers.*, vol. ii. p.
472, note *d*)—say that Henry while at Dublin received hostages from "Leinster,
Meath, Breffny, Oiriel and Uladh."   This leaves only Connaught and Aileach

a dwelling of wattle or wicker-work, after the manner of their country, outside the walls of Dublin, and there in their midst he held his Christmas court.[1]

Early in November two royal chaplains had been despatched to summon the Irish bishops to a council and claim their submission.[2] We hear not a word of Pope Adrian's bull ; but we can hardly doubt that its existence and its contents were in some way or other certified to the Irish prelates before, in response to the royal mandate, they met in council at Cashel in the first weeks of 1172.[3] The archbishop of Armagh absented himself on the plea of extreme age and infirmity ;[4] all his episcopal brethren, however, made full submission to Henry, pledged themselves to conform in all things to the pattern of the English Church,[5] gave written promises to support the English king and his heirs as lawful sovereigns of Ireland,[6] and joined with him

unsubdued. Gerv. Cant. (Stubbs, vol. i. p. 235) and the *Gesta Hen.* (Stubbs, vol. i. p. 25) lump all these submissions together, and the latter seems to place them all, as well as the submission of the bishops, during Henry's stay in Waterford. Rog. Howden (Stubbs, vol. ii. p. 30) not only does the same still more distinctly, but he does worse ; he places the submission of the bishops first, and then says that the lay princes submitted "exemplo clericorum." It is he, not Gerald or any one else, who is responsible for this misrepresentation, which the champions of the Irish Church have been justly denouncing ever since Dr. Lynch's time.

[1] *Gesta Hen.* (Stubbs), vol. i. pp. 28, 29. Rog. Howden (Stubbs), vol. ii. p. 32. Gerv. Cant. (Stubbs), vol. i. p. 236. Gir. Cambr. *Expugn. Hibern.*, l. i. c. 33 (Dimock, vol. v. p. 279).

[2] *Gesta Hen.* (as above), p. 28. Rog. Howden (as above), p. 31. The messengers were Nicolas, a chaplain of the king, and Ralf archdeacon of Landaff. They were sent out "circa festum S. Leonardi" (November 6). *Gesta Hen.* as above.

[3] The *Gesta Hen.* and Rog. Howden as above, both place this council before Christmas 1171. Gir. Cambr. as above, c. 35 (p. 281), and R. Diceto (Stubbs), vol. i. p. 351, date it 1172. It seems better to follow them, for though Gerald is certainly no chronologist, he is the only writer who gives a detailed and rational account of this synod ; and the summary given by R. Diceto also shews a fair knowledge of the subject, though he makes the synod meet at Lismore instead of Cashel.

[4] Gir. Cambr. as above (p. 283). He adds that the primate afterwards went to Dublin and there submitted to Henry ; but see Dr. Lanigan's comment, *Eccles. Hist. Ireland*, vol. iv. pp. 205, 206.

[5] Gir. Cambr. as above. R. Diceto (as above), pp. 350, 351.

[6] They sent him "litteras suas in modum cartæ extra sigillum pendentes :" *Gesta Hen.* (as above), p. 26. Cf. Rog. Howden (as above), pp. 30, 31. This is however placed by both writers some time before the council. See above, p. 114, note 6.

in sending to Rome a report of his proceedings and their
own.[1]

In all Ireland the king of Connaught was now the
only ruler, spiritual or temporal, who had not submitted
to Henry.[2]   Trusting to the inaccessible nature of his
country,[3] Roderic had at first refused all dealings with the
invader, declaring that he himself was the sole rightful
monarch of Ireland.[4]   It seems however that he afterwards
came to a meeting with William Fitz-Aldhelm and Hugh de
Lacy by the banks of the Shannon, on the frontier of
Connaught and Meath, and there promised tribute and fealty
like his fellow-kings.[5]   The promise was however worthless
until confirmed by his personal homage ; and this Henry
soon perceived was only to be extorted at the sword's point.
The impossibility of fighting to any advantage in the wet
Irish winter compelled him to postpone the attempt until
the spring;[6] and when spring came he found that his
intended campaign must be abandoned altogether.   From
the day when he left Milford he had received not one word
of tidings from any part of his dominions.[7]   This total
isolation, welcome at first as a relief from the load of cares

---

[1] Rog. Howden (Stubbs), vol. ii. p. 31, says that Henry sent copies of the
bishops' letters of submission to Rome.   Dr. Lanigan (*Eccles. Hist. Ireland*, vol.
iv. pp. 217, 218) objects that this can only have been done some time later, as
Henry's communications were cut off by the weather.   But this is not borne out
either by the words of R. Diceto (Stubbs, vol. i. p. 350) or by those of Gerald
(*Expugn. Hibern.*, l. i. c. 36, Dimock, vol. v. p. 284).   They both say distinctly
that a persistent contrary wind hindered all communication *from England to Ireland*.   For communication in the opposite direction such a wind would surely be
most favourable.   Moreover, it is quite certain that the Pope did, some time before
September 20, 1172, receive reports of Henry's proceedings in Ireland both from
Henry himself and from the Irish bishops, for he says so in three letters—one
addressed to Henry, another to the kings and bishops of Ireland, and the third to
the legate, Christian bishop of Lismore—all dated Tusculum, September 20, and
all printed in Hearne's *Liber Niger*, vol. i. pp. 42-48, as well as in the notes to
Macariæ Excidium (O'Callaghan), pp. 255-262.

[2] Perhaps we should add the chief of Aileach ; see above, p. 114, note 6.

[3] R. Diceto (Stubbs), vol. i. p. 348.

[4] *Gesta Hen.* (Stubbs), vol. i. pp. 25, 26.   Gerv. Cant. (Stubbs), vol. i. p. 235.

[5] Gir. Cambr. *Expugn. Hibern.*, l. i. c. 33 (Dimock, vol. v. p. 279).   See Dr.
Lanigan's refutation of Gerald's comment on the legal effect of this transaction,
Eccles. Hist. Ireland, vol. iv. pp. 203, 204.

[6] *Gesta Hen.* (as above), pp. 26, 29.

[7] Gir. Cambr. as above, c. 36 (p. 284).   R. Diceto as above, p. 350.

which indeed he had purposely left behind him,[1] became at the end of nineteen weeks a source of almost unbearable anxiety. On March 1 he removed from Dublin to Wexford;[2] there for nearly a month he remained eagerly watching for a ship from England ; none came until after Mid-Lent,[3] and then it was laden with such ill news that he could only take such hasty measures as were possible at the moment for maintaining his hold upon Ireland, and prepare to hurry out of it as soon as the wind would carry him.[4] Richard of Striguil was suffered to remain at Kildare[5] as earl of Leinster ; the general direction of government and administration throughout the king's Irish domains was intrusted to Hugh de Lacy,[6] who had already received a grant of Meath in fee,[7] and who was also left in command of the citadel of Dublin,[8] with a garrison of twenty knights, among whom were Maurice Fitz-Gerald[9] and Robert Fitz-Stephen.[10] The grants of territory made by Dermot to the half-brothers were of course annulled ; Waterford and Wexford were both garrisoned and placed in charge of an officer appointed by the king ;[11] and in each of these towns a fortress was either erected or repaired by his orders.[12]

A better mode of securing his authority in Dublin was probably suggested to him by the ravages which war and

---

[1] See Gervase of Canterbury's account of his motives for going to Ireland (Stubbs, vol. i. p. 235).

[2] *Gesta Hen.* (Stubbs), vol. i. p. 29 ; Rog. Howden (Stubbs), vol. ii. p. 33.

[3] Gir. Cambr. *Expugn. Hibern.*, l. i. c. 37 (Dimock, vol. v. p. 285).

[4] *Ib.* c. 37 (pp. 285, 286). In the Anglo-Norm. Poem (Michel), pp. 128, 129, Henry is made to receive the bad news before leaving Dublin, which is obviously too soon. Cf. *Gesta Hen.* as above, and Rog. Howden (as above), pp. 33, 34.

[5] Anglo-Norm. Poem (Michel), p. 132.

[6] " Constituit eum justitiarium Hyberniæ." Rog. Howden (as above), p. 34.

[7] *Ibid. Gesta Hen.* (as above), p. 30. Gir. Cambr. (as above), c. 38 (p. 286). Anglo-Norm. Poem (Michel), p. 130. See the charter of donation in Lyttelton, *Hen. II.*, vol. iv. p. 295.

[8] Gir. Cambr., *Gesta Hen.* and Rog. Howden, as above. Anglo-Norm. Poem (Michel), p. 129.   [9] Gir. Cambr. as above.

[10] Anglo-Norm. Poem, as above—adding Meiler Fitz-Henry and Miles Fitz-David.

[11] *Gesta Hen.*, Rog. Howden and Gir. Cambr. as above.

[12] *Gesta Hen.* and Rog. Howden, as above. If we may believe the Anglo-Norm. Poem (Michel, p. 130) Henry furthermore made a grant of Ulster to John de Courcy—" si à force la peust conquere."

famine had made among its population.   Eight years before
he had taken the burghers of Bristol, so long the medium of
trading intercourse between England and Ireland, under his
especial patronage and protection.[1]   He now granted to
them the city of Dublin, to colonize and to hold of him and
his heirs by the same free customs which they enjoyed in
their own town of Bristol.[2]   It is plain that Henry was
already aiming at something far other than a mere military
conquest of Ireland ; and the long and varied list of English
names, from all parts of the country, which is found in a roll
of the Dublin citizens only a few years later,[3] shews how
willingly his plans were taken up, not only at Bristol but
throughout his realm, by the class to which he chiefly and
rightly trusted for aid in their execution.   Unluckily, they
were scarcely formed when he was obliged to leave their
developement to other hands ; and the consequence was a
half success which proved in the end to be far worse than
total failure.   On Easter night[4] he sailed from Wexford ;[5] next day he landed at Portfinnan, hard by S. David's ;[6]
before the octave was out he had hurried through South

---

[1] In January 1164 " he granted a short charter of privileges to the burghers of
Bristol, whom as sovereign lord he calls *his* burgesses, although they were then
under the lordship of the earl of Gloucester.   This charter contains only an
exemption from toll and passage and other customary payments for themselves and
their goods through the king's own lands, with a confirmation of their existing
privileges and liberties" (Seyer, *Mem. of Bristol*, vol. i. p. 494, with a reference to
" Charters of Bristol, No. 1 ").

[2] Charter printed in Gilbert, *Hist. and Munic. Documents of Ireland*, p. 1.

[3] *Ib.* p. 3 *et seq.*

[4] R. Diceto (Stubbs), vol. i. p. 351, says at sunset on Easter day (April 16) ;
the Ann. Loch Cé, a. 1172 (Hennessy, vol. i. p. 147), say on Easter day " after
Mass." Gerald, *Expugn. Hibern.*, l. i. c. 38 (Dimock, vol. v. p. 286), the *Gesta
Hen.* (Stubbs), vol. i. p. 30, and Rog. Howden (Stubbs), vol. ii. p. 34, say he
sailed early on the Monday morning, the two latter adding a reason—he would not
travel on the feast-day, though he had suffered his household to do so.   Most
probably he sailed at midnight, as seems to have been often done.   The *Brut y
Tywys.* a. 1172 (Williams, p. 217), makes him reach Pembroke on Good Friday,
but this is impossible.

[5] *Gesta Hen.* as above, p. 30. Anglo-Norm. Poem (Michel), p. 131.   The
household had sailed from Croch to Milford ; *ibid.* Cf. Rog. Howden as above,
p. 34.

[6] *Gesta Hen.* and Rog. Howden, as above. R. Diceto (Stubbs), vol. i. p. 351.
The name of the place, Portfinnan, is given only in the Anglo-Norm. Poem (as
above).

Wales to Newport;[1] in a few days more he was at Portsmouth;[2] and before Rogation-tide he was once more in Normandy, ready to face the bursting of a storm whose consequences were to overshadow all his remaining years and to preclude all chance of his return to complete his conquest of Ireland.

---

[1] See the itinerary in Gir. Cambr. *Expugn. Hibern.*, l. i. cc. 38-40 (Dimock, vol. v. pp. 286-291), compared with *Brut y Tywys.* a. 1172 (Williams, pp. 217-219).

[2] *Gesta Hen.* (Stubbs), vol. i. p. 30. Rog. Howden (Stubbs), vol. ii. p. 34. It is Porchester in R. Diceto (Stubbs), vol. i. p. 351.

CHAPTER IV.

HENRY AND THE BARONS.

1166-1175.

FOR the last eight years Henry had been literally, throughout his English realm, over all persons and all causes supreme. From the hour of Thomas's flight, not a hand, not a voice was lifted to oppose or to question his will; England lay passive before him; the time seemed to have come when he might work out at leisure and without fear of check his long-cherished plans of legal, judicial and administrative reform. In the execution of those plans, however, he was seriously hampered by the indirect consequences of the ecclesiastical quarrel. One of these was his own prolonged absence from England, which was made necessary by the hostility of France, and which compelled him to be content with setting his reforms in operation and then leave their working to other hands and other heads, without the power of superintending it and watching its effects with his own eyes, during nearly six years. He had now to learn that the enemy with whom he had been striving throughout those years was after all not the most serious obstacle in his way;—that the most threatening danger to his scheme of government still lay, as it had lain at his accession, in that temper of the baronage which it had been his first kingly task to bring under subjection. The victory which he had gained over Hugh Bigod in 1156 was real, but it was not final. The spirit of feudal insubordination was checked, not crushed; it was only waiting an opportunity to lift its

head once more ; and with the strife that raged around S.
Thomas of Canterbury the opportunity came.

Henry's attitude towards the barons during these years
had been of necessity a somewhat inconsistent one. He
never lost sight of the main thread of policy which he had
inherited from his grandfather : a policy which may be
defined as the consolidation of kingly power in his own
hands, through the repression of the feudal nobles and the
raising of the people at large into a condition of greater
security and prosperity, and of closer connexion with and
dependence upon the Crown, as a check and counterpoise to
the territorial influence of the feudataries. On the other
hand, his quarrel with the primate had driven him to throw
himself on the support of those very feudataries whom it was
his true policy to repress, and had brought him into hostility
with the ecclesiastical interest which ought to have been, and
which actually had been until now, his surest and most
powerful aid. If it was what we may perhaps venture
to call the feudal side of the ecclesiastical movement—its
introduction of a separate system of law and jurisdiction,
traversing and impeding the course of his own uniform regal
administration—which roused the suspicions of the king, it
was its anti-feudal side, its championship of the universal
rights and liberties of men in the highest and widest sense,
that provoked the jealousy of the nobles. This was a point
which Henry, blinded for the moment by his natural instinct
of imperiousness, seems to have overlooked when at the
council of Northampton he stooped to avail himself of the
assistance of the barons to crush the primate. They doubtless saw what he failed to see, that he was crushing not so
much his own rival as theirs. The cause of the Church was
bound up with that of the people, and both alike were closely
knit to that of the Crown. Sceptre and crozier once parted,
the barons might strive with the former at an advantage
such as they had never had while Lanfranc stood beside
William and Anselm beside Henry I., such as they never
could have had if Thomas had remained standing by the
side of Henry II.[1]

[1] " The government party was made up of two elements—the higher order of

As yet, however, there was no token of the strife to come.   In February 1166, two years after the publication of the Constitutions of Clarendon, Henry assembled another council at the same place and thence issued an ordinance [1] for carrying out a reform in the method of bringing to justice criminals in general, similar to that which he had in the Constitutions sought to apply to criminals of one particular class.   By the Assize of Clarendon it was enacted that the king's justices and the sheriffs should in every shire throughout the kingdom make inquiry concerning all crimes therein committed "since our lord the king was king." [2] The method of their investigations was that of inquest by sworn recognitors chosen from among the " lawful men ' of each hundred and township, and bound by oath to speak the truth according to their knowledge of the fact in question.   This mode of legal inquiry had been introduced into England by William the Conqueror for fiscal purposes, such as the taking of the Domesday survey, and its employment for similar objects was continued by his successors.   Henry II. had in the early years of his reign applied the same principle to the uses of civil litigation by an ordinance known as the " Great Assize," whereby disputes concerning the possession of land might, if the litigants chose, be settled before the justices of the king's court by the unanimous oath of twelve lawful knights chosen according to a prescribed form from among those dwelling in the district where the land lay, and therefore competent to swear to the truth or falsehood of the claim.[3]   This proceeding seems to

---

the Clergy, who joined the king out of cowardice, having more at stake than they could make up their minds to lose ; and the higher order of the Laity, who in this instance sided with the king against the Church, that when they had removed this obstacle they might afterwards fight him single-handed." (R. H. Froude, *Remains*, vol. iv. p. 30).   Which is just what Arnulf of Lisieux saw from the first (Ep. clxii., Robertson, *Becket*, vol. v. pp. 309, 310), and what Henry learned to his cost in 1173.

[1] On the date see Bishop Stubbs' preface to *Gesta Hen.*, vol. ii. pp. lix.-lxi. The Assize is printed in an appendix to same preface, pp. cxlix-cliv, and in *Select Charters*, pp. 143-146.

[2] Assize of Clarendon, c. 1 (Stubbs, *Select Charters*, p. 143).

[3] Glanville, *De legibus Angliæ*, l. ii. c. 7 (*ib.* p. 161).   Cf. Stubbs, *Constit. Hist.*, vol. i. p. 616.

be assumed as already in use by the ninth Constitution of
Clarendon, which ordains its application to disputes concerning Church lands.[1] The Assize of Clarendon aimed at
bringing criminals to justice by the help of the same
machinery. It decreed that in every hundred of every shire
inquest should be made by means of twelve lawful men of
the hundred and four from each township, who should be
sworn to denounce every man known in their district as
a robber, thief or murderer, or a harbourer of such ; on their
presentment the accused persons were to be arrested by the
sheriff, and kept by him in safe custody till they could
be brought before the itinerant justices, to undergo the
ordeal of water and receive legal punishment according to
its results.[2] The inquest was to be taken and the session of
the justices held in full shire-court ; no personal privileges
of any kind were to exempt any qualified member of the
court from his duty of attendance and of service on the jury
of recognitors if required ;[3] and no territorial franchise or
private jurisdiction, whether of chartered town or feudal
" honour," was to shelter a criminal thus accused from the
pursuit of the sheriffs on the authority of the justices.[4]

As was the case with most of Henry's reforms, none of
the methods of procedure adopted in this Assize were new
inventions. Not only had the inquest by sworn recognitors
been in use for civil purposes ever since the Norman conquest ; it may even be that the germ of a jury of presentment in criminal cases, which in its modern shape appears
for the first time in the Assize of Clarendon, is to be traced
yet further back, to an ordinance of Æthelred II., whereby
the twelve senior thegns in every wapentake were made to
swear that they would " accuse no innocent man nor conceal any guilty one." [5] The mission of itinerant justices—
derived in principle from the early days of English kingship,
when the sovereign himself perambulated his whole realm,

---

[1] Constit. Clar. c. 9 (Stubbs, *Select Charters*, p. 139). See above, pp. 26, 27.
[2] Assize Clar. cc. 1, 2, 4, 6 (as above, pp. 143, 144).
[3] *Ib.* c. 8 (p. 144).   [4] *Ib.* cc. 9-11 (as above).
[5] Laws of Æthelred II., l. iii. c. 3 (Stubbs, *Select Charters*, p. 72). See
Stubbs, *Constit. Hist.*, vol. i. pp. 103, 115, 396, 611, 614.

hearing and deciding whatever cause came before him as he passed along—had been employed by Henry I., and revived by Henry II. immediately after his accession. A visitation of the greater part of England had been made by two of the chief officers of the Curia Regis in the first year of his reign, and again in the second ; another circuit seems to have been made in 1159 by William Fitz-John ; and in 1163 Alan de Neville held pleas of the forest in Oxfordshire, while the justiciar himself, Richard de Lucy, made a journey into Cumberland to hold the pleas of the Crown there, for the first time since the district had passed into the hands of the king of Scots.[1] From the date of the Assize of Clarendon, however, these journeys became regular and general,[2] and the work of the judges employed on them became far more extensive and important.

The first visitation under the assize was at once begun by Richard de Lucy and Geoffrey de Mandeville, earl of Essex ;[3] and the Pipe Roll of the year furnishes some indications of its immediate results. The sums credited to the treasury for the pleas of the Crown reach a far greater amount than in the earlier rolls, and its receipts are further swelled by the goods and chattels of criminals condemned under the assize,[4] which were explicitly declared forfeit to the king.[5] The clause binding all qualified persons to be ready to serve on the juries was strictly enforced ; one attempt to evade it was punished with a fine of five marks.[6] Another clause, enjoining upon the sheriffs the construction and repair of gaols for the detention of criminals, was carried into effect with equal vigour.[7] The work of the two justiciars was apparently not completed till the summer of 1167.[8] In that year pleas of the forest were held throughout the

[1] Stubbs, *Gesta Hen.*, vol. ii., pref. p. lxiv.   [2] *Ib.* pp. lxiii, lxiv.

[3] Stubbs, *Constit. Hist.*, vol. i. p. 470. *Gesta Hen.*, vol. ii., pref. pp. lxiv, lxv.   [4] See Stubbs, *Constit. Hist.*, vol. i. p. 471.

[5] Ass. Clar., c. 5 (Stubbs, *Select Charters*, pp. 143, 144).

[6] "Homines de Tichesoura debent v marcas quia noluerunt jurare assisam regis." Pipe Roll a. 1166, quoted in Stubbs, *Constit. Hist.*, vol. i. p. 470, note 1.

[7] " The expenses of gaols at Canterbury, Rochester, Huntingdon, Cambridge, Sarum, Malmesbury, Aylesbury and Oxford are accounted for in the Roll of 1166." *Ib.* p. 471, note 5.

[8] Stubbs, *Gesta Hen.*, vol. ii., pref. pp. lxiv, lxv and note 1.

country by Alan de Neville; and in 1168 seven barons of the Exchequer made a general visitation of the shires for the collection of an aid on the marriage of the king's eldest daughter.[1] This last was primarily a fiscal journey; the aid itself was a strictly feudal impost, assessed at one mark on every knight's fee.[2] It was however levied in a remarkable manner. The Domesday survey, which by a few modifications in practice had been made to serve as the rate-book of the whole kingdom for eighty years, was at last found inadequate for the present purpose. A royal writ was therefore addressed to all the tenants-in-chief, requiring from them an account of the knights' fees which they held and the services due upon them, whether under the "old infeoffment" of the time of Henry I., or under the "new infeoffment" since the resettlement of the country by his grandson.[3] The answers were enrolled in what is known as the *Black Book of the Exchequer*[4] and the aid was levied in accordance with their contents. The whole process occupied a considerable time; the preparations seem to have begun shortly after Matilda's betrothal, for we hear of the purchase of "a hutch for keeping the barons' letters concerning their knights" as early as 1166,[5] yet the collection of the money was not finished till the summer of 1169,[6] a year and a half after her marriage. The labours of the barons employed in it were however not confined to this one end; as usual, their travels were turned to account for judicial purposes,[7] and the system begun by the assize of Clarendon was by no means suffered to fall into disuse.

[1] Stubbs, *Constit. Hist.*, vol. i. p. 471 and note 6.

[2] *Ib.* p. 472. Madox, *Hist. Exch.*, vol. i. p. 572.

[3] The tenour of the king's writ is shewn by a typical answer, printed by Bishop Stubbs in his *Select Charters*, p. 146, from Hearne's *Liber Niger Scaccarii* (2d. ed.), vol. i. pp. 148, 149.

[4] *Liber Niger Scaccarii*, edited by Hearne. A roll of the Norman tenants-in-chivalry was compiled in the same manner in 1172; see Stapleton, *Magni Rotuli Scaccarii Normanniæ*, vol. i., *Observations*, p. xxxiv.

[5] Madox, *Hist. Exch.*, vol. i. p. 576, and Stubbs, *Constit. Hist.*, p. 471, note 7, from Pipe Roll a. 1166.

[6] Stubbs, as above, p. 472, and *Gesta Hen.*, vol. ii. pref. p. lxv and note 2. Eyton, *Itin. Hen. II.*, p. 117.

[7] Stubbs, *Gesta Hen.*, vol. ii., pref. p. lxv, note 2.

It was too soon as yet for the beneficial results of these measures to become evident to the people at large ; but it was not too soon for them to excite the resentment of the barons. The stringency with which in the assize of Clarendon every claim of personal exemption or special jurisdiction was made to give way before the all-embracing authority of the king's supreme justice shewed plainly that Henry still clave to the policy which had led him to insist upon the restoration of alienated lands and the surrender of unlicensed castles in England, to lose no opportunity of exercising his ducal right to seize and garrison the castles of his vassals in Normandy [1]—in a word, to check and thwart in every possible way the developement of the feudal principle. The assessment of the aid for his daughter's marriage seems indeed at first glance to have been based on a principle wholly favourable to the barons, for it apparently left the determination of each landowner's liabilities wholly in his own hands. But the commissioners who spent nearly two years in collecting the aid had ample power and ample opportunity to check any irregularities which might have occurred in the returns ; and the impost undoubtedly pressed very heavily upon the feudal tenants as a body. Its proceeds seem, however, not to have come up to Henry's expectations, and the unsatisfactory reports which reached him from England of the general results of his legal measures led him to suspect some failure in duty on the part of those who were charged with their execution.

A large share of responsibility rested with the sheriffs ; and the sheriffs were still for the most part, as they had been in his grandfather's days, the chief landowners in their respective shires, men of great local importance, and only too likely to have at once the will and the power to defeat the ends of the very measures which by their official position they were called upon to administer. Henry therefore on his return to England at Easter 1170 summarily deposed all sheriffs of counties and bailiffs of royal demesnes, pending an inquisition into all the details of their official conduct since his own departure over sea four years ago. The in-

---

[1] Stubbs, *Gesta Hen.*, vol. ii. pref. p. xlvii, note.

quiry was intrusted not to any of the usual members of
the King's Court and Exchequer, but to a large body of
commissioners specially chosen for the purpose from the
higher ranks of both clergy and laity.[1] These were to
take pledges of all the sheriffs and bailiffs that they would
be ready to appear before the king and make redress on
an appointed day; an oath was also to be exacted from
all barons, knights and freemen in every shire that they
would answer truthfully and without respect of persons to
all questions put to them by the commissioners in the
king's name.[2]

The subject-matter of these inquiries, as laid down in
the king's instructions, embraced far more than the conduct
of the sheriffs. Not only were the commissioners to examine
into all particulars of the sums received by the sheriffs and
bailiffs in the discharge of their functions, and the manner
and grounds of their acquisition,[3] and into the disposal of all
chattels and goods forfeited under the assize of Clarendon ;
they were also to ascertain whether the collection of the aid
pour fille marier had been honestly conducted ; they were
at the same time to investigate the administration of the
forests[4] and the condition of the royal demesnes ;[5] to find
out and report any persons who had failed to do homage to
the king or his son ;[6] and they were moreover to make inquisition into the proceedings of all the special courts of the
various franchises, whether held by archbishop or bishop,
abbot, earl or baron, as fully and minutely as into those of
the ordinary hundreds.[7] Only two months were allowed to
the commissioners for their work, which nothing but their
great number can have enabled them to execute in the time.
Unhappily, the report which they brought up to the king on
S. Barnabas's day is lost, and we have no record of its

---

[1] The list of commissioners for seven of the southern shires is in Gerv.
Cant. (Stubbs), vol. i. p. 216. See also Stubbs, *Constit. Hist.*, vol. i. p. 473 and
note 2.

[2] Inquest of sheriffs, Stubbs, *Select Charters*, p. 148. Gerv. Cant. (as above),
p. 217.

[3] Inquest of sheriffs, cc. 1, 4, 9, 10 (as above, pp. 148-150).

[4] *Ib.* cc. 5, 6, 7 (p. 149).   [5] *Ib.* c. 12 (p. 150).

[6] *Ib.* c. 11 (p. 150).   [7] *Ib.* cc. 2, 3 (pp. 148, 149).

results save in relation to one point: out of twenty-seven
sheriffs, only seven were allowed to retain their offices. The
rest, who were mostly local magnates owing their importance
rather to their territorial and family influence than to their
connexion with the court, were replaced by men of inferior rank, and of whom all but four were officials of the
Exchequer.[1]

This significant proof of Henry's determination to pursue
his anti-feudal policy was followed up next year by the last
step in that resumption of alienated demesnes which in
England had been virtually completed thirteen years ago,
but which had been enforced only by slower degrees on the
other side of the channel. In 1171 Henry ordered a
general inquisition into the extent and condition of the
demesne lands and forests held by his grandfather in Normandy, and into the encroachments since made upon them
by the barons; and we are told that the restitution which
resulted from the inquiry almost doubled his ducal revenue.[2]
The endurance of the barons was now almost at an end;
and moreover, their opportunity had now come. From that
same council at Westminster whence the decree had gone
forth for the inquest of sheriffs, there had gone forth also the
summons for the crowning of the young king; that other
assembly which on S. Barnabas's day saw the deposition of
the delinquent officers saw also, three days later, the new
and dangerously suggestive spectacle of two kings at once in
the land. When, six months later still, the first consequences
of that coronation appeared in the murder of S. Thomas, the
barons could not but feel that their hour was at hand. His
regal dignity no longer all his own, but voluntarily shared
with another—his regal unction washed out in that stream
of martyr's blood which cut him off from the support of the
Church—Henry seemed to be left alone and defenceless in
the face of his foes. The year which he spent in conquering
Ireland was a breathing-space for them as well as for him.
They used it to adapt to their purposes the weapon which
he had so lately forged for his own defence; they found a

---

[1] See the list, and Bishop Stubbs's analysis of it, in his preface to *Gesta Hen.*,
vol. ii. p. lxvii, note 3.   [2] Rob. Torigni, a. 1171.

rallying-point and a pretext for their designs against him in the very son whom he had left to cover his retreat and supply his place at home.

The younger Henry had passed over to Normandy just before his father quitted it, in July 1171.[1]   There he apparently stayed with his mother and her younger children till the opening of the next year, when he and his wife went to England, and there remained as titular king and queen until his father's return from Ireland.[2]   The youth's kingship, however, was scarcely more than nominal ; in his presence no·less than in his absence, the real work of government in England was done by the justiciars ; and his own personal interests lay chiefly beyond the sea.   The influences which surrounded him there were those of his father's open or secret foes :—of his wife's father, King Louis of France, of his own mother, Queen Eleanor, her kindred and her people; and Eleanor had ceased to be a loyal vice-gerent for the husband who had by this time forfeited his claims to wifely affection from her.   She seems to have taken for her political confidant her uncle, Ralf of Faye [3]—one of the many faithless barons of Poitou ; and it is said to have been at her instigation that Ralf and an Angevin baron, Hugh of Ste.-Maure, profited by Henry's absence in Ireland to whisper to her eldest son that a crown was worthless without the reality of kingly power, and that it was time for him to assert his claim to the substance of which his father had given him only the shadow.[4]   Young Henry, now seventeen years old, listened but too readily to such suggestions ; and it was a rumour of his undutiful temper, coupled significantly with a rumour of growing discontent among the barons, that called Henry back from Ireland [5] and made him carry his son with him to Normandy [6] in the spring of 1172.   After the elder king's reconciliation with the Church, however, and

---

[1] *Gesta Hen.* (Stubbs), vol. i. p. 24, note 2.

[2] Eyton, *Itin. Hen. II.*, pp. 162, 166.   He kept Christmas at Bures ; Rob. Torigni, a 1172 (*i.e.* 1171).

[3] Ep. ciii., Robertson, *Becket*, vol. v. p. 197.   Cf. Ep. cclxxvii., *ib.* vol. vi. p. 131.   [4] R. Diceto (Stubbs), vol. i. p. 350.

[5] Gir. Cambr. *Expugn. Hibern.*, l. i. c. 37 (Dimock, vol. v. p. 285).   Anglo-Norm. Poem (Michel), pp. 128, 129.   [6] *Gesta Hen.* (as above), p. 30.

the second coronation of the younger one, the danger seemed to have subsided ; and in November Henry, to complete the pacification, allowed his son to accompany his girl-wife on a visit to her father, the king of France.[1] When they returned,[2] the young king at once confronted his father with a demand to be put in possession of his heritage, or at least of some portion of it—England, Normandy, or Anjou—where he might dwell as an independent sovereign with his queen.[3] The father refused.[4] He had never intended to make his sons independent rulers of the territories allotted to them ; Richard and Geoffrey indeed were too young for such an arrangement to be possible in their cases ; and the object of the eldest son's crowning had been simply to give him such an inchoate royalty as would enable his father to employ him as a colleague and representative in case of need, and to feel assured of his ultimate succession to the English throne. The king's plans for the distribution of his territories and for the establishment of his children had succeeded well thus far. He had secured Britanny in Geoffrey's name before he quitted Gaul in 1171 ; and a month after his return, on Trinity Sunday (June 10) 1172, Richard was enthroned as duke of Aquitaine according to ancient custom in the abbot's chair in the church of S. Hilary at Poitiers.[5] One child, indeed, the youngest of all, was still what his father had called him at his birth—" John Lackland."[6] Even for John, however, though he was scarcely five years old,[7] a politic marriage was already in view.

[1] *Gesta Hen.* (Stubbs), vol. i. p. 34. This writer says they went over—young Henry much against his will—about All Saints' day, and were sent to the king of France both together. Rob. Torigni, a. 1172, says they crossed at Martinmas, and paid their visits to Louis separately, Henry at Gisors, Margaret at Chaumont.

[2] Summoned, it seems, by Henry, "timens fraudem et malitiam regis Franciæ, quas sæpe expertus fuerat." *Gesta Hen.* (as above), p. 35.

[3] *Ib.* p. 41. Cf. Gerv. Cant. (Stubbs), vol. i. p. 242. The *Gesta* say the demand was made "per consilium regis Francorum, et per consilium comitum et baronum Angliæ et Normanniæ, qui patrem suum odio habebant."

[4] *Gesta Hen.* and Gerv. Cant. as above.

[5] Geoff. Vigeois, l. i. c. 67 (Labbe, *Nova Biblioth.*, vol. ii. p. 318).

[6] " Quartum natu minimum Johannem Sine Terrâ agnominans." Will. Newb., l. ii. c. 18 (Howlett, vol. i. p. 146).

[7] There is some doubt as to the date of John's birth. Rob. Torigni (*ad ann.*) places it in 1167 ; R. Diceto (Stubbs, vol. i. p. 325) in 1166. The prose addition

One of the many branches of Henry's continental policy was the cultivation of an alliance with those small but important states which lay on the border-land between Italy, Germany, and that old Aquitanic Gaul over which he claimed dominion in his wife's name. The most important of these was the county of Maurienne, a name which in strictness represents only a small mountainous region encircled to east and south by the Graian and Cottian Alps, and to west and north by another chain of mountains bordering the outermost edges of two river-valleys, those of the Isère and the Arc, which again are severed from each other by a line of lesser heights running through the heart of the district. In the southern valley, that of the Arc, stood the capital of the county, S. Jean-de-Maurienne, the seat of a bishopric from the dedication of whose cathedral church the town itself took its name. In the northern valley, at the foot of the Little S. Bernard, some few miles above the source of the Isère, the counts of Maurienne were advocates of the abbey of S. Maurice, which long treasured the sacred symbol of the old Burgundian royalty, the spear of its patron saint. The power of the counts of Maurienne, however, was not bounded by the narrow circle of hills which stood like an impregnable rampart round about their native land. On the shore of the lake of Bourget they held Chambéry, guarding the pass of Les Echelles, through which southern Gaul communicated with the German lands around the lake of Geneva ; the county of Geneva itself was almost surrounded by their territories, for on its western side their sway extended from Chambéry across the valley of the Rhône northward as far as Belley, while eastward they held the whole southern shore of the lake. To north-east of Maurienne, again, the great highway which led from Geneva and from the German lands beyond it into Italy, through the vale of Aosta by the passes of the Pennine Alps or up the valley of the Isère by S. Maurice under the foot of the Little S. Bernard, was in

---

to Robert of Gloucester's Chronicle (Hearne, vol. ii. p. 484) says that he was born at Oxford on Christmas Eve. As Eleanor seems to have been in England at Christmas-tide in both years, this gives us no help. Bishop Stubbs (Introd. to *W. Coventry*, vol. ii. p. xvii, note 3) adopts the later date.

their hands ; for Aosta itself and the whole land as far
as Castiglione on the Dora Baltea belonged to them.
Across the Graian Alps, their possession of the extreme out-
posts of the Italian border, Susa and Turin, gave them the
title of " Marquises of Italy,"[1] and the command of the great
highway between Italy and southern Gaul by the valley of
the Durance and through the gap which parts the Cottian
from the Maritime Alps beneath the foot of the Mont
Genèvre ; while yet further south, on either side of the
Maritime Alps where they curve eastward towards the Gulf
of Genoa, Chiusa, Rochetta and Aspromonte all formed part
of their territories.[2]   In one word, they held the keys of
every pass between Italy and north-western Europe, from
the Great S. Bernard to the Col di Tenda.   Nominally
subject to the Emperor in his character of king of Burgundy,
they really possessed the control over his most direct lines
of communication with his Imperial capital ; while the intercourse of western Europe with Rome lay almost wholly at
their mercy ;[3] and far away at the opposite extremity of
Aquitania the present count Humbert of Maurienne seems
to have claimed, though he did not actually hold, one of the
keys of another great mountain-barrier, in the Pyrenean
county of Roussillon on the Spanish March.[4]

In 1171[5] Henry's diplomatic relations with the Alpine
princes bore fruit in a proposal from Humbert of Maurienne
for the marriage of his eldest daughter with the king's
youngest son.   Humbert himself had no son, and by the
terms of the marriage-contract his territories, Alpine and
Pyrenean, were to be settled upon his daughter and her

[1] "Comes Maurianensis et Marchio Italiæ" is Count Humbert's style in the
marriage-contract of his daughter with John : *Gesta Hen.* (Stubbs), vol. i. p. 36.

[2] All these places are named in the marriage-contract of John and Alice of
Maurienne ; *Gesta Hen.* (as above), pp. 36-40.

[3] As says Rob. Torigni, a. 1171 : " Nec aliquis potest adire Italiam, nisi per
terram ipsius " [sc. comitis].

[4] *Gesta Hen.* (as above), p. 37.   Humbert "concedit eis" [*i.e.* to John and
Alice, in case he himself should have a son who must oust them from Maurienne]
"in perpetuum et hæredibus eorum Russillun cum toto mandato suo sive pertinentiis
suis omnibus," as if he actually had it in his own hands.   I have however failed
to discover any connexion between Roussillon and Maurienne.

[5] Rob. Torigni *ad ann.*

future husband,[1] in return for five thousand marks of English silver.[2]   The contract was signed and ratified before Christmas 1172,[3] and soon afterwards Henry summoned his eldest son to join him in a journey into Auvergne for a personal meeting with Humbert.   They reached Montferrand before Candlemas, and were there met not only by Humbert and his daughter but also by the count of Vienne,[4] the count of Toulouse and the king of Aragon.[5]   How high the English king's influence had now risen in these southern lands may be judged by the fact that not only King Alfonso of Aragon, a son of his old ally Raymond-Berengar, but also his former enemy Raymond of Toulouse, could agree to choose him as arbiter in a quarrel between themselves.[6]   Raymond in truth saw in Henry's alliances with Aragon and Maurienne a death-blow to his own hopes of maintaining the independence of Toulouse.   Hemmed in alike to south and east by close allies of the English king whose own duchy of Aquitaine surrounded almost the whole of its north-western border, the house of St.-Gilles felt that it was no longer possible to resist his claim to overlordship over its territories.   Henry carried his guests back with him to Limoges ; there he settled the dispute between Raymond and Alfonso ; and there Raymond did homage to the two Henrys for Toulouse,[7] promising to do the like at Whitsuntide to Richard as duke of Aquitaine, and pledging himself to military service and yearly tribute.[8]

---

[1] *Gesta Hen.* (Stubbs), vol. i. pp. 36-40.   [2] *Ib.* p. 36.

[3] Rog. Howden (Stubbs, vol. ii. p. 44), in copying from the *Gesta Hen.* (as above, p. 40) an account of the ratification of the contract, heads the paragraph "De adventu nunciorum comitis Mauriensis *in Angliam.*" If he is right, it must have taken place in April ; but he may mean only "to the king of England."

[4] R. Diceto (Stubbs), vol. i. p. 353.

[5] *Ibid. Gesta Hen.* (as above), pp. 35, 36.

[6] This seems to be the meaning of *Gesta Hen.* (as above), p. 36 : "Venerunt etiam illuc ad regem rex Arragoniæ et comes de S. Ægidio, qui inimici erant ad invicem, et rex duxit eos secum usque Limoges, et ibi pacem fecit inter eos."

[7] *Ibid.* Rog. Howden (as above), p. 45. R. Diceto, as above, says only "fecit homagium 'regi Anglorum Henrico patri regis Henrici." Geoff. Vigeois, l. i. c. 67 (Labbe, *Nova Biblioth.*, vol. ii. p. 319), gives the date, the first Sunday in Lent, February 25.

[8] *Gesta Hen.* as above. "Sed quia Ricardus dux Aquitaniæ, cui facturus esset homagium comes S. Egidii, præsens non erat, usque ad octavas Pentecostes negotii

The infant heiress of Maurienne was now placed under the care of her intended father-in-law;[1] Henry's political schemes seemed to have all but reached their fulfilment, when suddenly Count Humbert asked what provision Henry intended to make for the little landless bridegroom to whom he himself was giving such a well-dowered bride.[2] That question stirred up a trouble which was never again to be laid wholly to rest till the child who was its as yet innocent cause had broken his father's heart. Henry proposed to endow John with the castles and territories of Chinon, Loudun and Mirebeau.[3] But the Angevin lands, with which the younger Henry had been formally invested, could not be dismembered without his consent; and this he angrily refused.[4] The mere request, however, kindled his smouldering discontent into a flame[5] which seems to have been fanned rather than quenched by the suggestions of Eleanor; yet so blind was the indulgent father that, if we may venture to believe the tale, nothing but a warning from Raymond of Toulouse opened his eyes to the danger which threatened him from the plots of his own wife and children. Then, by Raymond's advice, he started off at once with a small escort, under pretence of a hunting-party,[6] and carried his son back towards Normandy with the utmost possible speed. They reached Chinon about Mid-Lent; thence young Henry slipped away secretly by night to Alençon; his father flew after him, but when he reached Alençon on the next evening the son was already at Argentan; and thence before cock-crow he fled again over the French border, to the court of his father-in-law King Louis.[7]   Henry in vain sent messengers

---

complementum dilationem accepit," says R. Diceto (Stubbs, vol. i. pp. 353, 354). The *Gesta* and Rog. Howden make Raymond do homage to the two Henrys and to Richard all at once. They alone give full details of the services promised.

   [1] *Gesta Hen.* (Stubbs), vol. i. p. 36.   [2] *Ib.* p. 41.
   [3] *Ibid.*   Gerv. Cant. (Stubbs), vol. i. p. 242, turns these into "tria castella in Normanniâ."   [4] *Ibid.*
   [5] According to Rob. Torigni, a. 1173, the young king was further offended because his father removed from him some of his favourite counsellors and friends, Hasculf of St. Hilaire and some other young knights.
   [6] Geoff. Vigeois, l. i. c. 67 (Labbe, *Nova Biblioth.*, vol. ii. p. 319).
   [7] *Gesta Hen.* (as above), pp. 41, 42. R. Diceto (as above), p. 355. The chronology is here in great confusion. The *Gesta* tell us that the two kings

to recall him : " Your master is king no longer—here stands
the king of the English ! " was the reply of Louis to the
envoys.¹

Henry at once made a circuit of his Norman fortresses,
especially those which lay along the French border, put
them in a state of defence, and issued orders to all his
castellans in Anjou, Britanny, Aquitaine and England, to
do the like.² Before Lent had closed the old prophecy
which Henry's enemies were never weary of casting in his
teeth was fulfilled : his own " lion-cubs " were all openly
seeking to make him their prey.³ Whether sent by their
mother, with whom they had been left behind in Aquitaine,
or secretly fetched by their eldest brother in person,⁴ both
Richard and Geoffrey now joined him at the French court.⁵
Eleanor herself was caught trying to follow them disguised
as a man, and was by her husband's order placed in strict con-
finement.⁶ Louis meanwhile openly espoused the cause of the
rebels ; in a great council at Paris he and his nobles publicly
swore to help the young king and his brothers against their

reached Chinon just before Mid-Lent (which in 1173 was on March 16), that
young Henry was next day at Alençon, the day after that at Argentan, and that
on the third night, " circa gallicantum," he went off again, " octavâ Idus Martii,
feriâ quintâ ante mediam Quadragesimam." (In the printed edition by Bishop
Stubbs—vol. i. p. 42—the word *mediam* has been accidentally omitted ; see note
to his edition of R. Diceto, vol. ii. pref. p. xxxvi, note 6). It is of course impossible
to make anything of such a contradiction as this. On the other hand, R. Diceto
gives only one date, that of the young king's flight from Argentan, which he
places on March 23. Now in 1173 March 23 was the Friday after Mid-Lent
Sunday. Reckoning backwards from this—*i.e.* from the night of Thursday-
Friday, March 22-23, for it is plain that the flight took place before daybreak—
we should find the young king at Alençon on Wednesday, March 21, and at
Chinon on Tuesday, March 20 ; that is, four days after Mid-Lent. It looks very
much as if the author or the scribe of the *Gesta* had written " ante " instead of
" post " twice over.

¹ Will. Newb., l. ii. c. 27 (Howlett, vol. i. p. 170).
² *Gesta Hen.* (Stubbs), vol. i. p. 42.
³ See the quotation from Merlin's prophecy, and the comment on it, *ib.* pp.
42, 43.
⁴ The first is the version of the *Gesta Hen.* (as above) ; the second that of
Will. Newb. as above, pp. 170, 171).
⁵ *Gesta Hen.* (as above), p. 42. R. Diceto (Stubbs), vol. i. p. 355. Gerv.
Cant. (Stubbs), vol. i. p. 242.
⁶ Gerv. Cant. as above. He adds a comment : " Erat enim prudens femina
valde, nobilibus orta natalibus, sed instabilis."

father to the utmost of their power, while the three brothers
on their part pledged themselves to be faithful to Louis, and
to make no terms with their father save through his mediation and with his consent.[1] Young Henry at once began to
purchase allies among the French feudataries and supporters
among the English and Norman barons, by making grants
of pensions and territories on both sides of the sea : grants
for which the recipients did him homage and fealty,[2] and
which he caused to be put in writing and sealed with a new
seal made for him by order of Louis[3]—his own chancellor,
Richard Barre, having loyally carried back the original
one to the elder king who had first intrusted it to his
keeping.[4]

Nearly three months passed away before war actually
broke out ; but when the outburst came, the list of those
who were engaged in it shews that the whole Angevin
empire had become a vast hotbed of treason ; though, on
the other hand, it shews also that the treason was almost
entirely confined to one especial class.   Its local distribution, too, is significant.   The restless barons of Aquitaine,
still smarting under their defeat of 1169, were but too eager,
at the instigation of their duchess and their newly-crowned
duke, to renew their struggle against the king.   Foremost
among them were, as before, the count of Angoulême,[5] the
nobles of Saintonge, and Geoffrey of Lusignan, beside whom
there stood this time his young brother Guy, now to begin
in this ignoble strife a career destined to strange vicissitudes
in far-off Palestine.[6]   The heart of the old Angevin lands,
Anjou itself, was in the main loyal ; we find there the names
of only five traitors ; and three of these, Hugh, William
and Jocelyn of Ste.-Maure, came of a rebellious house, and

[1] *Gesta Hen.* (Stubbs), vol. i. p. 44.

[2] See the list, *ib.* pp. 44, 45 ; and cf. Gerv. Cant. (Stubbs), vol. i. p. 243.

[3] *Gesta Hen.* (as above), pp. 43 and 45.   [4] *Ib.* p. 43.   [5] *Ib.* p. 47.

[6] *Ib.* p. 46.   The other Aquitanian rebels, besides the count of Angoulême
and the two Lusignans, were Geoffrey of Rancogne, the lords of Coulonges and
Rochefort in Saintonge, of Blaye (" Robertus de Ble "—this might possibly be Blet
in Berry) and Mauléon in Gascony, and of Chauvigny in Poitou, with Archbishop William of Bordeaux and Abbot Richard of Tournay (*ib.* pp. 46, 47) ;
to whom we may add Ralf of Faye.

were only doing over again what their predecessors had
done in the days of Geoffrey Plantagenet's youth.[1] The
same may be said of Henry's native land, Maine ; this too
furnished only seven barons to the traitor's cause ; and five
of these again are easily accounted for. It was almost
matter of course that in any rising against an Angevin count
the lord of Sablé should stand side by side with the lord
of Ste.-Maure. Brachard of Lavardin had a fellow-feeling
with undutiful sons, for he was himself at strife with his
own father, Count John of Vendôme, a faithful ally of
Henry II., ; the same was probably the case of Brachard's
brother Guy.[2] Bernard of La Ferté represented a family
whose position in their great castle on the Huisne, close to
the Norman border, was almost as independent as that of
their neighbours the lords of Bellême, just across the frontier.
Hugh of Sillé bore a name which in an earlier stage of
Cenomannian history—in the days of the "commune," just
a hundred years before—had been almost a by-word for
feudal arrogance ; and whether or not he inherited anything
of his ancestor's spirit, he had a personal cause for enmity to
the king if, as is probable, he was akin to a certain Robert
of Sillé, whose share in the southern revolt of 1169 was
punished by Henry, in defiance of treaties, with an imprisonment so strict and cruel that it was speedily ended
by death.[3]

Across the western border of Maine, in Geoffrey's duchy,
Ralf of Fougères was once more at the head of a band of
discontented Breton nobles, chiefly, it seems, belonging to
that old seed-plot of disturbance, the county of Nantes.[4]

---

[1] *Gesta Hen.* (Stubbs), vol. i. pp. 46, 47. The other Angevin rebels are Vivian
and Peter of Montrévault : to whom may be added John of Lignières and Geoffrey
of La Haye in Touraine. *Ibid.* p. 46.　　　　　[2] *Ib.* pp. 47, 63.

[3] "Robertum de Selit quâdam occasione captum rex Henricus crudeliter ferro
indutum, pane arcto atque aquâ breve cibavit donec defecit." Geoff. Vigeois,
l. i. c. 66 (Labbe, *Nova Biblioth.*, vol. ii. p. 318). "Robertus de Silliaco redeat
in mentem . . . quem nec pacis osculum publice datum, nec fides corporaliter
regi Francorum præstita, fecit esse securum." Ep. dcx., Robertson, *Becket*, vol.
vii. p. 178. Cf. Epp. dcvi., dcxliv., *ib.* pp. 165, 247. The other Cenomannian
rebels are Gwenis of Palluau and Geoffrey of Brulon ; *Gesta Hen.* (as above),
p. 46.

[4] Hardwin of Fougerai, Robert of Tréguier, Gwiounon of Ancenis, Joibert of

The true centre and focus of revolt, however, was as of old the duchy of Normandy. Almost all the great names which have been conspicuous in the earlier risings of the feudal baronage against the repressive policy of William and of Henry I. re-appear among the partizans of the young king. The house of Montfort on the Rille was represented by that Robert of Montfort[1] whose challenge to Henry of Essex ten years before had deprived the king of one of his most trusty servants. The other and more famous house of Montfort—the house of Almeric and of Bertrada—was also, now as ever, in opposition in the person of its head, Count Simon of Evreux.[2] He, like his fellow-traitor the count of Eu,[3] to whom, as after-events shewed, may be added the count of Aumale, represented one of those junior branches of the Norman ducal house which always resented most bitterly the determination of the dukes to concentrate all political power in their own hands. The counts of Ponthieu[4] and of Alençon[5] inherited the spirit as well as the territories of Robert of Bellême. Count Robert of Meulan[6] was the son of Waleran who in 1123 had rebelled against Henry I., and the head of the Norman branch of the great house of Beaumont, which for more than half a century had stood in the foremost rank of the baronage on both sides of the sea. The chief of the English Beaumonts was his cousin and namesake of Leicester, soon to prove himself an unworthy son of the faithful justiciar who had died in 1168; while the countess of Leicester, a woman of a spirit quite as determined and masculine as her husband's, was the heiress of the proud old Norman house of Grandmesnil[7]—a granddaughter of that Ivo of Grandmesnil who had been banished by Henry I. for trying to bring into England the Norman practice of private warfare. Of the other English rebels, Hugh of Chester[8] was a son of the fickle Ralf, and had at

La Guerche; *Gesta Hen.* (Stubbs), vol. i. pp. 46, 47. To these we afterwards find added several others; *ib.* pp. 57, 58.

[1] *Gesta Hen.* (Stubbs), vol. i. p. 45.   [2] *Ib.* p. 47.   [3] *Ib.* p. 45.   [4] *Ibid.*

[5] Called simply "William Talvas" in the *Gesta Hen.* (as above), p. 46, and "John count of Sonnois" by R. Diceto (Stubbs), vol. i. p. 371. John was his real name.   [6] *Gesta Hen.* and R. Diceto, as above.

[7] Rob. Torigni, a. 1168.   [8] R. Diceto, as above.

stake besides his palatine earldom in England his hereditary viscounties of Bayeux and Avranches on the other side of the Channel. Hugh Bigod, the aged earl of Norfolk, untaught by his experiences of feudal anarchy in Stephen's day and undeterred by his humiliation in 1157, was ready to break his faith again for a paltry bribe offered him by the young king.[1] Earl Robert of Ferrers, Hamo de Massey, Richard de Morville, and the whole remnant of the great race of Mowbray—Geoffrey of Coutances, Roger de Mowbray and his two sons—were all men whose grandfathers had "come over with the Conqueror," and determined to fight to the uttermost for their share in the spoils of the conquest. All these men were, by training and sympathy, if not actually by their own personal and territorial interests, more Norman than English ; and the same may probably be said of the rebels of the second rank, among whom, beside the purely Norman lords of Anneville and Lessay in the Cotentin, of St.-Hilaire on the Breton frontier, of Falaise, Dives, La Haye and Orbec in Calvados, of Tillières, Ivry and Gaillon along the French border, we find the names of Ralf of Chesney, Gerald Talbot, Jordan Ridel, Thomas de Muschamp, Saher de Quincy the younger, Simon of Marsh, Geoffrey Fitz-Hamon, and Jocelyn Crispin, besides one which in after-days was to gain far other renown—William the Marshal.[2]

---

[1] Young Henry promised him, and received his homage for, the hereditary constableship of Norwich castle ; *Gesta Hen.* (Stubbs), vol. i. p. 45. This writer adds the honour of Eye ; Rog. Howden, however (Stubbs, vol. ii. p. 46), says this was granted to Matthew of Boulogne.

[2] All these names are given in the list of the young king's partizans in *Gesta Hen.* (as above), pp. 45-48. The remaining names are : William de Tancarville the chamberlain of Normandy, of whom more presently ; Eudo, William, Robert, Oliver and Roland Fitz-Erneis (see *Liber Niger*, Hearne, pp. 142, 295. and Eyton, *Itin. Hen. II.*, pp. 186 and 251) ; Robert of Angerville (he seems to have been the young king's steward or seneschal—see quotations from Pipe Roll a. 1172 in Eyton, as above, pp. 166, 167, 168) ; Solomon Hostiarius (probably also an attendant of young Henry); Gilbert and Ralf of Aumale: "Willelmus Patricius senior" (he appears in Pipe Rolls 3 Hen. II., Hunter, p. 81, 4 Hen. II., p. 118—Berks and Wilts); William Fitz-Roger (Pipe Roll 4 Hen. II., p. 172, Hants) ; Robert "de Lundres" (is this some mighty London citizen?) ; Peter of St.-Julien (may be either St.-Julien in Gascony, in eastern Touraine, or in the county of Nantes); Hugh "de Mota" (La Mothe on the lower Garonne,

One other rebel there was who stood indeed on a different footing from all the rest, and whose defection had a wider political significance. The king of Scots—William the Lion, brother and successor of Malcom IV.—had long been suspected of a secret alliance with France against his English cousin and overlord. The younger Henry now offered him the cession of all Northumberland as far as the Tyne for himself, and for his brother David confirmation in the earldom of Huntingdon,[1] with a grant of the earldom of Cambridge in addition, in return for the homage and services of both brothers :—offers which the king of Scots accepted.[2] Only three prelates, on either side of the sea, shewed any disposition to countenance the rebellion ; in the south, William, the new-made archbishop of Bordeaux ;[3] in the north, Arnulf of Lisieux[4] and Hugh of Durham. Arnulf's influence at court had long been on the wane ; all his diplomacy had failed, as far as his personal interest with King Henry was concerned ; but he possessed the temporal as well as the spiritual lordship of his see ; and the man's true character now shewed itself at last, justifying all Henry's suspicions, in an attempt to play the part of a great baron rather than of a bishop—to use his

La Motte Archard in the county of Nantes, or La Motte de Ger in Normandy) ; Robert of Mortagne (possibly the Norman Mortagne, possibly a place of the same name in Anjou close to the Poitevin border) ; William of " Tibovilla " (probably Thiberville in the county and diocese of Lisieux) ; John and Osbert " de Praellis " (possibly Pradelles in Auvergne, more likely Préaux in Normandy) ; Almeric Turel, Robert Bussun, Guy of Curtiran, Fulk Ribule, Adam de Ikobo, Robert Gerebert, William Hagullun, Baldric of Baudemont, Geoffrey Chouet, " Bucherius," and William de Oveneia, whom I cannot identify.

[1] To which, as will be seen later, there was a rival claimant who adhered to Henry II.

[2] *Gesta Hen.* (Stubbs), vol. i. p. 45. Jordan Fantosme, vv. 268, 269 (Michel, p. 14) adds Carlisle and Westmoreland to the young king's offers, and relates at great length how William hesitated before accepting them, how he sent envoys to the elder king begging for a new cession of Northumberland from him, and only upon Henry's defiant refusal, and after long debate with his own barons, entered upon the war. *Ib.* vv. 372-426 (pp. 14-22).

[3] " Willelmus archiepiscopus." *Gesta Hen.* (as above), p. 47. This can be no one else than William, formerly abbot of Reading, appointed to Bordeaux in February 1173 ; Geoff. Vigeois, l. i. c. 67 (Labbe, *Nova Biblioth.*, vol. ii. p. 319); but I find no further account of his political doings.

[4] *Gesta Hen.* (as above), p. 51, note 4.

diplomatic gifts in temporizing between the two parties, instead of seeking to make peace between them or to keep his straying flock in the path of loyalty as a true pastor should.   He did but imitate on a smaller scale and under less favourable conditions the example set by Hugh of Puiset in his palatine bishopric of Durham, where he had been throughout his career simply a great temporal ruler, whose ecclesiastical character only served to render almost unassailable the independence of his political position.   It was the pride of the feudal noble, not the personal sympathies of the churchman, that stirred up both Hugh and Arnulf to their intrigues against Henry.   Personal sympathies indeed had as yet little share in drawing any of the barons to the side of the boy-king.   What they saw in his claims was simply a pretext and a watchword which might serve them to unite against his father.   Young Henry himself evidently relied chiefly on his foreign allies—his father-in-law, the counts of Flanders and Boulogne, and the count of Blois, the last of whom was bribed by a promise of an annual pension and the restitution of Château-Renaud and Amboise ; while to Philip of Flanders was promised the earldom of Kent with a pension in English gold, and to Matthew of Boulogne the soke of Kirton-in-Lindsey and the Norman county of Mortain.[1]

The first hostile movement was made directly after Easter by a body of Flemings who crossed the Seine at Pacy ; but they had no sooner touched Norman soil than they were driven back by the people of the town, and were nearly all drowned in attempting to recross the river.[2]   Henry meanwhile, after spending Easter at Alençon,[3] had established his head-quarters at Rouen, where he remained till the end of June, apparently indifferent to the plots that were hatching around him, and entirely absorbed in the pleasures of the chase.[4]   In reality however he was transacting a good deal

---

[1] *Gesta Hen.* (Stubbs), vol. i. pp. 44, 45.   Roger of Howden, as has been said above (p. 139, note 1), adds the honour of Eye to Matthew's intended possessions.

[2] R. Diceto (Stubbs), vol. i. p. 367.   He says they were drowned because the bridge was "a quâdam mulierculâ effractus."

[3] *Gesta Hen.* (as above), p. 45.

[4] "Rex pater eo tempore morabatur Rothomagi, ut populo videbatur æquo

of quiet business, filling up vacant sees in England ;[1] appointing a new chancellor, Ralf of Varneville, to the office which had been in commission—that is, virtually, in the hands of Geoffrey Ridel—ever since S. Thomas had resigned it ten years before ;[2] and writing to all his continental allies to enlist their sympathies and if possible their support in the coming struggle.[3]   One of them at least, his future son-in-law William of Sicily, returned an answer full of hearty sympathy ;[4] neither he nor his fellow-kings, however, had anything more substantial to give.   The only support upon which Henry could really depend was that of a troop of twenty thousand Brabantine mercenaries, who served him indeed bravely and loyally, but by no means for nothing ;[5] and if we may trust a writer who, although remote from the present scene of action, seems to have had a more intimate acquaintance than most of his fellow-historians with all matters connected with the Brabantines, Henry's finances were already so exhausted that he was obliged to give the sword of state used at his coronation in pledge to these men as security for the wages which he was unable to pay them.[6] Yet he could trust no one else in Normandy ; and as yet he scarcely knew his own resources in England.

Early in June Robert of Leicester and William of Tancarville, the high-chamberlain of Normandy, sought license

animo ferens quæ fiebant in terrâ ; frequentius solito venatui totus indulgens " [see extracts from Pipe Roll 1173 illustrating this, in Eyton, *Itin. Hen. II.*, p. 173] ; " venientibus ad se vultum hylaritatis prætendens, aliquid extorquere volentibus patienter respondens." R. Diceto (Stubbs), vol. i. pp. 373, 374. Cf. Jordan Fantosme, vv. 118, 119 (Michel, p. 6).

[1] R. Diceto (Stubbs), vol. i. pp. 366-368.   Gerv. Cant. (Stubbs), vol. i. pp. 243, 245.   [2] R. Diceto (as above), p. 367.

[3] Rog. Howden (Stubbs), vol. ii. p. 47.   He says Henry wrote "*imperatoribus et regibus*," which we must take to include the Eastern Emperor.

[4] Letter in *Gesta Hen.* (Stubbs), vol. i. p. 55, note 2 ; Rog. Howden (as above), p. 48.

[5] Rog. Howden (as above), p. 47.   Cf. Will. Newb., l. ii. c. 27 (Howlett, vol. i. p. 172).   The latter does not mention their number ; Jordan Fantosme, v. 67 (Michel, p. 4) makes it only ten thousand ; the *Gesta Hen.* (as above), p. 51, says "plus quam decem millia."

[6] I suppose this to be the meaning of Geoff. Vigeois, l. i. c. 67 (Labbe, *Nova Biblioth.*, vol. ii. p. 319): " Adeo Rex multis thesauris exhaustis nauseatus est, ut Brabantionibus qui ei parebant pro mercede Spatham regiæ coronæ in gagium mitteret."

from the justiciars in London to join the king at Rouen. Immediately on landing, however, they hastened not to Henry II., but to his son.[1] The justiciar himself, Richard de Lucy, was in such anxiety that he seems to have had some thoughts of going in person to consult with the king.[2] The consultation however was to be held not in Normandy but in England. In the last days of June or the first days of July, while the counts of Flanders and Boulogne were easily overcoming the mock resistance of Aumale and Driencourt, and Louis of France was laying siege to Verneuil,[3] Henry suddenly crossed the sea, made his way as far inland as Northampton, where he stayed four days, collected his treasure and his adherents, issued his instructions for action against the rebels, and was back again at Rouen so quickly that neither friends nor foes seem ever to have discovered his absence.[4]

---

[1] R. Diceto (Stubbs), vol. i. p. 370. He gives no date ; but it must have been quite in the beginning of June, for Mr. Eyton says (*Itin. Hen. II.*, p. 172, note 5) : " The Dorset Pipe Roll of Michaelmas 1173 shews that the Earl of Leicester's manor of Kingston (now Kingston Lacy) had been confiscated four months previously (Hutchins, iii. 233)."

[2] " Et in liberacione ix navium quæ debuerunt transfretare cum Ricardo de Luci, et Ricardo Pictaviæ archidiacono, et Gaufrido Cantuariensi archidiacono et aliis baronibus, precepto Regis £13 : 15s. per breve Ricardi de Luci." Pipe Roll a. 1173 (Southampton), quoted by Eyton, *Itin. Hen. II.*, p. 174. See Mr. Eyton's comment, *ib.* note 4, which points to the conclusion that the ships made the voyage —doubtless with the other passengers—but that Richard " probably thought it wise to adhere to his post of viceroy."

[3] R. Diceto (as above), pp. 373, 374. *Gesta Hen.* (Stubbs), vol. i. p. 49. Rob. Torigni, a. 1173.

[4] " Et item in liberacione Esnaccæ quando transfretavit in Normanniam contra Regem £7 : 10s. per breve Regis. Et in liberacione xx. hominum qui fuerunt missi de cremento in Esnacchâ 40s. per breve Regis. Et in liberacione iv. navium quæ transfretaverunt cum Esnacchiâ £7 : 10s. per idem breve. Et pro locandis carretis ad reportandum thesaurum de Hantoniâ ad Wintoniam duabus vicibus 9s. Et pro unâ carretâ locandâ ad portandas Bulgas Regis ad Winton. 9d." Pipe Roll a. 1173 (Southampton), quoted in Eyton, *Itin. Hen. II.*, p. 173. " Et in corredio Regis apud Norhanton per iv dies £32 : 6 : 5 per breve Regis." Northampton, *ibid.* " Et in soltis per breve Regis ipsi vicecomiti [of Northamptonshire] £72 : 11 : 9, pro robbâ quam invenit Regi." *Ibid.* On the Southampton entries Mr. Eyton remarks : " The above charges, from their position on the roll, would seem to have been incurred after July 15." But surely if Henry had been in England during the siege of Leicester, which lasted from July 3 to July 28, we must have had some mention of his presence ; and there is scarcely time for it later, between the capture of Leicester and his own expedition to Conches on August 7.

Hurried, however, as was the king's visit to England, it did its work in bracing up the energies and determining the action of the vassals who were faithful to him there. In personal and territorial importance indeed these were very unequally matched with the rebels. The fidelity of the Welsh princes, David Ap-Owen and Rees Ap-Griffith,[1] could not balance the hostility of the King of Scots. Among the loyal English barons, the most conspicuous were a group of the king's immediate kinsmen, none of whom however ranked high among the descendants of the ducal house of Normandy :—his half-brother Earl Hameline of Warren, his uncle Reginald of Cornwall, his cousin William of Gloucester ;[2] besides Earl William of Arundel the husband of his grandfather's widow Queen Adeliza, his son William, and his kinsman Richard of Aubigny. The earl of Essex, William de Mandeville, was a son of that Geoffrey de Mandeville who had accepted the earldom of Essex from both Stephen and Matilda, and who had been one of the worst evil-doers in the civil war ; but the son was as loyal as the father was faithless ; he seems indeed to have been a close personal friend of the king, and to have well deserved his friendship.[3] The loyalty of Earl Simon of Northampton may have been quickened by his rivalry with David of Scotland for the earldom of Huntingdon. That of William of Salisbury was an inheritance from his father, Earl Patrick, who had earned his title by his services to the Empress, and had fallen honourably at his post of governor of Aquitaine in the rising of 1168. The loyal barons of lesser degree are chiefly representatives of the class which half a century before had been

Is it not much more natural to conclude that the visit took place earlier—at the end of June—and that the orders for the Leicester expedition, which Rog. Wend. (Coxe, vol. ii. p. 372) expressly says were given by the king, were issued to Richard de Lucy in a personal interview?

[1] In *Gesta Hen.* (Stubbs), vol. i. p. 51, note 4, the names are given as " David et Evayn reges Walliæ "—a blunder probably-caused by the writer's greater familiarity with David, owing to his later family alliance with the English king. In the present war, however, Rees proved the more active ally of the two, as we shall see later.

[2] It will however appear later that Gloucester's fidelity was somewhat doubtful.

[3] William de Mandeville is constantly found, 'hroughout his life, in the king's immediate company. See Eyton, *Itin. Hen. II. passim.*

known as the " new men "—men who had risen by virtue of
their services in the work of the administration, either under
Henry himself or under his grandfather. Such were the
justiciar Richard de Lucy and the constable Humfrey de
Bohun ; William de Vesci, son of Eustace Fitz-John, and
like his father a mighty man in the north ; his nephew John,
constable of Chester ;—the whole house of Stuteville, with
Robert de Stuteville the sheriff of Yorkshire at its head ;[1]—
and Ralf de Glanville,[2] sheriff of Lancashire, custodian of the
honour of Richmond,[3] and destined in a few years to wider
fame as the worthy successor of Richard de Lucy. The
Glanvilles, the Stutevilles and the de Vescis now wielded in
Yorkshire as the king's representatives the influence which
had been usurped there by William of Aumale before his
expulsion from Holderness ; while in Northumberland a
considerable share of the power formerly exercised by the
rebellious house of Mowbray had passed to servants of the
Crown such as Odelin de Umfraville[4] and Bernard de
Bailleul,[5] whose name in its English form of Balliol became
in after-times closely associated with that borne by two other
loyal northern barons—Robert and Adam de Bruce.[6] To
the same class of " new men " belonged Geoffrey Trussebut,
Everard de Ros, Guy de Vere, Bertram de Verdon, Philip de
Kime and his brother Simon.[7]

Some half-dozen of the king's English adherents—William of Essex, William of Arundel, Robert de Stuteville and
the elder Saher de Quincy, besides two who had lately come
over from Ireland, Richard of Striguil and Hugh de Lacy—

---

[1] All these names are in the list in the *Gesta. Hen.* (Stubbs), vol. i. p. 51,
note 4.

[2] *Ib.* p. 65. Rog. Howden (Stubbs), vol. ii. p. 60. Will. Newb., l. ii. c. 33
(Howlett, vol. i. p. 184).

[3] Escheated on the death of Duke Conan of Britanny.

[4] *Gesta Hen.* as above, pp. 51, note 4, 66.

[5] *Ib.* pp. 65, 66. Will. Newb. as above.

[6] *Gesta Hen.* as above, p. 51, note 4.

[7] *Ibid.* The Trussebuts, de Roses and de Veres appear under Henry I. Ber-
tram de Verdon and Philip de Kime were employed in the Curia Regis and
Exchequer under Henry II. ; see Eyton, *Itin. Hen. II.*, pp. 185, 76, 130, etc.
Another name among the loyalists in the *Gesta Hen.* (as above)—that of Richard
Louvetot—seems to have got in by mistake ; cf. *ib.* p. 57, where he appears
among the rebels at Dol.

either returned with him to Rouen or had joined him there already,[1] thus helping to swell the little group of loyalists who surrounded him in Normandy.   That group contained no Norman baron of the first rank, and consisted only of a few personal friends and ministers :—Richard of Hommet the constable of the duchy, with all his sons and brothers ;[2] William de Courcy the seneschal ;[3] Richard Fitz-Count, the king's cousin ;[4] Hugh de Beauchamp[5] and Henry of Neubourg,[6] sons of the loyal house of Beauchamp which in England looked to the earl of Warwick as its head ; Richard de Vernon and Jordan Tesson ;[7]—while two faithful members of the older Norman nobility, Hugh of Gournay and his son, had already fallen prisoners into the hands of the young king.[8]   It was in truth Henry's continental dominions which most needed his presence and that of all the forces which he could muster ; for the two chief English rebels, the earls of Leicester and Chester, were both beyond the Channel, and their absence enabled the king's representatives to strike the first blow before the revolt had time to break forth in England at all.   On July 3 the town of Leicester was besieged by Richard de Lucy and Earl Reginald of Cornwall at the head of " the host of England." [9]   After a three weeks' siege and a vast expenditure of money and labour,[10] the town was fired, and on July 28 it surrendered.[11]   The castle still

---

[1] Essex and Arundel had both been with him since the very beginning of the year, for they witnessed the marriage-contract of John and Alice of Maurienne ; *Gesta Hen.* (Stubbs), vol. i. p. 39.   Robert de Stuteville and Saher de Quincy seem to have been with him in the summer of 1173 (Eyton, *Itin. Hen. II.*, p. 174). Hugh de Lacy was at Verneuil, defending it for the king in July (*Gesta Hen.*, vol. i. p. 49) ; and Richard of Striguil was of the party which went to its relief in August (R. Diceto, Stubbs, vol. i. p. 375).

[2] *Gesta Hen.* as above, p. 51, note 4.

[3] *Ib.* p. 39.   Cf. Eyton, *Itin. Hen. II.*, pp. 170, 177.

[4] *Gesta Hen.* as above, p. 51.   [5] *Ib.* p. 49.

[6] *Ib.* p. 52.   [7] *Ib.* pp. 51, 52.

[8] Hugh of Gournay and his son, with eighty knights, fell into the young king's hands, " non tam inimicorum virtuti quam insidiis intercepti," quite early in the war ; R. Diceto (as above), p. 369.

[9] " Cum exercitu Angliæ," *i.e.* the national not the feudal host.   *Gesta Hen.* as above, p. 58.   The date comes from R. Diceto (as above), p. 376.

[10] See some illustrations in the Pipe Roll of 1173, as quoted by Eyton (as above), p. 175.

[11] R. Diceto (as above), p. 376.   He seems to make the fire accidental,

held out, its garrison accepting a truce until Michaelmas ;
the gates and walls of the city were at once thrown down ;
the citizens were suffered to go out free on payment of a
fine of three hundred marks ;[1] but it was only by taking
sanctuary in the great abbeys of S. Alban or S. Edmund
that their leaders could feel secure against the vengeance of
the king.[2]

Three days before the capture of Leicester, an arrow
shot by one of Henry's Brabantine cross-bowmen gave
Matthew of Boulogne his death-wound, and thereby caused
the break-up of the Flemish expedition against Normandy.[3]
A fortnight later Henry set out at the head of all his
available forces to the relief of Verneuil, which Hugh de
Lacy and Hugh de Beauchamp were defending against the
king of France.   By a double treachery Louis, under cover
of a truce, gained possession of the town, set it on fire, and
retreated into his own domains before Henry could overtake him.[4]   Henry marched back to Rouen, taking Gilbert
of Tillières's castle of Damville on the way,[5] and thence
despatched his Brabantines to check the plundering operations which Hugh of Chester and Ralf of Fougères were
carrying on unhindered throughout the border district which
lay between Fougères and Avranches.   The interception of
an important convoy and the slaughter of its escort by the
Brabantines drove the rebel leaders to retire into the fortress

and the surrender a consequence of it.   In the *Gesta Hen.* (Stubbs), vol. i. p. 58,
the victors seem to fire the town after they have captured it.

[1] R. Diceto (Stubbs), vol. i. p. 376.

[2] Mat. Paris, *Chron. Maj.* (Luard), vol. ii. p. 289.

[3] R. Diceto as above, p. 373.   He alone gives the date, attributes the
wound to a shot "a quodam marchione," and places the scene on the invaders'
march from Driencourt to Arques.   The *Gesta Hen.* as above, p. 49, Gerv.
Cant. (Stubbs), vol. i. p. 246, and Will. Newb., l. ii. c. 28 (Howlett, vol. i. p.
173) make it occur during the siege of Driencourt (William calls it by its more
modern name, "Châteauneuf"), but as the former has told us that this siege began
about July 6 and was ended within a fortnight, this is irreconcileable with the
date given by R. Diceto.   Gervase says Matthew was shot "a quodam arcu-
balistâ."

[4] See the details of the story, and the disgraceful conduct of Louis, in *Gesta
Hen.* as above, pp. 51-54 ; Rog. Howden (Stubbs), vol. ii. p. 50 ; R. Diceto
as above, p. 375 ; and another version in Will. Newb. as above (pp. 174, 175).

[5] *Gesta Hen.* as above, p. 56.

of Dol. Here they were blockaded by the Brabantines, backed by the populace of the district of Avranches,[1] who clearly had no sympathy with the treason of their viscount. The siege began on August 20 ; on the morrow Henry received tidings of it at Rouen ; on the 23d he appeared in the midst of his soldiers ; and on the 26th Dol and its garrison, with Ralf of Fougères and Hugh of Chester at their head, surrendered into his hands.[2] This blow crushed the Breton revolt ; the rest of the duchy submitted at once.[3] Louis of France was so impressed by Henry's success that he began to make overtures for negotiation, while Henry was holding his court in triumph at Le Mans. Shortly before Michaelmas a meeting took place near Gisors ; Henry shewed the utmost anxiety to be reconciled with his sons, offering them literally the half of his realms in wealth and honours, and declaring his willingness virtually to strip himself of everything except his regal powers of government and justice.[4] That, however, was precisely the reservation against which the French king and the disaffected barons were both alike determined to fight as Henry himself had fought against S. Thomas's reservation of the rights of his order. The terms were therefore refused, and the earl of Leicester in his baffled rage not only loaded his sovereign with abuse, but actually drew his sword to strike him. This outrage of course broke up the meeting.[5] Leicester hurried through Flanders, collecting troops as he went, to Wissant, whence he sailed for England on Michaelmas day.[6] Landing at Walton in

[1] Rob. Torigni, a. 1173. " Itaque obsessa est turris Doli a Brebenzonibus et militibus regis et plebe Abrincatinâ."

[2] R. Diceto (Stubbs), vol. i. p. 378 ; *Gesta Hen.* (Stubbs), vol. i. pp. 57, 58 ; Rob. Torigni, a. 1173 ; Will. Newb. l. ii. c. 29 (Howlett, vol. i. p. 176). The *Gesta Hen.* gives the date, and a list of the captured. According to Rob. Torigni, Ralf of Fougères escaped to the woods, and his two sons were taken as hostages. The Chron. S. Albin. a. 1173 (Marchegay, *Eglises*, p. 42), says he was taken, together with Hugh (whom the Angevin monk transforms into " comitem Sceptrensem ") and a hundred knights.

[3] Rog. Howden (Stubbs), vol. ii. p. 52.

[4] *Gesta Hen.* as above, p. 59. Rog. Howden as above, p. 53.

[5] Rog. Howden as above, p. 54.

[6] R. Diceto as above, p. 377. Gerv. Cant. (Stubbs), vol. i. p. 246, and *Gesta Hen.* as above, p. 60, say he came over about S. Luke's day ; but this ᵢₛ

Map to illustrate
the
REBELLION
of
1173.-1174.

Royal Strongholds underlined
thus: Alnwick.

Rebel Strongholds:
(S) *Scottish*
(HD)*Hugh of Durham*
(M) *Mowbrays*
(HB)*Hugh Bigod*
(HC)*Hugh of Chester*
(HM)*Hamo de Massey*
(RM)*Richard de Morville*
(RL)*Robert of Leicester*
(RF)*Robert of Ferrers*

Suffolk, he made his way to Hugh Bigod's castle of Framlingham ; here the two earls joined their forces ; and they
presently took and burned the castle of Haughley, which
Ralf de Broc held against them for the king.[1]

At the moment of Leicester's arrival the representatives
of the king were far away on the Scottish border. At the
close of the summer William of Scotland had gathered his
motley host of Lowland knights and wild Galloway High-
landers, marched unhindered through the territories of the
see of Durham, and was just beginning to ravage Yorkshire
after the manner of his forefathers when Richard de Lucy
and Humfrey de Bohun hastily reassembled their forces
and marched against him with such promptitude and vigour
that he was compelled to retreat not merely into Lothian
but into the safer shelter of the Celtic Scotland beyond it.
The English host overran Lothian,[2] and had just given
Berwick to the flames when tidings reached them of Earl
Robert's doings in Suffolk. The king of Scots was
begging for a truce ; the English leaders readily consented,
that they might hurry back to their duties in the south.[3]
Richard de Lucy returned to his post of viceroy, and the
supreme military command was left to the constable
Humfrey de Bohun, assisted by the earls of Cornwall and
Gloucester and by Earl William of Arundel,[4] who had now
come to give the help of his sword in England as he had
already given it in Normandy. The constable and the
three earls, with three hundred paid soldiers of the king,
posted themselves at S. Edmund's, ready to intercept Earl
Robert on his way from Framlingham to join the garrison

---

irreconcileable with R. Diceto's careful and minute chronology of the subsequent
campaign.   R. Niger (Anstruther), p. 175, says "in vigiliâ S. Mauricii," *i.e.*
September 20.

[1] *Gesta Hen.* (Stubbs), vol. i. pp. 60, 61, with an impossible date ; see *ib.*
p. 60, note 12.   Gerv. Cant. (Stubbs), vol. i. p. 246.   R. Diceto (Stubbs), vol. i.
p. 377, gives the correct date of the capture of Haughley, October 13.

[2] R. Diceto as above, p. 376.   Cf. *Gesta Hen.* as above, p. 61.

[3] *Gesta Hen.* as above, p. 61.   R. Diceto as above, p. 376.   Jordan
Fantosme, vv. 478-838 (Michel, pp. 22-38), has a long account of this first
Scottish invasion, but it is far from clear, and some parts of it, *e.g.* the statement
that Warkworth was taken by the Scots, seem incompatible with after-events.

[4] *Gesta Hen.* as above.

of Leicester.[1]   He made a circuit to the northward to
avoid them, but in vain.   They marched forth from S.
Edmund's beneath the banner of its patron saint, the famous
East-Anglian king and martyr, overtook the earl in a marsh
near the church of S. Geneviève at Fornham,[2] and in spite of
overwhelming odds defeated him completely.   His Flemish
mercenaries, who had gone forth in their insolent pride
singing " Hop, hop, Wilekin! England is mine and thine,"[3]
were cut to pieces not so much by the royal troops as by
the peasantry of the district, who flocked to the battle-field
armed with forks and flails, with which they either despatched them at once or drove them to suffocation in the
ditches.[4]   His French and Norman knights were all made
prisoners ;[5] he himself took to flight, but was overtaken and
captured ;[6] and his wife, who had accompanied him throughout his enterprise, was made captive with him.[7]   The
victors followed up their success by posting bodies of
troops at S. Edmund's, Ipswich and Colchester, hoping
that Hugh Bigod, thus confined within his own earldom,
would be unable to provide for the large force of Flemish
mercenaries still quartered in his various castles, and that

---

[1] R. Diceto (Stubbs), vol. i. p. 377. *Gesta Hen.* (Stubbs), vol. i. p. 61.
Rog. Howden (Stubbs), vol. ii. p. 54.

[2] *Gesta Hen.* as above. Rog. Howden (as above), p. 55. The date, according to R. Diceto (as above, p. 378) is October 17 ; the *Gesta* (as above, p. 62)
make it October 16.

[3] Mat. Paris, *Hist. Angl.* (Madden), vol. i. p. 381. " Hoppe, hoppe, Wilekin, hoppe, Wilekin, Engelond is min ant tin."

[4] Jordan Fantosme, vv. 1086-1091 (Michel, p. 50).

[5] R. Diceto as above, pp. 377, 378. *Gesta Hen.* as above, pp. 61,
62. Rog. Howden as above, p. 55. Gerv. Cant. (Stubbs), vol. i. p. 246. Will.
Newb., l. ii. c. 30 (Howlett, vol. i. p. 179). The number of Robert's Flemish
troops is surely exaggerated by all these writers ; still, even at the lowest computation, the odds seem to have been, as R. Diceto says, at least four to one.

[6] Gerv. Cant. as above.

[7] Will. Newb. as above. R. Diceto as above, p. 378. She had been with
her husband in France, and returned with him to England ; *ib.* p. 377. According to Jordan Fantosme, vv. 980-992 (Michel, p. 46), it was she who urged
him to the march which led to his ruin, in defiance of his own dread of the royal
forces. See also in Jordan, vv. 1070-1077 (Michel, p. 50) the story of her trying
to drown herself in a ditch to avoid being captured ; and that in Mat. Paris,
as above, of her throwing away her ring. This latter seems to be only another
version of Jordan's ; cf. his v. 1072.

these would be starved into surrender. The approach of winter however disposed both parties for a compromise ; a truce was arranged to last till the octave of Pentecost, Hugh consenting to dismiss his Flemings, who were furnished with a safe-conduct through Essex and Kent and with ships to transport them from Dover back to their own land.[1]

The earl and countess of Leicester were sent over to Normandy by the king's orders, there to be shut up in company with Hugh of Chester in prison at Falaise.[2] Their capture filled the French king and the rebel princes with dismay, and none of them dared to venture upon any opposition against Henry when at Martinmas he led his Brabantines into Touraine, forced some of its rebellious barons into submission,[3] reinstated his ally Count John of Vendôme in his capital from which he had been expelled by his own son,[4] and returned to keep the Christmas feast at Caen.[5] An attack upon Séez, made at the opening of the new year by the young king and the counts of Blois, Perche and Alençon, was repulsed by the townsfolk,[6] and led only to a truce which lasted till the end of March.[7] The truce made by Richard de Lucy with the king of Scots was prolonged to the same date — the octave of Easter — by the diplomacy of Bishop Hugh of Durham, who took upon himself to purchase this delay, apparently without authority and for his own private ends, by a promise of three hundred marks of silver to be paid to

---

[1] R. Diceto (Stubbs), vol. i. p. 378. He gives the number of these Flemings as fourteen hundred.

[2] *Gesta Hen.* (Stubbs), vol. i. p. 62. Rog. Howden (Stubbs), vol. ii. p. 55. See also quotations from Pipe Roll a. 1173 on this matter, in Eyton, *Itin. Hen. II.*, p. 177.

[3] *Gesta Hen.* as above, pp. 62, 63. The chief rebels were Geoffrey of La Haye—apparently that same La Haye which had formed part of the dower-lands of the first countess of Anjou, and is known now as La Haye Descartes—and Robert of " Ble " (see above, p. 136, note 6) who held Preuilly and Champigny. A list of the garrisons of these castles is given ; two names are worth noting— " Hugo le Danais " and " Rodbertus Anglicus."

[4] *Gesta Hen.* as above, p. 63.

[5] *Ibid.* Gerv. Cant. (Stubbs), vol. i. p. 246. According to Rob. Torigni, however (a. 1174—*i.e.* 1173 in our reckoning) he kept it at Bures.

[6] R. Diceto as above, p. 379.   [7] *Gesta Hen.* as above, pp. 63, 64.

the Scot king out of the lands of the Northumbrian barons.[1]

The issue proved that Hugh's real object was simply to gain time for the organization of a general rising in the north ; and in this object he succeeded. The old isolation of Yorkshire was not yet a thing of the past ; and its few lines of communication with southern England were now all blocked, at some point or other, by some stronghold of rebellion. Earl Hugh's Chester, Hamo de Massey's Dunham[2] and Geoffrey of Coutances' Stockport commanded the waters of the Dee and the Mersey. South of the Peak, in the upper valley of the Trent, the earl of Ferrers held Tutbury and Duffield ; further to south-east, on the opposite border of Charnwood Forest, lay the earl of Leicester's capital and his castles of Groby and Mount Sorrel.[3] By the time that the truce expired Robert de Mowbray had renewed the fortifications of Kinardferry in the Isle of Axholm,[4] thus linking this southern chain of castles with those which he already possessed at Kirkby Malzeard, or Malessart, and Thirsk ;[5] and Bishop Hugh had done the like at Northallerton.[6] Further north stood the great stronghold of Durham ; while all these again were backed, far to the north-westward, by a double belt of fortresses stretching from the mouths of the Forth and the Tweed to that of the Solway :—Lauder, held by Richard de Morville ; Stirling, Edinburgh, Berwick, Jedburgh, Roxburgh, Annan and Lochmaben, all in the hands of the king of Scots.[7]

Between this northern belt of rebel strongholds, however, and the southern one which stretched from Chester to Axholm, there lay along the river-valleys of Cumberland

[1] *Gesta Hen.* (Stubbs), vol. i. p. 64. King and bishop met in person at "Revedale"—or, as Rog. Howden (Stubbs), vol. ii. pp. 56, 57, says, "in confinio regnorum Angliæ et Scotiæ apud Revedene."

[2] *Gesta Hen.* as above, p. 48. Hamo de Massey had another castle called Ullerwood ; where was this?   [3] *Ibid.*

[4] *Ib.* p. 64. R. Diceto (Stubbs), vol. i. p. 379.

[5] *Gesta. Hen.* (Stubbs), vol. i. p. 48.

[6] Rog. Howden as above, p. 57.

[7] *Gesta Hen.* as above, p. 48. Annan and Lochmaben belonged to Robert de Bruce ; *ibid.* No doubt William had seized them when Bruce joined Henry.

and Northumberland a cluster of royal castles.   Nicolas de
Stuteville held Liddell, on the river of the same name.
Burgh [1] stood on the Solway Firth, nearly opposite Annan ;
the whole valley of the Eden was guarded by Carlisle,
whose castellan was Richard de Vaux,[2] and Appleby, which
like Burgh was held by Robert de Stuteville for the king.[3]
The course of the Tyne was commanded by Wark, under
Roger de Stuteville,[4] Prudhoe, under Odelin de Umfraville,[5]
and by the great royal fortress of Newcastle, in charge of
Roger Fitz-Richard ;[6] further north, between the valleys of
the Wansbeck and the Coquet, stood Harbottle, also held by
Odelin, with Roger Fitz-Richard's Warkworth[7] and William
de Vesci's Alnwick [8] at the mouths of the Coquet and the
Alne.   This chain of defences William of Scotland, when
at the expiration of the truce he again marched into England,
at once set himself to break.   While his brother David
went to join the rebel garrison of Leicester,[9] he himself
began by laying siege to Wark.   This fortress, held in the
king's name by Roger de Stuteville—apparently a brother
of the sheriff of Yorkshire—occupied a strong position in
the upper valley of the Tyne, on the site of an earlier
fortress which under the name of Carham had played a
considerable part in the Scottish wars of Stephen's time,
and had been finally taken and razed by William's grandfather King David in 1138.[10]   William himself had already
in the preceding autumn besieged Wark without success ;[11]
he prospered no better this time, and presently removed his
forces to Carlisle,[12] where he had also sustained a like repulse

---

[1] *Gesta Hen.* (Stubbs), vol. i. p. 65.   [2] *Ib.* p. 64.

[3] *Ib.* p. 65.   Jordan Fantosme, v. 1467 (Michel, p. 66), gives us the name
—a very interesting one—of the acting commandant—" Cospatric le fiz Horm,
un viel Engleis fluri."

[4] Jordan Fantosme, vv. 478-483 (Michel, pp. 22-24).

[5] *Ib.* vv. 594-603 (p. 28).   *Gesta Hen.* as above.

[6] Jordan Fantosme, vv. 566, 567 (Michel, p. 26).

[7] *Ib.* vv. 562-565 (p. 26).   *Gesta Hen.* as above, p. 65.   See above, p. 149,
note 3.   [8] Jordan Fantosme, vv. 538, 539 (as above).

[9] *Gesta Hen.* as above.   Cf. Jordan Fantosme, vv. 1113-1136 (Michel, p. 52).

[10] See above, vol. i. pp. 287, 292.

[11] Jordan Fantosme, vv. 478-530 (Michel, pp. 22, 26).

[12] *Ib.* vv. 1191-1351 (pp. 54-62).

six months before.[1]   Carlisle, as well as Wark, was in truth
almost impregnable except by starvation; and William,
while blockading it closely, detached a part of his host for
a series of expeditions against the lesser fortresses, Liddell,
Burgh, Appleby, Harbottle and Warkworth, all of which fell
into his hands.[2]   His brother's arrival at Leicester, meanwhile,
seemed to have revived the energies of its garrison; under
the command of Earl Robert of Ferrers they sallied forth
very early one morning, surprised and burned the town of
Nottingham, made a great slaughter of its citizens, and went
home laden with plunder and prisoners.[3]

Meanwhile the king's representatives in the south were
not idle.   Knowing however that he was powerless to rescue
the north, Richard de Lucy made an attempt to draw off in
another direction the forces both of the Scot king and of his
brother by laying siege to David's castle of Huntingdon.[4]
Huntingdon had been held ever since 1136 either by the
reigning king of Scots or by one of his nearest kinsmen, in
virtue of their descent from Waltheof, the last Old-English
earl of Huntingdon and Northampton, through his daughter
Matilda, the wife of King David.   In each case, however,
the fief seems to have been held not as an hereditary possession but by a special grant made to the individual holder for
his life.   The house of Northampton, sprung from an earlier
marriage of the same Matilda, were thus enabled to maintain a claim upon it which had never been entirely barred,
and which Earl Simon of Northampton now seized his
opportunity to urge upon the king.[5]   Henry answered that
Simon might keep Huntingdon if he could win it;[6] thus

---

[1] Jordan Fantosme, vv. 610-760 (pp. 28-36).

[2] *Gesta Hen.* (Stubbs), vol. i. pp. 64, 65. Rog. Howden (Stubbs), vol. ii. p.
60.   Will. Newb., l. ii. cc. 30, 31 (Howlett, vol. i. pp. 177, 180), seems to have
confused this campaign with that of the preceding autumn; and so has, apparently, Jordan Fantosme, vv. 1145-1511 (Michel, pp. 52-68). "Banesburc"
in v. 1158 (p. 54), though it looks like Bamborough, surely ought to be *Burgh*.

[3] *Gesta Hen.* as above, p. 69.   Nottingham was commanded by Reginald de
Lucy; what relation to the justiciar?   [4] R. Diceto (Stubbs), vol. i. p. 384.

[5] See the story in the tract "De Judithâ uxore Waldevi comitis," in M. F.
Michel's *Chroniques Anglo-Normandes*, vol. ii. pp. 128, 129.

[6] *Gesta Hen.* as above, p. 71.   The case seems to have been tried in the
Curia Regis; *ibid.*, and *Chron. Anglo-Norm.*, as above.

securing for Richard de Lucy his support and co-operation in the siege, which began on May 8.[1]   Three days before this, however, a severe blow had been dealt at the northern rebels.   The king's eldest son Geoffrey, who a year before had been appointed to the bishopric of Lincoln, gathered up the forces of Lincolnshire, led them into Axholm and laid siege to Kinardferry.   Robert of Mowbray, who was commanding there in person, seeing his garrison threatened with the want of water, slipped out to seek aid of his friends at Leicester, but was surrounded and made prisoner by the country-folk at Clay.[2]   On May 5 Kinardferry surrendered ; after razing it, Geoffrey marched northward to York ; here he was joined by the forces of the archbishop and of the shire ; with this united host he took Mowbray's castle of Malessart,[3] closely menaced that of Thirsk by erecting a rival fortification at Topcliff, and having intrusted the former to Archbishop Roger and the latter to William de Stuteville, marched back to Lincoln in triumph.[4]   His victory was scarcely won when a new peril arose in East-Anglia.   Three days after Pentecost some three hundred Flemish soldiers, forerunners of a great host with which Count Philip of Flanders had sworn to invade England at Midsummer on behalf of the young king, landed at the mouth of the Orwell.[5] Hugh Bigod, whose truce with the king's officers, made when he dismissed his other Flemish troops in the preceding autumn, expired four days later, at once received them into his castles.[6]   For a whole month, however, no further movement was made save by the garrison of Leicester, who after the close of Whitsun-week made a successful plundering raid upon the town of Northampton.[7]   On June 18 Hugh Bigod and his Flemings marched upon Norwich, took it by

---

[1] R. Diceto (Stubbs), vol. i. p. 384.

[2] "A rusticis del Clay." *Gesta Hen.* (Stubbs), vol. i. p. 68.   Rog. Howden (Stubbs), vol. ii. p. 58, alters "rusticis" into "hominibus."   The place is perhaps Clay Cross in Derbyshire.   [3] Kirkby or Kirby Malzeard, near Ripon.

[4] *Gesta Hen.* as above, pp. 68, 69.   Cf. R. Diceto as above, and Gir. Cambr., *Vita Galfr. Archiep.*, l. i. cc. 2, 3 (Dimock, vol. iv. pp. 364-367).

[5] "Apud Airewellam."   R. Diceto (as above), p. 381.

[6] *Ibid.*   Gerv. Cant. (Stubbs), vol. i. p. 247.

[7] *Gesta Hen.* as above, p. 68.

assault, committed a vast slaughter of men and women, and finally sacked and fired the city.[1]   They seem to have returned to Framlingham by way of Dunwich, which was still a flourishing seaport, of sufficient wealth to tempt their greed ; but its stout fisher-folk met them with such a determined front that they were compelled to retire.[2]

Richard de Lucy was all this while busy with the siege of Huntingdon.   Provoked apparently by a vigorous assault which he made upon it at midsummer,[3] the garrison set fire to the town ; Richard then built a tower to block their egress from the castle, and left the completion of the siege to the earl of Northampton.[4]   For himself it was time once more to lay down the knightly sword and resume that of justice.   While the justiciar's energies were absorbed in warfare with the barons, the burgher-nobles of the capital had caught from their feudal brethren the spirit of lawlessness and misrule, and London had become a vast den of thieves and murderers.   Young men, sons and kinsmen of the noblest citizens, habitually went forth by night in parties of a hundred or more, broke into rich men's houses and robbed them by force, and if they met any man walking in the streets alone, slew him at once.   Peaceable citizens were driven in self-defence to meet violence with violence.   One man, expecting an attack, gathered his armed servants around him in a concealed corner, surprised his assailants in the act of breaking into his house with crowbars, struck off with a blow of his sword the right hand of their leader

---

[1] *Gesta Hen.* (Stubbs), vol. i. p. 68.   R. Diceto (Stubbs), vol. i. p. 381 (to whom we owe the date).   Gerv. Cant. (Stubbs), vol. i. p. 248.

[2] Will. Newb., l. ii. c. 30 (Howlett, vol. i. p. 178).   "Insignum vicum maritimum, variis opibus refertum, qui dicitur Donewich," he calls it.   He gives an account of the entire East-Anglian campaign, but he has mixed up the doings of this summer of 1174 with those of the preceding autumn.   Jordan Fantosme, vv. 845-897 (Michel, pp. 40-42), has done the same.   He explains, however, the otherwise unaccountable facility with which Norwich was taken, by telling us that " Uns traïtres Lohereng la trahi, pur ço si fud surprise."

[3] "Appropinquante autem nativitate S. Johannis Baptistæ, Ricardus de Luci magnum congregavit exercitum et obsedit castellum de Huntendoniâ."   *Gesta Hen.* as above, p. 70.   Rog. Howden (Stubbs), vol. ii. p. 60, substitutes for the first words "in festo Nativitatis S. Johannis."   This is the first time that either writer mentions the siege, but see R. Diceto as above, p. 376.

[4] *Gesta Hen.* as above, p. 71.

Andrew Bucquinte, and raised an alarm which put the rest
to flight.   Bucquinte was captured and delivered next
morning to the justiciar; on a promise of safety for life
and limb he gave up the names of his accomplices ; some
fled, some were caught, and among the latter was one of the
noblest and richest citizens of London, John Oldman,[1] who
vainly offered five thousand marks of silver to the Crown to
purchase his escape from the gallows.[2]   The revelation of
such a state of things in the capital apparently drove
Richard de Lucy and his colleagues almost to desperation.
They had already sent messenger after messenger to intreat
that the king would return ; getting however no certain
answer, they now determined that one of their number
should go to Normandy in person to lay before him an
authentic account of the desperate condition of his realm.[3]

Henry had spent the spring in a successful progress
through Maine and Anjou to Poitiers, where he kept the
Whitsun feast.   He had just rescued Saintes from a band
of rebels who had seized it in Richard's name[4] when he
was called northward again by a rumour of the Flemish
count's scheme for the invasion of England.   By S. Barnabas's day he was back again on the borders of Britanny and
Anjou ; he took and fortified Ancenis, and then, leaving
Anjou to the charge of a faithful baron, Maurice of Craon,[5]
went to meet the castellans of the Norman border in a
council at Bonneville on Midsummer-day.   Their deliber-

---

[1] "Johannes Senex."

[2] *Gesta Hen.* (Stubbs), vol. i. pp. 155, 156. The story is there told in connexion with that of the murder of a brother of the earl of Ferrers in 1177, and
said to have happened "three years before." The wording of the latter part,
where it is said that John "obtulit quingentas marcas argenti *domino regi* . . .
sed . . . noluit denarios illos accipere, et præcepit ut judicium de eo fieret,"
seems to imply that the king himself came to England between the capture of
Bucquinte and the execution of John. In that case the date of the affair would
be about June or July 1174. Rog. Howden (Stubbs), vol. ii. p. 131, mentions
the hanging of John Oldman, but puts it after the murder of De Ferrers in 1177
and omits the whole story which in the *Gesta* intervenes, thereby also omitting
to shew the true sequence of events and chronology.

[3] R. Diceto (Stubbs), vol. i. p. 381.

[4] *Ib.* p. 380. Cf. *Gesta Hen.* as above, p. 71, and Chron. S. Albin. a. 1174
(Marchegay, *Eglises*, p. 43).

[5] R. Diceto and *Gesta Hen.* as above.

ations were interrupted by the appearance of Richard of
Ilchester—now bishop-elect of Winchester—on his errand
from England to recall the king.[1]   Richard's pleadings however were scarcely needed.   Henry knew that his eldest son
was at that very moment with the count of Flanders at
Gravelines, only awaiting a favourable wind to set sail for
the invasion of England,[2] and that, whatever might be the
risk to his continental realms, he must hasten to save the
island.[3]   He at once took measures for the security of the
Norman castles and for the transport of those prisoners and
suspected persons whom he dared not venture to leave behind him—his queen,[4] the earl and countess of Leicester,
the earl of Chester,[5] the young queen Margaret,[6] and the
affianced brides of his three younger sons ; besides the two
children who. were still with him, Jane and John.[7]   The
wind which thwarted the designs of his foes was equally
unfavourable to him ; it was not till July 7 that he himself embarked at Barfleur, and even then the peril of crossing seemed so great that the sailors were inclined to put
back.   Henry raised his eyes to heaven : " If I seek the
peace of my realm—if the heavenly King wills that my
return should restore its peace—He will bring me safe into
port.   If He has turned away His Face from me and
determined to scourge my realm, may I never reach its
shores !"   By nightfall he was safe [8] at Southampton.[9]

---

[1] R. Diceto (Stubbs), vol. i. pp. 381, 382.   Cf. Jordan Fantosme, vv. 1530-
1633 (Michel, pp. 70-74).

[2] *Gesta Hen.* (Stubbs), vol. i. p. 72.   Rog. Howden (Stubbs), vol. ii. p. 61.

[3] Gerv. Cant. (Stubbs), vol. i. p. 248.   Cf. Will. Newb., l. ii. c. 32 (Howlett,
vol. i. p. 181).

[4] R. Diceto as above, p. 382.   *Gesta Hen.* as above.

[5] R. Diceto (as above) has "comitem Cestrensem, Legecestrensem comitissam"; Mat. Paris, *Chron. Maj.* (Luard), vol. ii. p. 292, turns this into "comitem Legecestrensem et comitissam."   We may surely combine the two versions.

[6] R. Diceto and *Gesta Hen.* as above.

[7] R. Diceto as above, p. 382.   "Uxores filiorum suorum" must mean
Adela of France, Constance of Britanny and Alice of Maurienne, all of whom are
known to have been in Henry's custody.

[8] R. Diceto as above, pp. 382, 383.

[9] *Ib.* p. 383.   *Gesta Hen.* as above.   Cf. Pipe Roll a. 1173, quoted by
Itin. Hen. II., p. 180.   R. Niger (Anstruther), p. 176, puts the voyage two days
later.

His first care was to bestow his prisoners and hostages in safe custody.[1]   That done, he set off at once on a pilgrimage to the grave of his former friend and victim at Canterbury.   Travelling with the utmost speed, and feeding only on bread and water, he reached Canterbury on July 12 ; before the church of S. Dunstan, outside the west gate, he dismounted, exchanged his kingly robes for the woollen gown of a pilgrim, and made his way with bare and bleeding feet along the rough-paved streets to the cathedral church.   Here, surrounded by a group of bishops and abbots who seem to have come with him, as well as by the monks of the cathedral chapter and a crowd of wondering lay-folk, he threw himself in an agony of penitence and prayer on the martyr's tomb, which still stood in the crypt where his body had been hastily buried by the terrified monks immediately after the murder.   The bishop of London now came forward and spoke in the king's name, solemnly protesting that he had never sought the primate's death, and beseeching absolution from the assembled prelates for the rash words which had occasioned it.   The absolution was given ; the king then underwent a public scourging at the hands of the bishops and monks ; he spent the whole night in prayer before the shrine ; early on the morrow he heard mass and departed, leaving rich gifts in money and endowments, and rode back still fasting to London, which he reached on the following morning.[2]   The next few days were spent in collecting forces, in addition to a large troop of Brabantines whom he had brought over with him,[3] and in despatching a part of these into Suffolk against Hugh Bigod ;

[1] *Gesta Hen.* (Stubbs), vol. i. p. 72.   Eleanor was placed at Salisbury (Geoff. Vigeois, l. i. c. 67 ; Labbe, *Nova Bibl.*, vol. ii. p. 319) in charge of Robert Mauduit ; the younger queen "and the hostages" were sent to Devizes under the care of Eustace Fitz-Stephen. (Eyton, *Itin. Hen. II.*, p. 180, from Pipe Roll a. 1173.)

[2] For accounts of the penance see R. Diceto (Stubbs), vol. i. p. 383 ; Gerv. Cant. (Stubbs), vol. i. pp. 248, 249 ; *Gesta Hen.* as above ; Rog. Howden (Stubbs), vol. ii. pp. 61, 62 ; Will. Newb., l. ii. c. 35 (Howlett, vol. i. p. 18) ; E. Grim (Robertson, *Becket*, vol. ii.), pp. 445-447 ; Herb. Bosh. (*ib.* vol. iii.), pp. 545-547.

[3] R. Diceto as above, p. 382.   *Gesta Hen.* as above.   Rob. Torigni, a. 1174.

Henry himself lingering another day or two to recover from his excitement and fatigue.[1]

In the middle of the night of July 17 a courier from the north came knocking wildly for admittance at the palace-gate. The porters remonstrated with him in vain ; he bore, he said, good news which the king must hear that very night. He hurried to the door of the king's chamber, and, despite the expostulations of the chamberlains, made his way to the bedside and woke the king from his sleep. " Who art thou ?" demanded Henry. " A servant of your faithful Ralf de Glanville, and the bearer of good tidings from him to you." " Is he well ?" " He is well ; and lo ! he holds your enemy the king of Scots in chains at Richmond castle." Not till he had seen Ralf's own letters could Henry believe the tidings; then he burst into thanksgivings for the crowning triumph which had come to him, as he now learned, almost at the moment when his voluntary humiliation at Canterbury was completed.[2] The garrison of Carlisle had pledged themselves to surrender to the Scot king at Michaelmas if not previously relieved. In the interval William laid siege to Odelin de Umfraville's castle of Prudhoe on the Tyne.[3] Here he was rejoined by Robert de Mowbray, who had somehow escaped from his jailors, and now came to intreat the Scot king's aid in the recovery of his lost castles.[4] Meanwhile, however, the king's return had apparently brought with it the return of the sheriff of Yorkshire, Robert de Stuteville. Under his leadership and that of his son William the whole military forces of the shire, with those of William de Vesci, Ralf de Glanville, Bernard de Balliol and Odelin de Umfraville, and Archbishop Roger's men under his con-

[1] Will. Newb., l. ii. c. 35 (Howlett, vol. i. p. 189), says he stayed in London in order to be bled.

[2] *Ib.* (pp. 189, 190). On the coincidence of time see Mr. Howlett's note 3, p. 188. Cf. the more detailed, but far less vivid version of the story in Jordan Fantosme, vv. 1956-2029 (Michel, pp. 88-92). In the *Gesta Hen.* (Stubbs), vol. i. p. 72, Henry is said to have received the news on July 18. Taken in conjunction with the story given above, this must mean the night of July 17-18.

[3] *Gesta Hen.* as above, p. 65. Rog. Howden (Stubbs), vol. ii. p. 60. Cf. Will. Newb., l. ii. c. 32 (as above, p. 182) ; and Jordan Fantosme, vv., 1640-1650 (Michel, p. 74).   [4] Will. Newb. as above.

stable Ralf de Tilly, gathered and marched northward to
oppose the Scots.[1]   They reached Newcastle on July 12[2]—
the day of Henry's penitential entry into Canterbury—but
only to find that on the rumour of their approach William
the Lion had retired from Prudhoe, and was gone to besiege
Alnwick with his own picked followers, while the bulk of
his host, under the earls of Fife and Angus and the English
traitor Richard de Morville, dispersed over all Northumberland to burn, plunder and slay in the old barbarous Scottish
fashion which seems hardly to have softened since the days
of Malcolm Canmore.[3]   The English leaders now held a
council of war.   Their forces consisted only of a few hundred knights, all wearied and spent with their long and
hurried march, in which the foot had been unable to keep
up with them at all.   The more cautious argued that enough
had been done in driving back the Scots thus far, and that
it would be madness for a band of four hundred men to
advance against a host of eighty thousand.   Bolder spirits,
however, urged that the justice of their cause must suffice to
prevail against any odds ; and it was decided to continue
the march to Alnwick.   They set out next morning before
sunrise ; the further they rode, the thicker grew the mist ;
some proposed to turn back.   " Turn back who will," cried
Bernard de Balliol, "if no man will follow me, I will go on
alone, rather than bear the stain of cowardice for ever !"
Every one of them followed him ; and when at last the mist
cleared away, the first sight that met their eyes was the
friendly castle of Alnwick.   Close beside it lay the king of
Scots, carelessly playing with a little band of some sixty
knights.   Never dreaming that the English host would dare
to pursue him thus far, he had sent out all the rest of his

[1] *Gesta Hen.* (Stubbs), vol. i. p. 65, 66.   Cf. Rog. Howden (Stubbs), vol. ii.
p. 60.

[2] " Sexta Sabbati."   Will. Newb., l. ii. c. 33 (Howlett, vol. i. p. 183).

[3] *Gesta Hen.* as above, p. 66.   Cf. Rog. Howden as above; Will. Newb., l. ii.
c. 32 (as above, pp. 182, 183), and Jordan Fantosme, vv. 1671-1729 (Michel, pp.
76-78).   On the Scottish misdoings see also R. Diceto (Stubbs), vol. i. p. 376 ;
Gerv. Cant. (Stubbs), vol. i. p. 247 ; and *Gesta Hen.* as above, p. 64 ; this latter
writer can find no better way of describing them than by copying Henry of
Huntingdon's account of the Scottish invaders of 1138 (Hen. Hunt., l. viii. c. 6,
Arnold, p. 261).

VOL. II.

troops on a plundering expedition, and at the first appearance
of the enemy he took them for his own followers returning
with their spoils.   When they unfurled their banners he saw
at once that his fate was sealed.   The Scottish Lion, however, proved worthy of his name, and his followers proved
worthy of their leader.   Seizing his arms and shouting,
" Now it shall be seen who are true knights ! " he rushed
upon the English ; his horse was killed, he himself was
surrounded and made prisoner, and so were all his men.[1]
Roger de Mowbray and Adam de Port, an English baron
who had been outlawed two years before for an attempt on
King Henry's life, alone fled away into Scotland ;[2] not one
Scot tried to escape, and some even who were not on the
spot, when they heard the noise of the fray, rode hastily
up and almost forced themselves into the hands of their
captors, deeming it a knightly duty to share their sovereign's
fate.[3]

The capture of William the Lion almost put an end to
the rebellion.   A body of Flemings summoned by Bishop
Hugh of Durham landed the same day at Hartlepool ; but
at the tidings of the Scottish disaster, Hugh thought it safest
to pay them their forty days' wages and send them home
again at once.[4]   On the same day, too, the young king,
weary of waiting for a wind at Gravelines, left the count of
Flanders there alone and proceeded to Wissant with a body
of troops whom he succeeded in despatching from thence
into England, under the command of Ralf of La Haye, to the
assistance of Hugh Bigod.[5]   In London, meanwhile, the news
brought by Ralf de Glanville's courier raised to the highest
pitch the spirits both of Henry and of his troops.   On that
very day he set out for Huntingdon,[6] whose titular earl had

---

[1] Will. Newb., l. ii. c. 33 (Howlett, vol. i. pp. 183-185). Jordan Fantosme,
vv. 1731-1839 (Michel, pp. 78-84). Cf. *Gesta Hen.* (Stubbs), vol. i. p. 67 ; Rog.
Howden (Stubbs), vol. ii. p. 63 ; and Gerv. Cant. (Stubbs), vol. i. p. 249.

[2] Jordan Fantosme, vv. 1841-1849 (Michel, p. 84). Will. Newb. as above
(p. 185). On Adam de Port (whose presence on this occasion is mentioned by
Jordan only) see *Gesta Hen.* as above, p. 35 and note 2, and Stapleton, *Magn.
Rot. Sacc. Norm.* (Soc. Antiq.), vol. i., *Observ.*, p. clxi.

[3] Will. Newb. as above.   [4] *Gesta Hen.* as above, p. 67.

[5] R. Diceto (Stubbs), vol. i. p. 381.   Cf. *ib.* p. 385.

[6] *Gesta Hen.* as above, p. 72.

already fled back to Scotland;[1] at Huntingdon Geoffrey of
Lincoln came to meet him with a force of seven hundred
knights;[2] and three days later the garrison surrendered at
discretion.[3] The king then marched to S. Edmund's; here
he divided his host, sending half against Hugh Bigod's castle
of Bungay, while he himself led the other half to Framlingham, where Hugh was entrenched with five hundred knights
and his Flemish men-at-arms. The number of these, however, had dwindled greatly; when the royal host encamped
on July 24 at Sileham, close to Framlingham, Hugh felt
himself unable to cope with it; and next morning he
surrendered.[4] By the end of the month the whole struggle
was over. One by one the king's foes came to his feet as
he held his court at Northampton. The king of Scots was
brought, with his feet tied together under his horse's body,
from his prison[5] at Richmond.[6] On the last day of July
Bishop Hugh of Durham came to give up his castles of
Durham, Norham and Northallerton. On the same day the
earl of Leicester's three fortresses were surrendered by his
constables;[7] and Thirsk was given up by Robert of Mowbray.[8]
Earl Robert de Ferrers yielded up Tutbury and Duffield;[9]
the earl of Gloucester and his son-in-law Richard de Clare,
who were suspected of intriguing with the rebels, came to
offer their services and their obedience to the king;[10] and a

---

[1] Will. Newb., l. ii. c. 37 (Howlett, vol. i. p. 195).

[2] See Henry's remark at their meeting in Gir. Cambr. *Vita Galfr.*, l. i. c. 3
(Dimock, vol. iv. p. 368).

[3] *Gesta Hen.* (Stubbs), vol. i. p. 73. Cf. R. Diceto (Stubbs), vol. i. p. 384.

[4] *Gesta Hen.* as above. R. Diceto as above, p. 384, 385.

[5] Rog. Howden (Stubbs), vol. i. p. 64.

[6] Will. Newb., l. ii. c. 33 (as above, p. 185).

[7] *Gesta Hen.* as above. R. Diceto as above, p. 384, dates the surrender of
these three castles July 22—*i.e.* just as Henry was leaving Huntingdon for Suffolk.
The chronology of the *Gesta* seems much more probable. See in Will. Newb.,'l.
ii. c. 37 (as above, pp. 194, 195), how Henry frightened the constables into submission. Jordan Fantosme, vv. 2039-2046 (Michel, p. 92), has a different story about
Leicester. He makes David of Huntingdon its commandant, and says that as soon
as Henry received the news of the Scot king's capture, he forwarded it to David with
a summons to surrender; whereupon David gave up Leicester castle and himself
both at once.   [8] *Gesta Hen.* as above. R. Diceto (as above), p. 385.

[9] *Gesta Hen.* as above. Tutbury was being besieged by a host of Welshmen
under Rees Ap-Griffith; R. Diceto (as above), p. 384.

[10] R. Diceto as above, p. 385.

like offer came from far-off Galloway, whose native princes,
Uhtred and Gilbert, long unwilling vassals of the king of
Scots, had seized their opportunity to call home their men,
drive out William's bailiffs, destroy his castles and slaughter
his garrisons, and now besought his victorious English cousin
to become their protector and overlord.[1]   In three weeks
from Henry's landing in England all the royal fortresses
were again in his hands, and the country was once more at
peace.[2]

When England was secured, it was comparatively a light
matter to secure the rest.   Louis of France was so dismayed
at the sudden collapse of the rebellion in England—a collapse
which necessarily entailed a like fate upon the rebellion in
Normandy, since the leaders were the same men in both
cases—that he at once recalled the young king and the
count of Flanders from their project of invasion.   As a last
resource, all three concentrated their forces upon the siege of
Rouen.[3]   Its garrison held out gallantly until Henry had
time to recross the sea with his Brabantines and a thousand
Welshmen [4] who had already done good service under Rees
Ap-Griffith at the siege of Tutbury.[5]   On August 11, three
days after landing, he entered Rouen ;[6] a successful raid of
his Welshmen upon some French convoys, followed by an
equally successful sally of Henry himself against the besieging forces, sufficed to make Louis ask for a truce, under cover
of which he fled with his whole host back into his own
dominions.[7]   Some three weeks later [8] he and Henry met in

---

[1] Rog. Howden (Stubbs), vol. ii. p. 63.

[2] *Ib.* p. 65.   Rob. Torigni, a. 1174.

[3] *Gesta Hen.* (Stubbs), vol. i. p. 73.   Rog. Howden as above, p. 64.   Will.
Newb., l. ii. c. 36 (Howlett, vol. i. p. 190).   Gerv. Cant. (Stubbs), vol. i. p. 249.
R. Diceto (Stubbs), vol. i. p. 386.   [4] *Gesta Hen.* as above, p. 74.

[5] See R. Diceto as above, p. 384.   It seems most likely that these were
the same.   The Pipe Roll of 1174 (Eyton, *Itin. Hen. II.*, p. 183) has a charge of
£4 : 18 : 11 "in corredio Reis et aliorum Walensium qui venerunt ad regem in
expedicionem."

[6] R. Diceto as above, p. 385.   *Gesta Hen.* as above.   Rog. Howden as above,
p. 65.

[7] See the details of Louis's disgraceful conduct in *Gesta Hen.* as above, pp.
74-76, Rog. Howden as above, pp. 65, 66, R. Diceto as above, pp. 386, 387, Gerv.
Cant. as above, p. 250, and Will. Newb., l. ii. cc. 36 and 37 (as above, pp. 192-
196).   [8] On September 8.   *Gesta Hen.* as above, p. 76.

conference at Gisors and arranged a suspension of hostilities until Michaelmas on all sides, except between Henry and his son Richard, who was fighting independently against his father's loyal subjects in Poitou.[1] Henry marched southward at once ; Richard fled before him from place to place, leaving his conquests to fall back one by one into the hands of their rightful owner ; at last he suddenly returned to throw himself at his father's feet, and a few days before Michaelmas Henry concluded his war in Poitou [2] by entering Poitiers in triumph with Richard, penitent and forgiven, at his side.[3]

On the last day of September the two kings and all the princes met in conference between Tours and Amboise.[4] Henry's three elder sons accepted the endowments which he offered them ; in return, the young king gave his assent to a provision for John. A general amnesty was agreed upon ; all prisoners on both sides, except the king of Scots, the earls of Leicester and Chester and Ralf of Fougères, were released at once ; all the rebels returned to their allegiance, and were fully forgiven ; Henry claimed nothing from any of them save the restoration of their castles to the condition in which they had been before the war, and the right of taking such hostages and other security as he might choose.[5] These terms of course did not apply to England ; while, on the other hand, the king of Scots and his fellow-captives, whom Henry had brought back with him to Normandy and replaced in confinement at Falaise,[6] were excluded from them as prisoners of war.   It was at Falaise, on October 11, that Henry and his sons embodied their agreement in a written document.[7]   A few weeks later William of Scotland, with

---

[1] *Gesta Hen.* (Stubbs), vol. i. p. 76.   Rog. Howden (Stubbs), vol. ii. p. 66. Rob. Torigni, a. 1174.

[2] " Et sic finivit rex gwerram suam in Pictaviâ," comments the writer of the *Gesta Hen.* (as above) on the reconcilation.

[3] Rog. Howden as above, p. 67.

[4] *Ibid.   Gesta Hen.* as above.   Gerv. Cant. (Stubbs), vol. i. p. 250.   R. Diceto (Stubbs), vol. i. p. 394.   On the date given by this last see below, note 7.

[5] Treaty given at length in *Gesta Hen.* as above, pp. 77-79, and Rog. Howden as above, pp. 67-69 ; abridged in R. Diceto as above, pp. 394, 395.

[6] *Gesta Hen.* as above, p. 74.

[7] The treaty, as given in *Gesta Hen.* and Rog. Howden (see above), note

the formal assent of the bishops and barons of his realm, who had been allowed free access to him during his captivity, submitted to pay the price which Henry demanded for his ransom.   The legal relations between the crowns of England and Scotland had been doubtful ever since the days of William the Conqueror and Malcolm Canmore, if not since the days of Eadward the Elder and Constantine; henceforth they were to be doubtful no longer.   William the Lion became the liegeman of the English king and of his son for Scotland and for all his other lands, and agreed that their heirs should be entitled to a like homage and fealty from all future kings of Scots.   The castles of Roxburgh, Jedburgh, Berwick, Edinburgh and Stirling were required by Henry as security; and as soon as the treaty had been ratified at Valognes [1] William was sent over sea in a sort of honourable custody to enforce their surrender and thereby complete his own release.[2]

By the terms of Henry's treaty with France, all the English barons who held lands on both sides of the sea were to be at once re-instated in their continental possessions, except the castles over which the king resumed his ancient rights of garrison or of demolition.   Their English estates however were wholly at his mercy; but he made a very gentle use of his power over them.   He took in fact no personal vengeance at all; he exacted simply what was necessary for securing his own authority and the peace

---

5), is printed also in Rymer's *Fœdera*, vol. i. p. 30, with the addition of a date —Falaise—and the signatures of twenty-eight witnesses.   Among the latter is Geoffrey, bishop elect of Lincoln.   Now we know from R. Diceto (Stubbs), vol. i. p. 393, that Geoffrey came over from England to Normandy on October 8.   R. Diceto (*ib.* p. 394) gives the date of the meeting at which the treaty was made as October 11.   Is it not probable that he has substituted for the date of the making of the treaty that of its formal ratification at Falaise?

[1] This treaty, as given in *Gesta Hen.* (Stubbs), vol. i. pp. 96-99, and Rog. Howden (Stubbs), vol. ii. pp. 80-82 (and from them in Rymer's *Fœdera*, vol. i. pp. 30, 31), is dated at Falaise.   R. Diceto, however (Stubbs, vol. i. p. 396), who gives an abridgement of it, says it was made at Valognes, on December 8.   Now there is in Hearne's *Liber Niger*, vol. i. pp. 36-40, a copy of the treaty, differing from the former ones in having eighteen more witnesses (one cannot help noting the name of the last—" Roger Bacun ") and in its date, which is "Valognes."   No doubt the Falaise copy was made first, and this is the ratification of it.

[2] R. Diceto as above, p. 398.

of the realm—the instant departure of the Flemish mercenaries [1] and the demolition of unlicensed fortifications—and
for defraying the expenses of the war.   This was done by a
tax levied partly on the royal demesnes, partly on the estates
of the rebels throughout the country, on the basis of an
assessment made for that purpose during the past summer
by the sheriffs of the several counties, assisted by some
officers of the Exchequer.[2]   No ruinous sums were demanded;
even Hugh Bigod escaped with a fine of a thousand marks,
and lost none of the revenues of his earldom save for the
time that he was actually in open rebellion ; the third penny
of Norfolk was reckoned as due to him again from the third
day after his surrender, and its amount for two months was
paid to him accordingly at Michaelmas.[3]   Even the earls of
Leicester and Chester seem to have been at once set free ; [4]
and in little more than two years they were restored to all
their lands and honours, except their castles, which were
either razed or retained in the king's hands.[5]

This very clemency was in itself at once the strongest
proof of the completeness of Henry's victory and the surest
means of retaining the hold which he had now gained over
the barons.   The struggle whose course we have been trying
to follow has a special significance : it was the last struggle
in English history in which the barons were arrayed against
the united interests of the Crown and the people.   That
feudal pride which had revolted so often and so fiercely
against the determination of William the Conqueror and
Henry I. to enforce justice and order throughout their realm
stooped at last to acknowledge its master in Henry II.

---

[1] Hugh Bigod's Flemings and the knights sent over by the young king were
all sent out of the country immediately after Hugh's surrender, and the former
were made to swear that they would never set a hostile foot in England again.
R. Diceto (Stubbs), vol. i. p. 385.

[2] This is the "Assiza super dominica regis et super terras eorum qui recess-
erunt." Eyton, *Itin. Hen. II.*, pp. 184, 185.

[3] See extract from Pipe Roll 20 Hen. II. [a. 1174], and Mr. Eyton's comment
upon it, *Itin. Hen. II.*, p. 181, note 2.

[4] Hugh of Chester was probably released at the same time with the king of
Scots, for he signs among the witnesses to the treaty of Falaise. *Gesta Hen.*
(Stubbs), vol. i. p. 99. Rog. Howden (Stubbs), vol. ii. p. 82.

[5] *Gesta Hen.* as above, pp. 134, 135. Rog. Howden as above, p. 118.

In the unbroken tranquillity, the uninterrupted developement of reform in law and administration, the unchecked growth of the material and social prosperity of England during the remaining fifteen years of his reign, Henry and his people reaped the first-fruits of the anti-feudal policy which he and his predecessors had so long and so steadily maintained. Its full harvest was to be reaped after he was gone, not by the sovereign, but by the barons themselves, to whom his strong hand had at last taught their true mission as leaders and champions of the English people against a king who had fallen away from the traditions alike of the Norman and of the Angevin Henry.

CHAPTER V.

THE ANGEVIN EMPIRE.

1175–1183.

IN the seven years which followed the suppression of the barons' revolt Henry's prosperity reached its height. The rising in which all his enemies had united for his destruction had ended in leaving him seated more firmly than ever upon the most securely-established throne in Europe. Within the four seas of Britain he was master as no king had ever been master before him. The English people had been with him from the first, and was learning year by year to identify its interests more closely with his ; the Church, alienated for nearly ten years, was reconciled by his penance ; feudalism was beaten at last, and for ever. The Welsh princes were his obedient and serviceable vassals; the Scot king had been humbled to accept a like position ; a new subject-realm was growing up on the coast of Ireland. The great external peril which had dogged Henry's footsteps through life, the hostility of France, was for a while paralyzed by his success. Other external foes he had none ; the kings of Spain and of Sicily, the princes of the Western and even of the Eastern Empire, vied with each other in seeking the friendship, one might almost say the patronage, of the one sovereign in Europe who, safe on his sea-girt throne, could afford to be independent of them all. Within and without, on either side of the sea, all hindrances to the full and free developement of Henry's policy for the government of his whole dominions were thus completely removed.

In England itself the succeeding period was one of unbroken tranquillity and steady prosperous growth, social, intellectual, political, constitutional. Henry used his opportunity to make a longer stay in the island than he had ever made there before, save at the very beginning of his reign. He was there from May 1175 to August 1177 ; in the following July he returned, and stayed till April 1180 ; he came back again in July 1181, and remained till March 1182. Each of these visits was marked by some further step towards the completion of his judicial and administrative reforms. Almost as soon as he set foot in the country, indeed, he took up his work as if it had never been interrupted. The king and his eldest son went to England together on May 9, 1175 ;[1] on Rogation Sunday they publicly sealed their reconciliation with each other and with the Church in a great council which met at Westminster[2] under the presidence of a new archbishop of Canterbury, Richard, formerly prior of Dover, who after countless troubles and delays had been chosen just before the outbreak of the rebellion to fill S. Thomas's place,[3] and had come back from Rome in triumph, with his pallium and a commission as legate for all England, just as Henry was returning to Normandy from his success against Hugh Bigod.[4] From the council the two kings and the primate went all together on a pilgrimage to the martyr's tomb at Canterbury ;[5] at Whitsuntide the kings held a court at Reading,[6] and on S. Peter's day they met the Welsh princes in a great council at Gloucester.[7] Two days later the process, begun two years before, of filling up the vacant bishoprics and abbacies which had been accumulating during Thomas's exile was

---

[1] *Gesta Hen.* (Stubbs), vol. i. pp. 83, 84.   R. Diceto (Stubbs), vol. i. p. 399.

[2] *Gesta Hen.* as above, p. 84.   Gerv. Cant. (Stubbs), vol. i. p. 250.   R. Diceto as above, pp. 399-401.

[3] On the Canterbury troubles and Richard's election see Gerv. Cant. as above, pp. 239-242, 243-245, 247.

[4] *Ib.* p. 249.   R. Diceto as above, p. 391.   *Gesta Hen.* as above, p. 74.

[5] *Gesta Hen.* as above, p. 91.   Gerv. Cant. as above, p. 256.   R. Diceto as above, p. 399.

[6] *Gesta Hen.* as above.   [7] *Ib.* p. 92.

completed in another council at Woodstock.[1]   Thence, too,
was issued an edict for the better securing of order throughout the realm, and particularly around the person of the
king ; all his opponents in the late war were forbidden, on
pain of arrest as traitors, to come to the court without special
summons, and, under any circumstances, to come before sunrise or stay over night ; and all wearing of arms, knife, bow
and arrows, was forbidden on the English side of the Severn.
These prohibitions however were only temporary ;[2] and they
were, with one exception, the only measure of general
severity taken by Henry in consequence of the rebellion.
That exception was a great forest-visitation, begun by
Henry in person during the summer of 1175 and not
completed by his ministers, it seems, till Michaelmas 1177,
and from which scarcely a man throughout the kingdom,
baron or villein, layman or priest, was altogether exempt.
In vain did Richard de Lucy, as loyal to the people as to
the king, shew Henry his own royal writ authorizing the
justiciars to throw open the forests and give up the royal
fish-ponds to public use during the war, and protest against
the injustice of punishing the people at large for a trespass
to which he had himself invited them in the king's name and
in accordance, as he had understood it, with the king's expressed will.   The license had probably been used to a far
wider extent than Henry had intended ; the general excitement had perhaps vented itself in some such outburst of
wanton destructiveness as had occurred after the death of
Henry I. ; at any rate, the Norman and the Angevin blood
in Henry II. was all alike stirred into wrath at sight of
damage done to vert and venison ; the transgressors were
placed, in technical phrase, " at the king's mercy," and their
fines constituted an important item in the Pipe Roll of
1176.[3]

---

[1] *Gesta Hen.* (Stubbs), vol. i. p. 93.   Rog. Howden (Stubbs), vol. ii. pp. 78, 79.

[2] *Gesta Hen.* as above.   " Sed hæc præcepta parvo tempore custodita sunt."

[3] On the "misericordia regis pro foresta," as it is called in the Pipe Rolls, see
Gesta Hen. as above, pp. 92, 94 ; Rog. Howden as above, p. 79 ; R. Diceto
(Stubbs), vol. i. p. 402 ; Stubbs, *Constit. Hist.*, vol. i. p. 483 ; and the extracts
from the Pipe Rolls 22 and 23 Hen. II. (*i.e.* 1176 and 1177) in Madox, *Hist.
Exch.*, vol. i. pp. 541, 542.

In the beginning of that year the king assembled a great council at Northampton,[1] and thence issued an Assize which forms another link in the series of legal enactments begun at Clarendon just ten years before. The first three clauses and the twelfth clause of the Assize of Northampton are substantially a re-issue of those articles of the Assize of Clarendon which regulated the presentment, detention and punishment of criminals and the treatment of strangers and vagabonds.[2] The experience of the past ten years had however led to some modifications in the details of the procedure. The recognition by twelve lawful men of every hundred and four of every township, to be followed by ordeal of water, was re-enacted ; but the presentment was now to be made not to the sheriff, but direct to the king's justices. The punishments, too, were more severe than before ; the forger, robber, murderer or incendiary who under the former system would have suffered the loss of a foot was now to lose a hand as well, and to quit the realm within forty days.[3] The remaining articles dealt with quite other matters. The fourth declared the legal order of proceeding with regard to the estate of a deceased freeholder, in such a manner as to secure the rights of his heir and of his widow before the usual relief could be exacted by the lord ; and it referred all disputes between the lord and the heir touching the latter's right of inheritance to the decision of the king's justices, on the recognition of twelve lawful men[4] —a process which, under the name of the assize of *mort d'ancester*, soon became a regular part of the business transacted before the justices-in-eyre. Some of the other clauses

---

[1] On January 26. R. Diceto (Stubbs), vol. i. p. 404. Cf. *Gesta Hen.* (Stubbs), vol. i. p. 107, and Rog. Howden (Stubbs), vol. ii. p. 87. The *Gesta* date it merely "circa festum Conversionis S. Pauli"; Roger turns this into "in festo," etc., and adopts the reading "Nottingham" instead of "Northampton." Gerv. Cant. (Stubbs), vol. i. pp. 257, 258, confounds the Assize of Clarendon with the Constitutions.

[2] Cf. articles 1-3, 12 of Ass. Northampton (Stubbs, *Select Charters*, pp. 150, 151, 152), with Ass. Clarendon, cc. 1-4, 13, 15, 16 (*ib.* pp. 143, 144, 145). The Assize of Northampton is given in the *Gesta Hen.* as above, pp. 108-110, and by Rog. Howden as above, pp. 89-91.

[3] Ass. North. c. 1 (Stubbs, as above, p. 151).

[4] *Ib.* c. 4 (pp. 151, 152).

had a more political significance. They directed the justices to take an oath of homage and fealty to the king from every man in the realm, earl, baron, knight, freeholder or villein, before the octave of Whit-Sunday at latest, and to arrest as traitors all who refused it :[1]—to investigate and strictly enforce the demolition of the condemned castles ;[2] to ascertain and report by whom, how and where the duty of castle-guard was owed to the king ;[3] to inquire what persons had fled from justice and incurred the penalty of outlawry by failing to give themselves up at the appointed time, and to send in a list of all such persons to the Exchequer at Easter and Michaelmas for transmission to the king.[4] The tenth article was aimed at the bailiffs of the royal demesnes, requiring them to give an account of their stewardship before the Exchequer ;[5] and two others defined the justices' authority, as extending, in judicial matters, over all pleas of the Crown, both in criminal causes and in civil actions concerning half a knight's fee or less ; and in fiscal matters, over escheats, wardships, and lands and churches in royal demesne.[6]

The visitations of the justices by whom this assize was carried into effect were arranged upon a new plan, or rather upon a modified form of the plan which had been adopted two years before for the assessment of a tallage upon the royal demesnes, to meet the cost of the expected war. It was at that terrible crisis, when most men in Henry's place would have had no thought to spare for anything save the military necessities and perils of the moment, that he had first devised and carried into effect the principle of judicial circuits which with some slight changes in detail has remained in force until our own day. This tallage was levied by nineteen barons of the Exchequer, distributed into six companies, each company undertaking the assessment throughout a certain district or group of shires.[7] The

---

[1] Ass. North., c. 6 (Stubbs, *Select Charters*, p. 152).

[2] *Ib.* c. 8 (as above). [3] *Ib.* c. 11 (*ibid.*)

[4] *Ib.* c. 13 (pp. 152, 153). [5] *Ib.* c. 10 (p. 152).

[6] *Ib.* cc. 7 and 9 (*ibid.*).

[7] See the lists in Stubbs, *Gesta Hen.*, vol. ii., pref. p. lxv, note 5, and Eyton, *Itin. Hen. II.*, p. 176 ; from the Pipe Roll 19 Hen. II. (a. 1173).

abandonment of this scheme in the assizes of the two
following years was probably necessitated by the disturbed
state of the country.   But at the council of Northampton
the kingdom was again definitely mapped out into six divisions, to each of which three justices were sent.[1]   In the
report of their proceedings in the Pipe Roll of the year
they are for the first time since the Assize of Clarendon[2]
officially described by the title which they had long borne
in common speech, "*justitiæ itinerantes*" (or "*errantes*"),
justices-in-eyre ; and it is from this time that the regular
institution of itinerant judges is dated by modern legal
historians.[3]

This first distribution of circuits however was soon
altered.   In the very next year the same eighteen officers
made, in addition to their judicial circuits, a general visitation of the realm for fiscal purposes, in four companies
instead of six ;[4] and on Henry's return to England in the
summer of 1178 he made what at first glance looks like a
sweeping change in the organization of the Curia Regis.
"The king," we are told, "made inquiry concerning his
justices whom he had appointed in England, whether they
treated the men of the realm with righteousness and moder-
ation ; and when he learned that the country and the people
were sore oppressed by the great multitude of justices—for
they were eighteen in number—by the counsel of the wise
men of the realm he chose out five, two clerks and three
laymen, who were all of his private household ; and he
decreed that those five should hear all the complaints of
the realm, and do right, and that they should not depart
from the king's court, but abide there to hear the complaints
of his men ; so that if any question came up among them
which they could not bring to an end, it should be presented
to the king's hearing and determined as might please him
and the wise men of the realm."[5]   From the mention of the
number eighteen it appears that the persons against whom

---

[1] See lists in *Gesta Hen.* (Stubbs), vol. i. pp. 107, 108.
[2] Ass. Clar., c. 19 (Stubbs, *Select Charters*, p. 145).
[3] Stubbs, *Gesta Hen.*, vol. ii. pref. pp. lxix, lxx and notes.
[4] *Ib.* p. lxx and note 3.   [5] *Ib.* vol. i. pp. 207, 208.

were primarily directed both the complaint of the people
and the action of the king were the justices-in-eyre of the
last two years ; and this is confirmed by the fact that of all
these eighteen, only six were among the judges who went
on circuit in 1178 and 1179, while from 1180 onwards
only one of them reappears in that capacity, though many
of them retained their functions in the Exchequer.   In
1178 and 1179 moreover the circuits were reduced from
six to two, each being served by four judges.[1]   The enactment of 1178, however, evidently touched the central as
well as the provincial judicature, and with more important
results.   It took the exercise of the highest judicial functions
out of the hands of the large body of officers who made up
the Curia Regis as constituted until that time, and restricted it to a small chosen committee.   This was apparently the origin of a limited tribunal which, springing up thus
within the Curia Regis, soon afterwards appropriated its
name, and in later days grew into the Court of King's
Bench.   At the same time the reservation of difficult
cases for the hearing of the king in council points to the
creation, or rather to the revival, of a yet higher court of
justice, that of the king himself in council with his "wise
men " — a phrase which, while on the one hand it carries
us back to the very earliest form of the Curia Regis,
on the other points onward to its later developements
in the modern tribunals of equity or of appeal, the
courts of Chancery and of the Privy Council in its judicial
capacity.[2]

All these changes in the circuits and in the Curia Regis
had however another motive.   The chief obstacle to Henry's
judicial and legal reforms was the difficulty of getting them
administered according to the intention of their author.   It
was to meet this difficulty that Henry, as a contemporary
writer says, "while never changing his mind, was ever
changing his ministers."[3]   He had employed men chosen

---

[1] Stubbs, *Gesta Hen.*, vol. ii., pref. p. lxxi and note 2.
[2] Stubbs, *Constit. Hist.*, vol. i. pp. 486, 487, 601-603 ; *Gesta Hen.*, vol. ii.
pref. pp. lxxi, lxxiv-lxxvii.
[3] " Sic animum a proposito non immutans, circa personas mutabiles immut-

from every available class of society in turn, and none of his experiments had altogether brought him satisfaction. Feudal nobles, court officials, confidential servants and friends, had all alike been tried and, sooner or later, found wanting.[1] There was only one who had never yet failed him in a service of twenty-five years' duration—Richard de Lucy "the loyal"; but in the summer of 1179 Richard de Lucy, to his master's great regret, resigned his office of justiciar and retired to end his days a few months later as a brother of an Augustinian house which he had founded at Lesnes in Kent to the honour of S. Thomas of Canterbury.[2] Henry in this extremity fell back once more upon a precedent of his grandfather's time and determined to place the chief administration, for the moment at least, again in clerical hands. Instead of a single justiciar-bishop, however, he appointed three — the bishops of Winchester, Ely and Norwich;[3] all of whom, under their earlier appellations of Richard of Ilchester, Geoffrey Ridel and John of Oxford, had long ago acquired ample experience and shewn ample capacity for the work of secular administration.[4]

This arrangement was however only provisional. The number of judicial circuits was again raised to four, and to each of the three southern circuits was despatched one of the justiciar-bishops, with a royal clerk and three laymen to act as his subordinate assistants. The fourth circuit, which took in the whole district between the Trent and the Scottish border, was intrusted to six justices, of whom only two were clerks ; one of these, Godfrey de Lucy the archdeacon of Richmond, a brother of the late chief justiciar, stood nomin-

---

abilem semper sæpe mutavit sententiam." R. Diceto (Stubbs), vol. i. p. 434—part of a long passage which sets forth very fully the motives and the general aims and results of Henry's administrative changes.

[1] R. Diceto as above, pp. 434-435.

[2] *Gesta Hen.* (Stubbs), vol. i. p. 238. Cf. Rog. Howden (Stubbs), vol. ii. p. 190.   [3] R. Diceto as above, p. 435.

[4] Richard of Ilchester is well known as an active official of the Exchequer ; see below, pp. 193, 194. Geoffrey Ridel seems to have acted as vice-chancellor throughout S. Thomas's primacy and exile ; see Eyton, *Itin. Hen. II.*, p. 174, note 1. As for John of Oxford, his diplomatic talents are only too notorious.

ally at the head of the commission ; but there can be little
doubt that its real head was one of his lay colleagues—Ralf
de Glanville,[1] the faithful sheriff of Lancashire and castellan
of Richmond to whom William the Lion had given up his
sword at Alnwick in 1174 ;[2] and these six were appointed
to form the committee for hearing the complaints of the
people, apparently in succession to the five who had been
selected in the previous year.[3]   All four bodies of judges
brought up a report of their proceedings to the king at
Westminster on August 27,[4] and it seems to have been the
most satisfactory which he had yet received.   When he
went over sea in the following April, he left Ralf de Glanville to represent him in England as chief justiciar.[5]   Ralf's
business capacities proved to be at least as great, and his
honesty as stainless, as those of his predecessor ; and from
that time forth the management of the entire legal and
judicial administration was left in his hands.   Circuits,
variously distributed, continued to be made from year to
year and for divers purposes by companies of judges, ranging in total numbers from three to twenty-two ;[6] while the
King's Court and the Exchequer pursued their work on the
lines already laid down, without further interruption, till the
end of Henry's reign.

The last of Henry's great legal measures, with the exception of a Forest Assize issued in 1184, was an ordinance
published in the autumn of 1181 and known as the Assize
of Arms.   Its object was to define more fully and exactly
the military obligations of the people at large in the service
of the king and the defence of the country ;—in a word, to
put once again upon a more definite footing the old institu-

---

[1] See the lists in *Gesta Hen.* (Stubbs), vol. i. pp. 238, 239 ; Rog. Howden
(Stubbs), vol. ii. pp. 190, 191.

[2] Jordan Fantosme, v. 1811 (Michel, p. 82).

[3] "Isti sex sunt justitiæ in curiâ regis constituti ad audiendum clamores
populi." *Gesta Hen.* as above, p. 239. See on this Stubbs, *Gesta Hen.*, vol. ii.
pref. p. lxxiii, and *Constit. Hist.*, vol. i. pp. 601, 602.

[4] R. Diceto (Stubbs), vol. i. p. 436.

[5] Rog. Howden as above, p. 215.

[6] See notices of the circuits and of the sessions of the Curia Regis and Exchequer in Eyton, *Itin. Hen. II.*, pp. 236, 237, 243, 244, 247, 248, 249, 251,
253, 258, 259, 265, 272, 273, 281, 291.

tion of the " fyrd," which was the only effective counterpoise
to the military power of the barons, and whose services in
1173 and 1174 had proved it to be well worthy of the
royal consideration and encouragement.   The Assize of 1181
declared the obligation of bearing arms at the king's command to be binding upon every free layman in the realm.
The character of the arms with which men of various ranks
were required to provide themselves was defined according
to a graduated scale, from the full equipment of the knight
down to the mail-coat, steel-cap and spear of the burgher
and the simple freeman.[1]   The justices were directed to
ascertain, through the " lawful men " of the hundreds and
towns, what persons fell under each category, to enroll their
names, read out the Assize in their presence, and make them
swear to provide themselves with the proper accoutrements
before S. Hilary's day.[2]   Every man's arms were to be carefully kept and used solely for the royal service ; they were
not to be taken out of the country, or alienated in any way ;[3]
at their owner's death they were to pass to his heir ;[4] if any
man possessed other arms than those required of him by the
Assize, he was to dispose of them in such a manner that
they might be used in the king's service ;[5] and all this was
enforced by a stern threat of corporal punishment upon
defaulters.[6]

The freemen who were armed under this Assize had
little occasion to use their weapons so long as King Henry
lived.   Within the four seas of Britain there was almost
unbroken peace till the end of his reign.   The treaty with
Scotland was ratified by the public homage of William the
Lion to Henry and his son at York on August 10, 1175 ;[7]
and thenceforth Henry's sole trouble from that quarter was
the necessity of arbitrating between William and his unruly

---

[1] Ass. Arms, cc. 1-3 (Stubbs, *Select Charters*, p. 154; from *Gesta Hen.*,
vol. i. pp. 278-280.   The Assize is also given by Rog. Howden, vol. ii. pp.
261, 262).

[2] *Ib.* cc. 9 and 4 (Stubbs as above, pp. 155, 156, 154).

[3] *Ib.* cc. 4, 8 (pp. 154, 155).   [4] *Ib.* c. 5 (p. 155).

[5] *Ib.* cc. 6, 7 (as above).   [6] *Ib.* c. 10 (p. 156).

[7] *Gesta Hen.* (as above), pp. 94-96. Rog. Howden (Stubbs), vol. ii. p. 79.
Cf. Will. Newb., l. ii. c. 38 (Howlett, vol. i. p. 198).

vassals in Galloway,[1] and of advising him in his ecclesiastical difficulties with the Roman see. The western border of England was less secure than the northern ; yet even in Wales the authority of the English Crown had made a considerable advance since Henry's accession. His first Welsh war, directed against the princes of North Wales in 1157, had little practical result. A second expedition marched in 1163 against Rees Ap-Griffith, prince of South Wales, and a lucky incident at the outset insured its success. Directly in the king's line of march from Shrewsbury into South Wales, between Wenlock and Newport, there ran a streamlet called Pencarn—a mountain-torrent passable only at certain points. One of these was an ancient ford concerning which a prophecy attributed to the enchanter Merlin declared : "When ye shall see a strong man with a freckled face rush in upon the Britons, if he cross the ford of Pencarn, then know ye that the might of Cambria shall perish." The Welsh guarded this ford with the utmost care to prevent Henry from crossing it ; he, ignorant of the prophecy, sent his troops over by another passage, and was about to follow them himself, when a loud blast from their trumpets on the opposite bank caused his horse to rear so violently that he was obliged to turn away and seek a means of crossing elsewhere. He found it at the fatal spot, and as the Welsh saw him dash through the stream their hearts sank in despair.[2] He marched unopposed from one end of South Wales to the other, through Glamorgan and Carmarthen as far as Pencader ;[3] here Rees made his submission ;[4] and Rees himself, Owen of North Wales, and several other Welsh princes appeared and swore allegiance to King Henry and his heir in that famous council of Woodstock where the first quarrel arose between Henry and Thomas of Canterbury.[5]

[1] On the Galloway affair see *Gesta Hen.* (Stubbs), vol. i. pp. 67, 68, 79, 80, 99, 126, 313, 336, 339, 348, 349 ; Rog. Howden (Stubbs), vol. ii. pp. 63, 69, 105, 299, 309.   [2] Gir. Cambr. *Itin. Kambr.* l. i. c. 6 (Dimock, vol. vi. pp. 62, 63).   [3] *Ib.* l. ii. c. 10 (p. 138).   [4] Ann. Cambr. a. 1164 (Williams, p. 49). *Brut y Tywys.*, a. 1162 (Williams, p. 199). Both dates are self-evidently wrong ; the only possible one is the intermediate year.   [5] R. Diceto (Stubbs), vol. i. p. 311.

Next year Rees, provoked as he alleged by Henry's non-fulfilment of his promises and also by the shelter given to the slayer of his nephew by Earl Roger of Clare, harried the whole border and roused all Wales to fling off the yoke of the "Frenchmen," as the Welsh still called their Norman conquerors.[1]   Henry was obliged to delay his vengeance till the following summer, when it furnished him with an excellent pretext for escaping from his ecclesiastical and political entanglements on the continent.[2]   He set out from Oswestry[3] at the head of a vast army drawn from all parts of his dominions, both insular and continental, and reinforced by Flemish and Scottish allies.[4]   All the princes of Wales were arrayed against him, and both parties intended the campaign to be decisive.   But the wet climate of the Welsh hills proved a more dangerous foe than the mountaineers themselves ; and after remaining for some time encamped at Berwen, Henry was compelled to beat an ignominious retreat, completely defeated by the ceaseless rain,[5] and venting his baffled wrath against the Welsh in a savage mutilation of their hostages.[6]   For six years after this, as we have seen, he never had time to visit his island realm at all, and the daring "French" settlers in Wales or on its borders, such as the Geraldines or the De Clares, were free to fight their own battles and make their own alliances with the Welsh just as they chose ; it was not till Henry in 1171 followed them to their more distant settlement in Ireland that he again entered South Wales.   Then he used his

[1] Ann. Cambr. a. 1165 (Williams, pp. 49, 50).   *Brut y Tywys.*, a. 1163 (Williams, p. 199).   [2] See above, p. 56, note 3.

[3] Ann. Cambr. a. 1166 (*i.e.* 1165 ; Williams, p. 50).   *Brut y Tywys.*, a. 1164 (Williams, p. 201).   Gir. Cambr. *Itin. Kambr.*, l. ii. c. 10 (Dimock, vol. vi. p. 138).   According to the *Brut* (as above) Henry first "moved an army with extreme haste, and came to Rhuddlan, and purposed to erect a castle there, and stayed there three nights.   After that he returned into England, and collected a vast army," etc.   Following this, Mr. Bridgeman (*Princes of S. Wales*, p. 48) and Mr. Eyton (*Itin. Hen. II.*, pp. 79, 82) divide the Welsh campaign of 1165 into two, one in May and the other in July.   Neither the Ann. Cambr. nor Gerald, however, make any mention of the Rhuddlan expedition.

[4] Ann. Cambr. and *Brut y Tywys.* as above.

[5] *Brut y Tywys.*, a. 1164 (Williams, pp. 201, 203).

[6] *Ibid.* (p. 203).   Chron. Mailros a. 1165.

opportunity for a series of personal interviews with Rees,[1] which ended in a lasting agreement. Rees was left, in the phrase of his native chronicler, as the king's "justice" over all South Wales.[2] How far he maintained, along the border or within his own territories, the peace and order whose preservation formed the main part of an English justiciar's duty, may be doubted ; but in the rebellion of 1174 he shewed his personal loyalty to the king by marching all the way into Staffordshire to besiege Tutbury for him, and some of his followers did equally good service in the suppression of the Norman revolt.[3] David of North Wales, too, if he did nothing to help the king, at least resisted the temptation of joining his enemies ; and the war was no sooner fairly over than, anxious that some reflection of the glories of English royalty should be cast over his own house, he became an eager suitor for the hand of Henry's half-sister Emma— a suit which Henry found it politic to grant.[4] A few months later, in June 1175, the king made an attempt to secure the tranquillity of the border by binding all the barons of the district in a sworn mutual alliance for its defence.[5] The attempt was not very successful ; the border-warfare went on in much the same way as of old ; but it was not till the summer of 1184 that it grew serious enough to call for Henry's personal intervention, and then a march to Worcester sufficed to bring Rees of South Wales once more to his feet.[6]

It was the latest-won dependency of the English crown which during these years gave the most trouble to its wearer. If Henry found it hard to secure fit instruments for the work of government and administration in England, he found it harder still to secure them for the same work in Ireland. At the outbreak of the barons' revolt he had at once guarded against all danger of the rebels finding support in Ireland by recalling the garrisons which he had left in the

[1] See *Brut y Tywys.*, a. 1171, 1172 (Williams, pp. 213-219).
[2] *Ib.* a. 1172 (p. 219).   [3] See above, p. 164.
[4] R. Diceto (Stubbs), vol. i. pp. 397, 398.
[5] At the council held at Gloucester on June 29.   *Gesta Hen.* (Stubbs), vol. i. p. 92.   [6] *Ib.* p. 314.

Irish coast-towns and summoning the chief men of the new
vassal state, particularly Richard of Striguil and Hugh de
Lacy, to join him personally in Normandy.[1]   Richard served
him well in the war as commandant of the important border-
fortress of Gisors ;[2] and it may have been as a reward for
these services that he was sent back to Ireland as governor
in Hugh's stead[3] at the close of the year.   For the next
two years, while the king had his hands full in Normandy
and England, matters in Ireland went much as they had
gone before his visit there ; the Norman-English settlers
pursued their strifes and their alliances with their Irish
neighbours or with each other, and granted out to their
followers the lands which they won, entirely at their own
pleasure.[4]   But the lesson which Henry was meanwhile
teaching their brethren in England was not thrown away
upon them ; and at the close of 1175 it was brought home
to them in another way.   Roderic O'Conor, moved as it
seems by the fame of Henry's successes, and also perhaps
by two papal bulls—Adrian's famous " Laudabiliter," and
another from the reigning Pope Alexander—which Henry
had lately caused to be published at Waterford,[5] at last bent
his stubborn independence to send three envoys to the
English king with overtures for a treaty of peace.   The
treaty was signed at Windsor on October 6.   Roderic submitted to become Henry's liegeman, and to pay him a yearly
tribute of one hide "pleasing to the merchants " for every
ten head of cattle throughout Ireland ; on these conditions
he was confirmed in the government and administration of
justice over the whole island, except Leinster, Meath and
Waterford, and authorized to reckon upon the help of the
royal constables in compelling the obedience of his vassals
and collecting from them their share of the tribute.[6]

[1] Anglo-Norm. Poem (Michel), pp. 136-141. Cf. above, p. 145.

[2] Anglo-Norm. Poem (Michel), p. 137.

[3] Gir. Cambr. *Expugn. Hibern.*, l. i. c. 44 (Dimock, vol. v. p. 298).

[4] For the history of these years in Ireland see Four Masters, a. 1173-1175
(O'Donovan, vol. iii. pp. 9-23) ; Gir. Cambr. *Expugn. Hibern.*, l. ii. cc. 1-4
(Dimock, vol. v. pp. 308-314) ; Anglo-Norm. Poem (Michel), pp. 142 to end.

[5] Gir. Cambr. as above, c. 5 (pp. 315-319).

[6] *Gesta Hen.* (Stubbs), vol. i. pp. 101-103.   Rog. Howden (Stubbs), vol. ii.
pp. 83, 84.

This scheme might perhaps have answered at least as well as a similar plan had answered during a few years in South Wales, had it not been for the disturbed condition of the English settlement. The death of Richard of Striguil in 1176[1] left the command in the hands of his brother-in-law and constable, Raymond the Fat, who for some years had been not only the leader of his forces, but also his chief adviser and most indispensable agent in all matters political and military.[2] A jealous rival, however, had already brought Raymond into ill repute at court,[3] and the king's seneschal William Fitz-Aldhelm was sent to supersede him.[4] William appears to have been a loyal servant of the king, but his tact and wisdom did not equal his loyalty. At the moment of landing his suspicions were aroused by the imposing display of armed followers with which Raymond came to meet him ; the muttered words which he incautiously suffered to escape his lips—" I will soon put an end to all this !"—were enough to set all the Geraldines against him at once ; and the impolitic haste and severity with which he acted upon his suspicions, without waiting to prove their justice,[5] drove the whole body of the earlier settlers into such a state of irritation that early in the next year Henry found it necessary to recall him.[6] Meanwhile the aggressive spirit of the English settlers had made Henry's treaty with Roderic almost a dead letter. In defiance of the rights which that treaty reserved to the Irish monarch, they had profited by the mutual dissensions of the lesser native chieftains to extend their own power far beyond the limits therein laid down. A civil war in Munster had ended in its virtual subjugation by Raymond and his Geraldine kinsfolk ;[7] a like pretext had

---

[1] Gir. Cambr. *Expugn. Hibern.*, l. ii. c. 14 (Dimock, vol. v. p. 332). R. Diceto (Stubbs), vol. i. p. 407. Four Masters, a. 1176 (O'Donovan, vol. iii. p. 25). *Gesta Hen.* (Stubbs), vol. i. p. 125.

[2] Gir. Cambr. as above, cc. 1-3 (pp. 308-313).

[3] *Ib.* cc. 10, 11 (pp. 327, 328).

[4] *Gesta Hen.* as above. Rog. Howden (Stubbs), vol. ii. p. 100.

[5] Gir. Cambr. as above, c. 15 (pp. 334-337).

[6] *Ib.* c. 20 (p. 347). Gerald gives no date for the recall of William ; but it seems to have been before the nomination of John as king of Ireland in May 1177 ; see below, p. 184.

[7] Gir. Cambr. as above, cc. 7, 12, 13 (pp. 320-323, 329-332).

served for an invasion of Connaught itself by Miles Cogan ;[1] John de Courcy was in full career of conquest in Ulster.[2] Henry could scarcely have put a stop to all this, even had he really wished to do so ; and by this time he was probably more inclined to encourage any extension of English power in Ireland, for he had devised a new scheme for the government of that country.

The bride of John " Lackland," Alice of Maurienne, had died within a year of her betrothal.[3]   The marriage-contract indeed provided that in case of such an event her sister should take her place ; but the connexion had begun too inauspiciously for either Henry or Humbert to have any desire of renewing it ; and Henry now saw a possibility of more than repairing within his insular dominions the ill-luck which had befallen his plans of advancement on the continent for his favourite child.   In the autumn of 1176 John was betrothed to his cousin Avice, the youngest of the three daughters of Earl William of Gloucester, and Avice was made heiress to the whole of the vast estates in the west of England and South Wales which her father had inherited from his parents, Earl Robert of Gloucester and Mabel of Glamorgan.[4]   But a mere English earldom, however important, was not enough to satisfy Henry's ambition for his darling.   In his scheme Avice's wealth was to furnish her bridegroom with the means of supporting a loftier dignity. He had now, it was said, obtained Pope Alexander's leave to make king of Ireland whichever of his sons he might choose.   On the strength of this permission he seems to have reverted to his original scheme of conquering the whole island.[5]   In May 1177 he publicly announced his intention of bestowing the realm of Ireland upon his youngest son John,

---

[1] Four Masters, a. 1177 (O'Donovan, vol. iii. p. 35).   Ann. Loch Cé, a. 1177 (Hennessy, vol. i. p. 155).   Gir. Cambr. *Expugn. Hibern.*, l. ii. c. 19 (Dimock, vol. v. p. 346).

[2] Gir. Cambr. as above, c. 17 (pp. 338-343).   Four Masters, as above, pp. 29-33. Ann. Loch Cé, as above, pp. 155-157.   *Gesta Hen.* (Stubbs), vol. i. pp. 137, 138 Rog. Howden (Stubbs), vol. ii. p. 120.

[3] *Art de vérifier les Dates*, vol. xvii. p. 165.

[4] *Gesta Hen.* as above, p. 124.   Rog. Howden as above, p. 100.   Cf. R. Diceto (Stubbs), vol. i. p. 415.   [5] *Gesta Hen.* as above, p. 161.

FRANCE & BURGUNDY
cir. 1180.
Shewing the growth of the Angevin
Empire from the time of Fulk the Black.

*Anjou 987, Touraine 1044, Maine 1111, Normandy 1144,
Aquitaine and Gascony 1152, England 1154, Nantes 1158,
Quercy 1160, Britanny 1169, Overlordship of Toulouse
1173.*

| | Royal Domain (France) |
| --- | Royal Domain (France) |

Royal Domain (France).
House of St. Gilles (Tou-
louse)
Aragon
Provence
Maurienne

and parcelled out the southern half of the country among
a number of feudal tenants, who did homage for their new
fiefs to him and John in a great council at Oxford.[1] As
however John was too young to undertake the government
in person, his father was again compelled to choose a viceroy.
He fell back upon his earliest choice and re-appointed Hugh
de Lacy ;[2] and with the exception of a temporary disgrace in
1181,[3] it was Hugh who occupied this somewhat thankless
office during the next seven years. With the internal
history of Ireland during his administration and throughout
the rest of Henry's reign we are not called upon to deal
here ; for important as are its bearings upon the history of
England, their importance did not become apparent till a
much later time than that of the Angevin kings.

It is during these years of prosperity and peace that we
are able to get the clearest view of the scope and aims of
Henry's general scheme of home and foreign policy. That
policy, when fully matured in its author's mind, formed a
consistent whole ; it was however made up of two distinct
parts, originating in the twofold position of Henry himself.
His empire extended from the western shores of Ireland to
the Cévennes, and from the northernmost point of the mainland of Britain to the Pyrenees. But this empire was composed of a number of separate members over which his
authority differed greatly in character and degree. These

[1] *Gesta Hen.* (Stubbs), vol. i. pp. 162-165. Rog. Howden (Stubbs), vol. ii.
pp. 133-135.

[2] The *Gesta Hen.* as above, p. 161, seem to imply that the appointment
was given to Hugh of Chester. After relating the earl's restoration to his lands
and honours, they add : "Et postea præcepit ei [rex] ut iret in Hiberniam ad
subjiciendum eam sibi et Johanni filio suo . . . et præcepit prædicto comiti ut
debellaret reges et potentes Hiberniæ qui subjectionem ei facere noluerunt."
Hugh de Lacy is named simply in the general list of whose who were to accompany him. But Gerald (*Expugn. Hibern.*, l. ii. c. 20, Dimock, vol. v. p. 347),
says that Hugh de Lacy was re-appointed viceroy at this time. That he acted as
such for the next seven years is certain, while there is, as far as I know, no indication that his namesake of Chester ever was in Ireland at all. It seems therefore
that either the earl refused the office—or the king changed his mind—or the author
of the *Gesta*, confused by the identity of Christian names, has substituted one
Hugh for another.

[3] When he was superseded for about half a year by John de Vesci (the constable of Chester) and Richard de Pec. Gir. Cambr. as above, c. 23 (pp. 355,
356). *Gesta Hen.* as above, p. 270.

members, again, fell into two well-marked groups. Over
the one group Henry ruled as supreme head ; no other
sovereign had ever claimed to be his superior, none now
claimed to be even his equal, within the British Isles. In
the other group, however, he had at least a nominal superior
in the king of France. It was impossible to deal with these
two groups of states on one and the same principle ; and
Henry had never attempted to do so. The one group had
its centre in England, the other in Anjou. As a necessary
consequence, Henry's policy had also two centres throughout
his reign. The key to it as a whole lies in its blending of
two characters united in one person, yet essentially distinct :
the character of the king of England and supreme lord of
the British Isles, and the character of the head of the house
of Anjou. Henry himself evidently kept the two characters
distinct in his own mind. His policy as king of England,
however little it may have been consciously aimed at such a
result—and we should surely be doing a great injustice to
Henry's sagacity if we doubted that it was so aimed, at least
in some degree—certainly tended to make England a strong
and independent national state, with its vassal states, Scotland,
Wales and Ireland, standing around it as dependent allies.
If he had ever for a moment dreamed of reducing his insular
dominions to a mere subject-province of the empire which he
was building up in Gaul, when he thought of intrusting their
government to his boy-heir under the guardianship of Thomas,
that dream had been broken at once and for ever by the
quarrel which deprived the child of his guardian and the
king of his friend. But, on the other hand, Henry certainly
never at any time contemplated making his continental
empire a mere dependency of the English crown. It was
distinctly an Angevin empire, with its centre in the spot
whence an Angevin count had been promised of old that the
sway of his descendants should spread to the ends of the
earth. Henry in short had another work to carry on besides that of Cnut and William and Henry I. He had to
carry on also the work of Fulk the Black and Geoffrey
Martel and Fulk V.; and although to us who know how
speedy was to be its overthrow that work looks a compar-

atively small matter, yet at the time it may well have seemed
equally important with the other in the eyes both of Henry
and of his contemporaries. While what may be called the
English thread in the somewhat tangled skein of Henry's life
runs smoothly and uneventfully on from the year 1175 to
the end, it is this Angevin thread which forms the clue to
the political and personal, as distinguished from the social
and constitutional, interest of all the remaining years of his
reign. And from this interest, although its centre is at
Angers, England is not excluded. For the whole continental relations of Henry were coloured by his position as
.an English king ; and the whole foreign relations of England,
from his day to our own, have been coloured by the fact
that her second King Henry was also head of the Angevin
house when that house was at the height of its continental
power and glory.

The prophecy said to have been made to Fulk the
Good was now literally fulfilled. The dominions of his
posterity reached to the uttermost ends of the known world.
In the far east, one grandson of Fulk V. ruled over the little
strip of Holy Land which formed the boundary of Christendom against the outer darkness of unexplored heathendom.
In the far west, another of Fulk's grandsons was, formally at
least, acknowledged overlord of the island beyond which, in
the belief of those days, lay nothing but a sea without a
shore. Scarcely less remarkable, however, was the fulfilment of the prediction in a narrower sense. The whole
breadth of Europe and the whole length of the Mediterranean sea parted the western from the eastern branch of
the Angevin house. But in Gaul itself, the Angevin
dominion now stretched without a break from one end of
the land to the other. The Good Count's heir held in his
own hands the whole Gaulish coast-line from the mouth of
the Somme to that of the Bidassoa, and he could almost
touch the Mediterranean Sea through his vassal the count of
Toulouse. Step by step the lords of the little Angevin
march had enlarged their borders till they enclosed more
than two-thirds of the kingdom of France. Fulk Nerra
and Geoffrey Martel had doubled their possessions by the

conquest of Touraine to the south-east ; Fulk V. had tripled them by the annexation of Maine to the northward ; Geoffrey Plantagenet's marriage with the heiress of Normandy had brought him to the shores of the English Channel. The whole series of annexations and conquests whereby his son expanded his continental dominions to the extent which they covered thirty years after Geoffrey's death resulted simply from a continuation of the same policy which, a century and a half before, had laid the foundations of the Angevin empire. Count Henry Fitz-Empress stood in a figure, like Count Fulk the Black, upon the rock of Angers, looked around over his marchland and its borders, noted every point at which those borders might be strengthened, rounded off or enlarged, and set himself to the pursuit of Fulk Nerra's work in Fulk Nerra's own spirit. For such a survey indeed he needed a more wide-reaching vision than even that of the Black Falcon. The work had altered vastly in scale since it left the "great builder's" hands ; but it had not changed in character. Henry's policy in Gaul was essentially the same as Fulk's—a policy of consolidation, rather than of conquest. He clearly never dreamed, as a man of less cautious ambition might well have done in his place, of pitting the whole strength of his continental and insular dominions against that of the French Crown in a struggle for the mastery of Gaul ; he seems never to have dreamed even of trying to free himself from his feudal obedience to a sovereign far inferior to him in territorial wealth and power ; he never, so far as we can see, aspired to stand in any other relation to the French king than that which had been held by his forefathers. He aimed in fact simply at compacting and securing his own territories in Gaul, and maintaining the rank of the head of the Angevin house, as the most influential vassal of the Crown. If he ever saw, on a distant horizon, a vision of something greater than this, he kept his dream to himself and, like Fulk of old, left his successors to attempt its fulfilment.

An ambition so moderate as this entailed no very complicated schemes of foreign diplomacy. As a matter of fact, Henry was at some time or other in his reign in diplomatic relations with every state and every ruler in Christendom,

Map VI.

MAP OF
EUROPE
cir. 1180.

Abbreviations:
An.= Anjou
Au.= Auvergne
B = Burgundy
Bl.= Burk
Ch.= Quatres
Fr.= Frence
R.= Roussillon
T.= Tourainne
Verm.= Vermandois

London, Macmillan & Co.

from Portugal to Norway, and from the count of Montferrat
to the Eastern and Western Emperors. But these relations
sprang for the most part from his insular rather than from
his continental position ; or, more exactly, they arose from
his position as a king of England, but a king far mightier
than any who had gone before him. It was the knowledge
that Henry had at his back all the forces of the island-crown
which roused in Louis VII. such a restless jealousy of his
power in Gaul ; and it was the jealousy of Louis which
drove Henry into a labyrinth of diplomacy and of war,
neither of which was a natural result of Henry's own policy.
A very brief glance at Henry's foreign relations will suffice
to shew that they concerned England far more than Anjou.
A considerable part of them arose directly out of his quarrel
with the English primate. Such was the case with his
German and Italian alliances, designed to counterbalance
the French king's league with the Pope. The alliances
formed through the marriages of his daughters were all
strictly alliances made by the English Crown. The immediate occasion of Matilda's marriage with Henry of
Saxony was her father's quarrel with S. Thomas; in another
point of view, this union was only a natural continuation of
a policy which may be traced through the wedding of her
grandmother with Henry V. and that of Gunhild with Henry
III. back to the wedding of Æthelstan's sister Eadgifu with
Charles the Simple. The marriages of Eleanor and Jane
were first planned during the same troubled time ; in each
case the definite proposal came from the bridegroom, and
came in the shape of an humble suit to the king of England
for his daughter's hand ; and in the case of all three sisters,
the proposal was laid before a great council of the bishops
and barons of England, and only accepted after formal
deliberation upon it with them, as upon a matter which concerned the interests of England as a state.[1] When Jane
went to be married to the king of Sicily in 1176, the details

---

[1] On the marriages of Matilda and Eleanor see above, pp. 55, 59, 60, and the
references there given ; on that of Jane, *Gesta Hen.* (Stubbs), vol. i. pp. 116, 117;
Rog. Howden (Stubbs), vol. ii. p. 94; R. Diceto (Stubbs), vol. i. p. 408 : Rymer,
Fœdera, vol. i. p. 32.

of her journey to her new home and of the honours which she received on her arrival there were recorded in England as matters of national interest and national pride.[1] When in the following year her sister Eleanor's husband, Alfonso of Castille, submitted a quarrel between himself and his kinsman the king of Navarre to his father-in-law's arbitration, the case was heard in an assembly of the English barons and wise men at Westminster.[2] Henry's daughters in short were instruments of his regal, his national, his English policy ; for the carrying out of his Angevin, his family policy, he looked to his sons.

The arrangement by which he endeavoured to make them carry it out is however not very easy to understand or to account for. He had long since abandoned his early scheme of devoting himself entirely to continental politics and making England over to the hands of his eldest son. That scheme, indeed, had been frustrated in the first instance by his quarrel with Thomas ; although it seemed to have been revived in 1170, it was as a mere temporary expedient to meet a temporary need ; and the revolt of 1173 put an end to it altogether, by proving clearly to Henry that he must never again venture to delegate his kingly power and authority to any one, even for a season. But, on the other hand, it is not easy at once to see why, during the years which followed, he persistently refused to give to his eldest son as much real, though subordinate, power on the continent as he was willing to give to the younger ones—why young Henry was not suffered to govern Anjou and Normandy as Richard was suffered to govern Aquitaine and Geoffrey to govern Britanny, so soon as they were old enough, under the control of their father as overlord. So far as we can venture to guess at the king's motives, the most probable reason seems to be that he could not part with any share of authority over his ancestral dominions without parting at the same time with his ancestral dignities.

---

[1] R. Diceto (Stubbs), vol. i. pp. 414, 415, 418; *Gesta Hen.* (Stubbs), vol. i. pp. 120, 127, 157, 158, 169-172 ; Rog. Howden (Stubbs), vol. ii. pp. 95-98; Gerv. Cant. (Stubbs), vol. i. pp. 263-265.

[2] *Gesta Hen.* as above, pp. 139-154; Rog. Howden as above, pp. 120, 131.

From a strictly Angevin or Cenomannian point of view,
Aquitaine and Britanny were both simply appendages,
diversely acquired, to the hereditary Angevin and Cenomannian dominions.   Nay, from a strictly Norman point of view,
England itself was but an addition to the heritage of the
Norman ducal house.   Henry might make over all these to
his sons as under-fiefs to govern in subjection to him, and
yet retain intact his position as head of the sovereign houses
of Normandy and Anjou.   But to place his mother's duchy
and his father's counties in other hands—to reduce them to
the rank of under-fiefs, keeping for himself no closer connexion with them than a mere general overlordship—would
have been, in principle, to renounce his birthright ; while in
practice, it would probably have been equivalent to complete
abdication, as far as his continental empire was concerned.
Henry would have had as little chance of enforcing his
claim to overlordship without a territorial basis on which to
rest it, as a German Emperor without his hereditary duchy of
Saxony or Franconia or Suabia, or a French king without
his royal domain.   In short, when Henry found it impossible
to give England to his eldest son, he had nothing else to
give him, unless he gave him all ; and Henry Fitz-Empress
was no more inclined than William the Conqueror had been
to " take off his clothes before he was ready to go to bed."
All his schemes for the distribution of his territories, therefore, from 1175 onwards, were intended solely to insure a
fair partition among his sons after his own death ; his
general aim being that young Henry should step into exactly
his own position as king of England, duke of Normandy and
count of Anjou, and overlord of Britanny, Aquitaine, and
all other dependencies of the Angevin and Norman coronets
or of the English crown.

    None of the holders of these dependencies, however,
had as yet entered into full enjoyment of their possessions.
At the close of their first revolt, in 1175, the young king
was but just entering his twentieth year ; Richard was in his
eighteenth and Geoffrey in his seventeenth year ; and
although the one had been titular duke of Aquitaine and
the other titular duke of Britanny since 1169, the real

government of both duchies, as well as that of Normandy
and Anjou, had been until now in the hands of their father.
For the purposes of our story there is only one part of these
continental possessions of our Angevin king into whose
internal concerns we need enter at any great length ; a very
slight sketch may suffice for the others.   The part which lay
nearest to England, and which politically was most closely
connected with it—the duchy of Normandy—was •also
associated with it in many of Henry's legal, constitutional
and administrative reforms.   A comparison of dates indeed
would almost suggest that Henry, when contemplating a
great legal or administrative experiment in England, usually
tried it first in Normandy in order to test its working there
upon a small scale before he ventured on applying it to his
island realm.   An edict issued at Falaise in the Christmas-
tide of 1159-1160, ordaining " that no dean should accuse
any man without the evidence of neighbours who bore a
good character, and that in the treatment of all causes, the
magistrates of the several districts at their monthly courts
should determine nothing without the witness of the neighbours, should do injustice to no man and inflict nothing to
the prejudice of any, should maintain the peace, and should
punish all robbers summarily," [1] seems to contain a fore-
shadowing at once of some of the Constitutions of Clarendon
which created such excitement in England four years afterwards, and of the Assize which followed two years later still.
A commission of inquiry into the administration of the
Norman episcopal sees and viscounties in 1162 [2] was a sort
of forerunner of the great inquest into the conduct of the
English sheriffs in 1170.   This again was followed next
year, as we have seen, by an inquiry into the state of the
ducal forests and demesnes,[3] which has its English parallels
in the great forest assize of 1176 and in an inquest into the
condition of the royal demesnes ordered in the spring of
1177.[4]   On the other hand, a roll of the Norman tenants-in-

---

[1] Contin. Becc. (Delisle, *Rob. Torigni*, vol. ii. p. 180).   Stubbs, *Constit.
Hist.*, vol. i. pp. 459, 460.   [2] Rob. Torigni, a. 1162.
    [3] Rob. Torigni, a. 1171.   See above, p. 128.
    [4] *Gesta Hen.* (Stubbs), vol. i. p. 138.

chivalry compiled in 1172 seems to have been modelled
upon the English " Black Book " of 1168 ;[1] and when Henry
determined to institute a thorough reform in the whole
Norman administration, it was at the English exchequer-
table that he found his instrument for the work.　In 1176
William de Courcy, the seneschal of Normandy, died.　In
his stead the king appointed Richard of Ilchester.　Richard,
to judge by his surname, must have been an Englishman by
birth ; from the second year of Henry's reign he was
employed as a " writer " in the royal treasury ;[2] about 1163
he was made archdeacon of Poitiers, but his archidiaconal
functions sat as lightly upon him as upon a contemporary
whose name is often associated with his, Geoffrey Ridel,
archdeacon of Canterbury and vice-chancellor; and throughout the struggle with Archbishop Thomas he was one of the
most active agents of Henry's foreign diplomacy.[3]　Unlike
his colleagues Geoffrey Ridel and John of Oxford, he contrived, notwithstanding the ecclesiastical disgrace in which
he became involved through his dealings with the schismatic
Emperor and the antipope, to retain the general respect of
all parties among his fellow-countrymen.[4]　Throughout
the same period, when not absent from England on some
diplomatic mission, he frequently appears as an acting justice
of the King's Court and baron of the Exchequer.[5]　He
continued to fulfil the same duties after his elevation to the
see of Winchester in 1174; and the estimation in which he
was held is shewn by the fact that on his return from
Normandy, where he was replaced at the end of two years

[1] See above, p. 125.

[2] Pipe Roll 2 Hen. II., pp. 30, 31 ; 4 Hen. II., pp. 121, 122 (Hunter) ; 5
Hen. II., p. 20; 6 Hen. II., p. 57; 7 Hen. II., p. 48; 8 Hen. II., p. 21 (Pipe
Roll Soc.)　　　[3] See the Becket correspondence, *passim.*

[4] Except, of course, the immediate personal friends of the archbishop, to whom
he seems to have been even more obnoxious than the "*archidiabolus*" Geoffrey Ridel
—that is, supposing Mr. Eyton to be right in his theory that Richard of Ilchester
is the person designated in the private letters of Thomas and his friends as
" Luscus." Canon Robertson, however, took " Luscus " to mean Richard de
Lucy ; but the other interpretation seems on the whole more probable.

[5] Madox, *Formulare Anglic.*, p. xix (a. 1165). Eyton, *Itin. Hen. II.*, p.
130 (a. 1168, 1169). He was one of two custodians of the temporalities of the see
of Lincoln during the vacancy caused by Bishop Robert's death in 1167 ; *ib.* p.
99, note 5, from Pipe Roll 12 Hen. II.

by William Fitz-Ralf,[1] a special seat was assigned to him at the exchequer-table between the presiding justiciar and the treasurer, " that he might diligently examine what was written on the roll."[2]   He was evidently invested with far more authority in Normandy than that which usually appertained to a Norman seneschal—authority, in fact, more like that of an English justiciar ; indeed, he is actually called justiciar, and not seneschal, by contemporary English writers.[3] His work in the duchy seems to have been moreover specially connected with finance ;[4] and we may perhaps venture to see a trace of his hand in the organization of the Norman Court of Exchequer, which first comes distinctly to light in Henry's latter years, its earliest extant roll being that of the year 1180.[5]   The earlier stages of the legal and administrative organization of Normandy are, however, so lost in obscurity that neither constitutional lawyers in Henry's day nor constitutional historians in our own have been able to determine the exact historical relation of the Norman system to that of England ;[6] and the speedy severance of the political connexion between them makes the determination of the question, after all, of little practical moment.

Even more obscure than the internal history of Normandy under Henry II. is that of Anjou and of the two dependencies which may now be reckoned as one with it, Touraine and Maine.   There is in his time throughout the whole of his dominions, with the marked exception of England, a dearth of historical records.   Normandy cannot boast of a single historian such as those of the preceding generation, Orderic or William of Jumiéges ; the only Norman chronicle of any importance is that of Robert of Torigny, commonly known as " Robert *de Monte*," from the Mont-St.-Michel of which he was abbot ; and even his work is nothing more than a tolerably full and accurate chronicle

---

[1] See Rog. Howden (Stubbs), vol. ii. p. 100, and the editor's note 3.

[2] *Dialog. de Scacc.*, Stubbs, *Select Charters*, p. 178; cf. *ib.* p. 184.

[3] *Gesta Hen.* (Stubbs), vol. i. p. 124.   " Curiâ sibi totius Normanniæ deputatâ " says R. Diceto (Stubbs), vol. i. p. 415.   [4] R. Diceto as above.

[5] Edited by Mr. Stapleton for the Society of Antiquaries—*Magni Rotuli Scaccarii Normanniæ*, vol. i.

[6] *Dial. de Scacc.* as above, p. 176.   Stubbs, *Constit. Hist.*, vol. i. p. 438.

of the old-fashioned type, arranged on the annalistic plan
" according to the years of our Lord " which William
of Malmesbury had condemned long ago. The Breton
chronicles, always meagre, grow more meagre still as the
years pass on ; the same may be said of the chronicles of
Tours ; the " Acts of the bishops of Le Mans," our sole
native authority for the history of Maine, cease to record
anything save purely ecclesiastical details. In Anjou itself
the recent aggrandizement of the Angevin house stirred up
in Henry's early years a spirit of patriotic loyalty which led
more than one of his subjects to collect the floating popular
traditions of his race, as the ballads and tales of old England had been collected by Henry of Huntingdon and
William of Malmesbury, and weave them into a narrative
which passed for a history of the Angevin counts ; and one
of these writers supplemented his work with a special memoir
of Henry's father, Geoffrey duke of the Normans. But the
reign of Henry himself found no historian in the Marchland ;
and indeed the half-blank pages of the few monastic chronicles
which still dragged out a lingering existence in one or two
of the great Angevin abbeys shew us that under Count
Henry Fitz-Empress Anjou was once more, as of old under
Count Fulk the Good, happy in having no history.

Yet it is there, and there alone, that we can catch a
glimpse of one side of his character which, if we saw him
only in England or in Normandy, we should hardly have
discerned at all. Strange as it seems to us who know him
in his northern realms only as the enterprising and somewhat unscrupulous politician, the stern and vigorous ruler,
the hard-headed statesman, the uncompromising opponent
of the Church's claims, Henry is yet the one Angevin count
who completely reproduced in his Marchland, as a living
reality, the ideal which was represented there by the name
of the good count-canon of Tours. Fulk the Black and
Fulk the Fifth had both tried to reproduce it, each according
to his lights, during those few years when the pressure of
external politics and warfare left them free to devote their
energies for a while to their country's internal welfare. But
Henry's whole reign was, for his paternal dominions, a reign

of peace. If we drew our ideas of him solely from the traces and traditions which he has left behind him there, we could never have guessed that he was a greater warrior than Fulk Nerra ; we should rather have taken him for a quiet prince who, like Fulk the Good, " waged no wars." These traces and traditions lie scattered over the soil of Anjou, Touraine and Maine as thickly as the traces and the traditions of the Black Count himself. Henry is in fact the only one of the later Angevin counts who made upon the imagination of his people an impression even approaching in vividness to that left by Fulk the Black, and of whose material works there remains anything which can be compared with those of the "great builder" of the preceding century. But the memory which Anjou has retained of Henry differs much in character from that which she has kept of Fulk ; and it differs more widely still from that which Henry himself has left in his island-realm. In English popular tradition he appears simply as the hero of a foolish and discreditable romance, or as the man who first caused the murder of S. Thomas and then did penance at his grave ; and material traces of him there are literally none, for of his English dwelling-places not one stone is left upon another, and not a single surviving monument of public utility, secular or ecclesiastical, is connected with his name. In the valley of the Loire it was far otherwise. There the two great Angevin builders share between them the credit of well-nigh all the more important monuments which give life to the medieval history of the land—except the military constructions, which belong to Fulk alone. It is not in donjons such as that of Loches or Montrichard, but in palaces and hospitals, bridges and embankments, that we see our Angevin king's handiwork in his own home-lands. Almost every one of his many local capitals was adorned during his reign with a palace of regal dimensions and magnificence, reared by him in place of the lowlier " halls " which had served for the dwelling of the merely local rulers whom he succeeded. The rebuilding of the ducal palace at Rouen was begun in 1161 ;[1] that of Caen was nearly

[1] Rob. Torigni, a. 1161.

finished in 1180; its hall, which still exists, is the traditional seat of the Norman Exchequer.[1] At Tours a round
tower which still stands in the barrack-yard is the sole surviving fragment of a castle which Henry is said to have
built. His favourite abode in Touraine, however, was not
at Tours but at Chinon, where the little fortress above the
Vienne which had been the last conquest of Fulk Nerra and
the lifelong prison of Geoffrey the Bearded grew under
Henry's hands into a royal retreat of exquisite beauty and
splendour—a gem, even now in its ruin, worthy of its setting
in the lovely valley of the Vienne, with the background of
good greenwood which to Henry was probably its greatest
charm. Angers, again, almost put on a new face in the
course of Henry's lifetime. In the year before his birth it
had been visited by a fire which reduced to almost total
ruin its whole south-western quarter, including the palace of
the counts,[2] of which nothing but the great hall seems to
have remained. The work of reconstruction, begun no
doubt by Geoffrey Plantagenet, was completed on a regal
scale by his son, and before the close of Henry's reign
a visitor from England, Ralf de Diceto, could gaze in
admiration at the " vast palace," with its " newly-built
apartments, adorned with splendour befitting a king," which
rose at the foot of the vine-clad hills above the purple stream
of Mayenne.[3]

But the count-king did not build for himself alone. It
was, above all, with works of public usefulness that he
delighted to adorn his realms. His beneficence indeed took
a different shape from that of his predecessors. Church-
building and abbey-founding met with little sympathy from
him ; throughout his whole dominions, only six religious
houses, in the strict sense, could claim him as their founder ;
and even one of these was as much military as religious,
for it was a commandery of knights Templars.[4] But no

[1] *Mag. Rot. Scacc. Norm.* (Stapleton), vol. i. p. 56. *Ib.* Observ. pp. xxvii-
xxviii.   [2] Chron. S. Serg. a. 1132 (Marchegay, *Eglises d'Anjou*, p. 144).

[3] R. Diceto (Stubbs), vol. i. p. 292 (*Hist. Com. Andeg.*, Marchegay, *Comtes
d'Anjou*, p. 337).

[4] Founded in 1173, at Vaubourg in the forest of Roumare—an old hunting-
seat of his Norman grandfather ; Stapleton, *Mag. Rot. Scacc. Norm.*, vol. i.,

sovereign was ever more munificent in providing for the sick and needy. Not only do the Norman Exchequer-rolls contain frequent mention of sums set apart out of the ducal revenues for the support of lazar-houses and hospitals in the chief towns of the several bailiwicks ;[1] nineteen years before the completion of his own palace at Caen, he had founded an hospital for lepers outside the walls of the town ;[2] and a park and hunting-lodge which he had made for himself in the same year, 1161, at Quévilly by Rouen[3] were shortly afterwards given up by him to a colony of monks from Grandmont in Aquitaine, to be converted under their care into another great asylum for victims of the same disease.[4] At his own native Le Mans, the great hall of an almshouse

Observ., p. cxli. Of the other houses, three were Austin priories : S. Laurence at Beauvoir in the forest of Lions, founded while Henry was still only duke of Normandy (*ib.* p. cxiv); Newstead, in Sherwood Forest, founded before 1174 (its foundation-charter, dated at Clarendon, has no mention of day or year, but is witnessed by "Geoffrey archdeacon of Canterbury," who in 1174 became a bishop ; Dugdale, *Monast. Angl.*, vol. vi. pt. i. p. 474); and the priory "B. Mariæ Mellinensis," near La Flèche, founded in 1180 (*Gall. Christ.*, vol. xiv. col. 600. I cannot identify this place). The other two were Carthusian houses, Witham in the forest of Selwood and Le Liget in that of Loches, founded respectively in 1174 and 1175. (The date of Le Liget is traditional ; I cannot find any mention of the place in *Gall. Christ.*) Of all these, Witham is the only one of any consequence ; and the importance of even Witham lies chiefly in its connexion with S. Hugh. (For its history see *Magna Vita S. Hugonis*, Dimock, pp. 52 *et seq.*) The insignificance of the others is shewn by Gerald's account of Henry's religious foundations, in *De Instr. Princ.*, dist. ii. c. 7 (Angl. Christ. Soc., pp. 27, 28)—an account, however, which is by no means fair. Henry on his absolution for S. Thomas's death, in 1172, promised to go on a crusade of three years' duration (Rog. Howden, Stubbs, vol. ii. p. 37); this undertaking he was afterwards allowed to exchange for a promise that he would build three religious houses in his dominions. According to Gerald, he managed one of these by turning the nuns out of Amesbury and putting a colony from Fontevraud in their place (see *Gesta Hen.*, Stubbs, vol. i. pp. 134-136, 165), and another by turning the secular canons out of Waltham and putting regulars in their place (*ib.* pp. 134, 135, 173, 174, 316, 317. Both these transactions took place in 1177.) "Tertium vero," says Gerald (as above) "vel nullum, vel simile prioribus sibique prorsus inutile fecit ; nisi forte domum conventualem ordinis Cartusiensis de Witham, s. modicis sumptibus et exilem, ad hoc fecisse dicatur." No doubt Witham was one of the three. But the other two are easily found ; they were Newstead and Vaubourg or Le Liget. R. Niger (Anstruther, p. 168) is as unjust to Henry in this matter as Gerald ; but so he is on most others also.

[1] See Stapleton, *Mag. Rot. Scacc. Norm.*, vol. i., Observ., pp. lix., lxi., lxvii.
[2] *Ib.* p. ci. Rob. Torigni, a. 1161.   [3] Rob. Torigni, a. 1161.
[4] See Stapleton as above, pp. cxlvi-cxlvii.

or hospital outside the north-eastern boundary of the city, said to have been reared by him for the reception of its poor and sick folk, is still to be seen, though long since perverted to other uses. At Angers, on the other hand, it is only within the last half-century that the sick and disabled poor have exchanged for a more modern dwelling the shelter provided for them by Henry Fitz-Empress. Some time in the quiet years which followed the barons' revolt, Stephen,[1] the seneschal of Anjou, bought of the abbess and convent of our Lady of Charity at Angers a plot of ground which lay between their abbey and the river, and on which he designed to build an hospice for the poor. In the last days of 1180 or the first days of 1181 the count-king took under his own care the work which his seneschal had begun, granted to the new hospital a rich endowment in lands and revenues, exempted it from secular charges and imposts, and won from Pope Alexander a confirmation of its spiritual independence.[2] Four priests were appointed to minister to the spiritual needs of its inmates; the care of their bodies was undertaken at first, it seems, by some pious laymen bound by no special rule; some years later, however, the hospital became, like most other establishments of the kind, affiliated to the Order of S. Augustine.[3] The pretty little chapel—dedicated to S. John the Baptist, and still standing,—the cloisters and the domestic offices were all finished before Henry's death;[4] while of the two great pillared halls which now form the chief architectural glory of the suburb, one, the smaller and simpler, is clearly of his building; and the other, more vast and beautiful, is in all probability the last legacy of his sons to the home which was soon to be theirs no longer.[5]

This Hospice of S. John formed a third with Fulk Nerra's abbey of S. Nicolas and Hildegard's nunnery of our Lady of Charity in the group of pious and charitable found-

---

[1] Of Marçay—or Matha—or Turnham; authorities differ so much as to his identity that I dare not venture upon adopting either surname.

[2] C. Port, *Cartulaire de l'Hopital St. Jean d'Angers*, pp. 2-10, ii-vi.

[3] *Ib.* pp. 11-13. [4] *Ib.* p. xiv.

[5] On the hospital-buildings see an article by M. D'Espinay in *Revue de l'Anjou*, vol. xii. (1874), pp. 264-273.

ations round which there gathered, on the meadows that bordered the right bank of the Mayenne, the suburb now known as Ronceray or La Doutre,—a suburb which even before the close of Henry's reign had grown almost as populous as Angers itself, and was actually preferred to it as a residence by Ralf de Diceto.[1]   Twice in Henry's reign the bridge which linked it to the city was destroyed by fire ;[2] the present " Grand-Pont " probably owes its erection to him.   Fire was, however, by no means the most destructive element in the valleys of the Loire and its tributaries.   " Well-nigh disappearing in summer, choked within their sandy beds," these streams were all too apt, as Ralf de Diceto says of the Mayenne, to " rage and swell in winter like the sea ;"[3] and the greatest and most lasting of all Henry's material benefactions to Anjou was the embankment or " *Levée*"—a work which he seems characteristically to have planned and executed in the very midst of his struggle with the Church[4]— which stretches along Loire-side, from Ponts-de-Cé, just above the junction of the Mayenne and the Loire, some thirty miles eastward to Bourgueil.   Further south, in the valley of the Vienne, the legend of the " Pont de l'Annonain " illustrates the curious but not altogether unaccountable confusion which grew up in popular imagination between the two great builders of Anjou.   The " bridge," a long viaduct which stretched from Chinon across river and meadow southwestward to the village of Rivière, was in reality built by Henry to secure a safe transit from Chinon into Poitou across the low ground on the south bank of the Vienne, which in rainy seasons was an all but impassable swamp. Later ages, however, connected it with a dim tradition, which still lingered in the district, of the wonderful night-ride across Loire and Vienne whereby Fulk Nerra had won Saumur, and in the belief of the peasantry the Pont de l'Annonain

---

[1] R. Diceto (Stubbs), vol. i. p. 292 (*Hist. Com. Andeg.*, Marchegay, *Comtes d'Anjou*, p. 337).

[2] In 1167 and 1177.   Chron. S. Serg. a. 1167 and 1177, Chron. S. Albin. a. 1177 (Marchegay, *Eglises d'Anjou*, pp. 149, 151, 44).

[3] R. Diceto as above.

[4] It was certainly made before 1169; see Rob. Torigni *ad ann.*

became a "devil's bridge," built in a single night by the
Black Count's familiar demon[1]—a demon who is but a
popular personification of that spirit of dauntless enterprise
and ceaseless activity which, alike in their material and in
their political workmanship, was the secret of Henry's
success no less than of Fulk's.

One portion, however, of Henry's continental dominions
has during these years a political and military history of its
own, which is not without a bearing upon that of our own
land. Geographically remote as it was from England, still
more remote in the character of both country and people,
Aquitaine yet concerns us more than any other part of
Henry's Gaulish possessions. For not only was it a chief
source of the political complications which filled the closing
years of his life ; it was the only one of those possessions
whose connexion with England survived the fall of the
Angevin house. The heritages of Geoffrey and Matilda
were lost by their grandson ; the heritage of Eleanor remained, in part at least, in the hands of her descendants for
more than two hundred years.

It was in truth a dower at once valuable and burdensome that Henry had received with his Aquitanian wife.
She had made him master of a territory whose extent surpassed that of all his Norman and Angevin dominions put
together, and was scarcely equalled by that of England—a
territory containing every variety of soil and of natural
characteristics, from the flat, rich pastures of Berry and the
vineyards of Poitou and Saintonge to the rugged volcanic
rocks and dark chestnut-woods of Auvergne, the salt marshes,
sandy dunes, barren heaths and gloomy pine-forests of the
Gascon coast, and the fertile valleys which open between
the feet of the Pyrenees :—a territory whose population
differed in blood and speech from their fellow-subjects north
of Loire almost as widely as Normans and Angevins differed
from Englishmen ; while in temper and modes of thought
and life they stood so apart from the northern world that in
contradistinction to them Angevins and Normans and
English might almost be counted, and indeed were almost

---

[1] See Salies, *Foulques-Nerra*, note civ., pp. 429, 430.

ready to count themselves, as one people. It was a territory, too, whose political relations varied as much as its physical character, and were full of dangers which all Henry's vigilance and wisdom were powerless to guard against or overcome. Setting aside, for the moment, the internal difficulties of Aquitaine, its whole eastern frontier, from the banks of the Cher to the Pyrenees, was more or less in dispute throughout his reign. The question of Toulouse, indeed, was settled in 1173; thenceforth the county of Toulouse, with its northern dependencies Rouergue and Alby, became a recognized underfief of the Poitevin duchy of Aquitaine, to which its western dependency, Quercy or the county of Cahors, had been already annexed after the war of 1160. The north-eastern portions of the older Aquitania, Berry and Auvergne, were sources of more lasting trouble. Berry had long ago been split into two unequal portions, of which the larger had remained subject to the dukes of Aquitaine, while the smaller northern division formed the viscounty of Bourges, and was an immediate fief of the French Crown. Naturally, the king was disposed to use every opportunity of thwarting the duke in the exercise of his authority over southern Berry; and Henry was equally desirous to lose no chance of re-asserting his ducal rights over Bourges.[1] The feudal position of Auvergne was a standing puzzle which king and duke, count, clergy and people, all in vain endeavoured to solve. During the struggle for supremacy in southern Gaul between the houses of Poitiers and Toulouse, Auvergne, after fluc-tuating for nearly a hundred years between the rival dukedoms, had virtually succeeded in freeing itself from the control of both, and in the reign of Louis VI. it seems to have been regarded as an immediate fief of the French Crown, to which however it proved a most unruly and troublesome possession. But the dukes of Aquitaine had never relinquished their claim to its overlordship; and when a quarrel broke out between two rival claimants of the

---

[1] His first attempt to do so was made in 1170, when a pretext was given him by the declaration said—whether truly or falsely—to have been made by the dying archbishop Peter of Bourges, that his see belonged of right to Aquitaine. Nothing, however, came of the attempt. See *Gesta Hen.* (Stubbs), vol. i. pp. 10, 11.

county, it was naturally followed by a quarrel between Henry
and Louis VII. as to their respective rights, as overlord and
as lord paramount, to act as arbiters in the strife.[1]   During
five-and-twenty years it was a favourite device of Louis and
of his successor, at every adverse crisis in Henry's fortune,
to despatch a body of troops into Auvergne to occupy that
country and threaten Aquitaine through its eastern marches,[2]
just as they habitually threatened Normandy through the
marches of the Vexin.

Such a threat implied a far more serious danger in the
south than in the north.   The Aquitanian border was guarded
by no such chain of strongly-fortified, stoutly-manned ducal
castles as girt in the Norman duchy from Gisors to Tillières;
and Henry's hold over his wife's dominions was very different
from his grasp of the heritage of his mother.   Twenty years
of Angevin rule, which for political purposes had well-nigh
bridged over the channel that parted England from Gaul,
seem to have done nothing towards bridging over the gulf
that parted Aquitaine from France and Anjou.   If our
Angevin king sometimes looks like a stranger amongst us,
he was never anything but a stranger among the fellow-
countrymen of his wife.   Nowhere throughout his whole
dominions was a spirit of revolt and insubordination so rife
as among the nobles of Poitou and its dependencies; but it
was a spirit utterly unlike the feudal pride of the Norman
baronage.   The endless strife of the Aquitanian nobles with
their foreign duke and with each other sprang less from
political motives than from a love of strife for its own sake;
and their love of strife was only one phase of the passion
for adventure and excitement which ran through every fibre
of their nature and coloured every aspect of their social life.
The men of the south lived in a world where the most
delicate poetry and the fiercest savagery, the wildest moral
and political disorder, and the most refined intellectual
culture, mingled together in a confusion as picturesque as it

---

[1] See Rob. Torigni, a. 1167.

[2] *E.g.* in 1164 (Ep. lx., Robertson. *Becket*, vol. v. p. 115), 1167 (above, p. 58;
Rob. Torigni *ad ann.*), 1170 (Will. Fitz-Steph., Robertson, *Becket*, vol. iii. p. 116;
Ep. dccxxii., *ib.* vol. vii. p. 400), and again in 1188.

was dangerous.   The southern warrior was but half a knight
if the sword was his only weapon—if he could not sing his
battles as well as fight them.   From raid and foray and
siege he passed to the " Court of Love," where the fairest
and noblest women of the land, from the duchess herself
downwards, presided over contests of subtle wit, skilful rime
and melodious song, conducted under rules as stringent and
with earnestness as deep as if life and death were at stake
upon the issue; and in truth they sometimes were at stake,
for song, love and war all mingled together in the troubadour's
life in an inextricable coil which the less subtle intellects of
the north would have been powerless to unravel or comprehend.   The *sirvente* or poetical satire with which he stung
his enemies into fury or roused the slumbering valour of his
friends often wrought more deadly mischief than sharp steel
or blazing firebrand.   The nature of the men of the south
was like that of their country : it was made up of the most
opposite characteristics—of the lightest fancies, the stormiest
passions, the most versatile capabilities of body and mind,
the most indolent love of ease and pleasure, the most restless
and daring valour, the highest intellectual refinement and the
lowest moral degradation.   It was a nature which revolted
instinctively from constraint in any direction,—whose impetuosity burst all control of law and order imposed from
without upon its restless love of action and adventure, just
as it overflowed all conventional bounds of thought and
language with its exuberant play of feeling and imagination
in speech or song.[1]   We may see a type of it in the portrait,
drawn by almost contemporary hands, of one who played an
important part both in the social and in the political history
of Aquitaine throughout the closing years of Henry II. and
the reign of his successor.   "Bertrand de Born was of the
Limousin, lord of a castle in the diocese of Périgueux, by
name Hautefort.   He had at his command near a thousand
men.   And all his time he was at war with all his neigh-

---

[1] As John of Salisbury says—" auctor ad opus suum " :—
　　" De Pictavorum dices te gente creatum,
　　Nam licet his linguâ liberiore loqui."
　　　　　　　　　　(*Enthet. ad Polycrat.*, Giles, vol. iii. p. i.)

bours, with the count of Périgord, and the viscount of
Limoges, and with his own brother Constantine—whom he
would have liked to disinherit, had it not been for the king
of England—and with Richard, while he was count of Poitou.
He was a good knight, and a good warrior, and a good
servant of ladies, and a good troubadour of *sirventes;* he
never made but two songs, and the king of Aragon assigned
the songs of Guiraut de Borneil as wives to his *sirventes ;*
and the man who sang them for him was named Papiol.
And he was a pleasant, courteous man, wise and well-spoken,
and knew how to deal with good and evil.   And whenever
he chose, he was master of King Henry and his sons ; but
he always wanted them to be at war among themselves, the
father and the sons and the brothers one with another ; and
he always wanted the king of France and King Henry to be
at war too.   And if they made peace or a truce, he immediately set to work to unmake it with his *sirventes*, and
to shew how they were all dishonoured in peace.   And he
gained much good by it, and much harm."[1]

Until the dukedom of Aquitaine passed to a woman, as
were the vassals, so was their sovereign.   Eleanor's grandfather the crusader-duke William VIII. and her father
William IX. were simply the boldest knights, the gayest
troubadours and the most reckless adventurers in their duchy.
There can be no doubt that the submission of Aquitaine to
Louis VII., so far as it ever did submit to him, was due to
Eleanor's influence ; and it was the same influence which
chiefly contributed to preserve its obedience to her second
husband during those earlier years of their married life when,
at home and abroad, all things had seemed destined to
prosper in his hands.   But at the first symptom of a turn in
the tide of his fortunes, southern Gaul at one rose against its
northern master.   Eleanor's tact and firmness, Henry's wariness and vigour, were all taxed to the uttermost in holding
it down throughout the years of his struggle with the Church ;
and when Eleanor herself turned against him in 1173, the

---

[1] From the two old Provençal sketches of the life of Bertrand de Born, printed
and translated into French by M. Léon Clédat in his monograph *Du rôle hist-
orique de Bertrand de Born*, pp. 99-101.

chances of a good understanding between her subjects and her husband became very nearly desperate. Henry himself seems to have long ago perceived that a duke of Aquitaine, to be thoroughly sure of his ground, needed a different apprenticeship from that which might befit a king of England, a duke of Normandy or Britanny, or a count of Anjou. The very first step in his plans for the future of his children —a step taken several years before he seems even to have thought of crowning his eldest son—was the designation of the second as his mother's destined colleague and ultimate heir. Richard had been trained up ever since he was two years old specially for the office of duke of Aquitaine. After long diplomacy, and at the cost of a betrothal which became the source of endless mischief and trouble, the French king's sanction to the arrangement had been won ; and on Trinity-Sunday 1172 Richard, in his mother's presence, had been formally enthroned at Poitiers. He was probably intended to govern the duchy under her direction and advice ; if so, however, the plan was frustrated by Eleanor's own conduct and by the suspicions which it aroused in her husband. She was one of the very few captives whom at the restoration of peace in 1175 he still retained in confinement. Richard, on the other hand, had been like his brothers fully and freely forgiven ; and while his father and eldest brother went to seal their reconciliation in England, he was sent into Poitou charged with authority to employ its forces at his own discretion, and to take upon himself the suppression of all disturbance and disorder in Aquitaine.[1]

What had been the precise nature of Richard's training for his appointed work—what proportion of his seventeen years' life had been actually spent in Aquitaine, what opportunities he had had of growing familiar with the people over whom he was now set to rule—we have no means of determining. By his own natural temper, however, he was probably of all Eleanor's sons the one least fitted to gain the goodwill of the south. The " Cœur-de-lion " of tradition, indeed—the adventurous crusader, the mirror of knightly prowess and knightly courtesy, the lavish patron of verse

[1] *Gesta Hen.* (Stubbs), vol. i. p. 81.

and song, the ideal king of troubadours and knights-errant—
looks at first glance like the very incarnation of the spirit of
the south.　But it was only in the intellectual part of his
nature that his southern blood made itself felt ; the real
groundwork of his character was made of sterner stuff.　The
love of splendour and elegance, the delight in poetry and
music,[1] the lavish generosity, the passion for adventure, which
contrasted so vividly with his father's practical business-
like temper, came to him without doubt from his mother.
The moral deficiencies and evil tendencies of his nature he
himself charged, somewhat too exclusively, upon the demon-
blood of the Angevin counts.[2]　But we need not look either
to an ancestress so shadowy and so remote as the demon-
countess, nor to a land so far distant from us as Poitou, for
the source of Richard's strongest characteristics both of body
and of mind.　In him alone among Henry's sons can we see
a likeness to the Norman forefathers of the Empress Matilda.
His outward aspect, his lofty stature, his gigantic strength—
held in check though it was by the constantly-recurring ague
which " kept him, fearless, in a tremor as continual as the
tremor of fear in which he kept the rest of the world "[3]—
his blue eyes and golden hair, all proclaimed him a child of
the north.　And although he spent the chief part of his life
elsewhere, the slender share of local and national sympathies
which he possessed seems to have lain in the same direction.
The " lion-heart " chose its own last earthly resting-place at
Rouen, not at Poitiers ;[4] and the intimate friend and comrade whose name is inseparably associated with his by a
tradition which, whatever its historical value, is as famous as
it is beautiful, was no Poitevin or Provençal troubadour, but
a trouvère from northern France.[5]　The influence of his
northman-blood shewed itself more vividly still when on his

----

[1] See R. Coggeshall's description of Richard's love of church music : " clericos
sonorâ voce modulantes donis et precibus ad cantandum festivius instimulabat, atque
per chorum huc illucque deambulando, voce ac manu ut altius concreparent excit-
abat." R. Coggeshall (Stevenson), p. 97.

[2] Gir. Cambr. *De Instr. Princ.*, dist. iii. c. 27 (Angl. Christ. Soc., p. 154).

[3] *Ib.* c. 8 (p. 105).

[4] Rog. Howden (Stubbs), vol. iv. p. 84.

[5] That is, if the Blondel of tradition is to be identified with Blondel of Nesle.

voyage to Palestine, having lived to be more than thirty years old without possessing a skiff that he could call his own, or—unless indeed in early childhood he had gone a cruise round his father's island-realm—ever making a longer or more adventurous voyage than that from Southampton to Barfleur or Wissant, he suddenly developed not only a passionate love of the sea, but a consummate seamanship which he certainly had had no opportunity of acquiring in any way, and which can only have been born in him, as an inheritance from his wiking forefathers. When scarcely more than a boy in years, Richard was already one of the most serious and determined of men. His sternness to those who "withstood his will" matched that of the Conqueror himself; and Richard's will, even at the age of seventeen, was no mere caprice, but a fixed determination which overrode all obstacles between itself and its object as unhesitatingly as the old wiking-keels overrode the billows of the northern sea. He went down into Aquitaine fully resolved that the country should be at once, and once for all, reduced to submission and order. He set himself "to bring the shapeless into shape, to reduce the irregular to rule, to cast down the things that were mighty and level those that were rugged; to restore the dukedom of Aquitaine to its ancient boundaries and its ancient government."[1]   He did the work with all his might, but he did it with a straightforward ruthlessness untempered by southern craft or Angevin caution and tact. He would not conciliate; he could not wait. "He thought nothing done while anything still remained to do; and he cared for no success that was not reached by a path cut by his own sword and stained with his opponent's blood. Boiling over with zeal for order and justice, he sought to quell the audacity of this ungovernable people and to secure the safety of the innocent amid these workers of mischief by at once proceeding against the evil-doers with the utmost rigour which his ducal authority could enable him to exercise upon them."[2]   In a word, before Richard had been six months in their midst, the Aquitanians discovered that if their Angevin duke had chastised

---

[1] Gir. Cambr. *De Instr. Princ.*, dist. iii. c. 8 (Angl. Christ. Soc., p. 104).
[2] *Ibid.* (p. 105).

them with whips, the son of their own duchess was minded
to chastise them with scorpions.

He set off at once upon a furious campaign against the
strongholds of the unruly barons. "No mountain-side however steep and rugged, no tower however lofty and impregnable, availed to check his advance, as skilful as it was
daring, as steady and persevering as it was impetuous." [1]
By midsummer the castles of Poitou itself were mostly in
his hands, and the young conqueror was busy with the siege
of Castillonnes-sur-Agen, which surrendered to him in the
middle of August.[2] Before the winter was over he was
master of Périgueux, and had, in the phrase of a local writer,
well-nigh "disinherited" the barons of Périgord, the Quercy
and the Limousin. But in the spring their smouldering
resentment was kindled into a blaze by the incitements of
Bertrand de Born, whose brother Constantine, expelled by
him from the castle of Hautefort which the two brothers
had inherited in common, had appealed to Richard for
succour ; the signal for revolt, given by Bertrand in a
vigorous *sirvente*, was answered by all the malcontents of
the district,[3] and at the opposite end of Poitou by the count
of Angoulême ; and at Easter Richard found his position so
difficult that he went to seek advice and reinforcements from
his father in England.[4] Geoffrey of Britanny arrived at the
same time on a like errand. Henry bade his eldest son go
to the help of the younger ones ; the young king complied,[5]
somewhat unwillingly, and went to collect forces in France
while Richard hurried back into Poitou. The peril was
urgent ; in his absence Count Vulgrin of Angoulême had
invaded Poitou at the head of a host of Brabantines. The
invaders were however met and defeated with great slaughter
at Barbezieux by Richard's constable Theobald Chabot and
Bishop John of Poitiers.[6] By Whitsuntide Richard had

---

[1] Gir. Cambr. *De Instr. Princ.*, dist. iii. c. 8 (Angl. Christ. Soc., p. 105).

[2] *Gesta Hen.* (Stubbs), vol. i. p. 101.

[3] See Clédat, *Bertrand de Born*, pp. 29, 30.

[4] *Gesta Hen.* as above, pp. 114, 115.

[5] *Ib.* p. 115. Rog. Howden (Stubbs), vol. ii. p. 93.

[6] R. Diceto (Stubbs), vol. i. p. 407. He adds : "Sicque salus in manu clericorum data satis evidenter ostendit plerisque non animos deesse sed arma."

gathered a sufficient force of loyal Poitevins and stipend-
iaries from the neighbouring lands to march against Vulgrin
and his Brabantines and defeat them in a battle near the
border of the Angoumois and Saintonge.   He then turned
upon the viscount of Limoges, besieged and took his castle
of Aixe, and thence advanced to Limoges itself, which he
captured in like manner.   At midsummer he was rejoined
at Poitiers by his elder brother, and the two led their combined forces against Vulgrin of Angoulême.[1]   A fortnight's
siege had however scarcely made them masters of Châteauneuf on the Charente when the young king—seduced, it
was said, by some evil counsellor whom we may probably
suspect to have been Bertrand de Born[2]—suddenly abandoned the campaign and withdrew again to France.   Richard,
undaunted by his brother's desertion, pushed on to Moulin-
Neuf and thence to Angoulême itself, where all the leaders
of the rebellion were gathered together.   A six days' siege
sufficed to make Vulgrin surrender himself, his fellow-rebels,
his city and five of his castles to the mercy of the duke and
the English king.   Richard sent over all his prisoners to
his father in England ; Henry, however, sent them back
again, and Richard put them in prison to await their
sentence till the king should return to Gaul.[3]

Northern Aquitaine, or Guyenne, was now for the
moment subdued.   As soon as Christmas was over Richard
proceeded to the reduction of Gascony.   Dax, held against
him by its viscount Peter and by the count of Bigorre, and
Bayonne, defended by its viscount Ernald Bertram, submitted each after a ten days' siege ; S. Pierre-de-Cize, on
the Spanish frontier, fell in one day ; the Basques and
Navarrese were compelled to promise peace; the plunderings
habitually inflicted by the border-folk upon pilgrims to the
shrine of S. James at Compostella were suppressed ; and
from his court at Poitiers on Candlemas - day Richard
triumphantly reported to his father that he had pacified the
whole country.[4]   But the peace did not last long.   Trouble

---

[1] *Gesta Hen.* (Stubbs), vol. i. pp. 120, 121.
[2] See Clédat, *Bertrand de Born*, p. 35.
[3] *Gesta Hen.* as above, p. 121.   [4] *Ib.* pp. 131, 132.

was already threatening at the opposite end of the duchy.
Ralf of Déols, the wealthiest baron in Berry, had lately died
leaving as his heir an infant daughter.   She was of course,
according to feudal law, a ward of her overlord, King Henry;
but her relatives seized both her and her estates, and refused
to give up either.[1]   Henry, probably feeling that the boy-
duke of Aquitaine had already more than enough upon his
hands, charged his eldest son with the settlement of this
affair, bidding him take possession of all Ralf's lands without
delay, and significantly adding : " While I governed my
realms alone, I lost none of my rightful possessions ; it will
be shame to us all if aught of them be lost now that we are
several to rule them."   The young king took the hint,
marched with all his Norman and Angevin forces into Berry,
and laid siege to Châteauroux ;[2] but he seems to have had
no success ;[3] and there was no chance of help from Richard,
for not only was the Limousin again plunged in civil war,[4]
but all southern Aquitaine was in danger of a like fate—an
attempt of Count Raymond of Toulouse to exert his authority as overlord of Narbonne with greater stringency than
its high-spirited viscountess Hermengard was disposed to
endure having stirred up against him a league of all the
princes of Septimania and the Spanish border, under the
leadership of Hermengard herself and of Raymond's hereditary rivals, the king of Aragon and his brothers.[5]   The way
in which Raymond prepared to meet their attack supplies a
vivid illustration of southern character and manners.   He
sought an ally in Bertrand de Born, and he appealed to him
in his character not of knight but of troubadour.   He sent
a messenger to Hautefort to state his cause and to ask
Bertrand, not to fight for it, but simply to publish it to the

---

[1] *Gesta Hen.* (Stubbs), vol. i. p. 127.   [2] *Ib.* p. 132.

[3] The *Gesta Hen.*, as above, say Châteauroux was surrendered to him at
once ; but we hear nothing more of it till the autumn, and then we find that the
elder king has to besiege it himself ; so if the younger one ever did win it, he must
have lost it again as quickly.

[4] Geoff. Vigeois, l. i. cc. lxix., lxx. (Labbe, *Nova Biblioth.*, vol. ii. pp.
322, 323).

[5] See Vic and Vaissète, *Hist. du Languedoc* (new ed.), vol. vi. pp. 69, 70;
and the terms of the league, *ib.* vol. viii. cols. 325, 326.

world in a *sirvente*.   Bertrand answered readily to the appeal ; he was only too glad of any excuse for a *sirvente* which should " cause dints in a thousand shields, and rents in a thousand helms and hauberks."   " I would fain have the great barons ever wroth one with another !" is the characteristic exclamation with which he ends his war-song.[1]

The strife thus begun for the mastery in Septimania was continued at intervals between the houses of Toulouse and Aragon for many years to come.   The overlord of Toulouse, however, seems to have taken no part in it as yet ; and indeed, it had scarcely more than begun when Richard was summoned away to meet his father in Normandy.   Three times in the course of that spring and summer had King Henry collected his host in England for the purpose of going over sea to the help of his sons ; twice had he remanded it,[2] for the sake, as it seems, of continuing his legal and administrative work in England.   By midsummer however the tidings from Gaul were such that he dared not further prolong his absence.   Geoffrey wanted his help in Britanny ; Richard wanted it almost as much in Aquitaine ; the young king's unaccountable lack of vigour in their support, and in the prosecution of the war in Berry, was justly raising suspicions of his loyalty to the family cause ; and the treaty made with Louis of France at the close of the last war was proving, as such treaties too often did prove, only a source of fresh disputes.   Henry summoned Louis to fulfil his part of the agreement by handing over the Vexin to the young king and the viscounty of Bourges to Richard, according to his promise, as the dowries of their brides ;[3] Louis insisted that Henry should first complete his share of the engagement by allowing Adela, who had been in his custody ever since the treaty was signed, to be wedded to her promised bridegroom, Richard.   At last, in July, he succeeded in bringing the matter to a crisis by extorting from a papal legate who had been sent to deal with a heresy that had arisen in southern Gaul a threat of laying all Henry's dominions under interdict unless Richard and Adela were

[1] Clédat, *Bert. de Born*, pp. 38, 39.
[2] *Gesta Hen.* (Stubbs), vol. i. pp. 138, 160, 167, 168.   [3] *Ib.* p. 168.

married at once.[1]   The English bishops appealed against
the threat ;[2] while Henry hurried over to Normandy,[3] met first
his two elder sons,[4] then the legate,[5] then the French king,[6]
and once again contrived to stave off the threatening peril.
At Nonancourt, on September 25, the two kings made
a treaty containing not one word of marriages or dowries,
but consisting of an agreement to bury all their differences
under the cross.   They pledged themselves to go on crusade
together, to submit to arbitration the questions in dispute
between them about Auvergne and Berry, and to lay aside
all their other quarrels at once and for ever.[7]   Such a treaty
was in reality a mere temporary expedient ; but it served
Henry's purpose by securing him against French interference
while he marched against the rebels in Berry.   As usual, he
carried all before him ; Châteauroux surrendered without a
struggle ; the lord of La Châtre, who had stolen the little
heiress of Déols and was keeping her fast in his own castle,
hurried to make his peace and give up his prize.[8]   Henry
used his opportunity to advance into the Limousin and
exert his authority in punishing its turbulent barons ;[9] soon
after Martinmas he and Louis met at Graçay and made
another ineffectual attempt to settle the vexed question of
Auvergne ;[10] a month later he was again in Aquitaine,

---

[1] *Gesta Hen.* (Stubbs), vol. i. pp. 180, 181.   Rog. Howden (Stubbs), vol. ii. p. 143.
Gerv. Cant. (Stubbs), vol. i. p. 271.   [2] *Gesta Hen.* as above, p. 181.
    [3] In the night of August 17-18.   *Gesta Hen.* as above, p. 190.   R. Diceto
(Stubbs), vol. i. p. 421.   [4] Rob. Torigni, a. 1177.
    [5] On September 11.   *Gesta Hen.* as above, p. 190.
    [6] September 21.   *Ibid.*   Cf. Rog. Howden and Gerv. Cant. as above.
    [7] *Gesta Hen.* as above, pp. 191-194.   Rog. Howden (Stubbs), vol. ii. pp.
144-146 ; Gerv. Cant. as above, pp. 272-274 ; shorter in R. Diceto as above, pp.
421, 422.   The place and date are from this last authority.
    [8] *Gesta Hen.* as above, pp. 195, 196.   Cf. R. Diceto as above, p. 425.
    [9] *Gesta Hen.* as above, p. 196.
    [10] The proceedings on this occasion are worth notice.   Henry, it seems, tried
to substitute for the arbitration of three prelates and three laymen on each side
(which had been agreed upon at Nonancourt) his own favourite plan of sworn inquest.   He called together the barons of Auvergne, and required them to certify
what rights his predecessors the dukes of Aquitaine had enjoyed in their country.
They answered that by ancient right all Auvergne pertained to the ducal dominions,
except the bishopric (Clermont), which was dependent on the French Crown.   To
this definition Louis would not agree ; so they fell back upon the former scheme

purchasing the direct ownership of one of its under-fiefs, the county of La Marche, from the childless Count Adalbert who was purposing to end his days in Holy Land ;[1] and at Christmas he was back at Angers, where he kept the feast with his three elder sons amid such a gathering of knights as had never been seen at his court except at his own crowning or that of the young king.[2]

For six months there was peace, and in July the king ventured to return to England.[3] He knighted his son Geoffrey at Woodstock on August 6,[4] and when the lad hurried over sea, eager to flesh his maiden sword and emulate the prowess of his brothers, he could find no more serious field in which to exercise his warlike energies than a succession of tournaments on the borders of France and Normandy.[5] Richard however was again busy with more earnest fighting. The rivalry between the houses of Aragon and Toulouse had stirred up the petty chieftains of southern Gascony, whom the king of Aragon was seeking to enlist in his service ; and Richard was obliged to undertake a campaign against the count of Bigorre in particular, which seems to have occupied him till the end of the year. The defiant attitude of the nobles of Saintonge and the Angoumois, and especially of a powerful baron, Geoffrey of Rancogne, called him back at Christmas to Saintes ; as soon as the feast was over he laid siege to Geoffrey's castle of Pons ; after spending more than three months before the place, he left his constables to continue the blockade while he himself went to attack the other rebel castles. Five of them were taken and

---

of arbitration—which, however, seems never to have got any further. *Gesta Hen.* (Stubbs), vol. i. p. 196. This was apparently the last meeting (except the one in England ; see below, p. 216) between Henry and Louis, and must therefore be the one of which a curious account is given by Gir. Cambr. *De Instr. Princ.*, dist. iii. c. 1 (Angl. Christ. Soc., pp. 85, 86).

  [1] *Gesta Hen.* (Stubbs), vol. i. p. 197. Rog. Howden (Stubbs), vol. ii. pp. 147, 148. Rob. Torigni, a. 1177. R. Diceto (Stubbs), vol. i. p. 425, under a wrong year. Geoff. Vigeois, l. i. c. 70 (Labbe, *Nova Biblioth.*, vol. ii. p. 324). Henry received the homage of the under-tenants of La Marche (*Gesta Hen.* as above) ; but he did not really get what he paid for, as will be seen later.

  [2] Rob. Torigni, a. 1178.

  [3] *Gesta Hen.* as above, pp. 206, 207. R. Diceto as above, p. 426.

  [4] R. Diceto as above.   [5] *Gesta Hen.* as above, p. 207.

razed between Easter and Rogation-tide,[1] and then Richard
gathered up all his forces to assault Geoffrey of Rancogne's
mightiest stronghold, Taillebourg.   It stood a few miles
north of Saintes, on the crest of a lofty rock, three of whose
sides were so steep as to defy any attempt to scale them,
while the fourth was guarded by a triple ditch and rampart.
Three lines of wall, built of hewn stone and strengthened
with towers and battlements, encircled the keep, which was
stored with provisions and arms offensive and defensive, and
crowded with picked men-at-arms who laughed to scorn the
rashness of the young duke in attempting to besiege a fortress which all his predecessors had looked upon as well-nigh
unapproachable.   But he cleared its approaches with a
ruthless energy such as they little expected, cutting down
vineyards, burning houses, levelling every obstacle before
him, till he pitched his tents close to the castle walls under
the eyes of the astonished townsfolk.   A sally of the latter
only resulted in making a way for Richard's entrance into
the town ; three days later the castle surrendered, and
Geoffrey himself with it.[2]   Ten days' more fighting brought
all the rebels to submission and reduced Vulgrin of Angoulême himself to give up his capital city and his castle of
Montignac in Périgord ;[3] and at Whitsuntide Richard went
to report his success with his own lips to his delighted
father in England.[4]

He returned shortly before Michaelmas,[5] to witness the
opening of a new phase in the relations between the Angevin
house and the French Crown.   Philip of France, the only
son of Louis VII., was now fourteen years old, and his
father was desirous to have him crowned king.   Before the
appointed day arrived, however, he fell sick almost to death.[6]

---

[1] *Gesta Hen.* (Stubbs), vol. i. pp. 212, 213.

[2] R. Diceto (Stubbs), vol. i. pp. 431, 432.   Cf. *Gesta Hen.* as above, p. 213,
and Rob. Torigni, a. 1179.   [3] *Gesta Hen.* as above.

[4] *Ibid.*   R. Diceto as above, p. 432.

[5] So it appears from an entry in the Pipe Roll of 1179 ; Eyton, *Itin. Hen. II.*,
p. 227.

[6] *Gesta Hen.* as above, p. 240.   According to Rob. Torigni, a. 1179,
Rigord (Duchesne, *Hist. Franc. Scriptt.*, vol. v. p. 5), and Will. Armor., *Philippis*,
l. i. (*ib.* pp. 99, 100), the boy's sickness was the effect of a fright caused by an adventure in the forest of Compiègne, very like that of Geoffrey Plantagenet at Loches.

Louis, half wild with anxiety, dreamed that the martyr of Canterbury required him to visit his shrine as a condition of the boy's recovery.[1] He hurried across the Channel; Henry met him at Dover and conducted him to Canterbury, where they both spent three days in fasting and prayer before the shrine; and on the fourth day after his landing Louis re-entered his own country, to find that his prayers were answered.[2] His brief visit was long remembered in England, where no king of France had ever been seen before,[3] or was ever seen again save when John the Good was brought there as a prisoner in the days of Edward III. Scarcely, however, had Philip recovered when Louis himself was stricken down by paralysis.[4] This calamity made him all the more anxious for his son's coronation, which took place at Reims on All Saints' day. The archbishop of the province—a brother of Queen Adela —performed the rite, assisted by nearly all the bishops of Gaul ; all the great vassals of the kingdom were present, among them the young King Henry, who in his capacity of duke of Normandy carried the crown before his youthful overlord in the procession to and from the cathedral church, as Count Philip of Flanders carried the sword of state.[5] Like the crowning of young Henry himself, the crowning of Philip Augustus proved to be a beginning of troubles. His father's helpless condition left the boy-king to fall under the influence of whatever counsellor could first get at his ear. That one happened to be his godfather, Philip of Flanders ; and the policy of Flanders was to get the boy entirely under his own control by setting him against all his father's old friends,[6]

---

[1] *Gesta Hen.* (Stubbs), vol. i. pp. 240-241. Cf. Rog. Howden (Stubbs), vol. ii, p. 192.

[2] *Gesta Hen.* as above, pp. 241, 242 ; Rog. Howden, as above, pp. 192, 193 ; Will. Armor., *Philipp.*, l. i. (Duchesne, *Hist. Franc. Scriptt.*, vol. v.) pp. 100, 101. R. Diceto (Stubbs), vol. i. pp. 432, 433, relates the pilgrimage without any mention of its motive ; while Gerv. Cant. (Stubbs), p. 293, seems to think Louis came for the benefit of his own health, not his son's.

[3] R. Diceto, as above, p. 433.   [4] *Gesta Hen.* as above, p. 243.

[5] *Ib.* p. 242. Rog. Howden as above, pp. 193, 194. R. Diceto as above, p. 438. It is Roger who says that Henry bore the crown officially—"de jure ducatûs Normanniæ." Ralf explains away the matter as a mere act of courtesy and friendship.

[6] *Gesta Hen.* as above, p. 244. Rog. Howden as above, p. 196.

and even against his mother, whom he tried to rob of her
dower-lands and persecuted to such a degree that she was
compelled to leave his domains and fly to her brothers
for the protection which her husband was powerless to give
her.[1]   The united forces of Flanders and of the Crown—for
the latter were now wholly at Philip's command [2]—were,
however, more than a match for those of Champagne and
Blois ; and the house of Blois was driven to seek help of the
only power which seemed capable of giving it—the power
of their old rivals of Anjou.[3]

The days were long gone by when it had been a chief
part of the Angevin interest and policy to set the French
king and the house of Blois at variance with each other.   If
Henry had needed any proof that the rivalry of Blois was
no longer to be feared, he would have found it in the appeal
for succour thus sent to him by Queen Adela and her
brothers, and supported by his own eldest son, who at Mid-
Lent 1180 went over to England purposely to consult with
him on the state of affairs in France.   Before Easter father
and son both returned to Normandy, and there held a personal meeting with the French queen, her brothers Theobald
of Blois and Stephen of Sancerre, and several other victims
of young Philip's tyranny.   Pledges of good faith were exchanged, and summons were issued for a general levy of all
Henry's forces, on both sides of the sea, ready to attack
Philip after Easter.[4]   Before the attack could be made, however, Philip had got himself into such difficulties as to render
it needless.   As soon as Lent was over he went into
Flanders and there married a niece of its count, Elizabeth,
daughter of the count of Hainaut.[5]   He then summoned all

[1] Rog. Howden (Stubbs), vol. ii. p. 196.   R. Diceto (Stubbs), vol. ii. p. 6.
Cf. Gerv. Cant. (Stubbs), vol. i. p. 294.

[2] He had stolen his father's royal seal, to prevent all further exercise of
authority on the part of Louis.   R. Diceto, as above.

[3] *Gesta Hen.* (Stubbs), vol. i. p. 244.   Rog. Howden as above.

[4] *Gesta Hen.* as above, p. 245.   Rog. Howden as above.

[5] *Ibid.*   R. Diceto as above, p. 5.   Gerv. Cant. as above.   Rob. Torigni, a.
1181 (a year too late).   The bride is called Elizabeth by her husband's panegyrist,
Rigord (Duchesne, *Hist. Franc. Scriptt.*, vol. v. p. 7), and Isabel by another of
his biographers (*ib.* p. 258).   R. Diceto calls her Margaret.

the princes of his realm to meet him at Sens on Whit-Sunday for the coronation of himself and his queen.   The marriage had, however, given such offence that Philip of Flanders, in dread of opposition to his niece's crowning, persuaded the young king to anticipate the ceremony and have her crowned together with himself at S. Denis, early in the morning of Ascension-day, by the archbishop of Sens.[1]   The wrath of the great vassals knew no bounds ; and the wrath of the archbishop of Reims was almost more formidable still, for the exclusive right to crown the king of France was a special prerogative of his see, and he at once forwarded to Rome an indignant protest against the outrage done to him by his royal nephew.[2]   Philip of France and Guy of Sens had in fact put themselves into a position which might easily have become almost as full of peril as that into which Henry of England and Roger of York had put themselves by a somewhat similar proceeding ten years before.   As, however, William of Reims was not a Thomas of Canterbury, the consequences were less tragic; and Henry himself must have been tempted to smile at the turning of the tables which suddenly placed in his hands the task of shielding Philip from the consequences of his rashness, and reconciling him to the outraged Church and the offended people.

There was a story that young Henry of Anjou, standing close behind his brother-in-law Philip on his first coronation-

---

[1] *Gesta. Hen.* (Stubbs), vol. i. pp. 245, 246.   Rog. Howden (Stubbs), vol. ii. p. 197.   R. Diceto (Stubbs), vol. ii. p. 5.   Rob. Torigni, a. 1181.   This last writer, whose chronology has now become extremely confused, puts the event a year too late.   So does Rigord (Duchesne, *Hist. Franc. Scriptt.*, vol. v.), p. 7.   Rigord indeed gives an account of the matter so different from that of the English writers—*e.g.*—he represents it as taking place publicly, amid a great concourse of spectators—that one might almost suppose he was relating a second coronation, performed in the following year.   But there seems no other record of any such thing ; and there are some details in his story which point to a different conclusion.   Not only does he, too, name the archbishop of Sens as the consecrator—an outrage upon Reims which could not possibly have been repeated—but he betrays his own confusion by giving the date as June 1, 1181, and then describing the day as Ascension-day, which in 1181 fell on May 14, but which really was the day of the crowning in 1180 (May 29).   The truth is that the panegyrists of Philip Augustus are obliged to slur over this first disgraceful year of his reign as rapidly and confusedly as they can.

[2] *Gesta Hen.* as above, p. 246.   Rog. Howden as above.

day in Reims cathedral, had bent forward to hold the crown
upon the boy's head, and thus relieve him of its weight and
keep it safely in its place.[1] The little act of brotherly kind-
ness and protecting care may be taken as typical of the
political attitude which Henry's father actually assumed
towards the boy-king of the French, and which he faithfully
maintained until Philip himself rendered its maintenance
impossible. It was in truth no new thing for a count of
Anjou to act as the protector of a king of France. But we
may fairly question whether this traditional function of the
Angevin house had ever been fulfilled so honestly and un-
selfishly as it was by Henry during the first two years of
Philip's reign. It was Henry alone who, by his personal
influence and tact, brought Philip himself to reason and the
count of Flanders to submission.[2] Next year, when Philip had
been left sole king of France by the death of Louis VII.,[3] it
was Henry whose mediation checked an attempt of the Flemish
count to avenge by force of arms the loss of his influence at
court;[4] and when a few months later the house of Blois, with
characteristic inconstancy, made common cause with Flanders
against France, it was the prompt and vigorous action of
Henry's sons which alone saved ,the royal domain from
invasion on all sides at once, and enabled their young
sovereign to hold out against his assailants till Henry himself came over to patch up another settlement in the spring
of 1182.[5]

Other needs, however, than those of the French Crown
were once more calling for Henry's presence in Gaul. The
condition of Aquitaine only grew more unsatisfactory, in
spite or in consequence of Richard's efforts to improve it.

---

[1] R. Diceto (Stubbs), vol. i. p. 439. Rigord (Duchesne, *Hist. Franc.
Scriptt.*, vol. v.), p. 5, tells the same story more briefly, and it is amusing to see
how differently he colours it.

[2] *Gesta Hen.* (Stubbs), vol. i. pp. 246, 247. R. Diceto (Stubbs), vol. ii. p. 6.

[3] September 18, 1180; *Gesta Hen.* as above, p. 250; R. Diceto as above,
p. 7; Will. Armor., *Gesta Phil. Aug.* (Duchesne, *Hist. Franc. Scriptt.*, vol. v.),
p. 72. Rigord (*ib.*), p. 7, makes a confusion about the year.

[4] *Gesta Hen.* as above, p. 277. Rog. Howden (Stubbs), vol. ii. p. 260.

[5] *Gesta Hen.* as above, pp. 284-286. R. Diceto as above, pp. 9-11. Gerv.
Cant. (Stubbs), vol. i. pp. 297, 300. Gir. Cambr., *De Instr. Princ.*, dist. ii. cc.
15, 16 (Angl. Christ. Soc., pp. 42-47). Rob. Torigni, a. 1182.

Henry's bargain with Adalbert of La Marche had failed to secure him the possession of that county ; the brother-lords of Lusignan claimed it as next-of-kin to Adalbert as soon as the king's back was turned, and made good their claim by forcible occupation.[1] The Limousin was again threatening revolt ; the town-walls of Limoges were razed by Richard's order at midsummer 1181.[2] Almost at the same moment the death of Count Vulgrin of Angoulême opened a fresh source of strife ; his two brothers laid claim to his inheritance against his only daughter, whom Richard of course took into wardship as a feudal heiress, and on Richard's refusal to admit their claims they made common cause with Ademar of Limoges.[3] The mischief however did not end here. Richard's unbending resolve to bridle Aquitaine had gradually stirred up against him the bitter hatred of the whole people—a hatred for which his stern rule is quite sufficient to account, without admitting the blacker charges brought against him by the reckless tongues of the south.[4] The voice of Bertrand de Born had once more given the signal for a general rising. A *sirvente* which went forth from Hautefort in 1181 rang like a trumpet-call in the ears of the lords of Ventadour and Comborn and Périgord and Dax, of Angoulême and Pons and Taillebourg.[5] But even this was not all. Years before, it seems, there had flashed through the troubadour's quick brain a possibility of stirring up strife in higher quarters than among the petty princes of his native land. Now he distinctly saw the possibility of finding for the Aquitanian resistance to Richard a rallying-point and a leader in Richard's own brother.

One of the most puzzling figures in the history of the time is that of the younger Henry of Anjou—the "young king," as he is usually called. From the day of his crowning to that of his death not one deed is recorded of him save

[1] Geoff. Vigeois, l. i. c. 70 (Labbe, *Nova Biblioth.*, vol. ii. p. 324).

[2] *Ib.* c. 72 (p. 326).

[3] *Ibid.* He was their half-brother, the only son of their mother's first marriage.

[4] Cf. *Gesta Hen.* (Stubbs), vol. i. p. 292, with Gerv. Cant. (Stubbs), vol. i. p. 303, and Gir. Cambr., *De Instr. Princ.*, dist. iii. c. 8 (Angl. Christ. Soc., p. 105).

[5] Clédat, *Bert. de Born*, pp. 44, 45.

deeds of the meanest ingratitude, selfishness, cowardliness
and treachery.   Yet this undutiful, rebellious son, this
corrupter and betrayer of his younger brothers, this weak
and faithless ally, was loved and admired by all men while
he lived, and lamented by all men after he was gone.[1]   The
attraction exercised by him over a man so far his superior as
William the Marshal[2] is indeed well-nigh incomprehensible.
But the panegyrics of the historians, unaccountable as they
look at first glance, do throw some light on the secret of
young Henry's gift of general fascination.   It was a gift
which indeed, in varying degrees, formed part of the hereditary endowments of the Angevin house.   But the character which it took in Fulk Nerra or Henry Fitz-Empress
was very different from that which it assumed in Henry's
eldest son.   The essence of the young king's nature was
not Angevin.   He had little either of the higher talents or
of the stronger and sterner qualities of the Angevin race ; he
had still less of the characteristics of the Norman.   It is by
studying his portrait as drawn in contrast to that of Richard
by a hand equally favourable to both that we can best see
what he really was.   " The first was admired for his mild-
ness and liberality ; the second was esteemed for his serious-
ness and firmness.   One was commendable for graciousness,
the other for stateliness.   One gained praise for his courtesy,
the other for his constancy.   One was conspicuous for mercy,
the other for justice.   One was the refuge and the shield of
vagabonds and evil-doers, the other was their scourge.   One
was devoted to the sports of war, the other to war itself ;
one was gracious to strangers, the other to his own friends—
one to all men, the other only to good men."[3]   Henry in
fact was at bottom what Richard never was but on the
surface—a careless, pleasure-loving, capricious, but withal
most gracious and winning child of the south.   The most
philosophic English historian of the day was reduced to
account for the young king's popularity by the simple and
comprehensive explanation that " the number of fools is in-

---

[1] Except the ever-independent William of Newburgh ; see his l. iii. c. 7 (Howlett, vol. i. pp. 233, 234).   [2] See Rog. Howden (Stubbs), vol. ii. p. 279.
[3] Gir. Cambr., *De Instr. Princ.*, dist. iii. c. 8 (Angl. Christ. Soc. p. 106).

finite."[1]   But it was not folly, it was a shrewd perception of
their own interest, which led the Aquitanians writhing under
Richard's iron rule to see in his elder brother a prince after
their own hearts.[2]

It was not the first time that Bertrand de Born had
sought to kindle in the young king's mind the sparks of
jealousy and discontent which were always latent there.[3]
Now, he fed the flames with an unsparing hand. In words
of bitter satire he ridicules the position of the young king,
who bears the titles of a great sovereign, but has no authority
in his own land, and cannot even claim the tolls upon the
traffic along its roads : " Barons of Aquitaine, are we not all
of us better than a carter who leaves his cart to go as it
may, and counts his dues, if he counts any at all, with trembling fingers ? " " I prize a tiny tract of land with honour
above a great empire with disgrace ! "[4]   Richard, meanwhile,
was playing into his enemies's hands by an encroachment
upon territory which in name at least belonged to his
brother. He had built a castle at Clairvaux, between
Loudun and Poitiers, but on the Angevin side of the
frontier. If the thought of resentment did not occur to
Henry, Bertrand took care to suggest it : " Between Poitiers
and Ile-Bouchard and Mirebeau and Loudun and Chinon
some one has dared to rear, at Clairvaux, a fair castle in the
midst of the plain. I would not have the young king see
it or know of it, for it would not be to his taste ; but its
walls are so white, I doubt he will catch sight of their gleam
from Mateflon ! "[5]   The troubadour's shafts were well aimed,
and they rankled. When King Henry returned to Normandy in the spring of 1182 the Aquitanian rising was in
full career ; as soon as he had composed matters in France
he hurried to the help of Richard, who was fighting the
rebels in the Limousin ; at Whitsuntide the counts of Angou-

---

[1] " Quia ut scriptum est, Stultorum infinitus est numerus." Will. Newb., l. iii.
c. 7 (Howlett, vol. i. p. 234). The quotation is from the Vulgate version of Eccles-
iastes i. 15 ; the English A. V. conveys a wholly different idea.
    [2] Gerv. Cant. (Stubbs), vol. i. p. 303. See also Gerald's other account of
young Henry, *De Instr. Princ.*, dist. ii. c. 9 (Angl. Christ. Soc., pp. 31, 32).
    [3] See Clédat, *Bert. de Born.*, p. 36.   [4] *Ib.* p. 44.   [5] *Ibid.*

lême and Périgord and the viscount of Limoges came to
confer with him at Grandmont, but nothing came of the
negotiations ; Henry then went to attack Pierre-Buffière,
while Richard returned to the siege of Excideuil. At midsummer the king was back at Grandmont, and Geoffrey of
Britanny with him ; thence they went to rejoin Richard,
who was now busy with the siege of Périgueux.[1] Matters
were in this stage when the young king at last made up his
mind to advance into Aquitaine. He was joyfully welcomed
at Limoges on the festival of its patron S. Martial—the last
day of June. On the morrow, however, he joined his father
and brothers before Périgueux, and within a week peace was
made ; Périgueux surrendered, its count and the viscount of
Limoges submitted to Richard, and only the brother-counts
of Angoulême still remained in arms against him.[2]

Peace, however, never lasted long either in Aquitaine or
in King Henry's family. His eldest son now again grew
importunate for a definite and immediate share in the family
heritage. When this was refused, he fled to the court of
France, and was only recalled by a promise of an increased
pecuniary allowance for himself and his queen.[3] Aquitaine,
as soon as Henry had left it, drifted into a state of anarchy
more frightful than any that had ever been known there
before ; the sudden conclusion of the war had let loose all
over the country a crowd of mercenaries—commonly known
as " Brabantines," but really the off-scouring of every land
from Flanders to Aragon—who wrought, as a local writer
says, such havoc as had never been seen since the days of
the heathen northmen.[4] The evil in some measure brought
its own remedy with it, for it drove the common people to
take into their own hands the maintenance of peace and
order. A poor Auvergnat carpenter, urged by a vision of
the Blessed Virgin, set forth under the protection of the
diocesan bishop to preach the cause of peace in his native
district of Le Puy. Those who were like-minded with him,

---

[1] Strictly, of its suburb Puy-St.-Front.

[2] Geoff. Vigeois, l. ii. cc. 1, 2 (Labbe, *Nova Biblioth.*, vol. ii. pp. 330, 331).

[3] *Gesta Hen.* (Stubbs), vol. i. pp. 289, 291. Cf. Rog. Howden (Stubbs), vol.
ii. pp. 266, 267.

[4] Geoff. Vigeois, l. i. c. 73 (as above, p. 328).

no matter what their rank or calling, enrolled themselves in a society bound together by solemn pledges for mutual support in adherence to right and resistance to wrong in every shape ; and in a few years these " *Caputii*," as they were called from the linen capes or hoods which they always wore in fight, proved more than a match for the Brabantines.[1]

Meanwhile, however, the warlike barons of Aquitaine were exasperated at the failure of their league against Richard ; and their anger reached its height when at the conclusion of the Christmas festivities held by King Henry and his sons at Caen, the young king of his own accord renewed his oath of allegiance to his father, confessed his secret alliance with Richard's enemies, and offered to abandon it and make peace with his brother if his father would but insist upon the surrender of Clairvaux. Richard, after some hesitation, gave up to his father the fortress in dispute.[2] The incident apparently opened Henry's eyes to the necessity of clearly defining his sons' political relations with each other ; and while Bertrand de Born was giving a voice to the wrath of his fellow-barons at the young king's desertion of their cause,[3] Henry led his three sons back to Angers, made them all take an oath of obedience to him and peace with each other,[4] and then called upon the two younger to do homage to the eldest for their fiefs.[5] Geoffrey obeyed ;[6] Richard indignantly refused, declaring it was utterly unreasonable that there should be any distinction of rank between children of the same parents, and that if the father's heritage belonged of right to the eldest son, the mother's was equally due to the second.[7] The young king, on the other hand, was on account of his entanglements with the Aquitanian barons almost as unwilling to receive

[1] Geoff. Vigeois, l. ii. c. 22 (Labbe, *Nova Biblioth.*, vol. ii. p. 339). Rob. Torigni, a. 1183. Gerv. Cant. (Stubbs), vol. i. pp. 300, 301. Rigord (Duchesne, *Hist. Franc. Scriptt.*, vol. v.), pp. 11, 12.

[2] *Gesta Hen.* (Stubbs), vol. i. pp. 291, 294, 295.

[3] Clédat, *Bert. de Born*, p. 47.

[4] *Gesta Hen.* as above, p. 295. Cf. R. Diceto (Stubbs), vol. ii. p. 18.

[5] *Gesta Hen.* as above, p. 291. Rog. Howden (Stubbs), vol. ii. p. 273.

[6] *Ibid.* R. Diceto as above.

[7] R. Diceto (as above), pp. 18, 19. *Gesta Hen.* (as above), p. 292. Cf. Gerv. Cant. (as above), p. 303.

the homage as Richard was to perform it.[1] The end of the discussion was that Richard quitted the court, "leaving behind him nothing but threats and insults," and hurried into Poitou to prepare for defence and defiance.[2]

In the first burst of his anger Henry bade the other two brothers go and "subdue Richard's pride" by force of arms.[3] Immediately afterwards, however, he summoned all three, together with the aggrieved barons of Aquitaine, to meet him in conference at Mirebeau.[4] But the young king had already marched into Poitou and received a warm welcome there;[5] Geoffrey, to whom his father had intrusted his summons to the barons, led a motley force of Bretons, Brabantines and mercenaries of all kinds to Limoges;[6] soon afterwards young Henry joined him; with the viscount's help they threw themselves into the citadel,[7] and set to work to raise the whole country against Richard. He, in his extremity, appealed to his father;[8] and Henry at once hurried to the rescue. For six weeks he laid siege to the citadel of Limoges;[9] twice he was personally shot at, and narrowly escaped with his life; twice the young king came to him with offers of submission, and each time he was welcomed with open arms, but each time the submission was a mere feint, designed to keep Henry quiet and give the barons time to wreak their vengeance upon Richard.[10] By Easter matters were so far advanced that Bertrand de Born was openly calling for aid upon Flanders, France and Nor-

---

[1] R. Diceto (Stubbs), vol. ii. p. 18. *Gesta Hen.* (Stubbs), vol. i. p. 292. The two accounts do not exactly agree, Ralf placing at this point the young king's confession of his dealings in Aquitaine; while the story in the *Gesta* is extremely confused, because it is told twice over, in different forms (pp. 291, 292 and 294, 295). [2] *Gesta Hen.* as above, p. 292.

[3] R. Diceto as above, p. 19.

[4] *Gesta Hen.* as above, p. 295. [5] *Ib.* p. 292.

[6] *Ib.* pp. 293, 295. Geoff. Vigeois, l. ii. c. 6 (Labbe, *Nova Biblioth.*, vol. ii. p. 332).

[7] *Gesta Hen.* as above, pp. 293, 296. Geoff. Vigeois as above. Gerv. Cant. (Stubbs), vol. i. p. 304.

[8] Rog. Howden (Stubbs), vol. ii. p. 274.

[9] From Shrove Tuesday—March 1—to Easter. Geoff. Vigeois, l. ii. cc. 12, 16 (as above, pp. 334, 336).

[10] *Gesta Hen.* as above, pp. 296-298. Cf. Geoff. Vigeois, l. ii. c. 7 (as above, pp. 332, 333).

VOL. II.

mandy ;[1] and the dread of a rising in this last-named
quarter prompted Henry to send orders for the arrest of
those barons, both in Normandy and England, who had
been most conspicuous in the rebellion of 1173.[2]

The young king at the same time quitted Limoges to
make a diversion at Angoulême.　On his return, however,
he found it impossible to re-enter Limoges ; its townsfolk
had by this time so fully awakened to his real character and
to their own best interests that they drove him from their
walls with a volley of stones, shouting " We will not have
this man to reign over us !"[3]　He had already robbed them
of their wealth and stripped the shrine of their patron saint
to provide wages for his Brabantines ;[4] and the insult goaded
him to yet more unsparing plunder and yet more reckless
sacrilege.　From the castle of Aixe, which he took on the
Monday in Rogation-week, he advanced to Grandmont, a
religious house whose inmates enjoyed, amid the now general
decay of monastic sanctity, an almost unique reputation for
piety and virtue, and were known to be held by his father
in especial reverence and esteem.　He wrung from them all
the treasure they possessed, and forcibly carried off a golden
pyx, his father's gift, from the high altar itself.　He then
proceeded to Uzerches, where the duke of Burgundy and
the count of Toulouse met him with reinforcements on
Ascension-day ; from Uzerches he moved southward to
Donzenac and Martel, and thence to Rocamadour.[5]　Rocamadour was the most famous of the holy places of Aquitaine ;
besides the tomb of the hermit from whom its name was
derived, it boasted of a statue of the Virgin which attracted
as many pilgrims as the shrine of S. James at Compostella ;
and among the treasures of its church, which was said to
have been founded by Zacchæus the publican, was a sword
traditionally believed to be the famous " Durandal "—the
sword of the Paladin Roland, devoted by him to the Blessed
Virgin on the eve of his last campaign, and carried to her

---

[1] Clédat, *Bert. de Born*, p. 52.　　[2] *Gesta Hen.* (Stubbs), vol. i. p. 294.
[3] Geoff. Vigeois, l. ii. c. 16 (Labbe, *Nova Biblioth.*, vol. ii. p. 336).　*Gesta Hen.* as above, p. 299.
[4] Geoff. Vigeois, l. ii. cc. 13, 14 (pp. 335, 336).　　[5] *Ib.* c. 16 (p. 336).

shrine at Rocamadour after the disaster of Roncevaux. Heed-less alike of paladins and of saints, the young king stripped the shrine of S. Amadour[1] as he had stripped that of S. Martial ; and local tradition declares that he also carried off the hallowed sword, leaving his own dishonoured brand in its place.

He had been ailing ever since he left Uzerches ;[2] now, on his return to Martel, his baffled rage threw him into a fever, to which other complications were soon added.[3] Con-science awoke as death drew near. From the blacksmith's cottage[4] where he lay awaiting his end he sent a message to Limoges, imploring his father to come and speak with him once more.[5] Henry would have gone, but his friends, in their natural dread of another trick, prevented him ;[6] he sent, however, a bishop charged with a message of love and par-don,[7] and as a token of the genuineness of the commission, a precious ring, said to be an heirloom from Henry I.[8] The messenger was only just in time. On the Tuesday in Whitsun-week the young king called together the bishops and religious men who had gathered round him at the tidings of his sickness, confessed his sins first privately, then publicly, before all his followers, was absolved and received the Holy Communion.[9] For three more days he lingered, long enough to receive his father's message of forgiveness and to dictate a letter to him, pleading that the same clemency might be extended to his mother the captive Queen Eleanor, to his own young Queen Margaret, and to

---

[1] Rog. Howden (Stubbs), vol. ii. p. 278.

[2] Geoff. Vigeois, l. ii. c. 16 (Labbe, *Nova Biblioth.*, vol. ii. p. 336).

[3] *Ibid. Gesta Hen.* (Stubbs), vol. i. p. 300. Will. Newb., l. iii. c. 7 (How-lett, vol. i. pp. 233, 234).

[4] "In domo Stephani cognomine Fabri." Geoff. Vigeois, l. ii. c. 19 (as above, p. 337). Is this to be taken literally, or can it be merely a punning nickname applied to the lord of *Martel ?*

[5] *Gesta Hen.* as above. Will. Newb. as above (p. 234).

[6] Will. Newb. as above. Geoff. Vigeois, l. ii. c. 17 (as above, p. 337).

[7] *Gesta Hen.* as above.

[8] "Annulum preciosum . . . qui Henrici munifici Regis olim extitisse nar-ratur." Geoff. Vigeois as above. Cf. Will. Newb. as above, and Th. Agnellus, *De Morte Hen. Reg. jun.* (Stevenson, *R. Coggeshall*), pp. 265, 266.

[9] Geoff. Vigeois as above.

all his servants, friends, adherents and allies ;[1] beseeching also that his father would make atonement in his stead for the sacrileges which he had committed against the holy places of Aquitaine, and would cause his body to be buried at Rouen in the cathedral church of our Lady.[2]   In the early twilight of S. Barnabas's day he repeated his confession, after which he begged to be wrapped once more in his cloak, marked with the cross which he had taken at Limoges in petulance rather than in piety.   Now, however, he was in earnest, and when the sacred symbol had rested for a moment on his shoulder he gave it to his best-beloved knight, William the Marshal, charging him to bear it to the Holy Sepulchre and thus fulfil his vow in his stead.[3]   He then caused his attendants to strip him of his soft raiment, clothe him in a hair-shirt and put a rope round his neck ; with this he bade the assembled clergy drag him out of bed and lay him on a bed of ashes strewed for the purpose. There, lying as if already in his grave, with a stone at his head and another at his feet, he received the last sacraments ;[4] and there, an hour after nones,[5] kissing his father's ring he died.[6]

[1] Geoff. Vigeois, l. ii. c. 24 (Labbe, *Nova Biblioth.*, vol. ii. p. 339).   *Gesta Hen.* (Stubbs), vol. i. pp. 300, 301.   [2] Geoff. Vigeois as above.

[3] *Ib.* c. 17 (p. 337).   Rog. Howden (Stubbs), vol. ii. p. 279.   On young Henry's vow of crusade see *Gesta Hen.* as above, pp. 297, 298.

[4] Rog. Howden as above.

[5] Geoff. Vigeois, l. ii. c. 19 (as above, p. 338).

[6] Will. Newb., l. iii. c. 7 (Howlett, vol. i. p. 234).

CHAPTER VI.

THE LAST YEARS OF HENRY II.

1183-1189.

THE unexpected death of the young king was a catastrophe almost equally overwhelming to both parties in the war. Henry himself, when the news was brought to him by the prior of Grandmont, whither the body had been taken to be prepared for burial,[1] went almost out of his mind with grief.[2] For a moment indeed friends and foes alike seemed incapable of anything but mourning. Hero or saint could scarcely have won a more universal tribute of affection and regret than was showered upon this young king who, so far as we can see, had done so little to deserve it. Stern voices like that of Bertrand de Born, accustomed only to the bitterest tones of sarcasm, insult and angry strife, melted suddenly into accents of the deepest tenderness and lamentation.[3] Sober-minded churchmen and worldly-wise courtiers, though they could not deny or excuse the dead man's sins, yet betrayed with equal frankness their unreasoning attachment to his memory.[4] As his body, arrayed in the linen robe which

---

[1] Geoff. Vigeois, l. ii. c. 20 (Labbe, *Nova Bibloth.*, vol. ii. p. 338).

[2] *Gesta Hen.* (Stubbs), vol. i. p. 301. Cf. Rog. Howden (Stubbs), vol. ii. p. 279, and Gir. Cambr. *De Instr. Princ.*, dist. ii. c. 8 (Angl. Christ. Soc., p. 30).

[3] See Bertrand de Born's two elegies on the young king, Clédat, *Bert. de Born*, pp. 53, 54.

[4] See Pet. Blois, Ep. ii. (Giles, vol. i. pp. 3-5); Gir. Cambr. as above, c. 9 (pp. 31, 32); W. Map, *De Nug. Cur.*, dist. iv. c. i. (Wright, pp. 139, 140); and Th. Agnellus (Stevenson, *R. Coggeshall*), pp. 265-273. The tone of the real historians of the time is however somewhat different. The *Gesta Hen.* is perfectly colourless, and even on the young king's death the writer adds not

he had worn at his coronation—its white folds, hallowed by
the consecrating oil, made to serve for a winding-sheet—was
borne on an open bier upon the shoulders of his comrades-
in-arms from Grandmont northward through Anjou, the
people streamed forth from every castle and town and village
along the road to meet it with demonstrations of mourning
and tears ;[1] and at Le Mans, where it was deposited for a
night in the cathedral church, the bishops and citizens forcibly
took possession of it, refused to give it up, and buried their
beloved young king then and there by the side of his grand
father Geoffrey Plantagenet.[2]

The political tide, however, turned as soon as he was
gone.   The Aquitanian league suddenly found itself without
a head ; for Geoffrey of Britanny, although the wiliest and
most plausible of all the king's sons, was also the most
generally distrusted and disliked.[3]   The league broke up at
once ; on Midsummer-day Ademar of Limoges surrendered
his citadel and made his peace ;[4] and most of the other
rebels soon followed his example.   By the end of the month
Henry, having razed the walls of Limoges and garrisoned
with his own troops the castles which had submitted to him,
could venture to set out for Normandy ;[5] while King Alfonso
of Aragon, who had come to the help of his father's old

a word of comment, good or bad. Rog. Howden, on the other hand (Stubbs,
vol. ii. p. 279), openly gives vent to a feeling which may be expressed by " So
perish all the enemies of King Henry," and grows almost impatient with
Henry's grief. R. Diceto (Stubbs, vol. ii. pp. 19, 20) is as usual very cautious
in the expression of his personal opinions, but they also appear to be somewhat
opposed to the popular sentiment. The point of view taken by Gerv. Cant.
(Stubbs, vol. i. p. 305) is probably unique. The one really judicial commentator
on the whole affair is William of Newburgh (l. iii. c. 7—Howlett, vol. i. pp.
233, 234).

[1] R. Diceto (Stubbs), vol. ii. p. 20.   Cf. Th. Agnellus (Stevenson, *R. Coggeshall*), p. 268.

[2] R. Diceto as above. Th. Agnellus (as above), p. 269. *Gesta Hen.* (Stubbs),
vol. i. p. 303.

[3] See Gir. Cambr. *De Instr. Princ.*, dist. ii. c. 11 (Angl. Christ. Soc., p. 35).
The author of the *Gesta Hen.* seems to look upon Geoffrey as the instigator of all
his brothers' misdoings, and scarcely ever mentions his name without an epithet of
abuse.

[4] Geoff. Vigeois, l. ii. c. 18 (Labbe, *Nova Biblioth.*, vol. ii. p. 337). *Gesta
Hen.* as above, p. 302.   The date comes from Geoffrey.

[5] *Gesta Hen.* as above, p. 303.

ally, found nothing left for him to do but to join Richard in an expedition against the one baron who still persisted in his rebellion—Bertrand de Born.[1]   If Bertrand's story may be believed, it was Alfonso's treachery which, after a week's siege, compelled him to surrender Hautefort.[2]   What followed shewed plainly that the Aquitanian revolt was at an end.   Richard made over Hautefort to Constantine de Born, the troubadour's brother and lifelong rival;[3] Bertrand, instead of calling his fellow-barons to avenge him as of old, threw himself upon the generosity of his conqueror, and addressed Richard in a *sirvente* entreating that his castle might be restored to him.   Richard referred him to his father; Bertrand then hastened to the king, who greeted him sarcastically with an allusion to one of his own earlier *sirventes :* "You were wont to boast of possessing more wits than you ever needed to use—what has become of them now?"   "Sire, I lost them on the day that you lost your son."   Henry burst into tears ; Bertrand was forgiven, indemnified for the losses which he had sustained during the siege, and dismissed with a charter securing to him from that time forth the sole possession of Hautefort.[4]   As a natural consequence, his lyre and his sword were thenceforth both alike at the service of the ducal house to whom he had hitherto been such a troublesome and dangerous foe.

On his northward march Henry met with no opposition. The young king had drawn to himself followers from all parts of the Angevin dominions, as well as from those of the French Crown ;[5] but they had all been drawn by a purely personal attraction, or by the hope of gain ; their action had no political significance ; and the greater barons, warned by their experience of ten years before, had remained entirely aloof from the whole movement.   On reaching Le Mans, indeed, Henry found the old jealousy between Normandy and Maine on the point of breaking out over his son's dead body ; the clergy and people of Rouen, indignant

---

[1] Geoff. Vigeois, l. ii. c. 18 (Labbe, *Nova Biblioth.*, vol. ii. p. 337).

[2] On the story of this siege see Clédat, *Bert. de Born*, pp. 55-57, and Geoff. Vigeois as above.

[3] Geoff. Vigeois as above.   [4] Clédat, *Bert. de Born*, pp. 57, 58.

[5] W. Map, *De Nug. Cur.*, dist. iv. c. i. (Wright, p. 139).

at being defrauded of their young king's dying bequest, were
threatening to come and destroy the city of Le Mans and
carry off his body by force.   Henry was obliged to cause it
to be disinterred and conveyed to Rouen for re-burial,[1] while
he himself returned to Angers to meet Richard and to
receive Geoffrey's submission.[2]   The quarrel between the
Cenomannians and the citizens of Rouen was however only
the smallest part of the troubles which arose from the young
king's death.   As Margaret's only child had died in infancy,
her brother Philip of France at once demanded the restoration of her dowry, and especially the fortress of Gisors.
Henry refused to give it up ; conference after conference
was held without result ;[3] at last, in December, a compromise was made, Henry consenting to do homage to Philip
for all his transmarine dominions and to pay a money-compensation for Gisors, which was to be left in his hands
henceforth as the dowry not of Margaret, but of her sister
Adela, Richard's affianced bride.[4]

But a far worse difficulty remained.   All Henry's schemes
for the distribution of his territories were upset by the death
of his heir, and it was necessary to devise some new arrangement.   It really seems as if Henry's first thought about the
matter was that now at last he could provide as he chose
for his darling " Lackland " ; for he at once bade the English
justiciar Ralf de Glanville bring John over to meet him in
Normandy.   As soon as they arrived he sent for Richard and
unfolded his plan.   Richard was now the eldest son ; if he
lived, he must in due time succeed his father as head of the
Angevin house.   Henry had clearly no mind to venture a
second time upon the dangerous experiment of crowning his
heir during his own life.   But, although we have no actual

[1] *Gesta Hen.* (Stubbs), vol. i. pp. 303, 304.   Rog. Howden (Stubbs), vol. ii.
p. 280.   R. Diceto (Stubbs), vol. ii. p. 20.   Gerv. Cant. (Stubbs), vol. i. p. 305.
Th. Agnellus (Stevenson, *R. Coggeshall*), pp. 269-272.

[2] *Gesta Hen.* as above, p. 304.

[3] *Ib.* pp. 304, 305.   Cf. Rog. Howden as above, pp. 280, 281.   According
to the *Gesta*, one of Henry's contrivances for avoiding the restitution of the
dower-lands was to declare that he had bestowed them upon his own wife; and
he set her at liberty and made her go through the said lands to demonstrate the
fact.   If so, however, she was soon put in prison again.

[4] *Ib.* p. 306.   Cf. Rog. Howden, as above, pp. 281, 284.

statement of his intentions, it seems plain that he did intend
to place Richard, in every respect short of the coronation, in
the same position which had been held by the young king.
Under these circumstances, if the continental dominions of
the Angevin house were to be redistributed among the three
surviving brothers, there was only one possible mode of re-
distribution.   Geoffrey could not give up Britanny, for he
was now actually married to its duchess;[1] but Richard, in
consideration of his prospects as future king of England,
duke of Normandy and count of Anjou, might fairly be
asked to surrender to his youngest brother the duchy of
Aquitaine.   So at least it seemed from Henry's point of
view.   Richard however saw the matter in another light.
Not because he loved Aquitaine, but because he hated it—
because for eight years he had fought unceasingly to crush it
beneath his feet—now that it lay there prostrate, he could
not let it escape him.   Richard was generous ; but to give
up to other hands the reaping of a harvest which he had
sown with such unsparing labour and watered with such
streams of blood, was a sacrifice too great for his generosity
in his six-and-twentieth year.   He met his father's demand
with a request for time to think it over ; that evening he
mounted his horse and rode straight for Poitou ; and thence
he sent back a message that so long as he lived, no one but
himself should ever hold the duchy of Aquitaine.[2]

After threatening and beseeching him by turns all
through the winter, Henry so far lost patience that he gave
permission to John—now fifteen years old—to lead an
army into his brother's territories and win an heritage for
himself if he could.[3]   It does not appear, however, that any
such attempt was actually made till after Henry himself
had gone back to England in June 1184.[4]   As soon as his
back was turned, his two younger sons joined to harry the
lands of the eldest ; Richard retaliated by pushing across
the Angevin border and making a raid upon Britanny ; and

---

[1] Geoffrey and Constance were married in 1181 ; see a document in Morice,
Hist. Bret., preuves, vol. i. col. 687.   Rob. Torigni dates the marriage a year too
ate (Delisle, vol. ii. p. 104 and note 4).

[2] *Gesta Hen.* (Stubbs), vol. i. p. 308.   [3] *Ib.* p. 311.

[4] *Ib.* p. 312.   R. Diceto (Stubbs), vol. ii. p. 21.

in November Henry found it necessary to check the lawless doings of all three by summoning them to rejoin him in England.[1]   On S. Andrew's day a sort of public reconciliation of the whole family took place in a great council at Westminster; Eleanor was suffered to resume her place as queen, and the three sons were compelled formally at least to make peace among themselves.[2]   Geoffrey was at once sent back to Normandy;[3] Richard and John stayed to keep the Christmas feast with their father and mother amid a brilliant gathering of the court at Windsor.[4]   Soon afterwards Richard also returned to his troublesome duchy;[5] for Henry had now abandoned all idea of transferring it to John.   Falling back upon his earlier plans for his youngest child, on Mid-Lent Sunday 1185 he knighted John at Windsor, and thence despatched him as governor to Ireland.[6]

Meanwhile the king himself was again called over sea by fresh troubles in Gaul.   The king of France and the count of Flanders had been quarrelling for the last two years over the territories of the latter's deceased wife, the counties of Amiens and Vermandois;[7] Henry's last act before he left

---

[1] *Gesta Hen.* (Stubbs), vol. i. p. 319.

[2] *Ib.* pp. 319, 320. Rog. Howden (Stubbs), vol. ii. p. 288. Eleanor had been released in June in order that she might welcome her daughter, the duchess of Saxony ; *Gesta Hen.* as above, p. 313.

[3] *Gesta Hen.* as above, p. 320.   [4] *Ib.* p. 333.   [5] *Ib.* p. 334.

[6] *Ib.* p. 336. R. Diceto (Stubbs), vol. ii. p. 34. John sailed from Milford on April 24 and landed next day at Waterford. Gir. Cambr. *Expugn. Hibern.*, l. ii. c. 32 (Dimock, vol. v. p. 380).

[7] *Gesta Hen.* as above, pp. 311, 312. Gerv. Cant. (Stubbs), vol. i. p. 309. On this quarrel cf. Rigord (Duchesne, *Hist. Franc. Scriptt.*, vol. v.), pp. 12, 13, and Gir. Cambr. *De Instr. Princ.*, dist. iii. c. 2 (Angl. Christ. Soc., pp. 88-90). This last version is extremely confused in its chronology. The main facts of the case are these : Philip of Flanders and Isabel his wife had no children, and they had quarrelled (*Gesta Hen.* as above, pp. 99, 100). Philip's heir-presumptive was his sister Margaret, wife of Count Baldwin of Hainaut, and after her, her son, another Baldwin. In 1180, however, Philip proposed, instead of leaving all his dominions to his sister and her son, to settle the southern half of them, comprising Vermandois and Flanders south of the river Lys, upon her daughter Elizabeth, whom he had just given in marriage to Philip of France. (*Ib.* p. 245.) He meant to leave them to her on his own death ; but when his wife died, in 1182 (*ib.* p. 285), Philip Augustus laid claim to her two counties as lapsed fiefs. King and count went on quarrelling till 1186, when, as we shall see, the matter was

Normandy had been to arrange a truce between them.[1] Two
months later—in August 1184—while Philip of Flanders
was away in England on a pilgrimage to the martyr's tomb
at Canterbury, Philip of France broke the truce by stirring
up his father-in-law the count of Hainaut to attack Flanders
in his behalf: Philip of Flanders appealed for help to his
other overlord the Emperor Frederic; the archbishop of
Cöln, who had been his fellow-pilgrim, at once joined him in
a counter-invasion of Hainaut ;[2] and the incalculable dangers
of a war between France and Germany were only averted by
Frederic's wise reluctance to interfere, strengthened, we may
perhaps suspect, by the influence of the English king.   It
seemed indeed as if nothing but Henry's presence could
avail to keep order in Gaul.   When he returned thither, in
April 1185,[3] his first task was to pacify another quarrel
between his own sons.   This time the elder one seems to
have been the aggressor ; and Henry grew so angry that he
once more summoned Richard to give up Aquitaine altogether, not, however, to either of his brothers, but to its own
lawful lady, his mother, Queen Eleanor.   Despite all her
faults, Eleanor was reverenced by her sons; Richard especially
treated her throughout his life with the utmost respect and
affection ; and the demand thus made in her behalf met
with immediate submission.[4]   For nine months Henry's
dominions were quiet, and his hands were free to deal with
the quarrels of France and Flanders.   But before he had
succeeded in pacifying them, a further complication was
added.   King Bela of Hungary made suit to Philip of
France for the hand of his sister the widowed Queen
Margaret,[5] and this at once re-opened the question about her

settled by the immediate cession of Vermandois to Philip Augustus, who thereupon
agreed to wait for the rest till the Flemish count's death.

[1] *Gesta Hen.* (Stubbs), vol. i. p. 312.   Gerv. Cant. (Stubbs), vol. i. p. 309.

[2] *Gesta Hen.* as above, pp. 321, 322.   Cf. Rog. Howden (Stubbs), vol. ii. p.
288, and R. Diceto (Stubbs), vol. ii. p. 32.

[3] *Gesta Hen.* as above, p. 337.   R. Diceto as above, p. 34.

[4] *Gesta Hen.* as above, pp. 337, 338.   Cf. Rog. Howden as above, p. 304.

[5] Rigord (Duchesne, *Hist. Franc. Scriptt.*, vol. v.), p. 20.   Will. Armor.,
Gesta Phil. Aug. (ibid.), p. 73.   According to the *Gesta Hen.* as above, p. 346,
Bela's first suit was to Henry, for the hand of his granddaughter Matilda of

dower ; for the agreement made two years before had been conditional upon Richard's marriage with Adela, and as this event seemed as far off as ever, Philip again laid claim to the whole dowry, including Gisors.   He was however too much in need of Henry's assistance in his dispute with Flanders over the dower-lands of Isabel of Vermandois to risk a quarrel with him about those of the young queen ; and by Henry's tact and diplomacy both questions were settled in a conference at Gisors itself early in 1186.[1]   The count of Flanders gave up Vermandois to Philip Augustus,[2] while Philip and Margaret again consented, in return for a money-compensation from Henry, to make Gisors over to him on the old condition—that Richard should marry Adela without further delay.[3]   The condition however remained unfulfilled.   Richard was again despatched into Aquitaine, not indeed as its duke—for Henry had placed all its fortresses under officers of his own appointment [4]—but still as his father's representative, charged in his name with the maintenance of obedience and order.[5]   As for Eleanor, Henry had clearly never intended again to intrust her with any real authority ; and in April he carried her back with him to England.[6]

England was now his only refuge.   In these closing years of his reign, when the whole interest of the story centres round the person of the king, the character of those few incidents which take place on English ground is in striking contrast with the state of affairs which occupied him in Gaul.   While the Angevin dominions on the continent

Saxony ; but Henry, "ut mos suus erat," was so slow in answering that Bela, tired of waiting, transferred his proposals to Margaret. On the other hand, Gerv. Cant. (Stubbs), vol. i. pp. 336, 337, charges Henry with having contrived Margaret's marriage with Bela on purpose to get her to a safe distance, whence neither she nor her husband could reclaim the dowry.

[1] *Gesta Hen.* (Stubbs), vol. i. p. 343.   R. Diceto (Stubbs), vol. ii. p. 40.   The last gives the date as March 10 ; the *Gesta* make it just before Mid-Lent, which was February 26.

[2] Cf. Rigord (Duchesne, *Hist. Franc. Scriptt.*, vol. v.), p. 13, with R. Diceto as above.

[3] *Gesta Hen.* as above, p. 344.   Cf. R. Diceto as above.

[4] R. Diceto as above.   [5] *Gesta Hen.* as above, p. 345.

[6] *Ibid.*   R. Diceto as above.

were threatening disruption under their owner's very eyes,
each of his visits to England was marked by some fresh
indication of the firm hold which he had gained upon his
island realm and its dependencies, or of the lofty position
which England under him had acquired among the powers
of the world.   Of the internal affairs of England itself,
indeed, we hear absolutely nothing save a few ecclesiastical
details, and of Wales and Scotland scarcely more.   Henry's
first business after his landing in 1184 had been to lead
an army against South Wales ;[1] but at the mere tidings of
his approach Rees hurried to make submission at Worcester.[2]
William of Scotland was in still greater haste to meet the
English king with a suit for the hand of his granddaughter
Matilda of Saxony,[3] who was now in England with her
parents.   The project was foiled by the Pope's refusal to
grant a dispensation,[4] without which such a marriage was
impossible, owing to the descent of both parties from
Malcolm III. and Margaret.   Henry, however, on his
next visit to England in 1186, proposed that William
should wed in Matilda's place her kinswoman Hermengard
of Beaumont.[5]   Hermengard stood even nearer than Matilda
in descent from Henry I., but there was no obstacle to
her marriage with the king of Scots ; he therefore willingly embraced the offer ; and before the year closed the
alliance between the two kings was doubly cemented, first
at Carlisle by the final submission of Galloway to Henry,
William himself standing surety for its obedience ;[6] and
afterwards, at Woodstock on September 5, by the marriage
of Hermengard and William, to whom Henry restored
Edinburgh castle as his contribution to the dowry of the
bride.[7]

Henry is said to have received in the course of the
same year another proposal, from a more distant quarter, for
his granddaughter's hand.   According to one writer, Bela of
Hungary had at first desired the young Saxon princess for his
queen, and it was only Henry's long delay in answering his

[1] *Gesta Hen.* (Stubbs), vol. i. p. 314.   Gerv. Cant. (Stubbs), vol. i. p. 309.
[2] *Gesta Hen.* as above.   [3] *Ib.* p. 313.   [4] *Ib.* p. 322.
[5] *Ib.* p. 347.   [6] *Ib.* pp. 348, 349.   [7] *Ib.* p. 351.

suit which provoked him to transfer it to Margaret.[1]   Both
Matilda's suitors must have been attracted solely by the
ambition of forming a family connexion with her grandfather King Henry; and that attraction must have been a
very strong one, for at the time of William's suit, if not at
the time of Bela's, it had to counterbalance the fact that
Matilda herself, her parents, and all their other children,
were landless and penniless exiles.   To Henry's load of
family cares there had been added since 1180 that of the
troubles of his eldest daughter and her husband, Duke Henry
the Lion of Saxony.   During the retreat of the Imperial
forces from Italy in 1179 the duke fell under the displeasure
of his cousin the Emperor; next year he was deprived of
all his estates and placed under the ban of the Empire.   In
the summer of 1182 he and his family made their way to
the sole refuge left them, the court of his father-in-law; and
there for the most part they remained during the next two
years.   Towards the close of 1184 the English king's influence in Germany prevailed to obtain the duke's restoration
to his patrimonial duchy of Brunswick;[2] and another token
of the eagerness with which Henry's alliance was sought
may be seen in the fact that among the conditions demanded
by Frederic was the betrothal of one of his own daughters
to Richard of Poitou.[3]   This condition, which might have
added considerably to Henry's difficulties in France, was
annulled by the speedy death of the intended bride.[4]   On
the other hand, the restoration of the exiled duke was far
from complete; Brunswick was only a small part of the
vast territories which he had formerly possessed; although
he returned to Germany in 1185,[5] it was as a suspected and
ruined man; and before Henry's reign closed another sentence of banishment drove him and his wife again to seek
the shelter of her father's court.

Early in 1185 came a crowning proof of the estimation
in which the English king was held both at home and

---

[1] *Gesta Hen.* (Stubbs), vol. i. p. 346.   See above, p. 235, note 5.

[2] *Gesta Hen.* as above, pp. 249, 287, 288, 318, 319, 322, 323; cf. Rog. Howden
(Stubbs), vol. ii. pp. 199-201, 269, 288, 289.   [3] *Gesta Hen.* as above, p. 319.

[4] *Ib.* p. 322.   [5] R. Diceto (Stubbs), vol. ii. p. 38.

abroad.   King Baldwin III. of Jerusalem, the eldest son and
successor of Queen Melisenda and Fulk of Anjou, had died
in 1162, the year of Thomas Becket's appointment to the
see of Canterbury.   He was succeeded by his brother
Almeric, who died while Henry was struggling with his
rebellious barons in 1173.   During the twelve years which
had passed since then, Almeric's son, another Baldwin, had
fought on bravely against overwhelming odds to keep out
the Infidel foe.   But the struggle grew more hopeless year
by year and day by day.   The young king himself was in
natural temper as gallant a knight as ever sprang from the
blood of Anjou ; but he was crippled physically, socially and
politically by a disease which made his life a burthen—he
was a leper ; his kingdom was torn by the mutual jealousies
of the kinsmen on whom he was compelled to rely for its
government and defence ; while the political and military
power of the Turks was growing to a height such as it had
never before attained, under their famous leader Saladin.[1]
If the necessities of Palestine had been grievous when King
Baldwin II. had called upon Fulk to protect Melisenda on
her perilous throne—if they had been grievous when Melisenda sought the aid of the western princes for her infant
son Baldwin III.—they were far more grievous now.   But
times were changed in the west since Melisenda had been
obliged to rest content with a general appeal addressed to
Latin Christendom through the abbot of Clairvaux.   Independent of the claim of the king of Jerusalem to the sympathy and the succour of all Christian princes, Baldwin had
a direct personal claim upon one prince, and that one well-
nigh the mightiest of all.   He himself represented one
branch of the race whose power had spread from the black
rock of Angers to the ends of the earth ; the other, the elder
branch, was represented by Henry Fitz-Empress.   As Baldwin's nearest kinsman, as the foremost descendant alike of
Fulk the King and of Fulk the Canon, as head of the whole

---

[1] Will. Tyr., ll. xix.-xxii. l. xxi. ; containing a most moving account of Bald-
win.   See also Will. Newb., l. iii. c. 10 (Howlett, vol. i. pp. 240-247), and Bishop
Stubbs's elucidation of the whole story and its significance in his introduction to
Itin. Reg. Ric., pp. lxxxi. *et seq.*

Angevin race on both sides of the sea, it was to the Angevin king of England that the Angevin king of Jerusalem appealed, as a matter of right and almost of duty, for succour in his extremity.[1] And he threw his appeal into a shape which made it indeed irresistible. Henry was at Nottingham, on his way northward to York, in the last days of January 1185, when he was stopped by tidings that two of the highest dignitaries of the Latin Church in the east, Heraclius the Patriarch of Jerusalem and the Grand Master of the Hospital, had arrived at Canterbury on a mission from Holy Land.[2] He at once changed his course and hurried southward again to meet them at Reading.[3] With a burst of tears Heraclius laid at the feet of the English king the royal standard of Jerusalem, the keys of the city, those of the Tower of David and of the Holy Sepulchre itself, beseeching him in Baldwin's name to carry them back at the head of his crusading host.

The whole assembly wept with the Patriarch; and the king himself was deeply moved.[4] How many of his earlier projects of going on crusade—now to Spain, now to Holy Land, now alone, now with the king of France—had been mere political expedients, we cannot tell; there may have been more sincerity in them than one is at first disposed to imagine. Little as Henry cared for either war or adventure merely for its own sake, still there flowed in his veins, no less than in those of his young cousin Baldwin, the blood of Angevin pilgrims and crusaders. The lifelong dream of

---

[1] "Sicut ab eo ad cujus nutum regnum Jerosolymitanum de jure hæreditario prædecessorum suorum spectabat." *Gesta Hen.* (Stubbs), vol. i. p. 328.

[2] *Ib.* p. 335. They had come through France, and had been received in Paris by Philip on January 16; Rigord (Duchesne, *Hist. Franc. Scriptt.*, vol. v.), p. 14. They were at Canterbury on January 29, and it seems that even the Patriarch of Jerusalem, with the very keys of the Sepulchre itself in his hands, thought it well to stop and pay his devotions at the martyr's tomb; Gerv. Cant. (Stubbs), vol. i. p. 325. A third envoy, the Grand Master of the Temple, had died on the way at Verona; *Gesta Hen.* as above, p. 331; R. Diceto (Stubbs), vol. ii. p. 32.

[3] *Gesta Hen.* as above, p. 335; cf. R. Diceto as above. Gir. Cambr., *De Instr. Princ.*, dist. ii. c. 24 (Angl. Christ. Soc., p. 59) places the meeting at Winchester.

[4] *Gesta Hen.* as above, pp. 335, 336. R. Diceto as above, pp. 32, 33. Cf. Gir. Cambr. as above (pp. 59, 60).

Fulk Nerra and Fulk V. may have been also the dream of
Henry, although none of the three was a man to let his
dreams influence his conduct until he saw a clear possibility
of realizing them. Whether there was such a possibility
now, however, was a question whose decision did not rest
with Henry alone. If he was to head a crusade, he must
head it not merely as count of Anjou but as king of
England, with all England's powers and resources, material
and moral, at his back ; and this could only be if England
sanctioned his undertaking. The "faithful men of the
land"—the bishops and barons, the constitutional representatives of the nation—were therefore gathered together
in council at Clerkenwell on March 18 ; Henry bade them
advise him as they thought best for his soul's health, and
promised to abide by their decision. After deliberation,
they gave it as their unanimous judgement that he must
remain at home and not venture to abandon, for the sake of
giving his personal assistance in the east, the work to which
he was pledged by his coronation-oath, of keeping his own
realms in peace and order and securing them from external
foes.[1] Whether or not the decision thus arrived at was wise
for the interests of Christendom at large—whether or not it
redounds altogether to the honour of England—it was surely
the highest tribute she could pay to her Angevin king. A
ruler from whom his people were so unwilling to part had
clearly some better hold over them than that of mere
force. That they shrank with such dread from any interruption of his kingly labours is the best proof how greatly
they had benefited by those labours during the past thirty
years.

The Patriarch was bitterly disappointed, and vented his

---

[1] R. Diceto (Stubbs), vol. ii. pp. 33, 34. The author of *Gesta Hen.* (Stubbs),
vol. i. p. 336, dates the council eight days earlier than Ralf, and finds nothing
more to say about it than "cum diu tractâssent de itinere Jerosolimitanæ profec-
tionis, tandem placuit regi et consiliariis consulere inde Philippum regem Franciæ."
But the totally independent versions of Henry's answer to the Patriarch given by
Gir. Cambr., *De Instr. Princ.*, dist. ii. c. 27 (Angl. Christ. Soc., pp. 64, 65), and
Gerv. Cant. (Stubbs), vol. i. p. 32, both distinctly support Ralf thus far, that they
represent the king's refusal as grounded on the difficulty of reconciling the proposed expedition with the fulfilment of his duty to his own realms.

disappointment upon Henry in unmeasured terms.   In vain
did he intreat that at least John, the only one of the king's
sons then in England, might be sent to infuse some new
life into the rapidly-dying stock of the Angevin house in
Palestine.   John himself, it is said, was eager to go,[1] but
the king refused his consent, and six weeks later, as we
have seen, despatched him as governor to Ireland.   This
mission failed completely, through John's own fault.   He
was received with every demonstration of loyalty both by
the native princes and by the English settlers ; but in a
very few months he contrived to set them all against him.
He treated the English leaders with the most overbearing
insolence ; he insulted the Irish chieftains who came to
bring him their loyal greetings at Waterford more brutally
still, mocking at their dress and manners, and even pulling
their beards ;[2] he sent the mercenaries who had accompanied
him from England to make a raid upon North Munster, in
which they were repulsed with great loss,[3] and then exasperated them to mutiny by keeping them penniless while
he spent their wages upon his own pleasure.[4]   By September
he had brought matters to such a pass that his father was
obliged to recall him and bid John de Courcy undertake the
government of Ireland in his place.[5]   Henry however was
far from abandoning his cherished scheme.   Blinded by his
fatal partiality for his youngest child, he was willing to attribute John's failure to any cause except the true one ; he
determined that the lad should return to his post, but
clothed with fuller powers and loftier dignity.   Taking advantage of a change in the Papacy, he at once applied to
the new Pope, Urban III., for leave to have his son anointed
and crowned as king of Ireland.   Urban not only gave his
consent, but accompanied it with a gift of a crown made of
peacock's feathers set in gold.[6]   Next summer there came
to England news that "a certain Irishman had cut off the

---

[1] Gir. Cambr. *De Instr. Princ.*, dist. ii. c. 27 (Angl. Christ. Soc., p. 65).

[2] Gir. Cambr. *Expugn. Hibern.*, l. ii. c. 36 (Dimock, vol. v. p. 389).

[3] Four Masters, a. 1185 (O'Donovan, vol. iii. p. 67).

[4] *Gesta Hen.* (Stubbs), vol. i. p. 339.

[5] Gir. Cambr. *Expugn. Hibern.* as above (p. 392).

[6] *Gesta Hen.* as above.   Rog. Howden (Stubbs), vol. ii. pp. 306, 307.

head of Hugh de Lacy ";[1] Henry, seeing in this event an
opportunity of recovering for the Crown Hugh's vast estates
in Ireland, hurried John off thither at once [2] without waiting
to have him crowned, or possibly intending that the coronation should take place in Dublin.   But before John had
sailed, he was recalled by tidings of another death which
touched his father more nearly.

Geoffrey of Britanny had gone to visit the French king
in Paris ; there, on August 19, he died.[3]   No one regretted
him, unless it was his father, and Philip of France, who
caused him to be buried with regal honours in the cathedral
church of our Lady in Paris, and followed him to the grave
with every demonstration of mourning.[4]   If report spoke
true, Philip's grief was as sincere as it was selfish ; for
Geoffrey had been cut off in the midst of a plot whereby he
proposed, out of spite against his father and elder brother,
to withdraw from them his homage for Britanny and become
Philip's liegeman, receiving in return the title of grand
seneschal which in the year of his own birth had been
conferred upon his father as a warrant for intervention in
the affairs of the Breton duchy.[5]   Faithful servants of the
English king were inclined to see in Geoffrey's sudden end
a divine judgement upon this undutiful scheme.[6]   Philip however saw a means of making his own profit out of Geoffrey's
death, quite as readily as out of his life.   He at once
claimed, as overlord, the wardship of the infant heiress-

---

[1] *Gesta Hen.* (as above), p. 350.   Cf. *ib.* p. 361 ; Rog. Howden (Stubbs),
vol. ii. p. 309 ; Four Masters, a. 1186 (O'Donovan, vol. iii. pp. 71-75) ; Gir.
Cambr. *Expugn. Hibern.*, l. ii. c. 35 (Dimock, vol. v. p. 387) ; and R. Diceto
(Stubbs), vol. ii. p. 34.   This last gives the day, July 25, but places the event a
year too early.   [2] *Gesta Hen.* (Stubbs), vol. i. p. 350.

[3] R. Diceto as above, p. 41.   Rigord (Duchesne, *Hist. Franc. Scriptt.*,
vol. v.), p. 20.   Will. Armor., *Gesta Phil. Aug. (ibid.)*, p. 73.   The accounts of
the cause of death are very conflicting.   Rigord, Will. Armor. and Gerv. Cant.
(Stubbs, vol. i. 336) say he died of some malady not specified.   Gir. Cambr.,
De Instr. Princ., dist. ii. c. 10 (Angl. Christ. Soc., p. 34), makes him die " eodem
quo et frater antea morbo acutissimo, sc. febrili calore."   The *Gesta Hen.* as
above, and Rog. Howden (Stubbs), vol. ii. p. 309, attribute his death to
injuries received in a tournament ; but the *Gesta*, as we shall see, have an
alternative version.   [4] Gir. Cambr., Rigord and Will. Armor. as above.

[5] Cf. Gir. Cambr. as above (pp. 33, 34), with *Gesta Hen.* as above, and Will.
Newb., l. iii. c. 7 (Howlett, vol. i. p. 235).   [6] *Gesta Hen.* as above.

presumptive of Britanny — Eleanor, the only child of
Geoffrey and Constance [1]—and with it the administration
of her duchy till she should be old enough to be married.
Henry tried to temporize,[2] but the longer the negotiations
lasted the more complicated they became, as Philip kept
increasing his demands. First Aquitaine was dragged into
the dispute. Its northern portion was just now in a state
of unwonted tranquillity, for at the close of the year we
find Bertrand de Born complaining that he had witnessed
neither siege nor battle for more than twelve months.[3]
Richard was in fact busy in the south, at war with the
count of Toulouse.[4] Against this Philip remonstrated, as
an unjust aggression upon a loyal vassal of the French
Crown ;[5] he added to his remonstrance a demand for
Richard's homage to himself for Aquitaine, and also—all
prospect of Adela's marriage being now apparently at an
end—for the definite restitution of Gisors.[6] While the two
kings were negotiating, actual hostilities broke out between
some of their constables on the border ; the warlike zeal
of both parties, however, died down at the approach of
Christmas ;[7] Henry lingered in England to receive two
papal legates who were coming to crown John as king of
Ireland,[8] but the crowning never took place ; and at last, on
February 17, 1187, king and legates sailed together for
Normandy.[9]

When the two kings met at the Gué-St.-Rémy on April
5,[10] little Eleanor was no longer heiress of Britanny. On

---

[1] R. Diceto (Stubbs), vol. ii. p. 41, says they had two daughters ; but I can
find no trace of a second.   [2] *Gesta Hen.* (Stubbs), vol. i. pp. 353, 354.

[3] Clédat, *Bert. de Born*, pp. 68, 69.   [4] *Gesta Hen.* as above, p. 345.

[5] R. Diceto as above, pp. 43, 44.

[6] Rigord (Duchesne, *Hist. Franc. Scriptt.*, vol. v.), p. 23. Will. Armor.,
Gesta Phil. Aug. (*ibid.*), pp. 73, 74 ; *Philipp.*, l. ii. (*ibid.*), p. 118.

[7] *Gesta Hen.* as above, pp. 354, 355. R. Diceto as above, p. 44.

[8] Cardinal Octavian and Hugh of Nonant, bishop-elect of Chester ; *Gesta Hen.*
(Stubbs), vol. ii. pp. 3, 4 ; R. Diceto (as above), p. 47. They landed at Sandwich on Christmas-eve and kept the feast at Canterbury. Gerv. Cant. (Stubbs),
vol. i. p. 346.

[9] The *Gesta Hen.* as above, p. 4, and Rog. Howden (Stubbs), vol. ii. p. 317,
say they crossed together ; R. Diceto as above, p. 47, to whom we owe the date
of Henry's crossing, seems to think the legates had preceded him.

[10] *Gesta Hen.* (as above), p. 5.

Easter-day Constance had become the mother of a son,
whom the Bretons, in defiance of his grandfather's wish to
bestow upon him his own name, insisted upon calling after
the legendary hero of their race, Arthur[1]—thus at once
claiming him as the representative of their national existence and rights.   The child's birth made little difference in
the political situation ; Philip claimed the wardship of the
heir of Britanny just as he had claimed that of its heiress ;
the conference broke up, and both parties prepared for war.
Henry distributed his forces in four divisions ; one of these
was commanded by his eldest son, Geoffrey the chancellor,
who as bishop-elect of Lincoln had given good proof of his
military capacities in the revolt of 1174 ;—another was
intrusted to the king's faithful friend Earl William de Mandeville ; the other two were commanded respectively by
Richard and John, and it seems that both of these were at
once sent down into Berry, where Philip was expected to
begin his attack.   Soon after Whitsuntide Philip advanced
upon Berry,[2] took Issoudun and Graçay, and laid siege to
Châteauroux.[3]   Henry now followed his sons ; the three
together marched to the relief of Châteauroux, and Richard
apparently succeeded in making his way into the place,
where John afterwards rejoined him.[4]   For nearly a fortnight the two kings remained encamped on opposite sides
of the Indre, drawing up their forces every morning for
battle ;[5] but each day the battle was averted by some
means or other.   Now it was the mediation of the French
bishops in Philip's camp, or of the Roman legates in that
of Henry ;[6] now it was a miraculous judgement upon a
sacrilegious Brabantine in the French host, which scared

---

[1] R. Diceto (Stubbs), vol. ii. p. 48.   Will. Newb., l. iii. c. 7 (Howlett, vol.
i. p. 235).   *Gesta Hen.* (Stubbs), vol. i. pp. 358, 361.   Rog. Howden (Stubbs),
vol. ii. p. 315.   These two latter make the year 1186, which is nonsense, as they
both expressly say that the child was posthumous.

[2] *Gesta Hen.* (Stubbs), vol. ii. p. 6.

[3] Rigord (Duchesne, *Hist. Franc. Scriptt.*, vol. v.), p. 23 ; Will. Armor.
Gesta Phil. Aug. (ibid.), p. 74 ; *Philipp.*, l. ii. *(ibid.)*, p. 119.

[4] *Gesta Hen.* (as above), p. 5.   Cf. Gerv. Cant. (Stubbs), vol. i. p. 369.

[5] See Clédat, *Bert. de Born*, p. 71.

[6] *Ibid.   Gesta Hen.* as above, pp. 6, 7.

Philip into dismissing his mercenaries ;[1] now it was the
count of Flanders who, as soon as his peace with France
was made, turned against the peace-maker and sought to
stir Richard up to play over again the part of the young
king ; now it was Henry himself who opened negotiations
for a truce.[2] Finally, on Midsummer-eve,[3] a truce was
made for two years.[4] According to Bertrand de Born, it
was wrung from Philip by the discovery that the troops of
Champagne, which formed a considerable part of his army,
had been bought over by the English king.[5] Its actual
negotiator was Richard ;[6] and when Richard, instead of
returning to his father, rode away in the closest companion-
ship with the king of France, Henry naturally grew suspicious of the terms on which it had been won. His
suspicions were confirmed when Richard, under pretence of
obeying his summons to return, made his way to Chinon
and there seized the contents of the Angevin treasury,
which he immediately applied to the fortification of his
own castles in Poitou.[7] A partizan of Richard tells us
that Philip had communicated to him a letter in which
Henry proposed to make peace by marrying Adela to
John and constituting the latter heir to all his dominions
except England and Normandy.[8] If this scheme really
existed, it was foiled by Philip's own act ; and when Henry
and his elder son met soon afterwards at Angers, their dif-

---

[1] Cf. Gerv. Cant. (Stubbs), vol. i. pp. 369, 370 ; Rigord (Duchesne, *Hist.
Franc. Scriptt.*, vol. v.), pp. 23, 24 ; Will. Newb., l. iii. c. 14 (Howlett, vol. i.
p. 248) ; and Gir. Cambr. *De Instr. Princ.*, dist. iii. c. 2 (Angl. Christ. Soc.,
p. 92).   [2] Gerv. Cant. as above, pp. 371-373.
[3] R. Diceto (Stubbs), vol. ii. p. 49.
[4] *Gesta Hen.* (Stubbs), vol. ii. p. 7 ; R. Diceto and Gir. Cambr. as above ;
Rigord (as above), p. 23. Will. Armor., *Gesta Phil. Aug. (ibid.)*, p. 75, and
Philipp., l. ii. *(ibid.)*, p. 120, turns the truce into an abject submission of Henry
and Richard. Gerald says that one of the conditions of the truce was that
Auvergne, which Philip had conquered, should remain in his hands during the
period. But none of the other authorities mention Auvergne at all at this time ;
and Gerald's statement seems incompatible with the French accounts of Philip's
attack upon Auvergne, as if upon a hostile country, in 1188 (Rigord, as above,
p. 27 ; Will. Armor., *ibid.*, pp. 74, 122). Gerald and Rigord are however almost
equally untrustworthy for details, and especially for chronology.
[5] See Clédat, *Bert. de Born*, pp. 71, 72.   [6] Gerv. Cant. as above, p. 373.
[7] *Gesta Hen.* as above, p. 9.   [8] Gir. Cambr. as above (pp. 91, 92).

ferences were apparently settled for the moment by Richard's
reinstatement in the dukedom of Aquitaine ; for we are told
that he not only returned to his duty, but publicly renewed
his homage to the king.[1]

All these western quarrels again sank into the background before the tidings which came from Holy Land as
the year drew to a close.   Heraclius had gone home from
his unsuccessful mission to find Baldwin IV. delivered out
of all his troubles, and his throne occupied by his infant
nephew, the child of his sister Sibyl.   The little king
soon followed his uncle to the grave; and Sibyl, on whom
the representation of the royal house thus devolved, at once
bestowed her crown upon the man who had already been for
six years the bravest and most successful defender of the
distracted realm—her husband, Guy of Lusignan.[2]   Guy
sprang from a faithless race whom the Angevins had little
cause to love or trust in their western home; but in Palestine
he was hated simply because he had deservedly won the
affection and the confidence of both Baldwin and Sibyl.
Thwarted, baffled, deserted, betrayed by envious rivals, left
almost alone to face the Infidel foes whose advance grew
more threatening day by day, Guy fought on till in a great
battle at Tiberias, in July 1187, he was made prisoner by
the Turks ; the Christians were totally defeated, and the
relic of the Cross, which they had carried with them to the
fight, fell with the king into the hands of the unbelievers.[3]
The tidings of this disaster, when they reached Europe in
October, gave the death-blow to Pope Urban III.[4]   His
successor, Gregory VIII., opened his pontificate with an im-
passioned appeal to all Western Christendom for the rescue
of the Holy Land.[5]   The first response came from the young

---

[1] *Gesta Hen.* (Stubbs), vol. ii. p. 9.   [2] *Ib.* vol. i. pp. 358, 359.

[3] According to the pathetic story in *Itin. Reg. Ric.* (Stubbs), p.15, it was
rather the king who fell with the Cross, in a desperate effort to save it.   See also
Gesta Hen. (Stubbs), vol. ii. pp. 13, 22, 37 ; R. Coggeshall (Stevenson), p. 21 ;
Expugn. Terræ Sanctæ (ibid.), pp. 209-227.

[4] Cf. Will. Newb., l. iii. c. 21 (Howlett, vol. i. p. 267), and Rigord (Duchesne,
Hist. Franc. Scriptt., vol. v.), p. 24.

[5] Will. Newb. as above.   See also *Gesta Hen.* as above, p. 15, and Rog.
Howden (Stubbs), vol. ii. p. 322.

duke of Aquitaine ; without waiting to consult his father, at the earliest tidings of the catastrophe Richard took the cross at the hands of the archbishop of Tours.[1] Henry himself was so thunderstruck at the news that for four days he suspended all state business and refused to see any one.[2] He was in Normandy, and with him was Archbishop Baldwin of Canterbury, who had taken the cross two years before with the archbishop of Rouen, the veteran warrior-bishop Hugh of Durham, the justiciar Ralf de Glanville, and a crowd of other dignitaries of both Church and state, none of whom, however, had as yet actually started on their crusade. It was not King Henry who hindered them ; he had given every facility for the preaching of the crusade throughout his dominions ;[3] and even in Richard's case, although reproving the hastiness of the vow, he made no attempt to thwart its fulfilment, but on the contrary promised his son every assistance in his power.[4] Richard's project, however, roused up the king of France to insist once more upon his immediate marriage with Adela, or, failing this, the restitution of Gisors ; and Henry, on his way to England in January 1188, was recalled by tidings that Philip had gathered his host and was threatening to invade Normandy unless his demands were granted at once. The kings met at the old trysting-place between Gisors and Trie ;[5] but their conference had scarcely begun when it was interrupted by another messenger from Palestine, charged with news of a catastrophe more awful than even that of Tiberias. Three months after Guy's capture, in October 1187, Jerusalem itself had fallen into the hands of the Infidels ;[6] and the

---

[1] R. Diceto (Stubbs), vol. ii. p. 50. Cf. Will. Newb., l. iii. c. 23 (Howlett, vol. i. p. 271). Gir. Cambr. De Instr. Princ., dist. iii. c. 5 (Angl. Christ. Soc., p. 98).   [2] Gerv. Cant. (Stubbs), vol. i. p. 389.

[3] Rog. Howden (Stubbs), vol. ii. p. 302.   [4] Will. Newb. as above.

[5] Gesta Hen. (Stubbs), vol. ii. p. 29. Rog. Howden as above, p. 334. R. Diceto as above, p. 51. Gerv. Cant. as above, p. 406. Rigord (Duchesne, Hist. Franc. Script. vol. v.), p. 24. Will Armor. Gesta Phil. Aug. (ibid.), p. 74. The date is either S. Hilary's day, January 13 (Rigord and Will. Armor.), or that of S. Agnes, January 21 (Gesta Hen., Rog. Howden and R. Diceto). Gerv. Cant. makes it "about S. Vincent's day" (January 22).

[6] Gesta Hen. as above, p. 24. R. Coggeshall (Stevenson), pp. 22, 23. Expugn. Terræ Sanctæ (ibid.), pp. 241-248. Itin. Reg. Ric. (Stubbs), pp. 20-22.

archbishop of Tyre now came to tell with his own lips the sad and shameful story.

In his presence the selfish quarrel of the two kings was shamed into silence.   The king of France took the cross at once, and the king of England followed his example, this time without waiting for his people's consent ; the archbishops of Reims and Rouen, the counts of Flanders, Burgundy, Blois and Champagne, and a crowd of French and Norman barons did the like.[1]   The two kings set up a wooden cross, afterwards replaced by a church, to mark the spot, which they called the " Holy Field ";[2] then they separated to make their preparations.   Henry at once sent to request a safe-conduct for himself and his troops through the dominions of the king of Hungary and those of the Western and Eastern Emperors.[3]   Before the end of the month he issued from Le Mans an ordinance known as that of the " Saladin tithe," requiring every man in his dominions to give towards the expenses of the crusade a tithe of all his personal property, excepting only the necessary outfit of a knight or a priest.[4]   This was accompanied by eight other ordinances also relating to the crusade,[5] and was imitated two months later in France by Philip Augustus.[6]   On January 30 Henry returned to England ;[7] on February 11 he met the bishops and barons in council at Geddington near Northampton, to obtain their assent to the Saladin tithe and make arrangements for its collection.[8]   It was chiefly to superintend this that the king remained in England, while the archbishop of Canterbury went to preach the crusade in Wales.[9]

---

[1] R. Diceto (Stubbs), vol. ii. p. 51.   *Gesta Hen.* (Stubbs), vol. ii. p. 30.   Will. Newb., l. iii. c. 23 (Howlett, vol. i. p. 272).   Gerv. Cant. (Stubbs), vol. i. p. 406. Rigord (Duchesne, *Hist. Franc. Scriptt.*, vol. v.), p. 25.   [2] Rigord, as above.

[3] R. Diceto as above, pp. 51-54.

[4] *Gesta Hen.* as above, p. 31.   Rog. Howden (Stubbs), vol. ii. pp. 335, 336. Stubbs, *Select Charters*, p. 160.

[5] *Gesta Hen.* as above, pp. 31, 32.   Rog. Howden as above, pp. 336, 337. These latter ordinances were issued in all Christian realms by the Pope's desire ; ·
see Will. Newb. as above (pp. 273, 274).   [6] Rigord (as above), pp. 25, 26.

[7] *Gesta Hen.* as above, p. 33.   Gerv. Cant. as above.

[8] Gerv. Cant. as above, pp. 409, 410 (we are indebted to him for place and date).   *Gesta Hen.* as above.

[9] Henry seems to have intended going to Wales himself, but to have given it

Meanwhile Richard was eager to start without delay ; but his father refused his consent, insisting that their expedition should be made in common. The impatient "Lionheart," however, was not to be thus restrained, and in his father's absence he made all his preparations and wrote to bespeak the aid of his brother-in-law William of Sicily for the voyage which he was determined to begin as soon as the summer should arrive.[1] But his plans were checked by a fresh rising of the Poitevin barons, headed as usual by the count of Angoulême, Geoffrey of Rancogne and Geoffrey of Lusignan.[2] This last was the worst offender, having treacherously slain a personal friend of Richard's.[3] But, like Richard himself, he had taken the cross ; and it was doubtless owing to this protection that, before the summer was over, he was suffered to make his escape to the realm of his hapless brother in Palestine.[4] The other rebels were scarcely put down when Raymond of Toulouse seized and cruelly maltreated some Poitevin merchants who were passing through his territory. Richard at once avenged this outrage by an armed raid upon the frontier-districts of Toulouse, and presently managed to catch and imprison the count's chief adviser Peter Seilun, who was said to have instigated the seizure of the merchants. Raymond retaliated by capturing two knights attached to the household of the English king, Robert Poer and Ralf Fraser, on their way back from a pilgrimage to Compostella ; and neither Richard's protest against the sacrilege of keeping pilgrims in prison, nor even the express command of the king of France for their liberation out of reverence to S. James, could induce him to give them up on any condition save the release of Peter Seilun, which Richard firmly refused.[5] A heavy ransom offered by

up and sent the archbishop instead—an exchange which Baldwin gladly accepted. as he was at feud with his chapter, and greatly relieved to get away from it. Gerv. Cant. (Stubbs), vol. i. pp. 419-421.

[1] Gir. Cambr. *De Instr. Princ.*, dist. iii. c. 7 (Angl. Christ. Soc., pp. 102, 103).
[2] *Gesta Hen.* (Stubbs), vol. ii. p. 34.   [3] R. Diceto (Stubbs), vol. ii. p. 54.
[4] *Itin. Reg. Ric.* (Stubbs), p. 26.
[5] *Gesta Hen.* (as above), pp. 34, 35. Cf. Rog. Howden (Stubbs), vol. ii. pp. 339, 340. The date of this expedition of Richard's against Toulouse seems to have been about April ; see Will. Armor. *Gesta Phil. Aug.* (Duchesne, *Hist. Franc. Scriptt.*, vol. v.), p. 74.

the two English captives themselves shortly afterwards
changed Raymond's determination ;[1] but this was of course
no satisfaction to Richard, and after Whitsuntide he again
invaded Toulouse with fire and sword ; castle after castle
fell into his hands, till at last he began to threaten the capital
itself.[2]

In Aquitaine even more than elsewhere, the beginning
of strife was like the letting-out of water. This time the
strife of Richard and Raymond led to the outbursting of a
flood which ended by overspreading the whole Angevin
dominions and sweeping away Henry Fitz-Empress himself.
If Richard's story was true, neither he nor Raymond was
the real originator of the mischief ; it was Philip of France
who had secretly urged him to the attack ;[3] while another
rumour, which Richard was only too ready to believe,
accused Henry himself of stirring up the count of Toulouse
and the Aquitanian rebels against his son, in order to prevent
him from starting on the Crusade.[4] Little as we can credit
such a tale, it is easy to imagine how dexterously Philip
would use it to sow dissensions between father and son and
entangle the impetuous Richard in a coil such as only the
sword could cut. Openly, meanwhile, Philip was taking the
part of Toulouse, and peremptorily insisting that Henry
should put a stop to his son's aggressions in that quarter.[5]
Without waiting for Henry's reply, he marched upon Berry
and laid siege to Châteauroux, which surrendered to him on

---

[1] Rog. Howden. (Stubbs), vol. ii. p. 340.

[2] *Gesta Hen.* (Stubbs), vol. ii. p. 36. R. Diceto (Stubbs), vol. ii. p. 55. This
last writer says that Richard took seventeen castles, but he must be counting in
those which had been taken in the spring. The date of this second expedition
comes from Rigord (Duchesne, *Hist. Franc. Scriptt.*, vol. v.), p. 27, who places
it between Pentecost and midsummer. The new editors of Vic and Vaissète,
Hist. du Languedoc, vol. vii. p. 22, charge Rigord with false chronology here, and
insist upon following (as they suppose) that of Will. Armor., who tells us that
Richard began his campaign against Toulouse "modico elapso tempore" after
the Mid-Lenten council at Paris (*Gesta Phil. Aug.*, Duchesne, *Hist. Franc. Scriptt.*,
vol. v. p. 74). If, however, they had read the English authorities more carefully,
they would have seen that there were really two campaigns, and that while Will.
Armor. speaks of the first, Rigord is speaking of the second.

[3] Rog. Howden as above. Cf. *Gesta Hen.* as above, p. 39.

[4] R. Diceto as above. Gir. Cambr. *De. Instr. Princ.*, dist. iii. c. 7 (Angl.
Christ. Soc., p. 103).   [5] *Gesta Hen.* as above, p. 36.

June 16.[1] It was now Henry's turn to remonstrate against this breach of truce, all the more flagrant because committed against a brother-crusader.   He knew however that nothing but his own presence could make his remonstrances of any avail ; sending John over before him, on the night of July 10 he hurried across the sea to Barfleur, and thence went to muster his forces at Alençon.[2]   They consisted of the feudal levies of England and Normandy, and a multitude of Welsh under the command of Ralf de Glanville,[3] together with some Bretons and Flemish mercenaries,[4] and apparently some Angevins and Cenomannians.[5]   Henry was however very unwilling to resort to force ; his old scruple about making war upon his overlord seems not to have been yet quite extinguished, and moreover he shrank alike from the bloodshed and the expense of war.   During some weeks his forces were still kept idle, save for an occasional plundering-raid across the French border.[6]   Philip meanwhile was carrying all before him in Berry, and having conquered nearly the whole district, made a dash upon Auvergne.[7] Richard seized the opportunity for an attempt to regain Châteauroux, in which however he failed, and was only saved from capture or death by the help of a friendly butcher.[8]   His advance however had been enough to make Philip retire into his own domains.[9]   Soon afterwards the approach of the vintage-season compelled the French king to disband a part of his forces ; the remainder, under com-

---

[1] R. Diceto (Stubbs), vol. ii. p. 55.   Gerv. Cant. (Stubbs), vol. i. p. 432, seems to have confused this siege of Châteauroux with an earlier one. Cf. Will. Newb., l. iii. c. 25 (Howlett, vol. i. p. 276), Rigord (Duchesne, *Hist. Franc. Scriptt.*, vol. v.), p. 27, and Will. Armor., *Gesta Phil. Aug.* (*ibid.*), p. 74.

[2] *Gesta Hen.* (Stubbs), vol. ii. p. 40.   Cf. Gerv. Cant. as above, p. 433. R. Diceto (as above) dates the king's crossing "circa festum S. Jacobi," but this is clearly wrong.

[3] *Gesta Hen.* as above.   [4] R. Diceto as above.

[5] Rog. Howden (Stubbs, vol. ii. p. 343) adds some troops "from his other lands."   [6] Gerv. Cant. as above, pp. 433, 434.

[7] Rigord as above.   Will. Armor. as above ; *Philipp.*, l. iii. (*ibid.*), p. 122. Both these writers however throw some suspicion upon their account of Philip's successes by saying that Henry was flying before him all the while, and was finally chased back by him into Normandy—which in reality it seems plain that he had never quitted.

[8] Gerv. Cant. as above, p. 434.   [9] *Gesta Hen.* as above, p. 45.

mand of the bishop of Beauvais, went to ravage the Norman frontier-lands. Henry demanded reparation, and threatened to cast off his allegiance in default of it ; Philip retorted that he would not cease from the warfare which he had begun till all Berry and the Vexin were in his hands.[1]   At last, in the middle of August, the two kings met in person once more between Gisors and Trie ; but the meeting broke up in anger ; and when they parted, Philip in his rage cut down the great elm tree under which the conferences be-tween the rulers of France and Normandy had so long been held, vowing that no conference should ever be held there again.[2]

Richard had now rejoined his father,[3] and at his instig-ation an attack was made by their united forces upon Mantes, which was occupied by a small French force under William des Barres, lately the commandant of Châteauroux.   Richard succeeded in avenging his recent mishap at Châteauroux by taking William prisoner, but he made his escape immcd-iately, and nothing was gained by the expedition.[4]   Richard again went into Berry; Henry lingered on the Norman border, where soon afterwards he received from Philip a demand for another conference.   It took place at Châtillon on October 7, but again without result.   Philip now followed Richard, who thereupon opened negotiations on his own account, offering to submit his quarrel with Toulouse to the

---

[1] *Gesta Hen.* (Stubbs), vol. ii. pp. 45, 46.

[2] According to R. Diceto (Stubbs), vol. ii. p. 55, the conference began on August 16 and lasted three days.   The *Gesta Hen.* as above, p. 47, place it after September 1, but this is impossible.   Will. Armor., *Gesta Phil. Aug.* (Duchesne, *Hist. Franc. Scriptt.*, vol. v.), p. 74, and *Philipp.*, l. iii. (*ibid.*) pp. 123, 124, tells the story of the tree in a very odd shape.   He says the English were sitting comfortably under its shade, while the French were broiling in the sun, and the French grew so envious of the more agreeable situation of their foes that they made a dash at them, put them to flight, and then cut down the tree, which Henry had caused to be carefully enclosed, as a sort of symbol of his ownership in the soil.   R. Diceto, however, says that the ground on which the tree stood was French.

[3] Gir. Cambr. *De Instr. Princ.*, dist. iii. c. 10 (Angl. Christ. Soc., p. 111), makes them meet before Châteauroux.   He has confused this campaign with that of the previous year.

[4] Cf. *Gesta Hen.* as above, p. 46, with Will. Armor. *Philipp.*, l. iii. (as above), pp. 124-132.

judgement of the French king's court ;[1] but this also came
to nothing. Still the negotiations went on, and Henry's
difficulties were increasing. Chief among them was the
want of money to pay his soldiers. His realms had been
almost drained for the Saladin tithe ; his own treasury was
exhausted ; his troops, seeing no prospect of either wages
or plunder, began to slip away ; and at last he was obliged
to disband his mercenaries and send his Welsh auxiliaries
back to their own country.[2] Philip meanwhile was secretly
in communication with Richard ;[3] and Richard was growing
eager to bring matters to a crisis. The insidious whispers
of France and Flanders had done their work in his too
credulous mind. To the end of his life Richard was but
little of a statesman and less of a diplomatist ; it is therefore no wonder that he failed on the one hand to fathom
the subtle policy of his father, and on the other to see
through the wiles of Philip. His fault lay in this—that
while Henry's servants were content to trust him where they
could not understand him, his own son was ready to find a
ground of suspicion in every word and action of his father's
for which his own intelligence was incapable of accounting,
and to credit every calumny reported to him by his father's
enemies. More than a year ago they had contrived, as has
been seen, to awaken in his mind an idea that he was in
danger of being disinherited in favour of his youngest
brother ; and it was with a determination to ascertain once
for all the extent of this danger that he brought the two
kings to a meeting with each other and with himself near
Bonmoulins on November 18.[4]

The conference lasted three days ; and each day the
prospect of peace grew fainter.[5] Philip proposed that all
parties should return to the position which they had occupied before taking the cross ; Henry was ready to close with
this proposition, but Richard rejected it, as it would have

---

[1] *Gesta Hen.* (Stubbs), vol. ii. pp. 46, 48, 49.

[2] *Ib.* p. 50. Cf. Gerv. Cant. (Stubbs), vol. i. pp. 434, 435.

[3] Gerv. Cant. (as above), p. 435.

[4] *Ibid.* R. Diceto (Stubbs), vol. ii. p. 57. *Gesta Hen.* as above.

[5] Gerv. Cant. as above.

compelled him to give up his conquests won from Toulouse and worth a thousand marks or more as demesne lands, in exchange for Châteauroux and a few other castles over which he would have had only a precarious overlordship.[1] As far as the two kings were concerned, the meeting ended in a simple truce between them, to last till S. Hilary's day. No sooner however was this settled than Philip offered to restore all his conquests on condition that Henry should cause his subjects to do homage to Richard as his heir, and should allow his marriage with Adela to take place immediately. Henry refused.[2] The two kings were standing, with Richard and the archbishop of Reims, in the midst of a crowded ring of spectators. Richard himself now suddenly turned to his father, and demanded to be distinctly acknowledged as heir to all his dominions. Henry tried to put him off; he repeated his demand with the same result. "Now," he exclaimed, "I believe what hitherto seemed to me incredible." Ungirding his sword, he stretched out his hands to the king of France and offered him his homage and fealty for the whole continental heritage of the Angevin house; an offer which Philip readily accepted, promising in return to give back to Richard his recent conquests in Berry.[3] Henry drew back, speechless with amazement and consternation; the crowd, seeing the two kings thus separated, rushed in between them, and the duke of Aquitaine rode away in company with the French king, leaving Henry alone with his recollections of all the evils which had come of his eldest son's alliance with Louis VII., and his forebodings of worse mischief to come from this new alliance with Philip, who, as he well knew, was far more dangerous than Louis had ever been; for he had more brains and even fewer scruples.[4]

What little could be done to ward off the impending danger Henry did without delay. He sent the only one of his

[1] R. Diceto (Stubbs), vol. ii. p. 58.

[2] *Ibid.* Gerv. Cant. (Stubbs), vol. i. p. 435. *Gesta Hen.* (Stubbs), vol. ii. p. 50.

[3] Gerv. Cant. as above, pp. 435, 436. R. Diceto and *Gesta Hen.* as above. Cf. Rigord (Duchesne, *Hist. Franc. Scriptt.*, vol. v.), p. 27, and Gir. Cambr. *De Instr. Princ.*, dist. iii. c. 10 (Angl. Christ. Soc., p. 111).

[4] Gerv. Cant. as above, p. 436.

sons on whom he could really depend, Geoffrey the chancellor, to secure the fortresses of Anjou ; he himself went
to do the like in Aquitaine,[1] whence he returned to keep
Christmas at Saumur.   The feast must have been a dreary
one, even if both Geoffrey and John were with him ; yet,
deserted as he was, he managed to collect, for the last time,
some semblance of the old regal state.[2]   When the truce
expired, however, he postponed his intended meeting with
Philip, on the plea of illness, first to Candlemas-day, and
then till after Easter.   He hoped to make use of the delay
for winning Richard back ; but Richard turned a deaf ear
to every message of conciliation.[3]   He had in fact joined
Philip in an attack upon Henry's territories as soon as the
truce was expired ; and the ever-discontented Bretons had
been induced to lend their aid.[4]   After Easter Richard was
at length brought to a meeting with his father, on the
borders of Anjou and Maine ; but nothing came of the
interview.[5]   In vain did the Pope, fearing that these
quarrels in Gaul would put a stop to the crusade, send two
legates in succession to make peace.   The first, Henry of
Albano, who was sent early in 1188 to mediate between
Henry and Louis, unintentionally became the indirect cause
of a further addition to Henry's troubles.   Thinking it
safer to postpone his mediation till the meeting of the two
kings should take place, he in the meantime went to preach
the crusade in Germany and there persuaded the Emperor
himself to take the cross.[6]   By May 1189 Frederic was ready
to start ;[7] but before doing so he took a stern and summary
measure to secure the peace of the Empire during his
absence.   He ordered all those princes and nobles whose
loyalty he suspected either to accompany him or to quit
the country and take an oath not to set foot in it again till

---

[1] Gerv. Cant. (Stubbs), vol. i. p. 436.

[2] *Gesta Hen.* (Stubbs), vol. ii. pp. 60, 61.

[3] Gerv. Cant. as above, pp. 438, 439.   [4] *Gesta Hen.* as above, p. 61.

[5] Gir. Cambr. *De Instr. Princ.*, dist. iii. c. 13 (Angl. Christ. Soc., pp. 116, 117).

[6] Rog. Howden (Stubbs), vol. ii. pp. 355, 356.

[7] He took the cross at Mainz on March 27, 1188, and started on May 10, 1189. Ansbert (Dobrowsky), pp. 18, 21.

his return. Among those who thus incurred banishment was Henry the Lion. For the second time he and his wife sought shelter in England ; not finding the king there, they crossed over to Normandy in search of him,[1] but it does not appear that they ever reached him where he lay, sick and weary, at Le Mans.[2] Meanwhile Henry of Albano, after anathematizing Richard for his disturbance of the peace, had withdrawn to Flanders and there died.[3] His mission was taken up with a somewhat firmer hand by another legate, John of Anagni. Reaching Le Mans at Ascension-tide 1189,[4] John at once excommunicated all troublers of the peace except the two kings themselves, who were made to promise that they would submit their quarrels to his arbitration and that of the archbishops of Reims, Bourges, Canterbury and Rouen, and were threatened with excommunication if they should fail to redeem their promise.[5]

On the basis of this agreement a conference was held on Trinity Sunday, June 4, at La Ferté-Bernard. There were present, besides the two kings, Richard, and the legate, the four archbishops who were to assist him as arbitrators, most of the Norman bishops, those of Angers and Le Mans, four English and several French prelates, and a crowd of French, English and Norman barons.[6] Philip began by again demanding that Adela and Richard should be married at once ; that Richard should have security given him for his succession to his father's dominions ; and that John should be made to take the cross and accompany his brother to Palestine.[7] Richard repeated these demands for himself.[8] Henry refused, and made a counter-proposition to Philip— the same which he was said to have made at Châteauroux two years ago, for Adela's marriage with John ; but this

---

[1] *Gesta Hen.* (Stubbs), vol. ii. p. 62.

[2] The duchess died in that very summer, seven days after her father according to R. Diceto (Stubbs), vol. ii. p. 65, or nine days before him according to the Chron. Stederburg (Leibnitz, *Scriptt. Rer. Brunswic.*, vol. i. p. 861).

[3] *Gesta Hen.* as above, pp. 51, 55, 56. Rog. Howden (Stubbs), vol. ii. p. 355.

[4] *Epp. Cant.* cccvii. (Stubbs), p. 290.   [5] *Gesta Hen.* as above, p. 61.

[6] *Ib.* p. 66. The English bishops were Lincoln, Ely, Rochester and Chester.

[7] *Ibid.* Rog. Howden as above, p. 362.

[8] Gerv. Cant. (Stubbs), vol. i. p. 447.

Philip rejected in his turn.[1]   The legate now interposed with a threat to Philip that unless he would come to terms, his domains should be laid under interdict ; Philip defied the threat, and charged the legate with having been bribed by English gold.[2]   This explosion of course broke up the meeting.[3]   Henry went back to Le Mans, whence neither bishop nor archbishop, servant nor friend, could persuade him to move,[4] although Philip and Richard with their united forces were overrunning Maine at their will.   In five days the principal castles of its eastern portion were in their hands ; one of the most important, Ballon, only fifteen miles from Le Mans, fell on June 9.   There the conquerors paused for three days ;[5] and there, probably, they received the submission of the chief nobles of the western border— Geoffrey of Mayenne, Guy of Laval, Ralf of Fougères.[6]   But while the barons were false, the citizens were true.   Le Mans still clung with unswerving loyalty to the count whom she looked upon as her own child ; and Henry clung with equal attachment to the city which held his father's grave and had held his own cradle.[7]   He had little else to cling to now.   Where John was it is impossible to say ; he was clearly not at Le Mans ; and it is certain that, wherever he may have been, his proceedings were wholly unknown to Henry.[8]   Geoffrey the chancellor was still

[1] Rog. Howden (Stubbs), vol. ii. p. 363.

[2] *Ibid.   Gesta Hen.* (Stubbs), vol. ii. p. 66.

[3] R. Diceto (Stubbs), vol. ii. p. 62, says there were *two* meetings at La Ferté "after Easter." There seems to be no other notice of the second ; but Gerv. Cant. (Stubbs), vol. i. pp. 446, 447, has an account of a conference at Le Mans on June 9, which agrees almost to the letter with the report given in the *Gesta Hen.* and Rog. Howden of the proceedings at La Ferté on June 4. It seems most unlikely that either Philip or Richard would go to a conference at Le Mans itself ; and June 9 is an impossible date, for by that time, as we shall see, the war was in full career, and Philip and Richard were actually besieging Ballon. Gervase has probably mistaken both place and date.

[4] R. Diceto as above, p. 63.   [5] *Gesta Hen.* as above, p. 67.

[6] R. Diceto as above.   [7] *Gesta Hen.* as above.

[8] Will. Newb., l. iii. c. 25 (Howlett, vol. i. p. 277), says, after the king's retreat from Le Mans, "Tunc Johannes filius ejus minimus, quem tenerrime diligebat, recessit ab eo." But it is almost impossible that all the contemporary historians should have failed to mention John's presence with his father if he had really been there ; and Henry's horrified surprise at the final discovery of John's treachery shews that there had been no open desertion such as William seems to imply.

at his father's side, and so were some half-dozen faithful barons, as well as Archbishop Bartholomew of Tours.[1]
Beyond these the king had nothing but a small force
of mercenaries wherewith to defend either himself or Le
Mans.   The citizens were however willing to stand a
siege for his sake, and he in return had promised never to
desert them.[2]

On S. Barnabas's day—Sunday, June 11—Philip and
Richard appeared with their host before Le Mans.   They
made a feint of passing on in the direction of Tours ;
but next morning Philip suddenly drew up his forces
under the walls and prepared for an assault.   The defenders, conscious of the overwhelming odds against them,
adopted the desperate remedy of setting fire to the suburbs.   Unhappily, the wind carried the flames not into
the enemy's lines but into the city itself.[3]   The French
saw their opportunity and rushed at the bridge ; a gallant,
though unsuccessful, attempt to break it down was made
by some of Henry's troops, headed by a Cenomannian
knight, Geoffrey of Brulon, who thus honourably wiped
out the memory of his rebellion of sixteen years before ;
after a desperate fight, Geoffrey was wounded and made
prisoner with a number of his comrades, and the rest
were driven back into the city, the French rushing in
after them.[4]   Then at last Henry felt that he could not
keep his promise to the citizens of Le Mans, and with
some seven hundred knights he took to flight.[5]   The

[1] Besides Bartholomew (whom most of the English writers of the time call
William) there had been with him throughout the spring the archbishops of Canter-
bury and Rouen; Gir. Cambr. *De Instr. Princ.*, dist. iii. c. 13 (Angl. Christ.
Soc., pp. 115, 116).   It is clear that Bartholomew stayed with him to the end, for
he buried him.   But we hear nothing more of either Baldwin of Canterbury or
Walter of Rouen, except that Baldwin was at Rouen two or three days before
Henry's death ; *Epp. Cant.* cccxi. (Stubbs), p. 296.   See Bishop Stubbs's preface
to Rog. Howden, vol. ii. p. lxi, note 1.   Of the laymen more later.

[2] *Gesta Hen.* (Stubbs), vol. ii. p. 67.

[3] *Ibid.*   R. Diceto (Stubbs), vol. ii. p. 63.   Gir. Cambr. as above, c. 24 (p.
137).   Cf. Will. Newb., l. iii. c. 25 (Howlett, vol. i. p. 277).

[4] *Gesta Hen.* as above.

[5] *Ibid.*   Cf. Gerv. Cant. (Stubbs), vol. i. p. 447 ; R. Diceto and Will. Newb.
as above ; Gir. Cambr. as above (p. 138) ; Rigord (Duchesne, *Hist. Franc.
Scriptt.*, vol. v.), p. 28 ; and Will. Armor., *Gesta Phil. Aug.* (*ibid.*), p. 75.

French hurried in pursuit, but they did not carry it far. It may be that Geoffrey of Brulon's effort to break down the bridge saved the king although it could not save the city ; for the French are said to have been checked in their pursuit by the impossibility of fording the river,[1] and one can scarcely help conjecturing that the fugitives had crossed by the half-undermined bridge, and that it fell as soon as they had passed over it.[2]

Geoffrey however was not the only baron who after siding with Henry's enemies in his prosperous days had learned to stand by him in his last hour of need. Besides his one faithful son, Geoffrey the chancellor, his old friend Earl William de Mandeville, and William Fitz-Ralf the seneschal of Normandy, Henry was accompanied in his flight by an English baron, William the Marshal. William's father, John, who seems to have been marshal successively to Henry I. and to Stephen, had married a sister of Patrick of Salisbury and, like his brother-in-law, espoused the cause of the Empress in the civil war.[3] William himself first appears in history at the age of about six years, in 1152, when he was placed as a hostage in the hands of Stephen. Twice his life was forfeited by his father's defiance of the king, and twice it was saved by the unconscious fearlessness of the child, which so won Stephen's heart that he ended by making himself the little fellow's playmate instead of his slayer.[4] John's services to the Empress were rewarded on Henry's accession by his reinstatement in the office of marshal ; he afterwards became notorious through his quarrel with Thomas of Canterbury, which formed one of the pretexts for the archbishop's condemnation at Northampton.[5] After John's death his title and office seem to have been shared by his two sons.[6] The second, William,

[1] *Gesta Hen.* (Stubbs), vol. ii. p. 68.

[2] This is suggested by Bishop Stubbs's remark about "the breaking down of the bridge." *Rog. Howden*, vol. ii. pref. p. lxii.

[3] See extracts from *Hist. de Guillaume le Maréchal*, vv. 23-398, in *Romania*, vol. xi. (1882), pp. 47-52.

[4] *Hist. de Guill. le Mar.*, vv. 399-654 (as above, pp. 52-55).

[5] See above, pp. 32, 33.

[6] They seem to have both officiated at the crowning of Richard. *Gesta Ric.* (Stubbs, " Benedict of Peterborough," vol. ii.), p. 81.

we find in 1173 among the partizans of the young king's rebellion ; ten years later he appears as the young king's best-
beloved knight, and as charged by him with the last office of
friendship, the accomplishment in his stead of the crusading
vow which he had not lived to fulfil.[1]   Six years afterwards,
however, William was still in Europe, ready to stand to the
last by another perishing king, and to take the post of
honour as well as of danger among the little band of faithful
servants who watched over the last days of Henry Fitz-
Empress.   It was William who brought up the rear of the
little force which covered Henry's retreat from Le Mans.
Turning round as he heard the pursuers close behind him, he
suddenly found himself face to face with Richard, and
levelled his spear at him without hesitation.   " God's feet,
marshal ! " cried Richard with his wonted oath, " slay me
not !   I have no hauberk."   " Slay you ! no ; I leave that
to the devil," retorted William, plunging his spear into the
horse's body instead of the rider's.[2]   Richard was of course
compelled to abandon the chase, and at a distance of some
two miles from Le Mans the king felt himself sufficiently
out of danger to pause on the brow of a hill whence he
could look back for the last time upon his native city.   As
he saw its blazing ruins words of madness burst from his
lips : " O God, Thou hast shamefully taken from me this day
the city which I loved most on earth, in which I was born
and bred, where lies the body of my father and that of his
patron saint—I will requite Thee as I can ; I will withdraw
from Thee that thing in me for which Thou carest the
most." [3]   Another eighteen miles'[4] ride brought the fugitives

---

[1] See above, pp. 139 and 228.

[2] P. Meyer, in *Romania*, vol. xi. pp. 62, 63, from *Hist. de Guill. le
Mar.*, vv. 8833-8836. This is clearly the incident recorded briefly and without
a name by Gir. Cambr. *De Instr. Princ.*, dist. iii. c. 25 (Angl. Christ. Soc.,
p. 140).

[3] Gir. Cambr. as above, c. 24 (p. 138). He makes the distance two miles from
Le Mans ; in the *Gesta Hen.* (Stubbs), vol. ii. p. 67, the pursuit is said to have
extended to three miles.

[4] Will. Armor. *Philipp.*, l. iii. (Duchesne, *Hist. Franc. Scriptt.*, vol. v.),
p. 132, makes the day's ride twenty miles altogether ; but he carries it as far as
Alençon. See, however, Bishop Stubbs's pref. to Rog. Howden, vol. ii. pp.
lxii, lxiii and notes.

at nightfall to La Frênaye,[1] whose lord, the viscount of
Beaumont, was a kinsman of Henry, and the father of
Hermengard whose marriage with the king of Scots had
been arranged three years ago by Henry's influence. The
king found shelter in the castle ; his followers, already sadly
diminished in number in consequence of the overpowering
heat and fatigue of the day's ride, quartered themselves in
the little town as best they could ; the chancellor would
have remained with them to keep guard himself, but his
father would not be parted from him, and made him come
in to sup and spend the night. Geoffrey, whose baggage
had been all left in Le Mans, was glad to exchange his
travel-stained clothes for some which his father was able to
lend him ; Henry, with characteristic disregard of such
details, persisted in lying down to rest just as he was, with
his son's cloak thrown over him for a coverlet.[2]

From La Frênaye another day's ride would have brought
the king to the Norman border. His first intention on
leaving Le Mans had evidently been to fall back upon Normandy and there rally his forces—doubtless also to summon
help from England—to renew the struggle with Philip ; and
this was the course to which his followers still urged him on
the Tuesday morning. He, however, had changed his plans
in the night. He seems to have made up his mind that his
end was near ; and in consequence, he had also made up his
mind to go back to the Angevin lands. Since he had been
compelled to leave his own birthplace in the enemy's power,
he would at any rate stand to the last by the old home of
his father's house, and die at his hereditary post as count of
Anjou. He made William Fitz-Ralf and William de Mandeville swear that they would surrender the castles of Normandy to no one save John ; he bade Geoffrey take the
command of the troops, escort the barons with them as far
as Alençon, and then come back to rejoin him in Anjou.
Geoffrey, whose dominant feeling clearly was anxiety for his
father's personal safety, only stayed in Alençon long enough

---

[1] Gir. Cambr. *De Instr. Princ.*, dist. iii. c. 25 (Angl. Christ. Soc., p. 140) ;
Vita Galfr., l. i. c. 4 (Brewer, vol. iv. p. 369). See Stubbs, *Rog. Howden*, vol.
ii. pref. p. lxiii, note 5.   [2] Gir. Cambr. *Vita Galfr.* as above.

to secure the place and collect a fresh force of a hundred picked knights, and with these set off southward again to overtake his father. Henry meanwhile had started for Anjou almost alone. His son rejoined him at Savigny [1]— whether it was the village of that name near Chinon, or one of several others further north, there is no means of deciding ; but it is certain that by the end of the month Henry and his son were both safe at Chinon.[2] Whether the king had made his way alone, or whether he had been at once the leader and the guide of the little Norman force, through the Angevin woodlands which as a hunter he had learned to know so well, and where he was now in danger of being hunted down in his turn—in either case this sick and weary man had achieved an adventure equal in skill and daring to those of Fulk Nerra's most romantic days, or of his own youth. Once safe out of the enemy's reach, he made no further movement until Philip, having possessed himself of the citadel of Le Mans [3] and the remnant of the Cenomannian strongholds, and made his way southward by Chaumont and Amboise as far as Roche-Corbon,[4] sent him a proposal for a meeting to be held at Azay on the last day of June.[5] Henry apparently advanced from Chinon to Azay ; but on that very day an attack of fever was added to the malady from which he was already suffering, and he was unable to attend the conference.[6] It seems probable that he sent representatives to whom Philip and Richard made their propositions, and who may possibly have accepted them in his name.[7] Cer-

[1] Gir. Cambr. *Vita Galfr.*, l. i. c. 4 (Brewer, vol. iv. p. 369). See Stubbs, *Rog. Howden*, vol. ii. pref. pp. lxiv, lxv and notes.

[2] *Gesta Hen.* (Stubbs), vol. ii. p. 68.

[3] Some of Henry's troops had thrown themselves into the citadel, and held out there for three days after his flight. *Gesta Hen.* as above. Another body of troops in a tower by the north gate (this must be the Conqueror's Mont-Barbet— the "citadel" being the old palace or castle of the counts, near the cathedral) held out for a week longer still. R. Diceto (Stubbs), vol. ii. p. 63.

[4] *Gesta Hen.* as above, p. 69.

[5] Gir. Cambr. *De Instr. Princ.*, dist. iii. c. 25 (Angl. Christ. Soc., p. 140). R. Diceto, as above, p. 64, makes the day June 28 ; Bishop Stubbs (*Rog. Howden*, vol. ii. pref. p. lxv) follows Gerald.   [6] Gir. Cambr. as above.

[7] Rog. Howden (Stubbs), vol. ii. pp. 365, 366, gives, with the date " circa festum apostolorum Petri et Pauli, ad colloquium inter Turonim et Azai," a treaty identical with that which the *Gesta Hen.* as above, pp. 69, 70, give without

tainly, however, no truce was made ; for that same day Philip marched up to the southern bank of the Loire and drew up his host opposite the gates of Tours.[1]   Next day he forded the river—an easy exploit when it was half dried up by the summer's heat [2]—established his headquarters in the " borough of S. Martin " or Châteauneuf,[3] and began to invest the city.[4]   Henry, it seems, had now gone to Saumur ; [5] there on the Sunday—July 2—he was visited, according to one account at his own request, by the archbishop of Reims, the count of Flanders and the duke of Burgundy, endeavour- ing to arrange terms of peace.[6]   The visit was a failure ; it could not be otherwise, for the peacemakers were acting without Philip's sanction, and in spite of a distinct warning from him that, whatever tidings they might bring back, he would assault Tours next morning.[7]   The morning came ; the assault was made ; the walls which had kept out Fulk Nerra and Geoffrey Martel could not avail to keep out Philip Augustus, enabled as he was by his possession of Châteauneuf and by the lack of water in the Loire to bring up his machines against their weakest side ; and in a few hours he was master of Tours.[8]

The tidings were carried at once to Henry, with a final

any date at all, but after Philip's capture of Tours, and which we know to have been finally made at Colombières on July 4 (see below, p. 265).   R. Diceto (Stubbs), vol. ii. p. 63, also gives the substance of the treaty, adding (p. 64): " Facta sunt autem hæc in vigiliâ Apostolorum Petri et Pauli, scilicet inter Tur- onim et Azai."   It seems possible that the terms were arranged at Azay between Philip and Henry's representatives, subject to ratification by Henry himself.   See Stubbs, *Rog. Howden*, vol. ii. pref. p. lxv.

[1] On the date see Stubbs, *Rog. Howden*, vol. ii. pref. p. lxvi and note.

[2] This is the English account ; *Gesta Hen.* (Stubbs), vol. ii. p. 69, copied by Rog. Howden (Stubbs), vol. ii. p. 364.   But the French writers turn it into some- thing very like a miracle.   See Rigord (Duchesne, *Hist. Franc. Scriptt.*, vol. v.), p. 28 ; Will. Armor., *Gesta Phil. Aug.* (*ibid.*), p. 75, and *Philipp.*, l. iii. (*ibid.*), p. 133.   [3] *Gesta Hen.* as above.

[4] Gir. Cambr. *De Instr. Princ.*, l. iii. c. 25 (Angl. Christ. Soc., p. 140) says the investment began on the morrow of the Azay conference.

[5] *Gesta Hen.* as above.   See Stubbs, *Rog. Howden*, vol. ii. pref. p. lxvi and note.

[6] *Gesta Hen.* as above.   Gir. Cambr. as above (p. 141).   For the duke of Burgundy Gerald substitutes the count of Blois.   Bishop Stubbs (*Rog. Howden*, as above) adopts the former version.   [7] *Gesta Hen.* as above.

[8] *Ibid.*   Cf. Rigord and Will. Armor. as above, and *Philipp.* l. iii. (*ibid.*)., pp. 133, 134.

summons to meet the conqueror at Colombières, half-way
between Tours and Azay.[1]   Henry, at his wits' end, con-
sulted William the Marshal as to whether or not he should
respond to the summons ; William recommended him to
follow the counsel of his barons ; they advised that he should
go, and he went.   Most of his followers went with him ;
Geoffrey, however, feeling that he could not endure to see
his father's humiliation, besought and obtained permission to
remain where he was.[2]   Henry found a lodging in a small
commandery of Knights Templars at Ballan,[3] close to Colombières ; but he had no sooner reached it than he was seized
with racking pains in every limb and every nerve.   He
again called for William the Marshal, who did his best to
soothe him, and persuaded him to go to bed.   Philip and
Richard had always refused to believe that his sickness was
anything but a feint, and despite the pleadings of his friends
they still insisted that the conference should take place[4] on
the following day.[5]   When they saw him, however, they were
compelled to admit the truth of his excuse ; his sternly-set
and colourless face shewed but too plainly how acutely he
was suffering.   So evident was his weakness that they offered
him a seat—on a cloak spread upon the ground—but he
refused it ; he had not come there, he said, to sit down with
them ; he had come simply to hear and see what the French
king demanded of him, and why he had taken away his
lands.[6]   Philip formulated his demands with brutal bluntness ; he required that Henry should put himself, as a
conquered enemy, entirely at his mercy before he would
discuss any terms at all.[7]   Henry could not at once bring
himself to submit.   Suddenly, amid the breathless stillness
of the sultry July morning, a clap of thunder was heard, and

---

[1] *Hist. de Guill. le Mar.*, vv. 8935-8944 (*Romania*, vol. xi. p. 64).   The name
of Colombières is given only by Will. Armor., *Gesta Phil. Aug.* (Duchesne, *Hist.
Franc. Scriptt.*, vol. v.), p. 75, and *Philipp.*, l. iii. (*ibid.*), p. 134.

[2] Gir. Cambr. *Vita Galfr.*, l. i. c. 5 (Brewer, vol. iv. p. 370).

[3] *Hist. de Guill. le Mar.*, vv. 8947-8958 (as above).   M. Meyer (*ib.* p. 69) supplies the name of the commandery.   [4] *Ib.* vv. 8960-8997 (as above, p. 64).

[5] Will. Armor. *Philipp.*, l. iii. (as above), gives the date by saying Henry died
" post triduum."

[6] *Hist. de Guill. le Mar.*, vv. 9013-9028 (as above, p. 65).

[7] Gir. Cambr. *De Instr. Princ.*, dist. iii. c. 25 (Angl. Christ. Soc., p. 141).

the excited bystanders thought they actually saw a stroke of lightning fall out of the cloudless blue sky, directly between the two kings. Both started back in terror ; after a while they rode forward again, and immediately there was a second peal of thunder. Henry's shattered nerves gave way completely ; he nearly fell from his horse, and at once placed himself wholly at Philip's mercy.[1] Then the terms were dictated to him. He was made to do homage to Philip, and to promise that Adela should be placed under guardians chosen by Richard, who was to marry her on his return from Palestine ;—that Richard should receive the fealty of all the barons of the Angevin dominions, on both sides of the sea, and that all who had attached themselves to Richard's party in the late war should be suffered to remain in his service and released from their obligations to his father, at any rate until the latter should be ready to set forth on the crusade ; —that he would be thus ready, and would meet Philip and Richard at Vézelay, thence to start with them at Mid-Lent ;[2] —that he would renounce all claims upon Auvergne,[3] and pay Philip an indemnity of twenty thousand marks.[4] As security for the fulfilment of the treaty, Philip and Richard were to hold in pledge either three castles on the Norman border or two in Anjou, with the cities of Tours and Le Mans ; and all Henry's barons were to swear that they would hold their allegiance to him contingent only upon his fulfilment of these conditions.[5] Finally, he was compelled to acknowledge himself reconciled with Richard, and to give him the kiss of peace. The kiss was indeed given ; but it was accompanied by a whisper which Richard did not scruple to repeat for the amusement of the French court when the conference was over—" May I only be suffered to live long enough to take vengeance upon thee as thou deservest ! "[6]

One thing alone Henry asked and obtained in return for all this humiliation ; a written list of those among his sub-

---

[1] Rog. Howden (Stubbs), vol. ii. p. 366.

[2] *Gesta Hen.* (Stubbs), vol. ii. p. 70.

[3] R. Diceto (Stubbs), vol. ii. p. 64.   [4] *Ib.* p. 63. *Gesta Hen.* as above.

[5] *Gesta Hen.* as above, pp. 70, 71.

[6] Gir. Cambr. *De Instr. Princ.*, dist. iii. c. 26 (Angl. Christ. Soc., pp. 149, 150).

jects whose services were transferred to Richard.[1]   The list
was promised,[2] and Henry was carried back, worn out with
fatigue, suffering and shame, to the favourite home of his
brighter days at Chinon.[3]   By the time he reached it he was
too ill to do anything but lie down never to rise again.   He
sent back his vice-chancellor, Roger Malchat,[4] to fetch the
promised list of traitors ; and on Roger's return he bade
him sit down beside his bed and read him out the names.
With a sigh Roger answered : " Our Lord Jesus Christ help
me, sire ! the first written down here is Count John, your
son." [5]   The words gave Henry his death-blow.   " Say no
more," [6] he faltered, turning away his face.[7]   Yet the tale
seemed too horrible to be true, and he started up again :
" Can it be ?   John, my darling child, my very heart, for love
of whom I have incurred all this misery—has he indeed forsaken me ? "   It could not be denied ; he sank back again
and turned his face to the wall, moaning : " Let things go
now as they will ; I care no more for myself or for the
world." [8]

All through that day and the next he lay there, trembling

---

[1] Rog. Howden (Stubbs), vol. ii. p. 366.   *Hist. de Guill. le Mar.*, v. 9035
(*Romania*, vol. xi. p. 65).

[2] Rog. Howden says that it was given, and implies that it was read, then and
there, but we shall see that he is wrong.

[3] Rog. Howden as above.   *Hist. de Guill. le Mar.*, v. 3639 (as above).   Bishop
Stubbs (*Rog. Howden*, vol. ii. pref. p. lxviii)̈says " he returned to Azai," and makes
the reading of the fatal list take place there, before Henry went on to Chinon
(*ib.* p. lxx).   This seems to be the meaning of Gir. Cambr. *De Instr. Princ.*, dist.
iii. c. 25 (Angl. Christ. Soc., p. 148).   But Gerald evidently thought Henry had
been at Azay ever since the Friday, just as William of Armorica (*Philipp.*, l. iii.,
Duchesne, *Hist. Franc. Scriptt.*, vol. v. p. 134) thought he had been all the
while at Chinon ; whereas the *Gesta* and Roger shew that both are wrong in this.
On the other hand, the *Life of William the Marshal* seems distinctly to shew that
the place where Henry went to lodge before the meeting at Colombières was not
Azay, but Ballan ; and it also tells us that he went straight back from Colombières
to Chinon, and *there* read the list.   In the absence of further elucidations, I venture to follow this version.

[4] " . . . Mestre Roger Malchael,
          Qui lores portout son seel."
Hist. de Guill. le Mar., vv. 9051-9052 (as above, p. 65).   See M. Meyer's note,
ib. p. 69.

[5] *Hist. de Guill. le Mar.*, vv. 9040-9076 (as above, p. 65).

[6] " Asez en avez dit."   *Ib.* v. 9083 (as above).   [7] *Ib.* v. 9084 (p. 66).

[8] Gir. Cambr. as above.

from head to foot, sometimes appearing to see and hear nothing, and to be conscious of nothing but pain, murmuring broken words which no one could understand.[1] At other times his delirium shewed itself in frenzied curses upon himself and his sons, which the attendant bishops vainly besought him to revoke.[2] It was Geoffrey who at length managed to bring him to a somewhat calmer frame both of body and of mind. With his head on his son's shoulder and his feet on the knees of a faithful knight, Henry at last seemed to have fallen asleep. When he opened his eyes again and saw Geoffrey patiently watching over him and fanning away the flies which buzzed around his head, he spoke in accents very different from any that he had used for some days past. "My dearest son! thou, indeed, hast always been a true son to me. So help me God, if I recover of this sickness, I will be to thee the best of fathers, and will set thee among the chiefest men of my realm. But if I may not live to reward thee, may God give thee thy reward for thy unchanging dutifulness to me!" "O father, I desire no reward but thy restoration to health and prosperity" was all that Geoffrey could utter, as the violence of his emotion so overcame his self-control that he was obliged to rush out of the room.[3] The interval of calmness passed away, and the ravings of delirium were heard again; "Shame, shame upon a conquered king!" Henry kept muttering over and over again, till the third morning broke—the seventh day of the fever[4]—and brought with it the lightning before death. Once more Geoffrey, stifling his own distress, came to his father's side; once more he was rewarded by seeing Henry's eyes open and gaze at him with evident recognition; once more the dying king recurred wistfully to his plans, not this time of vengeance upon his rebellious sons, but of advancement for the loyal one, faintly murmuring in Geoffrey's ear how he had hoped to see him bishop of Winchester, or better still, archbishop of York;[5] but he knew that for himself all

---

[1] *Hist. de Guill. le Mar.*, vv. 9085-9094 (*Romania*, vol. xi. p. 66).
[2] Rog. Howden (Stubbs), vol. ii. p. 366.
[3] Gir. Cambr. *Vita Galfr.*, l. i. c. 5 (Brewer, vol. iv. pp. 370, 371).
[4] Gir. Cambr. *De Instr. Princ.*, l. iii. c. 26 (Angl. Christ. Soc., p. 150).
[5] Gir. Cambr. *Vita Galfr.* as above (p. 371).

was over.   He took off a gold finger-ring, engraved with a leopard[1]—the armorial device of the Angevin house—and handed it to Geoffrey, bidding him send it to the king of Castille, the husband of his daughter Eleanor ; he also gave directions that another precious ring which lay among his treasures should be delivered to Geoffrey himself, and gave him his blessing.[2]   After this he was, by his own desire, carried into the chapel of the castle and laid before the altar ; here he confessed his sins to the attendant bishops and priests, was absolved, and devoutly made his last Communion.   Immediately afterwards he passed away.[3]

Then followed one of those strange scenes which so often occurred after the death of a medieval king.   The servants who should have laid out the body for burial stripped it and left it naked on the ground ; and as during the three days that he lay dying they had plundered him of everything on which they could lay their hands, the few friends who were shocked at the sight could not find a rag wherewith to cover the dead king, till one of his knights, William de Trihan, took off his own cloak for the purpose.[4]   All this, however, was speedily set right by William the Marshal.   He at once took the command of the little party—a duty for which Geoffrey was evidently unfitted by the violence of his grief —sent to call as many barons as were within reach to attend the funeral, and gave directions for the proper robing of the corpse.[5]   It was no easy matter to arrange within four-and-twenty hours, and utterly without resources, anything like a

---

[1] "Pantera."   "The word is doubtful," notes Mr. Brewer (*Gir. Cambr.*, vol. iv. p. 371) ; Bishop Stubbs (*Rog. Howden*, vol. ii. pref. p. lxxi) renders it "panther."

[2] Gir. Cambr. *Vita Galfr.*, l. i. c. 5 (Brewer, vol. iv. p. 371).

[3] Rog. Howden (Stubbs), vol. ii. p. 367.   Gir. Cambr. *De Instr. Princ.*, dist. iii. c. 28 (Angl. Christ. Soc., p. 156), says there were no bishops with him at his death ; any way, there were two at his burial.   The date of death—July 6—is given by many authorities: *Gesta Hen.* (Stubbs), vol. ii. p. 71 ; Rog. Howden as above ; R. Diceto (Stubbs), vol. ii. p. 64 ; Gerv. Cant. (Stubbs), vol. i. p. 450, etc.

[4] *Hist. de Guill. le Mar.*, vv. 9027-9161 (*Romania*, vol. xi. p. 66).   Gir. Cambr. *De Instr. Princ.*, as above (pp. 156, 157), tells the same story, more highly coloured, but with less verisimilitude, as he has lost the name of William de Trihan and turned him into "puer quidam."

[5] *Hist. de Guill. le Mar.*, vv. 9165-9172, 9215-9220 (as above, pp. 66, 67).

regal burial for this fallen king.[1]   William, however, managed to do it ; and next day Henry Fitz-Empress, robed as if for his coronation, with a crown of gold upon his head, a gold ring on his finger, sandals on his feet, and a sceptre in his gloved right hand,[2] was borne upon the shoulders of his barons down from his castle on the rock of Chinon, across the viaduct which he himself had built over the swampy meadows beneath, and thence northward along the left bank of the silvery, winding Vienne to his burial-place at Fontevraud.[3]   He had wished to be buried at Grandmont ;[4] but this of course was impossible now.   " He shall be shrouded among the shrouded women "—so ran the closing words of a prophecy which during the last few months had been whispered throughout Henry's dominions as a token of his approaching end.   It was fulfilled now to the letter, as he lay in state in the abbey-church of Fontevraud, while the veiled sisters knelt by night and day murmuring their prayers and psalms around the bier.[5]

None of the dead king's friends had thought it necessary to wait for any instructions from his heir.   The marshal, however, had sent to apprise Richard of his father's death, and delayed the burial long enough to give him an opportunity of attending it if he chose to do so.   The other barons were in great dread of meeting the future king against whom they had been in arms ; and several of them were even more anxious for the marshal than for themselves, for they could not but imagine that Richard's heaviest

[1] Gir. Cambr. *De Instr. Princ.*, dist. iii. c. 28 (Angl. Christ. Soc., pp. 157, 158).

[2] *Gesta Hen.* (Stubbs), vol. ii. p. 71.   How hard it was to manage all this we learn from Gerald : " Vix annulus digito, vix sceptrum manu, vix capiti corona sicut decuit, quia de aurifrigio quodam veteri inventa fuit, vix ulla prorsus insignia regalia nisi per emendicata demum suffragia, eaque minus congruentia suppetiere." *De Instr. Princ.* as above (p. 158).   The chronicle of Laon, a. 1187, quoted in note (*ibid.*), adds that the gold fringe of which the crown was made came off a lady's dress.

[3] *Hist. de Guill. le Mar.*, vv. 9071-9223 (*Romania*, vol. xi. p. 67).   See a curious incident at the setting out of the funeral train, in vv. 9173-9214.

[4] He had given solemn directions to that effect, when he thought himself dying at La Motte-de-Ger, in 1170.   *Gesta Hen.* (Stubbs), vol. i. p. 7.

[5] *Hist. de Guill. le Mar.*, vv. 9229-9244 (as above).   For the prophecy and its application see *Gesta Hen.* (Stubbs), vol. ii. p. 55, and Rog. Howden (Stubbs), vol. ii. pp. 356, 367.

vengeance would fall upon the man who had unhorsed and
all but killed him at Le Mans.   More than one of them
offered to place himself and all his possessions at the service
of the comrade whom they all held in such reverence, if
thereby anything could be done to save him from Richard's
wrath.   But he only answered quietly : "Sirs, I do not
repent me of what I did.   I thank you for your proffers ;
but, so help me God, I will not accept what I cannot return.
Thanks be to Him, He has helped me ever since I was
made a knight ; I doubt not He will help me to the end." [1]
Before nightfall Richard overtook them.[2]   He came, it
seems, alone.   Vainly did the bystanders seek to read his
feelings in his demeanour ; he shewed no sign of either
grief or joy, penitence or wrath ; he "spoke not a word,
good or bad," [3] but went straight to the church and into the
choir, where the body lay.[4]   For awhile he stood motionless
before the bier ; [5] then he stepped to the head, and looked
down at the uncovered face.[6]   It seemed to meet his gaze
with all its wonted sternness ; but there were some who
thought they saw a yet more fearful sight—a stream of
blood which flowed from the nostrils, and ceased only on
the departure of the son who was thus proclaimed as his

---

[1] *Hist. de Guill. le Mar.*, vv. 9245-9290 (*Romania*, vol. xi. pp. 67, 68).

[2] The *Gesta Hen.* (Stubbs), vol. ii. p. 71, make Richard meet the corpse on
its way ; and Rog. Howden (Stubbs), vol. ii. p. 367, follows the *Gesta*. But
the *Hist. de Guill. le Mar.* and Gir. Cambr. *De Instr. Princ.*, dist. iii. c. 28
(Angl. Christ. Soc., p. 157) both distinctly say that he met it at Fontevraud.
The other version is intrinsically most improbable, for Richard can hardly have
been coming from anywhere else than Tours, and in that case he could not possibly meet the funeral train on its way from Chinon to Fontevraud.   That he should
reach Fontevraud some hours after it, on the other hand, is perfectly natural ;
and this is just what Gerald and the French *Life* imply ; for they both tell
us that the funeral started from Chinon on the day after the death—*i.e.* Friday,
July 7—and Gerald (as above, p. 158) implies that the actual burial took place
the day after Richard's arrival, while in the *Vita Galfr.*, l. i. c. 5 (Brewer, vol. iv.
p. 372), he seems to place it on the Saturday, July 8.   See Bishop Stubbs's preface
to Rog. Howden, vol. ii. p. lxix, note 1.   One of the MSS. of Mat. Paris, *Chron.
Maj.* (Luard, vol. ii. p. 344, note 8) has a curiously different version of Richard's
behaviour on the occasion.

[3] *Hist. de Guill. le Mar.*, vv. 9294-9298, 9300 (p. 68).

[4] Gir. Cambr. *De Instr. Princ.* as above.

[5] *Hist. de Guill. le Mar.*, vv. 9299, 9300 (as above).

[6] *Ib.* v. 9301.   Gir. Cambr. *De Instr. Princ.* and *Vita Galfr.* as above.

father's murderer.[1] Richard sank upon his knees ; thus he remained " about as long as one would take to say the Lord's Prayer ; "[2] then he rose and, speaking for the first time, called for William the Marshal. William came, accompanied by a loyal Angevin baron, Maurice of Craon. Richard bade them follow him out of the church ; outside, he turned at once to the marshal : " Fair Sir Marshal, you had like to have slain me ; had I received your spear-thrust, it would have been a bad day for both of us !" " My lord," answered William, " I had it in my power to slay you ; I only slew your horse. And of that I do not repent me yet." With kingly dignity Richard granted him his kingly pardon at once ;[3] and on the morrow they stood side by side while Henry Fitz-Empress was laid in his grave before the high altar by Archbishop Bartholomew of Tours.[4]

[1] Gir. Cambr. *De Instr. Princ.*, dist. iii. c. 28 (Angl. Christ. Soc., p. 157); *Vita Galfr.*, l. i. c. 5 (Brewer, vol. iv. p. 372). *Gesta Hen.* (Stubbs), vol. i. p. 71.

[2] Gir. Cambr. as above.

[3] *Hist. de Guill. le Mar.*, vv. 9304-9344 (*Romania,* vol. xi. pp. 68, 69).

[4] The day is given by Gir. Cambr. *De Instr. Princ.* as above (p. 158), and *Vita Galfr.* as above ; the name of the officiating prelate by R. Diceto (Stubbs), vol. ii. p. 65. Bartholomew was assisted by Archbishop Fulmar of Trier (*ibid.*)

CHAPTER VII.

RICHARD AND ENGLAND.

1189–1194.

ALL doubts as to the destination of Henry's realms after his death were settled at once by the discovery of John's treason. Throughout the Angevin dominions not a voice was raised to challenge the succession of Richard. The English marshal and the Angevin barons gathered at Fontevraud received him unquestioningly as their lord, and were at once accepted as loyal subjects. One of them indeed, the seneschal of Anjou, Stephen of Turnham or of Marçay, was flung into prison for failing to surrender the royal treasure ;[1] but the reason of his failure seems to have been simply that the treasury was empty.[2] According to one contemporary historian, Richard sealed his forgiveness of William the Marshal by at once despatching him to England with a commission to hold the country for him—in effect, to act as justiciar—till he could proceed thither himself.[3] In all probability, however, William was authorized to do nothing more than set Eleanor at liberty ; it was she who, by her son's desire, undertook the office of regent in England,[4] which she fulfilled without difficulty for the next six weeks. Geoffrey the chancellor resigned his seal into his half-brother's hands as soon as the funeral was over.[5] The

---

[1] *Gesta Ric.* ("Benedict of Peterborough," Stubbs, vol. ii.), p. 71. Cf. Ric. Devizes (Stevenson), p. 6.

[2] See *Hist. de Guill. le Mar.*, vv. 9198, 9199 (*Romania*, vol. xi. p. 67).

[3] *Ib.* vv. 9347-9354 (p. 69). [4] R. Diceto (Stubbs), vol. ii. p. 67.

[5] Gir. Cambr. *Vita Galfr.*, l. i. c. 5 (Brewer, vol. iv. p. 372).

promise of the Norman castellans to Henry that they would surrender to no one but John was of course annulled by later events. John himself hastened to join his brother; Richard gave him a gracious welcome, and they returned to Normandy together.[1] At Séez the archbishops of Canterbury and Rouen came to meet them, and absolved Richard from the excommunication[2] laid on him by the legate John of Anagni. Thence they all proceeded to Rouen. On July 20 Richard went in state to the metropolitan church, where Archbishop Walter girded him with the ducal sword and invested him with the standard of the duchy.[3] On the same day he received the fealty of the Norman barons,[4] and held his first court as duke of Normandy, and also, it seems, as king-elect of England, although there had been no formal election. He at once made it clear that the abettors of his revolt had nothing to hope from him—three of the most conspicuous had been deprived of their lands already[5]—and that his father's loyal servants had nothing to fear, if they would transfer their loyalty to him. He shewed indeed every disposition to carry out his father's last wishes; he at once nominated Geoffrey for the see of York, and confirmed Henry's last grant to John, consisting of the Norman county of Mortain and four thousand pounds' worth of land in England;[6] at the same time he bestowed upon William the Marshal the hand of Isabel de Clare, daughter and heiress of Earl Richard of Striguil, and upon the son of the count of Perche a bride who had already been sought by two kings —his niece, Matilda of Saxony.[7]

This last match was evidently intended to secure the attachment of the important little border-county of Perche in case of a rupture with France, which seemed by no means unlikely. The alliance of Philip and Richard had expired

---

[1] *Gesta Ric.* (Stubbs), p. 72.

[2] R. Diceto (Stubbs), vol. ii. p. 67. How had the archbishops power to cancel a legatine sentence?

[3] *Ibid. Gesta Ric.* (Stubbs), p. 73. (The date is from this last).

[4] *Gesta Ric.* as above.   [5] *Ib.* p. 72.

[6] *Ib.* p. 73. Will. Newb., l. iv. c. 3 (Howlett, vol. i. p. 301). On John and Mortain see Rog. Howden (Stubbs), vol. ii. p. 6 and note 2, and preface to vol. iii. p. xxiv, note 1.   [7] *Gesta Ric.* as above.

with King Henry; now that Richard stood in his father's
place, Philip saw in him nothing but his father's successor—
the head of the Angevin house, whose policy was to be
thwarted and his power undermined on every possible occasion and by every possible means.   This was made evident
at a colloquy held on S. Mary Magdalene's day to settle the
new relations between the two princes ; Philip greeted his
former ally with a peremptory demand for the restitution
of the Vexin.[1]   Richard put him off with a bribe of four
thousand marks, over and above the twenty thousand promised by Henry at Colombières ; and on this condition,
accompanied, it seems, by a vague understanding that Richard
and Adela were to marry after all,[2] Philip agreed to leave
Richard in undisturbed possession of all his father's dominions, including the castles and towns which had been
taken from Henry in the last war,[3] except those of Berry
and Auvergne.[4]   Thus secured, for the moment at least, in
Normandy, Richard prepared to take possession of his island
realm.   He had paved the way for his coming there by
empowering Eleanor to make a progress throughout England, taking from all the freemen of the land oaths of fealty
in his name, releasing captives, pardoning criminals, mitigat-
ing, so far as was possible without upsetting the ordinary
course of justice, the severe administration of the late king.
Richard himself now restored the earl of Leicester and the
other barons whom Henry had disseized six years before.[5]   The
next step was to send home the archbishop of Canterbury and
three other English prelates who were with him in Normandy.[6]
On August 12 they were followed by Richard himself.[7]

His politic measures of conciliation, executed by his
mother with characteristic intelligence and tact, had secured
him a ready welcome.   It was only by slow degrees, and
with the growing experience of years, that the English

---

[1] *Gesta Ric.* (Stubbs), pp. 73, 74.   Rog. Howden (Stubbs), vol. iii. pp. 3, 4.
[2] *Gesta Ric.* (Stubbs), p. 74.   [3] Rog. Howden as above, p. 4.
[4] Rigord (Duchesne, *Hist. Franc. Scriptt.*, vol. v.), p. 29.   Will. Armor.
Gesta Phil. Aug. (*ib.*), p. 75.   Gerv. Cant. (Stubbs), vol. i. p. 450.
[5] *Gesta Ric.* (Stubbs), pp. 74, 75.   [6] *Ib.* p. 75.
[7] Gerv. Cant. as above, p. 457.   The *Gesta Ric.*, as above, give a confused
date—"Idus Augusti, die dominicâ post Assumptionem B. Mariæ."

people learned how much they owed to the stern old king
who was gone.   At the moment they thought of him chiefly
as the author of grievances which his son seemed bent upon
removing.[1]   Richard's mother, with a great train of bishops
and barons, was waiting to receive him at Winchester ;[2] there,
on the vigil of the Assumption, he was welcomed in solemn
procession ;[3] and there, too, he came into possession of the
royal treasury, whose contents might make up for the de-
ficiencics in that of Anjou.[4]   So complete was his security
that instead of hastening, as his predecessors had done, to
be crowned as soon as possible, he left Eleanor nearly three
weeks in which to make the arrangements for that ceremony,[5]
while he went on a progress throughout southern England,[6]
coming back at last to be crowned by Archbishop Baldwin
at Westminster on September 3.[7]   No charter was issued
on the occasion.   The circumstances of the new king's
accession were not such as to make any special call for one ;
they were sufficiently met by a threefold oath embodied in
the coronation-service, pledging the sovereign to maintain
the peace of the Church, to put down all injustice, and to
enforce the observance of righteousness and mercy.[8]   In the
formal election by clergy and people which preceded the
religious rite,[9] and in the essentials of the rite itself, ancient
prescription was strictly followed.   The order of the procession and the details of the ceremonial were, however,
arranged with unusual care and minuteness ; it was the most
splendid and elaborate coronation-ceremony that had ever

[1] Cf. *Gesta Ric.* (Stubbs), pp. 75, 76 ; and Will. Newb., l. iv. c. 1 (Howlett,
vol. i. p. 293).   [2] Gerv. Cant. (Stubbs), vol. i. pp. 453, 454.

[3] *Ib.* p. 457.   R. Diceto (Stubbs), vol. ii. p. 67.   *Gesta Ric.* (Stubbs), p. 74.

[4] *Gesta Ric.* (Stubbs), pp. 76, 77.

[5] "Mater comitis Alienor regina de vocatione comitum, baronum, vicecomitum,
uit sollicita." R. Diceto as above, p. 68.

[6] *Gesta Ric.* (Stubbs), p. 77.   Gerv. Cant. as above, p. 457, says he went to
check the depredations of the Welsh.

[7] *Gesta Ric.* (Stubbs), pp. 78, 79.   Gerv. Cant. and R. Diceto as above.   Ric.
Devizes (Stevenson), p. 5.   R. Coggeshall (Stevenson), pp. 26, 27.   Will. Newb.
as above (p. 294).

[8] *Gesta Ric.* (Stubbs), pp. 81, 82.   R. Diceto as above.   This last was an
eye-witness for, the see of London being vacant, the dean had to fulfil in his
bishop's stead the duty of handing the unction and chrism to the officiating
primate. *Ib.* p. 69.   [9] R. Diceto as above, p. 68.

been seen in England, and it served as a precedent for all
after-time.[1]   Richard had none of his father's shrinking from
the pageantries and pomps of kingship ; he delighted in its
outward splendours almost as much as in its substantial
powers.[2]   He himself, with his tall figure, massive yet finely-
chiselled features, and soldierly bearing, must have been by
far the most regal-looking sovereign who had been crowned
since the Norman Conqueror ; and when Archbishop Baldwin
set the crown upon his golden hair, Englishmen might for a
moment dream that, stranger though he had been for nearly
thirty years to the land of his birth, Richard was yet to be in
reality what he was in outward aspect, a true English king.

Such dreams however were soon to be dispelled.   On
the second day after his crowning Richard received the
homage of the bishops and barons of his realm ;[3] he then
proceeded into Northamptonshire, and on September 15
held a great council at Pipewell.[4]   His first act was to fill
up the vacant sees, of which there were now four besides
that of York.   The appointments were made with considerable judgement.   London, whose aged bishop Gilbert Foliot
had died in 1187,[5] was bestowed upon Richard Fitz-Nigel,[6]
son of Bishop Nigel of Ely, and for the last twenty years
his successor in the office of treasurer ; while Ely, again
vacated scarcely three weeks ago by the death of Geoffrey
Ridel,[7] rewarded the past services and helped to secure the
future loyalty of Richard's chancellor, William of Longchamp.[8]   Winchester, vacated nearly a year ago by the
death of Richard of Ilchester,[9] was given to Godfrey de
Lucy, a son of Henry's early friend and servant Richard
de Lucy " the loyal " ;[10] Salisbury, which had been without

---

[1] See details in *Gesta Ric.* (Stubbs), pp. 80-83 ; and Rog. Howden (Stubbs),
vol. iii. pp. 9-12.

[2] We see this in the descriptions of his magnificent dress, brilliant armour, etc.
in the *Itinerarium Regis Ricardi.*   [3] *Gesta Ric.* (Stubbs), p. 84.

[4] *Ib.* p. 85.   R. Diceto (Stubbs), vol. ii. p. 69. Gerv. Cant. (Stubbs), vol.
i. p. 458.   [5] *Gesta Hen.* (Stubbs), vol. ii. p. 5.   R. Diceto as above, p. 47.

[6] *Gesta Ric.* (Stubbs), p. 85.   R. Diceto as above, p. 69.   Ric. Devizes
(Stevenson), p. 9.   [7] *Gesta Ric.* (Stubbs), p. 78.   R. Diceto as above, p. 68.

[8] *Gesta Ric.* (Stubbs), p. 85.   R. Diceto as above, p. 69.   Ric. Devizes as above.

[9] *Gesta Hen.* as above, p. 58.   R. Diceto as above, p. 58.

[10] *Gesta Ric.* (Stubbs), p. 84.   R. Diceto as above, p. 69.   Ric. Devizes as above.

a bishop ever since November 1184,[1] was given to Hubert Walter,[2] a near connexion of the no less faithful minister of Henry's later years, Ralf de Glanville. This last appointment had also another motive. Hubert Walter was dean of York ; he stood at the head of a party in the York chapter which had strongly disputed the validity of Geoffrey's election in the preceding August, and some of whom had even proposed the dean himself as an opposition candidate for the primacy.[3] Hubert's nomination to Salisbury cleared this obstacle out of Geoffrey's way, and no further protest was raised when Richard confirmed his half-brother's election in the same council of Pipewell.[4]

When, however, the king turned from the settlement of the Church to that of the state, it became gradually apparent that his policy in England had only two objects :—to raise money for the crusade, and to secure the obedience of his realm during his own absence in the East. These objects he endeavoured to effect both at once by a wholesale change of ministers, sheriffs and royal officers in general, at the council of Pipewell or during the ten days which elapsed between its dissolution and the Michaelmas Exchequer-meeting. The practice of making a man pay for the privilege either of entering upon a public office or of being released from its burthen was, as we have seen, counted in no way disgraceful in the days of Henry I., and by no means generally reprobated under Henry II. Richard however carried it to a length which clearly shocked the feelings of some statesmen of the old school,[5] if not those of the people in general. The first to whom he applied it was no less a person than the late justiciar, Ralf de Glanville. Ralf

---

[1] R. Diceto (Stubbs), vol. ii. p. 32.   *Gesta Hen.* (Stubbs), vol. i. p. 320.

[2] *Gesta Ric.* (Stubbs), p. 84.   R. Diceto as above, p. 69.   Ric. Devizes (Stevenson), p. 9.

[3] *Gesta Ric.* (Stubbs), pp. 77, 78.   Cf. Gir. Cambr. *Vita Galfr.*, l. i. c. 6 (Brewer, vol. iv. p. 373).   Hubert had indeed been proposed for the see as far back as 1186 ; *Gesta Hen.* as above, p. 352.   See also Bishop Stubbs's preface to Rog. Howden, vol. iv. pp. xxxix–xlvi.

[4] Gir. Cambr. as above (p. 374).

[5] This appears from the tone in which his sales of office, etc., are described by Richard Fitz-Nigel in the *Gesta Ric.* (Stubbs), pp. 90, 91, and by Roger of Howden (Stubbs), vol. iii. p. 13.

was, like Richard himself, under a vow of crusade, which
would in any case have rendered it impossible for him to
retain the justiciarship after the departure of the English
host for Palestine.[1]   The king, however, insisted that his
resignation should take effect at once,[2] and also that it
should be paid for by a heavy fine—a condition which was
also required of the Angevin seneschal, Stephen of Turnham,
as the price of his release from prison.[3]   Worn out though
he was with years and labours,[4] Ralf faithfully kept his
vow.[5]   If all the intending crusaders had done the same, it
would have been no easy matter to fill his place or to make
adequate provision for the government and administration of
the realm.   Both king and Pope, however, had learned that
for eastern as well as western warfare money was even more
necessary than men ; Richard had therefore sought and
obtained leave from Clement III. to commute crusading
vows among his subjects for pecuniary contributions towards
the expenses of the war.[6]   By this means he at once raised
a large sum of money, and avoided the risk of leaving England deprived of all her best warriors and statesmen during
his own absence.   Instead of Ralf de Glanville he appointed
two chief justiciars, Earl William de Mandeville and Bishop
Hugh of Durham ;[7] under these he placed five subordinate
justiciars, one of whom was William the Marshal.[8]   The
bishop-elect of London, Richard Fitz-Nigel, was left undisturbed in his post of treasurer, where his services were too
valuable for the king to venture upon the risk of forfeiting
them ; but the bishop-elect of Ely, although a favourite
servant and almost a personal friend of Richard, had to pay
three thousand pounds for his chancellorship.   On the other
hand, Richard proved that in this instance he was not

---

[1] He had taken the cross in 1185 ; Rog. Howden (Stubbs), vol. ii. p. 302.
The *Gesta Ric.* (Stubbs), p. 87, and Will. Newb. l. iv. c. 4 (Howlett, vol. i. p.
302) say distinctly that Ralf himself wished to resign in order to fulfil his vow.
[2] *Gesta Ric.* (Stubbs), p. 90.   Ric. Devizes (Stevenson), p. 7, says he even
put him in ward.   [3] Ric. Devizes (Stevenson), pp. 6, 7.   [4] *Ib.* p. 9.
[5] He died at the siege of Acre before October 21, 1190. *Epp. Cant.* ccclvi.
(Stubbs, p. 329).   [6] Rog. Howden (Stubbs), vol. iii. p. 17.
[7] *Gesta Ric.* (Stubbs), p. 87.   Hugh paid a thousand marks for the remission
of his crusading vow, to enable him to undertake the office. *Ib.* p. 90.
[8] Rog. Howden as above, p. 16.

actuated solely by mercenary motives, by refusing a still higher bid from another candidate.[1] All the sheriffs were removed from office; some seven or eight were restored to their old places, five more were appointed to shires other than those which they had formerly administered ;[2] the sheriffdom of Hampshire was sold to the bishop-elect of Winchester,[3] that of Lincolnshire to Gerard de Camville, those of Leicestershire, Staffordshire and Warwickshire to Bishop Hugh of Chester ;[4] and the earldom of Northumberland was granted on similar terms to the justiciar-bishop of Durham.[5]

Two other matters had to be dealt with before Richard's preparations for departure were completed. To guard his realm from external disturbance, he must secure the fealty of the vassal-rulers of Scotland and Wales. To guard it against internal treason, he must, if such a thing were possible, secure the loyalty of the brother whom he was leaving behind him. The first was at once the less important and the easier matter of the two. Rees of South Wales had indeed profited by the change of rulers in England to break the peace which he had been compelled to maintain with King Henry, and after the council of Pipewell Richard sent John against him at the head of an armed force. The other Welsh princes came to meet John at Worcester and made submission to him as his brother's representative ;[6] Rees apparently refused to treat with any one but the king in person, and accordingly he came back with John as far as Oxford, but Richard would not take the trouble to arrange a meeting, and was so unconcerned about the matter that he let him go home again without an audience, and, of course, in a state of extreme indignation.[7]

---

[1] Ric. Devizes (Stevenson), p. 9.

[2] Stubbs, *Rog. Howden*, vol. iii. pref. p. xxix.

[3] Ric. Devizes (Stevenson), p. 10.

[4] Stubbs as above, pp. xxviii, xxix, and Madox, *Hist. Exch.*, vol. i. p. 458, from Pipe Roll 2 Ric. I.

[5] Pipe Roll 2 Ric. I. (Stubbs, as above, p. xxviii, note 3). *Gesta Ric.* (Stubbs), p. 90. Ric. Devizes (Stevenson), p. 8. Will. Newb., l. iv. c. 5 (Howlett, vol. i. p. 304). Geoff. Coldingham, c. 9 (*Scriptt. Dunelm. III.*, Raine, p. 14). The grant itself, dated November 25, is in *Scriptt. Dunelm. III.*, App. p. lxii.

[6] *Gesta Ric.* (Stubbs), pp. 87, 88.   [7] *Ib.* p. 97.

His threatening attitude served as an excuse for raising a scutage, nominally for a Welsh war ;[1] but the expedition was never made.   The king of Scots was otherwise dealt with.   Early in December, while Richard was at Canterbury on his way to the sea, William the Lion came to visit him, and a bargain was struck to the satisfaction of both parties.   Richard received from William a sum of ten thousand marks, and his homage for his English estates, as they had been held by his brother Malcolm ; in return, he restored to him the castles of Roxburgh and Berwick, and released him and his heirs for ever from the homage for Scotland itself, enforced by Henry in 1175.[2]

Richard's worst difficulty however was still unsolved : how to prevent John from trying to supplant him in his absence.   Richard knew that this lad, ten years younger than himself, had been his rival ever since he was of an age to be a rival to any one ; and he knew his brother's character as, perhaps, no one else did know it as yet—for their mother had scarcely seen her youngest child since he was six years old.   In the light of later history, it is impossible not to feel that Richard's wisest course, alike for his own sake and for England's, would have been to follow the instinct which had once prompted him to insist that John should go with him to the crusade.   In this case however he was now led astray by the noblest feature in his character, his unsuspecting confidence and generosity.   From the hour of their reconciliation after their father's death, Richard's sole endeavour respecting John was to gain his affection and gratitude by showering upon him every honour, dignity and benefit of which it was possible to dispose in his favour.   The grant of the county of Mortain made him the first baron of Normandy, and it was accompanied by a liberal provision in English lands.   To these were added, as soon as the brothers reached England, a

---

[1] Madox, *Hist. Exch.*, vol. i. p. 664, from Pipe Roll 2 Ric. I.

[2] *Gesta Ric.* (Stubbs), p. 98.   Richard's charter of release to William is in Rymer, *Fœdera*, vol. i. p. 30 ; *Gesta Ric.* as above, pp. 102, 103 ; Rog. Howden (Stubbs), vol. iii. pp. 25, 26.   It is dated (in Rymer's copy) December 5.   On this transaction see also R. Diceto (Stubbs), vol. ii. p. 72, and Will. Newb., l. iv. c. 5 (Howlett, vol. i. p. 304).

string of "honours"—Marlborough, Luggershall, Lancaster, each with its castle; the Peak, Bolsover, and the whole honour of Peverel; those of Wallingford and Tickhill, and that of Nottingham, including the town; and the whole shire of Derby;[1] besides the honour of Gloucester, which belonged to John's betrothed bride Avice, and which Richard secured to him by causing him to be married to her at Marlborough on August 29,[2] in spite of Archbishop Baldwin's protests against a marriage between third cousins without dispensation from the Pope.   Baldwin at once laid all the lands of the young couple under interdict; but John appealed against him, and a papal legate who came over in November to settle Baldwin's· quarrel with his own monks confirmed the appeal and annulled the sentence of the primate.[3]   At the same time Richard bestowed upon his brother four whole shires in south-western England—Cornwall, Devon, Somerset and Dorset—with the ferms and the entire profits of jurisdiction and administration.[4]   More than this even Richard could not give; if more was needed to hold John's ambition in check, he could only trust to the skilful management of Eleanor.   She was left, seemingly without any formal commission, but with the practical authority of queen-regent, and with the dowries of two former queens in addition to her own.[5]

One important part of Richard's administrative arrangements was however already upset: William de Mandeville, having gone to Normandy on business for the king, died there on November 14.[6]   Earl of Essex by grant of Henry II., count of Aumale by marriage with its heiress, William had been through life one of Henry's most faithful friends; he was honoured and esteemed by all parties on both sides of the sea; there was no one left among the barons who could command anything like the same degree

---

[1] *Gesta Ric.* (Stubbs), p. 78.   See also Stubbs,' *Rog. Howden*, vol. iii., pref. p. xx.
[2] *Gesta Ric.* as above, p. 78.   [3] R. Diceto (Stubbs), vol. ii. pp. 72,'73.
[4] *Gesta Ric.* as above, p. 99.   Stubbs as above, p. xxv.   Cf. Will. Newb., l. iv. c. 3 (Howlett, vol. i. p. 301), and his comments on the subject (*ib.* p. 302).
[5] *Gesta Ric.* as above.
[6] R. Diceto as above, p. 73.   *Gesta Ric.* as above, p. 92.   The day comes from Ralf.   R. Coggeshall (Stevenson), p. 26, makes it December 12.

of general respect ; and Richard for the moment saw no
means of filling his place.   He therefore left Bishop Hugh
of Durham as sole chief justiciar ; but he made a change in
the body of subordinate justiciars appointed at Pipewell.
Two of them were superseded ; one was replaced by Hugh
Bardulf, and the other, it seems, by the chancellor William of
Longchamp, who, in addition to the office which he already
held, was put in charge of the Tower of London, and
intrusted with powers which virtually made him equal in
authority to the chief justiciar.[1]

None of these appointments was in itself unwise ; but
two worse-matched yokefellows than the justiciar and the
chancellor it would have been difficult to find.   Hugh of
Puiset—or " Pudsey," as his English flock called him—had
stood high in both Church and state ever since the days of
the civil war.   Through his mother he was a great-grandson
of the Conqueror, and thus cousin in no remote degree to
Henry Fitz-Empress and Richard Cœur-de-Lion, as well as
to Philip of France.   We saw him more than forty years
ago, as archdeacon and treasurer of York, meeting the
ecclesiastical censures of his metropolitan with a retort on
equal terms, and wielding not unsuccessfully the weapons
both of spiritual and temporal warfare in the cause of his
cousin William of York and his uncle Henry of Winchester.
Since 1153 he had been bishop of Durham ; certainly not
an ideal successor of S. Cuthbert ; yet his appointment had
been sanctioned by the saintly archbishop Theobald ; and
throughout his long episcopate he shewed himself by no
means ill-fitted, on the whole, for his peculiar position.   That
position, it must be remembered, had more than that of any
other English bishop an important political side.   The bishop
of Durham was earl palatine of his shire ; its whole administration, secular as well as ecclesiastical, was in his hands.
His diocesan jurisdiction, again, extended over the whole of
Northumberland, and thus brought him into immediate con-

---

[1] On these appointments cf. *Gesta Ric.* (Stubbs), p. 101 ; Rog. Howden
(Stubbs), vol. iii. p. 28 ; Ric. Devizes (Stevenson), pp. 8, 11 ; Will. Newb., l. iv.
c. 5 (Howlett, vol. i. p. 306) ; and Bishop Stubbs's note, pref. to Rog. Howden as
above, p. xxx.

tact with the Scots across the border. His diocese was in fact a great marchland between England and Scotland ; he was the natural medium of communication or negotiation between the two realms ; and on him depended in no small degree the security of their relations with each other. For such a post it was well to have a strong man, in every sense of the words ; and such a man was Hugh of Puiset. His strength was not based solely upon an unscrupulous use of great material and political resources. He was a popular man with all classes ; notwithstanding his unclerical ways, he never fell into any ecclesiastical disgrace except with his own metropolitan, for whom he was generally more than a match ; and he was one of the very few prelates who managed to steer their way through the Becket quarrel without either damaging their reputation as sound churchmen or forfeiting the confidence of Henry II. His intrigues with the Scot king and the rebel barons in 1174 failed so completely and so speedily that Henry found it scarcely worth while to punish them in any way ; and on the other hand, Hugh's position was already so independent and secure that he himself never found it worth while to renew them. In his own diocese, whatever he might be as a pastor of souls, he was a vigorous and on the whole a beneficent as well as magnificent ruler ; the men of the county palatine grumbled indeed at his extravagance and at the occasional hardships brought upon them by his inordinate love of the chase, but they were none the less proud of his splendid buildings, his regal state, and his equally regal personality. His appearance and manners corresponded with his character and his rank ; he was tall in stature, dignified in bearing, remarkably attractive in look, eloquent and winning in address.[1] Moreover, he had lived so long in England, and all his interests had so long been centred there, that for all practical purposes, social as well as political, he was a thorough Englishman—certainly far more of an Englishman than his young English-born cousin, King Richard. For the last eight

---

[1] On Hugh of Durham see Will. Newb., l. v. c. 10 (Howlett, vol. ii. pp. 436-438), Geoff. Coldingham, cc. 1, 4, 11, 14 (*Scriptt. Dunelm. III.*, Raine, pp. 4, 8, 9, 11, 12, 14), and Stubbs, *Rog. Howden*, vol. iii. pref. pp. xxxiii.-xxxvii.

years, indeed, he had held in the north much the same position as had belonged in earlier times to the archbishops of
York ; for the northern province had been without a metropolitan ever since the death of Roger of Pont-l'Evêque in
November 1181,[1] and the supreme authority, ecclesiastical
as well as secular, had thus devolved upon the bishop of
Durham.   He was now threatened with the loss of this pre-
eminence ; but he had no intention of giving it up without
a struggle, in which his chances of success were at least as
good as those of his rival the archbishop-elect ; and whatever the result might be with respect to his ecclesiastical
independence, he had secured a formidable counterpoise to
the primate's territorial influence by his purchase of Northumberland, which made him sole head, under the Crown, of
the civil administration of the whole country between the
Tweed and the Tees.

Alike in himself and in his antecedents Hugh of Puiset
was the very antithesis to William of Longchamp.   William
had nothing of the stately presence and winning aspect
which distinguished the bishop of Durham ; on the contrary,
he laboured under personal disadvantages which should have
entitled him to sympathy, but which one of his political
opponents was heartless enough to caricature, after his fall,
in order to make him an object of vulgar contempt and disgust.   His stature was diminutive, his countenance swarthy
and ill-favoured, his figure mis-shapen, and he was moreover
very lame.[2]   His origin was as lowly as his person.   His
father was a certain Hugh of Longchamp who in 1156 received from the king a grant of lands in Herefordshire,[3] and
about the time of the barons' revolt was fermor of the
honour of Conches in Normandy.[4]   His grandfather was
said to have been a French serf who had fled from the
justice of his lord and found a refuge in the Norman village

---

[1] *Gesta Hen.* (Stubbs), vol. i. p. 283.   R. Diceto (Stubbs), vol. ii. p. 10.
Will. Newb., l. iii. c. 5 (Howlett, vol. i. p. 225).

[2] Cf. Ric. Devizes (Stevenson), p. 11, with the horrible caricature in Gir.
Cambr. *Vita Galfr.*, l. ii. c. 19 (Brewer, vol. iv. p. 420).

[3] Pipe Roll 2 Hen. II. (Hunter), p. 51.

[4] *Mag. Rot. Scacc. Norm.* (Stapleton), vol. i. p. 74.   Cf. Stubbs, *Rog. Howden,*
vol. iii. pref. p. xxxviii.

whence his descendants took their name.[1]   In Henry's latter
years Hugh of Longchamp was deep in debt and disgrace,[2]
and his six sons had to make their way in the world as
best they could under the shadow of the king's displeasure.[3]
William, whose physical infirmities must have shut him out
from every career save that of a clerk, first appears under
the patronage of Geoffrey the chancellor, as his official in
one of his many pieces of Church preferment, the archdeaconry of Rouen.[4]   The king, however, remonstrated
strongly with his son on the danger of associating with
a man whom he declared to be " a traitor, like his
father and mother before him."[5]   The end of his remonstrances was that, shortly before the last outbreak,
William fled from Geoffrey to Richard, and, according to
one account, became the chief instigator of Richard's rebellion.[6]   However this may be, it is certain that Richard, while
still merely duke of Aquitaine, employed William as his
chancellor,[7] and that he was not only so well satisfied with
his services as to retain him in the same capacity after his
accession to the crown, but had formed such a high opinion
of his statesmanship and his fidelity as to make him his
chief political adviser and confidant.   Richard, like his father,
was constant in his friendships, and very unwilling to discard
those to whom he had once become really attached ; his
trust in William remained unshaken to the end of his life,
and in some respects it was not misplaced.   William seems
to have been thoroughly loyal to his master, and his energy
and industry were as unquestionable as his loyalty.   As
Richard's most intimate companion, confidential secretary,
and political adviser in foreign affairs, William was in his

---

[1] Letter of Hugh of Nonant, in *Gesta Ric.* (Stubbs), p. 216 (also in Rog.
Howden, Stubbs, vol. iii. p. 142).   Gir. Cambr. *Vita Galfr.*, l. ii. c. 18 (Brewer,
vol. iv. p. 418).
[2] *Mag. Rot. Scacc. Norm.* (Stapleton), vol. i. p. 74.   Stubbs, *Rog. Howden,*
vol. iii. pref. pp. xxxviii, xxxix and notes.
[3] Stubbs, as above, pp. xxxix, xl.   [4] Gir. Cambr. as above, c. 1 (p. 388).
[5] *Ibid.* Cf. c. 19 (pp. 420, 421).   It does not seem to be known exactly who
William's mother was ; but she brought to her husband in dower a knight's fee in
Herefordshire under Hugh de Lacy.   See *Lib. Nig. Scacc.* (Hearne), p. 155, and
Stubbs, as above, p. xxxviii, note 4.   [6] Gir. Cambr. as above, c. 19 (p. 421).
[7] Ric. Devizes (Stevenson), p. 6.

right place ; but he was by no means equally well fitted to be Richard's representative in the supreme government and administration of England. He had the primary disqualification of being a total stranger to the land, its people and its ways. Most likely he had never set foot in England till he came thither with Richard in 1189 ; he was ignorant of the English tongue ;[1] his new surroundings were thoroughly distasteful to him ; and as he was by no means of a cautious or conciliatory temper, he expressed his contempt and dislike of them in a way which was resented not only by the people, but even by men whose origin and natural speech were scarcely more English than his own.[2] He had in short every qualification for becoming an extremely unpopular man, and he behaved as if he desired no other destiny. The nation at large soon learned to return his aversion and to detest him as a disagreeable stranger ; his colleagues in the administration despised him as an upstart interloper ; the justiciar, in particular, keenly resented his own virtual subordination to one whom he naturally regarded as his inferior in every way.[3] It was sound policy on Richard's part to place a check upon Hugh of Durham ; and it was not unnatural that he should select his chancellor for that purpose. The seven happiest years of Henry Fitz-Empress had been the years during which another chancellor had wielded a power almost as great as that which Richard intrusted to William of Longchamp. But, on the other hand, any one except Richard might have seen at a glance that of all statesmen living, William of Longchamp was well-nigh the least fitted to reproduce the career of Thomas of London.

The king left England on December 11.[4] William was consecrated, together with Richard Fitz-Nigel, on December 31,[5] and on the feast of the Epiphany he was enthroned at Ely.[6] Immediately afterwards he began to assert his temporal authority. At a meeting of the Court of Exchequer

[1] Letter of Hugh of Nonant in *Gesta Ric.* (Stubbs), vol. ii. p. 219.
[2] See Gir. Cambr. *Vita Galfr.*, l. ii. c. 19 (Brewer, vol. iv. p. 424).
[3] *Gesta Ric.* (Stubbs), p. 101.   Rog. Howden (Stubbs), vol. iii. p. 29.
[4] *Gesta Ric.* as above.   R. Diceto (Stubbs), vol. ii. p. 73, makes it December 14.
[5] R. Diceto as above, p. 75.   Ric. Devizes (Stevenson), p. 11.
[6] R. Diceto as above.

the bishop of Durham was turned out by the chancellor's orders ; presently after he was deprived of his jurisdiction over Northumberland.   Soon after this, Bishop Godfrey of Winchester was dispossessed not merely of his sheriffdom and castles, but even of his own patrimony.[1]   For this last spoliation there is no apparent excuse ; that a man should hold a sheriffdom together with a bishopric was, however, contrary alike to Church discipline and to sound temporal policy ; and the non-recognition of Hugh's purchase of Northumberland might be yet further justified by the fact that the purchase-money was not yet paid.[2]   In February 1190 Richard summoned his mother, his brothers and his chief ministers to a final meeting in Normandy ;[3] the chancellor, knowing that complaints against him would be brought before the king, hurried over in advance of his colleagues, to justify himself before he was accused,[4] and he succeeded so well that Richard not only sent him back to England after the council with full authority to act as chief justiciar as well as chancellor,[5] but at the same time opened negotiations with Rome to obtain for him a commission as legate[6]—an arrangement which, the archbishop of Canterbury being bound on crusade like the king, would leave William supreme both in Church and state.

The new justiciar's first act on his return was to fortify the Tower of London ;[7] his next was to punish a disturbance which had lately occurred at York.   During the last six months the long-suppressed hatred which the Jews inspired had broken forth into open violence.   The first pretext had been furnished by a misunderstanding on the coronation-day. Richard, who had some very strict ideas about the ceremonials of religion, had given orders that no Jew should approach him on that solemn occasion ; in defiance or ignorance of the prohibition, some rich Jews came to offer gifts to the new sovereign ; the courtiers and the people seized the

---

[1] Ric. Devizes (Stevenson), p. 11.

[2] See Stubbs, *Rog. Howden*, vol. iii. pref. p. xxxi. and note 3.

[3] *Gesta Ric.* (Stubbs), pp. 105, 106.   [4] Ric. Devizes (Stevenson), p. 12.

[5] *Gesta Ric.* (Stubbs), p. 106.   Cf. Ric. Devizes as above, and Will. Newb., l. iv. c. 14 (Howlett, vol. i. p. 331).

[6] *Gesta Ric.* as above.   [7] *Ibid.*

excuse to satisfy at once their greed and their hatred ; the unwelcome visitors were driven away, robbed, beaten, some even slain ;[1] and the rage of their enemies, once let loose, spent itself throughout the night in a general sack of the Jewish quarter.   Richard, engaged at the coronation-banquet, knew nothing of what had happened till the next day,[2] when he did his best to secure the ringleaders, and punished them severely.[3]   When he was gone, however, the spark thus kindled burst forth into a blaze in all the chief English cities in succession, Winchester being almost the sole exception.[4]   Massacres of Jews took place at Norwich on February 6, at Stamford on March 7, at S. Edmund's on March 18, Palm Sunday.[5]   A day before this last, a yet worse tragedy had occurred at York.   The principal Jews of that city, in dread of a popular attack, had sought and obtained shelter in one of the towers of the castle, under the protection of its constable and the sheriff of Yorkshire.[6]   Once there, they refused to give it up again ; whereupon the constable and the sheriff called out all the forces of city and shire to dislodge them.   After twenty-four hours' siege the Jews offered to ransom themselves by a heavy fine ; but the blood of the citizens was up, and they rejected the offer.   The Jews, in desperation, resolved to die by their own hands rather than by those of their Gentile enemies ; the women

---

[1] The *Gesta Ric.* (Stubbs), p. 83, lay the blame on "curiales"; with Rog. Howden (Stubbs), vol. iii. p. 12, the source of the mischief is "plebs superbo oculo et insatiabili corde "; R. Diceto (Stubbs), vol. ii. p. 69, is so ashamed of the whole business that he tries to shift the responsibility off all English shoulders alike—" Pax Judæorum, quam ab antiquis temporibus semper obtinuerant, ab alienigenis interrumpitur." Cf. the very opposite tone of R. Coggeshall (Stevenson), p. 28, and the judicial middle course characteristically steered by Will. Newb., l. iv. cc. 1 and 9 (Howlett, vol. i. pp. 297, 298, 316, 317).

[2] R. Diceto as above.

[3] *Gesta Ric.* (Stubbs), p. 84. Rog. Howden as above. Both take care to assure us that Richard's severity was owing not to any sympathy for the Jews, but to the fact that in the confusion a few Christians had suffered with them. Cf. a slightly different version in Will. Newb., l. iv. c. 1 (as above, pp. 297-299).

[4] Ric. Devizes (Stevenson), p. 5.

[5] R. Diceto as above, p. 75. Cf. Will. Newb., l. iv. cc. 7, 8 (as above, pp. 308-312), who adds Lynn to the series.

[6] *Gesta Ric.* (Stubbs), p. 107, and a more detailed account in Will. Newb., l. iv. c. 9 (as above, pp. 312-314). From him we learn that the Jews of Lincoln did the same, and with a more satisfactory result.

VOL. II.

and children were slaughtered by their husbands and fathers, who flung the corpses over the battlements or piled them up in the tower, which they fired.[1] Nearly five hundred Jews perished in the massacre or the flames;[2] and the citizens and soldiers, baulked of their expected prey, satiated their greed by sacking and burning all the Jewish houses and destroying the bonds of all the Jewish usurers in the city.[3] At the end of April or the beginning of May[4] the new justiciar came with an armed force to York to investigate this affair. The citizens threw the whole blame upon the castellan and the sheriff; William accordingly deposed them both.[5] As the castle was destroyed, he probably thought it needless to appoint a new constable until it should be rebuilt ; for the sheriff—John, elder brother of William the Marshal—he at once substituted his own brother Osbert.[6] Most of the knights who had been concerned in the tumult had taken care to put themselves out of his reach ; their estates were, however, mulcted and their chattels seized;[7] and the citizens only escaped by paying a fine[8] and giving hostages who were not redeemed till three years later, when all thought of further proceedings in the matter had been given up.[9] Even the clergy of the minster had their share of punishment, although for a different offence : William, though his legatine commission had not yet arrived, claimed already to be received as legate, and put the church under interdict until his claim was admitted.[10]

For the moment William's power was undisputed even

---

[1] *Gesta Ric.* (Stubbs), p. 107. For date—March 16—see R. Diceto (Stubbs), vol. ii. p. 75.   [2] R. Diceto as above.

[3] *Gesta Ric.* as above. Rog. Howden (Stubbs), vol. iii. p. 34. Cf. the somewhat different version of Will. Newb., l. iv. cc. 9, 10 (Howlett, vol. i. pp. 314-322), and also R. Coggeshall (Stevenson), pp. 27, 28.

[4] The *Gesta Ric.* (Stubbs), p. 108, say merely " post Pascha " ; Will. Newb., l. iv. c. 11 (as above, p. 323), says " circa Dominicæ Ascensionis solemnia," which fell on May 4.   [5] *Gesta Ric.* as above.

[6] Rog. Howden as above.

[7] Will. Newb. as above (p. 323). Cf. Pipe Roll 2 Ric. I., quoted in Stubbs, *Rog. Howden*, vol. iii. pref. pp. xliv., notes 4, 5, xlv., note 1.

[8] Will. Newb. as above.

[9] Pipe Roll 5 Ric. I. in Stubbs, *Rog. Howden*, vol. iii. pref. p. xliv., note 7. Will. Newb., as above (p. 324), says that nothing further was ever done in the matter.   [10] *Gesta Ric.* (Stubbs), pp. 108, 109.

in the north ; for Hugh of Durham was still in Gaul.	Now,
however, there came a notice from the king that he was
about to send Hugh back to England as justiciar over the
whole country north of the Humber.[1]	Hugh himself soon
afterwards arrived, and hurried northward, in the hope, it
seems, of catching the chancellor on the further side of the
Humber and thus compelling him to acknowledge his
inferiority.[2]	In this hope he was disappointed ; they met
at Blyth in Nottinghamshire.[3]	Hugh, impetuous in old age
as in youth, talked somewhat too much as the chancellor
had acted—" as if all the affairs of the realm were dependent
on his nod." [4]	At last, however, he produced the commission
from Richard upon which his pretensions were founded ;[5]
and William, who could read between the lines of his royal
friend's letters, saw at once that he had little to fear.[6]	He
replied simply by expressing his readiness to obey the king's
orders,[7] and proposing that all further discussion should be
adjourned to a second meeting a week later at Tickhill.
There Hugh found the tables turned.	The chancellor had
reached the place before him ; the bishop's followers were
shut out from the castle ; he was admitted alone into the
presence of his rival, who, without giving him time to speak,
put into his hands another letter from Richard, bidding all
his English subjects render service and obedience to " our
trusty and well-beloved chancellor, the bishop of Ely," as
they would to the king himself.	The letter was dated June
6—some days, if not weeks, later than Hugh's credentials ;[8]
and it seems to have just reached William together with his
legatine commission, which was issued on the previous day.[9]
He gave his rival no time even to think.	" You had your
say at our last meeting ; now I will have mine.	As my
lord the king liveth, you shall not quit this place till you

---

[1] *Gesta Ric.* (Stubbs), p. 109.	This appointment is mentioned (*ib.* p. 106)
among those made at the council of Rouen, where William himself was appointed ;
but it seems plain that it was not ratified till some time later.

[2] Ric. Devizes (Stevenson), p. 12.	[3] *Gesta Ric.* as above, p. 109.

[4] Ric. Devizes as above.	[5] *Ib.* p. 13.	*Gesta Ric.* as above.

[6] Ric. Devizes as above.	[7] *Gesta Ric.* as above.

[8] Cf. R. Diceto (Stubbs), vol. ii. p. 83, with Ric. Devizes as above.

[9] R. Diceto as above.

have given me hostages for the surrender of all your castles.
No protests! I am not a bishop arresting another bishop;
I am the chancellor, arresting his supplanter."[1]   Hugh was
powerless; yet he let himself be dragged all the way to
London before he would yield. Then he gave up the
required hostages,[2] and submitted to the loss of all his
lately-purchased honours—Windsor, Newcastle, Northumberland, even the manor of Sadberge which he had bought of
the king for his see[3]—everything, in short, except his
bishopric. For that he set out as soon as he was liberated;
but at his manor of Howden he was stopped by the chancellor's orders, forbidden to proceed further, and again
threatened with forcible detention. He promised to remain
where he was, gave security for the fulfilment of his promise,
and then wrote to the king his complaints of the treatment
which he had received.[4]   All the redress that he could get,
however, was a writ commanding that Sadberge should be
restored to him at once and that he should suffer no further
molestation.[5]

The chancellor's first rival was thus suppressed; but
already he could see other stumbling-blocks arising in his
path, not a few of them placed there by the shortsighted
policy of his royal master. Richard's reckless bestowal of
lands and jurisdictions would, if left undisturbed, have put
the administration of at least ten whole shires practically
beyond the control of the central government. The bishops
of Durham, Winchester and Coventry or Chester would have
had everything their own way, in temporal matters no less
than in spiritual, throughout their respective dioceses. To
this state of things William had summarily put an end in
the cases of Northumberland and Hampshire; in those of

---

[1] Ric. Devizes (Stevenson), p. 13.

[2] *Gesta Ric.* (Stubbs), p. 109.   Rog. Howden (Stubbs), vol. iii. p. 35, places
the submission at Southwell.

[3] *Gesta Ric.* as above.   On Sadberge see Rog. Howden as above, p. 13.

[4] *Gesta Ric.*, pp. 109, 110.

[5] The *Gesta Ric.*, p. 110, say Richard ordered the restitution of Newcastle and
Sadberge; for Newcastle Rog. Howden, as above, p. 38, substitutes "comitatum
Northumbriæ"; but the king's letter, given by Roger himself (*ib.* pp. 38, 39),
mentions nothing except Sadberge. For its date see *ib.* pp. 37 note 1, 39 note 3,
and *Gesta Ric.* as above, p. 112, note 1.

Leicestershire, Staffordshire and Warwickshire the primate had been induced to remonstrate with Hugh of Coventry upon the impropriety of a bishop holding three sheriffdoms, and Hugh had accordingly given up two of them, though he managed to get them back after Baldwin's death at the close of 1190.[1] There were however still four shires in the south-west and one in Mid-England over which the king's justiciar was not only without practical, but even without legal jurisdiction. In these, and in a number of " honours " scattered over the midland shires from Gloucester to Nottingham, the whole rights and profits of government, administration and finance belonged solely to John ; for his exercise of them he was responsible to no one but the king ; and thus, as soon as Richard was out of reach, John was to all intents and purposes himself king of his own territories. For the present indeed he was unable to set foot in his little realm : Richard in the spring had made both his brothers take an oath to keep away from England for three years.[2] It was however easy enough for John to govern his part of England, as the whole of it had often been governed for years together, from the other side of the Channel. He had his staff of ministers just like his brother—his justiciar Roger de Planes,[3] his chancellor Stephen Ridel,[4] his seneschal William de Kahaines, and his butler Theobald Walter ;[5] the sheriffs of his five counties and the stewards or bailiffs of his honours were appointed by him alone, and exercised their functions solely for his advantage, without reference to the king's court or the king's exchequer.[6] It is evident that, even though as yet the sea lay between them, John had already the power to make himself, if he were so minded, a serious obstacle to the chancellor's plans of governing England for Richard. Moreover, before Richard finally quitted Gaul, his mother persuaded him to release John from his oath of absence ;[7]

---

[1] See R. Diceto (Stubbs), vol. ii. pp. 77, 78, and Stubbs, *Rog. Howden,* vol. iii. pref. p. xxxi. and note 5.

[2] *Gesta Ric.* (Stubbs), p. 106. Ric. Devizes (Stevenson), p. 15.

[3] R. Diceto as above, p. 99.   [4] *Gesta Ric.* as above, p. 224.

[5] Rymer, *Fœdera,* vol. i. p. 55.

[6] See Stubbs, *Rog. Howden,* vol. iii. pref. pp. xxxiii and lii.

[7] *Gesta Ric.* and Ric. Devizes as above.

and William of Longchamp himself, in his new character of legate, was obliged to confirm the release with his absolution.[1] In view of the struggle which he now saw could not be far distant, William began to marshal his political forces and concert his measures of defence. On August 1 he held a Church council at Gloucester, in the heart of John's territories ;[2] on October 13 he held another at Westminster ;[3] and he seems to have spent the winter in a sort of half legatine, half vice-regal progress throughout the country, for purposes of justice and finance and for the assertion of his own authority. This proceeding stirred up a good deal of discontent. Cripple though he was, William of Longchamp seems to have been almost as rapid and restless a traveller as Henry II.; one contemporary says he "went up and down the country like a flash of lightning." [4] It may be however that these words allude to the disastrous effects of the chancellor's passage rather than to its swiftness and suddenness ; for he went about in such state as no minister except Henry's first chancellor had ever ventured to assume. His train of a thousand armed knights, besides a crowd of clerks and other attendants, was a ruinous burthen to the religious houses where he claimed entertainment ; and the burthen was made almost unbearable by the heavy exactions, from clerk and layman alike, which he made in his master's name.[5]

That master was now with Philip of France at Messina,[6] preparing for his departure from Europe. When he would come back—whether he ever would come back at all—was felt by all parties to be doubtful in the extreme. With his

---

[1] Gir. Cambr. *De rebus a se gestis*, l. ii. c. 23 (Brewer, vol. i. p. 86). Ric. Devizes (Stevenson), p. 15, says the arrangement was that John "in Angliam per cancellarium transiens staret ejus judicio, et ad placitum illius vel moraretur in regno vel exularet." But with Eleanor in England to back her son, William could really have no choice in the matter.

[2] R. Diceto (Stubbs), vol. ii. p. 83. On the version of this in Ric. Devizes (as above, pp. 13, 14), see Stubbs, *Rog. Howden*, vol. iii. pref. p. xlix.

[3] R. Diceto as above, p. 85. Gerv. Cant. (Stubbs), vol. i. p. 488, makes it October 16.   [4] Ric. Devizes (Stevenson), p. 14.

[5] *Gesta Ric.* (Stubbs), p. 214. Rog. Howden (Stubbs), vol. iii. p. 72. Will. Newb., l. iv. c. 14 (Howlett, vol. i. pp. 333, 334).

[6] Richard was there from September 23, 1190, to April 10, 1191. *Gesta Ric.* (Stubbs), pp. 125, 162 ; R. Diceto as above, pp. 84, 91.

ardent zeal, rash valour and peculiar health, he was little
likely to escape both the chances of war and the effects of
the eastern climate ;[1] and the question of the succession was
therefore again becoming urgent.   There was indeed not
much latitude of choice ; the male line of Anjou, already
extinct in Palestine, had in Europe only three representatives
—Richard himself, John, and their infant nephew Arthur of
Britanny.   By the strict feudal rule of primogeniture, Arthur,
being Geoffrey's son, would have after Richard the next
claim as head of the Angevin house.   By old English constitutional practice, John, being a grown man and the reigning sovereign's own brother, would have a much better
chance of recognition as his successor than his nephew,
a child not yet four years old.   Neither alternative was
without drawbacks.   Richard himself had made up his
mind to the first ; early in November 1190 he arranged a
marriage for Arthur with a daughter of King Tancred of
Sicily, on a distinct understanding that in case of his own
death without children Arthur was to succeed to all his
dominions ;[2] while at the same time William of Longchamp
was endeavouring to secure the Scot king's recognition of
Arthur as heir-presumptive to the English crown.[3]   The
queen-mother was unwilling to contemplate the succession
of either Arthur or John ; she was anxious to get Richard
married.   Knowing that he never would marry the woman
to whom he had been so long betrothed, she took upon
herself to find him another bride.   Her choice fell upon
Berengaria, daughter of King Sancho VI. of Navarre ;[4] it

---

[1] See Will. Newb., l. iv. c. 5 (Howlett, vol. i. p. 306).

[2] Treaty in *Gesta Ric.* (Stubbs), pp. 133-136, and Rog. Howden (Stubbs),
vol. iii. pp. 61-64.   It is dateless, but on November 11 Richard wrote to the
Pope telling him of its provisions and asking for his sanction. *Gesta Ric.* as
above, pp. 136-138 ; Rog. Howden as above, pp. 65, 66.

[3] Will. Newb., l. iv. c. 14 (as above, pp. 335, 336).   William represents this
as an unauthorized proceeding of the chancellor's, contrived in his own interest as
against John.   He seems to place it at a later date.

[4] " Puella prudentior quam pulchra " says Ric. Devizes (Stevenson), p. 25 ;
but he seems to be contrasting her with Eleanor.   On the other hand, Will.
Newb., l. iv. c. 19 (as above, p. 346), calls her " famosæ pulchritudinis et
prudentiæ virginem."   According to the *Itin. Reg. Ric.* (Stubbs), p. 175, this had
been Richard's own choice for many years past.

was accepted by Richard ; early in February 1191 [1] she went over to Gaul ; there she met her intended daughter-in-law, whom she carried on with her into Italy, and by the end of March they were both with Richard at Messina.[2] On the very day of their arrival Philip had sailed.[3] After long wrangling with him, Richard had at last succeeded in freeing himself from his miserable engagement to Adela ; [4] he at once plighted his troth to Berengaria ; and when his mother, after a four days' visit, set out again upon her homeward journey,[5] his bride remained with him under the care of his sister the widowed queen Jane of Sicily [6] till the expiration of Lent and the circumstances of their eastward voyage enabled them to marry. The wedding was celebrated and the queen crowned at Limasol in Cyprus on the fourth Sunday after Easter.[7]

On her way home Eleanor stopped to transact some diplomatic business at Rome, and she seems to have remained in Gaul until the beginning of the next year. Long before she returned to England there were evident tokens that when Richard had proposed to keep John out of it, he had for once been wiser than his mother. Early in the year John, profiting by the liberty which her intercession had procured him, came over to England and there set up his court in such semi-regal state as to make it a source of extreme irritation, if not of grave anxiety, to the chancellor.[8] Eleanor's departure thus left William of Longchamp face to face with a new and most formidable rival ; while about the same time he saw his power threatened on another side. In March 1191 tidings came that Archbishop Baldwin had died at Acre in the foregoing November.[9] If a new primate

---

[1] Richard sent ships to meet her at Naples before the end of that month. *Gesta Ric.* (Stubbs), p. 157.

[2] They arrived on March 30. *Gesta Ric.* as above, p. 161.   [3] *Ibid.*

[4] *Gesta Ric.* as above, pp. 160, 161. Rog. Howden (Stubbs), vol. iii. p. 99. R. Diceto (Stubbs), vol. ii. p. 86. Ric. Devizes (Stevenson), p. 26. The actual treaty between Richard and Philip, of which more later, is in Rymer, *Fœdera*, vol. i. p. 54.

[5] She sailed on April 2. *Gesta Ric.* as above, p. 161. Cf. R. Diceto as above.

[6] *Ibid.* Ric. Devizes (Stevenson), p. 28.

[7] *Gesta Ric.* as above, pp. 166, 167. Ric. Devizes, p. 39. *Itin. Reg. Ric.* (Stubbs), pp. 195, 196.   [8] See Stubbs, *Rog. Howden*, vol. iii. pref. pp. li., lii.

[9] Gerv. Cant. (Stubbs), vol. i. pp. 488, 490.

should be appointed, it was to be expected as a matter of course that the bishop of Ely would lose the legation ; he could hope to retain it only by persuading Richard either to nominate him to the primacy, or to keep it vacant altogether. Richard's notions of ecclesiastical propriety were however too strict to admit the latter alternative ; from the former he would most likely be deterred by his father's experiences with another chancellor ; so, to the astonishment of everybody, he nominated for the see of Canterbury a Sicilian prelate, one of his fellow-crusaders, William archbishop of Monreale.[1] Meanwhile John and the chancellor were quarrelling openly ; popular sympathy, which William had alienated by his arrogance and his oppressions, was on the side of John ; even the subordinate justiciars, who had stood by William in his struggle with Hugh of Durham,[2] were turning against him now; from one and all complaints against him were showering in upon the king ;[3] till at the end of February Richard grew so bewildered and so uneasy that he decided upon sending the archbishop of Rouen to investigate the state of affairs in England and see what could be done to remedy it.[4]

The archbishop of Rouen—Walter of Coutances—was a man of noble birth and stainless character who had been successively archdeacon of Oxford, treasurer of Rouen cathedral and vice-chancellor to Henry II. ;[5] in this last capacity he had for eight years done the whole work of head of the chancery for his nominal chief Ralf of Varneville,[6] till Ralf was succeeded in 1182 by the king's son Geoffrey, and next year the vice-chancellor was promoted to the see of Lincoln, which Geoffrey had resigned. A year later Walter was advanced to the primacy of Normandy.[7] He was now with Richard, on his way to Holy Land, but commuted his vow to serve the king.[8]   He was a very quiet,

---

[1] Gerv. Cant. (Stubbs), vol. i. pp. 493, 494 ; date, January 25 [1191].
[2] See Ric. Devizes (Stevenson), pp. 11, 12.
[3] *Gesta Ric.* (Stubbs), p. 158.   Rog. Howden (Stubbs), vol. iii. pp. 95, 96.
[4] *Gesta Ric.* as above.   Rog. Howden as above, p. 96.   We get the date approximately from Richard's letter in R. Diceto (Stubbs), vol. ii. p. 90.
[5] Gir. Cambr. *Vita Galfr.*, l. ii. c. 10 (Brewer, vol. iv. p. 408).
[6] R. Diceto (Stubbs), vol. i. p. 367.   [7] *Ib.* vol. ii. pp. 10, 14, 21.
[8] Ric. Devizes (Stevenson), p. 27—very unfairly coloured.

unassuming person, and certainly not a vigorous statesman ; but his integrity and disinterestedness were above question ;[1] and the position in which he was now placed was one in which even a Thomas Becket might well have been puzzled how to act. The only commission given him by Richard of which we know the date was issued on February 23 ;[2] but it was not till April 2 that he was allowed to leave Messina ;[3] and during the interval Richard, in his reluctance to supersede the chancellor, seems to have been perpetually changing his mind and varying his instructions, some of which were sent direct to England and some intrusted to Walter, till by the time the archbishop started he was laden with a bundle of contradictory commissions, addressed to himself, to William and to the co-justiciars, and apparently accompanied by a verbal order to use one, all or none of them, wholly at his own discretion.[4]

Before he reached England John and the chancellor were at open war. On Mid-Lent Sunday they met at Winchester to discuss the payment of John's pensions from the Exchequer and the possession of certain castles within his territories.[5] The discussion clearly ended in a quarrel ; and this served as a signal for revolt against the unpopular minister. Gerard de Camville, sheriff of Lincolnshire by purchase from the king, was also constable of Lincoln castle in right of his wife Nicolaa de Haye. He was accused of harbouring robbers in the castle, and when summoned before the king's justices he refused to appear, declaring

---

[1] Cf. Gir. Cambr. *Vita Galfr.*, l. ii. c. 10 (Brewer, vol. iv. p. 408), and Will. Newb., l. iv. c. 15 (Howlett, vol. i. p. 336). In this place William calls Walter "virum prudentem et modestum"; but in l. iii. c. 8 (*ib.* p. 236) he displays a curiously bitter resentment against him for his abandonment of the see of Lincoln for the loftier see of Rouen.

[2] R. Diceto (Stubbs), vol. ii. p. 90. Gir. Cambr. as above, c. 6 (p. 401), gives the date as February 20.

[3] He and Eleanor left Messina together. *Itin. Reg. Ric.* (Stubbs), p. 176.

[4] This seems the only possible explanation at once of Walter's conduct and of the conflicting accounts in R. Diceto as above, pp. 90, 91 ; Gir. Cambr. as above (pp. 400, 401); *Gesta Ric.* (Stubbs), p. 158 ; Rog. Howden (Stubbs), vol. iii. pp. 96, 97 ; Ric. Devizes (Stevenson), pp. 27-29 ; and Will. Newb. as above. See Stubbs, *Rog. Howden*, vol. iii. pref. pp. lx., lxi., note 1.

[5] Ric. Devizes (Stevenson), p. 26.

that he had become John's liegeman and was answerable only to him.[1] At the opposite end of England Roger de Mortemer, the lord of Wigmore—successor to that Hugh de Mortemer who had defied Henry II. in 1156— was at the same moment found to be plotting treason with the Welsh. Against him the chancellor proceeded first, and his mere approach so alarmed Roger that he gave up his castle and submitted to banishment from the realm for three years.[2] William then hurried to Lincoln; but before he could reach it Gerard and Nicolaa had had time to make their almost impregnable stronghold ready for a siege, and John had had time to gain possession of Nottingham and Tickhill[3]—two castles which the king had retained in his own hands, while bestowing upon his brother the honours in which they stood. Nicolaa was in command at Lincoln, and was fully equal to the occasion; her husband was now with John, and John at once sent the chancellor a most insulting message, taunting him with the facility with which the two castles had been betrayed,[4] and threatening that if the attempt upon Lincoln was not at once given up, he would come in person to avenge the wrongs of his liegeman.[5] William saw that John was now too strong for him; he knew by this time that Pope Clement was dead,[6] and his own legation consequently at an end; he must have known, too, of the mission of Walter of Rouen; he therefore, through some of his fellow-bishops,[7] demanded a personal meeting with John, and proposed that all their differences should be submitted to arbitration. John burst into a fury at what he chose to call the impudence of this proposal,[8] but he ended by accepting it, and on April 25 the meeting took place at Winchester.

---

[1] Cf. Ric. Devizes (Stevenson), p. 30, with Rog. Howden (Stubbs), vol. iii. pp. 242, 243, and Will. Newb., l. iv. c. 16 (Howlett, vol. i. pp. 337, 338), and see Stubbs, *Rog. Howden*, vol. iii. pref. pp. lvi., lvii. [2] Ric. Devizes as above.

[3] *Ibid. Gesta Ric.* (Stubbs), p. 207. Will. Newb. as above (p. 338).

[4] Ric. Devizes as above. [5] *Ibid. Gesta Ric.* as above.

[6] He died on the Wednesday before Easter—April 10—and his successor Celestine III. was elected on Easter-day. *Gesta Ric.* as above, p. 161.

[7] Ric. Devizes (Stevenson), p. 31, makes Walter of Rouen the mediator, but we shall see that this is chronologically impossible. [8] *Ibid.*

The case was decided by the bishops of London, Winchester
and Bath, with eleven lay arbitrators chosen by them from
each party. Their decision went wholly against the chancellor. He was permitted to claim the restitution of Nottingham and Tickhill, but only to put them in charge of two
partizans of John ; his right to appoint wardens to the other
castles in dispute was nominally confirmed, but made
practically dependent upon John's dictation ; he was compelled to reinstate Gerard de Camville, and moreover to
promise that in case of Richard's death he would do his
utmost to secure the crown for John.[1]

Two days later Walter of Rouen landed at Shoreham.[2]
He was evidently not wanted now to act as a check upon
William of Longchamp ; he might almost expect to be soon
wanted as a check upon John ; but meanwhile, he could
only stand aside and watch the effect of the new arrangements. His passive attitude gave, however, an indirect
support to the chancellor ; after midsummer, therefore, the
latter ventured to repudiate the concessions wrung from
him at Winchester ; he again advanced upon Lincoln, and
formally deprived Gerard of the sheriffdom, which he conferred upon William de Stuteville.[3] Once more the other
bishops interposed, backed now by the Norman primate.
Another assembly met at Winchester on July 28,[4] and here
a fresh settlement was made. Gerard was reinstated in the
sheriffdom of Lincolnshire, pending his trial in the king's
court ; William and John were both bound over to commit
no more forcible disseizures ; the disputed castles were to be
again put in charge for the king, but through the medium of
the archbishop of Rouen instead of the chancellor, and John
was allowed no voice in the selection of the castellans, who

---

[1] Ric. Devizes (Stevenson), pp. 32, 33. On the date see Bishop Stubbs's notes
to *Gesta Ric.*, p. 208, and Rog. Howden, vol. iii. p. 134, and pref. to latter, pp.
lviii., lix.

[2] Gerv. Cant. (Stubbs), vol. i. p. 497, says he landed about midsummer, and
the printed text of R. Diceto (Stubbs), vol. ii. p. 90, makes the date June 27 ; but
see note in latter place. Bishop Stubbs (*Rog. Howden*, vol. iii. pref. p. lix.) adopts
the earlier date.   [3] *Gesta Ric.* (Stubbs), p. 207.

[4] The date comes from Ric. Devizes (Stevenson), p. 32, who however mis-
applies it. See Bishop Stubbs's notes to *Gesta Ric.*, p. 208, and Rog. Howden,
vol. iii. p. 134.

were chosen by the assembly then and there.   If the chancellor should infringe the agreement, or if the king should die, these castles were to be given up to John ; but all reference to his claims upon the succession to the throne was carefully omitted.[1]   The contest almost seemed to have ended in a drawn battle.   It was strictly a contest between individuals, involving no national or constitutional interests. The barons, as a body, clearly sided with John ; but, just as clearly, they sided with him from loyal motives.   The authority of the Crown was never called in question ; the question was, who was fittest to represent and uphold it —the king's chancellor, or his brother.   Of treason, either to England or to Richard, there was not a thought, unless— as indeed is only too probable—it lurked in the mind of John himself.

A drawn battle, however, could not possibly be the end of a struggle between two such men as John of Mortain and William of Longchamp.   In the autumn a new element was added to the strife by the return of Archbishop Geoffrey of York.   For thirty-five years Geoffrey had been the eldest living child, if indeed he was not actually the first-born, of Henry Fitz-Empress ;[2] but of the vast Angevin heritage there fell to his share nothing, except the strong feelings and fiery temper which caused half the troubles of his life. As a child he had been brought up at court almost on equal terms with his half-brothers ;[3] he seems indeed to have been his father's favourite, till he was supplanted by the little John.   When he grew to manhood, however, Henry could see no way of providing for him except by forcing him into

---

[1] Rog. Howden (Stubbs), vol. iii. pp. 135-137.

[2] In the first chapter of his *Life* by Gerald (Brewer, vol. iv. p. 363), we are told that Geoffrey was scarcely twenty when elected to Lincoln, *i.e.* in 1173.   But in l. i. c. 13 (*ib.* p. 384), Gerald says that he was consecrated to York "anno ætatis quasi quadragesimo," in 1191.   These two dates, as is usual with Gerald in such cases, do not agree, and neither of them pretends to be more than approximate.   Still it seems plain that Geoffrey's birth must fall somewhere between 1151 and 1153.   Even if we adopt the latest date, he must have been born in the same year as Eleanor's first son—the baby William who died in 1156—and must have been at least two years older than the young king, four years older than Richard, and fourteen years older than John.

[3] Gir. Cambr. *Vita Galfr.*, l. i. c. 1 (Brewer, vol. iv. p. 363).

a career for which he had no vocation. At an early age he
was put into deacon's orders and made archdeacon of Lincoln ;[1] in 1173, when about twenty years of age, he was
appointed to the bishopric of the same place.[2] The Pope,
however, demurred to the choice of a candidate disqualified
alike by his youth and his birth ; and when the former
obstacle had been outlived and the latter might have been
condoned, Geoffrey voluntarily renounced an office in which
he would have been secure for life, but which he had never
desired and for which he felt himself unfit,[3] in order to
become his father's chancellor and constant companion
during the last eight years of his life. It was Henry's last
regret that this son, the only one of his sons whose whole
life had been an unbroken course of perfect filial obedience,
had to be left with his future entirely at the mercy of his
undutiful younger half-brother. Richard received him with
a brotherly welcome ;[4] when, however, he nominated him to
the see of York, he was indeed carrying out their father's
last wishes, but certainly not those of Geoffrey himself.
Richard seems to have thought that he was held back by
other motives than those of conscience or of preference for a
secular life ; he suspected him of cherishing designs upon
the crown.[5] It can only be said that Geoffrey, so far as
appears, never did anything to justify the suspicion, but
shewed on the contrary every disposition to act loyally
towards both his brothers, if they would but have acted with
equal loyalty towards him. As soon however as the tonsure
had marked him irrevocably for a priestly life,[6] Richard's
zeal for his promotion cooled. The bishop of Durham, who

---

[1] Gir. Cambr. *Vita Galfr.*, l. i. c. 1 (Brewer, vol. iv. p. 363).
[2] *Ib.* p. 364. Will. Newb., l. ii. c. 22 (Howlett, vol. i. p. 154).
[3] *Gesta Hen.* (Stubbs), vol. ii. pp. 271, 272. Gir. Cambr. as above, c. 4
(p. 368). The resignation was formally completed at Epiphany 1182. R. Diceto
(Stubbs), vol. ii. p. 10.   [4] Gir. Cambr. as above, c. 5 (p. 372).
[5] *Ib.* c. 8 (p. 379). In c. 7 (p. 374) Gerald actually represents Geoffrey as
entertaining some hope of surviving and succeeding both his younger brothers ;
but this is a very different thing from plotting against them during their lives.
See Stubbs, *Rog. Howden*, vol. iii. pref. p. lxvi. As it turned out, the first part,
at any rate, of this dream of Geoffrey's was not so mad as it seemed, for he died
only four years before John.
[6] He was ordained priest September 23, 1189. *Gesta Ric.* (Stubbs), p. 88.

was striving to make his see independent of the metropolitan,[1] and a strong party in the York chapter with whom Geoffrey had quarrelled on a point of ecclesiastical etiquette, easily won the king's ear;[2] it was not till the very eve of Richard's departure from England that Geoffrey was able to buy his final confirmation both in the see of York and in the estates which his father had bequeathed to him in Anjou;[3] and in March he was summoned over to Normandy and there, like John, made to take an oath of absence from England for three years.[4]

According to Geoffrey's own account, he followed his brother as far as Vézelay, and there won from him a remission of this vow.[5] It is certain that by April 1191 Richard had so far changed his mind again as to be desirous of Geoffrey's speedy consecration. The Pope's consent was still lacking; and the negotiations for obtaining this were undertaken by the person who, from Geoffrey's very birth, had been his most determined enemy—Queen Eleanor. When she went from Messina to Rome to plead his cause with Clement III. or his successor Celestine,[6] it is plain that natural feeling gave way to motives of policy. She could now see that an archbishop of York might become very useful in England, in holding the balance between Hugh of Durham and William of Ely. His canonical authority and personal influence might furnish, not indeed a counterpoise, but at least a check to the now unlimited powers of the legate. On the other hand, it was the long vacancy of York which more than anything else had tended to Hugh's exaltation. For ten years the bishop of Durham, with no metropolitan over him, had virtually been himself metropolitan of northern England. He strongly resented the filling of the vacant see, and had actually obtained from

---

[1] *Gesta Ric.* (Stubbs), p. 146.   Rog. Howden (Stubbs), vol. iii. p. 74.

[2] *Gesta Ric.* as above, pp. 88, 91, 99.   Rog. Howden as above, pp. 17, 18, 27.   Gir. Cambr. *Vita Galfr.*, l. i. c. 8 (Brewer, vol. iv. pp. 377, 378).

[3] *Gesta Ric.* as above, p. 100.   Cf. Gir. Cambr. as above (p. 379).

[4] Gir. Cambr. as above. *Gesta Ric.* as above, p. 106.   Ric. Devizes (Stevenson), p. 15.   [5] Gir. Cambr. as above, c. 11 (p. 382).

[6] Rog. Howden as above, p. 100.   The change in the Papacy must have occurred while she was there.

Clement III. a privilege of exemption from its jurisdiction.¹
If the archbishop of York could be reinstated in his proper
constitutional position, his own interests would lead him to
use it for those of the kingdom and the king.

Geoffrey's qualifications and disqualifications for such a
task may be very easily summed up. He had the Angevin
fearlessness, energy, persistence and thoroughness, with a fair
share of the versatile capabilities of the family ; he had all
their impetuosity, but very little of their wariness and tact.
Mingled with the Angevin fire, there seems to have run in
his veins the blood, and with it the spirit, of a totally different race. If we may credit on such a point the gossip of
his father's court, Geoffrey was through his mother a child
of the people—seemingly the English people—and of its
very lowest class.² This consideration has more interest at
a later stage of Geoffrey's career, when he stands forth as a
champion of constitutional liberty. Until then, there is, so
far as we can see, no evidence of any special sympathy
between him and the English people. Yet the plebeian and
probably English element in him existed, or was believed to
exist ; and if it did not become, as it easily might have done,
an important element in his political career, it was at any
rate not unlikely to have exercised some influence upon his
character.

Eleanor's mission to Rome succeeded. Geoffrey's election and his claim to the obedience of the bishop of Durham
were both confirmed by Pope Celestine ;³ he was consecrated

---

¹ *Gesta Ric.* (Stubbs), p. 146.

² W. Map, *De· Nugis Cur.*, dist. v. c. 6 (Wright, pp. 228-235). Walter is
the only writer who tells us anything about Geoffrey's mother ; as he does not
say she was a foreigner, it seems most probable that he looked upon her as an
Englishwoman. The name which he gives to her—" Ykenai " or " Hikenai "—
tells nothing either way, in itself. But Mr. Dimock (in his preface to the seventh
volume of Gerald's works, p. xxxvii) throws doubt upon Walter's whole account
of her except her name, and suggests that she may have belonged to a knightly
family of *Akeny* (*i.e.* Acquigny) in Normandy. This, however, is a question to
be investigated by a biographer of Geoffrey or a student of his later political
career rather than by an historian of the Angevin kings. The doubts which W.
Map tries to throw upon his connexion with them are probably affected, and clearly
unfounded. Few specimens of the Angevin race are more unmistakeable than
Geoffrey ; one might perhaps add, few more creditable.

³ *Gesta Ric.* as above, p. 209. See Celestine's letter (date, May 11) in

at Tours by Archbishop Bartholomew on August 18, and
received his pall on the same day.[1]   He at once put himself in
communication with John, to secure a protector on his return
to his see ;[2] for William of Longchamp, having had no notice
from Richard of the remission of Geoffrey's vow of absence,
refused to believe in it,[3] and had not only issued orders for
the archbishop's arrest as soon as he should land in England,[4]
but had agreed with the countess of Flanders that no Flemish
ship should be allowed to give him a passage.   The countess,
however, evaded her agreement by letting him sail from
Wissant in an English boat.[5]   He landed at Dover on Holy
Cross day,[6] having changed his clothes to avoid recognition.[7]
The constable of Dover, Matthew de Clères, was absent ; his
wife Richenda was a sister of William of Longchamp ; her
men-at-arms surrounded the archbishop the moment he
touched the shore, recognized him in spite of his disguise,
and strove to arrest him, but he managed to free himself
from their hands and make his way to the priory of S. Martin, just outside the town.   Here for five days Richenda's
followers vainly endeavoured to blockade and starve him
into surrender.[8]   On the fifth day a band of armed men
rushed into the priory-church, and in the chancellor's name
ordered Geoffrey to quit the country at once.   Geoffrey,
seated by the altar, clad in his pontifical robes and with his

Monasticon Angl., vol. vi. pt. iii. col. 1188, and Stubbs, *Rog. Howden*, vol. iii.
pref. p. lxvii, note 2.

[1] R. Diceto (Stubbs), vol. ii. p. 96.   Cf. *Gesta Ric.* (Stubbs), p. 209 ; Gir.
Cambr. *Vita Galfr.*, l. i. c. 13 (Brewer, vol. iv. p. 384).   Will. Newb., always
hostile to Geoffrey, declares that "ordine præpostero" he got his pallium before
he was consecrated ; l. iv. c. 17 (Howlett, vol. i. pp. 339, 340).

[2] Ric. Devizes (Stevenson), p. 34.

[3] His disbelief was evidently shared by Roger of Howden (Stubbs, vol. iii. p.
138); but Roger's authority, the treasurer, does not commit himself to any opinion
on the subject.   *Gesta Ric.* (Stubbs), p. 210.

[4] See the chancellor's writ—dated Preston, July 30—in R. Diceto as above, and
Gir. Cambr. as above, l. ii. c. 1 (p. 389); and cf. Ric. Devizes and *Gesta Ric.* as above.

[5] Gir. Cambr. as above (p. 388).   Cf. *Gesta Ric.* as above.   The countess—
Isabel of Portugal, second wife of Count Philip—was governing her husband's
territories during his absence on crusade, where he died.

[6] R. Diceto as above, p. 97.   Gerv. Cant. (Stubbs), vol. i. p. 504.

[7] *Gesta Ric.* as above.

[8] Gir. Cambr. as above (pp. 388-390).   Cf. R. Diceto and *Gesta Ric.* as above,
and Will. Newb., l. iv. c. 17 (Howlett, vol. i. p. 340).

archiepiscopal cross in his hand, set them and their chancellor at defiance.[1]   They dragged him out of the church by the hands and feet ; and as nothing would induce him to mount a horse which they brought for him, they dragged him on, still in the same array, still clinging to his cross and excommunicating them as they went, all through the town to the castle, where they flung him into prison.[2]

This outrage roused up all parties alike in Church and state.   England had had quite enough of persecuted and martyred archbishops.   Protests and remonstrances came pouring in upon the chancellor from the most opposite quarters :—from the treasurer and bishop of London, Richard Fitz-Nigel[3]—from the aged bishop of Norwich, John of Oxford,[4] and from the Canterbury chapter,[5] both of whom had had only too much experience, in different ways, of the disasters which might result from such violence to an archbishop.   The most venerated of living English prelates, S. Hugh of Lincoln, at once excommunicated Richenda, her husband and all her abettors, with lighted candles at Oxford.[6] John remonstrated most vehemently of all,[7] and his remonstrances procured Geoffrey's release,[8] but only on condition that he would go straight to London and there remain till the case between him and the chancellor could be tried by an assembly of bishops and barons.[9]   This of course satisfied nobody.   John had no mind to lose his opportunity of crushing his enemy once for all.   From Lancaster, where he was laying his plans with the help of Bishop Hugh of Coventry—a nephew of the old arch-plotter Arnulf of

[1] Gir. Cambr. *Vita Galfr.*, l. ii. c. 1 (Brewer, vol. iv. p. 391).

[2] *Ibid.* (pp. 391, 392).   Ric. Devizes (Stevenson), pp. 35, 36.   R. Diceto (Stubbs), vol. ii. p. 97.   *Gesta Ric.* (Stubbs), p. 111.   Gerv. Cant. (Stubbs), vol. i. p. 505.   Will. Newb., l. iv. c. 17 (Howlett, vol. i. p. 340).

[3] R. Diceto as above.   Gir. Cambr. as above, c. 2 (pp. 393, 394).

[4] Gir. Cambr. as above (p. 394).

[5] Gerv. Cant. as above, pp. 505, 506.

[6] Gir. Cambr. as above (p. 393).

[7] *Ibid.* (p. 394).   *Gesta Ric.* (Stubbs), p. 211.   Rog. Howden (Stubbs), vol. iii. p. 139.

[8] On September 26 ; R. Diceto (Stubbs), vol. ii. p. 97.   Cf. Gir. Cambr. as above, c. 4 (p. 395), Gerv. Cant. as above, p. 507, and Ric. Devizes (Stevenson), p. 36.   [9] Gir. Cambr. as above.

Lisieux—he hurried to Marlborough, and thence sent out summons to all the great men whom he thought likely to help him against the chancellor. He was not disappointed. The co-justiciars hastened up from the various shires where they were apparently busy with their judicial or financial visitations—William the Marshal from Gloucestershire, William Bruère from Oxfordshire, Geoffrey Fitz-Peter from Northamptonshire ; the bishops were represented by Godfrey of Winchester and Reginald of Bath, and the sovereign himself by Walter of Rouen ; S. Hugh of Lincoln joined the train as it passed through Oxford to Reading. From Reading John sent to call his half-brother to his side. Geoffrey, who was beginning to be looked upon and to look upon himself as something like another S. Thomas, had made a sort of triumphal progress from Dover to London ; tied by his parole, he was obliged to ask the chancellor's consent to his acceptance of John's invitation, and only gained it on condition of returning within a given time.[1]

The chancellor meanwhile was at Norwich ;[2] and thither John and the justiciars had already sent him a summons to appear before them and answer for his conduct towards both Geoffrey of York and Hugh of Durham, at an assembly to be held at the bridge over the Lodden, between Reading and Windsor, on Saturday October 5.[3] William retorted by a counter-summons to all who had joined the count of Mortain to forsake him as an usurper and return to their obedience• to the king's chosen representative.[4] He hurried, however, to Windsor in time for the proposed meeting ; but when the Saturday morning came, the earls of Arundel, Warren and Norfolk appeared at the trysting-place in his stead, pleading ill-health as an excuse for his absence.[5] As Saturday was accounted an unlucky day for contracts or

---

[1] Gir. Cambr. *Vita Galfr.*, l. ii. cc. 4, 5 (Brewer, vol. iv. pp. 395-397).

[2] *Ib.* cc. 2, 5 (pp. 393, 394, 397).

[3] *Ib.* c. 5 (p. 397). Ric. Devizes (Stevenson), p. 37, giving the date, which is confirmed by one of the summons—that addressed to the bishop of London—given by R. Diceto (Stubbs), vol. ii. p. 98. Cf. also *Gesta Ric.* (Stubbs), p. 212.

[4] Gir. Cambr. as above.

[5] *Ib.* c. 6 (p. 398). Cf. R. Diceto, Ric. Devizes and *Gesta Ric.* as above.

settlements of any kind,[1] no one regretted the delay ; John and the barons, sitting amid a ring of spectators in the meadows by the Lodden, spent the day in discussing all the complaints against the chancellor, and also, apparently, in looking through such of the Norman primate's bundle of royal letters as he chose to shew them, and deliberating which would be most appropriate to the present state of affairs. On one point all were agreed ; the chancellor must be put down at once.[2] Early next morning he tried to bribe John into reconciliation, but in vain.[3] At the high mass in Reading parish church the whole body of bishops lighted their candles and publicly excommunicated all who had been, whether by actual participation, command or consent, concerned in Archbishop Geoffrey's arrest ;[4] and at nightfall the chancellor was compelled to swear that, come what might, he would be ready to stand his trial at the bridge of Lodden on the morrow.[5]

Scarcely had he set out on the Monday morning when he was met by a report that his enemies were marching upon London.[6] The report was true in substance ; John and the barons, instead of waiting for him at the Lodden bridge, crossed it, and then divided their forces into two bodies ; the smaller, consisting of the bishops and barons with John himself, proceeded towards Windsor to meet the chancellor; the larger, comprising the men-at-arms and the servants in charge of the baggage, was sent on by the southern road to Staines.[7] Such a movement was quite enough to justify William in hurrying back to Windsor and thence on to London as fast as horses could carry him.[8] Before he could reach it he met

---

[1] R. Diceto (Stubbs), vol. ii. p. 98.
[2] Gir. Cambr. *Vita Galfr.*, l. ii. c. 6 (Brewer, vol. iv. pp. 398-401).
[3] *Ib.* c. 7 (p. 402).   [4] *Ibid.* R. Diceto as above.
[5] Gir. Cambr. as above.
[6] *Ibid.* c. 8 (pp. 402, 403). Ric. Devizes (Stevenson), p. 37. *Gesta Ric.* (Stubbs), p. 212.
[7] Cf. Gir. Cambr. as above (pp. 403, 404), and R. Diceto as above, p. 99. Ric. Devizes, as above, says plainly what the other writers leave us to guess, that these followers were meant to go on to London.
[8] Gir. Cambr. as above (p. 403). Ric. Devizes (Stevenson), p. 38. R. Diceto and *Gesta Ric.* as above. Cf. Will. Newb., l. iv. c. 17 (Howlett, vol. i. pp. 341, 342).

John's men-at-arms coming up by the other road from Staines; a skirmish took place, in which John's justiciar Roger de Planes was mortally wounded, but his followers seem to have had the best of the fight,[1] although they could not prevent the chancellor from making his way safe into London. Here he at once called a meeting of the citizens in the Guildhall, and endeavoured to secure their support against John.[2] He found, however, a strong party opposed to himself. On the last day of July [3]—three days after the second award between John and William at Winchester—the citizens of London had profited by the king's absence and his representative's humiliation to set up a *commune*. They knew very well that, as a contemporary writer says, neither King Henry nor King Richard would have sanctioned such a thing at any price ;[4] and they knew even better still that Richard's chancellor would never countenance it for a moment. With John they might have a chance, and they were not disposed to lose it by shutting their gates in his face at the bidding of William of Longchamp. William, seeing that his cause was lost in the city, shut himself up in the Tower.[5]

By this time John and his companions were at the gates; a short parley ended in their admittance.[6] Next morning barons and citizens came together in S. Paul's.[7] One after another the chancellor's victims, with the archbishop of York at their head, set forth their grievances.[8] Archbishop Walter of Rouen and William the Marshal then produced the king's letter of February 20, addressed to the Marshal, and accredit-

---

[1] R. Diceto (Stubbs), vol. ii. p. 99. *Gesta Ric.* (Stubbs), p. 212. Gir. Cambr. *Vita Galfr.*, l. ii. c. 8 (Brewer, vol. iv. p. 404).

[2] Gir. Cambr. as above. Cf. Ric. Devizes (Stevenson), p. 38.

[3] "Ipsâ die"—the day on which Philip of France set out homeward from Acre. Ric. Devizes, p. 53.

[4] *Ib.* pp. 53, 54. Yet Richard had once said that he would sell London altogether, if he could find anybody who would give him his price for it. *Ib.* p. 10, and Will. Newb., l. iv. c. 5 (Howlett, vol. i. p. 306).

[5] Ric. Devizes (Stevenson), p. 38. R. Diceto as above. *Gesta Ric.* as above, p. 212, 218. Will. Newb. as above, c. 17 (p. 342).

[6] Gir. Cambr. as above (p. 404).

[7] Ric. Devizes (Stevenson), p. 38, says "in ecclesiâ S. Pauli"; R. Diceto as above, "in capitulo"; the *Gesta Ric.* as above, p. 213, and Rog. Howden (Stubbs), vol. iii. p. 140, say "in atrio."

[8] Ric. Devizes as above. *Gesta Ric.* as above, pp. 213, 218.

ing Walter to him and his fellow-justiciars, and bidding them, in case of any failure of duty on the chancellor's part, follow Walter's direction in all things.[1] John and the barons agreed to act in accordance with these instructions ; they won the assent of the citizens by swearing to maintain the commune ;[2] the whole assembly then swore fealty to Richard, and to John as his destined successor.[3] According to one account they went a step further : they appointed John regent of the kingdom, and granted him the disposal of all the royal castles except three, which were to be left to the chancellor.[4] Upon the latter they now set out to enforce their decision at the sword's point. His forces were more than sufficient to defend the Tower ; they were in fact too numerous ; they had had no time to revictual the place, they were painfully overcrowded, and before twenty-four hours were over they found their position untenable.[5] On the Wednesday William tried to bribe John into abandoning the whole enterprise, and he very nearly succeeded ; Geoffrey of York and Hugh of Coventry, however, discovered what was going on, and remonstrated so loudly that John was obliged to drop the negotiation and continue the siege.[6] In the afternoon, at the chancellor's own request, four bishops and four earls went to speak with him in the Tower.[7] Five days of intense excitement had so exhausted his feeble frame that when they told him what had passed at the meeting on the previous day, he dropped senseless at their feet, and when brought to himself could at first do nothing but implore their sympathy and mediation.[8] The brutal insolence of Hugh of Coventry,[9] however, seems

---

[1] *Gesta Ric.* (Stubbs), pp. 213, 218.

[2] *Ib.* p. 213. R. Diceto (Stubbs), vol. ii. p. 99.

[3] *Gesta Ric.* as above, p. 214.   [4] Ric. Devizes (Stevenson), pp. 37, 38.

[5] Will. Newb., l. iv. c. 17 (Howlett, vol. i. p. 342).

[6] Gir. Cambr. *Vita Galfr.*, l. ii. c. 9 (Brewer, vol. iv. p. 406).

[7] Gerald (*ib.* p. 405), says "quartâ vero¦feriâ." Ric. Devizes (Stevenson), p. 39, says " Dies ille nefastus declinabat ad vesperam," which, taken in connexion with what precedes, ought to mean Tuesday evening ; but he seems to have lost count of the days just here. It is he alone who mentions the earls ; while it is Gerald alone who gives the names of the bishops—London, Lincoln, Winchester and Coventry.

[8] Cf. Ric. Devizes as above, and Gir. Cambr. as above, who tries to colour this scene differently.   [9] Gir. Cambr. as above (pp. 405, 406).

to have stung him into his wonted boldness again. With flashing eyes he told them that the day of reckoning was yet to come, when they and their new lord would have to account for their treason with Richard himself ; and he sent them away with a positive refusal to surrender either his castles or his seal.[1]   Late at night, however, as he lay vainly endeavouring to gain a little rest, his friends came and implored him to abandon the useless struggle with fate; and at last his brother Osbert and some others wrung from him an unwilling permission to go and offer themselves as hostages for his submission on the morrow.[2]

On the Thursday morning the barons assembled in the fields east of the Tower,[3] and there William of Longchamp went forth to meet them.   The instant he appeared Hugh of Coventry stepped forward, recited the whole indictment against him, and pronounced with brutal bluntness the sentence of the assembly.[4]   William was to be deposed from all secular authority, to keep nothing but his bishopric and the castles of Dover, Cambridge and Hereford; he must give hostages for his future good behaviour ; then let him begone wherever he would.   The assembly broke into a chorus of approval which seemed intended to give William no chance of reply ; but his dauntless spirit had by this time regained its mastery over his physical weakness ; he stood quietly till they had all talked themselves out, and then they had to listen in their turn.   He denied every one of the charges against him ; he refused to recognize either the moral justice or the legal validity of his deposition; he agreed to surrender the castles, because he no longer had power to hold them, but he still lifted up his protest, as King Richard's lawful chancellor and justiciar, against all the proceedings and the very existence of the new ministry.[5]   Walter of Rouen was

    [1] Ric. Devizes (Stevenson), p. 39.

    [2] *Ib.* p. 40.   Gir. Cambr. *Vita Galfr.*, l. ii. c. 9 (Brewer, vol. iv. p. 406).

    [3] Ric. Devizes (as above).   Gir. Cambr. as above.   R. Diceto (Stubbs), vol. ii. p. 100.   [4] Ric. Devizes as above.

    [5] *Ib.* pp. 40-42.   Cf. Gir. Cambr. and R. Diceto as above ; *Gesta Ric.* (Stubbs), p. 214 ; and Will. Newb., l. iv. c. 17 (Howlett, vol. i. p. 341).

at once proclaimed ·justiciar in his stead.[1]   The keys of the
Tower and of Windsor castle, and the hostages, were delivered
up next morning, and William was then allowed to withdraw
to Bermondsey, whence on the following day he proceeded to
Dover.[2]   Thence, apparently in a desperate hope that his
men might yet be able to hold the castles till he could gather
means to relieve them, he twice attempted to escape over sea,
first in the disguise of a monk, then in that of a pedlar-
woman.   His lameness, however, and his ignorance of
English were fatal to his chances of flight ; he was detected,
dragged back into the town, and shut up in prison till all the
castles were surrendered.   Then he was set at liberty, and
sailed for Gaul on October 29.[3]

His opponents, however, were not rid of him yet.   The
king was now practically out of reach of his remonstrances
and appeals for succour ;[4] but the Pope was not.   William
was a bishop ; and the harshness with which he had been
treated enabled him now to pose in his turn as a consecrated
victim of profane violence.   Celestine III. warmly took up
his cause ; he distinctly acknowledged him as legate, whether
with or without a formal renewal of his commission ;[5] and
on December 2 he issued a brief addressed to the English bishops, bidding them excommunicate all who had
taken part in William's deposition, and put their lands under
interdict till he should be reinstated.[6]   William, as legate,
followed this up by excommunicating twenty-six of his chief
enemies by name, with the archbishop of Rouen at their head,
and, with the Pope's sanction, threatening to treat John in
like manner, if he did not amend before Quinquagesima.[7]

---

[1] *Gesta Ric.* (Stubbs), p. 213. Will. Newb., l. iv. c. 18 (Howlett, vol. i. p. 344).

[2] R. Diceto (Stubbs), vol. ii. p. 100.   Gir. Cambr. *Vita Galfr.*, l. ii. c. 9
(Brewer, vol. iv. p. 407).   Ric. Devizes (Stevenson), p. 42.

[3] Ric. Devizes as above.   R. Diceto as above, pp. 100, 101. Gir. Cambr.
as above, cc. 12, 13 (pp. 410-413).   *Gesta Ric.* (Stubbs), pp. 219, 220.   Will.
Newb. as above, c. 17 (p. 343).   The date comes from R. Diceto.

[4] He had written to complain of John's insubordination, but Richard did not
get the letter till six months after the writer's fall.   *Itin. Reg. Ric.* (Stubbs),
p. 333.   [5] See *Epp. Cant.* (Stubbs), introd. p. lxxxiii, note 1.

[6] Letter of Celestine III. in *Gesta Ric.* (Stubbs), pp. 221, 222.

[7] Letter of William "bishop of Ely, legate and chancellor," *ib.* pp. 222-
224 ; and Rog. Howden (Stubbs), vol. iii. pp. 152-154.

The bishops, however, took no notice of his letters, and the justiciars retorted by sequestrating his see ;[1] they all held him bound by the sentences pronounced against him at Reading and at London for his persecution of Geoffrey of York, and their view was upheld by the suffragans of Rouen, who all treated him as excommunicate.[2]   Geoffrey was now the highest ecclesiastical authority in England ; but he was not the man to rule the English Church.   He had more than enough to do in ruling his own chief suffragan.   As soon as he was enthroned at York,[3] he summoned Hugh of Durham to come and make his profession of obedience ; Hugh, who having been reinstated in his earldom of Northumberland[4] felt himself again more than a match for his metropolitan, ignored the summons, whereupon Geoffrey excommunicated him.[5]   This did not deter John from keeping Christmas at Howden with the bishop ; in consequence of which John himself was for a while treated as excommunicate by his half-brother.[6]   The momentary coalition, formed solely to crush the chancellor, had in fact already split into fragments.   The general administration, however, went on satisfactorily under the new justiciar's direction, and his influence alone—for Eleanor was still on the continent[7] —sufficed to keep John out of mischief throughout the winter.

Richard's continental dominions had thus far been at peace—a peace doubly secured by the presence of Eleanor and the absence of Philip of France.   Shortly before Christmas 1191, however, Philip returned to his kingdom.[8]   In January 1192 he called the seneschal and barons of Normandy to a conference, and demanded from them, on the strength of a document which he shewed to them as the

---

[1] *Gesta Ric.* (Stubbs), p. 225.

[2] *Ib.* p. 221.   Cf. Ric. Devizes (Stevenson), p. 43.

[3] On All Saints' day [1191]. Gir. Cambr. *Vita Galfr.*, l. ii. c. 11 (Brewer, vol. iv. p. 410).	[4] Ric. Devizes (Stevenson), p. 39.

[5] *Gesta Ric.* (Stubbs), p. 225. Rog. Howden (Stubbs), vol. iii. pp. 168, 169. See the excellent summary of this affair in Will. Newb., l. iv. c. 27 (Howlett, vol. i. pp. 371, 372).	[6] *Gesta Ric.* (Stubbs), pp. 235, 236.

[7] She kept Christmas at Bonneville.   *Ib.* p. 235.   Rog. Howden as above, p. 179.

[8] Will. Armor. *Gesta Phil. Aug.* (Duchesne, *Hist. Franc. Scriptt.*, vol. v.), p. 76.

treaty made between himself and Richard at Messina, the restitution of his sister Adela and her dower-castles in the Vexin, as well as the counties of Eu and Aumale. The seneschal, rightly suspecting the paper to be a forgery, answered that he had no instructions from Richard on the subject, and would give up neither the lands nor the lady.[1] Philip threatened war, and all Richard's constables prepared for defence.[2] Meanwhile, Philip offered to John the investiture of all Richard's continental dominions, if he would accept Adela's hand with them.[3] That John had a wife already was an obstacle which troubled neither the French king nor John himself.   He was quite ready to accept the offer ; but meanwhile it reached his mother's ears, and she hurried to England to stop him.[4] Landing at Portsmouth on Quinquagesima Sunday,[5] she found him on the point of embarking ; the archbishop of Rouen and the other justiciars gladly welcomed her back to her former post of regent, and joined with her in forbidding John to leave the country, under penalty of having all his estates seized in the king's name.[6] They then held a series of councils, at Windsor, Oxford, London and Winchester ;[7] in that of London the barons renewed their oath of fealty to the king, but to pacify John they were obliged to do the like to him as heir,[8] and the immediate consequence was that he persuaded the constables of Windsor and Wallingford to surrender their castles into his hands.[9] William of Longchamp thought his opportunity

[1] *Gesta Ric.* (Stubbs), p. 236. Cf. Ric. Devizes (Stevenson), p. 56. It is certain that Philip told and acted a downright lie ; for the treaty of Messina is extant, and its main provisions are these : Richard shall be bound to surrender Adela only within one month after his own return to Gaul, and the whole Norman Vexin, including its castles, shall remain to him and his heirs male for ever. Only in case of his death without male heir is it to revert to the French Crown ; and as for Aumale and Eu, there is not a word about them. Rymer, *Fœdera*, vol. i. p. 54.   [2] *Gesta Ric.* as above. Ric. Devizes (Stevenson), p. 55.
[3] *Gesta Ric.* as above.   [4] *Ibid.* Ric. Devizes (Stevenson), p. 57.
[5] Ric. Devizes (Stevenson), p. 55.   This was February 11 [1192].
[6] *Gesta Ric.* as above, p. 237.
[7] Ric. Devizes (Stevenson), p. 57.
[8] *Gesta Ric.* as above. Rog. Howden (Stubbs), vol. iii. p. 187.
[9] Ric. Devizes as above. In Rog. Howden (as above), p. 204, the betrayal of these castles is placed a year later. Roger's account of the first few months of 1193 has, however, somewhat the look of a repetition of the history of 1192, and

had come.   He managed to gain Eleanor's ear and to bribe John ;[1] both connived at his return to Dover, and thence he sent up his demand for restoration to a council gathered in London towards the close of Lent.[2]   It seems plain that he had won the favour of the queen ; for the justiciars, whose original purpose in meeting had been to discuss the misdoings of John, now saw themselves obliged to fetch John himself from Wallingford to support them, as they expected, in their resistance to the chancellor's demands.   To their dismay John told them plainly that he was on the point of making alliance with his old enemy for a consideration of seven hundred pounds.[3]   They saw that their only chance was to outbid William.   They gave John two thousand marks out of the royal treasury ;[4] Walter of Rouen helped to persuade the queen-mother,[5] and the chancellor was bidden to depart out of the land.[6]

Shortly afterwards, two cardinal-legates arrived in France to settle his dispute with the archbishop of Rouen.   When they attempted to enter Normandy, the seneschal refused them admittance and shut the gates of Gisors in their faces, pleading that the subjects of an English king were forbidden by ancient custom to admit legates into any part of his dominions without his consent.   The legates on this excommunicated the seneschal and laid all Normandy under interdict.[7]   William had done the same to his own diocese before

his story is much less consistent and circumstantial than Richard's, which I have therefore ventured to follow.

[1] *Gesta Ric.* (Stubbs), p. 239.   Rog. Howden (Stubbs), vol. iii. p. 188.   Cf. Gir. Cambr. *Vita Galfr.*, l. ii. c. 14 (Brewer, vol. iv. p. 413) ; Ric. Devizes (Stevenson), p. 56 ; and Gerv. Cant. (Stubbs), vol. i. p. 512.

[2] Gir. Cambr., as above, says he landed about April 1, *i.e.* the Wednesday before Easter.   But the other writers seem to place this council soon after Mid-Lent.   Gerv. Cant., as above, says the chancellor came " mediante mense Martio."

[3] Ric. Devizes (Stevenson), pp. 58, 59.

[4] " 2000 marks, £500 of which were to be raised from the chancellor's estates" is Bishop Stubbs's interpretation (*Rog. Howden*, vol. iii. pref. p. xc.) of *Gesta Ric.*, p. 239, and Ric. Devizes (Stevenson), p. 59.

[5] *Gesta Ric.* as above.

[6] *Ibid.*   Ric. Devizes as above.   Gir. Cambr. as above (p. 415).   Cf. Will. Newb., l. iv. c. 18 (Howlett, vol. i. pp. 345, 346).   According to the first authority, William sailed again on Maunday Thursday, April 2.

[7] *Gesta Ric.* (Stubbs), pp. 246, 247.   Ric. Devizes (Stevenson), pp. 43, 44.

leaving England.[1] Archbishop Walter, the English justiciars,
even the queen-mother, were all at their wits' end : Philip
was openly threatening to invade the Norman duchy ; the
obstacle which had prevented him until now—the unwillingness of the French barons to attack the territories of a
crusader[2]—would be considerably lessened by the interdict;
the only person who could be found in England capable of
undertaking a negotiation with the legates was Hugh of
Durham ; but Hugh declined to go till his own quarrel with
his metropolitan was settled,[3] and this was not accomplished
till the middle of October.[4] Then indeed he went to France,
and succeeded in obtaining the removal of the interdict.[5]
But in other quarters the prospect grew no brighter. Aquitaine, held in check for a while by the presence of its
duchess, had risen as soon as she was out of reach. Count
Ademar of Angoulême marched into Poitou with a large
body of horse and foot ; taken prisoner by the Poitevins, he
appealed to the French king for deliverance.[6] A revolt of
the Gascon barons was with difficulty suppressed by the
seneschal, assisted by young Sancho of Navarre,[7] brother of
Richard's queen ; and the victors rashly followed up their
success by a raid upon Toulouse, which, though it went
unpunished for the moment, could only lead to further mischief.[8] In England John was still defying the justiciars ;
and they dared not proceed to extremities with him, for
they now saw before them an imminent prospect of having
to acknowledge him as their king.

Richard's adventures in the East lie outside the sphere
of English history. The crusade of which he was the chief
hero and leader had indirectly an important effect upon
English social life ; but it was in no sense a national under-

[1] Gir. Cambr. *Vita Galfr.*, l. ii. c. 15 (Brewer, vol. iv. p. 414). Ric. Devizes
(Stevenson), pp. 42, 43, puts this in the previous October.

[2] *Gesta Ric.* (Stubbs), p. 236.   Rog. Howden (Stubbs), vol. iii. p. 187.

[3] *Gesta Ric.* (Stubbs), p. 247.

[4] Gerv. Cant. (Stubbs), vol. i. p. 513.   Rog. Howden as above, pp. 170
note, 172.   [5] *Gesta Ric.* as above, p. 250.

[6] Chron. S. Albin, a. 1192 (Marchegay, *Églises*, p. 50). The sequel of this
story, however, clearly belongs to the following year ; so it may be that the whole
of it is antedated.   [7] Rog. Howden as above, p. 194.

[8] *Ibid.* Cf. Ric. Devizes (Stevenson), p. 55.

taking ; every man in the host was, like the king himself,
simply a volunteer, not sent out by his country or representing it in any way.   Richard's glory is all his own ; to us,
the practical interest of the crusade in which he won it consists in the light which it throws upon his character, and on
his political relations with the other princes who took part
in the enterprise.   The story, as it comes out bit by bit,
oddly intermingled with the dry details of home affairs, in
the English historians of the time, and as it is told at full
length in the "Itinerary" composed by one of his fellow-
crusaders, reads more like an old wiking-saga than a piece of
sober history, and its hero looks more like a comrade of S. Olaf
or Harald Hardrada than a contemporary of Philip Augustus.
Nothing indeed except Richard's northman-blood can account
for the intense love of the sea, and the consummate seamanship,
as sound and practical as it was brilliant and daring, which he
displayed on his outward voyage.   No sea-king of old ever
guided his little squadron of "long keels" more boldly, more
skilfully and more successfully through a more overwhelming
succession of difficulties and perils than those through which
Richard guided his large and splendid fleet on its way from
Messina to Acre.[1]   Not one had ever made a conquest at
once as rapid, as valuable and as complete as the conquest
of Cyprus, which Richard made in a few days, as a mere
episode in his voyage, in vengeance for the ill-treatment
which some of his ship-wrecked sailors had met with at the
hands of the Cypriots and their king.[2]   But it was a mere
wiking-conquest ; Richard never dreamed of permanently
adding this remote island to the list of his dominions ;
within a few months he sold it to the Templars,[3] and afterwards, as they failed to take possession, he made it over to
the dethroned king of Jerusalem who had helped him to
conquer it, Guy of Lusignan.[4]   The same love of adventure

---

[1] See the details of the voyage in *Itin. Reg. Ric.* (Stubbs), pp. 177-209 ; *Gesta Ric.* (Stubbs), pp. 162-169 ; Rog. Howden (Stubbs), vol. iii. pp. 105-112.

[2] *Itin. Reg. Ric.* (Stubbs), pp. 188-204.   *Gesta Ric.* (Stubbs), pp. 163-168. Rog. Howden as above, pp. 105-112.   Ric. Devizes (Stevenson), pp. 47-49. Will. Newb., l. iv. c. 20 (Howlett, vol. i. pp. 350, 351).

[3] Rigord (Duchesne, *Hist. Franc. Scriptt.*, vol. v.), p. 35.

[4] *Ibid.   Itin. Reg. Ric.* (Stubbs), p. 351.   R. Coggeshall (Stevenson), p. 36.

for its own sake colours many of his exploits in the Holy Land itself. But there we learn, too, that his character had yet another and a higher aspect. We find in him, side by side with the reckless northern valour, the northern endurance, patience and self-restraint, coupled with a real disinterestedness and a self-sacrificing generosity for which it would be somewhat hard to find a parallel among his forefathers on either side.[1] Alike in a military, a political and a moral point of view, Richard is the only one among the leaders of the crusading host, except Guy, who comes out of the ordeal with a character not merely unstained, but shining with redoubled lustre. And this alone would almost account for the fact that, before they separated, nearly every one of them, save Guy, had become Richard's open or secret foe.

Envy of a better man than themselves was however not the sole cause of their hostility. The office of commander-in-chief of the host fell to Richard's share in consequence of a catastrophe which altered the whole balance of political parties in Europe. That office had been destined for the Emperor Frederic Barbarossa, who for more than thirty years had stood as high above all other Christian princes in political capacity, military prowess, and personal nobility of character, as in titular dignity and territorial power. Frederic set out for Palestine as early as May 1189;[2] he fought his way through the treacheries of the Greek Emperor and the ambushes of the Turkish sultan of Iconium, only to be drowned in crossing a little river in Asia Minor on June 10, 1190.[3] These tidings probably met Richard on his arrival at Messina in September. There he had to deal with the consequences of another death which had occurred in the previous November, that of his brother-in-law King William of Sicily.[4] William was childless; after a vain attempt to

---

[1] It is impossible to give illustrations here; the whole *Itinerarium*, from his arrival at Acre (p. 211) onwards, is in fact one long illustration.

[2] Ansbert (Dobrowsky), p. 21. Most of the English writers give a wrong date.

[3] See the story of Frederic's expedition and death in Ansbert (Dobrowsky), p. 21 *et seq.; Itin. Reg. Ric.* (Stubbs), pp. 43-55; *Gesta Ric.* (Stubbs), pp. 56, 61, 62, 88, 89; Rog. Howden (Stubbs), vol. ii. p. 358; Monach. Florent., vv. 245-330 (*ib.* vol. iii. app. to pref. pp. cxiv.-cxvii.).

[4] *Gesta Ric.* (Stubbs), pp. 101, 102.

induce his father-in-law Henry II. to accept the reversion of his crown,[1] he had bequeathed it to his own young aunt Constance, who was married to Henry of Germany, the Emperor's eldest son.[2]   It was, however, seized by Tancred, a cousin of the late king.[3]   Richard's alliance with Tancred, though on the one hand absolutely necessary to secure the co-operation of Sicily for the crusade, was thus on the other a mortal offence to the new king of Germany, who moreover had already a grudge against England upon another ground : —Henry the Lion had in this very summer extorted from him almost at the sword's point his restoration to his forfeited estates.[4]   Thus when Richard at last reached Acre in June 1191,[5] he was already in ill odour with the leaders of the German contingent, the Emperor's brother Duke Frederic of Suabia and his cousin Duke Leopold of Austria.

This, however, was not all.   Isaac, the tyrant of Cyprus, whom Richard had brought with him as a captive, was also connected with the Suabian and Austrian houses ;[6] his capture was another ground of offence.   Next, when the siege of Acre, which the united forces of eastern and western Christendom had been pressing in vain for nearly two years, came to an end a month after Richard joined it,[7] Richard and Leopold quarrelled over their shares in the honour of the victory ; Leopold—so the story goes—set up his banner on the wall of the conquered town side by side with that of the English king, and Richard tore it down again.[8]   Besides all this, as Richard's superior military capacity made him an object of perpetual jealousy to the

---

[1] "Vidimus, et præsentes fuimus, ubi regnum Palæstinæ, regnum etiam Italiæ patri vestro aut uni filiorum suorum, quem ad hoc eligeret, ab utriusque regni magnatibus et populis est oblatum." Pet. Blois, Ep. cxiii. (Giles, vol. i. p. 350— to Geoffrey of York).   Bishop Stubbs (*Rog. Howden*, vol. ii. pref. p. xciii.) interprets "regnum Italiæ" as representing Sicily.

[2] *Gesta Ric.* (Stubbs), pp. 102, 202.   Rog. Howden (Stubbs), vol. iii. pp. 29, 164 and note.   [3] *Gesta Ric.* (Stubbs), p. 102.

[4] See *ibid.* p. 145 and note.   [5] *Ib.* p. 169.

[6] R. Coggeshall (Stevenson), p. 59.   Ansbert (Dobrowsky), p. 114.

[7] On July 12, 1191.   *Itin. Reg. Ric.* (Stubbs), pp. 232, 233.   *Gesta Ric.* (Stubbs), p. 178, etc.

[8] See the different versions of this story in Otto of S. Blaise, c. 36 (Wurstisen, *Germ. Hist. Illustr.*, vol. i. p. 216) ; Gerv. Cant. (Stubbs), vol. i. p. 514 ; R.

other princes, so his policy in Holy Land was in direct opposition to theirs. Since the death of Queen Sibyl in October 1189,[1] they had one and all aimed at transferring the crown from her childless widower Guy of Lusignan to the lord of Tyre, Conrad, marquis of Montferrat. Montferrat was an important fief of the kingdom of Italy; Conrad's mother was aunt both to Leopold of Austria and to Frederic Barbarossa;[2] he thus had the whole Austrian and imperial influence at his back; and that of Philip of France was thrown into the same scale, simply because Richard had espoused the opposite cause. Guy of Lusignan, with a fearlessness which speaks volumes in his favour as well as in Richard's, had thrown himself unreservedly on the generosity and justice of the prince against whom all his race had for so many years been struggling in Aquitaine; his confidence was met as it deserved, and from the hour of their meeting in Cyprus to the break-up of the crusade, Richard and Guy stood firmly side by side. But they stood alone amid the ring of selfish politicians who supported Conrad, and whose intrigues brought ruin upon the expedition. Philip, indeed, went home as soon as Acre was won, to sow the seeds of mischief in a field where they were likely to bring forth a more profitable harvest for his interests than on the barren soil of Palestine. But the whole body of French crusaders whom he left behind him, except Count Henry of Cham-

Coggeshall (Stevenson), p. 59; Ric. Devizes (Stevenson), p. 52; Rigord (Duchesne, *Hist. Franc. Scriptt.*, vol. v.), p. 35; and Mat. Paris, *Chron. Maj.* (Luard), vol. ii. p. 384.   [1] *Epp. Cant.* cccxlvi. (Stubbs, p. 329).

[2] Frederic's father and Leopold's father were half-brothers, sons of the two marriages of Agnes of Franconia, daughter of the Emperor Henry IV. Conrad's mother, Judith, was a child of Agnes's second marriage with Leopold, marquis of Austria. Conrad's father was the Marquis William of Montferrat who had been one of Henry II.'s allies in his struggle with the Pope (see above, p. 60); and his elder brother had been the first husband of Queen Sibyl. On his own iniquitous marriage, if marriage it is to be called, with her half-sister and heiress, Isabel—an affair which seems to have actually broken the heart of Archbishop Baldwin of Canterbury—see *Itin. Reg. Ric.* (Stubbs), pp. 119-124; *Expugn. Terræ Sanctæ* (Stevenson, *R. Coggeshall*), p. 256; *Gesta Ric.* (Stubbs), p. 141; Rog. Howden (Stubbs), vol. iii. pp. 70, 71. Conrad's antecedents are told by Rog. Howden (Stubbs), vol. ii. pp. 320, 321. Considering, however, the case of Guy of Lusignan, it is perhaps hardly safe to admit a charge of homicide against any claimant to the throne of Palestine on Roger's sole authority.

pagne, made common cause with the Germans and the partizans of Conrad in thwarting every scheme that Richard proposed, either for the settlement of the Frank kingdom in Palestine or for the reconquest of its capital. Twice he led the host within eight miles of Jerusalem, and twice, when thus close to the goal, he was compelled to turn away.[1] Conrad fell by the hand of an assassin in April 1192 ;[2] but Guy's cause, like that of Jerusalem itself, was lost beyond recovery ; all that Richard could do for either was to compensate Guy with the gift of Cyprus,[3] and sanction the transfer of the shadowy crown of Jerusalem to his own nephew, Henry of Champagne.[4] Harassed by evil tidings from England and forebodings of mischief in Gaul, disappointed in his most cherished hopes and worn out with fruitless labour, sick in body and more sick at heart, he saw that his only chance of ever again striking a successful blow either for east or west was to go home at once. After one last brilliant exploit, the rescue of Joppa from the Turks who had seized it in his absence,[5] on September 2 he made a truce with Saladin for three years ;[6] on October 9 he sailed from Acre.[7]

Stormy winds had again parted the king's ship from the rest of his fleet when, within three days' sail of Marseille, he learned that Count Raymond of Toulouse was preparing to

[1] *Itin. Reg. Ric.* (Stubbs), pp. 285-312, 365-396 ; Rog. Howden (Stubbs), vol. iii. pp. 174, 175, 179 ; R. Coggeshall (Stevenson), pp. 37-40. See also the characteristic and pathetic account of Richard's distress at the last turning-back, in Ric. Devizes (Stevenson), pp. 75-77.

[2] *Itin. Reg. Ric.* (Stubbs), pp. 339, 340. R. Diceto (Stubbs), vol. ii. p. 104. R. Coggeshall (Stevenson), p. 35. Rog. Howden (as above), p. 181. Will. Newb., l. iv. c. 24 (Howlett, vol. i. p. 363).

[3] Rigord (Duchesne, *Hist. Franc. Scriptt.*, vol. v.), p. 35, makes it a sale ; but it is hard to conceive where poor Guy could have found money for the purchase.

[4] *Itin. Reg. Ric.* (Stubbs), pp. 342, 346, 347. R. Diceto and Rog. Howden as above. R. Coggeshall (Stevenson), pp. 35, 36. Will. Newb. as above, c. 28 (p. 374). Henry of Champagne was son of Count Henry "the Liberal" and Mary, daughter of Louis VII. and Eleanor.

[5] *Itin. Reg. Ric.* (Stubbs), pp. 403-424. R. Coggeshall (Stevenson), pp. 41-51. This is really the most splendid of all Richard's wiking exploits.

[6] *Itin. Reg. Ric.* (Stubbs), p. 249. R. Coggeshall (Stevenson), p. 52. Rog. Howden (as above), p. 184.

[7] *Itin. Reg. Ric.* (Stubbs), pp. 441, 442. R. Diceto (as above), p. 106. Rog. Howden (as above), p. 185, makes it a day earlier.

seize him on his landing,[1] no doubt in vengeance for the attack made upon Toulouse a few months before by the seneschal of Gascony. Capture by Raymond meant betrayal to Philip of France, and Richard knew Philip far too well to run any needless risk of falling into his hands. Under more favourable conditions, he might have escaped by sailing on through the strait of Gibraltar direct to his island realm ; but contrary winds made this impossible, and drove him back upon Corfu, where he landed about Martinmas.[2] Thence, in his impatience, he set off in disguise with only twenty followers[3] on board a little pirate-vessel[4] in which, at imminent risk of discovery, he coasted up the Adriatic till another storm wrecked him at the head of the Gulf of Aquileia.[5] By this time his German enemies were all on the look-out for him, and whatever his plans on leaving Corfu may have been, he had now no resource but to hurry through the imperial dominions as rapidly and secretly as possible. His geographical knowledge, however, seems to have been at fault, for he presently found himself at Vienna, whither Leopold of Austria had long since returned. In spite of his efforts to disguise himself, Richard was recognized, captured and brought before the duke ;[6] and three

---

[1] R. Coggeshall (Stevenson), p. 53.

[2] R. Diceto (Stubbs), vol. ii. p. 106. *Itin. Reg. Ric.* (Stubbs), p. 442. Rog. Howden (Stubbs), vol. iii. p. 185. R. Coggeshall as above.· The two first supply the dates.

[3] Rog. Howden as above. The *Itin. Reg. Ric.* (as above) says four, but there were at least nine with him after his landing. See Rog. Howden (as above), p. 195.

[4] *Itin. Reg. Ric.* as above. R. Coggeshall (Stevenson), pp. 53-54, gives some details highly characteristic of Richard. The pirates began by attacking the king's ship, whereupon he, "for their praiseworthy fortitude and boldness," made friends with them, and took his passage in their company. This is authentic, for the writer had it from one of Richard's companions, the chaplain Anselm. *Ib.* p. 54.

[5] This is the Emperor's account, given in a letter to Philip of France ; Rog. Howden (as above), p. 195. Cf. Ansbert (Dobrowsky), p. 114 ; Will. Newb., l. iv. c. 31 (Howlett, vol. i. p. 383) ; *Itin. Reg. Ric.* (Stubbs), p. 42 ; R. Diceto as above ; R. Coggeshall (Stevenson), p. 54 ; and Rog. Howden (as above), p. 185 and note 7.

[6] He was captured December 20, 1192; *Itin. Reg. Ric.* (Stubbs), p. 443 ; R. Diceto (as above), p. 107. R. Coggeshall (Stevenson), p. 56, makes it a day later. Otto of S. Blaise, c. 38 (Wurstisen, *Germ. Hist. Illustr.*, vol. i. p. 217), gives the most detailed account of the capture—an account which looks too char-

days after Christmas the Emperor sent to Philip of France the welcome tidings that their common enemy was a prisoner in Leopold's hands.[1]

Philip at once forwarded the news to John, with a renewal of the proposal which he had made to him a year before. John hurried over sea and formally did homage to the French king for all his brother's continental dominions ; but the seneschal and barons of Normandy refused to acknowledge the transaction, and he hastened back again to try his luck in England.[2] There he met with no better success. He called the justiciars to a council in London, assured them that the king was dead, and demanded their homage ; they refused it ; he withdrew in a rage to fortify his castles, and the justiciars prepared to attack them.[3] Before Easter a French fleet sailed to his assistance, but was repulsed by the English militia assembled at the summons of Archbishop Walter.[4] While the justiciars laid siege to Windsor, Geoffrey of York fortified Doncaster for the king, and thence went to help his gallant old suffragan and rival, Hugh of Durham, who was busy with the siege of Tickhill.[5] The castles had all but fallen, and John was on the eve of submission, when the victorious justiciars suddenly grew alarmed at their own success. Richard's fate was still so uncertain that they dared

acteristic not to be true. According to him, Richard stopped to dine at a little inn just outside Vienna, and to avoid recognition, set to work to broil some meat for himself. He was holding the spit with his own hands, utterly forgetful that one of them was adorned with a magnificent ring, when a servant of the duke chanced to look in, noticed the incongruity, then recognized the king whom he had seen in Palestine, and hurried off to report his discovery ; whereupon the duke came in person and seized his enemy on the spot, in the middle of his cooking. The story of R. Coggeshall (Stevenson), pp. 55, 56, is somewhat more dignified. Cf. also Will. Newb., l. iv. c. 31 (Howlett, vol. i. p. 383) ; Rog. Howden (Stubbs), vol. iii. pp. 186, 195 ; and Ansbert (Dobrowsky), p. 114.

[1] The letter is in Rog. Howden (as above), pp. 195, 196. "Gratissimum illi super aurum et topazion . . . nuntium destinavit," says Will. Newb. as above, c. 32 (p. 384).

[2] Rog. Howden (as above), p. 204. Cf. R. Diceto (Stubbs), vol. ii. p. 106. John's treaty with Philip is in Rymer, *Fœdera*, vol. i. p. 57 ; date, February 1193.

[3] Rog. Howden (as above), pp. 204, 205. Cf. Will. Newb. as above, c. 34 (p. 390).

[4] Rog. Howden (as above), p. 205. Gerv. Cant. (Stubbs), vol. i. pp. 514, 515.

[5] Rog. Howden (as above), pp. 206, 208.

not humiliate his heir ; and at Eleanor's instigation they made a truce with John, to last until All-Saints' day.[1]

The six months of tranquillity thus gained were spent in negotiations for the king's release. As soon as the justiciars heard of his capture they had despatched Bishop Savaric of Bath to treat with the Emperor, and the abbots of Boxley and Robertsbridge to open communications, if possible, with Richard himself ;[2] this however was a difficult matter, for of the place of his confinement nothing was known except that it was somewhere in the Austrian dominions, and these were to most Englishmen of that day a wholly undiscovered country. How the captive was first found history does not say. Tradition filled the blank with the beautiful story of the minstrel Blondel, wandering through Europe till he reached a castle where there was said to be a prisoner whose name no one could tell—winning the favour of its lord and thus gaining admittance within its walls—peering about it on every side in a vain effort to catch a glimpse of the mysterious captive, till at last a well-known voice, singing " a song which they two had made between them, and which no one knew save they alone," fell upon his delighted ear through the narrow prison-window whence Richard had seen and recognized the face of his friend.[3] It may after all have been Blondel who guided the two abbots to the spot ; we only know that they met Richard at Ochsenfurt on his way to be delivered up on Palm Sunday to the Emperor Henry at Speyer.[4] Thenceforth the negotiations proceeded without intermission ; but it took nearly a year to complete them. Personal jealousy, family interest, and pride at finding himself actually arbiter of the fate of the most illustrious living hero in Christendom, all tempted Henry VI. to throw as many obstacles as possible in the way of his captive's release. Taking advantage of his own position as titular head of western Christendom, he demanded satisfaction for all the wrongs which the various princes of the Empire had received,

---

[1] Rog. Howden (Stubbs), vol. iii. p. 207. Gerv. Cant. (Stubbs), vol. i. p. 516, says Michaelmas.

[2] Rog. Howden (as above), pp. 197, 198.

[3] Récits d'un ménestrel de Reims (ed. N. de Wailly, Soc. de l'Hist. de France), cc. 77-81 (pp. 41-43).   [4] Rog. Howden (as above), p. 198.

or considered themselves to have received, at Richard's hands, and for all his alleged misdoings on the Crusade, from his alliance with Tancred to the death of Conrad of Montferrat, in which it was suggested that he had had a share.[1] Not one of the charges would bear examination; but they served Henry as an excuse for playing fast and loose with Richard on the one side and Philip of France on the other, and for making endless changes in the conditions required for Richard's liberation. These were ultimately fixed at a ransom of a hundred and fifty thousand marks, the liberation of Isaac of Cyprus, and the betrothal of Eleanor of Britanny to a son of the Austrian duke.[2]

The duty of superintending the collection of the ransom and the transmission of the hostages required by the Emperor for its payment had been at first intrusted by Richard to his old friend and confidant, the chancellor William of Longchamp. William, however, found it impossible to fulfil his instructions; before the justiciars would allow him to set foot in England at all, they made him swear to meddle with nothing outside his immediate commission; when compelled to meet him in council at S. Albans, Walter of Rouen refused him the kiss of peace, and the queen-mother and the barons all alike refused to trust him with the hostages.[3] Prompt and vigorous measures were however taken for raising the money. An "aid for the king's ransom" was one of the three regular feudal obligations, which in strict law fell only upon the tenants-in-chivalry; but all the knights' fees in Richard's whole dominions would have been unable to furnish so large a sum as was required in his case. In addition therefore to an aid of twenty shillings on the knight's fee, the justiciars imposed a wholly new tax: they demanded a fourth part of the revenue and of the moveable goods of every man, whether layman or clerk, throughout

---

[1] The charges are summed up in R. Coggeshall (Stevenson), pp. 58, 59. On the death of Conrad see Stubbs, *Itin. Reg. Ric.*, pref. pp. xxii, xxiii.

[2] Treaty in Rog. Howden (Stubbs), vol. iii. pp. 215, 216. Roger dates it S. Peter's day; *ib.* p. 215. R. Diceto (Stubbs), vol. ii. p. 110, makes it July 5. Cf. Will. Newb., l. iv. c. 37 (Howlett, vol. i. p. 398).

[3] Gir. Cambr. *Vita Galfr.*, l. ii. c. 17 (Brewer, vol. iv. pp. 415, 416). Cf. Rog. Howden as above, pp. 211, 212.

the realm. Severe and unprecedented as was this demand, it provoked no opposition, even from the clergy ;[1] it had indeed the active co-operation of the bishops, under the direction of a new primate—Hubert Walter, the bishop of Salisbury, who had been one of Richard's fellow-crusaders, and was now at Richard's desire elected to the see of Canterbury.[2] The nation seems to have responded willingly to the demands made upon it ; yet the response proved inadequate, and the deficiency had to be supplied partly by a contribution from the Cistercians and Gilbertines of a fourth part of the wool of the flocks which were their chief source of revenue, and partly by confiscating the gold and silver vessels and ornaments of the wealthier churches.[3] Similar measures were taken in Richard's continental dominions, and they were so far successful that when the appointed time arrived for his release, in January 1194, the greater part of the ransom was paid.[4] For the remainder hostages were given, of whom one was Archbishop Walter of Rouen.[5] This selection left the chief justiciarship of England practically vacant, and accordingly Richard, before summoning the Norman primate to Germany, superseded him in that office by bestowing it upon the new archbishop of Canterbury, Hubert Walter.[6]

---

[1] Except at York, where the resistance was prompted by spite against the archbishop. Rog. Howden (Stubbs), vol. iii. p. 222.

[2] Elected May 29, 1193 ; R. Diceto (Stubbs), vol. ii. pp. 108, 109. Gerv. Cant. (Stubbs), vol. i. p. 518.

[3] On the ransom, and how it was raised, see Rog. Howden as above, pp. 210, 211, 222, 225 ; R. Diceto as above, p. 110 ; Will. Newb. l. iv. c. 38 (Howlett, vol. i. pp. 399, 400) ; and Bishop Stubbs's explanations of the matter, in his preface to Rog. Howden, vol. iv. pp. lxxxii-lxxxvi, and *Constit. Hist.*, vol. i. p. 501.

[4] Rog. Howden as above, p. 225.

[5] *Ib.* p. 233. Will. Newb., l. iv. c. 41 (Howlett, vol. i. p. 404), and R. Diceto as above, p. 113. According to this last, another of the hostages was William the chancellor ; but his name does not appear in Rog. Howden's list. One MS. of Ralf has in its place that of Baldwin Wake. As Baldwin certainly was a hostage on this occasion, perhaps William was selected first, and Baldwin afterwards substituted for him. One at least of the hostages was released before the whole ransom was paid : Archbishop Walter came back to England on May 19. R. Diceto as above, p. 115.

[6] Rog. Howden as above, p. 226. R. Diceto as above, p. 112. Gerv. Cant. (Stubbs), vol. i. p. 523.

The new justiciar immediately had his hands full of trouble.   At the prospect of Richard's return John grew half frantic with rage and dismay.   As early as July 1193, when it became known that Richard and the Emperor had come to terms, Philip had sent warning to John—" Beware, the devil is loose again ! " and John, without stopping to reflect that the " devil " could not be really loose till his ransom was paid, had hurried over sea to seek shelter from his brother's wrath under the protection of the French king. Richard, however, at once made overtures of reconciliation to both ;[1] the terms which he offered to John were indeed so favourable that the Norman constables refused to execute them, and thereby put an end to the negotiation.[2]   In January Philip and John made a last effort to bribe the Emperor either to keep Richard in custody for another year, or actually to sell him into their hands.[3]   When this failed, John in the frenzy of desperation sent a confidential clerk over to England with letters to his adherents there, bidding them make all his castles ready for defence against the king. The messenger's foolish boasting, however, betrayed him as he passed through London ; he was arrested by order of the mayor, his letters were seized, and a council was hurriedly called to hear their contents.   Its prompt and vigorous measures were clearly due to the initiative of the new justiciar-archbishop.   John was excommunicated and declared disseized of all his English tenements, and the assembly broke up to execute its own decree by force of arms.   The old bishop of Durham returned to his siege of Tickhill; the earls of Huntingdon, Chester and Ferrers led their forces against Nottingham ; Archbishop Hubert himself besieged Marlborough, and took it in a few days ; Lancaster was given up to him by its constable, who happened to be his own brother ; and S. Michael's Mount in Cornwall —a monastery whose site, not unlike that of its great Norman namesake, had tempted one of John's partizans to drive out the monks and fortify it in his interest—surrendered on the death of its commander, who is said to have

---

[1] Rog. Howden (Stubbs), vol. iii. pp. 216-220.   [2] *Ib.* pp. 227, 228.
[3] *Ib.* p. 229.   Will. Newb., l. iv. c. 40 (Howlett, vol. i. p. 402).

died of terror at the news of the king's approach.[1]   Richard
had been set free on February 4.[2]   After a slow progress
through Germany and the Low Countries, he embarked at
Swine, near Antwerp, and landed at Sandwich on March 13.[3]
Following the invariable practice of his father, he hastened
first to the martyr's shrine at Canterbury;[4] next day he
was met by the victorious archbishop hastening to welcome
him home,[5] and three days later he was solemnly received
in London.[6]   As soon as the defenders of Tickhill were
certified of his arrival they surrendered to the bishop of
Durham.[7]   As Windsor, Wallingford and the Peak had been
in the queen-mother's custody since the truce of May 1193,[8]
only Nottingham now remained to be won.   Richard at
once marched against it with all his forces ; the archbishop
followed, Hugh of Durham brought up his men from Tickhill ; in three days the castle surrendered, and Richard was
once again undisputed master in his realm.[9]

It must have seemed, to say the least, an ungracious
return for the sacrifices which England had made in his
behalf, when the king at once demanded from the English
knighthood the services of a third of their number to accompany him into Normandy, from the freeholders a contribution
of two shillings on every carucate of land, and from the
Cistercians the whole of their wool for the current year.[10]
In view of a war with France, of which it was impossible to
calculate either the exigencies or the duration, Richard
undoubtedly needed money ; but his needs pressed heavily
upon a country which had already been almost drained to

[1] Rog. Howden (Stubbs), vol. iii. pp. 236-238.
[2] *Ib.* p. 233. R. Diceto (Stubbs), vol. ii. pp. 112, 113. R. Coggeshall
(Stevenson), p. 62, dates it February 2.
[3] Rog. Howden as above, p. 235 ; R. Coggeshall as above. Gerv. Cant.
(Stubbs), vol. i. p. 524, dates it March 12, and R. Diceto as above, p. 114, March
20.   [4] Gerv. Cant. as above. R. Coggeshall (Stevenson), p. 63.
[5] Gerv. Cant. as above, p. 524.
[6] R. Diceto and R. Coggeshall as above.
[7] Rog. Howden as above, p. 238.   [8] *Ib.* p. 207.
[9] *Ib.* pp. 238-240. R. Diceto and R. Coggeshall as above. Will. Newb.,
l. iv. c. 42 (Howlett, vol. i. pp. 407, 408).
[10] Rog. Howden as above, p. 242. Cf. Will. Newb., l. v. c. 1 (vol. ii. pp.
416, 417).

provide his ransom.   In justice to him, it must however be
added that the "carucage," as the new land-tax came to be
called, seems to have been levied not for his personal profit,
but as a supplement to the measures taken by the justiciars
in the previous year, to complete the sum still due to Henry
VI.   It was in reality an old impost revived under a new
name, for the carucate or ploughland was in practice
reckoned as equivalent to the ancient hide,[1] and the sum
levied upon it was precisely that which the hide had furnished for the Danegeld of earlier times.[2]   Its re-imposition
in these circumstances, under a new appellation and for the
payment of what the whole nation regarded as a debt of
honour, met with no resistance.   The Cistercians, however,
remonstrated so strongly against the demand for their wool
that they were allowed to escape with a money-compensation.[3]   The taxes were imposed in a great council held at
Nottingham at the end of March and beginning of April,[4]
where measures were also taken for the punishment of the
traitors and the reconstruction of the administrative body.
These two objects were accomplished both at once, and both
were turned to account for the replenishment of the royal
coffers.   Except John, Bishop Hugh of Chester, and Gerard
de Camville, who were cited before the king's court on a
charge of high treason,[5] none of the delinquents were even
threatened with any worse punishment than dismissal from
office.   This was inflicted upon most of those who had taken
part in the 'proceedings against the chancellor.   Several of
the sheriffs indeed were only transferred from one shire to

---

[1] That it was so in the reign of Henry I. seems plain from Orderic's story about
Ralf Flambard re-measuring for William Rufus "omnes carrucatas, quas Angli
hidas vocant" (Ord. Vit., Duchesne, *Hist. Norm. Scriptt.*, p. 678)—a statement
which, whether the story itself be correct or not, shews that Orderic himself was
accustomed to hear carucates and hides identified.   The settlement of the carucates
at a hundred acres in 1198 points to the same identification.

[2] And seemingly, to the "dona" which took the place of the Danegeld after its
abolition *eo nomine* in 1163.   On the carucage of 1194 see Stubbs, pref. to Rog.
Howden, vol. iv. pp. lxxxii-lxxxiv and notes, lxxxvi.   See also the account of it
given by Will. Newb., l. v. c. i (Howlett, vol. ii. p. 416).

[3] Rog. Howden (Stubbs), vol. iii. p. 242.

[4] March 30—April 2. *Ib.* pp. 240-243.

[5] *Ib.* pp. 241, 242.   Cf. the account of John's condemnation in Ann. Margam,
a. 1199 (Luard, *Ann. Monast.*, vol. i. p. 24).

another ;[1] but Gerard de Camville was ejected without compensation from the sheriffdom of Lincolnshire, and Hugh Bardulf, one of the subordinate justiciars who had joined the party of John, from those of Yorkshire and Westmoreland. These three offices Richard at once put up for sale, and, with a strange inconsistency, William of Longchamp, whose well-grounded resistance to the accumulation of sheriffdoms in episcopal hands had been the beginning of his troubles, now sought to buy the two former, and also that of Northamptonshire, for himself. He was however outbid by Archbishop Geoffrey of York, who bought the sheriffdom of Yorkshire for three thousand marks and a promise of a hundred marks annually as increment.[2] This purchase made Geoffrey the most influential man in the north, for Hugh of Durham, apparently finding himself powerless to hold Northumberland, had resigned it into the king's hands.[3] William of Scotland immediately opened negotiations with Richard for its re-purchase, as well as for that of Cumberland, Westmoreland, Lancaster, and the other English lands held by his grandfather David. The barons, however, before whom Richard laid the proposal in a council at Northampton, resented it strongly ; Richard's own military instinct led him to refuse the cession of the castles, and as William would not be satisfied without them, the scheme came to nothing.[4]

Richard meanwhile had been making a progress through Mid-England,[5] similar to that which he had made before his crowning in 1189, and ending at Winchester, where he solemnly "wore his crown" in the cathedral church on the first Sunday after Easter.[6] This ceremonial was in itself merely a revival of the old regal practice which Henry II. had formally abandoned in 1158 ; but its revival on this occasion was prompted by other motives than Richard's love of pomp and shew. As a concession to the Emperor's

[1] Stubbs, *Constit. Hist.*, vol. i. p. 503.

[2] Rog. Howden (Stubbs), vol. iii. p. 241.

[3] *Ib.* p. 249. Will. Newb., l. v. c. 1 (Howlett, vol. ii. p. 416).

[4] Rog. Howden as above, pp. 243-245, 249, 250.   [5] *Ib.* pp. 243-246.

[6] *Ib.* p. 247. R. Diceto (Stubbs), vol. ii. p. 114. R. Coggeshall (Stevenson), p. 64. Gerv. Cant. (Stubbs), vol. i. pp. 524, 525. Will. Newb., l. iv. c. 42 (Howlett, vol. i. p. 408).

vanity—for we can scarcely conceive any other motive—
Richard had accepted from Henry VI. the investiture of the
kingdom of Burgundy ; " over which," says a contemporary
English writer, " be it known that the Emperor had really
no power at all," but for which, nevertheless, he had received
Richard's homage.[1]   The homage was, of course, as empty
as the gift for which it was due ; but insular pride, which
had always boasted that an English king, alone among
European sovereigns, had no superior upon earth, was offended
by it none the less ; and although the story that Richard
had formally surrendered England itself into Henry's hands
and received it back from him as a fief of the Empire[2] may
perhaps be set down as an exaggeration, still it seems to have
been felt that the majesty of the island-crown had been so
far dimmed by the transactions of his captivity as to require
a distinct re-assertion.[3]   As he stood in his royal robes,
sceptre in hand and crown on head,[4] amid the throng of
bishops and barons in the " Old Minster " where so many of
his English forefathers lay sleeping, past shame was forgotten,
and England was ready once again to welcome him as a new
king.[5]   But the welcome met with no response.   On May 12
—just two months after his landing at Sandwich—Richard
again sailed for Normandy ;[6] and this time he went to return
no more.

[1] Rog. Howden (Stubbs), vol. iii. p. 226.

[2] *Ib.* pp. 202, 203.   He seems to be the only writer who mentions it. ;

[3] See R. Diceto (Stubbs), vol. ii. p. 113 ; and on the whole question of this
coronation, Bishop Stubbs's note to Rog. Howden, vol. iii. p. 247, and his
remarks in *Constit. Hist.*, vol. i. pp. 504, 561, 562.   Richard himself seems to
have resented the popular view, for R. Coggeshall (Stevenson, p. 64) says he went
through the ceremony " aliquantulum renitens."

[4] Rog. Howden (as above), p. 247.   See the details of the ceremony in Gerv.
Cant. (Stubbs), vol. i. pp. 524-526.

[5] " Detersâ captivitatis ignominiâ quasi rex novus apparuit."   Will. Newb.,
l. iv. c. 42 (Howlett, vol. i. p. 408).

[6] Rog. Howden as above, p. 251.   R. Diceto as above, p. 114.   Gerv. Cant.
as above, p. 527.

CHAPTER VIII.

THE LATER YEARS OF RICHARD.

1194-1199.

THE political history of England during the four years which followed Richard's departure over sea is simply the history of the administration of Hubert Walter. Richard never again interfered in the concerns of his island realm, save for the purpose of obtaining money from it; and even the method whereby the money was to be raised he left, like all other details of administration, wholly to the justiciar's discretion. Hubert in fact, as justiciar and archbishop, wielded during these years a power even more absolute than that which William of Longchamp had wielded during the king's absence on crusade. But Richard's second experiment in governing England by deputy succeeded far otherwise than the first. It was, indeed, attended with far less risk; for the king himself was never really out of reach, and could at any moment have returned to take up the reins of government in person, had there been any need to do so. Moreover, the man whom he now left as viceroy had far other qualifications for the office than William of Longchamp.

Hubert Walter had been trained under the greatest constitutional lawyer and most successful administrator of the age, Ralf de Glanville. He was nephew to Ralf's wife,[1] and

---

[1] Hubert's mother and Ralf's wife were sisters; cf. the Glanville family history in Dugdale, *Monast. Angl.*, vol. vi. pt. i., p. 380, and the foundation-charter of Arklow, given by Hubert's brother Theobald, *ib.* pt. ii. p. 1128. Hubert and his brothers seem to have been brought up by their aunt and her husband;

had been a clerk or chaplain in Ralf's household until 1186, when he was appointed dean of York.[1]   A few months later he was one of five persons nominated by the York chapter in answer to a royal mandate for election to the vacant see.[2] King Henry, however, refused all five, and Hubert remained dean of York for three years longer.   He seems to have held, besides his deanery, an office at court, either as protonotary or as vice-chancellor under Geoffrey; for during the last few months of Henry's life he is found in Maine attending upon the king, and apparently charged with the keeping of the royal seal.[3]   Consecrated to Salisbury by Archbishop Baldwin on October 22, 1189,[4] he immediately afterwards set out with him for Palestine ; there he won universal esteem by the zeal and ability with which he exerted himself to relieve the wants of the poorer crusaders;[5] on Baldwin's death Hubert virtually succeeded to his place as the chief spiritual authority in the host ;[6] and after Richard's arrival he made himself no less useful as the king's best adviser and most trusty diplomatic agent in Palestine.[7]   It was Hubert who headed in Richard's stead the first body of pilgrims whom the Turks admitted to visit the Holy Sepulchre ;[8] and it seems to have been he, too, who led back the English host from Palestine to Europe after Richard's departure.   He hastened as early as possible to visit the king in his captivity;[9] and Richard lost no time in sending him to England to be made archbishop, and to help the justiciars in collecting the

Hubert, when dean of York, founded a Premonstratensian house at West Dereham " pro salute animæ meæ, et patris, et matris meæ, et domini Ranulphi de Glanvillâ, et dominæ Bertriæ uxoris ipsius, qui nos nutrierunt." *Ib.* vol. vi. pt. ii. p. 899.

[1]   *Gesta Hen.* (Stubbs), vol. i. 360.   Rog. Howden (Stubbs), vol. ii. p. 310.

[2]   *Gesta Hen.* as above, p. 352.

[3]   See Stubbs, *Rog. Howden*, vol. iv. pref. p. xli. note 1.

[4]   R. Diceto (Stubbs), vol. ii. p. 71.

[5]   *Itin. Reg. Ric.* (Stubbs), pp. 134-137.   *Gesta Ric.* (Stubbs), p. 145.

[6]   R. Diceto as above, p. 88.   The Patriarch Heraclius had become discredited in the eyes of all the right-minded crusaders by his share in the divorce and remarriage of Queen Isabel, which broke Baldwin's heart.

[7]   Will. Newb., l. iv. c. 29 (Howlett, vol. i. p. 378).

[8]   *Ibid.   Itin. Reg. Ric.* (Stubbs), pp. 437, 438.

[9]   Will. Newb. as above, c. 33 (p. 388).   Cf. Rog. Howden (Stubbs), vol. iii. p. 209.

ransom.[1]   They had refused the help of William of Longchamp, but they could not reject that of Hubert ; for they
knew that, as a contemporary historian says, "the king had
no one so like-minded with himself, whose fidelity, prudence
and honesty he had proved in so many changes of fortune."[2]
Hubert was one of the commissioners appointed to have the
custody of the ransom ;[3] and there can be little doubt that
the scheme by which it was raised was in part at least
devised by his financial genius, and carried into execution
by his energy and skill—qualities which he displayed no less
effectively in dealing with the revolt which was finally quelled
by the return of Richard himself.

Hubert entered upon his vice-royalty—for it was nothing
less—under more favourable conditions than William of
Longchamp.   He came to it not as an upstart stranger, but
as an Englishman already of high personal and official
standing, thoroughly familiar and thoroughly in sympathy
with the people whom he had to govern, intimately acquainted
with the principles and the details of the system which he
was called upon to administer ; his qualifications were well
known, and they were universally acknowledged.   Moreover,
there was now no one capable of heading any serious opposition to his authority, at least in secular affairs.   William of
Longchamp was still chancellor ; but like the royal master
to whose side he clave for the rest of his life, he had left
England for ever.   From John there was also nothing to
fear.   His intended trial never took place, for he threw
himself at Richard's feet at the first opportunity, and was
personally forgiven ; but the king was wise enough to leave
untouched the sentence of forfeiture passed by the justiciar,
and to keep his brother at his own side, a dependent upon
his royal bounty, for nearly twelve months ;[4] and then he
restored to him nothing but the counties of Mortain and
Gloucester and the honour of Eye, but without their castles,
giving him in compensation for the latter and for his other

---

[1] Will. Newb., l. iv. c. 33 (Howlett, vol. i. p. 388).   Cf. Gerv. Cant. (Stubbs),
vol. i. pp. 516, 517.   [2] Will. Newb. as above.
  [3] Rog. Howden (Stubbs), vol. iii. p. 212.
  [4] Cf. Rog. Howden as above, pp. 252 and 286, and also R. Coggeshall
(Stevenson), p. 64.

estates a yearly pension of eight thousand pounds Angevin.[1]
Even John's capacities for mischief-making were so far
paralyzed by this arrangement that he seems to have made
no further attempt to meddle in English politics so long as
Richard lived. The one man in whom Hubert saw, or
fancied he saw, a possible rival on personal and ecclesiastical
grounds, he swept roughly out of his path. The two primates
had already quarrelled over the privileges of their respective
sees, and nothing but the king's presence had availed to keep
peace between them.[2] The northern one had been at feud
with his own chapter ever since his appointment, and they
were now prosecuting an appeal against him at Rome. In
June 1194, backed, it can hardly be doubted, by Hubert's
influence, they obtained from the Pope a sentence which
practically condemned Geoffrey without trial ;[3] and before
these tidings reached England in September, a committee of
royal justices, sent by Hubert to deal with the case in its
temporal aspect, had already punished Geoffrey's refusal to
acknowledge their jurisdiction by confiscating all his archiepiscopal estates except Ripon.[4] He went over sea and
appealed to the king, but in vain ;[5] and for the next five
years there was again but one primate in the land. One
northern bishop, however, was still ready to defy Hubert as
he had defied William of Longchamp and his own metropolitan. When the newly appointed sheriff of Northumberland, Hugh Bardulf, sought to enter upon his office shortly
after Richard's departure, he found that Hugh of Durham
had already made a fresh bargain with the king, whereby he
was to retain the county on a payment of two thousand
marks. He tried, however, as before, to evade the necessity
of payment, and was in consequence forcibly disseized by
Richard's orders.[6] Still he was unwilling to give up the

---

[1] Rog. Howden (Stubbs), vol. iii. p. 286.
[2] *Ib.* pp. 246, 247, 250 ; vol. iv. pref. pp. lix, lx.
[3] *Ib.* vol. iii. pp. 272, 273, 278-286 ; vol. iv. pref. pp. lxii, lxiv.
[4] *Ib.* vol. iii. pp. 261, 262 ; vol. iv. pref. pp. lxi, lxii.
[5] Richard in November ordered his restoration, but the order was not carried
out ; the brothers went on quarrelling, and next year Richard again declared the
archiepiscopal estates forfeited, and this time finally. *Ib.* vol. iii. pp. 273, 287 ;
vol. iv. pref. pp. lxiv, lxix.   [6] *Ib.* vol. iii. pp. 260, 261 ; cf. p. 249.

game ; and in the spring of 1195 he made another attempt
to regain the territorial influence in the north which Geoffrey's
fall seemed to have placed again within his reach. The
story went in Yorkshire that he actually succeeded in once
more obtaining from Richard—of course on Richard's usual
terms—a commission as co-justiciar with Hubert.[1] Such a
commission can hardly have been given otherwise than in
mockery; yet the aged bishop, untaught by all his experience
of the king's shifty ways, once again set out from York,
where he had just been excommunicating some of Geoffrey's
partizans,[2] to publish his supposed triumph in London.
Sickness, however, overtook him on the way; from Doncaster
he was compelled to turn back to his old refuge at Howden,
and there on March 3 he died.[3] His palatinate was of
course taken into the custody of the royal justiciars.[4] A
fortnight later Celestine III. sent to Archbishop Hubert a
commission as legate for all England ;[5] and thenceforth he
was undisputed ruler alike in Church and state.

Like most of the higher clergy of Henry's later years,
Hubert was distinctly more of a statesman than a churchman. His pontificate left no mark on the English Church ;
as primate, his chief occupation was to quarrel with his
chapter. No scruples such as had moved Archbishop
Thomas to resign the chancellorship, or had made even
Bishop Roger of Salisbury seek a papal dispensation before
he would venture to undertake a lay office,[6] held back
Hubert Walter from uniting in his own person the justiciarship and the primacy of all England. He was, however,
a statesman of the best school of the time, steeped in the
traditions of constitutional and administrative reform which
had grown up during Henry's later years under the inspiration
of the king himself and the direction of Ralf de Glanville.
The task of developing their policy, therefore, could not have

---

[1] Will. Newb., l. v. c. 10 (Howlett, vol. ii. pp. 438, 439).
[2] Rog. Howden (Stubbs), vol. iii. p. 284.
[3] *Ibid.* Will. Newb. as above (p. 439).
[4] Rog. Howden as above, p. 285.
[5] Dated March 18 [1195]. *Ib.* pp. 290-293. R. Diceto (Stubbs), vol. ii. pp.
125-127.
[6] Will. Malm. *Gesta Reg.*, l. v. c. 408 (Hardy, p 637).

fallen to more competent hands ; and as Richard was totally destitute of his father's business capacities, it was well that Hubert was left to fulfil it according to his own judgement and on his own sole responsibility for nearly four years.

The justiciar's first act after his sovereign's departure was to despatch the judges itinerant upon their annual visitation-tour with a commission[1] which struck the key-note of his future policy.   It was the note which had been struck by Henry II. in the Assizes of Clarendon and North-ampton ; but the new commission shewed a great advance in the developement of the principles which those measures embodied.   The jurisdiction of the justices is defined with greater fulness and extended over a much wider sphere. The "pleas of the Crown" with which they are empowered to deal include, besides those formerly recognized under this head, such various matters as the number and condition of churches in the king's gift,[2] escheats, wardships and mar-riages ;[3] forgers[4] and defaulters ;[5] the harbouring of male-factors ;[6] the arrears of the ransom ;[7] the use of false meas-ures ;[8] the debts of the murdered Jews ; the fines due from their slayers,[9] from the adherents of John, and from his debtors, as well as from his own forfeited property ;[10] the disposal of the chattels of dead usurers, and also of crusaders who had died before setting out on their pilgrimage ;[11] and the taking of recognitions under the Great Assize con-cerning land worth not more than five pounds a year.[12]   In all these proceedings the chief object evidently was to procure money for the royal treasury ; a tallage which the judges were also directed to assess upon all cities, towns and royal demesnes[13] being deemed insufficient to supply its

---

[1] "Forma qualiter procedendum est in placitis Coronæ Regis." Rog. Howden (Stubbs), vol. iii. pp. 262-267 ; Stubbs, *Select Charters*, pp. 259-263.

[2] *Forma procedendi*, c. 4 (Stubbs, *Select Charters*, p. 259).

[3] *Ib.* cc. 3, 5, 6, 23 (pp. 259, 260, 261).   [4] *Ib.* c. 8 (p. 260).

[5] *Ib.* c. 19 (as above).   [6] *Ib.* c. 7 (as above).

[7] *Ib.* c. 10 (as above).

[8] *Ib.* c. 16 (as above).   Richard had at the beginning of his reign caused all weights and measures to be reduced to one standard ; Mat. Paris, *Chron. Maj.* (Luard), vol. ii. p. 351.   [9] *Forma proced.*, c. 9 (as above).

[10] *Ib.* cc. 11-14 (as above).   [11] *Ib.* cc. 15, 17 (as above).

[12] *Ib.* c. 18 (as above).   [13] *Ib.* c. 22 (p. 261).

needs. The details of this multifarious business are however of less historical importance than the method employed
for its transaction. Every item of it was to be dealt with
on the presentment of what may now be called the "grand
jury"—the jury of sworn recognitors in every shire, whose
functions, hitherto confined to the presentment of criminals,
were thus extended to all branches of judicial work. This
growth in the importance of the jury was marked by
the introduction of a new ordinance for its constitution.
The Assizes of Clarendon and Northampton simply ordered
that the jury should consist of twelve lawful men of every
hundred and four of every township, without specifying
how they were to be selected. Most probably they were
nominated by the sheriff.[1] The recognitors employed in the
civil process known as the Great Assize, however, were from
the first appointed in a special manner prescribed in the
Assize itself. Four knights of the shire were summoned by
the sheriff, and these four elected the twelve recognitors.[2]
By the "Form of proceeding in the pleas of the Crown"
delivered to the justices-errant in 1194, this method of election was applied to the jury of presentment in all cases, with
a modification which removed the choice yet one step further
from the mere nomination of the sheriff. Four knights were
first to be chosen out of the whole shire ; these were to elect
two out of every hundred or wapentake, and these two were
to choose ten others, who with them constituted the legal
twelve.[3] Whether or not the choice of the first four was
actually, as seems most probable, transferred from the sheriff
to the body of the freeholders assembled in the county-court,[4]
still this enactment shews a distinct advance in the principles
of election and representation, as opposed to that of mere
nomination by a royal officer. Another step in the same
direction was the appointment of three knights and a clerk
to be "elected in every shire to keep the pleas of the

---

[1] Stubbs, *Rog. Howden*, vol. iv. pref. pp. xcvi, xcvii.

[2] R. Glanville, *De Legg. Angl.*, l. xiii. c. 3.

[3] *Forma proced.*, introductory chap., Stubbs, *Select Charters*, p. 259; Rog.
Howden (Stubbs), vol. iii. p. 262.

[4] Stubbs, *Rog. Howden*, as above, pp. xcvii-xcix.

Crown."[1]   This was the origin of the office afterwards
known as that of coroner.   It had the effect of depriving
the sheriff of a considerable part of his judicial functions ;
and his importance was at the same time yet further limited
by an order that no sheriff should act as justiciar in his own
shire, nor in any shire which he had held at any time since
the king's first crowning.[2]   The difficulty of checking the
abuse of power in the hands of the sheriffs, which Henry
had been unable to overcome, had certainly not been lessened by Richard's way of distributing the sheriffdoms in his
earlier years.   It had indeed become so serious that in this
very year either the new justiciar, or possibly the king himself, proposed an inquisition similar to that made by Henry
in 1170, into the administration of all servants of the Crown,
whether justices, sheriffs, constables, or foresters, since the
beginning of the reign.   When the king was gone, however,
it seems to have been felt that such an undertaking would
add too heavily to the labours of the judges-errant ; and the
inquiry was accordingly postponed for an indefinite time by
the archbishop's order.[3]

The principle of co-operation between the government
and the people for maintaining order and peace, which under-
lies all Henry's reforming measures, and of which the new
regulations for election of the grand jury are a further recognition, was again enunciated yet more distinctly in the following
year.   An edict was published requiring every man above
the age of fifteen years to take an oath that he would do
all that in him lay for the preservation of the king's peace ;
that he would neither be a thief or robber, nor a receiver
or accomplice of such persons, but would do his utmost to
denounce and deliver them to the sheriff, would join to the
uttermost of his power in the pursuit of malefactors when
hue and cry was raised against them, and would deliver up
to the sheriff all persons who should have failed to perform
their share in this duty.[4]   The obligation binding upon every

---

[1] *Forma proced.*, c. 20 (Stubbs, *Select Charters*, p. 260).
[2] *Ib.* c. 21 (as above).   [3] *Ib.* c. 25 (p. 263).
[4] *Edictum Regium.* Rog. Howden (Stubbs), vol. iii. pp. 299, 300 ; Stubbs,
Select Charters, p. 264.

member of the state to lend his aid for the punishment of
offences against its peace had been declared, in words which
are almost echoed in this edict, as long ago as the reign of
Cnut.[1]   The difficulty of enforcing it caused by the disorganized condition of society which had grown up during
the civil war was probably the reason which led Henry, in
framing his Assizes of Clarendon and Northampton, at once
to define it more narrowly and to lay the responsibility of
its execution upon a smaller body of men specially appointed
for the purpose in every shire.   The completeness of organization which the system introduced by these Assizes had
now attained, however, gave scope for a wider application of
the principle through one of those revivals of older custom
in which the enduring character of our ancient national institutions and their capacity for adaptation to the most diverse
conditions of national life are so often and so strikingly displayed.   The edict of 1195 forms a link between the usage
of Cnut's day and that of modern times.   It directed that
the oath should be taken before knights assigned for the
purpose in every shire ; out of the office thus created there
seems to have grown that of conservators of the peace ; and
this again developed in the fourteenth century into that of
justices of the peace, which has retained an unbroken existence down to our own age.[2]

The same year was marked by the only important
ecclesiastical act of Hubert's pontificate.   Having received
in the spring his commission as legate, he made use of it to
hold a visitation of the northern province—now, by Geoffrey's
absence and Hugh of Puiset's death, deprived of both its
chief pastors—and a council in York minster at which
fifteen canons were passed [3] to remedy the general relaxation
of Church discipline which had been growing ever since
Thomas's flight.   At the close of the year Hubert was

---

[1] "And we will that every man above xii years make oath that he will neither
be a thief nor cognizant of theft."   Cnut, Secular Dooms, c. 21, Stubbs, *Select
Charters*, p. 74.

[2] Stubbs, *Select Charters*, p. 263 ; *Constit. Hist.*, vol. i. p. 507 ; pref. to Rog.
Howden, vol. iv. pp. c, ci.

[3] Rog. Howden (Stubbs), vol. iii. pp. 293-298.   Cf. R. Diceto (Stubbs), vol.
pp. 146-148, and Will. Newb., l. v. c. 12 (Howlett, vol. ii. p. 442).

again at York, upon a different errand : the negotiation of
a fresh treaty with Scotland, on the basis of a marriage
between the Scot king's eldest daughter and Richard's
nephew Otto of Saxony.[1] The marriage never took place,
but the alliance of which it was to be the pledge lasted
throughout Richard's reign ; and it is a noteworthy proof at
once of the growth of friendly relations between the two
countries, and of the success of Hubert's recent ordinance
for the preservation of peace and order in England, that in
the following year a similar edict, evidently modelled upon
the English one, was issued in Scotland by William the
Lion.[2]

Neither the renewal of order in the Church, nor the
securing of the external tranquillity of the realm by alliance
with its neighbour-states, nor the organization of justice and
police within its own borders, was however the most
laborious part of Hubert's task. One thing only was
required of him by his royal master ; but that was precisely
the one thing which cost him the most trouble to obtain.
From a country which must, as it seems, have been almost
drained of its financial resources over and over again during
the last ten years, he was perpetually called upon to extract
supplies of money such as had never been furnished before
to any English king. That he contrived to meet Richard's
ceaseless demands year after year without either plunging
the nation into helpless misery or provoking it to open
revolt, is the strongest proof not only of his financial genius
and tact, but also of the increase in material prosperity and

---

[1] William the Lion had been sick almost to death, and having no son, had
proposed to leave his crown to his eldest daughter, under the protection of Richard,
whose nephew he wished her to marry. The opposition of his barons, and the
restoration of his own health, caused him to drop the scheme of bequest (Rog.
Howden (Stubbs), vol. iii. pp. 298, 299). That of the marriage however was still
pursued, and accepted by Hubert in Richard's name, on somewhat singular conditions : Lothian, as the bride's dowry, was to be given over to Richard's custody,
while Northumberland and the county of Carlisle were to be settled upon Otto
and made over to the keeping of the king of Scots. The negotiation, however,
dragged on for a year, and was again checked by the hope of an heir to the Scottish
crown (*ib.* p. 308); and the fulfilment of this hope in August 1198 led to its abandonment. *Ib.* vol. iv. p. 54.

[2] Rog. Howden (Stubbs), vol. iv. p. 33. He says William issued his proclamation " de bono sumens exemplum."

national contentment which had been fostered by Henry's rule, and of the success of Hubert's own efforts in carrying out the policy which Henry had begun. By Michaelmas 1194 it seems that the whole of the complicated accounts for the ransom, including the carucage imposed in the spring, were closed.[1] In the same year the country had borne the additional burthen of a tallage upon the towns. This, however, added to the sums raised by sales of office during the king's visit and to the proceeds of the judges' visitation, failed to satisfy the wants of Richard. He therefore resorted to two other methods of raising money, both apparently of his own devising, and both harmonizing very ill with the constitutional policy of his justiciar. Save during the disorderly reign of Stephen, the practice of tournaments had been hitherto unknown in England. Both Henry I. and Henry II. were too serious and practical-minded to encourage vain shews of any kind, far less to countenance the reckless waste of energy and the useless risk of life and limb which these entertainments involved, which had moved Pope after Pope to denounce them as perilous alike to body and soul,[2] and, in spite of a characteristic protest from Thomas Becket, to exclude those who were slain in them from the privileges of Christian burial.[3] The Church had indeed been unable to check this obnoxious practice in Gaul ; backed, however, by the authority of the Crown, she had as yet succeeded in keeping it out of England. But in 1194 a fresh prohibition, issued by Pope Celestine in the previous year,[4] was met by Richard with a direct defiance. On August 20 he issued a license for the holding of tournaments in England, on condition that every man who took part in them should pay to the Crown a specified sum, varying according to his rank. Five places were appointed where tournaments might be held, and no one was allowed to enter the lists until he had paid for his license.[5] The

---

[1] See Stubbs, *Rog. Howden,* vol. iv. pref. pp. lxxxii-lxxxiv and notes.

[2] Will. Newb., l. v. c. 4 (Howlett, vol. ii. pp. 422, 423).

[3] Ep. xxiv., Robertson, *Becket,* vol. v. p. 36.

[4] Rymer, *Fœdera,* vol. i. p. 56.

[5] Writ in Rymer, as above, p. 65, and in Stubbs, *R. Diceto,* vol. ii., app. to pref. pp. lxxx, lxxxi ; this latter copy is dated August 22. Cf. Rog. Howden

collection of this new item of revenue was evidently looked upon as an important matter, for it was intrusted to the justiciar's brother Theobald Walter.[1] Whatever may have been Hubert's share in this measure, he was clearly in no way responsible for the other and yet more desperate expedient to which Richard, almost at the same time, resorted for the replenishment of his treasury. On pretext of a quarrel with his chancellor, he took away the seal from him, ordered another to be made, and declared all acts passed under the old one to be null and void, till they should have been brought to him for confirmation :[2] in other words, till they should have been paid for a second time.

In the following spring a fit of characteristic Angevin penitence—fervent and absorbing while it lasted, but passing away all too soon—moved the king to make some amends for his extortions as well as for his other sins ; he began to replace the church-plate which had been given up for his ransom ;[3] no fresh tax was imposed till late in the year, and then it was only a scutage of the usual amount—twenty shillings on the knight's fee—for the war in Normandy.[4] Next year, however, the king's mood again changed. He was now resolved to carry into effect, with or without Hubert's assent, the inquiry into the financial administration which Hubert had postponed in 1194. For this purpose he sent over to England Robert, abbot of S. Stephen's at Caen, who, notwithstanding his monastic profession, had acquired great experience as a clerk of the Norman exchequer, and seems to have there enjoyed a high reputation for knowledge and skill in all matters of finance.[5] The abbot, accompanied

(Stubbs), vol. iii. p. 268, Will. Newb., l. v. c. 4 (Howlett, vol. ii. pp. 422, 423), and R. Diceto (Stubbs), vol. ii. p. 120.

[1] Rog. Howden (Stubbs), vol. iii. p. 268.

[2] *Ib.* p. 267. Cf. R. Coggeshall (Stevenson), p. 93. Rog. Howden's very confused account of the seals is made clear by Bishop Stubbs, *Constit. Hist.*, vol. i. p. 506 note.

[3] Rog. Howden as above, p. 290. Cf. *Itin. Reg. Ric.* (Stubbs), pp. 449, 450.

[4] See Madox, *Hist. Exch.*, vol. i. pp. 637, 638. That it was imposed late in the year seems implied by so much of it not being accounted for till the next year ; see Stubbs, pref. to Rog. Howden, vol. iv. p. lxxxviii and note 3.

[5] Will. Newb., l. v. c. 19 (Howlett, vol. ii. p. 464). Cf. Rog. Howden (Stubbs), vol. iv. p. 5.

by the bishop-elect of Durham, Philip of Poitiers,[1] reached London in Lent 1196, and demanded Hubert's co-operation in fulfilling the royal orders. The justiciar, though displeased and hurt, had no choice but to comply, and an order was issued in the king's name bidding all sheriffs and officers of the Crown be ready to give an account of their stewardship in London on a certain day—apparently the day of the usual Exchequer-meeting in Easter-week.[2] Before Easter came, the abbot of Caen himself was gone to his last account ; he was seized with illness while dining with Archbishop Hubert on Passion Sunday, and five days later he died.[3] The intended inquisition never took place ; but the mere proposal to conduct it thus through the medium of a stranger from over sea was a direct slight offered to the justiciar by the king ;[4] and it coincided with a disturbance which warned Hubert of a possible danger to his authority from another quarter.

Strive as he might to equalize the burthens of taxation, he could not prevent them from pressing upon the poorer classes with a severity which grew at last well-nigh intolerable. The grievance was felt most keenly in London. The substitution of the "commune" for the older shire-organization of London in 1191 was a step towards municipal unity, and thus indirectly towards local independence and self-government ; but it had done nothing for the poorer class of citizens. It had placed the entire control of civic administration, including the regulation of trade and the assessment of taxes, in the hands of a governing body consisting of a mayor and aldermen, one of whom presided over each of the wards into which the whole city was divided, the head of them all being the mayor.[5] This corporation was the repre-

---

[1] Rog. Howden (Stubbs), vol. iv. p. 5. He seems to imply that Philip shared in the abbot's commission ; but he evidently made no attempt to act upon it after Robert's death.   [2] Will. Newb., l. v. c. 19 (Howlett, vol. ii. p. 465).

[3] Rog. Howden as above. " Nec cum eis quos evocaverat post Pascha positurus, sed ante Pascha rationem superno Judici de propriis actibus redditurus." Will. Newb. as above.

[4] On April 15, four days after the abbot's death, Richard wrote a sort of apology to the justiciar. See Stubbs, *R. Diceto*, vol. ii. app. to pref. pp. lxxix, lxxx.

[5] In the *Liber de Antiquis Legibus* (a chronicle of the mayors and sheriffs of London, compiled in 1274, and edited by Mr. Stapleton for the Camden Soc.), p.

sentative of the merchant-gild, which had thus absorbed into itself all the powers and privileges of the earlier ruling class of territorial magnates, in addition to its own.   As might be expected, the rule of this newly-established oligarchy over the mass of its unenfranchized fellow-citizens was at least as oppressive as that of the sheriffs and "barons of the city" which had preceded it ; and it was less willingly borne, owing to the jealousy which always existed between the craftsmen and the merchant-gild.   As the taxes grew more burthensome year by year, a suspicion began to spread that they were purposely assessed in such a manner as to spare the well-filled pockets of the assessors, and wring an unfair proportion of the required total from the hard-earned savings of the poor.[1]   Whether the injustice was intentional or not, the grievance seems to have been a real one ; and it soon found a spokesman and a champion.   William Fitz-Osbert —" William with the Long Beard," as he was commonly called — was by birth a member of the ruling class in the city.[2]   He seems to have shared with a goldsmith named Geoffrey the leadership of a band of London citizens who in 1190 formed part of the crusading fleet, and did good service, not indeed, so far as we know, in Holy Land, but like their brethren forty-three years earlier, in helping to drive the Moors out of Portugal.[3]   Since his return, whether

1, the first mayor, Henry Fitz-Aylwine, is said to have been appointed "anno gratie M? centesimo lxxxviii, anno primo regni Regis Ricardi ;" and the document known as Fitz-Aylwine's Assize (*ib.* p. 206) purports to have been issued "Anno Domini M? C? lxxxix, scilicet primo anno regni illustris Regis Ricardi, existente tunc Henrico filio Aylewini Maiore, qui fuit primus Maiorum Londoniarum." On this however Bishop Stubbs remarks : "It is improbable that London had a recognized mayor before 1191, in which year the communa was established . . . and there is I believe no mention of such an official in a record until some three years later." Introd. to *Annales Londonienses* ("Chronicles of Ed. I. and Ed. II."), p. xxxi.

[1] Rog. Howden (Stubbs), vol. iv. p. 5.   Mat. Paris, *Chron. Maj.* (Luard), vol. ii. p. 418.   Will. Newb., l. v. c. 20 (Howlett, vol. ii. p. 466).

[2] "Willelmus cum Barbâ," Rog. Howden as above, pp. 5, 6 ; "agnomen habens a barbâ prolixâ," Will. Newb. (as above); "cognomento cum-Barbâ," "dictus Barbatus vel Barba," Mat. Paris (as above), pp. 418, 419.   Will. Newb. thinks he wore the unusual appendage simply to make himself conspicuous ; Mat. Paris explains "cujus genus avitum ob indignationem Normannorum radere barbam contempsit," on which see Freeman, *Norm. Conq.*, vol. v. p. 900.

[3] *Gesta Ric.* (Stubbs), pp. 116-118.

fired by genuine zeal for the cause of the oppressed, or, as some of his contemporaries thought, moved by the hope of acquiring power and influence which he found unattainable by other means,[1] he had severed himself from his natural associates in the city to become the preacher and leader of another sort of crusade, for the deliverance of the poorer classes from the tyranny of their wealthy rulers. At every meeting of the governing body he withstood his fellow-aldermen to the face, remonstrating continually against their corrupt fiscal administration. They could not silence and dared not expel him, for they knew that his whispers were stirring up the craftsmen ; and although the rumour that he had more than fifty thousand sworn followers at his back must have been an exaggeration, yet there could be no doubt of the existence of a conspiracy sufficiently formidable to excuse, if not to justify, the terror of the civic rulers.[2] When after a visit to Normandy William began openly to boast of the king's favour and support, the justiciar thought it time to interfere. He called the citizens together, endeavoured to allay their discontent by reasonings and remonstrances, and persuaded them to give hostages for their good behaviour.[3] William however set his authority at defiance. Day after day, in the streets and open spaces of the city, and at last even in S. Paul's itself,[4] this bold preacher with the tall stately form, singular aspect and eloquent tongue gathered round him a crowd of eager listeners to whom he proclaimed himself as the " king and saviour of the poor." One of his audience afterwards reported to a writer of the time his exposition of a text from Isaiah : " With joy shall ye draw water out of the wells of the Saviour." [5] " I," said William, " am the saviour of the poor. Ye poor who have felt the heavy hand of the rich, ye shall draw from my wells the water of wholesome doctrine, and that with joy, for the time of your visitation

---

[1] Rog. Howden (Stubbs), vol. iv. pp. 5, 6, and Mat. Paris, *Chron. Maj.* (Luard), vol. ii. pp. 418, 419, represent the former view ; Will. Newb., l. v. c. 20 (Howlett, vol. ii. pp. 467, 468), and R. Diceto (Stubbs), vol. ii. p. 143, the latter.

[2] Will. Newb. as above (p. 468).   [3] *Ib.* (pp. 468, 469).

[4] R. Diceto as above.

[5] " Of salvation," A. V. ; " de fontibus Salvatoris," Vulg. Is. xii. 3.

is at hand. For I will divide the waters from the waters. The people are the waters ; and I will divide the humble and faithful people from the proud and perfidious people. I will divide the elect from the reprobate, as light from darkness." [1]

Powerless to deal with these assemblies within the city, Hubert determined at least to check the spread of such teaching as this, and issued orders that any citizen of the lower class found outside the walls should be arrested as an enemy to king and kingdom. Some chapmen from London were accordingly arrested at Mid-Lent at Stamford fair.[2] A day or two afterwards—the justiciar's fears being perhaps quickened by the arrival of the abbot of Caen, which William might easily interpret as the effect of his own remonstrances with the king—an attempt was made to call William himself to account for his seditious proceedings. The bearer of the summons found him surrounded by such a formidable array of followers that he dared not execute his commission, and a forcible arrest was decided on. Guided by two citizens who undertook to catch him at unawares, a party of armed men was sent to seize him ;[3] one of the guides was felled with a blow of a hatchet by William himself, the other was slain by his friends; William, with a few adherents, took sanctuary in the church of S. Mary-at-Bow. The justiciar, after surrounding the church with soldiers, ordered it to be set on fire,[4] and William, driven out by the smoke and the flames, was stabbed on the threshold by the son of the man whom he had killed an hour before.[5] The wound however was not immediately fatal ; the soldiers seized him and carried him to the Tower for trial before the justiciars, who at once condemned him to death ; he was stripped, tied to a horse's tail, thus dragged through the city, and hanged with eight of his adherents.[6] The rest of the malcontents were so overawed

---

[1] Will. Newb., l. v. c. 20 (Howlett, vol. ii. p. 469).
[2] Rog. Howden (Stubbs), vol. iv. p. 6.   [3] Will. Newb. as above (p. 470).
[4] *Ibid.* Rog. Howden as above ; Mat. Paris, *Chron. Maj.* (Luard) vol. ii. p. 419. R. Diceto (Stubbs), vol. ii. p. 143, makes William himself fire the church, but this seems nonsense, as he clearly had no intention of dying in it.
[5] Will. Newb. as above. Cf. Rog. Howden as above.
[6] Will. Newb., l. v. c. 20 (Howlett, vol. ii. p. 471) says nine. Eight is the

by this spectacle that they at once made complete submission.[1] The justiciar had triumphed ; but his triumph was
dearly bought at the cost of what little still remained to
him of personal popularity and ecclesiastical repute. The
common people persisted in reverencing William Longbeard
as a martyr ;[2] the clergy were horrified at the sacrilege
involved in the violation of the right of sanctuary and the
firing of a church, a sacrilege all the more unpardonable
because committed by an archbishop ; while his own chapter
seized upon it as the crowning charge in the already long
indictment which they were preparing against their primate.[3]
Thus overwhelmed with obloquy on all sides, Hubert in
disgust for a moment threw up the justiciarship, but resumed it as soon as he was once more assured of Richard's
confidence.[4] For two more years he toiled on at his thankless task. The budget of 1196 was made up by the safe
expedient of another scutage.[5] Next year the sole legislative act ventured upon by the justiciar was an attempt to
enforce uniformity of weights and measures throughout the
kingdom by means of an Assize,[6] whose provisions however
turned out to be so impracticable that, like a similar ordinance issued earlier in the reign, it seems to have remained
inoperative, and six years later was abolished altogether.[7]
In the autumn Hubert went over to Normandy, where he
was occupied for some weeks in diplomatic business for the
king.[8] A month after his return the crisis came.

number given by Rog. Howden (Stubbs), vol. iv. p. 6.   Cf. R. Diceto (Stubbs),
vol. ii. p. 143 ; Gerv. Cant. (Stubbs), vol. i. pp. 533, 534 ; and Mat. Paris, *Chron.
Maj.* (Luard), vol. ii. p. 419.   Gervase calls the place of execution " ad ulmos,"
Mat. Paris "ad Ulmetum " [" the Elms in Smithfield " notes Mr. Luard in the
margin].   R. Diceto calls it Tyburn ; the other writers give it no name at all.   We
are indebted to Gervase (as above, p. 533) for the date of this affair ; Saturday,
April 6—the day before the abbot of Caen fell sick ; see above, p. 344.
    [1] Rog. Howden and R. Diceto, as above.
    [2] See Will. Newb. as above, c. 21 (pp. 471, 472).   Mat. Paris (as above)
heartily shared in their opinion.
    [3] Rog. Howden as above, p. 48.   [4] *Ib.* pp. 12, 13.
    [5] Stubbs, *Rog. Howden*, vol. iv. pref. p. lxxxviii and note 3.   Madox, *Hist.
Exch.*, vol. i. pp. 637, 638.   [6] Rog. Howden as above, pp. 33, 34.
    [7] *Ib.* p. 172.   Stubbs, *Constit. Hist.*, vol. i. p. 509.
    [8] R. Diceto as above, p. 158.   Gerv. Cant. as above, pp. 544, 545.   The
dates do not exactly agree.

Richard, at the height of his struggle with Philip of France, found himself short not only of money but of men,[1] at any rate of men whom he could trust. He called upon Hubert to send him over from England either a force of three hundred knights to serve him at their own charges for a year, or a sum which would enable him to enlist the same number of mercenaries for the same period, at the rate of three English shillings a day.[2] For some reason or other it seems that Hubert, somewhat unwisely, at once decided to ignore the second alternative ; in a great council held at Oxford on December 7[3] he simply proposed, in his own name and that of his colleagues in the government, that the barons of England, among whom the bishops were to be reckoned, should come to the rescue of their distressed sovereign by supplying him with three hundred knights to serve him at their own cost for a year. Hubert himself, in his character of archbishop, declared his readiness to take his share of the burthen ; so did the bishop of London, Richard Fitz-Nigel the treasurer. The bishop of Lincoln, Hugh of Avalon, was then asked for his assent. "O ye wise and noble men here present," said the Burgundian saint, "ye know that I came to this land as a stranger, and from the simplicity of a hermit's life was raised to the office of a bishop. When therefore my inexperience was called to rule over the church of our Lady, I set myself carefully to learn its customs and privileges, its duties and burthens; and for thirteen years I have not strayed from the path marked out by my predecessors, in preserving the one and fulfilling the other. I know that the church of Lincoln is bound to do the king military service, but only in this land ; outside the boundaries of England she owes him no such thing. Wherefore I deem it meeter for me to go back to my native land and my hermit's cell, rather than, while holding a bishopric here, to bring upon my church the loss of her ancient immunities and the infliction of unwonted burthens."[4]

---

[1] *Magna Vita S. Hugonis* (Dimock), p. 248.

[2] Rog. Howden (Stubbs), vol. iv. p. 40.

[3] Cf. Gerv. Cant. (Stubbs), vol. i. p. 549, and *Mag. Vita S. Hug.* (Dimock), p. 251.   [4] *Mag. Vita S. Hug.* (Dimock), pp. 249, 250.

Hugh of Lincoln was the universally - acknowledged leader of the English Church in all matters of religion and morals ; he had exercised in Henry II.'s later years such an influence over the king as no one, except perhaps Thomas Becket, had ever possessed ; the whole Church and nation reverenced him as it had never reverenced any man since the death of S. Anselm.   When he took up the position of Thomas and Anselm as a champion of constitutional liberty, the victory was sure.   Strangely enough, his action seems to have taken the primate completely by surprise.   For a moment Hubert stood speechless ; then he turned to Bishop Herbert of Salisbury, and with quivering lips asked what he was minded to do for the king's assistance.   As a son of Richard of Ilchester and a kinsman of the great ministerial house founded by Roger of Salisbury,[1] Herbert represented the traditions of an old and venerated political school, as Hugh represented those of the best school of ecclesiastics. The statesman's reply was an echo of the saint's : " It seems to me that, without grievous wrong to my church, I can neither do nor say aught but what I have heard from my lord of Lincoln."   The justiciar, hurling a torrent of reproaches at Hugh, broke up the assembly, and wrote to the king that his plan had been foiled through Hugh's opposition.[2]   Richard in a fury ordered the property of the two recalcitrant bishops to be confiscated ; in the case of Salisbury this was done, but no Englishman dared lay a finger on anything belonging to the saint of Lincoln, " for they feared his curse like death itself."   In vain did the king reiterate his command, till at last his own officers begged Hugh to put an end to the scandal by making his peace, for their sakes if not for his own ; Hugh therefore went to seek Richard in Normandy, and literally forced him into a reconciliation on S. Augustine's day.   Herbert, on the other hand, had to purchase his restoration at a heavy price ;[3] but the king and his justiciar were none the less completely

---

[1] On Herbert's antecedents and connexions see Stubbs, *Rog. Howden*, vol. iv. pref. p. xci, note 4.

[2] *Mag. Vita S. Hug.* (Dimock), p. 250.   Cf. the brief account in Rog. Howden (Stubbs), vol. iv. p. 40.   [3] *Mag. Vita S. Hug.* (Dimock), p. 251.

beaten.   The death of Rees Ap-Griffith and a dispute
between his sons for the succession in South Wales gave
Hubert an opportunity of renewing his fading laurels by a
brilliant expedition to the Welsh marches, where he succeeded in restoring tranquillity and securing the border-
fortresses for the king.[1] He had however scarcely had time
to recover from his political defeat before he was overwhelmed
by the bursting of an ecclesiastical storm which had long
been hanging over his head.   Pope Celestine died on
January 8, 1198.   On the morrow the cardinals elected as
his successor a young deacon named Lothar, who took the
name of Innocent III., and began at once to sweep away the
abuses of the Roman court and to vindicate the rights of his
see against the Roman aristocracy with a promptness and
vigour which were an earnest of his whole future career.[2]
The monks of Canterbury lost no time in sending to the new
Pope their list of grievances against their primate ; and at
the head of the list they set a charge which, in the eyes of
such a pontiff as Innocent, could admit of no defence.
Hubert, said they, had violated the duties and the dignity
of his order by becoming the king's justiciar, acting as
a judge in cases of life and death, and so entangling himself
in worldly business that he was incapable of paying due
attention to the government of the Church.   Innocent
immediately wrote to the king, charging him, if he valued
his soul's health, not to suffer either the archbishop of
Canterbury or any other priest to continue in any secular
office ; and at the same time he solemnly forbade the acceptance of any such office by any bishop or priest throughout
the whole Church.   Discredited as Hubert now was in the
eyes of all parties, he had no choice but to resign, and this
time Richard had no choice but to accept his resignation.[3]

---

[1] On Rees's death his two sons quarrelled over the succession, and Hubert had
to go to the "fines Gwalliæ" and make peace between them. Rog. Howden
(Stubbs), vol. iv. p. 21. At Christmas he was at Hereford, where he took the
castle into his own hands, turning out its custodians and putting in new ones,
"ad opus regis"; he did the same at Bridgenorth and Ludlow. *Ib.* p. 35. See
also Gerv. Cant. (Stubbs), vol. i. p. 543, Gerald's letter to Hubert after his victory, and Hubert's reply : Gir. Cambr. *De Rebus a se gestis*, l. iii. cc. 5, 6
(Brewer, vol. i. pp. 96-102).

[2] Rog. Howden as above, pp. 41-44.   [3] *Ib.* pp. 47, 48.

The last few months of his justiciarship were however occupied with the projection, if not the execution, of a measure of great constitutional importance. Early in the spring he had, in his master's name, laid upon England a carucage to the amount of five shillings upon every carucate or ploughland. The great increase in the rate of taxation, as compared with that of 1194, was not unjustifiable ; for since that year the socage-tenants, on whom the impost fell, had paid no direct taxes at all, while two scutages had been exacted from the tenants-in-chivalry. But a far more important change was made in the assessment of the new impost. Until now, the carucate, like the hide, had been a term of elastic significance. It represented, as the literal meaning of the word implied, the extent of land which could be cultivated by a single plough ; and this of course varied in different parts of the country according to the nature of the soil, and the number and strength of the plough-team. In general, however, a hundred acres seem to have been reckoned as the average extent both of the carucate and of the hide. In order to avoid the endless complications and disputes which under the old system had made the assess-ment of the land-tax a matter of almost more trouble than profit, Hubert Walter adopted this average as a fixed standard, and ordered that henceforth, for purposes of tax-ation, the word " carucate " should represent a hundred acres. It followed as a necessary consequence that the whole arable land of England must be re-measured. The old customary reckoning of hides, based upon the Domesday survey, would no longer answer its purpose : the venerable rate-book which had been in use for more than a hundred years, partially superseded since 1168 by the Black Book of the Exchequer, was now to be superseded entirely. Hubert therefore issued in the king's name a commission for what was virtually a new Domesday survey. Into every shire he sent a clerk and a knight, who, together with the sheriff and certain lawful men chosen out of the shire, were, after swearing that they would do the king's business faith-fully, to summon before them the stewards of the barons of the county, the lord or bailiff of every township and the reeve and four lawful men of the same, whether free or villein, and two lawful knights of the hundred ; these persons were to declare upon oath what ploughlands there were in every township—how many in demesne, how many in villenage, how many in alms, and who was responsible for these last. The carucates thus ascertained were noted in a roll of which four copies were kept, one by each of the two royal commissioners, one by the sheriff, and the other divided among the stewards of the local barons. The collection of the money was intrusted to two lawful knights and the bailiff of every hundred ; these were responsible for it to the sheriff; and the sheriff had to see that it agreed with his roll, and to pay it into the Exchequer. Stern penalties were denounced against witnesses, whether free or villein, who should be detected in trying to deceive the commissioners. No land was to be exempted from the tax, except the free estates belonging to the parish churches, and lands held of the king by serjeanty or special service ; even these last, however, were to be included in the survey, and their holders were required to come and prove their excuses at its conclusion, in London at the octave of Pentecost.[1]

This was Hubert's last great administrative act, and it had a far more important significance than he himself probably knew. In form, the application of the process of jury-inquest to the assessment of an impost on the land was only a return to the precedent of Domesday itself. In reality, however, it was something much more important than this. The jury-inquest had been introduced by the Conqueror in 1086 under exceptional circumstances, and for an exceptional purpose which could be attained by no other means. So far as its original use was concerned, the precedent had remained a wholly isolated one for more than a hundred years. But during those years the principle which lay at the root of the jury-inquest had made its way into every branch of legal, fiscal and judicial administration. It had been applied to the purposes of private litigation by the Great Assize, to the determination of individual liability to military duty by the Assize of Arms, to the assessment

[1] Rog. Howden (Stubbs), vol. iv. pp. 46, 47.

of taxation on personal property by the ordinance of the Saladin tithe ; it had penetrated the whole system of criminal procedure through the Assizes of Clarendon and Northampton ; and it had gained a yet fuller recognition in the judicial ordinances of 1194. Viewed in this light, its application to the assessment of taxation on real property was another highly important step in the extension of its sphere of work. But this was not all. The chief value of the jury-system lay in its employment of the machinery of local representation and election, whereby it was a means of training the people to the exercise of constitutional self-government. The commission of 1198 shews that, although doubtless neither rulers nor people were conscious of the fact, this training had now advanced within measurable distance of its completion. The machinery of the new survey was not identical with that used in 1086. The taxpayers were represented, not only by the witnesses on whose recognition the assessment was based. but by the " lawful men chosen out of the shire " who took their place side by side with the king's officers as commissioners for the assessment, and by the bailiff and two knights of the hundred who were charged with the collection of the money. The representative principle had now reached its furthest develope-ment in the financial administration of the shire. Its next advance must inevitably result in giving to the taxpayers a share in the determination, first of the amount of the impost, and then of the purposes to which it should be applied, by admitting them, however partially and indirectly, to a voice in the great council of the nation.[1]

We must not credit Hubert Walter with views so lofty or so far-reaching as these. The ´chief aim of his policy doubtless was to get for his master as much money as he could, although he would only do it by what he regarded as just and constitutional methods. Unluckily the com-missioners' report is lost, and there is not even any proof that it was ever presented ; for before Whitsuntide the new Pope's views had become known, and on July 11 a royal writ

---

[1] On this " Great Carucage " see Stubbs, *Constit. Hist.*, vol. i. pp. 510, 511, and pref. to Rog. Howden, vol. iv. pp. xci-xcv.

announced Hubert's retirement from the justiciarship and
the appointment of Geoffrey Fitz-Peter in his stead.[1] Like
Hubert, Geoffrey Fitz-Peter came of a family which had
long been engaged in administrative work. His elder
brother Simon had in Henry's early years filled the various
offices of sheriff, justice-in-eyre, and king's marshal.[2] Geoffrey
himself had been sheriff of Northampton throughout the last
five years of Henry's reign, and had during the same period
acted occasionally as an ordinary justice of assize, and more
frequently as a judge of the forest-court.[3] In 1189 Richard
appointed him one of the assistant-justiciars, and in this
capacity he supported Walter of Rouen in the affair of
William of Longchamp's deposition.[4] In the early days of
William's rule, however, Geoffrey had made use of the latter's
influence to secure for himself the whole English inheritance
of the earl of Essex, William de Mandeville, upon which his
wife had a distant claim.[5] Such a man was likely to be
controlled by fewer scruples, as well as hampered by fewer
external restraints, than those which had beset the justiciar-archbishop ; and in truth, before the year was out,
both clergy and people had cause to regret the change of
ministers. Some of the religious orders refused to pay their
share of the carucage ; their refusal was met by a royal edict
declaring the whole body of clergy, secular as well as monastic, incapable of claiming redress for any wrongs inflicted
on them by the laity, while for any injury done by a clerk
or a monk to a layman satisfaction was exacted to the
uttermost farthing. The archbishop of Canterbury could
hardly have published what was virtually a decree of outlawry against his own order ; the new justiciar published it

---

[1] Rymer, *Fœdera*, vol. i. p. 71.

[2] He was sheriff of Northamptonshire, Bedfordshire and Buckinghamshire
from 1156 till 1160, and of Northamptonshire again from Michaelmas 1163 till
Easter 1170. See the list of sheriffs in index to Eyton's *Itin. Hen. II.*, pp. 337,
339. He appears as marshal in 1165 (Madox, *Form. Angl.*, p. xix), and as
justice-errant in Bedfordshire, A.D. 1163, in the story of Philip de Broi (above,
p. 21).

[3] Eyton, *Itin. Hen. II.*, list of sheriffs, p. 339 ; *ib.* pp. 265, 273, 281, 291,
298. Pipe Roll I. Ric. I. (Hunter) *passim*.

[4] Rog. Howden (Stubbs), vol. iii. pp. 16, 28, 96, 153.

[5] Stubbs, *Rog. Howden*, vol. iii., pref. p. xlviii, note 6.

seemingly without hesitation, and the recalcitrant monks were compelled to submit.[1] This act was followed by a renewal of the decree requiring all charters granted under the king's old seal to be brought up for confirmation under the new one[2]—a step which seems to imply that Richard's former command to this effect had not been very strictly enforced by Hubert. Meanwhile three justices-errant, acting on a set of instructions modelled upon those of 1194, were holding pleas of the Crown in the northern shires ;[3] "so that," says King Henry's old chaplain Roger of Howden, " with these and other vexations, just or unjust, all England from sea to sea was reduced to penury. And these things were not yet ended when another kind of torment was added to confound the men of the kingdom, through the justices of the forest," who were sent out all over England to hold a great forest-assize, which was virtually a renewal of that issued by Henry in 1184.[4]

Stern and cruel, however, as was the administration of the last eight months of Richard's reign, it was still part of a salutary discipline. The milder chastenings which Richard's English subjects had endured from Hubert Walter, the scorpion-lashes with which he chastised them by the hands of Geoffrey Fitz-Peter, were both alike stages in the training which Richard's predecessor had begun, and whose value they were to learn when left face to face with the personal tyranny of his successor. For nearer at hand than they could dream was the day when English people and Angevin king were to stand face to face indeed, more closely than they had ever stood before. The nine generations of increasing prosperity promised to Fulk the Good were all numbered and fulfilled, and with their fulfilment had come the turn of the tide. The power of the Angevins had

---

[1] Rog. Howden (Stubbs), vol. iv. p. 66.

[2] *Ibid.* Mat. Paris, *Chron. Maj.* (Luard), vol. ii. p. 451. Ann. Waverl. a. 1198 (Luard, *Ann. Monast.*, vol. ii. p. 251).

[3] Instructions in Rog. Howden (as above), pp. 61, 62. The judges were Hugh Bardulf, Roger Arundel and Geoffrey Hacket ; they held pleas in Lincolnshire, Nottinghamshire, Derbyshire, Yorkshire, Northumberland, Westmoreland, Cumberland and Lancashire.

[4] Rog. Howden (as above), pp. 62-66.

reached its destined limit, and had begun to recede again.
From the sacred eastern land all trace of it was already
swept away ; in the west it was, slowly indeed as yet, but
none the less surely falling back.   Five years were still to
pass before the tide should be fairly out ; then it was to
leave the Good Count's heir stranded, not on the black rock
of Angers, but on the white cliffs of England.

Richard had spent the first half of his reign in fighting
for a lost cause in Palestine ; he spent the other half in
fighting for a losing cause in Gaul.   The final result of the
long series of conquests and annexations whereby the Angevin counts, from Fulk the Red to Henry Fitz-Empress,
had been enlarging their borders for more than two hundred
years, had been to bring them into direct geographical contact and political antagonism with an enemy more formidable than any whom they had yet encountered.   In their
earliest days the king of the French had been their patron ;
a little later, he had become their tool.   Now, he was their
sole remaining rival ; and ere long he was to be their conqueror.   Since the opening of the century, a great change
had taken place in the political position of the French
Crown ; a change which was in a considerable measure
due to the yet greater change in the position of the Angevin
house.   When Louis VI. came to the throne in 1109, he
found the so-called "kingdom of France" distributed somewhat as follows.   The western half, from the river Somme
to the Pyrenees, was divided between four great fiefs—Normandy, Britanny, Anjou and Aquitaine.   Four others—
Champagne, Burgundy, Auvergne and Toulouse—covered
its eastern portion from the river Meuse to the Mediterranean
Sea ; another, Flanders, occupied its northernmost angle,
between the sources of the Meuse, the mouth of the Scheld,
and the English Channel.   The two lines of great fiefs were
separated by an irregular group of smaller territories, amid
which lay, distributed in two very unequal portions, the royal
domain.   Its northern and larger half, severed from Flanders
by the little counties of Amiens and Vermandois, was flanked
on the east by Champagne and on the north-west by Normandy, while its south-western border was ringed in by the

counties of Chartres, Blois and Sancerre, which parted it
from Anjou, and which were all linked together with Champagne under the same ruling house. Southward, in the
upper valleys of the Loire and the Cher, a much smaller
fragment of royal domain, comprising the viscounty of
Bourges and the territory afterwards known as the Bour-
bonnais, lay crowded in between Auvergne, the Aquitanian
district of Berry, and the Burgundian counties of Mâcon and
Nevers and that of Sancerre, which parted it from the larger
royal possessions north of the Loire. The whole domains
of the Crown thus covered scarcely more ground than the
united counties of Anjou, Touraine and Maine, scarcely so
much as the duchy of Normandy. Within these limits,
however, Louis VI. had in his twenty-nine years' reign contrived to establish his absolute authority on so firm a basis
that from thenceforth the independence of the Crown was
secured. To destroy that of the great feudataries, and to
bring them one by one into a subjection as absolute as that
of the royal domain itself, was the work which he bequeathed
to his successors.

We may set aside the temporary annexation of Aquitaine through the marriage of Louis VII. and Eleanor as
forming no part of this process of absorption. In the plans
of Louis VI. it was doubtless meant to be a very important
part ; but as a matter of fact, its historical importance proved
to be of a wholly different kind. The marriage of Louis
and Eleanor contributed to the final acquisition of Guienne
and Gascony by the French Crown not a whit more than
the marriage of Geoffrey Martel and Agnes had contributed
to their acquisition by the house of Anjou. The Parisian
king, like his Angevin follower of old, had work to do on
his own side of the Loire before he might safely attempt the
conquest of the south. By the middle of the century, the
map of Gaul had undergone a marked transformation. Its
eastern and central portions indeed remained unchanged ;
but the western half was utterly metamorphosed. Its four
great divisions had been virtually swept away, and the whole
land had become Angevin. In face of this altered state of
things, the remaining powers of northern Gaul were of

FRANCE
AND THE
ANGEVIN DOMINIONS.
To illustrate the wars of Richard and
John with Philip Augustus.

▨ *Royal Domain of Philip, A.D. 1194.*

Abbreviations
E.= Evreux
G.= Gamaches
Gail.= Gaillon
Lou.= Louviers
V.= Vaudreuil

Wagner & Debes' Geog^l Estab^t Leipsic.

London, Macmillan & Co.

necessity driven into union, as a counterpoise to this enormous growth of Anjou ; and the only possible centre of union, alike in a political and a geographical point of view, was the king of the French.   He alone could claim to match in rank and dignity the crowned masters of the west ; and under his leadership alone was it possible to face them all along the line from the mouth of the Somme to the source of the Cher with a front as unbroken as their own.   The old Angevin march had ceased to be a marchland at all ; its original character was now transferred to the counties of Chartres and Blois ; while to north and south of these, from Nonancourt to Aumale and along the whole course of the Cher above Vierzon, the royal domain itself was the sole bulwark of north-eastern Gaul against the advancing power of Anjou.   To secure Chartres and Blois was the first necessity for the king : but their counts needed his pro-tection even more than he needed their fidelity, for the whole width of his domains parted them from Champagne, where the bulk of their strength lay.   Accordingly Louis VII., by the matrimonial alliances which he formed first for his daughters and lastly for himself with the house of Blois and Champagne, easily succeeded in binding them to a com-munity of personal interests with the royal house of France, whereby their subservience to the French Crown was for the future secured.   The chain was too strong to be broken by the boyish wilfulness of Philip Augustus ; and from the moment of his reconciliation with his mother and uncles in 1180, the whole military and political strength of Blois, Chartres and Champagne may be reckoned at his command as unreservedly as that of his own immediate domains.

Since that time, the royal power had made an important advance to the northward.   At the opening of Philip's reign the dominions of the count of Flanders stretched from the Channel to the borders of Champagne, covered the whole northern frontier of the royal domain, and touched that of Normandy at its junction with Ponthieu.   Twelve years later, more than half this territory had passed, either by cession or by conquest, into the hands of the king.   Ver-

mandois was given up to him in 1186; and in 1191 the
death of the Flemish count Philip made him master of all
Flanders south of the river Lys, which had been promised to
him as the dowry of his first queen, Elizabeth of Hainaut,
niece of the dead count and daughter of his successor.[1]
This was in several respects a most valuable acquisition.
Not only did it bring to the Crown a considerable accession
of territory, including the whole upper valley of the Somme,
the famous fortress of Péronne, and the flourishing towns of
Amiens and Arras; but the power of Flanders, which a few
years before had threatened to overshadow every other power
in northern Gaul, was completely broken; and the effect
upon the political position of Normandy was more important
still.   While Vermandois and Amiens were in Flemish
hands, a league between the Flemish count and the ruler
of Normandy would at any moment not only place the
whole north-western border of France at their mercy, but
would enable them to call in the forces of the imperial
Crown to a junction which the French king could have no
power to hinder, and which must almost certainly lead to
his ruin.   Now, on the other hand, such a junction was
rendered well-nigh impossible; the whole territory between
Normandy, Ponthieu and the German border was in the
king's own hands, and all that was left of Flanders lay in
almost complete isolation between the Lys and the sea.   In
fine, as the dukes of Burgundy had for several generations
been obedient followers of their royal kinsmen, now that
Blois, Champagne and Vermandois were all secured, the
power and influence of the French Crown north of the
Loire was fully a match in territorial extent for that of the
house of Anjou.   South of the Loire the balance was less
equal.   The extensive possessions of the house of S. Gilles
may indeed be left out of both scales; their homage for
Toulouse was now secured to the dukes of Aquitaine, but it
was a mere formality which left them practically still independent of both their rival overlords.   It was indeed at the
expense of Toulouse that the Angevin rulers of Poitou had
made their last conquest, that of the Quercy.   But since

[1] See above, p. 234, note 7.

then the French king, too, had been gaining territory in Aquitaine ; and his gains were made at the expense of the Poitevin duke.   Richard had found it needful to buy Philip's assent to his peaceful entrance upon his ancestral heritage after his father's death by a renunciation of all claims upon Auvergne and a cession of two important lordships in Berry, Graçay and Issoudun.[1]   The sacrifice was trifling in itself, but it was significant.   It marked Richard's own consciousness that a turning-point had come in the career of his house.   Hitherto they had gone steadily forward ; now it was time to draw back.   The aggressive attitude which had been habitual to the counts of Anjou for nearly three hundred years must be dropped at last.   Henceforth they were to stand on the defensive in their turn against the advance of the French Crown.

It was not the strength of that advance itself which made it so formidable to Richard ; it was the knowledge that, side by side with the process of consolidation in France, there had been and still was going on in the Angevin dominions a process of disintegration which his father had been unable to check, and against which he himself was well-nigh helpless.   The French monarchy was built up around one definite centre, a centre round which all the subordinate parts of the structure grouped themselves unquestioningly as a matter of course.   Paris and its king, even when his practical authority was at the lowest ebb, had always been in theory the accepted rallying-point of the whole kingdom, the acknowledged head of the body politic, none of whose members had ever dreamed of establishing any other in its place.   But the empire of Richard Cœur-de-Lion had no centre ; or rather, it had three or four rival ones.   In Angevin eyes its centre was Angers ; in Norman eyes it was Rouen ; to the men of the south, it was Poitiers.   Even Henry Fitz-Empress had felt at times the difficulty of fulfilling two such opposite parts as those of duke of Normandy and count of Anjou without rousing the jealous resentment of either country against himself as the representative of the other ; while as for

---

[1] Rigord (Duchesne, *Hist. Franc. Scriptt.*, vol. v.) p. 29.   Will. Armor. *Gesta Phil. Aug. (ibid.)*, p. 75.

Britanny and Aquitaine, he had only been able to keep an uncertain hold over them by sheer force, until Britanny was appeased by the marriage of Constance, and Aquitaine subdued by the vigour of Richard.   But for Richard in his father's place the difficulty was far greater.   Chafe as they might against the yoke which bound them together—dispute as they might over their respective shares in their common ruler and their respective claims upon him—neither Angevin nor Norman could fail to recognize his own natural sovereign and national representative in the son of Geoffrey and Matilda.   But the chances of this recognition being extended to the next generation expired with the young king.   If the two Henrys were strangers in Britanny and in Aquitaine, yet on the banks of the Seine, the Loire and the Mayenne they were felt to be at home.   But Richard was at home nowhere, though he was master everywhere, from the Solway to the Pyrenees.   His Aquitanian subjects for the most part, if they counted him as a fellow-countryman, counted him none the less as an enemy ; his subjects north of Loire counted him as a southern stranger.   Normans and Angevins still saw in him, as they had been taught to see in him for the first twenty-six years of his life, the representative not of Hrolf and William or of Fulk the Red and Geoffrey Martel, but simply of his mother's Poitevin ancestors.   The Bretons saw in him the son of their conqueror, asserting his supremacy over them and their young native prince only by the right of the stronger.   As Suger had laid it down as an axiom, more than half a century ago, that " Englishmen ought not to rule over Frenchmen nor French over English," so now we begin to discern growing up in Richard's continental dominions a feeling that Normans should not rule over Angevins, nor Angevins over Normans, nor either over Bretons and Poitevins, nor Poitevins over any of the rest ; and that if one and all must needs submit to the loss of their ancient independence, it would be more natural and less humiliating to lay it down at the feet of the prince who had always been acknowledged in theory as the superior of all alike, the king of the French.

This feeling, however, had scarcely come into existence, much less risen to the surface of politics, when Philip Augustus came home from the Crusade at Christmas 1191. It is scarcely probable that any plan of actual conquest had as yet taken shape in Philip's mind. But the very audacity of the demand which he made upon the credulity of the Norman constables when in the following spring he asked them to believe that Richard had ceded to him not only the whole Vexin, but also the counties of Aumale and Eu—a cession for which there was not a shadow of reason either in past history or in present circumstances, and which if carried into effect would have cut off the Norman communications with Ponthieu and Flanders, and given him at once a foothold upon the Channel and an invaluable coign of vantage for an attempt upon Rouen—seems to indicate that he was already forming some more definite design against the Angevins' power than the simple system of lying in wait to steal from them any territorial or political advantage that could be stolen with impunity, with which he, like his father, had hitherto been content. The terms of his treaty with John in the following year point still more strongly in the same direction. As the price of John's investiture with the rest of his brother's dominions, Philip reserved to himself the whole Norman territory on the right bank of the Seine, except the city of Rouen ; on the left bank, nearly half the viscounty of Evreux, including the castles of Vaudreuil, Verneuil and Ivry ; and from the older Angevin patrimony, all that was most worth having in Touraine—Tours itself, Azay, Montbazon, Montrichard, Amboise and Loches— besides the transfer of the Angevin fiefs in the Vendômois from the count of Anjou to the count of Blois.[1] Owing to the disorganized state of Richard's dominions caused by his captivity, Philip's endeavours to carry this bargain into effect by conquering Normandy in John's interest and his own met for a while with considerable success. His first attempt at invasion was indeed repulsed by the Norman barons under the leadership of Earl Robert of Leicester ;[2] but a few weeks

---

[1] Treaty in Rymer, *Fœdera*, vol. i. p. 57.
[2] Rog. Howden (Stubbs), vol. iii. p. 205.

later treason opened to him the gates of Gisors and Neaufle ; the rest of the Vexin was easily won,[1] and secured thus against attack in his rear, he marched northward to the capture of Aumale and Eu.[2] Thence he turned back to besiege Rouen, but soon retreated again into his own terri- tories,[3] taking Pacy and Ivry on his way.[4] In July, finding that, according to his own phrase, the Angevin demon was after all to be let loose upon him once more, he thought it advisable to accept Richard's overtures of peace; and Richard on his part—being still in prison—deemed it wise for the moment to sanction the French king's recent conquests in Normandy and the liberation of Ademar of Angoulême, and also to let Philip have temporary possession of Loches, Châtillon-sur-Indre, Driencourt and Arques, as pledges for the payment of twenty thousand marks, due within two years of his own release.[5]

Whether he intended to keep or to break these engage- ments is practically no matter ; for, if he meant to break them, Philip took care to anticipate him. Seven months after the treaty was signed he again crossed the Norman border, took Evreux,[6] which he handed over to John's cus- tody,[7] and marched up by way of Neubourg and Vaudreuil, both of which he captured, to besiege Rouen. Thence, however, he again retired—scared, it may be, by tidings of Richard's approach—and hurrying back to the southern border laid siege to Verneuil on May 10.[8] Two days later

---

[1] Rog. Howden (Stubbs), vol. iii. p. 206. Will. Newb., l. iv. c. 34 (Howlett, vol. i. pp. 389, 390). Rigord (Duchesne, *Hist. Franc. Scriptt.*, vol. v.), p. 36. Will. Armor. *Gesta Phil. Aug. (ibid.)*, p. 77.

[2] Will. Newb. as above (p. 390).

[3] *Ibid.* Rog. Howden, as above. Cf. Chron. Rothom., a. 1193 (Labbe, *Nova Biblioth.*, vol. i. p. 369).

[4] Will. Newb. as above.

[5] Rog. Howden as above, pp. 217-220. These were apparently the twenty thousand marks promised in 1189 and not yet paid.

[6] Will. Newb. as above, c. 40 (p. 403). Rigord (as above), p. 37. Will. Armor. *Gesta Phil. Aug.* as above ; *Philipp.*, l. iv. *(ibid.)* p. 143.

[7] Will. Armor. *Philipp.* as above.

[8] Rigord as above. Will. Armor. *Gesta Phil. Aug.* as above. Cf. *Philipp.* as above ; Rog. Howden (as above), pp. 251, 252 ; R. Diceto (Stubbs), vol. ii. pp. 114, 115; and Will. Newb., l. v. c. 2 (Howlett, vol. ii. p. 418). The date of the siege of Verneuil comes from Rog. Howden.

Richard landed at Barfleur,[1] and by the end of another
fortnight he was encamped at L'Aigle,[2] within a few miles
of Verneuil. His presence there, coupled with the defection
of John who had contrived to join him on the road,[3] and
the surprise and slaughter of the French garrison of Evreux
by a body of Norman troops,[4] alarmed Philip so much that
on Whitsun Eve, May 28, he again fled into his own
dominions.[5] Richard was busy strengthening the walls of
Verneuil. when tidings came to him that "the Angevins
and Cenomannians" were besieging Montmirail,[6] a castle on
the borders of Perche and Maine, famous as the scene of
a stormy conference between Henry II. and S. Thomas.
Who the besiegers actually were, or what was the ground
of their hostility either to William of Montmirail[7] or to his
overlord King Richard, must remain undecided. It is
plain, however, that in Richard's ears the tidings sounded as
a warning of disaffection in his patrimonial dominions. He
hurried to the relief of Montmirail, but found it levelled with
the ground.[8] He wasted no time in pursuit of its destroyers,
but pushed on direct to Tours, took up his quarters in
Châteauneuf,[9] and shewed his suspicions concerning the

---

[1] Rog. Howden (Stubbs), vol. iii. p. 251. R. Diceto (Stubbs), vol. ii. p. 114.

[2] Will. Newb., l. v. c. 2 (Howlett, vol. ii. p. 418).

[3] Rog. Howden (as above), p. 252. R. Diceto, as above, says they met "apud
Bruis."

[4] This is all that Rigord says about the disaster (Duchesne, *Hist. Franc.
Script.*, vol. v. p. 37). In the hands of the poet William of Armorica it becomes
a horrible romance, wherein John, as commandant of Evreux, invites the unsuspecting Frenchmen to a banquet, and then brings in his "armed Englishmen" to
massacre them (*Philipp.*, l. iv., *ib.* p. 143 ; *Gesta Phil. Aug.*, *ib.* p. 77). John
has so many undoubted crimes to answer for that it probably seemed a mere trifle
to add one more to the list, but for that very reason one cannot admit it on the
sole testimony of the poet-historiographer. The English writers say nothing of
the whole matter.

[5] Rog. Howden and Will. Newb. as above. R. Diceto (as above), p. 115.
Cf. Rigord and Will. Armor. as above.

[6] "Andegavenses et Cenomannenses" says Rog. Howden as above. R. Diceto
(as above), p. 116, has "Andegavenses" only; the Chron. S. Albin. a. 1192
(Marchegay, *Eglises*, p. 49), has "Andegavenses et alii."

[7] William "Gohet" as R. Diceto calls him ; *i.e.* (see Bishop Stubbs's note,
ibid.), "William of Perche Gouet, Goeth, or le petit Perche."

[8] Rog. Howden as above. R. Diceto as above, p. 117. Cf. Chron. S. Albin.
a. 1192 (as above).   [9] R. Diceto as above.

origin of the new mischief by driving the canons of S. Martin out of the abbey where they dwelt under the special protection of the French king.[1] The burghers, on the other hand, made proof of their loyalty by a free-will offering of two thousand marks.[2] Determined now to redeem his pledges to Philip not with gold but with steel, Richard marched on to Beaulieu,[3] to join a body of Navarrese and Brabantines, sent by his brother-in-law Sancho of Navarre, in blockading the castle of Loches ;[4] a few days after his arrival, on June 13, it was surrendered by its French garrison.[5] He was however standing between two fires. Bertrand de Born was again stirring up the south, singing and fighting ostensibly in Richard's interest against his disaffected neighbours in the Limousin, but in reality kindling into a fresh blaze all the reckless passions and endless feuds which had been smouldering too long for the warrior-poet's pleasure.[6] Philip meanwhile was again threatening Rouen ;[7] the Norman archbishop and seneschal attempted to negotiate with him in Richard's name, but without result ;[8] and at the end of the month he marched southward to meet Richard himself. On July 4 the two kings were within a few miles of each other—Richard at Vendôme, Philip at Fréteval.[9] What followed is told so diversely by the English and French historians of the time that it seems impossible to reconcile the rival accounts or to decide between them. All that we know for certain is that Philip suddenly struck his tents and withdrew into the territories of the count of Blois ; that Richard set off in pursuit, missed Philip himself, but fell at unawares upon the troops who were convoying

---

[1] Rigord (Duchesne), *Hist. Franc. Scriptt.*, vol. v. p. 38.

[2] "Dono spontaneo," Rog. Howden (Stubbs), vol. iii. p. 252 ; "nullâ coactione præmissâ," R. Diceto (Stubbs), vol. ii. p. 117. The "burgenses" in question, as appears from R. Diceto, were those of Châteauneuf, not the *cives* of Tours proper.

[3] R. Diceto as above.

[4] Rog. Howden (as above), pp. 252, 253.

[5] *Ib.* p. 253 (with the date). R. Diceto as above. Cf. Chron. S. Albin. a. 1192 (Marchegay, *Eglises*, p. 49).

[6] Clédat, *Bert. de Born*, pp. 83, 84.

[7] Rog. Howden as above, p. 253. R. Diceto, p. 116.

[8] Rog. Howden as above, pp. 253-255.

[9] R. Diceto as above.

his baggage towards Blois, routed them, and captured all the French king's most precious possessions, including his royal seal and the treasury-rolls of the whole kingdom, besides a number of valuable horses, an immense quantity of money and plate, and—what would be scarcely less· useful to Richard for political purposes—the charters of agreement between Philip and all the Norman, Angevin and Poitevin rebels who had plotted treason with him and John against their lord.[1]

The repairing of this disaster gave Philip sufficient occupation for the rest of the year, and Richard was free to march upon the Aquitanian rebels. Sancho of Navarre was already wasting the lands of the ringleaders, Geoffrey of Rancogne and Ademar of Angoulême ;[2] and by July 22 Richard was able to report to his justiciar in England that he was master of all the castles of the Angoumois and all the lands of Geoffrey.[3] From Angoulême he marched northward again, took measures for the security of Anjou and Maine,[4] and then returned to Normandy, where he found that his representatives, headed by the chancellor, had just concluded a truce with the French king to last till All Saints' day[5]—a proceeding which served him as the pretext for that withdrawal of the seal from William and repudiation

---

[1] Cf. Rog. Howden (Stubbs), vol. iii. pp. 255, 256 ; R. Diceto (Stubbs), vol. ii. pp. 117, 118 ; Will. Newb., l. v. c. 2 (Howlett, vol. ii. p. 419); Rigord (Duchesne, *Hist. Franc. Scriptt.*, vol. v.), p. 38 ; Will. Armor. *Gesta Phil. Aug. (ibid.)*, p. 77 ; *Philipp.*, l. iv. *(ibid.)*, p. 144 ; and Chron. S. Albin. a. 1192 (Marchegay, *Eglises*, p. 49). Rog. Howden alone mentions the charters, and Will. Armor. the treasury-rolls and seal.

[2] R. Diceto as above, p. 117. Will. Newb. as above.

[3] Letter of Richard to Hubert Walter (date, Angoulême, July 22) in Rog. Howden as above, pp. 256, 257. Cf. R. Diceto as above, pp. 118, 119. Will. Newb. as above (p. 420).

[4] " Rediit in Andegaviam, et redemit omnes baillivos suos, id est, ad redemptionem coegit. Similiter fecit in Cenomanniâ." Rog. Howden as above, p. 267. At Le Mans " convocavit magnates omnes suæ jurisdictioni subpositos," and apparently tried to shame them into more active loyalty—or more liberal gifts— by eulogy of their English brethren : " ubi fidem Anglorum in adversitate suâ semper sibi gratiosam, integram et probabilem plurimum commendavit," R. Diceto as above, p. 119.

[5] Rog. Howden as above, pp. 257-260. Cf. R. Diceto as above, p. 120, and Will. Newb., l. v. c. 3 (as above). This last gives a wrong date ; that of the document in Rog. Howden is July 23.

of all engagements made under it, which has been mentioned already.[1] No further movement was however made by either party until the spring. Then the wearisome story of fruit-less negotiations alternating with indecisive warfare begins again, and goes on unceasingly for the next four years. Save for an occasional attempt to make a diversion in Berry, the actual fighting between the two kings was confined to the Norman border.[2] Normandy was the chief object of Philip's attack, partly no doubt because, owing to its geographical position, he could invade it with more ease and less risk than any other part of Richard's dominions, but also because it was the key to all the rest. A French conquest of Normandy would sever Richard's communica-tions not only with Flanders and Germany, but also with England ; and the strength of the Angevins in Gaul now rested chiefly upon the support of their island-realm. Neither assailant nor defender, however, was able to gain any decisive advantage in the field. The armed struggle between them was in fact of less importance than the diplomatic rivalry which they carried on side by side with it ; and in this, strangely enough, Richard, who had hitherto shewn so little of the far-sighted statecraft and political tact of his race, proved more than a match for his wily antagonist.

That the foes in Richard's own household should league themselves against him with Philip, as he had done in earlier days against his own father, was, so far as Richard himself is concerned, no more than retributive justice. Philip's alliance with John had proved a failure ; but it was not long before he saw a chance of securing a more useful tool in the person of little Arthur of Britanny. English histor-ians tell us that when Richard and Philip made their treaty at Messina in March 1191 Richard obtained a formal acknowledgement of his rights, as duke of Normandy, to the

---

[1] Rog. Howden (Stubbs), vol. iii. p. 267.   See above, p. 343.

[2] It may be followed in Rog. Howden (Stubbs), vol. iii. pp. 301-305, vol. iv. pp. 3-7, 14, 16, 19-21, 24, 54-61, 68, 78-81 ; Rigord (Duchesne, *Hist. Franc. Scriptt.*, vol. v.), pp. 38-40, 42 ; Will. Armor. *Gesta Phil. Aug. (ibid.)*, pp. 78, 79 ; *Philipp.*, l. v. (*ib.*), pp. 146-154.

overlordship of Britanny and the liege homage of its duke.[1]
The text of the treaty of Messina, however, contains not a
word on this subject ; the agreement, if made at all, must
have been drawn up in a separate form ; and it seems to
have remained a dead letter, like another agreement made
at the same place a few months earlier—the treaty with
Tancred whereby Richard had engaged to recognize Arthur
of Britanny as his successor in default of direct heirs.
Although after five years of marriage Queen Berengaria was
still childless, no such recognition had yet been made.
Richard on his return to Europe probably perceived that
Arthur's succession would be impossible in England, and in
Gaul would be fatal to the independence of the Angevin
house. Accordingly, he was once more doing all in his
power to win the attachment of John ; and John, having at
length discovered that his own interests could be better
served by supporting his brother than by intriguing against
him, proved an active and useful ally in the war against
Philip.[2]   On the other hand, Richard seems never to have
received Arthur's homage for Britanny ; and those who had
the control of political affairs in that country were determined that he never should.   The dispute between Henry
and Philip for the wardship of the two children of Geoffrey
and Constance had apparently ended in a compromise.
Eleanor, the elder child, was now under the care of her
uncle Richard ;[3] but Constance seems to have succeeded in
keeping her infant boy out of the reach of both his
would-be guardians, and, moreover, in governing her duchy
without any reference to either of them, for nearly seven
years after the death of her father-in-law King Henry.
She had been given in marriage by him, when scarcely
twelve months a widow, to Earl Ralf of Chester,[4] son and
successor of Earl Hugh who had been one of the leaders in
the revolt of 1173.   As the earls of Chester were hereditary viscounts of the Avranchin—the border-district of

---

[1] *Gesta Ric.* (Stubbs), p. 161. Rog. Howden (Stubbs), vol. iii. pp. 99, 100.

[2] See *e.g.* Rog. Howden (Stubbs), vol. iv. pp. 5, 16, 60 ; Rigord (Duchesne,
Hist. Franc. Scriptt., vol. v.), p. 38 ; Will. Armor. *Gesta Phil. Aug.* (*ibid.*), p.
77.   [3] Rog. Howden (Stubbs), vol. iii. pp. 275, 278.

[4] *Gesta Hen.* (Stubbs), vol. ii. p. 29.

Normandy and Britanny—this marriage would have furnished an excellent means of securing the Norman hold
upon the Breton duchy, if only Ralf himself could have
secured a hold upon his wife. In this however he completely failed. Safe in her hereditary dominions, with her
boy at her side, and strong in the support of her people
rejoicing in their newly-regained independence, Constance
apparently set Ralf, Richard and Philip all alike at defiance,
till in 1196 Richard summoned her to a conference with himself in Normandy, and she set out to obey the summons.
Scarcely had she touched the soil of the Avranchin at
Pontorson when she was caught by her husband and imprisoned in his castle of S. James-de-Beuvron.[1] It is hard
not to suspect that Richard and Ralf had plotted the
capture between them ; for Richard, instead of insisting
upon her release, at once renewed his claim to the wardship
of Arthur, and prepared to enforce it at the sword's point.
The Bretons first hurried their young duke away to the
innermost fastnesses of their wild and desolate country under
the care of the bishop of Vannes,[2] and then, after a vain
attempt to liberate his mother, intrusted him to the protection of the king of France,[3] who of course received him
with open arms, and sent him to be educated with his own
son.[4]

Philip had now got the old Angevin patrimony between
two fires ; but the Bretons were so little accustomed to act
in concert even among themselves, far less with any other
power, that he found it impossible to make any real use of
them as allies either for military or political purposes. The
independent warfare which they carried on with Richard
across the south-western border of Normandy[5] had little
effect upon that which Richard and Philip were carrying on
along its eastern border ; and upon the Angevin lands which
lay directly between Britanny and France the Breton revolt
had no effect at all. To the end of Richard's life, we hear

[1] Rog. Howden (Stubbs), vol. iv. p. 7.
[2] Will. Armor. *Philipp.*, l. v. (Duchesne, *Hist. Franc. Scriptt.*, vol. v.), p.
149.   Will. Newb., l. v. c. 18 (Howlett, vol. ii. pp. 463, 464).
[3] Rog. Howden as above.   [4] Will. Armor. as above.
[5] Will. Newb. as above, c. 30 (p. 491). Rog. Howden as above.

of no further troubles in Maine or Anjou.   Nay more, we
hear of no further troubles in Aquitaine.   If Philip had in
some sense turned Richard's flank in the west, Richard had
turned Philip's flank far more effectually in the south.   The
unwonted tranquillity there may indeed have been partly due
to the fact that one of the chief sources of disturbance was
removed in 1196 by the withdrawal of Bertrand de Born
into a monastery ;[1] but it was also in great measure owing
to Richard's quickness in seizing an opportunity which
presented itself, in that same eventful year, of forming a
lasting alliance with the house of Toulouse.   His old enemy
Count Raymond V. was dead ;[2] he now offered the hand of
his own favourite sister, the still young and handsome Queen
Jane of Sicily, to the new Count Raymond VI.;[3] and thenceforth the eastern frontier of his Aquitanian duchy was as secure
under the protection of his sister's husband as its southern
frontier under that of his wife's brother, the king of Navarre.

Nor were Richard's alliances confined within the boundaries of Gaul.   His year of captivity in Germany had not
been all wasted time.   When he parted from his imperial
jailor in the spring of 1194, they were, at any rate in outward semblance, close political allies ; and at the same time
Richard had succeeded in gaining over his bitterest foe,
Leopold of Austria, by an offer of his niece Eleanor of
Britanny as wife to Leopold's son.[4]   The marriage-contract
was however not yet executed when the Austrian duke met
with a fatal accident and died in agony, owning with his
last breath that his miserable end was a just retribution for
his conduct towards the English king.[5]   The impression
made by this event deepened the feeling of respect and awe
which the captive lion had already contrived to inspire in
the princes of the Empire.   Meanwhile Henry VI. had

---

[1] Clédat, *Bert. de Born*, p. 92.

[2] In 1194, according to Rigord (Duchesne, *Hist. Franc. Scriptt.*, vol. v.),
p. 38.

[3] Rog. Howden (Stubbs), vol. iv. p. 13.   Will. Newb., l. v. c. 30 (Howlett,
vol. ii. p. 491).   R. Coggeshall (Stevenson), p. 70.

[4] Rog. Howden (Stubbs), vol. iii. p. 275.   See above, p. 325.

[5] Rog. Howden as above, pp. 276, 277.   R. Diceto (Stubbs), vol. ii. p. 124.
Will. Newb. as above, c. 8 (pp. 431-434).   R. Coggeshall (Stevenson), pp. 65, 66.

made himself master of Sicily ;[1] and now the old dream by which the German Emperors never quite ceased to be haunted, the dream of re-asserting their imperial supremacy over Gaul, was beginning to shape itself anew in his brain. In the summer of 1195 he sent to Richard a golden crown and a message charging him, on his plighted faith to the Emperor and on the very lives of his hostages, to invade the French kingdom at once, and promising him the support and co-operation of the imperial forces. Richard, suspecting a trap, despatched William of Longchamp to inquire into the exact nature, extent and security of Henry's promised assistance ; Philip vainly tried to intercept the envoy as he passed through the royal domains ;[2] and the negotiations proved so far effectual that Henry remitted seventeen thousand marks out of the ransom, as a contribution to Richard's expenses in his struggle with Philip.[3] When, on Michaelmas Eve 1197, Henry VI. died,[4] the use of that homage on Richard's part which his English subjects had resented so bitterly was made apparent to them at last. While the English king was holding his Christmas court at Rouen there came to him an embassy from the princes of Germany, summoning him, as chief among the lay members of the Empire [5] by virtue of his investiture with the kingdom of Arles, to take part with them in the election of a new Emperor at Cöln on February 22.[6] Richard himself could not venture to leave Gaul ; but the issue proved that his presence at Cöln was not needed to secure his interests there. He wished that the imperial crown should be given to his nephew Duke Henry of Saxony, eldest son and successor of Henry the Lion. This scheme, however, when laid before the other electors by the envoys whom he sent to represent him at Cöln, was rejected on account of the duke's absence in Holy Land.[7] The representatives of the English king then proposed Henry's brother Otto, for whom Richard had long been vainly endeavouring to find satis-

---

[1] In the autumn of 1194. Rog. Howden (Stubbs), vol. iii. pp. 268-270. Cf. R. Diceto (Stubbs), vol. ii. pp. 123, 124.

[2] Rog. Howden (as above), pp. 300, 301.   [3] *Ib.* pp. 303, 304.

[4] *Ib.* vol. iv. p. 31.   [5] "Sicut præcipuum membrum imperii." *Ib.* p. 37.

[6] *Ibid.*   [7] *Ib.* pp. 37, 38.

factory provision on either side of the sea,[1] and who seems
really to have been his favourite nephew. The result was
that, on the appointed day, Otto was elected Emperor of the
Romans,[2] and on July 12 he was crowned king of the
Germans at Aachen by the archbishop of Cöln.[3]
For a moment, at the mere prospect of beholding a
grandson of Henry Fitz-Empress seated upon the imperial
throne of the west, there had flashed across the mind of at
least one friend of the Angevin house a fancy that the world-
wide dominion which seemed to be passing away from the
heirs of Fulk the Good was to be renewed for yet one more
generation.[4] There was indeed an opposition party in
Germany, who set up a rival Emperor in the person of
Philip of Suabia, a brother of Henry VI.;[5] and he at once

---

[1] He appointed him earl of York in 1190, but as the grant was made after
the king left England, some of the Yorkshire folk doubted its genuineness, and
Otto never succeeded in obtaining possession. Rog. Howden (Stubbs), vol. iii. p.
86. The elaborate scheme for his endowment in the north, projected in 1195, has
already been mentioned (above, p. 341). This having also failed, Richard in 1196
gave him the investiture of Poitou. Rog. Howden (Stubbs), vol. iv. p. 7; cf. *ib.*
vol. iii. p. 86, and R. Coggeshall (Stevenson), p. 70.

[2] Rog. Howden (Stubbs), vol. iv. pp. 37-39. R. Diceto (Stubbs), vol. ii. p.
163.   [3] R. Diceto as above.

[4] R. Diceto tells the story of the prophecy made to Fulk the Good in two
places; in the *Abbreviationes Historiarum* (Stubbs, vol. i. p. 149) and in the
Opuscula (vol. ii. pp. 267, 268). In the latter place he adds: "Quod quon-
dam probavit regnum Jerosolimitanum; quod adhuc ostendit regnum Anglorum;
quod suo tempore declarabit Romanum imperium." This, as Bishop Stubbs notes,
"looks like an anticipation of the election of Otto IV. to the empire. . . . As
Bishop Longchamp died in 1197, before which date we must suppose MS. R
to have been written" [the MS. from which the *Opuscula* are printed, and which
begins with a dedication to William of Longchamp], "it can scarcely be a prophecy after the event." As William of Longchamp died January 31, 1197
(R. Diceto, vol. ii. p. 150; February 1 according to Gerv. Cant., Stubbs,
vol. i. p. 543), it seems indeed to shew that the possibility of one or other of
Richard's nephews becoming Emperor at the next vacancy was already in contemplation more than eight months before the death of Henry VI. Or was Ralf
dreaming rather of a transfer of the imperial crown to Richard himself? for it is
to be observed that Otto can be included within the "nine generations" only by
excluding from them Fulk the Good himself; but this mode of computing would
fail if applied to the eastern branch of the Angevin house, where it would give
only eight generations, so that we can hardly suppose it to have been adopted by
Ralf. According to R. Coggeshall (Stevenson), p. 88, and Gerv. Cant. as above,
p. 545, a party among the electors actually did choose Richard, and—much more
strangely—another party chose Philip of France.

[5] Rog. Howden as above, p. 39.

made common cause with his French namesake.[1] This
Suabian alliance, however, and the support of the count of
Ponthieu—purchased two years before with the hand of the
unhappy Adela, whom Richard had at last restored to her
brother[2]—could not much avail Philip Augustus against
such a league as was now gathering around the English
king. The vast sums which Hubert Walter had been sending, year after year, to his royal master over sea were
bringing a goodly interest at last. Flanders, Britanny,
Champagne, had all been secretly detached from the French
alliance and bought over to the service of Richard;[3] the
Flemish count had already drawn Philip into a war in which
he narrowly escaped being made prisoner;[4] and in the summer
of 1198, when the imperial election was over, not only Baldwin
of Flanders, Reginald of Boulogne, Baldwin of Guines, Henry
of Louvain, Everard of Brienne, Geoffrey of Perche and Raymond of Toulouse, but even the young count Louis of Blois
and the boy-duke Arthur of Britanny himself, one and all
leagued themselves in an offensive and defensive alliance with
Richard against the French king.[5] The immediate consequence
was that Philip begged Hubert Walter, who being just released
from his justiciarship had rejoined his sovereign in Normandy,
to make peace for him with Richard ; and he even went so far
as to offer the surrender of all the Norman castles which he had
won, except Gisors. Richard however would listen to no terms
in which his allies were not included.[6] At last, in November,
a truce was made, to last till the usual term, S. Hilary's day.[7]
When it expired the two kings held a colloquy on the Seine

[1] Treaty in Rymer, *Fœdera*, vol. i. p. 70 ; date, June 29 [1197].

[2] Rog. Howden (Stubbs), vol. iii. p. 303. Rigord (Duchesne, *Hist. Franc.
Scriptt.*, vol. v.), p. 38. Will. Armor. *Gesta Phil. Aug. (ibid.)* p. 77.

[3] Cf. Rog. Howden (Stubbs), vol. iv. p. 19, R. Coggeshall (Stevenson), p. 77,
and Will. Newb., l. v. c. 32 (Howlett, vol. ii. p. 495). Richard's treaty with
Flanders is in R. Diceto (Stubbs), vol. ii. pp. 152, 153, and Rymer, as above,
pp. 67, 68 ; it has no date, but as R. Diceto (as above, p. 158) tells us that it
was drawn up by Hubert Walter, and also that Hubert was in Gaul from September 14 (or 28, according to Gerv. Cant., Stubbs, vol. i. p. 574) to November 8
[1197], it must fall in that interval.

[4] Rog. Howden as above, pp. 20, 21. Will. Newb. as above. R. Coggeshall
(Stevenson), pp. 77, 78.   [5] Rog. Howden as above, p. 54.

[6] *Ib.* p. 61.   [7] *Ib.* p. 68.

LES ANDELYS
AND
CHATEAU-GAILLARD.
(From Deville, "Histoire du Château-Gaillard.")

Norgate's "England under the Angevin Kings"

London, Macmillan & Co.

Wagner & Debes' Geog¹. Estab¹. Leipsic.

between Vernon and Les Andelys, Richard in a boat on the river, Philip on horseback on the shore ;[1] this meeting was followed by another, where, by the mediation of a cardinal-legate, Peter of Capua, who had lately arrived in Gaul, they were persuaded to prolong their truce for five years.[2]

Yet all the while, there lurked in Richard's heart a mis-giving that, in the last resort, his diplomacy would prove to have been in vain ; that, strive as he might to turn away the tide of war from his own borders by stirring up north and east and south to overwhelm the Crown of France, still, after all, the day must come when the Angevins would have to stake their political existence solely upon their own military resources, and to stand at bay, unaided, unsup-ported, alone, behind whatever bulwark they might be able to devise by their own military genius.   It was the genius and the foresight of Richard himself which insured that when the crisis came, the bulwark was ready, even though it were doomed to prove unavailing in the end.   The last and mightiest of the many mighty fortresses reared by Angevin hands since the first great builder of the race had begun his castle-building in the Loire valley was the Château-Gaillard, the " saucy castle " of Richard the Lion-heart.   He " fixed its site where the Seine bends suddenly at Gaillon in a great semicircle to the north, and where the valley of Les Andelys breaks the line of the chalk cliffs along its banks. Blue masses of woodland crown the distant hills ; within the river curve lies a dull reach of flat meadow, round which the Seine, broken with green islets and dappled with the grey and blue of the sky, flashes like a silver bow on its way to Rouen." [3]   Some three-quarters of a league from the right bank of the river, in a valley opening upon it from the east-ward and watered by the little stream of Gambon, stood the town of Andely.   Between the town and the river stretched a lake, or rather perhaps a marsh,[4] through which the Gam-bon and another lesser rivulet descending from the hills to

---

[1] Rog. Howden (Stubbs), vol. iv. pp. 79, 80.
[2] *Ib.* p. 80.   Rigord (Duchesne, *Hist. Franc. Scriptt.*, vol. v.), p. 42.
[3] I copy Mr. Green's picture, *Hist. of the English People*, vol. i. p. 187.
[4] Now dried up.   See Deville, *Hist. du Château-Gaillard*, pp. 27, 28.

the north of Andely found their way by two separate issues into the Seine, nearly opposite two islets, of which the larger and more northerly was known as the Isle of Andely.[1] The space enclosed between the three rivers and the marsh seems to have been a tract of waste land, occupied only by a toll-house for the collection of dues from the vessels passing up and down the Seine[2]—dues which formed one of the most important items in the revenue of the archbishop of Rouen, to whom Andely and its neighbourhood belonged.[3] Over against this spot, on the southern bank of the Gambon, in the angle formed by its junction with the Seine, a mass of limestone crag rose abruptly to the height of three hundred feet. Its western side, almost perpendicular, looked down upon the great river, the northern, scarcely less steep, over the Gambon and the lake beyond ; to the north-east and south-west its rocky slopes died down into deep ravines, and only a narrow neck of land at its south-eastern extremity connected it with the lofty plateau covered with a dense woodland known as the Forest of Andely, which stretches along the eastern side of the Seine valley between Andely and Gaillon. One glance at the site was enough to rivet a soldier's gaze. If, instead of the metropolitan church of Normandy, a lay baron had owned the soil of Andely, we may be sure that long ago that lofty brow would have received its fitting crown ; if the power of Fulk the Builder had reached to the banks of the Seine, we may doubt whether the anathemas of the Norman primate would not have availed as little to wrest such a spot from his grasp as those of the archbishop of Tours had availed to wrest from him the site of Montrichard. But a greater castle-builder than Fulk Nerra himself was the architect of Château-Gaillard.

---

[1] " Est locus Andelii qui nunc habet insula nomen." Will. Armor. *Philipp.*, l. vii. v. 29 (Deville, *Château-Gaillard*, p. 126 ; Duchesne, *Hist. Franc. Scriptt.*, vol. v. p. 169).

[2] See a charter of Archbishop Malger (11th century) and one of Pope Eugene III., a. 1148, quoted in Deville as above, p. 26, note 2.

[3] The archbishops seem to have looked upon Andely as their most profitable territorial possession ; Rotrou called it his " unicum vivendi subsidium " (Rotr. Ep. xxiv., *Rer. Gall. Scriptt.*, vol. xvi. p. 632); Walter called it "patrimonium ecclesiæ solum et unicum " (R. Diceto, Stubbs, vol. ii. p. 148).

Richard's historical connexion with the "rock of Andely" has its ill-omened beginning in a ghastly story of the fate of three French prisoners whom he flung from its summit into the ravine below, in vengeance for the slaughter of some Welsh auxiliaries who had been surprised and cut to pieces by the French king's troops in the neighbouring valley.[1] By the opening of 1196, however, he had devised for it a more honourable use.   In a treaty with Philip, drawn up in January of that year, the fief of Andely was made the subject of special provisions whereby it was reserved as a sort of neutral zone between the territories of the two kings, and a significant clause was added : "Andely shall not be fortified."[2]   As by the same treaty the older bulwarks of Normandy—Nonancourt, Ivry, Pacy, Vernon, Gaillon, Neufmarché, Gisors—were resigned into Philip's hands, this clause, if strictly fulfilled, would have left the Seine without a barrier and Rouen at the mercy of the French king.   The agreement in short, like all those which bore the signatures of Philip and Richard, was made only to be broken ; both parties broke it without delay ; and while Philip was forming his league with the Bretons for the ruin of Anjou, Richard was tracing out in the valley of the Gambon and on the rock of Andely the plan of a line of fortifications which were to interpose an insurmountable barrier between his Norman capital and the French invader.   His first act was to seize the Isle of Andely.[3]   Here he built a lofty octagonal tower, encircled by a ditch and rampart, and threw a bridge over the river from each side of the island, linking it thus to either shore.[4]   On the right, beyond the eastern bridge, he traced out the walls of a new town, which took the name of the New or the Lesser Andely,[5] a secure stronghold whose

[1] Will. Armor. *Philipp.*, l. v. (Duchesne, *Hist. Franc. Scriptt.*, vol. v.), p. 151.

[2] Treaty in Rymer, *Fœdera*, vol. i. p. 66.   For date see Rigord (Duchesne as above), p. 39.

[3] Letter of Walter of Rouen (a. 1196), R. Diceto (Stubbs), vol. ii. pp. 148, 149.   Cf. Rog. Howden (Stubbs), vol. iv. p. 14, and Will. Newb., l. v. c. 34 (Howlett, vol. ii. p. 499).

[4] Will. Armor. *Philipp.*, l. vii. vv. 29-43 (Deville, *Château-Gaillard*, p. 126 ; Duchesne as above, p. 169).

[5] A poet of the thirteenth century, William Guiart, calls it "le Nouvel-Andeli."   It is known now as "le Petit-Andely."   Deville as above, p. 26.

artificial defences of ramparts and towers were surrounded
by the further protection of the lake on its eastern side, the
Seine on the west, and the two lesser rivers to north and
south, a bridge spanning each of these two little streams
forming the sole means of access from the mainland.[1]   The
southern bridge, that over the Gambon, linked this New
Andely with the foot of the rock which was to be crowned
with the mightiest work of all.   Richard began by digging
out to a yet greater depth the ravines which parted this
rock from the surrounding heights, so as to make it wholly
inaccessible save by the one connecting isthmus at its south-
eastern extremity.   On its summit, which formed a plateau
some six hundred feet in length and two hundred in breadth
at the widest part, he reared a triple fortress.   The outer
ward consisted of a triangular enclosure ; its apex, facing the
isthmus already mentioned, was crowned by a large round
tower,[2] with walls ten feet in thickness ; the extremities of
its base were strengthened by similar towers, and two
smaller ones broke the line of the connecting curtain-wall.
This was surrounded by a ditch dug in the rock to a depth
of more than forty feet, and having a perpendicular counterscarp.   Fronting the base of this outer fortress across the
ditch on its north-western side was a rampart surmounted
by a wall ninety feet long and eight feet thick, also flanked
by two round towers ; from these a similar wall ran all
round the edges of the plateau, where the steep sides of the
rock itself took the place of rampart and ditch.   The wall
on the south-west side—the river-front—was broken by
another tower, cylindrical without, octagonal within ; and its
northern extremity was protected by two mighty rectangular
bastions.   Close against one of these stood a round tower,
which served as the base of a third enclosure, the heart and
citadel of the whole fortress.   Two-thirds of its elliptical
outline, on the east and south, were formed by a succession
of semicircular bastions, or segments of towers, seventeen in
number, each parted from its neighbour by scarcely more

---

[1] Will. Armor. *Gesta Phil. Aug.* (Duchesne, *Hist. Franc. Scriptt.*, vol. v.),
p. 81.   Deville, *Château-Gaillard*, p. 27.
[2] Now known as "tour de la Monnaie." Deville as above, p. 30, note 1.

CHÂTEAU-GAILLARD

(From Deville, "Histoire du Château-Gaillard").

A-Outer ward, B-second ward, C-citadel, D-keep, a-wells, b-bastions, c-staircase, communicating with d-outworks leading to river, e-dwelling-apartments, f-entrance to casemates, g-ditches, h-bridge leading into citadel, i-cellar and chapel (built by John, A.D. 1202).

River Seine

than two feet of curtain-wall—an arrangement apparently imitated from the fortress of Cherbourg, which was accounted the greatest marvel of military architecture in Normandy, until its fame was eclipsed by that of Richard's work.[1] This portion of the enclosure was built upon a rampart formed by the excavation of a ditch about fifteen to twenty feet in width ; the counterscarp, like that of the outer ditches, was perpendicular ; and a series of casemates cut in the rock ran along on this side for a distance of about eighty feet. On the western side of the citadel stood the keep, a mighty circular tower, with walls of the thickness of twelve feet, terminating at an angle of twenty feet in depth where it projected into the enclosure ; it had two or perhaps three stages,[2] and was lighted by two great arched windows, whence the eye could range at will over the wooded hills and dales of the Vexin, or the winding course of the river broadening onward to Rouen. Behind the keep was placed the principal dwelling-house, and under this a staircase cut out of the rock gave access to an underground passage leading to some outworks and a tower near the foot of the hill, whence a wall was carried down to the river-bank, just beyond the northern extremity of a long narrow island known as the " isle of the Three Kings "—doubtless from some one of the many meetings held in this district by Louis VII. or Philip Augustus and the two Henrys.[3] The river itself was barred by a double stockade, crossing its bed from shore to shore.[4]

All this work was accomplished within a single year.[5] Richard, who had watched over its progress with unremitting care, broke into an ecstasy of delight at its completion ; he

[1] See Deville, *Château-Gaillard*, p. 34, and the passage there quoted from *Hist. Gaufr. Ducis* (Marchegay, *Comtes d'Anjou*, p. 300).

[2] See Deville as above, p. 38, note 2.

[3] *Ib.* p. 36. The island is now joined to the mainland ; *ib.* note 1.

[4] For description see Will. Armor. *Gesta Phil. Aug.* (Duchesne, *Hist. Franc. Scriptt.*, vol. v.), p. 81 ; *Philipp.*, l. vii. vv. 48-85 (*ib.* pp. 169, 170 ; Deville as above, pp. 126, 127), and Deville as above, pp. 25-40.

[5] That is, the castle on the rock, built 1197-1198. See the story of the rain of blood in May 1198 (R. Diceto, Stubbs, vol. ii. p. 162), which fixes its completion after that date. The tower on the island and the Nouvel-Andely were the work of the previous year, 1196-1197.

called his barons to see "how fair a child was his, this child but a twelvemonth old ";[1] he called it his "saucy castle," "Château-Gaillard,"[2] and the name which he thus gave it in jest soon replaced in popular speech its more formal title of "the Castle on the Rock of Andely."[3]   The hardness of the rock out of which the fortifications were hewn was not the sole obstacle against which the royal builder had had to contend. Richard had no more thought than Fulk Nerra would have had of asking the primate's leave before beginning to build upon his land ; the work therefore was no sooner begun than Archbishop Walter lifted up his protest against it ; obtaining no redress, he laid Normandy under interdict and carried his complaint in person to the Pope.[4]   Richard at once sent envoys to appeal against the interdict and make arrangements for the settlement of the dispute.[5]   Meanwhile, however, he pushed on the building without delay. Like Fulk of old, the seeming wrath of Heaven moved him as little as that of its earthly representatives ; a rain of blood which fell upon the workmen and the king himself, though it scared all beside, failed to shake his determination ; "if an angel had come down out of the sky to bid him stay his hand, he would have got no answer but a curse."[6]   He had now, however, made his peace with the Church ; in the

[1] "Ecce quam pulcra filia unius anni !"   J. Bromton, Twysden, *X. Scriptt.*, col. 1276.

[2] "Totamque munitionem illam vocavit Gaillardum, quod sonat in Gallico petulantiam."   Will. Armor. *Gesta Phil. Aug.* (Duchesne, *Hist. Franc. Scriptt.*, vol. v.), p. 81.

[3] "Castrum" or "castellum de Rupe Andeleii" or "Andeliaci," it is called in the charters of Richard and John.   The first document in which it appears as "Château-Gaillard" is a charter of S. Louis, "actum in castro nostro Gaillard," A.D. 1261 ; Deville, *Château-Gaillard*, p. 40.   Will. Armor. however uses the name, and other writers soon begin to copy him.

[4] Rog. Howden (Stubbs), vol. iv. p. 14.   Cf. Will. Newb., l. v. c. 28 (Howlett, vol. ii. pp. 487, 488), R. Coggeshall (Stevenson), p. 70, and Gerv. Cant. (Stubbs), vol. i. p. 544.

[5] The envoys were William of Longchamp, William bishop of Lisieux and Philip elect of Durham ; Rog. Howden (as above), pp. 16, 17.   They must have started early in 1197, for William of Longchamp died on the journey, at Poitiers, on January 31 or February 1 ; see above, p. 373, note 4.

[6] Will. Newb., l. v. c. 34 (as above, p. 500).   This is William's last sentence. R. Diceto (Stubbs), vol. ii. p. 162, also tells of the portent, and gives its date, May 8, 1198.

spring of 1197 he offered to the archbishop an exchange of land on terms highly advantageous to the metropolitan see ; and on this condition the Pope raised the interdict in May of the same year.[1] The exchange was carried through on October 16,[2] and ratified by John in a separate charter, a step which seems to indicate that John was now recognized as his brother's heir.[3]

It was probably about the same time that the treaty with Flanders, the corner-stone of the league which Richard was forming against the king of France, was signed within the walls of the new fortress.[4] Yet, as has been already seen, the coalition was not fully organized till late in the following summer ; and even then the complicated weapon hung fire. Want of money seems to have been Richard's chief difficulty, now as ever—a difficulty which after Hubert Walter's defeat in the council at Oxford and his resignation in the following July must have seemed well-nigh insurmountable. At last, however, in the spring of 1199, a ray of hope came from a quarter where it was wholly unexpected. Richard was leading his mercenaries through Poitou to check the viscount of Limoges and the count of Angoulême in a renewal of their treasonable designs[5] when he was met

---

[1] Rog. Howden (Stubbs), vol. iv. pp. 17-19. Will. Newb., l. v. c. 34 (Howlett, vol. ii. pp. 499, 500).

[2] Richard's charter, of which Deville gives a fac-simile in his *Château-Gaillard*, p. 18, and a printed copy in his "pièces justificatives," *ib.* pp. 113-118, is also in R. Diceto (Stubbs), vol. ii. pp. 154-156. According to this last writer (*ib.* pp. 158, 159), and Gerv. Cant. (Stubbs, vol. i. p. 544), the settlement was due to the mediation of Archbishop Hubert.

[3] See Deville, as above, pp. 21, 22. John's charter is in the "pièces justificatives," *ib.* pp. 119-123.   [4] R. Diceto (as above), p. 153.

[5] Rog. Howden as above, p. 80, says merely that Richard was on his way to Poitou. R. Coggeshall (Stevenson), p. 94, says he was marching against the viscount of Limoges, to punish him for a treasonable alliance with the French king. The writer of the *Mag. Vita S. Hug.* (Dimock), p. 280, says "expeditionem direxerat adversus comitem Engolismensem"; and that Angoulême had some share in the matter appears also from the confused story of Gerv. Cant. (as above), pp. 592, 593, who makes Richard receive his death-wound while besieging "castrum comitis Engolismi, quod Nantrum erat appellatum." A joint rebellion of the lords of Limoges and Angoulême would be very natural, for they were half-brothers. On the other hand, the two men were very likely to be confounded by historians, for they both bore the same name, Ademar. See above, p. 220 and note 3.

by rumours of a marvellous discovery at Châlus in the
Limousin. A peasant working on the land of Achard, the
lord of Châlus, was said to have turned up with his plough
a treasure [1] which popular imagination pictured as nothing
less that "an emperor with his wife, sons and daughters, all
of pure gold, and seated round a golden table." [2] In vain
did Achard seek to keep his secret and his prize to himself.
Treasure-trove was a right of the overlord, and it seems to
have been at once claimed by the viscount Ademar of
Limoges, as Achard's immediate superior. His claim, however, had to give way to that of his own overlord, King
Richard ; but when he sent to the king the share which he
had himself wrung from Achard, Richard indignantly rejected it, vowing that he would have all. This Achard and
Ademar both refused, and the king laid siege to Châlus.[3]

This place, not far from the western border of the
Limousin, is now represented by two villages, known conjointly as Châlus-Chabrol, and built upon the summits of
two low hills, at whose foot winds the little stream of Tar-
doire. Each hill is crowned by a round tower of late twelfth-
century work ; the lower one is traditionally said to be the
keep of the fortress besieged by Richard with all his forces
at Mid-Lent 1199.[4] In vain did Achard, who was utterly
unprepared to stand a siege, protest his innocence and offer
to submit to the judgement of the French king's court, as
supreme alike over the duke of Aquitaine and over his
vassals ; in vain did he beg for a truce till the holy season

---

[1] Will. Armor. *Philipp.*, l. v. (Duchesne, *Hist. Franc. Scriptt.*, vol. v.), p.
155.   Rigord (*ib.* p. 42) describes the finder as a soldier.

[2] "Qui posteris, quo tempore fuerant, certam dabant memoriam," adds Rigord
(as above), p. 43.   Is it possible that the thing can have been a real relic of some
of the old Gothic kings of Aquitania?

[3] This seems to be the only way of reconciling the different accounts in Rog.
Howden (Stubbs), vol. iv. p. 82, Rigord (as above), p. 42, Will. Armor. as
above, and R. Coggeshall (Stevenson), p. 94.

[4] Will. Armor (as above) says the treasure was discovered *after* Mid-Lent. But
Rog. Howden (as above, p. 84), Gerv. Cant. (Stubbs, vol. i. p. 593), R. Coggeshall (Stevenson, p. 95), and the Ann. of Margam, Winton. and Waverl. a. 1199
(Luard, *Ann. Monast.*, vol. i. p. 24, vol. ii. pp. 71, 251), all tell us that Richard
received his death-wound on March 26—Friday, the morrow of Mid-Lent—and
R. Coggeshall adds that this was the third day of the siege, which must therefore
have begun on Wednesday, March 24.

should be past ; in vain, when the outworks were almost
wholly destroyed and the keep itself undermined,[1] did he
ask leave to surrender with the honours of war for himself
and his men. Richard was inexorable ; he swore that he
would hang them all.[2] With the courage that is born of
despair, Achard, accompanied by six knights and nine
serving-men, retired into the keep, determined to hold it
until death.[3] All that day—Friday, March 26 [4]—Richard
and his lieutenant Mercadier, the captain of his mercenaries,[5]
prowled vainly round the walls, seeking for a point at which
they could assault them with safety.[6] Their sappers were
all the while undermining the tower.[7] Its defenders, finding themselves short of missiles, began throwing down beams
of wood and fragments of the broken battlements at the
miners' heads.[8] They were equally short of defensive arms ;
one of the little band stood for more than half the day upon
a turret, with nothing but a frying-pan for a shield against
the bolts which flew whistling all around him, yet failed to
drive him from his post.[9] At last the moment came for
which he had been waiting so long and so bravely. Just as
Richard, unarmed save for his iron head-piece, paused within

---

[1] Will. Armor. *Philipp.*, l. v. (Duchesne, *Hist. Franc. Scriptt.*, vol. v.), p. 155.
[2] Rog. Howden (Stubbs), vol. iv. p. 82. Cf. Gerv. Cant. (Stubbs), vol. i. p. 593.
[3] Will. Armor. as above.   [4] See above, p. 382, note 4.
[5] On this man's history see an article by H. Géraud—"Mercadier ; les Routiers
au xiii⁴ siècle "—in *Bibl. de l'Ecole des Chartes*, ser. i. vol. iii. pp. 417 *et seq.*
The writers of his own time call him " Marcadeus," " Mercaderius," in every possible variety of spelling ; in a charter of his own, printed by Géraud (as above, p.
444), his style is " ego Merchaderius " ; it seems best therefore to adopt the form
"Mercadier," which Géraud uses. He was a Provençal by birth (Mat. Paris,
Chron. Maj., Luard, vol. ii. p. 421). He makes his first historical appearance in
1183, in Richard's service, amid the disorders in Aquitaine after the death of the
young king (Geoff. Vigeois, l. ii. c. 25, Labbe, *Nova Biblioth.*, vol. ii. p. 340).
He reappears by Richard's side at Vendôme in 1194 (Rog. Howden, Stubbs, vol.
iii. p. 256) ; about this time Richard endowed him with the lands of Bainac in
Périgord (see his own charter, a. 1195, as referred to above, and Géraud's
comments, *ib.* pp. 423-427). He played a considerable part in Richard's wars
with Philip (see authorities collected by Géraud, as above, pp. 428-431), remained,
as we shall see, with Richard till his death, and afterwards helped Eleanor to regain Anjou for John. He was slain at Bordeaux in April 1200 (Rog. Howden,
Stubbs, vol. iv. p. 114).   [6] Rog. Howden (as above), p. 82.
[7] R. Coggeshall (Stevenson), p. 94.
[8] *Ibid.* Will. Armor. as above.   [9] R. Coggeshall, p. 95.

bow-shot of the turret, this man caught sight of an arrow which had been shot at himself from the besieging ranks— seemingly, indeed, by Richard's own hand—and had stuck harmlessly in a crevice of the wall within his reach. He snatched it out, fitted it to his cross-bow, and aimed at the king.[1] Richard saw the movement and greeted it with a shout of defiant applause ; he failed to shelter himself under his buckler ; the arrow struck him on the left shoulder, just below the joint of the neck, and glancing downwards penetrated deep into his side.[2] He made light of the wound,[3] gave strict orders to Mercadier to press the assault with re-doubled vigour,[4] and rode back to his tent as if nothing was amiss.[5] There he rashly tried to pull out the arrow with his own hand.[6] The wood broke off, the iron barb remained fixed in the wound ; a surgeon attached to the staff of Mercadier was sent for, and endeavoured to cut it out ; un-luckily, Richard was fat like his father, and the iron, buried deep in his flesh, was so difficult to reach that the injuries caused by the operator's knife proved more dangerous than that which had been inflicted by the shaft of the hostile crossbow-man.[7] The wounded side grew more swollen and inflamed day by day ; the patient's constitutional restless-ness, aggravated as it was by pain, made matters worse ;[8] and at last mortification set in.[9]

---

[1] Will. Armor. *Philipp.*, l. v. (Duchesne, *Hist. Franc. Scriptt.*, vol. v.), p. 156. Cf. Rog. Howden (Stubbs), vol. iv. p. 82.

[2] "Percussitque regem super humerum sinistrum juxta colli spondilia, sicque arcuato vulnere telum dilapsum est deorsum ac lateri sinistro immersum." R. Coggeshall (Stevenson), p. 95. See also the briefer accounts of the scene and the wound in Rog. Howden and Will. Armor. as above, and Gerv. Cant. (Stubbs), vol. i. p. 593.   [3] R. Coggeshall as above.

[4] Rog. Howden as above.   [5] *Ibid.* R. Coggeshall as above.

[6] R. Coggeshall as above. Rog. Howden (as above), p. 83, lays the blame of this unskilful operation upon the doctor.

[7] Rog. Howden and R. Coggeshall as above.

[8] The English writers—Rog. Howden and R. Coggeshall—try to shift the blame of their king's death as much as possible upon the foreign surgeon. Will. Armor. (as above) attributes it wholly to Richard's disregard of the doctor's orders ; and even R. Coggeshall (Stevenson, p. 96) is obliged to add at last "rege . . . . præcepta medicorum non curante." Rog. Wendover. (Coxe), vol. iii. p. 135, says the arrow was poisoned, but this seems to be only an inference from the result.

[9] R. Coggeshall as above.

Then Richard, face to face with death, came to his better self once more, and prepared calmly and bravely for his end. Until then he had suffered no one to enter the chamber where he lay save four barons whom he specially trusted, lest the report of his sickness should be bruited about,[1] to discourage his friends or to rejoice his foes. Now, he summoned all of his followers who were within reach to witness his solemn bequest of all his dominions to his brother John, and made them swear fealty to John as his successor.[2] He wrote to his mother, who was at Fontevraud, requesting her to come to him ;[3] he bequeathed his jewels to his nephew King Otto, and a fourth part of his treasures to be distributed among his servants and the poor.[4] By this time Châlus was taken and its garrison hung, according to his earlier orders—all save the man who had shot him, and who had apparently been reserved for his special judgement. Richard ordered the man to be brought before him. " What have I done to thee," he asked him, " that thou shouldest slay me ? " " Thou hast slain my father and two of my brothers with thine own hand, and thou wouldst fain have killed me too. Avenge thyself upon me as thou wilt ; I will gladly endure the greatest torments which thou canst devise, since I have seen thee upon thy death-bed." " I forgive thee," answered Richard, and he bade the guards loose him and let him go free with a gift of a hundred shillings.[5] The

---

[1] R. Coggeshall (Stevenson), p. 96.

[2] Rog. Howden (Stubbs), vol. iv. p. 83. And this, although he and John had parted on bad terms shortly before. R. Coggeshall (Stevenson), p. 99. *Mag. Vita S. Hug.* (Dimock), p. 287.   [3] R. Coggeshall (Stevenson), p. 96.

[4] Rog. Howden as above.

[5] *Ibid.* Cf. the different account of the captive's demeanour in Gerv. Cant. (Stubbs), vol. i. p. 593. It seems impossible to make out who this man really was. R. Diceto (Stubbs), vol. ii. p. 166, the Ann. Margam, a. 1199 (Luard, *Ann. Monast.*, vol. i. p. 24), the anonymous continuator of Geoff. Vigeois (Labbe, *Nova Biblioth.*, vol. ii. p. 342) and Rog. Wend. (Coxe), vol. iii. p. 135, call him Peter Basilius or Basilii. Gervase calls him John Sabraz ; Rog. Howden, Bertrand de Gourdon ; and Will. Armor. *Philipp.*, l. v. (Duchesne, *Hist. Franc. Scriptt.*, vol. v. p. 156), Guy, without any surname at all. But as Géraud proves (art. " Mercadier," in *Bibl. de l'Ecole des Chartes*, ser. i. vol. iii. pp. 433, 434, 442), it cannot have been Bertrand de Gourdon ; for the only man who is known to have borne that name was still living in 1231, while Rog. Howden himself tells us that Richard's pardon did not avail to save the life

story went that Richard had not communicated for nearly seven years, because he could not put himself in charity with Philip.[1]   Now, on the eleventh day after his wound—April 6, the Tuesday in Passion-week [2]—he made his confession to one of his chaplains, and received the Holy Communion. His soul being thus at peace, he gave directions for the disposal of his body.   It was to be embalmed ; the brain and some of the internal organs were to be buried in the ancient Poitevin abbey of Charroux ; the heart was to be deposited in the Norman capital, where it had always found a loyal response ; the corpse itself was to be laid, in token of penitence, at his father's feet in the abbey-church of Fontevraud.[3] Lastly, he received extreme unction ; and then, " as the day drew to its close, his day of life also came to its end." [4] His friends buried him as he had wished.   S. Hugh of Lincoln, now at Angers on his way to protest against a fresh spoliation of his episcopal property, came to seal his forgiveness by performing the last rites of the Church over this second grave at Fontevraud,[5] where another Angevin king was thus " shrouded among the shrouded women "—his own

of his slayer.   Mercadier detained the man till the king was dead, and then had him flayed and hanged ; Rog. Howden (Stubbs), vol. iv. p. 84 ;—or, according to another account, he sent him to Jane, and it was she who took this horrible vengeance for her brother's death.   Ann. Winton. a. 1199 (Luard, *Ann. Monast.*, vol. ii. p. 71).

[1] R. Coggeshall (Stevenson), p. 96.   This must be, at any rate, an exaggeration ; for Richard had certainly communicated upon at least one occasion within the last five years—at his crowning at Winchester in April 1194.   Gerv. Cant. (Stubbs), vol. i. p. 526.

[2] R. Diceto (Stubbs), vol. ii. p. 166 ; Gerv. Cant. (as above), p. 593 ; Rog. Howden as above ; Rog. Wend. (Coxe), vol. iii. p. 136 ; Ann. Winton. and Waverl. a. 1199 (Luard as above, pp. 71, 251); Geoff. Vigeois Contin. (Labbe, *Nova Biblioth.*, vol. ii.), p. 342.   R. Coggeshall as above, and the Chron. S. Flor. Salm. a. 1199 (Marchegay, *Eglises*, p. 194), make it April 7 ; on the part of R. Coggeshall, however, this is clearly a mere slip, for he rightly places the death on the eleventh day after the wound.   Rigord (Duchesne, *Hist. Franc. Scriptt.*, vol. v.), p. 42, and the Chron. S. Serg. a. 1199 (Marchegay, *Eglises*, p. 151), date it April 8, and the Ann. Margam. a. 1199 (Luard, as above, vol. i. p. 24), April 10.

[3] Rog. Howden as above.   Cf. Rog. Wend. as above.

[4] " Cum jam dies clauderetur, diem clausit extremum."   R. Coggeshall as above.

[5] *Mag. Vita S. Hug.* (Dimock), p. 286.   The funeral was on Palm Sunday ; *ibid.*

mother, doubtless, in their midst.[1]   He was laid to sleep in the robes which he had worn on his last crowning-day in England, five years before.[2]   His heart was enclosed in a gold and silver casket, carried to Rouen, and solemnly deposited by the clergy among the holy relics in their cathedral church ;[3] and men saw in its unusual size[4] a fit token of the mighty spirit of him whom Normandy never ceased to venerate as Richard Cœur-de-Lion.

[1] She seems not to have got his letter in time to see him alive.   Berengaria was at Beaufort in Anjou, whither S. Hugh turned aside to visit and comfort her on his way from Angers to Fontevraud ; and the state of intense grief in which he found her supplies another proof of Richard's capacity for winning love which he did not altogether deserve.   *Mag. Vita S. Hug.* (Dimock), p. 286.

[2] Ann. Winton. a. 1199 (Luard, *Ann. Monast.*, vol. ii. p. 71).

[3] Will. Armor. *Philipp.*, l. v. (Duchesne, *Hist. Franc. Scriptt.*, vol. v.), p. 157.

[4] Gerv. Cant. (Stubbs), vol. i. p. 593.   According to the Ann. Winton. as above, it was "paulo majus pomo pini."

CHAPTER IX.

THE FALL OF THE ANGEVINS.

1199–1206.

"IN the year 1199," says a contemporary French writer, "God visited the realm of France; for King Richard was slain."[1] Richard's death was in truth the signal for the break-up of the Angevin dominions to the profit of the French Crown. John, who was at the moment in Britanny, hurried southward as soon as he heard the news. Three days after the funeral—on April 14, the Wednesday before Easter—he arrived at Chinon, the seat of the Angevin treasury; the wardens of the castle[2] welcomed him as their lord in his brother's stead; the household of the late king came to meet him and acknowledged him in like manner, after receiving from him a solemn oath that he would carry out Richard's testamentary directions and maintain the customs of the lands over which he was called to rule.[3] On this understanding the treasury was given up to him by the Angevin seneschal, Robert of Turnham.[4] After keeping Easter at Beaufort,[5] he proceeded into Normandy; here he was received without opposition, and on the Sunday after Easter was invested with the sword, lance and coronet of

---

[1] Will. Armor. *Gesta Phil. Aug.* (Duchesne, *Hist. Franc. Scriptt.*, vol. v.), p. 80.

[2] "A proceribus quibusdam *Anglorum* castrum ipsum servantibus." *Mag. Vita S. Hug.* (Dimock), p. 287.   [3] *Ibid.*

[4] Rog. Howden (Stubbs), vol. iv. p. 86.   R. Coggeshall (Stevenson), p. 99.

[5] Rog. Howden as above, p. 87.

the duchy by Archbishop Walter at Rouen.[1] As the lance
was put into his hands he turned with characteristic levity to
join in the laughing comments of the young courtiers behind
him, and in so doing let the symbol of his ducal authority
fall to the ground. His irreverent behaviour and refusal to
communicate on Easter-day had already drawn upon him a
solemn warning from S. Hugh ; and this fresh example of
his profane recklessness, and its consequence, were noted as
omens which later events made but too easy of interpretation.[2]
For the moment, however, the Normans were willing to
transfer to Richard's chosen successor the loyalty which they
had shewn towards Richard himself; and so, too, were the
representatives of the English Church and baronage who
happened to be on the spot, Archbishop Hubert and William
the Marshal.[3] But in the Angevin lands Philip's alliance
with the Bretons, fruitless so long as Richard lived, bore
fruit as soon as the lion-heart had ceased to beat. While
Philip himself invaded the county of Evreux and took its
capital,[4] Arthur was at once sent into Anjou with a body of
troops ;[5] his mother, released or escaped from her prison,
joined him at the head of the Breton forces ;[6] they marched
upon Le Mans, whence John himself only escaped the night
before it fell into their hands;[7] Angers was given up to them
by its governor, a nephew of the seneschal Robert of Turnham ;[8] and on Easter-day,[9] while John was actually holding
court within fifteen miles of them at Beaufort, the barons of
Anjou, Touraine and Maine held a council at which Arthur
was unanimously acknowledged as lawful heir to his uncle
Richard according to the customs of the three counties, and
their capital cities were surrendered to him at once.[10] At Le

[1] R. Diceto (Stubbs), vol. ii. p. 166. ˙ Rog. Howden (Stubbs), vol. iv. pp. 87,
88. R. Coggeshall (Stevenson), p. 99. *Mag. Vita S. Hug.* (Dimock), p. 293.
[2] *Mag. Vita S. Hug.* (Dimock), pp. 291-294.
[3] Rog. Howden as above, p. 86.
[4] Rigord (Duchesne, *Hist. Franc. Scriptt.*, vol. v.), p. 43. Will. Armor. *Gesta
Phil. Aug. (ibid.)*, p. 80. Cf. R. Coggeshall as above.   [5] Rigord as above.
[6] Cf. R. Coggeshall as above, and *Mag. Vita S. Hug.* (Dimock), p. 296, with
Rog. Howden as above, p. 87.   [7] *Mag. Vita S. Hug.* as above.
[8] Rog. Howden as above, p. 86.
[9] Chron. S. Albin. a. 1199 (Marchegay, *Eglises*, p. 50).
[10] Rog. Howden as above, pp. 86, 87. Cf. R. Coggeshall as above.

Mans he met the French king and did homage to him for his new dominions, Constance swearing fealty with him.[1] Shortly afterwards, at Tours, Constance formally placed her boy, who was now twelve years old, under the guardianship of Philip ; and Philip at once took upon himself the custody and the administration of all the territories of his ward.[2]

Neither in personal influence nor in political skill, however, was Constance a match for her mother-in-law. Eleanor was, as has been seen, at Fontevraud when Richard died. Feeling and policy alike inclined her to favour the cause of his chosen successor, her own only surviving son, rather than that of a grandson whom most likely she had never even seen. She therefore effected a junction with Mercadier and his Brabantines as soon as they had had time to march up from Châlus, and the whole band of mercenaries, headed by the aged queen and the ruthless but faithful Provençal captain, overran Anjou with fire and sword to punish its inhabitants for their abandonment of John.[3] Having given this proof of her undiminished energy, Eleanor, to take away all pretext for French intermeddling in the south, went to meet Philip at Tours and herself did homage to him for Poitou.[4] By this means Aquitaine was secured for John. John himself had made a dash into Maine and burned Le Mans in vengeance for the defection of its citizens.[5] He could, however, venture upon no serious attempt at the reconquest of the Angevin lands till he had secured his hold upon Normandy and England ; and for this his presence was now urgently needed on the English side of the Channel.

Archbishop Hubert and William the Marshal had already returned to England charged with a commission from John to assist the justiciar Geoffrey Fitz-Peter in maintaining order there until the new king should arrive.[6] The precaution was far from being a needless one. The news of

---

[1] Rigord (Duchesne, *Hist. Franc. Scriptt.*, vol. v.), p. 43.
[2] Rog. Howden (Stubbs), vol. iv. p. 87. The Chron. S. Albin. a. 1200 (Marchegay, *Eglises*, p. 51) places this a year later.
[3] Rog. Howden as above, p. 88.   [4] Rigord as above.
[5] Rog. Howden as above, p. 87.   R. Coggeshall (Stevenson), p. 99.
[6] Rog. Howden as above, p. 86.

Richard's death reached England on Easter Eve ; and its consequences appeared the very next morning, when some of the nobles and knights went straight from their Easter feast to begin a course of rapine and depredation which recalls the disorders after the death of Henry I., and which was only checked by the return of the primate.   Hubert at once excommunicated the evil-doers,[1] and, in concert with the Marshal, summoned all the men of the realm to swear fealty and peaceable submission to John, as heir of Henry Fitz-Empress.   The peace, however, was not so easy to keep now as it had been during the interval between Henry's death and Richard's coronation.   Since then John himself had set an example which those whom he now claimed as his subjects were not slow to follow.   All who had castles, whether bishops, earls or barons, furnished them with men, victuals and arms, and assumed an attitude of defence, if not of defiance ; and this attitude they quitted only when the archbishop, the marshal and the justiciar had called all the malcontents to a conference at Northampton, and there solemnly promised that John should render to all men their rights, if they would keep faith and peace towards him.   On this the barons took the oath of fealty and liege homage to John.   The king of Scots refused to do the like unless his lost counties of Northumberland and Cumberland were restored to him, and despatched messengers charged with these demands to John himself ; the envoys were, however, intercepted by the archbishop and his colleagues, and the Scot king was for a while appeased by a promise of satisfaction when the new sovereign should arrive in his island-realm.[2]

On May 25 John landed at Shoreham ; next day he reached London ;[3] on the 27th—Ascension-day—the bishops and barons assembled for the crowning in Westminster abbey.[4] John's coronation is one of the most memorable in English history.   It was the last occasion on which the old English doctrine of succession to the crown was formally asserted

---

[1] R. Coggeshall (Stevenson), p. 98.
[2] Rog. Howden (Stubbs), vol. iv. pp. 88, 89.   [3] *Ib.* p. 89.
[4] *Ib.* pp. 89, 90.   R. Diceto (Stubbs), vol. ii. pp. 166.   R. Coggeshall (Stevenson), pp. 99, 100.

and publicly vindicated, and that more distinctly than it had ever been since the Norman conquest. In the midst of the crowded church the archbishop stood forth and spoke : " Hearken, all ye that are here present ! Be it known unto you that no man hath any antecedent right to succeed another in the kingdom, except he be unanimously chosen by the whole realm, after invocation of the Holy Spirit's grace, and unless he be also manifestly thereunto called by the pre-eminence of his character and conversation, after the pattern of Saul the first anointed king, whom God set over his people, although he was not of royal race, and likewise after him David, the one being chosen for his energy and fitness for the regal dignity, the other for his humility and holiness ; that so he who surpassed all other men of the realm in vigour should also be preferred before them in authority and power. But indeed if there be one of the dead king's race who excelleth, that one should be the more promptly and willingly chosen. And these things have I spoken in behalf of the noble Count John here present, the brother of our late illustrious King Richard, now deceased without direct heir ; and forasmuch as we see him to be prudent and vigorous, we all, after invoking the Holy Spirit's grace, for his merits no less than his royal blood, have with one consent chosen him for our king." The archbishop's hearers wondered at his speech, because they could not see any occasion for it; but none of them disputed his doctrine; still less did they dispute its immediate practical application. " Long live King John !" was the unanimous response;[1] and, disregarding a protest from Bishop Philip of Durham against the accomplishment of such an important rite in the absence of his metropolitan Geoffrey of York,[2] Archbishop Hubert proceeded to anoint and crown the king. A foreboding which he could not put aside, however, moved him to make yet another significant interpolation in the ritual. When he tendered to the king-elect the usual oath for the defence of the Church, the redressing of wrongs and the maintenance of justice, he added a solemn personal adjuration to John, in

[1] Mat. Paris, *Chron. Maj.* (Luard), vol. ii. pp. 454, 455.
[2] Rog. Howden (Stubbs), vol. iv. p. 90.

Heaven's name, warning him not to venture upon accepting the regal office unless he truly purposed in his own mind to perform his oath. John answered that by God's help he intended to do so.[1] But he contrived to omit the act which should have sealed his vow. For the first and last time probably in the history of Latin Christendom, the king did not communicate upon his coronation-day.[2]

On that very day he made his arrangements for the government of the realm which he was already anxious to leave as soon as he could do so with safety. Geoffrey Fitz-Peter was confirmed in his office of justiciar, William in that of marshal, and both were formally invested with the earl-doms whose lands and revenues they had already enjoyed for some years — Geoffrey with the earldom of Essex, William with that of Striguil. At the same time, in defiance alike of precedent, of ecclesiastical propriety, and of the warnings of an old colleague in the administration, Hugh Bardulf, Archbishop Hubert undertook the office of chan-cellor.[3] Next day John received the homage of the barons, and went on pilgrimage to S. Alban's abbey ;[4] he afterwards visited Canterbury and S. Edmund's,[5] and thence proceeded to keep the Whitsun feast at Northampton.[6] An inter-change of embassies with the king of Scots failed to win either the restitution of the two shires on the one hand, or the required homage on the other ; William threatened to invade the disputed territories if they were not made over to him within forty days ; John retorted by giving them in charge to a new sheriff, the brave and loyal William de Stuteville, and by appointing new guardians to the tempor-alities of York, as security for the defence of the north against the Scots,[7] while he himself hurried back to the sea, and on June 20 sailed again for Normandy.[8]

[1] Rog. Wend. (Coxe), vol. iii. p. 140.

[2] *Mag. Vita S. Hug.* (Dimock), p. 293.

[3] Rog. Howden (Stubbs), vol. iv. pp. 90, 91.

[4] Rog. Wend. as above.   [5] R. Diceto (Stubbs), vol. ii. p. 166.

[6] *Ibid.* Rog. Howden as above, p. 91, says *Nottingham ;* but John was at Northampton on Whit-Monday according to Sir T. D. Hardy's *Itin. K. John,* a. 1 (*Introd. Pat. Rolls*).   [7] Rog. Howden as above, pp. 91, 92.

[8] *Ib.* p. 92. R. Diceto (as above) says June 19, but Sir T. D. Hardy's *Itinerary,* a. 1 (as above), shews John at Shoreham on the 20th.

On Midsummer-day he made a truce with Philip for three weeks.[1] At its expiration the two kings held a personal meeting ; John's occupation of his brother's territories without previous investiture from and homage to Philip was complained of by the latter as an unpardonable wrong ; and John was required to expiate it by the cession of the whole Vexin to Philip in absolute ownership, and of Poitou and the three Angevin counties for the benefit of Arthur. This John refused.[2] His fortunes were not yet so desperate as to compel him to such humiliation. He had already secured the alliance of Flanders ;[3] his nephew Otto, now fully acknowledged by the Pope as Emperor-elect, was urging him to war with France and promising him the aid of the imperial forces ;[4] and his refusal of submission to Philip was at once followed by offers of homage and mutual alliance from all those French feudataries who had been in league with Richard against their own sovereign.[5] The war began in September, with the taking of Conches by the French king ; this was followed by the capture of Ballon. Philip, however, chose to celebrate these first successes by levelling Ballon to the ground. As the castle stood upon Cenomannian soil, it ought, according to the theory proclaimed by Philip himself, to have been handed over by him to Arthur ; Arthur's seneschal William des Roches therefore remonstrated against its demolition as an injury done to his young lord. Philip retorted that "he would not for Arthur's sake stay from dealing as he pleased with his own acquisitions." The consequence was a momentary desertion of all his Breton allies. William des Roches not only surrendered to John the city of Le Mans, which Philip and Arthur had intrusted to him as governor, but contrived to get the boy-duke of Britanny out of Philip's custody and bring him to his uncle, who received him into seeming favour and peace.[6] That very day, however, a

---

[1] Rog. Howden (Stubbs), vol. iv. p. 93.   [2] *Ib.* pp. 94, 95.

[3] The count of Flanders did homage to John at Rouen on August 13 [1199]. *Ib.* p. 93.   [4] *Ib.* pp. 95, 96.   [5] *Ib.* p. 95.

[6] *Ib.* p. 96. This must have been on September 22 ; see Hardy, *Itin. K. John*, a. 1 (*Intr. Pat. Rolls*).

warning reached Arthur of the fate to which he was already
doomed by John ; and on the following night he fled away
to Angers with his mother and a number of their friends.
Among the latter was the viscount Almeric of Thouars, who
had just been compelled to resign into John's hands the
office of seneschal of Anjou and the custody of the fortress
of Chinon, which he held in Arthur's name ; and it seems
to have been shortly afterwards that Constance, apparently
casting off Ralf of Chester without even an attempt at
divorce, went through a ceremony of marriage with Almeric's
brother Guy.[1]

   The year's warfare again ended in a truce, made in
October to last till S. Hilary's day.[2]   Its author was that
Cardinal Peter of Capua[3] who had negotiated the last truce
between Philip and Richard, and who now found another
occupation in punishing the matrimonial sins of the French
king :—Philip having sent away his queen Ingebiorg of
Denmark immediately after his marriage with her in 1193,
and three years later taken as his wife another princess,·
Agnes of Merania.[4]   At a Church council at Dijon on
December 6, 1199, the legate passed a sentence of interdict
upon the whole royal domain, to be publicly proclaimed on
the twentieth day after Christmas[5]—the very day on which
Philip's truce with John would expire.   It was no doubt
the prospect of this new trouble which moved Philip, when
he met John in conference between Gaillon and Les
Andelys,[6] to accept terms far more favourable to the English
king than those which he had offered six months before.
As a pledge of future peace and amity between the two
kings, Philip's son Louis was to marry John's niece Blanche,

---

   [1] Rog. Howden (Stubbs), vol. iv. pp. 96, 97.   The marriage of Guy and
Constance must however have been legalized somehow, for their child was ultimately
acknowledged as heiress of Britanny.
   [2] *Ib.* p. 97.   Rigord (Duchesne, *Hist. Franc. Scriptt.*, vol. v.) p. 43, says S.
John's day.   [3] Rog. Howden as above.
   [4] Rog. Howden (Stubbs), vol. iii. pp. 224, 306, 307.   R. Diceto (Stubbs),
vol. ii. p. 111.   Rigord (as above), pp. 36, 37, 40, 42.   Will. Armor. *Gesta Phil.
Aug. (ibid.)*, pp. 77, 78.   "Merania" is Moravia.   Rigord and William both
call the lady Mary, but all scholars seem agreed that Agnes was her real name.
   [5] Rigord (as above), p. 43.   Will. Armor. (as above), p. 80.   Cf. R. Diceto
(as above), pp. 167, 168.   [6] Rog. Howden (Stubbs), vol. iv. p. 106.

a daughter of his sister Eleanor and her husband King
Alfonso of Castille ; John was to bestow upon the bride, by
way of dowry, the city and county of Evreux and all those
Norman castles which had been in Philip's possession on the
day of Richard's death ; he was also to give Philip thirty
thousand marks of silver, and to swear that he would give
no help to Otto for the vindication of his claim to the
Empire. The formal execution of the treaty was deferred
till the octave of midsummer ; and while the aged queen-
mother Eleanor went to fetch her granddaughter from
Spain, John at the end of February took advantage of the
respite to make a hurried visit to England,[1] for the purpose
of raising the thirty thousand marks which he had promised
to Philip. This was done by means of a carucage or aid
of three shillings on every ploughland.[2] As a scutage of a
most unusual amount—two marks on the knight's fee—
had already been levied since John's accession, this new
impost was a sore burthen upon the country. The abbots
of some of the great Cistercian houses in Yorkshire withstood it as an unheard-of infringement of their rights, to
which they could not assent without the permission of a
general chapter of their order. John in a fury bade the
sheriffs put all the White Monks outside the protection of
the law. The remonstrances of the primate compelled him
to revoke this command ; but he rejected all offers of compromise on the part of the monks, and "breathing out
threatenings and slaughter against the disciples of the
Lord" went over sea again at the end of April.[3] As
France had been suffering the miseries of an interdict ever
since January,[4] Philip was now growing eager for peace.
He therefore met John at Gouleton, between Vernon and
Les Andelys, on May 22, and there a treaty was signed.
Its solid advantages were wholly on the side of John. In

---

[1] Rog. Howden (Stubbs), vol. iv. pp. 106, 107. John crossed on February 24 ;
Ann. Winton, a. 1200 (Luard, *Ann. Monast.*, vol. ii. p. 73).

[2] R. Coggeshall (Stevenson), p. 101. Rog. Howden as above, p. 107.

[3] R. Coggeshall (Stevenson), pp. 102, 103. The date of John's crossing lies
between April 28 and May 2. Hardy, *Itin. K. John*, a. 1 (*Intr. Pat. Rolls*).

[4] Rigord (Duchesne, *Hist. Franc. Scriptt.*, vol. v.), p. 43 ; Rog. Howden as
above, p. 112. R. Diceto (Stubbs), vol. ii. p. 168, says only since Mid-Lent.

addition to the concessions made in January, he did indeed resign in favour of Blanche and her bridegroom his claims upon the fiefs of Berry ; but the thirty thousand marks due to Philip were reduced to twenty thousand ; Arthur was acknowledged as owing homage to his uncle for Britanny ; and John was formally recognized by the French king as rightful heir to all the dominions of his father and his elder brother.[1] On the morrow Louis and Blanche were married, by the archbishop of Bordeaux, and on Norman soil, in con-sequence of the interdict in France ;[2] and on the same day, at Vernon, John received in Philip's presence Arthur's hom-age for Britanny,[3] Philip having already accepted that of John for the whole continental dominions of the house of Anjou.[4]

The next six weeks were spent by John in a triumphant progress southward, through Le Mans, Angers, Chinon, Tours and Loches, into Aquitaine, where he remained until the end of August.[5] While there, he received the homage of his brother-in-law Count Raymond of Toulouse for the dower-lands of Jane,[6] who had died in the preceding autumn.[7] Of all these successes, however, John went far to cast away the fruit by a desecration of the marriage-bond almost as shameless and quite as impolitic as that which had brought upon Philip the wrath of Rome. He persuaded the Aqui-

---

[1] Treaty in Rymer, *Fœdera*, vol. i. p. 79, and Rog. Howden (Stubbs), vol. iv. pp. 148-151. Its date is not quite clear; the document itself bears only "mense Maii"; Rigord (Duchesne, *Hist. Franc. Scriptt.*, vol. v. p. 43) says it was made on Ascension-day (May 18); Rog. Howden (as above, p. 114) begins by placing it at the date for which it had been originally fixed—the octave of S. John Baptist—but in the next page corrects this into "xi kalendas Junii, feria secunda," *i.e.* Monday, May 22. R. Coggeshall (Stevenson), p. 103, believed the thirty thousand marks to have been paid in full. The remission of ten thousand of them clearly made no difference to England ; they were pocketed by John.

[2] Rog. Howden as above, p. 115. He says it was at Portmort, on the morrow of the treaty—*i.e.* according to his reckoning, on Tuesday, May 23. Rigord however (as above), p. 44, dates it "at the same place, on the Monday after [Ascension]," *i.e.* Gouleton, May 22. Hardy's *Itinerary*, a. 2, shews John at La Roche-Andelys (Château-Gaillard) daily from May 17 to May 25. The places however are all close together.   [3] Rog. Howden as above.

[4] R. Coggeshall (Stevenson), p. 101.

[5] See Hardy, *Itin. K. John*, a. 2 (*Intr. Pat. Rolls*).

[6] Rog. Howden as above, p. 124.   [7] *Ib.* p. 96.

tanian and Norman bishops to annul his marriage with his
cousin Avice of Gloucester, apparently by making them
believe that the dispensation granted by Clement III. had
been revoked by Innocent.[1] Instead however of restoring
to Avice the vast heritage which had been settled upon her
at her betrothal, he gave her county of Gloucester to her
sister's husband Count Almeric of Evreux as compensation
for the loss of his Norman honour,[2] and apparently kept the
remainder of her estates in his own hands. These proceedings were enough to excite the ill-will of a powerful section
of the English baronage. John's next step was a direct
challenge to the most active, turbulent and troublesome
house in all Aquitaine. He gave out that he desired to
wed a daughter of the king of Portugal, and despatched an
honourable company of ambassadors, headed by the bishop
of Lisieux, to sue for her hand ; after these envoys had
started, however, and without a word of notice to them, he
suddenly married the daughter of Count Ademar of Angoulême.[3] Twenty-nine years before, Richard, as duke of
Aquitaine, had vainly striven to wrest Angoulême from
Ademar in behalf of Matilda, the only child of Ademar's
brother Count Vulgrin III. Matilda was now the wife of
Hugh "the Brown" of Lusignan, who in 1179 or 1180
had in spite of King Henry made himself master of La
Marche,[4] and whose personal importance in southern Gaul
was increased by the rank and fame which his brothers
Geoffrey, Guy and Almeric had won in the kingdoms of
Palestine and Cyprus. His son by Matilda—another Hugh
the Brown—had through Richard's good offices been betrothed in boyhood to his infant cousin Isabel, Ademar's
only child ; the little girl was educated with her future hus-

---

[1] R. Coggeshall (Stevenson), p. 103, says the divorce was made "per man-
datum domini Papæ . . . propter consanguinitatis lineam." But R. Diceto
(Stubbs), vol. ii. p. 167, says it was made because John was "sublimioris thori
spe raptatus," and adds : "unde magnam summi pontificis, scilicet Innocentii
tertii, et totius curiæ Romanæ indignationem incurrit." He dates it 1199, and
attributes it to the Norman bishops ; Rog. Howden (Stubbs), vol. iv. p. 119,
places it in 1200, and names only the archbishop of Bordeaux and the bishops of
Poitiers and Saintes.   [2] R. Coggeshall (Stevenson), p. 101.

[3] R. Diceto as above, p. 170.   [4] See above, p. 220.

band, and it was hoped that in due time their marriage
would heal the family feud and unite the lands of Angoulême and La Marche without possibility of further dissension. No sooner however did Count Ademar discover
that a king wished to marry his daughter than he took her
away from her bridegroom ; and at the end of August she
was married to John at Angoulême by the archbishop of
Bordeaux.[1]

Heedless of the storm which this marriage was sure to
raise in Aquitaine, John in the first days of October carried
his child-queen with him to England, and on the 8th was
crowned with her at Westminster.[2] His first business in
England was to renew his persecution of the Cistercians ;[3]
the next was to arrange a meeting with the king of Scots.
This took place in November at Lincoln, where John, defying the tradition which his father had carefully observed,
ventured to present himself in regal state within the cathedral church.[4] The two kings held their colloquy on a hill
outside the city; William performed his long-deferred homage,[5] although his renewed demand for the restitution of
the northern shires was again put off till Whitsuntide.[6]
Next day the king of England helped with his own hands
to carry the body of the holy bishop Hugh to its last resting-place in the minster which he had himself rebuilt.[7]
Some haunting remembrance of Hugh's saintlike face, as
he had seen it in London only a few weeks before the good
bishop's death,[8] may have combined with a sense that the
White Monks were still too great a power in the land to be

---

[1] Rog. Howden (Stubbs), vol. iv. pp. 119, 120. Cf. R. Coggeshall (Stevenson), p. 103. No one gives a date ; but John was at Angoulême on August 26
(Hardy, *Itin. K. John*, a. 2, *Intr. Pat. Rolls*) ; and "his settlement on Isabella
is dated Aug. 30. *Rot. Chart.*, p. 75" (Stubbs, *Rog. Howden*, vol. iv. p. 168,
note 1). Rog. Howden and R. Coggeshall both say this marriage was advised
by Philip.

[2] Rog. Howden as above, p. 139. R. Diceto (Stubbs), vol. ii. p. 170. R.
Coggeshall as above, with a wrong date.

[3] R. Coggeshall (Stevenson), pp. 103, 104.

[4] Rog. Howden as above, pp. 140, 141. [5] *Ib.* p. 141.

[6] *Ib.* p. 142.

[7] *Ibid.* R. Diceto as above, p. 171. *Mag. Vita S. Hug.* (Dimock), pp. 370,
371. [8] Rog. Howden as above, pp. 140, 141.

defied with impunity, and moved John on the following
Sunday to make full amends to the Cistercian abbots, promising to seal his repentance by founding a house of their
order [1]—a promise which he redeemed by the foundation of
Beaulieu abbey, in the New Forest.[2]   After keeping Christmas at Guildford [3] he came back again to Lincoln, and
quarrelled with the canons about the election of a new
bishop.[4]   He thence went northward, accompanied by his
queen, through Lincolnshire, Yorkshire, Northumberland and
Cumberland, taking fines everywhere for offences against the
forest-law.   At Mid-Lent he was at York,[5] and on Easter-
day he and Isabel wore their crowns at Canterbury.[6]   A
few days later, rumours of disturbances in Normandy and in
Poitou caused him to issue orders for the earls and barons
of England to meet him at Portsmouth at Whitsuntide,
ready with horses and ships to accompany him over sea.
The earls however held a meeting at Leicester, and thence
by common consent made answer to the king that they
would not go with him " unless he gave them back their
rights." It is clear that they already looked upon personal
service beyond sea as no longer binding upon them without
their own consent, specially given for a special occasion.
John retorted by demanding the surrender of their castles,
beginning with William of Aubigny's castle of Beauvoir,
which William was only suffered to retain on giving his son
as a hostage.[7]   This threat brought the barons to Portsmouth on the appointed day ; but the quarrel ended in a
compromise. After despatching his chamberlain Hubert de
Burgh, with a hundred knights, to act as keeper of the
Welsh marches, and sending William the Marshal and Roger

---

[1] R. Coggeshall (Stevenson), pp. 107-110.   *Mag. Vita S. Hug.* (Dimock),
pp. 377, 378.

[2] On Beaulieu see R. Coggeshall (Stevenson), p. 147 ; Ann. Waverl. a. 1204
(Luard, *Ann. Monast.*, vol. ii. p. 256) ; and Dugdale, *Monast. Angl.*, vol. v. pp.
682, 683.

[3] R. Diceto (Stubbs), vol. ii. p. 172.   Rog. Howden (Stubbs), vol. iv. p. 156.

[4] Rog. Howden as above.

[5] *Ib.* p. 157.   See details of his movements in Hardy, *Itin. K. John*, a. 2
(*Intr. Pat. Rolls*).

[6] Rog. Howden as above, p. 160.   R. Diceto (Stubbs), vol. ii. p. 172.

[7] Rog. Howden as above, pp. 160, 161.

de Lacy, each with a hundred mercenaries, to resist the enemies in Normandy, John took from the remainder of the host a scutage in commutation of their services, and bade them return to their own homes.[1] On Whit-Monday the queen crossed to Normandy, and shortly afterwards her husband followed.[2]

After a friendly meeting near the Isle of Andelys,[3] Philip invited John to Paris, where he entertained him with the highest honours, vacating his own palace for the reception of his guest, and loading him with costly gifts.[4] From Paris John went to meet his sister-in-law, Richard's queen Berengaria, at Chinon,[5] where he seems to have chiefly spent the rest of the summer. He came back to Normandy in the autumn,[6] and the Christmas feast at Argentan[7] passed over in peace ; but trouble was fast gathering on all sides. Philip was at last free of his ecclesiastical difficulties, for Agnes of Merania was dead, and he had taken back his wife.[8] John was now in his turn to pay the penalty for his unwarrantable divorce and his lawless second marriage. As if he had not already done enough to alienate the powerful house of Lusignan by stealing the plighted bride of its head,[9] he had now seized the castle of Driencourt, which belonged to a brother of Hugh the Brown, while its owner was absent in England on business for the king himself ;[10] and he had further insulted the barons of Poitou by summoning them to clear themselves in his court from a general

---

[1] Rog. Howden (Stubbs), vol. iv. p. 163.   [2] *Ib.* p. 164.

[3] *Ibid.* John was at the Isle June 9-11, and again June 25-27 [1201]. Hardy, *Itin. K. John*, a. 3 (*Intr. Pat. Rolls*).

[4] Rigord (Duchesne, *Hist. Franc. Scriptt.*, vol. v.), p. 44. Rog. Howden as above ; on the date see Bishop Stubbs's note 1, *ibid.*

[5] Rog. Howden as above. The purpose was to settle with her about her dowry ; *ibid.*, and p. 172 and note 2.

[6] See Hardy as above.

[7] Rog. Wend. (Coxe), vol. iii. p. 167.

[8] Rigord as above. Will. Armor. *Gesta Phil. Aug.* (*ibid.*), p. 81. Rog. Howden as above, pp. 146-148.

[9] Strictly speaking, its future head. The elder Hugh, father of Isabel's bridegroom, lived till 1206.

[10] Will. Armor. *Philipp.*, l. vi. (Duchesne, as above), p. 159. This was Ralf of Issoudun, a brother of the elder Hugh, and count of Eu in right of his wife.

VOL. II.

charge of treason against his late brother and himself, by ordeal of battle with picked champions from England and Normandy. They scorned the summons,[1] and appealed to the king of France, John's overlord as well as theirs, to bring John to justice for their wrongs.[2] On March 25 Philip met John at Gouleton,[3] and peremptorily bade him give up to Arthur all his French fiefs, besides sundry other things, all of which John refused.[4] Hereupon Philip sent, through some of the great French nobles,[5] a citation to John, as duke of Aquitaine, to appear in Paris fifteen days after Easter at the court of his lord the king of France, to stand to its judgement, to answer to his lord for his misdoings, and to undergo the sentence of his peers.[6] John made no attempt to deny Philip's jurisdiction ; but he declared that, as duke of Normandy, he was not bound to obey the French king's citation to any spot other than the traditional trysting-place on the border. Philip replied that his summons was addressed to the duke of Aquitaine, not to the duke of Normandy, and that his rights over the former were not to be annulled by the accidental union of the two dignities in one person.[7] John at length yielded so far as to promise that on the appointed day he would present himself before the court in Paris, and would give up to Philip the two castles of Tillières and Boutavant as security for his abiding by the settlement then to be made. The day however came and went without either the surrender of the forts or the appearance of John.[8] The court of the

---

[1] Rog. Howden (Stubbs), vol. iv. p. 176.

[2] R. Coggeshall (Stevenson), p. 135. Will. Armor. *Gesta Phil. Aug.* (Duchesne, *Hist. Franc. Scriptt.*, vol. v.), p. 81 ; *Philipp.*, l. vi. (*ibid.*) p. 159.

[3] R. Diceto (Stubbs), vol. ii. p. 174.

[4] Rog. Wend. (Coxe), vol. iii. p. 167.

[5] " Per proceres regni Francorum." R. Coggeshall as above.

[6] *Ib.* pp. 135, 136. The date fixed for the trial—April 29 [1202]—is from Rigord (Duchesne as above), p. 44. This writer and Will. Armor. (*Gesta Phil. Aug.* as above) give a version somewhat different from Ralf's, saying that Philip summoned John to do right to Philip himself for the counties of Anjou, Touraine and Poitou. William however in the *Philipp.* (as above) substantially agrees with the English writer as to the ground of Philip's complaint.

[7] R. Coggeshall (Stevenson), p. 136.

[8] Will. Armor. as above, pp. 81, 161.

French peers condemned him by default, and sentenced him to be deprived of all his lands.[1]

Philip at once marched upon Normandy to execute the sentence by force of arms. He began by taking Boutavant[2] and Tillières ;[3] thence he marched straight up northward by Lions,[4] Longchamp, La Ferté-en-Bray,[5] Orgueil and Morte-mer,[6] to Eu ;[7] all these places fell into his hands. Thus master of almost the whole Norman border from the Seine to the sea, he turned back to lay siege on July 8 to Rade-pont on the Andelle, scarcely more than ten miles from Rouen. Dislodged at the end of a week by John,[8] he again withdrew to the border. The castle of Aumale and the rest of its county were soon in his hands.[9] Hugh of Gournay alone, the worthy bearer of a name which for generations had been almost a synonym for loyalty to the Norman ducal house, still held out in his impregnable castle ; Philip however, by breaking down the embankment which kept in the waters of a reservoir communicating with the river and the moat, let loose upon the castle a flood which undermined its walls and almost swept it away, thus compelling its defenders to make their escape and take shelter as best they could in the neighbouring forest.[10] At Gournay Philip bestowed upon Arthur the hand of his infant daughter Mary,[11]

---

[1] R. Coggeshall (Stevenson), p. 136.

[2] *Ibid.* Rog. Wend. (Coxe), vol. iii. p. 168. Rigord (Duchesne, *Hist. Franc. Scriptt.*, vol. v.), p. 45. Will. Armor. *Gesta Phil. Aug. (ibid.)*, p. 81 ; *Philipp.*, l. vi. *(ibid.)*, p. 161. Boutavant was a small fortress built by Richard in 1198, on the Seine, four miles above Château-Gaillard, on the border-line between Normandy and France (Will. Armor. *Gesta Phil. Aug.* as above. Rog. Howden, Stubbs, vol. iv. p. 78). Philip had retorted by building hard by it a rival fortress which he called Gouleton (Rog. Howden as above)—the scene of his treaty with John in May 1202 ; see above, p. 396.   [3] Will. Armor. as above.

[4] Rog. Wend. and Will. Armor. *Philipp.* as above.

[5] Will. Armor. as above.

[6] *Ibid.* *Gesta Phil. Aug. (ibid.)*, p. 81. Rigord *(ibid.)*, p. 45.

[7] Rog. Wend. as above.

[8] *Ibid.* p. 167 ; he says Philip besieged Radepont for eight days. John got there on July 15 ; Hardy, *Itin. K. John*, a. 4 *(Intr. Pat. Rolls)*.

[9] R. Coggeshall as above.

[10] Rog. Wend. as above, pp. 167, 168. Will. Armor. *Gesta Phil. Aug.* as above ; *Philipp. (ibid.)*, pp. 161, 162.

[11] Will. Armor. *Gesta Phil. Aug.* as above, p. 82 ; *Philipp. (ibid.)*, p. 162. Cf. R. Coggeshall (Stevenson), p. 137. Mary (or Jane, as Rigord calls her) was

the honour of knighthood,[1] and the investiture of all the
Angevin dominions except the duchy of Normandy,[2] which
he evidently intended to conquer for himself and keep by
right of conquest. What John had been doing all this time it is difficult to
understand. Between the middle of May and the end of
June he had shifted his quarters incessantly, moving through
the whole length of eastern Normandy, from Arques to Le
Mans ; throughout July he was chiefly in the neighbourhood
of Rouen ;[3] but, except in the one expedition to Radepont,
he seems to have made no attempt to check the progress of
his enemies. After the knighting of Arthur at Gournay,
however, he tried to make a diversion by sending a body
of troops into Britanny. With their duchess dead[4] and
their young duke absent, the Bretons were in no condition
for defence; Dol and Fougères were taken by John's soldiers,
and the whole country ravaged as far as Rennes.[5] This
attack stung Arthur into an attempt at independent action
which led to his ruin. He and Philip divided their forces ;

one of the two children of Agnes of Merania, legitimatized by Innocent III.; cf.
Will. Armor. *Gesta Phil. Aug.* (Duchesne, *Hist. Franc. Scriptt.*, vol. v.), p. 81,
and Rigord (*ibid.*), p. 44.

[1] R. Coggeshall (Stevenson), p. 137. Rigord as above, p. 45 ; Will. Armor.
Gesta Phil. Aug. (*ibid.*), p. 82 ; *Philipp.* (*ibid.*), p. 162. Rog. Howden (Stubbs),
vol. iv. p. 94, says that Arthur was knighted by Philip when he first did him
homage in 1199.

[2] Rigord as above. The order of the campaign above described is not easy to
make out, for no two contemporary writers name the castles in the same order.
Taking geography for a guide, it would at first glance seem more natural that
Philip should have gone to Radepont from Tillières, and that the whole northward expedition should come afterwards. But it is certain that the siege of
Radepont happened July 8-15 (see above, p. 403, note 8); and on the one hand,
the northern campaign, or at any rate part of it, seems needed to fill up the
interval between the breaking-out of the war at the beginning of May and July
8 ; while on the other, it seems impossible to crowd in the whole campaign
between July 15 and the knighting of Arthur, which clearly took place before
that month had expired. Lions, however, was not taken till after May 29, for
on that day John was there ; Hardy, *Itin. K. John*, a. 4 (*Intr. Pat. Rolls*).

[3] See Hardy, as above, a. 3, 4 (*ibid.*)

[4] Constance died September 3 or 4, 1201. Chronn. Britt. *ad ann.* (Morice,
Hist. Bret., preuves, vol. i. cols. 6, 106).

[5] Will. Armor. *Philipp.* as above, p. 163. In the *Gesta Phil. Aug.* (as above)
he places this after Arthur's capture. In both works he says that *John* did all this
in Britanny ; but Hardy's *Itinerary* (as above) shews that John did it vicariously.

while the French king led the bulk of his army northward to the siege of Arques,[1] Arthur with two hundred knights[2] moved southward to Tours,[3] sending forward a summons· to the men of his own duchy and those of Berry to meet him there for an expedition into Poitou.[4]   At Tours he was met by the disaffected Aquitanian chiefs :—the injured bridegroom young Hugh of La Marche, and two of his uncles, Ralf of Issoudun the dispossessed count of Eu, and Geoffrey of Lusignan, the inveterate fighter who had taken a leading part in every Aquitanian rising throughout the last twenty-two years of Henry's reign, who after being Richard's bitterest foe at home had been one of his best supporters in Palestine, and who had come back, it seems, to join in one more fight against his successor.   The three kinsmen, however, brought together a force of only seventy-five knights ; to which a Gascon baron, Savaric of Mauléon, added thirty more, and seventy men-at-arms.[5]   Arthur, mere boy of fifteen though he was, had enough of the hereditary Angevin wariness to shrink from attempting to act with such a small force, and in accordance with Philip's instructions proposed to wait for his expected allies.[6]   But the Poitevins would brook no delay ; and a temptation now offered itself which was irresistible alike to them and to their young leader.   On her return from Castille with her granddaughter Blanche in the spring of 1200, Queen Eleanor, worn out with age and fatigue, had withdrawn to the abbey of Fontevraud,[7] where she apparently remained throughout the next two years. The rising troubles of her duchy, however, seem to have brought her forth from her retirement once more, and she

[1] Rigord (Duchesne, *Hist. Franc. Scriptt.*, vol. v.), p. 45.   R. Coggeshall (Stevenson), p. 138.   Rog. Wend. (Coxe), vol. iii. p. 169.

[2] Rog. Wend. as above, p. 168.

[3] Will. Armor. *Philipp.*, l. vi. (Duchesne, *Hist. Franc. Scriptt.*, vol. v.), p. 162.   Rigord as above.

[4] Will. Armor. *Gesta Phil. Aug.* (Duchesne as above), p. 82.   To the Bretons and the men of Berry he adds "Allobroges."   What can they have had to do in the case, or what can he mean by the name?

[5] Will. Armor. *Philipp.* as above.   He says Geoffrey brought twenty picked knights, Ralf forty, and Hugh fifteen.   R. Coggeshall (Stevenson), p. 137, makes the total force of Arthur and the Poitevins together two hundred and fifty knights.

[6] Will. Armor. as above, p. 163.   [7] Rog. Howden (Stubbs), vol. iv. p. 114.

was now in the castle of Mirebeau, on the border of Anjou and Poitou. All John's enemies knew that his mother was, in every sense, his best friend. She was at once his most devoted ally and his most sagacious counsellor, at least in all continental affairs ; moreover, in strict feudal law, she was still duchess of Aquitaine in her own right, a right untouched by the forfeiture of John ; and she therefore had it in her power to make that forfeiture null and void south of the Loire, so long as she lived to assert her claims for John's benefit.[1] To capture Eleanor would be to bring John to his knees ; and with this hope Arthur and his little band laid siege to Mirebeau.[2]

John, however, when once roused, could act with all the vigour and promptitude of his race. On July 30, as he was approaching Le Mans, he received tidings of his mother's danger ; on August 1 he suddenly appeared before Mirebeau.[3] The town was already lost, all the gates of the castle save one were broken down, and Eleanor had been driven to take refuge in the keep ; the besiegers, thinking their triumph assured, were surprised and overpowered by John's troops, and were slain or captured to a man, the Lusignans and Arthur himself being among the prisoners.[4] Philip, who was busy with the siege of Arques, left it and hurried southward on hearing of this disaster ;[5] John however at once put an end to his hopes of rescuing Arthur by

---

[1] On the relations of Eleanor, John, and Aquitaine see Bishop Stubbs's note to W. Coventry, vol. ii., pref. p. xxxiv, note 1. His conclusion is that "certainly the legal difficulties were much greater than Philip's hasty sentences of forfeiture could solve."

[2] Will. Armor. *Philipp.*, l. vi. (Duchesne, *Hist. Franc. Scriptt.*, vol. v.), p. 164 ; *Gesta Phil. Aug. (ibid.)*, p. 82. R. Coggeshall (Stevenson), p. 137. Rog. Wend. (Coxe), vol. iii. p. 168.

[3] These dates are given by John himself in a letter to the barons of England, inserted by R. Coggeshall (Stevenson), pp. 137, 138. Hardy's *Itin. K. John*, a. 4 (*Intr. Pat. Rolls*), shews John at Bonport on July 30, and then gives no further indication of his whereabouts till August 4, when he appears at Chinon.

[4] R. Coggeshall as above. Rog. Wend. as above, p. 169. Cf. Rigord (Duchesne as above), p. 45 ; Will. Armor. *Gesta Phil. Aug.* as above ; and *Philipp. (ibid.)*, pp. 164, 165. According to this last, John got into Mirebeau by night, by a fraudulent negotiation with William des Roches.

[5] Rog. Wend., Rigord, and Will. Armor. *Gesta Phil. Aug.*, as above.

sending the boy to prison at Falaise ;[1] and Philip, after taking and burning Tours,[2] withdrew into his own domains.[3] John in his turn then marched upon Tours, and vented his wrath at its capture by completing its destruction.[4]   Shortly afterwards he had the good luck to make prisoner another disaffected Aquitanian noble, the viscount of Limoges.[5]   It was however growing evident that he would soon have nothing but his own resources to depend upon.   His allies were falling away ; the counts of Flanders, Blois and Perche and several of the other malcontent French barons had taken the cross and abandoned the field of western politics to seek their fortunes in the East ;[6] he had quarrelled with Otto of Germany ;[7] William des Roches, after pleading in vain for Arthur's release, was organizing a league of the Breton nobles which some of the Norman border-chiefs were quite ready to join, and by the end of October the party thus formed was strong enough to seize Angers and establish its head-quarters there.[8]   It was probably the knowledge of all this which in the beginning of 1203 made John transfer his captive nephew from the castle of Falaise to that of Rouen.[9] Sinister rumours of Arthur's fate were already in circulation, telling how John had sent a ruffian to blind him at Falaise, how the soldiers who kept him had frustrated the design, and how their commandant, John's chamberlain Hubert de Burgh, had endeavoured to satisfy the king by giving out

[1] Rog. Wend. (Coxe), vol. iii. pp. 169, 170.   Will. Armor. *Philipp.*, l. vi. (Duchesne, *Hist. Franc. Scriptt.*, vol. v.), p. 165.

[2] Rigord (Duchesne, as above), p. 45.   Will. Armor. *Gesta Phil. Aug.* (*ibid.*), p. 82.

[3] Rog. Wend. (as above), p. 170.   He adds "residuum anni illius imbellis peregit."

[4] Rigord as above.   Will. Armor. *Gesta Phil. Aug.* as above.   R. Coggeshall (Stevenson), p. 138.

[5] Rigord as above.   This was Guy, son and successor to Ademar, who had been slain in 1199 by Richard's son Philip in vengeance for the quarrel which had led to Richard's death.   Rog. Howden (Stubbs), vol. iv. p. 97.

[6] Rigord and Will. Armor. as above.

[7] In 1200 Otto had demanded the lands and the jewels bequeathed to him by Richard ; John had refused to give them up.   Rog. Howden as above, p. 116.

[8] Chron. S. Albin. a. 1202 (Marchegay, *Eglises*, p. 51).   R. Coggeshall (Stevenson), p. 139.   The former gives the date, Wednesday before All Saints' day.

[9] R. Coggeshall (Stevenson), p. 143.   Rog. Wend. as above.   Will. Armor. *Philipp.* as above, p. 166.

that Arthur had died of wounds and grief and ordering funeral services in his memory, till the threats of the infuriated Bretons drove him to confess the fraud for the sake of John's own safety.[1] How or when Arthur really died has never yet been clearly proved. We only know that at Easter 1203 all France was ringing with the tidings of his death, and that after that date he was never seen alive. In his uncle's interest an attempt was made to suggest that he had either pined to death in his prison, or been drowned in endeavouring to escape across the Seine;[2] but the general belief, which John's after-conduct tends strongly to confirm, was that he had been stabbed and then flung into the river by the orders, if not actually by the hands, of John himself.[3]

The fire which had been smouldering throughout the winter in Britanny now burst into a blaze. The barons and prelates of the duchy, it is said, held a meeting at Vannes, and thence sent to the king of France, as overlord alike of Arthur and of John, their demand for a judicial inquisition before the peers of the realm—that is, before the supreme feudal court of France—into John's dealings with their captive duke.[4] A citation was accordingly sent to John, as duke of Normandy, either to present Arthur alive,[5] or to come and stand his trial before the French king's court on a charge of murder. John neither appeared nor sent any defence; the court pronounced him worthy of death, and sentenced him and his heirs to forfeiture of all the lands and honours which he held of the Crown of France.[6] The trial seems to have been held shortly after Easter. The legal force of the sentence need not be discussed here.[7] Its moral justice can

---

[1] R. Coggeshall (Stevenson), pp. 139-141.

[2] Mat. Paris, *Hist. Angl.* (Madden), vol. ii. p. 95.

[3] On Arthur's death see note at end of chapter.

[4] Le Baud, *Hist. de Bretagne*, pp. 209, 210, with a reference to Robert Blondel, a writer of the fifteenth century. On the value of this account see Bishop Stubbs, pref. to W. Coventry, vol. ii. p. xxxii, note 3.

[5] R. Coggeshall (Stevenson), pp. 143-145.

[6] Proclamation of Louis of France, a. 1216, in Rymer, *Fœdera*, vol. i. p. 140. Ann. Margam, a. 1204 (Luard, *Ann. Monast.*, vol. i. p. 27). Rog. Wend. (Coxe), vol. iii. p. 373. Le Baud as above, p. 210. Stubbs, *W. Coventry*, vol. ii. pref. p. xxxii.

[7] Bishop Stubbs's remark (*W. Coventry*, vol. ii. pref. p. xxxiv, note 1), quoted

hardly be disputed, so far as John himself is concerned; and
Philip's action did little more than precipitate the consequences which must sooner or later have naturally resulted
from John's own deed.   John in committing a great crime
had committed an almost greater blunder.   Arthur's death
left him indeed without a rival in his own house.   It left him
sole survivor, in the male line, alike of the Angevin and
Cenomannian counts and of the ducal house of Normandy.
Even in the female line there was no one who could be set
up against him as representative of either race.   Eleanor of
Britanny, the only remaining child of his brother Geoffrey,
was a prisoner in her uncle's keeping.   The sons of his
sister Matilda had cast in their lot with their father's country
and severed all ties with their mother's people; the children
of his sister Eleanor were still more complete strangers to
the political interests of northern Gaul, and the only one of
them who was known there at all was known only as the
wife of the heir to the French crown.   But these very facts
set John face to face with a more dangerous rival than any
of the ambitious kinsmen with whom the two Williams or
the two Henrys had had to contend.   They drove his disaffected subjects to choose between submission to him and
submission to Philip Augustus.   The barons of Anjou, of
Maine, of Britanny or of Normandy had no longer any
chance of freeing themselves from the yoke of the king
from over-sea who had become a stranger to them all alike,
save by accepting in its stead the yoke of the king with whom
they had grown familiar through years of political and personal intercourse, and whom, in theory at least, even their own
rulers had always acknowledged as their superior.   Anjou,
Maine and Britanny had all resolved upon Richard's death
that they would not have John to rule over them; Normandy
was now fast coming to the same determination.   Under the
existing circumstances it would cost them little or no sacrifice
to accept their titular overlord as their real and immediate
sovereign.   So long as Arthur lived, Philip had been compelled to veil his ambition under a shew of zeal for Arthur's

above, p. 406, note 1, applies to this case also.   On the vexed question as to the
composition of the court I do not feel bound to enter here at all.

rights ; now he could fling aside the veil, and present himself almost in the character of a deliverer.   If the barons did
not actually hail him as such, they were at any rate for the
most part not unwilling to leave to him the responsibility of
accomplishing their deliverance, and to accept it quietly from
his hands.

Philip took the field as soon as the forfeiture was proclaimed.   Within a fortnight after Easter he had taken
Saumur[1] and entered Aquitaine ; there he seems to have
spent some weeks in taking sundry castles, with the help of
the Bretons and the malcontent Poitevin nobles.[2]   One great
Norman baron, the viscount of Beaumont, had already openly
joined the league against John ;[3] and as Philip turned northward again, the count of Alençon formally placed himself
and all his lands at the disposal of the French king.[4]   Thus
secure of a strong foothold on the southern frontier of
Normandy, and already by his last year's conquests master
of its north-eastern border from Eu to Gisors, Philip set
himself to win the intervening territory—the remnant of the
viscounty of Evreux.   One by one its castles—Conches,[5]
Vaudreuil[6] and many others—fell into his hands.   Messenger
after messenger came to John as he sat idle in his palace at
Rouen,[7] all charged with the same story : " The king of
France is in your land as an enemy, he is taking
your castles, he is binding your seneschals to their horses'
tails and leading them shamefully to prison, and he is
dealing with your goods according to his own will and
pleasure."   " Let him alone," John answered them all
alike ; " I shall win back some day all that he is taking
from me now."   The barons who still clave to him

---

[1] Chron. S. Albin. a. 1203 (Marchegay, *Eglises*, p. 52).
[6] Rigord (Duchesne, *Hist. Franc. Scriptt.*, vol. v.), p. 46.   Will. Armor.
Gesta Phil. Aug. (ibid.), p. 82 ; both under a wrong year, viz. 1202 instead of 1203.
[3] R. Coggeshall (Stevenson), p. 139.
[4] Rigord and Will. Armor. as above.   [5] Rigord as above.
[6] *Ibid.*   R. Coggeshall (Stevenson), p. 143.
[7] John was not literally there all the while ; but he only quitted it for short
excursions, never going further than Moulineaux, Pont-de-l'Arche, Orival or
Montfort, from the middle of May till the beginning of August, when he suddenly
went as far west as Caen, and thence as suddenly south again to Falaise and
Alençon.   Hardy, *Itin. K. John*, a. 5 (*Intr. Pat. Rolls*).

grew exasperated as they watched his unmoved face and
heard his unvarying reply ; some of them began to attribute
his indifference to the effects of magic ; all, finding it impossible to break the spell, turned away from him in despair.
One by one they took their leave and withdrew to their
homes, either passively to await the end, or actively to join
Philip.   Even Hugh of Gournay, who had held out so
bravely and so faithfully a year ago, now voluntarily gave up
his castle of Montfort.[1]   Not till near the middle of August
did John make any warlike movement ; then he suddenly
laid siege to Alençon ; but at Philip's approach he fled in a
panic ;[2] an attempt to regain Brezolles ended in like manner,[3]
and John relapsed into his former inactivity.   That the
conqueror did not march straight to the capture of Rouen,
that he in fact made no further progress towards it for six
whole months, was owing not to John but to his predecessor.
Richard's favourite capital was safe, so long as it was sheltered
behind the group of fortifications crowned by his "saucy
castle" on the Rock of Andely.

Upon the winning of Château-Gaillard, therefore, Philip
now concentrated all his energies and all his skill.   There
was no hope of voluntary surrender here ; John had given
the fortress in charge to Roger de Lacy the constable of
Chester, an English baron who had no stake in Normandy,
whose private interests were therefore bound up with those of
the English king, and who was moreover a man of dauntless
courage and high military capacity.[4]   The place was only to
be won by a regular siege.   Crossing the Seine higher up,
perhaps at Vernon, Philip led his troops along its left bank,
and encamped in the peninsula formed by the bend of the
river just opposite Les Andelys.   The garrison of the fort in
the Isle of Andely no sooner beheld his approach than they
destroyed the bridge between the island and the left bank.
Philip was thus deprived of the means not only of reaching

[1] Rog. Wend. (Coxe), vol. iii. pp. 171, 172.
[2] Will. Armor. *Gesta Phil. Aug.* (Duchesne, *Hist. Franc. Scriptt.*, vol. v.), p.
82. John was at Alençon August 11-15 ; Hardy, *Itin. K. John*, a. 5 (*Intr. Pat.
Rolls*).
[3] Will. Armor. as above.
[4] R. Coggeshall (Stevenson), p. 144.   Rog. Wend. as above, p. 180.

them, but also of opening communications with the opposite
shore ; for this could only be done with safety at some point
below Château-Gaillard, and the transport of the materials
needful for the construction of a bridge or pontoon was
barred by the stockade which crossed the river-bed directly
under the foot of the castle-rock. The daring of a few young
Frenchmen, however, soon cleared this obstacle away. While
the king brought up his engines close to the water's edge
and kept the garrison of the island-fort occupied with the
exchange of a constant fire of missiles, a youth named
Gaubert of Mantes with a few bold comrades plunged into
the water, each with an axe in his hand, and, regardless of
the stones and arrows which kept falling upon them from
both sides, hewed at the stockade till they had made a breach
wide enough for boats to pass through in safety. A number
of the broad flat-bottomed barges used for transport were
then hastily collected from the neighbouring riverside towns,
and moored side by side across the stream ; these served as
the foundation of a wooden bridge, which was further supported with stakes and strengthened with towers, and by
means of which Philip himself, with the larger part of his
host, crossed the river to form a new encampment under the
walls of the Lesser Andely. The garrison of the Isle were
thus placed between two fires ;[1] and the whole Vexin was
laid open as a foraging-ground for the besieging army, while
the occupants of the Lesser Andely and of Château-Gaillard
itself found their communications and their supplies cut off on
all sides.[2]

John was now again hovering about at a safe distance
in the neighbourhood.[3] To the peril of Château-Gaillard
his fatuous indifference was at last beginning to yield. A

[1] Will. Armor. *Gesta Phil. Aug.* (Duchesne, *Hist. Franc. Scriptt.*, vol. v.),
pp. 82, 83 ; *Philipp.*, l. vii. vv. 86-131 (*ib.* p. 170 ; Deville, *Château-Gaillard*,
pp. 127-129).

[2] Will. Armor. *Philipp.*, l. vii. vv. 132-139 (Duchesne, p. 170 ; Deville, p.
129).

[3] "Non multum distabat a loco illo" says Will. Armor. *Gesta Phil. Aug.*
(Duchesne, as above), p. 83. The date must fall between August 16, when John
was at Alençon, and September 5, when he was at Bonneville. His whereabouts
during the interval vary between Chambrai, Trianon, Montfort and Rouen.
Hardy, *Itin. K. John*, a. 5 (*Intr. Pat. Rolls*).

year ago he had shewn some appreciation of his brother's
work, by making an addition to the buildings in the second
ward ;[1] and he had shewn his sense of the military importance of the place yet more significantly, by appointing
Roger de Lacy as its commander. He now gathered up
all his remaining forces—still, it seems, a formidable array [2]
—with the apparent intention of dislodging the French
from Les Andelys. As Philip's biographer remarks, however, John feared and hated the light ; he resolved, according to his wont, upon a night attack ; and even that attack
he did not lead in person.[3] He intrusted its command
indeed to a far braver man than himself, but a man who
was better fitted for action in the light of day than for such
deeds of darkness as John delighted in. William the
Marshal, the favourite comrade-in-arms of the younger King
Henry, the faithful friend and servant of the elder one even
unto death, the honoured minister of Richard, still clave to
the last survivor of the house which he had loved so long
and so well. To him John confided his plan for the relief
of Les Andelys. The marshal was to lead a force of three
hundred knights, three thousand mounted serving-men and
four thousand foot, with a band of mercenaries under a chief
called Lupicar,[4] along the left bank of the Seine, and to fall
under cover of darkness upon the French camp in the
peninsula. Meanwhile seventy transport-vessels, constructed
by Richard to serve either for sea or river-traffic, and as
many more as could be collected, were to be laden with
provisions for the besieged garrison of the Isle, and con-

---

[1] Will. Armor. *Gesta Phil. Aug.* (Duchesne, *Hist. Franc. Scriptt.*, vol. v.), p.
84 ; *Philipp.*, l. vii. vv. 737-746 (*ib.* p. 181 ; Deville, *Château-Gaillard*, p. 145).

[2] "Maximum congregaverat exercitum." Will. Armor. *Gesta Phil. Aug.*, as
above, p. 83.

[3] *Ibid.* ; *Philipp.*, l. vii. vv. 140-143, 188-194 (*ib.* pp. 170, 171 ; Deville as
above, pp. 129, 130).

[4] On this man see Géraud, *Les Routiers* (*Bibl. de l'Ecole des Chartes*, ser. i.
vol. iii. p. 132). In his native tongue he was called "Lobar"; in Latin he appears as "Lupicarius," "Lupescarus," "Lupatius." M. Géraud calls him in
French "Louvart"; the name was doubtless an assumed one, meaning "wolf."
He was a fellow-countryman and old comrade-in-arms of Mercadier ; Mat. Paris
introduces them both at once, in 1196, as "natione Provinciales"—"qui duces
fuerunt catervæ quam ruttam vocamus, militantes sub comite Johanne regis fratre."

voyed up the river by a flotilla of small war-ships, manned
by pirates [1] under a chief named Alan, and carrying, besides
their own daring and reckless crews, a force of three thousand
Flemings. Two hundred strokes of the oar, John reckoned,
would bring these ships to the French pontoon ; they must
break it if they could ; if not, they could at least co-operate
with the land-forces under the Marshal in cutting off the
northern division of the French army from its comrades and
supplies on the left bank, and throw into the island-fort
provisions enough to save it from the necessity of surrender
till John himself should come to its relief.

The flower of the French host, as John knew, had
crossed the river with its king. Those who remained in
the peninsula were hampered by the presence of a crowd of
unwarlike serving-men, sutlers and camp-followers, many of
whom, after spending the day in drunken revelry, were lying
asleep in the fields outside the camp. The night was
drawing to its close—for the cock had crowed thrice—when
the Marshal's troops fell upon these sleepers and slew more
than two hundred of them as they lay. The soldiers within
the camp quickly caught the alarm ; in their terror they
rushed to the pontoon in such numbers that it broke under
their weight, and they sought safety in swimming across the
river to join their comrades on the opposite shore. These
however had now been aroused by the tumult ; the bravest
of the French knights, headed by William des Barres, confronted the fugitives with indignant reproaches for their
cowardice, and drove them back across the stream. By the
light of torches and fires, hastily kindled, the whole host was
soon got under arms, the bridge repaired, and the Marshal's
troops, surprised in their turn while groping about in the
darkness of the deserted camp, were routed with heavy loss.
The victors, thinking the fight was over, went back to their

Chron. Maj. (Luard), vol. ii. p. 421. Lupicar however had made his first historical appearance some years earlier than Mercadier, as a leader of the Brabantines in the Limousin, about 1177. See Geoff. Vigeois, l. i. c. 70 (Labbe, *Nova
Biblioth.*, vol. ii. p. 324).

[1] It seems a strange return to long-past times to hear of "*pirates*" sailing up
the Seine to attack a king of the French. Of what nationality are these men
likely to have been ?

sleeping-quarters, but had scarcely reached them when they were roused up again, to see, in the dim light of the August sunrise, the hostile fleet bearing down upon them. In a few minutes the two river-banks and the pontoon were lined with armed Frenchmen. Still the boats held on their course till the foremost of them touched the bridge ; and despite a ceaseless shower of arrows from either shore, and of stones, iron missiles, and boiling oil and pitch from the engines mounted on the wooden turrets of the bridge, the crews began to hew at the cables and stakes in a desperate effort to break it down, and kept its defenders at bay till the Seine ran red with blood. At last an enormously heavy oaken beam fell directly upon the two foremost ships and sank them. The rest, stricken with sudden terror, rowed away in disorder as fast as oars could move them. Gaubert of Mantes and three other gallant French sailors sprang each into a little boat, set off in pursuit, and succeeded in capturing two of the fugitive ships, which they brought back in tow, with their stores and all of their crews who survived.[1] The delay in the arrival of the fleet, caused by the difficulties of navigation in the Seine,[2] had ruined John's plan for the relief of the Isle of Andely. The fate of its garrison was soon decided ; and again the hero of the day was Gaubert of Mantes. The fort was encircled by a double palisade or rampart of wood, outside the walls. Gaubert tied a rope round his waist, took in his hand two iron vessels coated with pitch and filled with burning charcoal,[3] swam to the easternmost point of the island, which the garrison, trusting to the proximity of Château-Gaillard on this side, had ventured to leave unguarded, and threw these missiles against the palisade. The wood instantly caught fire ; the wind carried the flames all round the ramparts and into the fort itself. Some of the garrison made their escape by swimming or on rafts ; some were stifled in the cellars and

---

[1] Will. Armor. *Philipp.*, l. vii. vv. 144-335 (Duchesne, *Hist. Franc. Scriptt.*, vol. v. pp. 171-174 ; Deville, *Château-Gaillard*, pp. 129-134). Cf. *Gesta Phil. Aug.* (Duchesne as above), p. 83.

[2] Will. Armor. as above, vv. 206, 207 (Duchesne as above, p. 172 ; Deville as above, p. 131).

[3] See Deville's note, *Château-Gaillard*, p. 66.

galleries in which they sought a refuge from the fire ; the rest surrendered to the French king. Philip lost no time in repairing and garrisoning the fort and rebuilding the bridge on its western side. At the sight of his success the whole population of the Lesser Andely fled in a body to Château-Gaillard ; Philip entered the town in triumph, sent for new inhabitants to fill the places of the fugitives, and intrusted its defence to two companies of mercenaries, whose strength may be estimated from the statement that the leader of one of them, Cadoc by name, received from the royal treasury a thousand pounds daily for himself and his men.[1]

Philip's mastery of the river was still precarious and incomplete without the reduction of Château-Gaillard. For an attack upon the Saucy Castle itself, however, his courage seems as yet to have failed ; and striking north-westward by the road which leads from Les Andelys into the valley of the Andelle, on the last day of August he again sat down before Radepont. In two or three weeks it surrendered.[2] This time John made no attempt to save it, but fled away to the depths of his own old county of Mortain,[3] leaving Rouen to its fate. Philip however dared not advance upon Rouen with Château-Gaillard still unconquered in his rear ; and at the opening of the vintage-season he moved back to Les Andelys and girded himself up for his task. A brief survey of the Rock convinced him that assault was wellnigh hopeless ; his best chance was in a blockade. On the north the Lesser Andely occupied by his mercenaries, on the west the river commanded by his troops in the island-fort, sufficed to imprison the garrison. The next step was to dig

---

[1] Will. Armor., *Philipp.*, l. vii. vv. 336-398 (Duchesne, *Hist. Franc. Scriptt.*, vol. v. pp. 174, 175 ; Deville, *Château-Gaillard*, pp. 134-136). Cf. *Gesta Phil. Aug.* (Duchesne as above), p. 83.

[2] Rigord (Duchesne as above), p. 47, says the siege of Radepont began on the last day of August and lasted fifteen days. Will. Armor. *Gesta Phil. Aug.* (*ibid.*), p. 82, makes it last three weeks ; in *Philipp.*, l. vii. vv. 399, 400 (*ib.* p. 175 ; Deville, *Château-Gaillard*, p. 136), he extends its duration to a month.

[3] He went to Falaise on September 13—the day after the fall of Radepont, according to Rigord's reckoning. Thence he went on the 17th to Mortain, on the 19th to Dol, and back to Mortain again on the 22d. Hardy, *Itin. K. John*, a. 5 (*Intr. Pat. Rolls*).

out a double trench two hundred feet deep, starting from the brow of the hill over against the south-eastern extremity of the castle-rock, extending northward to the margin of the lake of Andely and westward to the bank of the Seine, and completely enclosing the two ravines which furrowed the sides of the rock.   Each line of entrenchment was garnished with seven *bretasches* or wooden forts, placed at regular intervals, each surrounded by a ditch of its own, furnished with a wooden draw-bridge, and filled with as many soldiers as it could hold.   The rest of the army took up their quarters in the trenches, where they built themselves little huts of wood and thatch for a shelter against the wet and cold of the coming winter—shelter against other foes they needed none, for they were out of bowshot from the castle [1] —and whiled away their time in jesting and making songs in mockery of the straits to which the Saucy Castle was reduced — " So many thousands girt about with a single girdle,"—" The eyrie overcrowded with nestlings, who will have to turn out when the spring comes." [2] The greater part of the " nestlings " were turned out before the spring came.   The blockade once formed, Roger de Lacy soon perceived the terrible blunder he had made in admitting within his walls the townsfolk of the Lesser Andely.   According to one computation, the number of these non-combatants now huddled within the castle-enclosure was no less than two thousand two hundred souls ; at the lowest reckoning, they seem to have amounted to fourteen hundred —all, in a military point of view, simply useless mouths, devouring in a few weeks the stores of food that should have furnished rations for a year and more to the little garrison which was amply sufficient to hold the castle for John.   One day, therefore, Roger opened the castle-gate and turned out five hundred of the oldest and weakest.   They were suffered to pass unmolested through the blockading lines, and were followed a few days later by five hundred more.   Philip

---

[1] Will. Armor. *Gesta Phil. Aug.* (Duchesne, *Hist. Franc. Scriptt.*, vol. v.), pp. 83, 84 ; *Philipp.*, l. vii. vv. 414-450 (*ib.* pp. 175, 176 ; Deville, *Château-Gaillard*, pp. 136, 137).

[2] Will. Armor. *Philipp.*, l. vii. vv. 451-456 (Duchesne, p. 176 ; Deville, p. 137).

however, who meanwhile had returned to his own dominions, no sooner heard what was going on than he issued strict orders that every man, woman or child, of whatever age or condition, who might issue from the castle should be driven back again without mercy. A large number still remained of whom Roger was as eager to be rid as Philip was anxious that he should be obliged to keep them. He took account of his stores, and found that he had enough to feed the regular garrison for a whole year. Hereupon he called together all the remaining non-combatants, and sent them forth, as they thought, to rejoin their families and friends. To their horror, as soon as they approached the French lines, they were overwhelmed with a volley of arrows. They rushed back to the castle-gate, only to find it closed against them. For three months this multitude of people dragged out a wretched existence in the ravines around the fortress, with no shelter against the wet and the cold but what they might find in the clefts of the rock, and no food but the dry leaves and scant herbage which they could pick up at its foot, and the flesh of the dogs which the garrison soon let loose for the purpose of yet further economizing their rations. This last resource was exhausted, and the horrors of cannibalism were already reached, when Philip came back to see how the siege was progressing. As he was crossing the bridge to the island-fort these unhappy beings caught sight of him and lifted up their voices in agonizing appeal ; the king, moved with a tardy compassion, and perhaps also by fear of the not improbable outbreak of a pestilence which might easily have spread into his own entrenchments, ordered that immediate relief should be given to all who survived. These however amounted to no more than half of the original number, which seems to have been something over four hundred ; and most of them had been so long without food that their first meal proved fatal.[1]

The last act of this tragedy must have taken place soon after Christmas. For three months the whole military power

---

[1] Cf. Will. Armor. *Gesta Phil. Aug.* (Duchesne, *Hist. Franc. Scriptt.*, vol. v.), p. 84, and *Philipp.*, l. vii. vv. 467-606 (*ib.* pp. 176-179 ; Deville, *Château-Gaillard*, pp. 138-142).

of the French Crown had been concentrated on the investment of Château-Gaillard ; and in all this time John had
done absolutely nothing. From his expedition to the Breton
border he had indeed returned to Rouen for a few days in
the beginning of October. Not a hand did he lift, however, to check the progress of the blockade which was being
formed almost before his eyes. Soon he was again far away
in the Bessin ; thence he suddenly moved across the duchy
to Verneuil, and in the second week of November he was
once more at Rouen.[1] It was probably during one of these
visits to the capital that he wrote to Roger de Lacy : " We
thank you for your good and faithful service, and desire that,
as much as in you lies, you will persevere in the fealty and
homage which you owe us, that you may receive a worthy
meed of praise from God and from ourselves, and from all
who know your fidelity to us. If, however, which God forbid,
you should find yourselves in such straits that you can hold out
no longer, then do whatsoever our trusty and well-beloved
Peter of Préaux, William of Mortemer and Hugh of Howels
our clerk shall bid you in our name."[2] Whether this letter
ever found its way through the blockading lines into the
castle it is scarcely worth while to inquire. If it did, it failed
to shake the courage or the loyalty of the garrison, although
it must have proved to them what they doubtless guessed
already, that their sovereign had forsaken them, and that
they were serving him for nought. Of the crowning proof
of his desertion they probably remained unconscious until
all was over for them. After dismantling Pont-de-l'Arche,
Moulineaux and Montfort,[3] John, on November 12, again
left Rouen ; for three weeks he flitted aimlessly up and down
the country, from Bonneville and Caen to Domfront and Vire,
and back again to Barfleur and Cherbourg ;[4] on December 6
he quitted Normandy altogether ;[5] and while the burghers of

---

[1] Hardy, *Itin. K. John*, a. 5 (*Intr. Pat. Rolls*).

[2] Letter in Duchesne, *Hist. Norm. Scrippt.*, p. 1059.

[3] Will. Armor. *Philipp.*, l. vii. vv. 826-828 (Deville, *Château-Gaillard*, pp. 147,
148; Duchesne, *Hist. Franc. Scriptt.*, vol. v. p. 182).   [4] Hardy as above.

[5] Rog. Wend. (Coxe), vol. iii. p. 173, says he landed at Portsmouth on S.
Nicolas's day. The *Itinerary* (as above) shews him at Barfleur on December 5
and at Portsmouth on the 7th.

the Lesser Andely were starving and freezing to death in the
valleys round Château-Gaillard, and the garrison of the castle
were anxiously reckoning how much longer their provisions
would enable them to hold out for his sake, he was keeping
his Christmas feast at Canterbury at the expense of Archbishop Hubert.[1]

By the end of February 1204[2] Philip grew impatient of
the blockade of Château-Gaillard, and probably also uneasy
lest John should return from England with an overwhelming
force for its relief. He therefore resolved to try whether it
could not, after all, be taken by assault. He himself took
up his station at the central point of the entrenchment, on
the crest of the hill, facing the narrow neck of land by which
it was joined to the castle-rock. This isthmus, the only
direct approach to the castle itself, he caused to be levelled
and widened till he could erect upon it a wooden gallery or
covered way leading from his own lines up to the edge of the
outermost ditch of the fortress. When, with considerable
difficulty and loss of life, this was accomplishcd, he caused a
beffroy or wooden tower on wheels to be carried through the
gallery, set up when it reached the further end, and moved
along the edge of the fosse, the cross-bowmen with whom it
was filled doing deadly execution upon the soldiers on the
ramparts, who however made a gallant defence. Meanwhile,
the French were bringing through their covered way earth,
wood, stones, turf, everything they could find to fill up the
ditch. Before it was half full they lost patience and adopted
a quicker method of approach. They dropped down the
perpendicular counterscarp by means of their scaling-ladders,
and set these up again on the sloping inner side of the ditch,
under the foot of the great round tower which formed the
head of the first ward. The ladders were too short for the
ascent ; but despite a heavy fire of stones and arrows from
the tower, the storming-party scrambled up, crawling on
hands and knees, or using their swords and daggers by way

---

[1] " H. archiepiscopo omnia necessaria festivitati regiæ ministrante." Rog.
Wend. (Coxe), vol. iii. p. 174.

[2] " Superveniente cathedrâ S. Petri" (February 22). Rigord (Duchesne, *Hist.
Franc. Scriptt.*, vol. v.), p. 47.

of Alpine-staves, till the base of the wall was reached. Then, while a shower of missiles rattled down upon the shields held over them by their comrades, the sappers dug and hewed at the foundations till the tower was undermined; the fuse was inserted and fired, and the miners had just had time to withdraw when a large portion of the wall fell crashing into the ditch. The French rushed to the breach ; Roger de Lacy, seeing that the first ward was lost, ordered the wooden buildings within it to be fired; he and his men withdrew across the drawbridge into the second ward, and when the fire died down, they saw the ruined fragment of the tower crowned by the banner of Cadoc.[1]

The French were one step nearer to the goal ; but the next step looked as impracticable as ever. Between them and the besieged there yawned another ditch as wide and deep, there rose another rampart as mighty and as inaccessible as the first. In vain they prowled about the edge of the fosse seeking for a point at which they could venture upon an attack, till a young squire or man-at-arms, by name Peter, but more commonly known in the camp as " Bogis " or " Snub-nose," caught sight of a little window just above the wall at the south-eastern corner of the rampart.[2] This window was the sole external opening in John's new building, which was otherwise accessible only on the inner side, by two doors, one leading into the storehouse which formed the lower story, one into the chapel above it, and both opening towards the courtyard. Bogis at once communicated his discovery to a few trusty comrades ; they reconnoitred the ditch till they found a somewhat shallower place on its southern side, where it was possible to scramble down ; thence they crawled along the bottom till they were directly

---

[1] Will. Armor. *Gesta Phil. Aug.* (Duchesne, *Hist. Franc. Scriptt.*, vol. v.), p. 84 ; *Philipp.*, l. vii. vv. 612-726 (*ib.* pp. 179-181 ; Deville, *Château-Gaillard*, pp. 142-145).

[2] I cannot understand M. Deville's idea of this window. In his plan of the castle he marks it about the middle of the south-western side of John's building— the side looking towards the river. But Will. Armor. *Gesta Phil. Aug.* (as above), p. 85, says it was "in latere orientali." And if it had not been there, how could Bogis, from the foot of the rampart of the first ward, ever have seen it at all ?

under the window, and then clambered up the sloping side to the foot of the wall. By standing on the shoulders of a comrade Bogis managed to reach the window ; he found it unbarred, unguarded, and wide enough for his body to pass through ; he sprang in, let down to his companions a rope which he had brought for the purpose, and drew them up one by one till they were all safe inside the building, which proved to be the storehouse under the chapel.[1] Finding the door locked, they began to hammer at it with the hilts of their daggers. This noise and the shouts with which they accompanied it soon alarmed the garrison. They, thinking that the French had entered the new building and occupied it in force, hastily set it on fire ; unhappily, the wind caught the flames and spread them in a few minutes over the whole enclosure. The garrison fled to their sole remaining refuge, the citadel ; Bogis and his companions escaped out of the blazing ruins into the casemates ; the bulk of the French host, anxiously watching the scene from the opposite side of the ditch, thought they had all perished; but when the flames died down and the smoke began to clear away, Bogis himself appeared at the gate and let down the drawbridge for the army to pass over in triumph.[2]

Philip's engines and their own too hastily-kindled fires had made havoc among the besieged garrison ; they were now reduced to a hundred and eighty fighting-men.[3] Even this small number, however, might have sufficed to hold for an indefinite time the remains of Richard's matchless fortress, but for one strange error on the part of the royal architect. Richard had indeed taken the precaution of making the sole gate of his citadel open not directly towards the courtyard of the second ward, but at a much less accessible point to

---

[1] So says M. Deville (*Château-Gaillard*, p. 82), following the *Philippis ;* but in the *Gesta Phil. Aug.* William makes it the chapel, *i.e.* the upper instead of the lower story. One would naturally expect the solitary window to be in the chapel rather than in the storehouse under it.

[2] Will. Armor. *Gesta Phil. Aug.* (Duchesne, *Hist. Franc. Scriptt.*, vol. v.), p. 85 ; *Philipp.*, l. vii. vv. 727-791 (*ib.* pp. 181, 182 ; Deville, *Château-Gaillard*, pp. 145-147).

[3] Will. Armor. *Philipp.*, l. vii. v. 775 (Duchesne as above, p. 181 ; Deville, p. 146).

the north-eastward, where only a narrow strip of ground intervened between the counterscarp of the ditch and the outer rampart. Most unaccountably, however, instead of furnishing this gate with a drawbridge, he left a portion of the rock itself to serve as a natural passage over the ditch hollowed out beneath it. Across this immovable bridge a machine known by the name of " cat "—a sort of tent upon wheels, moved by the men inside it—was, as the epic bard of the siege expresses it, " made to crawl " close up to the gate, which the sappers, hidden under this shelter, at once began to undermine. Roger de Lacy, alarmed no doubt by the fate of the first tower which had been thus dealt with, tried the effect of a countermine, which was so far successful that the French were for a moment compelled to retire ; but the " cat " was speedily replaced by a mighty engine discharging heavy stones with immense force. At the third discharge, the wall, undermined as it was from both sides, suddenly fell in. The French troops poured through the breach ; Roger and his little band were quickly surrounded, and it was no fault of theirs that they were not slaughtered to a man, for every one of them refused to yield, and was only disarmed by main force. The hundred and twenty men-at-arms and thirty-six knights who still remained were, however, made prisoners without further bloodshed; and thus, on March 6, 1204, Philip became master of Château-Gaillard.[1]

On that March day the king of England really lost not only his Saucy Castle, but his whole continental dominions north of Loire. Thenceforth all resistance in Normandy was at an end ; and in three months the whole duchy laid

---

[1] Will. Armor. *Philipp.*, l. vii. vv. 792-811 (Duchesne, *Hist. Franc. Scriptt.*, vol. v. p. 182; Deville, *Château-Gaillard*, p. 147). Cf. *Gesta Phil. Aug.* (Duchesne as above), p. 85. The date is from Rigord (*ibid.*), p. 47 (who, however, puts it under a wrong year, 1202), and Rog. Wend. (Coxe), vol. iii. p. 180. This last writer has a wholly different version of the capture, but it is not worthy of consideration. The number of prisoners is stated by Will. Armor. in the *Gesta Phil. Aug.* as forty knights, a hundred and twenty men-at-arms, "and many others." (By his own account in *Philipp.*, l. vii. v. 775, these "many" cannot have been more than twenty. See above, p. 422). Rigord speaks only of the knights, whom he reduces to thirty-six, saying that four had been slain during the siege.

itself without a struggle at the victor's feet. Soon after John's departure over sea Philip had opened negotiations with the citizens of the chief Norman towns, representing to them that the king of England had deserted them, that he himself was their rightful overlord and sovereign, and bidding them either receive him as such, or prepare to be all hanged or flayed alive when he should have overcome their resistance by force. After some discussion they made a truce with him for a year, promising that if no succour came from England within that time, they would submit to him without reserve.[1] On the fall of Château-Gaillard they all, together with the constables of the remaining fortresses throughout John's trans-marine dominions, sent messages to John setting forth the difficulties of their position and remonstrating earnestly with him on his tardiness in coming to their aid. He bade them look for nothing from him, but do each of them whatsoever they might think good.[2] A few weeks later he despatched the bishops of Norwich and Ely with the earls of Pembroke and Leicester to see if there was any possibility of coming to terms with the king of France.[3] But it was too late. Philip sarcastically retorted that the first preliminary to peace must be the restoration of Arthur ;[4] and on the Sunday after Easter he marched again into Normandy. Falaise surrendered after a week's siege ;[5] Domfront, Séez, Lisieux, Caen, Bayeux, Barfleur, Cherbourg, Coutances,[6] opened their gates at his mere approach. Meanwhile Guy of Thouars, who had been governing Britanny since Arthur's death,[7] with four hundred knights and an immense host of Bretons attacked and burned the Mont-St.-

---

[1] Rog. Wend. (Coxe), vol. iii. pp. 173, 174.   [2] Ib. pp. 180, 181.

[3] " Post mediam Quadragesimam," i.e. in the beginning of April. R. Coggeshall (Stevenson), p. 144. The earl of Pembroke (or Striguil), it will be remembered, was William the Marshal.   [4] R. Coggeshall (Stevenson), p. 145.

[5] Ibid. Will. Armor. Philipp., l. viii. (Duchesne, Hist. Franc. Scriptt., vol. v. p. 183) ; Gesta Phil. Aug. (ibid.), p. 85. Rigord (ibid.), p. 47. The dates come from the two last, both of whom however make the year 1203 instead of 1204.

[6] Cf. Rigord as above ; Will. Armor. Gesta Phil. Aug. as above ; Philipp. l. viii. (ibid.), pp. 183, 184 ; and R. Coggeshall as above.

[7] As guardian of his own daughter by Constance, the infant Alice, whom the Bretons and the French recognized as heiress of Britanny, in place of her half-sister Eleanor, who was in the custody of John.

Michel, sacked Avranches, and marched ravaging and burning through the Bessin to join the king at Caen. Philip
sent them back again, together with the count of Boulogne,
William des Barres, a large body of French knights, and a
troop of John's mercenaries who had changed sides after the
surrender of Falaise, to finish the subjugation of Mortain
and the Avranchin,[1] while he himself returned to complete
his conquest of eastern Normandy. Only three important
places were still unsubdued there : Arques on the northern
coast, Verneuil on the southern border, and Rouen itself.
The three bodies of soldiers and townsfolk came to a mutual
understanding whereby those of the capital, on the Tuesday
in Rogation-week—June 1—made a truce with Philip for
thirty days, stipulating that their brethren at Arques and
Verneuil should receive the same benefit if they applied
for it within a certain time, and promising in the name of all
alike that if no succour came from John within the specified
interval, they would give themselves up unreservedly to the
king of France.[2] None of them, however, waited for the
expiration of the truce. On midsummer-day Rouen opened
its gates ;[3] Arques and Verneuil followed its example,[4] and
Normandy was won.

Cadoc and his mercenaries had established their head-
quarters at Angers ;[5] the whole of Anjou and Touraine,
except the strongholds of Chinon and Loches, was already
secured ; Aquitaine alone still remained to be conquered.
This, indeed, was likely to prove a more difficult task ; for
however bitterly the men of the south might hate their
Norman or Angevin rulers, their chances of regaining or
preserving their independence under a sovereign who must
henceforth be parted from them by the whole width of the
Bay of Biscay would be obviously so much better than under
one whose direct sway now stretched all along the northern

[1] Will. Armor. *Gesta Phil. Aug.* (Duchesne, *Hist. Franc. Scriptt.*, vol. v.),
p. 85. *Philipp.*, l. viii. (*ibid.*), pp. 184, 185.
[2] Duchesne, *Hist. Norm. Scriptt.*, pp. 1057-1059.
[3] R. Coggeshall (Stevenson), p. 146. Rigord (Duchesne, *Hist. Franc. Scriptt.*,
vol. v.), p. 47, giving the date. Cf. Will. Armor. *Gesta Phil. Aug.* (*ibid.*), p. 85,
and *Philipp.*, l. viii. (*ibid.*), p. 186. [4] R. Coggeshall as above.
[5] Will. Armor. as above, pp. 86 and 188.

bank of the Loire from its mouth almost to its source, that they were certain to veer round at once to the side of John, simply for the purpose of keeping Philip out. Such was in fact the result throughout the whole country south of the Dordogne ; Savaric of Mauléon, lately John's enemy and prisoner, at once became his most energetic and devoted champion ;[1] while Angoulême was secured for John as the heritage of his queen Isabel. But the link which had bound Guyenne to the Angevin house was broken at last ; Queen Eleanor had died on April 1.[2] There was no longer any legal obstacle to the execution of the sentence of forfeiture passed two years ago ; and on S. Laurence's day Philip assembled his host for the conquest of Poitou.[3] Robert of Turnham, John's seneschal,[4] did what he could in its defence, but he was powerless against the indifference of the people and the active hostility of William des Roches and the Lusignans.[5] Poitiers was soon taken ; and in a few weeks all Poitou, except La Rochelle, Niort and Thouars, submitted to Philip as its liege lord.[6] At the approach of winter Philip returned to his own dominions, leaving a body of troops to blockade Chinon, which was held for John by Hubert de Burgh, and another to form the siege of Loches, no less bravely defended by Gerald of Atie.[7] At Easter 1205 the king marched with a fresh host upon Loches and took it by assault.[8] On midsummer-eve Chinon fell in like

---

[1] R. Coggeshall (Stevenson), p. 146.

[2] Ann. Waverl. a. 1204 (Luard, *Ann. Monast.*, vol. ii. p. 256). R. Coggeshall (Stevenson), p. 144, and Mat. Paris, *Hist. Angl.* (Madden), vol. ii. pp. 102, 103, give the same year ; the latter takes occasion to describe Eleanor as "admiribalis domina pulchritudinis et astutiæ," and says she died at John's newly-founded abbey of Beaulieu. The Chron. S. Albin. (Marchegay, *Eglises*, p. 53) places her death a year earlier, and at Poitiers.

[3] Rigord (Duchesne, *Hist. Franc. Scriptt.*, vol. v.), p. 47.

[4] Brother of Stephen of Turnham, and apparently seneschal of Anjou at the close of Richard's reign ; transferred to Poitou in 1201. Rog. Howden (Stubbs), vol. iv. pp. 86, 142, 176.   [5] R. Coggeshall as above.

[6] *Ibid.* Rigord as above. Will. Armor. *Gesta Phil. Aug.* (*ibid.*), p. 86. Rog. Wend. (Coxe), vol. iii. p. 181.

[7] R. Coggeshall and Rigord as above. Will. Armor. as above ; *Philipp.*, l. viii. (*ibid.*), pp. 189, 190.

[8] Rigord (as above), pp. 47, 48, and Will. Armor. *Gesta Phil. Aug.* as above ; both under a wrong year. R. Coggeshall (Stevenson), p. 152.

manner.[1] Robert of Turnham had already been made prisoner by the French ;[2] the viscount of Thouars now made
his submission to Philip, and received from him the seneschal-
ship of Poitou in Robert's stead ;[3] Niort and La Rochelle
were left alone in their resistance to the French king.

John, however, was now at last threatening an attack
from over sea. Three weeks after his return to England, in
January 1204, he had held a council at Oxford and compelled all the tenants-in-chief, including the bishops and
abbots, to promise a scutage of two marks and a half on the
knight's fee,[4] and a contribution, from which even the parish
churches were not exempt, of a seventh of all moveable
goods ;[5] all under the plea of gathering a great host for the
recovery of his lost dominions.[6] In May he held a council
at Northampton,[7] which resulted in a summons to the fleet
and the host to meet him at Porchester at Whitsuntide,
prepared to accompany him over sea. When all was ready,
however, the expedition was countermanded, at the urgent
entreaty, it was said, of Archbishop Hubert and William the
Marshal, the latter of whom had lately returned from Gaul,
and might therefore be supposed to know the condition of
affairs there better than the king could know it himself.
John, after a great shew of resistance, yielded to their entreaties ; the soldiers and sailors were made to pay a fine
in commutation of their services, and dismissed, grumbling
bitterly, to their homes.[8] The king gained a considerable
sum of money by the transaction ; and the primate and the
marshal, in their boundless loyalty, were content to take
upon themselves the burthen of its shame, which John felt,
or affected to feel, so keenly that he actually put to sea with
a small escort several days after the dispersion of the fleet.

---

[1] Rog. Wend. (Coxe, vol. iii.), pp. 182, 183 ; R. Coggeshall (Stevenson), pp.
154, 155 ; cf. Rigord (Duchesne, *Hist. Franc. Scriptt.*, vol. v.), p. 48 ; Will.
Armor. *Gesta Phil. Aug. (ibid.)*, p. 86 ; and Chron. S. Albin. a. 1203 (Marchegay,
Eglises, p. 54).   [2] R. Coggeshall (Stevenson), p. 152.
[3] Will. Armor. as above.   [4] Rog. Wend. as above, p. 175.
[5] Mat. Paris, *Chron. Maj.* (Luard), vol. ii. p. 483.
[6] R. Coggeshall (Stevenson), p. 144.
[7] *Ibid.* Date, May 21-25 ; Hardy, *Itin. K. John*, a. 7 (*Intr. Pat. Rolls*).
[8] R. Coggeshall (Stevenson), pp. 152, 153. Cf. Rog. Wend. as above, p. 183.

He landed again, however, at Wareham on the third day,[1] and contented himself with sending his half-brother Earl William of Salisbury and his own son Geoffrey with a body of knights to reinforce the garrison of La Rochelle.[2] A year later he again assembled his fleet at Portsmouth ;[3] and this time he led it in person direct to La Rochelle. He landed there on June 7,[4] and marched to Montauban, which he besieged and captured ;[5] the fickle viscount of Thouars, being now in revolt against Philip, speedily joined him ;[6] they advanced to Angers together, won it on September 6,[7] ravaged Anjou with fire and sword, and were doing the like in south-eastern Britanny[8] when Philip again crossed the Loire and harried the viscounty of Thouars under their very eyes.[9] John at once proposed a truce ; the terms were formally drawn up at Thouars on October 26 ;[10] but when the English king's signature was required, he was no longer to be found. He had slipped away the night before, and was out of reach at La Rochelle ;[11] and thence, on December 12, he sailed for England once more.[12]

Of the two devoted English ministers who had stood by him through so much obloquy, only the Marshal was now left. A month after the humiliating scene at Porchester in 1205, Archbishop Hubert died.[13] " Now for the first time

---

[1] R. Coggeshall (Stevenson), p. 154. Rog. Wend. (Coxe), vol. iii. 183. This happened June 13-15 ; see note 1 to R. Coggeshall as above, and Hardy, *Itin. K. John*, a. 7 (*Intr. Pat. Rolls*).   [2] R. Coggeshall as above.

[3] Rog. Wend. (as above), p. 186. John was at Porchester from Whit-Monday, May 22, to Friday, May 26. Hardy, *Itin. K. John*, a. 8 (*Intr. Pat. Rolls*).

[4] He crossed from Stoke to Yarmouth on Trinity Sunday, May 28, and thence to La Rochelle on Wednesday, June 7 ; cf. Hardy, as above, with Rog. Wend. as above, who has twice written " Julii " for " Junii."

[5] On August 1, after fifteen days' siege, says Rog. Wend. (as above), p. 187 ; but see Hardy as above.

[6] Rigord (Duchesne, *Hist. Franc. Scriptt.*, vol. v.), p. 48. Will. Armor. *Gesta Phil. Aug.* (*ibid.*), p. 86.

[7] *Ibid.* Date from Chron. S. Albin. a. 1206 (Marchegay, *Eglises*, pp. 54, 57).

[8] Will. Armor. as above.

[9] Rigord (*ibid.*), p. 48. Chron. S. Albin. a. 1206 (as above, pp. 56, 57).

[10] Rymer, *Fœdera*, vol. i. p. 95.

[11] Will. Armor. as above. He was at La Rochelle on October 25 ; Hardy as above.   [12] Rog. Wend. as above, p. 188.

[13] *Ib.* p. 183. R. Coggeshall (Stevenson), p. 156.

am I truly king of England!" was the comment of his ungrateful master upon the tidings of his death.[1] The words were words of ill omen for John himself, even more than for his people. He was indeed king of England, and of England alone. The prophecy of Merlin, which had been working itself out for a hundred years in the history of the Norman and Angevin houses, was fulfilled in yet one more detail: "the sword was parted from the sceptre."[2] The sword of Hrolf the Ganger and William the Conqueror, of Fulk the Red and Fulk the Black, had fallen from the hand of their unworthy descendant. The sceptre of his English forefathers was left to him. But the England over which he had to wield it was no longer the exhausted and divided country which had been swallowed up almost without an effort in the vast dominions of the young Count Henry of Anjou. It was an England which was once more able to stand alone—a new England which had been growing up under the hands of Henry himself, of his ministers, and of the ministers of his successor, silently and imperceptibly, they themselves knew not when or how; and between this new England and its stranger-king the day of reckoning was now to come.

Note.

THE DEATH OF ARTHUR.

Only two contemporary writers even pretend to give a circumstantial account of Arthur's death: the Annalist of Margam and William of Armorica. The former tells us that John, " post prandium, ebrius et dæmonio plenus " [did John, as well as Richard, make the demon-blood answerable for his sins?], slew Arthur with his own hand, and having tied a great stone to the body, flung it into the Seine; thence it was drawn up in a fisherman's net, recognized, and buried secretly, "propter metum tyranni," in Notre-Dame-des-Prés (Ann. Margam, a. 1204; Luard, *Ann. Monast.*, vol. i. p. 27). William allows the murderer no such excuse, if excuse it be, but works up the story into a long and horrible romance, in which John deliberately and of set purpose takes Arthur out alone with him by night in a boat on the Seine, plunges a sword into his body, and

[1] Mat. Paris, *Hist. Angl.* (Madden), vol. ii. p. 104.
[2] R. Coggeshall (Stevenson), p. 146.

then rows along for three miles before he flings the corpse over-board (Will. Armor. *Philipp.*, l. vi.; Duchesne, *Hist. Franc. Scriptt.*, vol. v. pp. 166, 167). Both these writers place the scene at Rouen. The Chron. Brioc. (Morice, *Hist. Bret., preuves*, vol. i. col. 39) transfers it to Cherbourg : " Apud Cæsaris-burgum duxit, et ibi pro-ditorie et tyrannice eum in mare submersit." Rigord says not a word of the matter. R. Coggeshall (Stevenson, p. 145) only speaks of it incidentally, saying that Philip " sæviebat . . . permaxime pro nece Arthuri, quem in Sequanâ submersum fuisse audierat." Rog. Wend. (Coxe, vol. iii. p. 170) says merely " subito evanuit." Mat. Paris in *Chron. Maj.* (Luard, vol. ii. p. 480) copies this, and adds : " modo fere omnibus ignorato ; utinam non ut fama refert." In *Hist. Angl.* (Madden, vol. ii. p. 95) he gives three stories as cur-rently reported : accidental drowning, death from grief, and the third, " ipsum manibus vel præcepto regis Johannis fuisse peremptum " —this last being the assertion of the French, " quibus propter hos-tilitatem plena fides non est adhibenda." But his own words in the *Chron. Maj.* shew that he could not wholly reject the unavoidable conclusion of John's guilt.

The date of Arthur's disappearance or death is given only by the Margam annalist. He places it on Maunday Thursday ; but unluckily he has damaged his own authority on chronological mat-ters by putting the whole affair a year too late, viz. in 1204 instead of 1203. Will. Armor., on the other hand, tells us that for three days before the murder John was at Moulineaux, near Rouen. These two chronological indications do not exactly agree, for in 1203 Maunday Thursday was April 3, and the *Itin. K. John*, a. 4 (Hardy, *Intr. Pat. Rolls*), shews that the king was at Moulineaux on Wednesday, April 2, but on the two preceding days he was at Rouen. It is however plain from the after-history that the deed must have been done shortly before Easter.

CHAPTER X.

THE NEW ENGLAND.

1170-1206.

IN the eyes of all contemporary Europe the most striking and important event in English history during the half-century which had passed away since the accession of Henry II. was the murder of Archbishop Thomas. The sensation which it produced throughout western Christendom was out of all proportion both to the personal influence of its victim during his lifetime and to its direct political results. The popular canonization bestowed upon the martyr was ratified by Rome with almost unprecedented speed, in little more than two years after his death ;[1] the stream of pilgrims which flowed to his shrine, from the east and from the west, from the north and from the south, was such as had hardly been seen even at the "threshold of the Apostles" or at the Holy Sepulchre itself ; and it flowed on without a break for more than three hundred years. Yet Pope and pilgrims all alike were probably as blind as Thomas himself had been to the true significance for England of his life and his death. The great ecclesiastical struggle of which he was the hero and the martyr marks a turning-point in the social history of the reign of Henry II. even more than in its political history. With the quarrel between Henry and Thomas the direction of the moral and intellectual revival whose growth we have in earlier chapters endeavoured to trace from the accession

---

[1] He was canonized by Alexander III. on Ash-Wednesday, February 21, 1173. Epp. dcclxxxiii.-dcclxxxvi., Robertson, *Becket*, vol. vii. pp. 544-550.

of Henry I. to the death of Archbishop Theobald passed altogether out of the hands in which it had prospered so long and so well—the hands of the higher clergy and the monastic orders. The flight of Thomas scattered to the winds the little band of earnest churchmen who had been sharers with him in the inheritance of Theobald's policy and Theobald's work, and left the reforming party in the Church without a rallying-point and without a leader. One man alone still remained among the higher clergy who under more favourable circumstances might have taken up the work with a far more skilful hand than that of Thomas himself; but the leadership of Gilbert Foliot was made impossible by the subsequent course of events, which ranged all the religious opinion and all the popular sympathies of England on the side of the persecuted and martyred primate, and set Gilbert, as the primate's most conspicuous adversary, in the light of an enemy to the Church, a rebel against her divine authority, and almost a denier of her faith.[1]

The final settlement of the controversy was in some sense a defeat of both parties; but the one which seemed to have gained the victory really suffered the heaviest loss. The king was indeed compelled to abandon his scheme for reforming the morals of the priesthood by the strong hand of his royal justice; the privilege of the clergy was saved, to fall at last before another King Henry four centuries later. Yet its staunchest champions must surely have felt their cause reduced well-nigh to an absurdity when they found that the first result of its triumph was to secure the primate's very murderers from the penalty due to their crime;[2] and

---

[1] The story of Gilbert's dream, in Mat. Paris, *Chron. Maj.* (Luard), vol. ii. p. 240, was probably suggested by a line in the French *Life of S. Thomas:*

—" Gilebert Foliot,
De lettres sout assez e servi Astarot "—

(Garnier, ed. Hippeau, p. 77)—where again in all likelihood the last words were prompted by nothing more than the exigencies of rime. That some such charges were however brought against Foliot we have seen above, p. 70, note 5.

[2] Henry, not knowing what to do with the archbishop's murderers, counselled or connived at their flight into Scotland. The Scot king and people, however, shewed such a strong disposition to hang them that they were driven to re-cross the border (MS. Lansdown., Robertson, *Becket,* vol. iv. p. 162). They then, it seems, took refuge at Knaresborough, and there lay hid till hunger compelled

far greater than the seeming gain of Henry's surrender at Avranches was the loss to the English Church involved in the break-down of Theobald's plans for the reform of the episcopate. The cowardice of the bishops during the struggle left them at its close wholly at the mercy of the king. The vacant sees, of which there were eight besides Canterbury, were filled after long delays with secular clerks wholly subservient to the royal will ; and before the end of Henry's life the English episcopate was as completely secularized as it had been in the worst days of his grandfather. The inevitable consequences followed. As were the bishops, so, and even worse, were the lower clergy. The cry against the extortion and tyranny of the diocesan officials which rang at the opening of Henry's reign through the *Polycraticus* of John of Salisbury rang yet more loudly and bitterly at its close through the pages of Walter Map and Gerald de Barri ; the immorality which had once stirred the indignant zeal of Henry himself grew more widespread and more frightful year by year, as a direct result of his own shortsighted and selfish ecclesiastical policy. To that policy there were, indeed, two honourably marked exceptions. In 1186 Henry raised to the bishopric of Lincoln one of the holiest and wisest men then living, Hugh of Avalon. His dealings with the important and difficult question of the succession to the metropolitan see itself appear to have been prompted by equally disinterested motives. It was not the apathy or procrastination of the king, but the determination of the monks of Christ Church to use to the uttermost the favourable opportunity for asserting their independence, and the difficulty of finding any willing candidate for such a siege-perilous as the chair

them to issue from their lurking-place. Finding themselves everywhere shunned like wild beasts, they at last in desperation gave themselves up to the mercy or the vengeance of the king. But the murderer of a priest was legally amenable to none save an ecclesiastical tribunal ; Henry could do nothing with them but send them on to the Pope ; and all that the Pope could do with them was to sentence them to lifelong exile and penance in Holy Land. Will. Newb., l. ii. c. 25 (Howlett, vol. i. pp. 163, 164); cf. MS. Lansdown (as above), pp. 162, 163. See also a minor illustration of the inconveniences attaching to this other side of the clerical immunities, in a letter of Archbishop Richard to some of his suffragans ; Ep. dccxciv., Robertson, *Becket*, vol. vii. pp. 561-564.

of S. Thomas was felt to be, that delayed the election of his successor for two years and a half, and his consecration for nine months longer still.[1]   The new Archbishop Richard was a monk of unblemished character, and though possessed of little talent or learning, fulfilled his office creditably for ten years ;[2] while Baldwin, who took his place in 1185, was a Cistercian of the best type—a type which, however, was now rapidly passing away.

The monastic revival which had shed such brightness over the earlier half of the twelfth century died down long before its close.   S. Bernard had not yet been seven years in his grave when John of Salisbury, certainly not a hostile witness, was compelled to acknowledge that the love of power and the greed of gain had infected the whole monastic body, not excepting even the White Monks.   Rome herself soon found it needful to make an attempt, although a vain one, to curb the arrogance of the military orders.[3] Reformers in the next generation vied with each other in denouncing the vices and crimes of the Cluniacs and those of the " white-robed herd, the abominable order " of Cîteaux.[4]   The fall of the Cistercians indeed was the most terrible of all ;   within the space of two generations their name, once the symbol of the highest moral and spiritual perfection which the men of their day were capable of conceiving, had become a by-word for the lowest depths of wickedness and corruption.   Startling as was the change, its causes are not far to seek.   Pledged though they were by the origin and primitive constitution of their order to be a standing protest against the wealth and luxury of the

[1] Gerv. Cant. (Stubbs), vol. i. pp. 239-245, 247.

[2] "Homo quidem mediocriter literatus, sed laudabiliter innoxius, et, ne ambularet in magnis, modulo suo prudenter contentus."   Will. Newb., l. iii. c. 8 (Howlett, vol. i. pp. 235, 236).

[3] See a canon of the third Lateran Council (A.D. 1179), in Will. Newb., l. iii. c. 3 (as above, pp. 221-223).   On the Templars and Hospitaliers see also W. Map, *De Nug. Cur.*, dist. i. c. 23 (Wright, pp. 36-38).

[4] See especially Gir. Cambr. *Spec. Eccles.*, distt. ii. and iii. (Brewer, vol. iv. pp. 29 *et seq.*).   " Grex albus, ordo nefandus," is a description of the Cistercians quoted apparently from W. Map by his opponent W. Bothewald ; Wright, *Latin Poems attributed to W. Mapes*, introd. p. xxxv.   See also King Richard's opinion of these two orders and of the Templars, in Gir. Cambr. as above, dist. ii. c. 12 (p. 54).

Benedictines, they had nevertheless become, in less than a hundred years from their first appearance in England, the richest and most powerful body of monks in the realm. At the time of their coming, almost the whole extent of arable land throughout the country was already occupied ; the only resource open to the new-comers was the yet unexhausted and, as it seemed in England at least, well-nigh inexhaustible resource of pasturage. They brought to their sheep-farming the same energy, skill and perseverance which characterized all their undertakings ; and their well-earned success in this pursuit, together with the vast increase of the wool-trade which marked the same period, made them in a few years masters of the most productive branch of English industry. Temptation came with prosperity. But the more obvious temptations of wealth, the temptations to ease and vanity and luxurious self-indulgence, had little power over the stern temper of the White Monks ; it was a deeper and a deadlier snare into which they fell; not sloth and gluttony, but avarice and pride, were their besetting sins. In the days of Richard and John, when we find them struggling and bargaining almost on equal terms with the king's ministers and the king himself, they were indeed a mighty power both in Church and state ; but the foundation on which their power now rested was wholly different from that upon which it had first arisen ; its moral basis was gone. As an element in the nation's spiritual life the Order of Cîteaux, once its very soul, now counted for worse than nothing.

Still the monastic impulse which had guided so many religious movements in the past was not wholly dead. On the continent it was giving indeed fresh proofs of its vitality in the growth of two remarkable orders, those of Grandmont and of the Chartreuse, both of earlier origin than that of Cîteaux, but overshadowed until now by its transcendent fame. These however had little influence upon English religious life. The " Good Men " of Grandmont—as the brotherhood were commonly called — although special favourites of King Henry, never set foot in his island realm ; the Carthusians reached it only in his last years, and the few settlements which they formed there never rose

to any great importance.[1] Out of all the English mon-
asteries, of various orders, whose dates of foundation are
known, only one hundred and thirteen arose during the
thirty-five years of Henry's reign, while a hundred and
fifteen owed their origin to the nineteen troubled winters of
his predecessor. In Yorkshire alone no less than twenty
new houses had been founded under Stephen ; only eleven
were founded there under Henry.[2] Towards the close of
the century, indeed, the reputation of English monachism
had fallen so low that in the high places of the Church a
reaction in favour of secular clerks began to set in once
more. One bishop, Hugh of Coventry, not only ventured
to repeat the experiment which had been vainly tried elsewhere under the Confessor and the Conqueror, of turning
the monks out of his cathedral and replacing them by
secular canons, but actually proposed that all the cathedral
establishments served by monks should be broken up and
put upon a new foundation of a like secular character.
Hugh himself was however scarcely the man to meet with
general recognition in the capacity of a reformer ; and his
bold anticipation of the ecclesiastical revolution which was
to come four centuries later ended in ignominious failure.[3]

[1] On Grandmont (founded in 1176, by Stephen of Tierny, near Muret in the
diocese of Limoges) see *Gall. Christ.*, vol. ii. col. 645 ; *Vita S. Steph. Muret.*
(Labbe, *Nova Biblioth.*, vol. ii. pp. 674-683) ; Bern. Guidon, *De Ordine Grandi-
mont.* (*ib.* p. 275 *et seq.*) ; W. Map, *De Nug. Curial.*, dist. i. cc. 17, 27 (Wright,
pp. 28, 29, 58, 59) ; and Gir. Cambr. *Spec. Eccles.*, dist. iii. c. 21 (Brewer, vol. iv.
p. 254). Henry's reverence for the brethren showed itself not only in frequent
visits and benefactions to their house, and also in his desire to be buried there
(above, p. 270), but also by the remarkable way in which he deferred to their
suggestions and sought their counsel on grave matters of policy. Examples of
this are frequent during the Becket controversy ; another may be seen in *Gesta
Hen.* (Stubbs), vol. i. p. 194. For the Chartreuse (diocese of Grenoble—founded
in 1084 or 1086 by Bruno of Cöln, a canon of Reims) see W. Map, *De Nug. Cur.*,
dist. i. cc. 16 and 28 (Wright, pp. 26-28, 59, 60) ; Gir. Cambr. *Spec. Eccles.*, dist.
iii. c. 20 (as above, pp. 248-252) ; *Gall. Christ.*, vol. xvi. cols. 268, 269. The
history of the English Carthusian houses is in Dugdale's *Monasticon*, vol. vi. pt. i. ;
a full account of one, Witham, is given in the Life of S. Hugh of Lincoln, who
had been its first prior.

[2] These figures are from Mr. Howlett's introduction to Will. Newb., vol. i.
pp. xiii, xiv.

[3] Gir. Cambr. *Spec. Eccles.*, dist. ii. c. 23 (as above, pp. 65, 67). Ric. Devizes
(Stevenson), pp. 65-67. Gerv. Cant. (Stubbs), vol. i. pp. 470, 488, 489, 550.

It was, however, no less a personage than Archbishop Baldwin himself who in 1186 proposed to endow out of his archiepiscopal revenues a college of secular priests at Hackington by Canterbury, with the avowed object of providing a dwelling-place and a maintenance for the scholarship which monkish jealousy and monkish sloth had all but driven out of the cloisters where from the days of Theodore to those of Theobald it had found a home. This scheme was at once met by a determined opposition on the part of the monks of Christ Church, who suspected, perhaps not without reason, that it was part of a design for curtailing the privileges and destroying the independence of the metropolitan chapter. They instantly appealed to Rome, and the appeal opened a contest which absorbed the unlucky primate's energies throughout the remainder of his life. He was steadily supported by the king ; but the weight of the whole monastic body, except his own order, was thrown into the opposite scale ; the general drift of ecclesiastical feeling still lay in the same direction ; and after nearly four years of wearisome litigation at Rome and almost open warfare at Canterbury, the building of the new college was stopped by order of the Pope. The undaunted primate transferred his foundation to a new site at Lambeth, where it might have seemed less open to suspicion of rivalry with the Canterbury chapter ; but the jealousy of the monks pursued it with relentless hatred, and Baldwin's absence and death in Holy Land enabled them to secure an easy victory a year later. The next archbishop, Hubert Walter, took up his predecessor's scheme with a zeal doubtless quickened by the fact that he was himself a secular clerk. The dispute dragged on for five more years, to end at last in the defeat of the primate, and, with him, of the last attempt made in England systematically to utilize the superfluous wealth of a great monastic corporation for the promotion of learning and the endowment of study.[1] The attempt was made under unfavourable circumstances, perhaps by unskilful hands ; and

---

[1] The history of this quarrel is told at wearisome length by Gervase of Canterbury, and in the *Epistolæ Cantuarienses*. It is summed up and explained by Bishop Stubbs in his preface to the last-named book.

it was moreover made too soon.   In English national sentiment, monachism was inseparably bound up with Christianity
itself.   To the monastic system England owed her conversion, her ecclesiastical organization, her earliest training as a
nation and as a Church.   Even if the guides to whom she
had so long trusted were failing her at last, the conservatism
and the gratitude of Englishmen both alike still shrank from
casting aside a tradition hallowed by the best and happiest
associations of six hundred years.   The bent of popular
sympathy was strikingly shewn by an episode in Baldwin's
quarrel with his monks, when their insolent defiance of his
authority provoked him to cut off all their supplies, in the
hope of starving them into submission.   For eighty-four
weeks not a morsel of food reached them save what was
brought by their friends or by the pilgrims who crowded to
the martyr's shrine ; so great however was the amount of
these contributions, some of which came even from Jews,
that—if we may believe the tale of one who was himself an
inmate of the convent at this time—the brethren were able
out of their superabundance to give a daily meal to two
hundred poor strangers.[1]   As a spiritual force, however,
monachism in England was well-nigh dead.   Though it
still kept a lingering hold upon the hearts of the people,
it had lost its power over their souls.   It might produce individual saints like Hugh of Lincoln ; but its
influence had ceased to mould the spiritual life of the
nation.   The time was almost ripe for the coming of the
Friars.

Meanwhile the decay of holiness and learning in the
cloister was brought into more vivid light by a great outburst of intellectual vigour of a wholly new type.   The
literary activity of the reign of Henry I. had been all but
quenched by the troubles of Stephen's reign.   Chronicler
after chronicler lays down his pen, as if in disgust or despair,
in the middle of the dreary story, till Henry of Huntingdon
and the nameless English annalist at Peterborough are left
to struggle almost alone through the last years of anarchy
to welcome the new king ; and he is no sooner crowned

[1] Gerv. Cant. (Stubbs), vol. i. p. 405.

than they, too, pass away into silence.[1] The first half of Henry's reign has no contemporary historian at all. The other branches of literature continued equally barren ; and a promise of better things had scarcely dawned in the miscellaneous treatises of John of Salisbury when the whole intellectual horizon was darkened by the great ecclesiastical storm. No sooner had it subsided, however, than the literary impulse revived under wholly changed conditions. Its bent was still mainly historical ; and, as might be expected, the first subject-matter upon which it seized was the history of the new martyr. Within twenty years of his death, no less than ten different biographies of S. Thomas were composed by writers of the most diverse characters—his old comrade John of Salisbury, three of his own confidential clerks, a Benedictine abbot of Peterborough, an Augustinian prior of Oxford, a monk of Canterbury who was probably an Irishman by blood, a French poet who had seen the primate in his chancellor-days, a Cambridge clerk who had joined him on the eve of his martyrdom. But meanwhile a new school of English history was springing up in the court instead of the cloister. Modern research has ascertained that the book which may fairly be called the foundation-stone of this new school, as well as the primary authority for English political history from the death of S. Thomas to the third year of Richard Cœur-de-Lion—the "Acts of King Henry and King Richard," long attributed to Benedict abbot of Peterborough—is really the work of Richard Fitz-Nigel, bishop of London and treasurer. Its continuator, Roger of Howden, was a clerk of the royal chapel and an active and trusted officer of the royal administration under both Henry and Richard.[2] A third chronicler of the period, Ralf de Diceto, was archdeacon of Middlesex from 1153 to 1180, when he became dean of S. Paul's, an office of great political as well as ecclesiastical importance, which he filled with distinction until his death in the fourth year of King John.[3] The

---

[1] Henry of Huntingdon, we know, intended to "devote a new book to the new king " ; but it seems that this intention was not fulfilled.

[2] On the *Gesta Hen.* and Rog. Howden see Bishop Stubbs's prefaces to his editions of them in the Rolls series.

[3] Stubbs, *R. Diceto*, vol. i. pref. pp. xxvi-lxxxiii.

works of these three writers are examples of a species of
historical composition which is one of the most valuable
literary products of the later twelfth century.   They are
chronicles in the strictest sense of the word :—records of
facts and events arranged year by year in orderly chronological sequence, and for the most part without any attempt
at illustration, comment or criticism.   But the gap which
parts them from the ordinary type of monastic chronicle is
as wide as that which parted the highly-placed ecclesiastical
dignitary, the trusted minister of the Crown, or the favourite
court-chaplain from the obscure monk who had spent, it may
be, well-nigh his whole life in copying manuscripts in the
scriptorium of Burton or Dunstable or Waverley.   Their
writers were not merely chroniclers ; they were statesmen
and diplomatists as well.   Their position as members of the
royal administration, dwelling in the capital or at the court,
placed them in constant and intimate communication with
the chief actors in the events which they narrate, events
of which not only were they themselves frequently eye-
witnesses, but in which they even took a personal, though
it might be subordinate, share ; it gave them access to the
most authentic sources of political intelligence, to the official
records of the kingdom, to the state-papers and diplomatic
correspondence of the time, whereof a considerable part, if
not actually drawn up by themselves, must at any rate
have passed through their hands in the regular course of
their daily business.   The fulness and accuracy, the balance
of proportion, the careful order which characterize the work
of these statesmen-chroniclers are scarcely more remarkable
than its cosmopolitan range ; Henry's historiographers, like
Henry himself, sweep the whole known world into the wide
circle of their intelligence and their interest ; the internal
concerns of every state, from Norway to Morocco and from
Ireland to Palestine, find a place in the pages of Richard
Fitz-Nigel and Roger of Howden, side by side with the
narrative of their sovereign's wars with France or with the
text of the various assizes whereby he was reforming the
legal and judicial administration of their own native land.
While, however, the first works of this new historical school

thus rose far above the level of mere annals, they still stood
far below the literary standard of history in the higher sense,
which had been set up by a monk at Malmesbury half a
century before. The only writer who in the latter half of
the twelfth century, like William of Malmesbury in its earlier
half, looked at history in its true light, not as a mere record
of facts, but according to its old Greek definition, as " philosophy teaching by examples," must be sought after all not
in the court but in the cloister. William indeed had left no
heir to his many-sided literary genius ; but if some shreds
of his mantle did fall upon any historian of the next generation, they fell upon one who bore his name, in an Augustinian priory among the Yorkshire moors.

William of Newburgh was born in 1136 at Bridlington,
a quiet little town lying under the southern escarpment of
the York Wolds, not far from Flamborough Head. Here,
between the bleak uplands and the cold northern sea, a
priory of Austin canons had been founded by Walter de
Gant in the reign of Henry I. ;[1] from this house a colony
went forth in the early years of Stephen to settle, under the
protection of Roger de Mowbray, first at Hode near Thirsk,
and afterwards, in 1145, at Newburgh near Coxwold.
William entered the new house as a child—probably, therefore, almost at its foundation ; there he passed his whole
life ; and there, as the reign of Richard Cœur-de-Lion drew
towards its close, he wrote his *English History*, from the
Norman conquest to his own day. The actual composition
of the book seems to have occupied little more than two
years ; it can scarcely have been begun earlier than 1196,
and it breaks off abruptly in the spring of 1198. The
surroundings of its writer offered comparatively few advantages
for the pursuit of historical study. No atmosphere of venerable antiquity, no traditions of early scholarship and poetry,
no hallowed associations with the kings and saints and
heroes of old, hung around Newburgh priory ; the house was
younger than its historian ; the earliest and well-nigh the
only memory that can attract a pilgrim to its now desolate
site is the memory of William himself. No crowd of

[1] Dugdale, *Monast. Angl.*, vol. vi. pt. 1, pp. 284, 285.

devotees from all parts of the realm came thither year by
year to bring their offerings and their news, as they came to
the shrine of S. Ealdhelm ; no visit of king or prince is likely
ever to have startled the inmates of Newburgh out of the
quiet routine of their daily life ; its prior held no such place
among the ecclesiastical dignitaries of his province as the
abbot of Malmesbury had held for ages among the prelates
of the south ; he and his canons could have little or no
business with the outside world, and it is hardly conceivable
that any of them would ever have occasion to travel further
than to the mother-house at Bridlington, unless indeed his
own love of enterprise and thirst for a wider knowledge of
the world should drive him further afield.   Even in such a
case, however, the undertaking would have been beset with
difficulties ; travelling in Yorkshire was still, even under
Henry Fitz-Empress and his son, a more arduous and
dangerous matter than travelling in Wessex under his grandfather.   William, too, had grown up amid those terrible
days when peaceable folk could find no shelter save within
convent-walls, and even that shelter sometimes proved unavailing—when the men of the north were only too thankful
to wrap themselves in that comparative isolation which
saved them at any rate from sharing in the worst miseries
that overwhelmed their brethren in southern England.   The
memories of his boyhood were little calculated to arouse in
him such a spirit of enterprise as had fired the young
librarian of Malmesbury.   He seems, indeed, never to have
set a foot outside his native shire ; we might almost fancy
that like the first and most venerable of all our historians,
he never set a foot outside his own monastery.   The vivid
sketches of town and country which give such a picturesque
charm to the writings of William of Malmesbury are wholly
absent from those of William of Newburgh ; there is but one
bit of local description in his whole book, and even that one
—a brief account of Scarborough[1]—contains no distinct proof
of having been drawn from personal knowledge of the place.
The brotherhood of Newburgh had, however, ample opportunities of obtaining authentic, though indirect, intelligence

[1] Will. Newb., l. ii. c. 3 (Howlett, vol. i. p. 104).

from the outer world.   Their home, in a sheltered spot
under the western slope of ·the Hambledon Hills, was quiet
and peaceful, but not lonely ; for it lay on an old road
leading from York to the mouth of the Tees, and within
easy reach of a whole group of famous monastic establishments which had sprung up during the early years of the
religious revival in the little river-valleys that open around
the foot of the moors.   A few hours' journey down the vale
of Pickering would bring the canons of Newburgh to brethren
of their own order at Kirkham and Malton ; some ten or
twelve miles of hill and moor lay between them and the
famous abbey of Rievaux ; another great Cistercian house,
Byland, rose only a mile from their own home.   With the
two last-named houses, at least, they were clearly in frequent
and intimate communication ; it was indeed at the desire of
Abbot Ernald of Rievaux that William undertook to write
his history ; and remembering the important part which the
Cistercians, and especially those of Yorkshire, had played
for more than half a century in English politics, secular
as well as ecclesiastical, we can readily see that his external
sources of information were likely to be at once copious and
trustworthy.

The literary resources of Newburgh itself, however, must
have been of the very poorest ; its library, if it possessed
one at all, could only be in process of formation even in
William's mature years.   He himself gives us no clue to its
contents.   His style is that of a man of education and taste,
but he shews little trace of the classical scholarship which
may be detected in William of Malmesbury.   Only three
earlier writers are mentioned by name in his preface ; with
two of these—Bæda and Gildas—he has of course no
ground in common ; while the third, Geoffrey of Monmouth,
is named only to be overwhelmed with scorn.   It is plain,
however, that William largely used the works of Simeon of
Durham and Henry of Huntingdon ; while the fact that his
sketch of the reigns of Henry I. and Stephen is founded
upon the last-named writer seems to shew that his literary
ambition had never been quickened by a sight of the *Gesta
Regum* and *Historia Novella*, of which nevertheless his book

is the sole worthy continuation. Compared with the works
of Richard Fitz-Nigel and Roger of Howden, its faults are
obvious ; its details are vague and inaccurate, it is full of
mistakes in names, pedigrees and suchlike small matters, and
its chronology is one long tangle of inconsistencies, confusions
and contradictions. But in the eyes of William of Newburgh, as in the eyes of William of Malmesbury, the office of
an historian is not so much to record the' events of the past
as to explain them, to extract from them their moral and
political significance for the instruction of the present and
the future. His work is not a chronicle ; it is a commentary
on the whole history of England, political, ecclesiastical and
social, throughout the twelfth century.[1] Such a commentary,
written at such a time and by such a man, is for later
students above all price. The one short chapter in which
William sums up the causes and effects of the anarchy under
Stephen[2] is of more real historical worth than the whole
chaos of mere disjointed facts which is all that the chroniclers
have to give us, and in which he alone helps us to discover a
meaning and a moral. The same might be said of many of
his reflections upon men and things, both at home and
abroad. In some respects indeed he contrasts favourably
even with his greater namesake of Malmesbury. If he is
less anxious for the entertainment of his reader, he is more
in earnest about the philosophical bearings of his subject ;
he cares less for artistic effect and more for moral impressions ; his stories are less amusing and less graphically told,
but they are untinged with Malmesbury's love of gossip and
scandal ; his aim is always rather to point a moral than to
adorn a tale ; he has a feeling for romance and a feeling for
humour,[3] but he will ruthlessly, though quietly, demolish a
generally-accepted story altogether, if he knows it to be
false.[4] Only once does the judicial calmness of his tone
change into accents of almost passionate indignation ; and it

[1] On Will. Newb. and his work see Mr. Howlett's preface to vol. i. of his
edition of the *Historia Anglicana* in the Rolls series.

[2] Will. Newb., l. i. c. 22 (Howlett, vol. i. pp. 69, 70).

[3] See *e.g.*, l. ii. c. 10, and l. iv. c. 32 (as above, pp. 123-125, 385, 386), l. v.
cc. 6 and 14 (vol. ii. pp. 424-427, 451-453).

[4] L. i. c. 26 (vol. i. p. 81).

is this outburst which above all has gained for him in our
own day the title of "the father of historical criticism,"[1] for
it is the earliest protest against a rising school of pseudo-
historical writers who seemed in a fair way to drive true
history altogether out of the literary field.

Nowhere, perhaps, has the marvellous vitality of the
ancient Celtic race shewn itself more strikingly than in the
province of literature. Of all the varied intellectual elements
that went to the making of the new England, the Celtic
element rose to the surface first. The romantic literature of
England owes its origin to a Welsh monk, Geoffrey of Monmouth, who became bishop of S. Asaph's about two years
before the accession of Henry II. Long before that time—
probably in the days when poets and men of letters of every
type were thronging to the court of Henry's grandmother
the good Queen Maude—Walter Calenius, archdeacon of
Oxford, had picked up during a journey in Britanny "a very
ancient book, containing a history of the Britons, from Brut
to Cadwallader son of Cadwallon;" this book he carried
home to England and presented to his friend Geoffrey, begging him to translate it out of Welsh into Latin.[2] Some
years after the death of Henry I. Geoffrey's translation was
given to the world. Its original cannot now be identified ;
but Geoffrey may fairly take to himself the whole credit of
the *History of the British Kings* to which his name is
attached. The book is an elaborate tissue of Celtic myths,
legends and traditions, scraps of classical and Scriptural
learning, and fantastic inventions of the author's own fertile
brain, all dexterously thrown into a pseudo-historical shape
and boldly sent forth under the imposing name of History.
The success of Geoffrey's venture was amazing. The dedication of the book was accepted by the foremost lay scholar
of the day, William of Malmesbury's friend and patron,
Earl Robert of Gloucester ; its fame spread rapidly through
all sections and classes of society. A Yorkshire priest,
Alfred of Beverley, tells us how some of the clergy of the
diocese, when suspended from the usual occupations of their

---

[1] From Mr. Freeman, in the *Contemporary Review*, vol. xxxiii. (1878), p. 216.
[2] Geoff. Monm. *Hist. Reg. Brit.*, l. i. c. 1 (Giles, Caxton Soc., pp. 1, 2).

calling—doubtless by one of the many interdicts which fell upon them during the struggle between S. William and Henry Murdac—beguiled their time by discussing the stories which they had heard or read about the ancient British kings ; how, his curiosity aroused by their talk, he with some difficulty borrowed a copy of the new book which had set them talking ; and how he longed to transcribe it at length, but lacking time and means was obliged to content himself with an abridgement.[1]   Norman barons and ladies heard of the wondrous book and became eager to read it in their own tongue ; a copy was borrowed from Earl Robert himself by no less a personage than Walter Lespec, that he might lend it in his turn to a friend of his own, Ralf Fitz-Gilbert, whose wife wanted her household-minstrel Geoffrey Gaimar to translate it into French verse for her entertainment.[2]

The version of Gaimar was superseded in a few years by that of Wace, a Norman poet who did a better service to the cause of history by his later work, the *Roman de Rou* or riming chronicle of the Norman dukes from Hrolf to Henry II.   Neither Alfred nor Gaimar nor Wace seems to have had any suspicion of the true character of Geoffrey's book of marvels ; they all alike treated it as genuine history, and from the point where it closes, at the death of Cadwallon in 689, carried on their narratives without a break down to the times of the Norman kings.   It was against this blurring of the line between truth and falsehood, this obliteration of the fundamental distinction between history and romance, that William of Newburgh lifted up his well-grounded and eloquent protest in the preface to his *Historia Anglicana*.[3] Notwithstanding that protest, the fabulous tales of the *Brut* (as Geoffrey's book is commonly called, from the name of the first British king mentioned in it) continued to pass current as an integral part of the history of Britain for many generations after him.   The fraud was in fact countenanced in high places for political ends ; Henry himself was quick to

---

[1] Alf. Beverl. (Hearne), pp. 1-3.

[2] Geoff. Gaimar, vv. 6436-6460 (Wright, Caxton Soc., pp. 224, 225).

[3] Will. Newb. procem. (Howlett, vol. i. pp. 11-18).

seize upon it as a means of humouring the national vanity and soothing the irritated national feelings of those Celtic vassals who were generally among the most troublesome of his subjects, but who were also not unfrequently among the most necessary and useful of his allies. On one occasion he is said, though on doubtful authority, to have conciliated the Bretons by consenting to enter into a diplomatic .correspondence with their long-departed, yet still mysteriously living monarch, Arthur, and by proposing to hold Britanny as Arthur's vassal.[1] In his last years, however, he turned the new Arthurian lore to account in a far more significant way in the island Britain : he set the monks of Glastonbury to find the grave of the British hero-king. In the cemetery of S. Dunstan's old abbey stood two pyramidal stones, of unknown age, and covered with inscriptions so old and worn that nothing could be read in them save, as it was thought, Arthur's name. Between these stones, sixteen feet below the surface of the ground, Henry—so the monks afterwards declared—guided by what he had heard from an old Welsh bard and read in the histories of the Britons,[2] bade them look for a wooden sarcophagus containing Arthur's mortal remains. The discovery was made in 1191 ; a coffin, hollowed as Henry had said out of the solid trunk of an oak-tree, was dug up on the spot indicated ; let into a stone at its foot was a leaden cross, which when taken out proved to

---

[1] " Hanc [sc. Britanniam] sub jure tuo, sub pace tuâ, teneamus ;
     Jus tibi, pax nobis, totaque terra simul "—
ends Henry's letter to Arthur in the *Draco Norm.*, l. ii. c. 22, vv. 1279, 1280 (Howlett, *Will. Newb.*, vol. ii. p. 707). See above, p. 57, note 2. The whole story is extremely curious ; but I feel too doubtful about the character of the source from which it comes to venture upon any discussion of its possible significance.

[2] " Sicut ab historico cantore Britone audierat antiquo," Gir. Cambr. *De Instr. Princ.* (Angl. Christ. Soc.), p. 192. " Ex gestis Britonum et eorum cantoribus historicis," *Spec. Eccles.*, dist. ii. c. 9 (Brewer, vol. iv. p. 49). These pyramids were there in William of Malmesbury's day, when one of them was already threatening to fall " præ nimiâ vetustate." They were covered with "antiquitatis nonnulla spectacula, quæ plane possunt legi licet non plane possunt intelligi." These were pictures of bishops and kings, with old English names written under them ; Arthur, however, is not in the list. William thought that the persons represented were buried underneath. Will. Malm. *Gesta Reg.*, l. i. c. 21 (Hardy, pp. 34, 35).

bear upon its inner face the words, "Here in the isle of
Avalon lies buried the renowned King Arthur, with Guine-
vere his wife." In the coffin were found a few rotten bones,
and a "cunningly-braided tress of golden hair," which however crumbled into dust in the hand of a monk who snatched
it up too eagerly. The bones were carefully preserved and
solemnly re-buried under a marble tomb before the high
altar in the abbey-church.[1]

It is easy to see what was, at any rate in Henry's mind,
the political significance of this transaction. When Arthur
could be thus publicly exhibited as dead and buried, it was
because the long-cherished dreams of Celtic national independence, of which his name had been the symbol and the
watchword, were dead and buried too. But the scene thus
enacted at Glastonbury in 1191 had also another meaning
of which perhaps none of the actors in it could be fully
aware. It marked the final "passing of Arthur" out of
the sphere of politics into a wholly new sphere of pure intel-
lect and philosophical romance. If Geoffrey of Monmouth
corrupted the sources of British history, he atoned for his
crime by opening to the poets of the generation succeeding
his own a fount of inspiration which is hardly exhausted
yet. Their imagination seized upon the romantic side of
these old-world legends, and gradually wove them into a
poetic cycle which went on developing all through the later
middle ages not in England alone, but over the whole of
civilized Europe. But in the hands of these more highly-
cultured singers the wild products of bardic fancy took a
new colour and a new meaning. As usual, it was the
Church who first breathed into the hitherto soulless body
the breath of spiritual and intellectual life. The earliest of

---

[1] See the various accounts of the invention and translation of Arthur in Gir.
Cambr. *Spec. Eccles.*, dist. ii. cc. 9, 10 (Brewer, vol. iv. pp. 48-51), and *De Instr.
Princ.* (Angl. Christ. Soc.), pp. 191, 192; R. Coggeshall (Stevenson), p. 36; Rog.
Wend. (Coxe), vol. iii. p. 48, and Ann. Margam, a. 1190 (Luard, *Ann. Monast.*,
vol. i. pp. 21, 22). Gerald seems to have been present himself. He tells us the
"translation" was made by the king's order; and indeed his account, taken by
itself, would leave an impression that the whole thing occurred during King
Henry's lifetime; but R. Coggeshall and Rog. Wend. both distinctly give the
date, 1191; the Margam Annals place it only a year earlier; and in both those
years the reigning king was far away.

the Arthurian romances, as we possess them now, is a wholly
new creation of the religious mysticism of the twelfth century, the story of the Holy Grail—

> " The cup, the cup itself, from which our Lord
> Drank at the last sad supper with His own.
> This, from the blessed land of Aromat—
> After the day of darkness, when the dead
> Went wandering o'er Moriah—the good saint,
> Arimathæan Joseph, journeying brought
> To Glastonbury, where the winter thorn
> Blossoms at Christmas, mindful of our Lord.
> And there awhile it bode ; and if a man
> Could touch or see it, he was heal'd at once,
> By faith, of all his ills.   But then the times
> Grew to such evil that the holy cup
> Was caught away to Heaven, and disappear'd."

As one by one the older legends of Arthur and Merlin, the
later stories of Lancelot and Tristan and Gawaine, were
moulded into literary form, a link to bind them all together
was found in the " quest of the Grail," vowed by the whole
company of Arthur's knights assembled at the Table Round,
achieved only by one, the Galahad whose pure figure has
gleamed upon all after-time, as it flashed first upon the corrupt court of the Angevins, the mirror of ideal Christian
chivalry.

The greater part—certainly the noblest part—of this
vast fabric of romance seems to have been woven by the
genius of one man.[1]   Every side of the intellectual movement which throughout the latter half of the twelfth century
was working a revolution in English thought and life is
reflected in Walter Map.   Born on the marches of England
and Wales, probably in the early years of the civil war, he
studied at Paris under Gerard la Pucelle, and came home
again, while Thomas Becket was still chancellor, to occupy
some post at court, doubtless that of chaplain to the king.

[1] On these Arthur-romances and Walter Map's share in them see Sir F.
Madden's introduction to his edition of *Sir Gawayne* (Bannatyne Club), and that
of M. Paulin Paris to the first volume of his *Manuscrits Français de la
Bibliothèque du Roi*, summarized in Mr. H. Morley's *English Writers*, vol. i. pp.
562-569.

He came of a family which had already done good service to
the Crown ; but once in personal contact with Henry himself,
Walter can have needed no passport to the royal favour save
his own versatile genius.   At once a scholar, a theologian
and a poet, an earnest political and ecclesiastical reformer
and a polished man of the world, shrewd and practical, witty
and wise, he soon rose high in the king's confidence and
esteem.   Henry employed him in the most varied capacities
—as a justice-itinerant in England, as an ambassador to the
court of France, as a representative of English orthodoxy
and theological learning at the Lateran council of 1179 ;
while in the intervals of these missions he was in close and
constant attendance upon the king himself.   In addition to
his post in the royal household he held several ecclesiastical
preferments—a canonry at S. Paul's, the parsonage of West-
bury in Gloucestershire, and the precentorship of Lincoln,
which he resigned in 1196 to become archdeacon of Oxford.[1]
By that time his literary work was probably for the most part
done.   The only book now extant which actually bears his
name, the treatise *De Nugis Curialium*—"Courtiers' Triflings"
—is a fruit of the busy years spent in attendance upon King
Henry from 1182 to 1189.   By its title and origin it recalls
the *Polycraticus ;* and the difference between the two books
marks the change which had come over the tone of educated
English thought in the quarter of a century that lay between
them.   Walter Map was, in all likelihood, as ripe a scholar
as John of Salisbury ; but there is nothing scholastic in his
treatment of his subject.   His book is far less elaborate in
form and methodical in arrangement than John's ; it has, in
fact, no visible arrangement at all ; it is a collection of
miscellaneous notes—scraps of folklore from the Welsh
marches, tales brought home by pilgrims and crusaders from
Byzantium or Jerusalem, stories from the classics, sayings
from the Fathers, fragments of information gleaned from the
by-ways of history, personal anecdotes new and old, sketches
of contemporary life and manners in the world and the
Church, court-news, court-gossip, court-scandal—all, as it

---

[1] For the life of Walter Map see Mr. Wright's *Biog. Britt. Litt.*, vol. ii. pp.
295-298, and his preface to *De Nug. Cur.* (Camden Soc.) pp. i.-viii.

seems, picked out at random from the writer's private com-
monplace-book and flashed in picturesque confusion before
the eyes of the literary public of his day. Yet the purpose
of it all is as earnest as that of the *Polycraticus*, though
veiled under a shew of carelessness. Walter appeals to a
wider circle than John ; he writes not for a chosen band of
kindred souls, but for all sorts and conditions of men who
know Latin enough to read him, for courtiers and men of the
world who have neither time nor patience to go through a
course of philosophical reasonings and exhortations, but who
may be caught at unawares by "truth embodied in a tale,"
and are the more likely to be caught by it the more unexpected the shape in which it comes. When Walter stops to
point the moral of his stories—for a moral they always have
—he does it with the utmost tact ; more often he leaves his
readers to find the moral for themselves. "I am your
huntsman; I bring you the game; dress the dishes for
yourselves!" he tells them.[1] But he strikes down the quarry
—if we may venture to borrow his own metaphor—with a
far more unsparing hand than his predecessor. King Henry
himself, indeed, never was spared in his own court ; but it is
in the satirist's attitude towards the Church that we find the
most significant sign of the times. The grave tone of
righteous indignation, the shame and grief of the Theobaldine
reformers at the decay of ecclesiastical purity, has given place
to bitter mockery and scathing sarcasm. Where John lifts
up his hands in deprecation of Heaven's wrath against its
unworthy ministers, Walter points at them the finger of
scorn. John turns with eager hope from the picture of
decaying discipline and declining morality, which he paints
with firm hand but with averted face, to the prospect of a reformation which is to be the spontaneous work of the clergy
and the "religious" themselves; Walter has seen this dream of
reform buried in the grave of S. Thomas—perhaps we should
rather say of Theobald—and now sees no way of dealing
with the mass of corruption but to fling it bodily into the
furnace of public criticism and popular hatred. The mightiest

---

[1] "Venator vester sum, feras vobis affero, fercula faciatis." W. Map, *De Nug.
Cur.*, dist. ii. c. 32 (Wright, p. 106).

creation of his genius is the "Bishop Goliath" whose gigantic figure embodies all the vice and all the crime which were bringing disgrace upon the clerical order in his day. The "Apocalypse" and "Confession" of this imaginary prelate have been ascribed to Walter Map by a constant tradition whose truth it is impossible to doubt, although it rests upon no direct contemporary authority.[1] The satire is in fact so daring, so bitter, and withal so appallingly true to life, that the author may well have deemed it wiser to conceal his name. He is the anonymous spokesman of a new criticism which has not yet fully discovered its own power; of a public opinion which is no longer held in check by external authority, but which is beginning to be itself an independent force; which dares to sling its pebble at abuses that have defied king and Pope, and will dare one day to sling it at king and Pope themselves. That day, however, was still far distant. Walter's ideal of perfection in Church and state is one with John of Salisbury's, only it is set forth in a different shape. The moral lesson which lies at the heart of the Arthurian romances comes home to us the more forcibly as we remember that the hand which drew Sir Galahad was the same hand which drew Bishop Goliath.

Side by side with Walter Map, in the foremost rank of this new school of critics and satirists, stands his probably younger contemporary, Gerald de Barri. Gerald was born in 1147 in the castle of Manorbeer, some three miles from Pembroke. He has left us a vivid picture of his childhood's home—its ramparts and towers crowning a lofty hill-top exposed to all the winds that swept over the stormy Irish Sea, whirled up the creek that ran up from the Bristol Channel to westward of the castle, and ruffled with ceaseless wavelets the surface of the little stream that flowed through the sandy valley on its eastern side;—its splendid fishponds at the northern foot of the hill, the enclosed tract of garden-ground beyond, and at the back of all, the protecting belt of woodland whose precipitous paths and lofty nut-trees were perhaps alike attractive to Gerald and his brothers in their

---

[1] They have been edited, under the title of *Latin Poems ascribed to Walter Mapes*, by Mr. T. Wright for the Camden Society.

boyish days.[1] His father, William de Barri, the lord of Manorbeer, represented one of those Norman families of knightly rank who had made for themselves a home in South Wales, half as conquerors, half as settlers, in the days of Henry I. His mother, Angareth, was a granddaughter of Rees Ap-Tewdor, prince of South Wales—a child of his daughter Nest by her marriage with Gerald the constable of Pembroke ; and the fiery Celtic spirit as well as the quick Celtic wit which the boy inherited from her shews itself alike in every act of his life and in every page of his writings. On both sides he came of a race of fighting-men, and he was certainly not the least pugnacious of his family. The countless battles of his life were, however, to be fought with other weapons than the sword which had won Manorbeer for his paternal ancestors, and which was soon to win for some of his mother's nearest kinsmen—for her half-brother Robert Fitz-Stephen, her nephews Meiler and Robert and Raymond, her own brother Maurice Fitz-Gerald—a wider heritage and a more lasting fame beyond the Irish Sea. Gerald's bent towards the clerical profession shewed itself in his earliest years ; as a child he was known at Manorbeer as " the little bishop." At three different periods before he reached the age of twenty-five, he spent some years in study at Paris, where he also lectured upon rhetoric with considerable success. He finally came home in 1172, just as King Henry, having twice passed through South Wales on his way to and from Ireland, was planning out a new scheme for the government of the principality. One part of this scheme was, as we have seen, the delegation of the supreme authority to the young Welsh prince Rees Ap-Griffith. Another part was the revival of the policy begun by the Norman kings of managing the Welsh people through the instrumentality of the Church, and, to this intent, filling the ranks of the clergy in Wales with as many foreign priests as possible. Experience had, however, shewn that men of pure English or Norman blood were not always the fittest instruments for such a purpose. A year after Gerald's birth a compromise had been tried in the appointment to the

---

[1] Gir. Cambr. *Itin. Kambr.*, l. i. c. 12 (Dimock, vol. vi. p. 92).

bishopric of S. David's of a prelate who was half Norman and half Welsh:—David, son of Gerald of Pembroke and Nest, brother of Maurice Fitz-Gerald and of Angareth the wife of William de Barri. When Angareth's son Gerald came home from Paris in 1172, therefore, the influence of her family was at its height. The foremost man in South Wales was her cousin Rees Ap-Griffith ; the second was her brother the bishop of S. David's. It was only natural that Gerald, sharing with his uncle the qualification of mingled Welsh and Norman blood, and already known as a distinguished scholar of the most famous seat of learning in Europe, should be at once selected for employment in the business of reforming his native land. Gerald himself was eager for the work ; he had no difficulty in obtaining from Archbishop Richard a commission to act as his legate and representative in the diocese of S. David's ; thus armed, he began a vigorous campaign against the evil doings of clergy and laity alike—forcing the people to pay their tithes of wool and cheese, a duty which the Welsh were always very unwilling to fulfil ; compelling the priests to abandon the lax system of discipline which they had inherited from the ancient British Church, and had contrived to retain in spite of Lanfranc and Anselm and Theobald ; excommunicating the sheriff and deposing the archdeacon of Brecknock themselves when they dared to resist his authority, and receiving in 1175, as the reward of his zeal, the appointment to the vacated archdeaconry.

Early in the next year his uncle, Bishop David, died. The young archdeacon had just issued victorious from a sharp struggle in behalf of the see against the bishop of S. Asaph's, who had attempted to encroach upon its rights ; the darling wish of his heart was to see it restored to its ancient metropolitical rank ; and he had managed to kindle in his fellow-canons a spark of the same ambition. They saw in him the only man capable of bringing their desire to fulfilment, and made a bold attempt to obtain him for their bishop. By this time, however, both King Henry and Archbishop Richard had learned enough of Gerald's character to perceive that, however useful he might be as an archdeacon in Wales, he was not at all the man to suit their purposes as bishop of any Welsh see, least of all as bishop of S. David's. Henry, with a burst of fury, summarily refused the nomination of the chapter; a long wrangle ended in the appointment of Peter de Leia, prior of the Cluniac house of Much Wenlock, to the vacant see. Peter, being a foreigner, a monk, and a man of no great intellectual capacity, was utterly unable either to rule his turbulent Welsh flock or to cope with his self-willed and quick-witted Welsh canons; Gerald undertook to teach him his duties, but found him such an unsatisfactory pupil that he soon gave up the task in disgust, and again betook himself to Paris. There he remained, studying civil and canon law, and lecturing at the same time with great success, till the summer of 1180, when he returned to England, was received by the chapter of Canterbury at a great banquet on Trinity Sunday, and thence proceeded into Wales. He found Bishop Peter at his wits' end, and the diocese in utter confusion, which he at once set himself to remedy after his own fashion. Thus matters went on till 1184, when Henry on his last hurried visit to England found time to intervene once more in the troubled affairs of South Wales. He called a council on the border, summoned Gerald to meet him there, and employed him to arrange the final submission of his cousin Rees to the English Crown; and then he dexterously removed the over-zealous archdeacon from a sphere where he was likely henceforth to be more dangerous than useful, by making him one of his own chaplains, and sending him next year to Ireland in attendance upon John. John came back in September; Gerald lingered till the following Easter. Two books were the fruit of this visit: a *Topography of Ireland*, published in 1187, and dedicated to the king; and the *Conquest of Ireland*, which came out under the patronage of Count Richard of Poitou in 1188. Towards the close of that year, when Archbishop Baldwin went to preach the Crusade in Wales, Gerald accompanied him half as interpreter, half as guide. An *Itinerary of Wales* forms the record of this expedition, which was followed by a journey over sea, still in the company of the archbishop, with whom Gerald seems to have remained in more or less close attendance upon Henry's movements until the final catastrophe in July 1189. He then offered his services to Richard, who sent him home once more to his old task of helping to keep order in South Wales. For a while he found favour with all parties ;[1] William of Longchamp offered him the bishopric of Bangor, John, in his day of power after William's fall, offered him that of Landaff. Gerald however refused them both, as he had already refused two Irish sees ; he cared in fact for no preferment short of the metropolitan chair of S. David. Shut out of Paris by the war between Richard and Philip Augustus, he withdrew to Lincoln and resumed his theological studies under its chancellor William, whom he had known in his earlier college days on the Mont-Ste.-Geneviève, till in the summer of 1198 he was roused to action once more by the death of Bishop Peter de Leia. The fight began at once ; the chapter of S. David's nominated Gerald for the vacant see ; the archbishop of Canterbury, Hubert Walter, set his face against the nomination ; they defied his authority and appealed to king and Pope ; Gerald himself fought his own battle and that of the see with indomitable courage, at home and abroad, for nearly four years ; but the canons were less resolute than their bishop-elect, he found himself at last fighting alone against the world, and in 1202 he gave up the struggle and withdrew to spend the rest of his life in the quiet pursuit of letters.[2]

For nearly thirty years it had been the aim of Gerald's highest ambition to be the S. Thomas of his native land. He had struggled and suffered for the privileges of S. David's in the same spirit in which Thomas had struggled and suffered for those of Canterbury, and it is by no means unlikely that had the occasion ever arisen, he would have been found ready to follow his model even

---

[1] Gerald himself goes so far as to say, with respect to Richard's appointment of William of Longchamp as justiciar, " cui archidiaconum adjunxit " (*De Rebus a se gestis*, dist. ii. c. 21, Brewer, vol. i. p. 84). We find however no hint of such a thing elsewhere.

[2] Gerald's life may be studied in his own book, *De Rebus a se gestis*, published in the first volume of the Rolls edition of his works ; and, more conveniently, in Mr. Brewer's preface to the same volume.

unto death.[1]   But, unlike Thomas, he knew when to yield ;
and instead of dying for a lost cause, was content to live for
posterity.   Both men have had their fitting reward.   Gerald
the Welshman—" Giraldus Cambrensis "—still lives in his
writings under the title won for him by his ardent patriotism ; he lives however for us not as the champion of Welsh
ecclesiastical independence, but as what he has been called
by a writer of our own day—" the father of our popular
literature." [2]   Gerald's first essay in authorship was made at
the age of twenty ; he was still busy with his pen when past
his seventieth year ;[3] and all through the intervening half-
century, every spare moment of his active, restless career was
devoted to literary composition.   His last years were spent
in revising and embellishing the hasty productions of these
earlier and briefer intervals of leisure.   Even in their more
finished shape, however, they still bear the impress of their
origin.   They breathe in all its fulness a spirit of which we
catch the first faint indications in William of Malmesbury,
and which may be described in one word as the spirit of
modern journalism.   Gerald's wide range of subjects is only
less remarkable than the ease and freedom with which he
treats them.   Whatever he touches—history, archæology,
geography, natural science, politics, the social life and thought
of the day, the physical peculiarities of Ireland and the
manners and customs of its people, the picturesque scenery
and traditions of his own native land, the scandals of the
court and of the cloister, the petty struggle for the primacy
of Wales and the great tragedy of the fall of the Angevin
empire—is all alike dealt with in the bold, dashing, offhand
style of a modern newspaper or magazine-article.   His first
important work, the *Topography of Ireland*, is, with due
allowance for the difference between the tastes of the twelfth
century and those of the nineteenth, just such a series of
sketches as a special correspondent in our own day might
send from some newly-colonized island in the Pacific to

---

[1] That Thomas was Gerald's chosen model may be seen all through his writings.   He harps upon the martyr's life and death somewhat as Thomas himself
harped upon the life of Anselm.   [2] Green, *Hist. Eng. People*, vol. i. p. 172.
[3] Gir. Cambr. *De Jure Menev. Eccles.*, dist. vii. (Dimock, vol. iii. pp.
372, 373).

satisfy or to whet the curiosity of his readers at home. The book made no small stir in the contemporary world of letters. Sober, old-fashioned scholars stood aghast at this daring Welshman's disregard of all classical traditions and literary conventionalities, at the colloquialisms of his style, and still more at the audacity of his stories.[1] For Gerald, determined to entertain his readers no matter by what means, and secure in their universal ignorance of the country which he professed to be describing, had raked together all the marvellous and horrible tales that could be found in Irish traditionary lore or devised by the inventive genius of his Irish informants ; and the more frightful and impossible these stories were, the more greedily did he seize upon them and publish them. Irish scholars, almost from that day to this, have justly declaimed against Gerald for his atrocious libels upon their country and its people; yet the fact remains that, in the words of one of his latest editors, " to his industry we are exclusively indebted for all that is known of the state of Ireland during the whole of the middle ages."[2] His treatise *De Expugnatione Hiberniæ* is by far the most complete and authentic account which we possess of the English or Norman conquest of Ireland. The *Topographia*, despite its glaring faults, has a special merit of its own ; its author " must " (as says the writer already quoted) " take rank with the first who descried the value, and, in some respects, the proper limits of descriptive geography."[3]

A far better specimen of his work in this direction is his *Welsh Itinerary*, followed some three or four years later by a *Description of Wales*.[4] Here Gerald is on familiar and congenial ground, dealing with a subject which he thoroughly knows and understands, describing a country which he ardently loves and a people with whom, although by no means blind or indulgent to their faults, he is yet heartily in sympathy, because he is one of themselves. In these treatises therefore we see him at his very best, both as a writer and as a man. In his own opinion the best of all

---

[1] Gir. Cambr. *Expugn. Hibern.*, introit. (Dimock, vol. v. p. 209).
[2] Brewer, *Gir. Cambr.*, vol. i. pref. p. xl.
[3] *Ibid.*   [4] Dimock, vol. vi.

his works was the *Gemma Ecclesiastica*,[1] or *Jewel of the Church*, a handbook of instructions on the moral and religious duties of the priesthood, compiled for the clergy of his own archdeaconry of Brecknock. To modern readers it is interesting only for the glimpse which it affords of the social, moral and intellectual condition of the South-Welsh clergy in his day. In his *Mirror of the Church*[2] the general state of religious society and ecclesiastical discipline, at home and abroad, is reflected as unsparingly as in the satires of Walter Map. The remainder of Gerald's extant works are of the most miscellaneous character—a half-finished autobiography, a book of *Invectives* against his enemies political and ecclesiastical, a collection of letters, poems and speeches, a treatise on the *Rights of the Church of S. David's*, some Lives of contemporary bishops, a tract nominally *On the Education of Princes*, but really occupied for the most part with a bitter attack upon the characters of Henry II. and his sons.[3] All of them are, more or less, polemical pamphlets, coloured throughout by the violent personal antipathies of the writer,[4] but valuable for the countless side-lights which they cast upon the social life of the period. As we read their bold language, we can scarcely wonder at Archbishop Hubert's relentless determination to put down their author by every means in his power. But though Gerald the bishop-elect of S. David's was no match for the primate of all England, Gerald the pamphleteer wielded a force against which the religious authority of the metropolitan and the hostility of the older race of scholars were both alike powerless. He and his colleagues in the new school of literature had at their back the whole strength of the class to which they belonged, a class of men who were rapidly taking the place of the clergy as leaders of the intellectual life and thought of the nation.

---

[1] Brewer, vol. ii.   [2] *Speculum Ecclesiæ* (Brewer, vol. iv.).

[3] Gerald's works have all been edited for the Rolls series by Mr. Brewer and Mr. Dimock, except the *Vitæ Sex Episcoporum*, which are in Wharton's *Anglia Sacra*, vol. ii., and *De Instructione Principum*, which has been published by the Anglia Christiana Society.

[4] It is only fair to note that Gerald at the close of his life published a little book of *Retractations*, printed in first volume of his works (ed. Brewer).

When old-fashioned critics lifted up their protest against Gerald's *Irish Topography*, he boldly carried the book down to Oxford, "where the most learned and famous English clerks were then to be found," and read it out publicly to as many as chose to come and hear it. "And as there were three distinctions or divisions in the work, and each division occupied a day, the readings lasted three successive days. On the first day he received and entertained at his lodgings all the poor of the town ; on the next day all the doctors of the different faculties, and such of their pupils as were of fame and note ; on the third day the rest of the scholars, with the knights, townsmen and many burgesses."[1] If some of the elder teachers shook their heads, it mattered little to Gerald ; their murmurs were lost in the applause of a younger generation which hailed him as one of its own most distinguished representatives.

The spirit which breathes through the pages of Gerald and Walter is the spirit of the rising universities. The word "university" indeed, as applied to the great seats of learning in the twelfth century, is somewhat of an anachronism ; the earliest use of it in the modern sense, in reference to Oxford, occurs under Henry III. ;[2] and the University of Paris appears by that name for the first time in 1215,[3] the year of our own Great Charter. But although the title was not yet in use, the institution now represented by it was one of the most important creations of the age. The school of Bologna sprang into life under the impulse given by Irnerius, a teacher who opened lectures upon the Roman civil law in 1113.[4] Nearly forty years later, when Gratian had published his famous book on the Decretals, a school of canon law was instituted in the same city by Pope Eugene III. ; and in 1158 the body of teachers who formed what we call the University won a charter of privileges from the

---

[1] Gir. Cambr. *De Rebus a se gestis*, l. ii. c. 16 (Brewer, vol. i. pp. 72, 73). I have availed myself of Mr. Brewer's translation of the passage, in his preface to the same volume, p. xlvii.

[2] Anstey, *Munimenta Academica*, vol. i. introd. p. xxxiv.

[3] Mullinger, *Univ. Cambridge*, p. 71 (from Savigny, *Gesch. des Röm. Rechts*, c. xxi. sec. 127).   [4] *Ib.* pp. 36, 37, 72.

Emperor Frederic Barbarossa.[1] We have already, in the course of our story, had more than one glimpse of the great school of arts and theology which was growing up during the same period in Paris. There, where the study of divinity had long found a congenial home under the shadow of the cathedral church, William of Champeaux in 1109—the year of S. Anselm's death—opened on the Mont-Ste.-Geneviève a school of logic which in a few years became the most frequented in Europe. Under his successors, Abelard and Peter Lombard (the latter of whom was made bishop of Paris in 1159), the schools of Paris became the centre of the intellectual life of Christendom.[2] Teachers and scholars from every nation met on equal terms, as fellow-citizens of a new and world-wide commonwealth of learning, on the slopes of the " Mount," and went forth again to carry into the most distant lands the instruction which they had acquired. There a Wiltshire lad could begin a lifelong intimacy with a youth from Champagne ;— could pass from the lectures of Abelard to those of a master who, though disguised under the title of " Robert of Melun," was in reality a fellow-countryman of his own ; could enter the *quadrivium* under the guidance of a German teacher, make acquaintance with Aristotle by the help of another learned Englishman, and complete his theological studies, it may be, under the same Robert Pulein whom we saw lecturing at Oxford some twelve or thirteen years before.[3] There a scholar from the Welsh marches could sit at the feet of the English master Gerard La Pucelle,[4] and another from the depths of Pembroke could give lectures on rhetoric and could study theology with William of Blois, who in after-days came at the call of the Burgundian S. Hugh to undertake the direction of a school at Lincoln.[5] There Ralf de Diceto was a fellow-student with Arnulf of Lisieux ;[6] there, in all likelihood, John of Salisbury met Nicolas Breakspear and Thomas Becket. Thence, we cannot doubt, came through some of these wandering scholars the impulse

[1] Mullinger, *Univ. Camb.*, p. 73.		[2] *Ib.* pp. 75-77.
[3] See above, vol. i. pp. 480-483.		[4] See above, p. 449.
[5] *Ib.* pp. 453, 456.		[6] Arn. Lisieux, Ep. 16 (Giles, pp. 100, 101).

which called the schools of Oxford into being. The first token of their existence is the appearance of Robert Pulein in 1133. From that time forth the intellectual history of Oxford is again blank till the coming of Vacarius in 1149; and it is not till the reign of Henry II. has all but closed that we begin to discern any lasting result from the visits of these two teachers. Then, however, the words of Gerald would alone suffice to shew that the University was to all intents and purposes full - grown. It had its different "faculties" of teachers, its scholars of various grades; and the little city in the meadows by the Isis, famous already in ecclesiastical legend and in political and military history, had by this time won the character which was henceforth to be its highest and most abiding glory, as the resort of all "the most learned and renowned clerks in England."

On a site less favoured by nature, Oxford's future rival was more slowly growing up. A lift of slightly higher ground above the left bank of the river Grant—better known to us now as the Cam—on the southern margin of what was then and for five hundred years afterwards a vast tract of flood-drowned fen stretching northward as far as the Wash, there stood at the close of the seventh century—long before Oxford makes its first appearance in history — a "little waste chester"[1] representing what had once been the Roman city of Camboritum. At the coming of the Norman the place was known as Grantebridge, and contained some three or four hundred houses, twenty-seven of which were pulled down by the Conqueror's orders to make room for the erection of a castle.[2] It may be that here, as at Lincoln, the inhabitants thus expelled went to make for themselves a new home beyond the river; and a church of S. Benet which still survives, and whose tower might pass for a twin-sister of Robert D'Oilly's tower of S. Michael's at Oxford, may have been the nucleus of a new town which sprang up half a mile to the south-east of the old one, on the right bank of the Cam. Around this new town there gathered in the course of the following century a fringe of religious foundations. The "round church" of the Holy

[1] Bæda, *Hist. Eccles.*, l. iv. c. 19.   [2] Domesday, vol. i. p. 189.

Sepulchre, clearly a work of the time of Henry I., was probably built by some crusader whose imagination had been
fired by the sight of its prototype at Jerusalem. A Benedictine nunnery, part of whose beautiful church now serves
as the chapel of Jesus College, was established under the
invocation of S. Radegund early in the reign of Stephen;
an hospital dedicated to S. John the Evangelist was founded
at some time between 1133 and 1169 under the patronage
of Bishop Nigel of Ely. This hospital, like most institutions
of the kind, may have been served by canons regular of the
order of S. Augustine. Some years before this, however,
the Augustinians had made a more important settlement in
the same neighbourhood. As early as 1092 Picot the
sheriff of Cambridgeshire had founded within the older
town on the left bank of the river a church of S. Giles, to
be served by four regular canons. In 1112 this little
college was removed to Barnwell, some two miles to the
north-eastward, on the opposite side of the river, where it
grew into a flourishing Austin priory. Wherever there were
Austin canons a school was sure to spring up ere long ; so,
too, we cannot doubt, it was at Cambridge. Whether the
seeds of learning were first sown in the cloisters of S. John's
or of Barnwell, or under the shadow of that old S. Benet's
which seems to have been the original University church[1]—
who it was that played here the part which had been played
at Oxford by Robert Pulein—we know not ; but we do
know that by the middle of the following century the old
Grantebridge had sunk into a mere suburb of the new town
beyond the river, and the existence of the schools of Cambridge had become an established fact.[2]

The student-life of the twelfth century—whether it were
the life of scholar or of teacher—had nothing either of the

[1] See Mullinger, *Univ. Camb.*, p. 299, note 3 ; and Willis and Clark, *Archit.
Hist. Cambr.*, vol. i. p. 276 and note 3.

[2] On the rise of Cambridge — town and university—see Mullinger, *Univ.
Camb.*, pp. 332-334. The schools were not formally recognized as an "University" till 1318 ; *ib.* p. 145. For S. Radegund's see Dugdale, *Monast. Angl.*,
vol. iv. pp. 215, 216 ; for Barnwell, *ib.* vol. vi. pt. i. pp. 83-87 ; for S. John's
Hospital, *ib.* pt. ii. p. 755. The present S. John's College stands on the site of
the hospital.

ease or the dignity which we associate with the college life of to-day. Colleges in the modern sense there were indeed none. Students of all ranks and ages, from boys of ten or twelve years to men in full priestly orders, lodged as they could in a sort of dames'-houses or hostels scattered up and down the streets and lanes of the city. The schools were entirely unendowed ; there was no University chest, no common fund, no pecuniary aid of any kind for either scholars or teachers. The sole support of both was, at first, the power under whose sheltering wings the school had grown up—the Church. Every book, even, had to be either bought out of their own private purses or borrowed from the library of some religious establishment. We may perhaps gather some idea of what this latter resource was likely to furnish in the great educational centres from a catalogue which has been preserved to us of the library attached to Lincoln minster, at the time when the Lincoln school of theology was at the height of its fame under Gerald's friend William of Blois and the saintly bishop Hugh. Five-and-thirty years before Hugh's appointment to the see, the church of Lincoln possessed, in addition to the necessary service-books which were under the care of the treasurer, some thirty or forty books in the chancellor's keeping. Among these we find, besides a number of Psalters, works of the Latin Fathers, Epistles, Gospels, and a complete Bible in two volumes, the Canons, Statutes and Decretals of the Popes ;—the Decretals edited by Ivo of Chartres ;—the works of Vergil : a copy of the military treatise of Vegetius, bound up with the Roman History of Eutropius, " which volume Master Gerard gave in exchange for the Consolations of Boëthius, which he lost";— Priscian's Grammar :—a " Mappa Mundi": and a *Book of the Foundation of Lincoln Minster*, with a collection of its charters. Of nine books presented by Bishop Robert de Chesney, who died in 1166, the most noticeable were the works of Josephus and of Eusebius, and the *Sentences* of Peter Lombard. Somewhat later, one Warin of Hibaldstow presented to the chapter a " book of Aristotle "—doubtless a Latin version of his treatise on logic or on natural philosophy —and seven volumes, whose contents are not stated, were given by Master "Radulphus Niger" or Ralf the Black, known to us as one of the minor chroniclers of King Henry's later years. A copy of Gratian's great book of Decretals was presented about the same time by an archdeacon of Leicester ; Gerald de Barri, probably during his residence at Lincoln at the close of Richard's reign, added another law-book called *Summula super Decreta*, a copy of S. Anselm's treatise *Cur Deus Homo*, and three of his own works, the *Topographia Hiberniæ*, the *Life of Bishop Remigius*, and the *Gemma Sacerdotalis* or *Ecclesiastica ;* and the list closes with another copy of the *Sentences*, acquired seemingly in the early years of the following century.[1]

The head of the scholastic body was the chancellor, who was an officer of the diocesan bishop — in the case of Oxford, the bishop of Lincoln. From him those who had reached a certain degree of proficiency in the schools received their license to become teachers in their turn ; and it was an established rule that all who had attained the rank of Master or Doctor should devote themselves for a certain time to the work of instructing others. They gave their lectures how and where they could, in cloister or church-porch, or in their own wretched lodgings, their pupils sitting literally at their feet, huddled all together on the bare ground ; their living depended solely on their school-fees, and these were often received with one hand only to be paid away again with the other, for many an ardent young teacher of logic or rhetoric was, like John of Salisbury and Gerald de Barri, at one and the same time giving lectures in these arts to less advanced scholars and pursuing his own studies under some great doctor of theology. The course of study was much the same everywhere. From the fifth century downwards it had consisted of two divisions, *trivium* and *quadrivium*. Under the former head were comprised Grammar, defined by an early teacher as the art of "writing and reading learnedly, understanding and judging skilfully ;"[2]

---

[1] See the Catalogues of Lincoln cathedral library in the twelfth century, in *Gir. Cambr. Opp.*, vol. vii. (Dimock and Freeman), App. C., pp. 165-171.

[2] "Docte scribere legereque, erudite intelligere probareque." Martianus Capella, quoted by Mullinger, *Univ. Camb.*, pp. 24, 25.

VOL. II.

Dialectics, including logic and metaphysics; and Rhetoric, by which were meant the rules and figures of the art, chiefly derived from Cicero. The Quadrivium included Geometry, not so much the science now known by that name as what we call geography; Arithmetic, which in the middle ages meant the science of mystical numbers; Music, in other words metre and harmony; and Astronomy, of course on the Ptolemaic system, although as early as the fifth century a theory had been put forth which is said to have given in after-days the clue to Copernicus.[1] There was a separate faculty of Theology, and another of Law. Between these different faculties there seems to have been a good deal of jealousy. The highest authorities of the Western Church, while encouraging by every means in their power the study of the canon law, set their faces steadily against the civil law of imperial Rome; the "religious" were over and over again forbidden to have anything to do with it: and on the continent the two branches of the legal profession were followed by different persons. As, however, the procedure of the canon law was founded upon that of the Theodosian code, the English clerical lawyers in Stephen's time and in Henry's early years found their account in combining the two studies; by degrees both together passed out of the hands of the clergy into those of a new class of lay lawyers; and in later days, while on the continent the canon law fell into neglect with its exclusively clerical professors, in England it was preserved by being linked with the civil law under the care of lay *doctores utriusque juris.*[2]

Theology had, however, a yet more formidable rival in the schools of logic. The text-book commonly used in these schools was a Latin translation, made by Boëthius in the sixth century, of part of Aristotle's treatise upon logic. Early in the twelfth century the natural philosophy of Aristotle was in some measure rendered accessible to western students through translations made by travelled scholars such as Adelard of Bath from Arabic versions which they had picked up in the schools of Salerno or of the remoter East. Of the " Ethics " nothing was known save a few frag-

---

[1] Mullinger, *Univ. Camb.*, pp. 24-26.   [2] *Ib.* pp. 37-39.

ments imbedded in the works of Latin writers, until a
hundred years later, when they found their way back to
Europe, probably in the train of the returning crusaders,
and certainly in a very strange shape—that of a Latin
translation from a Hebrew version of what was, after all,
nothing more than an Arabic commentary founded upon a
Syriac version of the original Greek text.[1] Garbled as it
was, however, this new Aristotelian lore revolutionized the
schools of western Christendom by laying open to them
wholly new fields of criticism and speculation. The spirit of
free inquiry in which Adelard had begun to deal with
physical science invaded every region of intellectual thought
and knowledge, while the spread of legal studies helped to
the invention of new methods of argument and disputation.
In vain did Peter Lombard, in the famous book which gained
for him his title of " Master of the Sentences," strive to stem
the rising tide and counterwork the influence of the rational-
izing dialecticians by applying to the purposes of theology
the methods of their own favourite science. The "Sentences"
remained the accepted text-book of theology down to the
cataclysm in the sixteenth century ; but their effect was
precisely the opposite to that which their author had desired.[2]
The endless " doubtful disputations," the hair-splittings, the
" systems of impossibilities," which had already taken possession of the logic-schools in John of Salisbury's day, were
even more irritating to the practical mind and impetuous
temper of Gerald de Barri. They were in fact ruining both
theology and letters. " Our scholars," Gerald complains,
" for the sake of making a shew, have betaken themselves to
subjects which rather savour of the quadrivium :—questions
of single and compound, shadow and motion, points and
lines, acute and obtuse angles—that they may display a
smattering of learning in the quadrivium, whereof the studies
flourish more in the East than in the West ; and thence they
have proceeded to the maintaining of false positions, the pro-
pounding of insoluble problems, the spinning of frivolous and
long-winded discourses, not in the best of Latin, hereby
holding up in their own disputations a warning of the conse-

[1] Mullinger, *Univ. Camb.*, pp. 94-96 and notes.   [2] *Ib*. pp. 58-62.

quences ensuing from their abandonment of the study of letters."[1] Yet it was from those very schools that Gerald himself, and men like him, had caught the fearless temper, the outspoken, unrestrained tone, in which they exposed and criticized not only every conspicuous individual, but every institution and every system, alike in the world and in the Church of their day. The democratic spirit of independence which had characterized the strictly clerical reformers of an earlier day had passed from the ranks of the priesthood into those of the universities, and had taken a mightier developement there. It was mainly through them that the nation at large entered in some degree into the labours of Theobald and his fellow-workers ; it was they themselves who entered into the labours of Thomas Becket. A large proportion of both students and teachers—a proportion which grew larger and larger as time went on—were laymen ; but an inveterate legal fiction still counted them all as " clerks." The schools had grown up under the wings of the Church, and when they reached their full stature, they were strong enough both to free themselves from the control of the ecclesiastical authorities and to keep the privileges for which the clergy had fought. A priest of the English Church in our own day is as completely subject to the ordinary law of the land as any of his flock ; but the chancellor's court of the University of Oxford still possesses sole cognizance over all causes whatsoever, in all parts of the realm, which concern any resident member of the University.[2]

Not the universities, however, but the towns, were the true strongholds of English freedom. The struggle of the English towns for municipal liberty which we have seen beginning under Henry I. was renewed under Henry II. and Richard with increased vigour and success. Henry Fitz-Empress was far too clear-sighted a statesman to undervalue the growing importance of this element in English social and political life. Most of his town-charters, however, date

---

[1] Gir. Cambr. *Gemma Eccles.*, dist. ii. c. 37 (Brewer, vol. ii. p. 355). Cf. *ib.* pp. 350, 351, and *Spec. Eccles.*, dist. i. prooem. (vol. iv. pp. 4-9).

[2] This privilege was secured by a charter of Edward III.; it was successfully asserted as lately as January 1886.

from the earlier years of his reign, and scarcely any of them contain anything more than a confirmation of the liberties enjoyed in his grandfather's time, with the addition in some cases of a few new privileges, carefully defined and strictly limited.[1] In the great commercial cities, where the municipal movement had probably received a fresh impulse from the extension of trade and intercourse with the continent which was a natural consequence of Henry's accession to the crown, the merchant-gilds soon began openly to aim at gathering into their own hands the whole powers of local government and administration, and acquiring the position of a French "commune." The French kings encouraged the growth of the communal principle as a possible counterpoise to the power of the feudal nobles; Henry, who had little need of it for such a purpose, saw the dangers which it threatened to his system of government and held it steadily in check. In 1170 Aylwine the Mercer, Henry Hund and "the other men of the town" paid a heavy fine to the treasury for an attempt to set up a commune at Gloucester;[2] six years later one Thomas "From-beyond-the-Ouse" paid twenty marks for a like offence at York.[3] Owing to the close connexion between the organization of the commune and that of the gilds, every developement of this latter institution also was watched by the Crown with jealous care; in 1164 the burghers of Totnes, those of Lidford and those of Bodmin were all fined for setting up gilds without warrant from the king;[4] and in 1180 no less than eighteen "adulterine gilds" in London met with a similar punishment.[5] Once established, however, they seem to have been permitted to retain their existence, for in the first Pipe Roll of Richard we find them again paying their fines "as they are set down in the twenty-sixth Roll of King Henry II."[6] A bakers' gild in London, a weavers' gild at Nottingham, one of the same craft and another of fullers at Winchester, make their

---

[1] Stubbs, *Select Charters*, pp. 165-168.
[2] Madox, *Hist. Exch.*, vol. i. p. 563, from Pipe Roll 16 Hen. II.
[3] Madox, *Firma Burgi*, p. 35, from Pipe Roll 22 Hen. II.
[4] Madox, *Hist. Exch.*, vol. i. pp. 562, 563.
[5] *Ib.* p. 562, from Pipe Roll 26 Hen. II.
[6] Pipe Roll 1 Ric. I. (Hunter), p. 226.

appearance as authorized bodies at the opening of Henry's reign ;[1] among the "adulterine gilds" of London were those of the butchers, goldsmiths, grocers, clothiers and pilgrims.[2] The golden days of English borough-life, however, began with the crowning of Henry's successor. "When History drops her drums and trumpets and learns to tell the story of Englishmen"—as he who wrote these words has told it— "it will find the significance of Richard, not in his crusade or in his weary wars along the Norman border, but in his lavish recognition of municipal life."[3] In his first seven years alone, we find him granting charters to Winchester, Northampton, Norwich, Ipswich, Doncaster, Carlisle, Lincoln, Scarborough and York. Some of these towns were only beginning their career of independence, and were content with the first step of all, the purchase of the *firma burgi;* some bought a confirmation of privileges already acquired ; Lincoln in 1194 had got so far as to win from the king a formal recognition of its right to complete self-government in a clause empowering its citizens to elect their own reeve every year.[4] King of knights-errant and troubadours as he seemed, Richard, it is plain, could read the signs of the times as clearly and act upon their warnings as promptly and as wisely as any of his race ; and we may be very sure that this bold advance upon his father's cautious policy towards the towns was dictated by a sound political instinct far more than by the mere greed of gain. John went still further in the same direction ; the first fifteen years of his reign afford examples of town-charters of every type, from the element-ary grant of the *firma burgi* and the freedom of the

[1] Pipe Roll 2 Hen. II. (Hunter), pp. 4, 39, 52.

[2] "Aurifabrorum," "Bocheiorum," "Piperariorum," "Parariorum," "Pere-grinorum." There are four gilds "de Ponte"; one "de S. Lazaro"; one "de Haliwell"; the rest are described simply as "the gild whereof So-and-so is alderman." Madox, *Hist. Exch.*, vol. i. p. 562, note *z.*

[3] Green, *Stray Studies*, p. 216.

[4] Northampton bought the *firma burgi* in 1191, Norwich in 1192, Ipswich and Doncaster in 1194 (Madox as above, pp. 399, 400, from Pipe Rolls) ; Winchester bought a confirmation of its liberties in 1190 (Stubbs, *Select Chart.*, pp. 265, 266), Carlisle in 1194, York and Scarborough in 1195 (Madox as above). The Lincoln charter is given by Bishop Stubbs, as above, pp. 266, 267 ; for its date see Pipe Roll 6 Ric. I., quoted by Madox, as above, p. 400.

merchant-gild to the little Cornish borough of Helston[1] up to the crowning privilege bestowed upon the "barons of our city of London" in 1215, of electing their own mayor every year.[2]

From the charter of Henry I. to the establishment of the commune under Richard the constitutional history of London is shrouded in obscurity. The charter granted by Henry II. to the citizens, some time before the end of 1158, is simply a confirmation of his grandfather's.[3] During the first fifteen years of his reign two sheriffs of London appear annually in the Pipe Rolls; in 1171 there were four, as there had been in the thirty-first year of Henry I.; but in the twentieth year of Henry II., 1171, we find that their number was again reduced to two; and from 1182 onwards there seems to have been only one, till at Michaelmas 1189 the accounts were rendered by Richard Fitz-Reiner and Henry of Corn- hill, both of whom continued in office till 1191.[4] In that year, as we have seen, the commune won its legal recogni- tion from John and Archbishop Walter of Rouen as representatives of the absent king;[5] and although the charter which Richard issued to the citizens of London, shortly before his final departure from England in 1194, is a mere echo of his father's,[6] yet the existence of the new corporation is thenceforth a recognized fact. John's first charter to London was issued from Normandy six weeks after his crowning. It renewed the old grant of the sheriffdom of London and Middlesex, with all rights and customs there- unto belonging, to the citizens and their heirs, to have and

[1] Stubbs, *Select Charters*, pp. 313, 314.

[2] *Ib.* pp. 314, 315. John's town-charters are all in the *Rotuli Chartarum*, edited by Sir T. D. Hardy for the Record Commission. See also extracts from Pipe Rolls in Madox, *Hist. Exch.*, vol. i. pp. 400 *et seq.*

[3] Charter in Riley's *Munimenta Gildhallæ*, vol. ii. part i. pp. 31, 32. It is witnessed by "archiepiscopo Cantuariæ" and "Ricardo episcopo Londoniarum"; *i.e.* Richard of London who died in May 1162, and Theobald who died in April 1161. As it is certain that neither of these two prelates ever crossed the sea after Henry's accession, the charter must have been issued in England, and therefore before Henry went abroad in August 1158.

[4] Stubbs, *Constit. Hist.*, vol. i. p. 629.   [5] Above, p. 301.

[6] Riley, *Munim. Gildh.*, vol. ii. pt. i. pp. 248, 249. Date, Winchester, April 23, 1194.

to hold of the king and his heirs for ever. They were to appoint as sheriffs any of their own number whom they might choose, and to remove them at their pleasure ; and for this privilege they were to pay, through the said sheriffs, three hundred pounds a year to the Treasury.[1] The establishment of the commune had reduced the sheriffs to the rank of mere financial officers, and the real head of the civic administration was the mayor. The first mayor of London, Henry Fitz-Aylwine, retained his office for life ; and his life extended beyond the limits of our present story. Yet the true significance of that story is strikingly illustrated by the next step in the history of London, a step which followed two years after Fitz-Aylwine's death. On May 9, 1215, John granted to the "barons of the city of London" the right of annually electing their mayor.[2] Five weeks later the barons of England compelled him to sign, in the meadows of Runnymede, the Great Charter which secured the liberties not of one city only but of the whole English people ; and among the five-and-twenty men whom they chose from among themselves to enforce its execution was Serlo the Mercer, mayor of London.[3]

Little, indeed, as the burghers themselves may have dreamed of any such thing, the highest importance of their struggle for municipal liberty lies in this, that its fruits were to be reaped by a far larger community than was inclosed within the town-walls. It was from the burghers that their brethren in the rural districts caught once more the spirit of freedom which ages of oppression had well-nigh crushed out of their hearts. " ' Ketel's case ' " at Bury S. Edmund's— the case of a tenant of the abbey who, dwelling "outside the gate," was hanged for a theft of which he had been found guilty by the Norman process of the judicial duel usual in the manor-courts, and over whose fate the townsmen, rejoicing in the Old-English right of compurgation which they still retained, grew so bitterly sarcastic that the abbot and the "saner part of the convent" were driven by

---

[1] Riley, *Munim. Gildh.*, vol. ii. pt. i. pp. 249-251. Date, Bonneville, July 5, 1199.   [2] Stubbs, *Select Charters*, pp. 314, 315.

[3] Mat. Paris, *Chron. Maj.* (Luard), vol. ii. p. 605.

terror of a peasant revolt to admit their rural tenants to a
share in the judicial franchise of the town [1]—was in all
probability only one out of many.   The history of this same
abbey of S. Edmund's shews us how even the villeins were
rising into a position more like that of their free brethren,
how the old badges of serfdom, the heavy labour-rents, the
hard customs, were vanishing one by one, and how in this
process of enfranchisement the boroughs led the way.[2]   "The
ancient customs belonging to the cellarer's office, as we have
seen them "—that is, as Jocelyn of Brakelond, who was a
monk of S. Edmund's from 1172 to 1211, had seen them
in the old custom-roll of the house—"were these : The
cellarer had his messuage and barn by the well of Scurun,
where he solemnly held his court for the trial of thieves and
of all pleas and quarrels ; and there he received the pledges
of his men, and enrolled them, and renewed them every
year, and got gain by it, as the reeve did in the portmannimot.   This messuage was the homestead of Beodric, who
of old time was lord of this township, whence it was called
Beodricesworth ; whose demesne lands are now in the
demesne of the cellarer ; and what is now called the *aver-
land* was the land of his rustics.   Now the sum of his
tenements and those of his men was three hundred and
thirty acres, which are lands still belonging to the township,
whereof the services, when the town was made free, were
divided into two parts ; so that the sacristan or the reeve
should receive the quit-rent, that is, twopence on every acre ;
and the cellarer should have the ploughings and other
services, that is, the ploughing of one rood for every acre,
without food (which custom is observed still) ; he was also
to have the folds wherein all the men of the township (except the seneschal, who has his own fold) were bound to put
their sheep (this custom, too, is observed still).   He was
also to have the *aver-penny*,[3] that is twopence for every

---

[1] Joc. Brakelond (Rokewode), p. 74.   See Mr. Green's *Stray Studies*, pp.
222-224, and *Hist. Eng. People*, vol. i. pp. 219, 220.

[2] On all this see Mr. Green's *Abbot and Town*, in *Stray Studies*, pp. 213-229.

[3] "The money paid by the tenant in commutation of the service (*avera*) of
performing any work for his lord by horse or ox, or by carriage with either."
Greenwell, Glossary to *Boldon Buke* (Surtees Soc.).

thirty acres; this custom was changed before the death of
Abbot Hugh (1180). For the men of the township had to
go at the cellarer's bidding to Lakenheath, to fetch a load
of eels from Southrey, and often they came back with their
carts empty, and so they had their trouble without any
benefit to the cellarer; wherefore it was agreed between
them that every thirty acres should pay a penny a year, and
the men should stay at home. At the present time, however,
these lands are so cut up that scarcely anybody knows from
whom the payment is due; so that whereas I have seen the
cellarer receive twenty-seven pence in a year, now he can
hardly get tenpence farthing. Moreover, the cellarer used
to have control over the roads outside the township, so that
no one might dig chalk or clay without his leave. He was
also wont to summon the fullers of the township to lend
cloths for carrying his salt; otherwise he would forbid them
the use of the waters, and seize whatever cloths he found
there; which customs are observed unto this day." "Moreover the cellarer alone ought, or used, to have one bull free
in the fields of this township; but now several persons have
them." "Moreover the cellarer used to warrant those who
owed service to his court, so that they were exempt from
scot and tallage; but now it is not so, because the burghers
say that those who do service at the court ought to be exempt for their service, but not for the burgage which they
hold in the town, and forasmuch as they and their wives do
publicly buy and sell in the market."[1] After the affair of
Ketel, in fact, the cellarer's court was merged in that of the
town; "it was decreed that his men should come to the
toll-house with the others, and there renew their pledges,
and be written in the reeve's roll, and there give to the
reeve the penny which is called *borth-silver*, and the cellarer
should have half of it (but he gets nothing at all of it
now); and all this was done, that all might enjoy equal
liberty."[2]

"That all might enjoy equal liberty"—Jocelyn's words
had a significance wider and deeper than he himself could
know, wider and deeper than could be known perhaps even

[1] Joc. Brakelond (Rokewode), pp. 75, 76.   [2] *Ib.* p. 74.

to his abbot from whom they were probably echoed; although it is clear from almost every page of Jocelyn's story that Abbot Sampson of S. Edmund's was a far more enlightened and far-seeing statesman than most of the great landowners of his day, whether secular or tonsured. The rural tenants of S. Edmund in his time had evidently made a good deal more progress towards enfranchisement than those of some other great houses, such as, for example, the abbey of Abingdon. In 1.185, on the death of Abbot Roger of Abingdon, a dispute between the "obedientiaries," or officers of the convent to whose support various portions of its revenues were assigned, and the steward appointed by the king to take charge of the abbot's property during the vacancy of his office, led to the drawing-up of a consuetudinary,[1] which it would be interesting to compare with the earlier "Black Book" of Peterborough. A large proportion of the tenants' dues were paid in money; but there were still considerable remnants of the older system. The chamberlain of the abbey, for instance, had an acre of land at Culham, which the men of that township were bound to reap and carry to make beds for the monks. The hay to be laid "under the monks' feet when they bathed" was supplied in like manner from a meadow at Stockgrave. A tenant named Daniel of Colebrook was bound, besides paying a rent of five shillings, to furnish the chamberlain whenever he went to London with hay for his horses, with wood and salt, and with straw for his bed. At Welsford, near Newbury, there were twenty-two "cotset-lands," whose tenants held them by their services as swineherds, bedels (or messengers of the chamberlain's court), shepherds, hedgewards and such like. Of eleven rent-paying tenants in the same township, one owed, besides his rent of twenty-seven pence, his personal service for getting in hay and stacking corn in August. As the whole township was in demesne, its inhabitants paid a tribute to the lord—in this case the chamberlain of the abbey—for the pannage of their pigs; they had also to furnish the services of one man for harvesting in August, and to lend their ploughs for bene-work. The men of Boxhole, Benham,

[1] *Hist. Mon. Abingdon* (Stevenson), vol. ii. pp. 297, 298.

Easton and Weston did the like.   At Boxhole, out of twelve tenants, eight were bound, besides paying their rent, to plough an acre of the demesne and sow it with their own seed ; and seven of these had moreover to carry hay and corn.   One Berner and his sons held a "cotset-land" by a rent of six sextaries of honey to the cellarer and thirty-one pence to the chamberlain.[1]   There were twenty-six tenants withdrawn from demesne, of whom six owed work in August, in addition to their rent; and there were five acres of meadow which had to be mowed and carried by five men of the township.   At Benham, out of twenty-four tenants, eleven were "cotsetles";· three of these were servants of the chamberlain, holding their lands by their service ; the rest were to hold by rent or by work, as the lord might choose[2]—an arrangement which applied also to the cotters of Boxhole.[3] Of the remaining thirteen tenants at Benham, six paid rent only ; the rest were bound also to plough and sow an acre or half an acre apiece, and to carry corn and hay.[4]   One was excused the ploughing and sowing, doubtless in consideration of her sex and condition—she was " Ernive a widow."[5]   The whole township owed a customary payment or church-shot of forty-six hens.[6]

On the manor of Weston the dues were thus distributed: Robert of Pont-de-l'Arche held four acres of the abbot "by the service of half a knight."   One acre belonged to the church of the township ; half a hide was held by John of S. Helen's, on what terms we are not told.   Of the remainder, over which the chamberlain was lord, half a hide was in demesne ; the rest was distributed in ten portions, held by thirteen tenants—a hide or half a hide being in three cases held by two persons conjointly.   Two hides and a half were for work or for gavel, at the option of the lord ; in actual practice, however, there were only two cotters who owed labour instead of, or in addition to, their money-rent.   On

---

[1] *Hist. Mon. Abingdon* (Stevenson), vol. ii. pp. 300-302.

[2] *Ib.* pp. 303-305.   [3] *Ib.* p. 303.

[4] And this though one of them was no less a personage than *Gaufridus vice-comes !* What can this mean ? *Hist. Mon. Abingdon* as above, pp. 304, 305.

[5] *Ib.* p. 304.   [6] *Ib.* p. 305.

the other hand, the right of poundage, or exemption from
impounding of cattle, was paid for in this village by the
ploughing of two acres.[1]   The township of Berton and
several others were bound to furnish sumpter-horses for conveying fish to the abbey-kitchen thrice a year ; the persons
responsible for this service had to pay their own travelling
expenses and those of their horses; but they got each a loaf
from the abbey when they left ; and those who could not
fulfil the service were allowed to compound for it with the
kitchener " as best they could."   The same manors rendered
each five hundred eggs on the feast of the Nativity of the
Blessed Virgin, at Christmas, Easter, Rogation-tide and
Pentecost ; and three hundred at Candlemas and Quinquagesima, besides eighteen hens apiece at the festivals of
S. Martin and at Christmas.   They also gave on the Wednesday before Easter a hundred herrings, which on the following
Thursday were distributed to the poor ;[2] and each of them
sent moreover to the monks' kitchen, in the course of the
year, besides the eggs and hens already enumerated, twenty-
four bushels of beans.[3]   Eight fisheries were bound to furnish
each a certain number of eels on Ash-Wednesday ;[4] the
fishermen who carried the eels to the hall were entitled to
receive thence two loaves apiece.[5]   From another fishery a
money-rent of seventeen shillings was due, paid in three
terms ; and its holder owed church-shot of twelve hens.[6]
Berton furnished five loads of straw, and Culham as many of
hay, three times a year—on Christmas Eve, Easter Eve, and
All Saints' Eve—for strewing the refectory.[7]   When the
chamberlain went to Winchelcombe fair, the men of Dumble-
ton were bound to bring home for him whatever he purchased
there ; the same duty fell to the tenantry of Welford when
he went to the fair at Winchester.[8]

If we compare this Abingdon consuetudinary of 1185
with the Peterborough Black Book of 1128, the main result
seems to be this : the Abingdon dues are quite as heavy, if

---

[1] *Hist. Mon. Abingdon* (Stevenson), vol. ii. pp. 305, 306.
[2] *Ib.* pp. 307, 308.   [3] *Ib.* p. 323.
[4] *Ib.* pp. 308, 323.   [5] *Ib.* p. 308.
[6] *Ib.* p. 309.   [7] *Ib.* p. 313.   [8] *Ib.* pp. 326, 327.

not heavier, but the labour-services are much lighter. We must not indeed assume that the difference is wholly owing to progress made during the half-century which elapsed between the compilation of the two books ; the customs of different localities varied in all ages, and those of Abingdon may never have been so hard as those of Peterborough. On the estates of the bishop of Durham, on the other hand, when Hugh of Puiset took account of his dues in 1183, the old labour-rents and customs seem to have subsisted almost without alteration. A large proportion of the villeins on the bishop's manors were holders of two bovates or oxgangs of thirty acres each, for which each man paid two shillings and sixpence for scot-pennies, half a chalder of oats, sixteen pence for aver-pennies, five cart-loads of wood, two hens and ten eggs ; he had to work for the lord three days every week throughout the year except Easter-week, Whitsun-week and the twelve days of Christmas ; moreover, he and all his family, except the house-wife, had to do in autumn four days boon-work in reaping ; besides this, he had to reap three roods of *averipe* (ripe oats), and plough and harrow three roods of *averere* (oat-stubble). Each villein plough had to plough and harrow two acres ; on this occasion the villeins had a corrody from the bishop, and so they had on occasion of a great boon-work. They were to harrow whenever required ; to perform services of carting, for which they got every man a loaf ; to make each one booth for the fair of S. Cuthbert ; "and when they make lodges" (possibly for the bishop's hunting) "and cart wood, they are free of other work." These were the services due from twenty-two out of the thirty-six tenants on the manor of Boldon. Of the remainder, twelve were "cotmen," holding each twelve acres and working throughout the year, except at the above-named seasons, two days a week, and rendering twelve hens and sixty eggs. One man held two oxgangs of thirty-seven acres, at a rent of half a mark ; another was the pounder, who held twelve acres, received from each plough one thrave of corn, and rendered twenty-four hens and five hundred eggs. The mill paid five marks and a half. The villeins were bound to give their labour every year, if required, for

the building of a house (perhaps a hunting-lodge) forty feet
long and fifteen feet wide ; in that case they were forgiven
fourpence for aver-pennies. The whole township rendered
seventeen shillings for cornage, and one cow.[1] Clevedon
and Whitburn contained twenty-eight villeins and twelve
cotmen whose services were the same as at Boldon ; besides
these and the pounder, there were four other tenants ; one
held two bovates of twenty-four acres at a rent of sixteenpence, and " went on the bishop's errands "; one held sixty
acres and a toft at eightpence, and fulfilled the same duty ;
the other two held their lands at a money-rent only.[2] At
Sedgefield there were fifty-one tenants, of whom twenty were
villeins holding and labouring on the same terms as their
brethren at Boldon ; twenty more were " farmers," holding
two bovates apiece, paying five shillings, ploughing and
harrowing half an acre, and finding two men to mow, two to
reap, and two to make hay, for two days, and also one cart
for two days to carry corn, and the same to cart hay ; they
also did four days' boon-work in autumn with all their families
except the housewives.   The reeve, the smith and the
carpenter held land by their service ; the pounder got his
thraves of corn and paid his dues in hens and eggs as on the
other manors.   Five *bordarii* held five tofts, paid five shillings,
and did four days' boon-work.   William of Oldacres and
Uhtred of Butterwick held lands, whose extent is not specified,
at a rent of sixteen shillings and half a mark respectively.[3]
At Norton there were thirty villeins holding and labouring
like those of Boldon, save that for lack of pasture-land they
owed no cornage ; and twenty farmers, whose tenure was
much the same as that of the farmers of Sedgefield.   Alan of
Normanton held one carucate for ten shillings, and had to
find thirty-two men for a day's work when required, four
carts for one day or two for two days for carrying corn, and
the same for carting hay ; besides which his men, if he had
any, were to work four boon-days in autumn with all their
families except the housewives, but Alan himself and his

---

[1] *Boldon Buke* (Greenwell), pp. 3, 4.   Cornage was a " payment made in
commutation of a return of cattle " (*ib.* Glossary).
[2] *Ib.* p. 5.   [3] *Ib.* p. 11.

own household were free of this service. Adam, son of
Gilbert of Hardwick, held a large piece of land by a money-
rent. There was a mill, with eight acres and a meadow, and
rendering twenty marks ; a pounder, holding on the usual
terms ; and there were twelve cotmen, holding tofts and crofts,
and paying partly in money, partly in work.[1] The palatine
bishopric, it is clear, was an old-fashioned district where
innovations of any kind were slow to penetrate. Even here,
however, the newer system of money-payment in commutation of service was beginning to make its appearance. The
tenures on the manor of Whickham had undergone a sweeping
change, apparently not long before Bishop Hugh's survey
was drawn up. On this manor there were thirty-five villeins,
holding each an oxgang of fifteen acres. Each of these had
been wont to pay sixteenpence, and to work three days a
week throughout the year, three boon-days in autumn
with all his family except his wife, and a fourth boon-day
with two men; in their ordinary work they had to mow the
grass, to cut and carry the hay, to reap and carry the corn;
and over and above this, they had to plough and harrow two
acres of *averere* with each plough ; for this, however, they
had a corrody. They had also, in the course of their work,
to " make a house " forty feet long and fifteen feet wide, to
make three fisheries in the Tyne, and to do carting and
carrying like the villeins of Boldon ; they gave nine shillings
cornage, one cow, and for every oxgang one hen and ten
eggs. " Now, however," adds the record, " the said manor
of Whickham is at farm "—demesne, villeins, mill, fisheries
and all :—it may possibly, like its neighbour Ryton, have been
let at farm to the tenants themselves ; but at any rate, its
entire services and dues, except a small tribute of hens and
eggs, were commuted for a rent of six-and-twenty pounds.[2]

On the whole, the glimpses which we get of the condition of the rural population of England under the Angevin
kings seem to indicate that they were by no means excluded
from a share in the progress of the kingdom at large. Even
if their dues had grown heavier, this surely points to an
advance in agricultural prosperity and of the material ease

---

[1] *Boldon Buke* (Greenwell), pp. 12, 13.   [2] *Ib.* pp. 33, 34.

and comfort which are its natural results. The spread of industry shewed itself in many ways. In the towns we can trace it in the growing importance of the handicraftsmen, proved by the jealousy with which their gilds were regarded by the central government and still more by the civic authorities. The weavers seem to have been special objects of civic dislike ; in most of the great towns they were treated as a sort of outcasts by the governing body ; and in 1201 the London citizens bought of John, at the price of twenty silver marks a year and sixty marks down, a charter authorizing them to turn the weavers out of the city altogether. The sequel of this bargain is eminently characteristic of John ; but it is equally significant of the growing influence of the craftsmen. The king took the citizens' money and gave them the charter which they desired, but he made it null and void by granting his protection to the weavers as before, merely exacting from them an annual payment of twenty marks instead of eighteen.[1]

Hand in hand with the growth of industry went the growth of trade. Markets and fairs were springing up everywhere, and a keen commercial rivalry sprang up with them. The little borough of S. Edmund's set up a " merchant-gild," whose members insisted that all who did not belong to it must pay toll in their market.[2] The great success of Abingdon fair in Henry's early years stirred up the jealousy of both Wallingford and Oxford, and their remonstrances compelled the king to order that inquisition should be made, through twenty-four of the old men of the shire " who were living in his grandfather's time," whether the obnoxious little township had in those days enjoyed the privilege of a market. The case was tried in full shire-moot at Farnborough; the twenty-four elders were duly elected, and swore that Abingdon had had a full market in the time of King Henry the First. The jurors were however challenged by the opposing party, whereupon Henry ordered " the men of Wallingford and the whole county of Berkshire " to meet before his justices at Oxford, and there to choose fresh recognitors.

[1] Riley, *Munim. Gildh.*, vol. ii. pt. i. introd. pp. lxi-lxiii.
[2] Joc. Brakelond (Rokewode), p. 74.

This time the jury could not agree among themselves. The Wallingford jurors swore that they remembered nothing sold at Abingdon in the first King Henry's reign except bread and ale.; the Oxford men admitted more than this, but not a "full market"—nothing brought by cart or boat (there was an old-standing quarrel between Oxford and Abingdon about boat-cargoes and river-tolls); the shiremen acknowledged that there had been a "full market," but doubted whether goods were carried thither by any boats save those belonging to the abbot himself. The justiciar, Earl Robert of Leicester, who was presiding over the court in person, transmitted these various opinions to the king without venturing to decide the case. As it chanced, however, he could —so at least the Abingdon story ran—add to them an useful reminiscence of his own childhood : he had himself seen a full market at Abingdon not only in the days of King Henry I., but as far back as the days of King William, when he, Earl Robert, was a little boy in the abbey-school. And so the men of Abingdon won their case.[1]

Disputes of this kind, however, were not always so peacefully settled. Some forty years later—in 1201—the monks of Ely set up, under the protection of a royal charter, a market at Lakenheath, within the " liberties " of S. Edmund's abbey. The chapter of S. Edmund's, " together with their friends and neighbours," sent to Ely an amicable remonstrance against this proceeding, adding that they would willingly make good the fifteen marks which the monks of Ely had paid for their charter, if these latter would consent to forego the use of it. The remonstrance however produced no effect. The brotherhood of S. Edmund's therefore demanded a recognition to declare whether the new market had been set up to their injury, and to the injury of the market at their own town. The verdict of the recognitors decided that it was so. The next step was to inform the king, and ascertain from him the exact tenour of his charter

---

[1] *Hist. Mon. Abingdon* (Stevenson), vol. ii. pp. 227-229. This happened 1158-1161. Mr. Eyton (*Itin. Hen. II.*, pref. pp. v, vi) denies on chronological grounds the authenticity of Earl Robert's supposed witness to the state of affairs in the Conqueror's time. He does not adduce his proofs ; I can therefore only leave this part of the matter undecided, and take the Abingdon story as I find it.

to Ely; search was made in the royal register, and it was found that the market had been granted only on condition that it should not damage the interests of other markets in the neighbourhood. Hereupon the king, for a promise of forty marks, gave to S. Edmund's a charter providing that no market should thenceforth be set up within the liberties of the abbey save by the abbot's consent; and he issued orders to the justiciar, Geoffrey Fitz-Peter, for the abolition of the market at Lakenheath. The justiciar sent on the order to the sheriff of Suffolk; and the sheriff, having no jurisdiction within the liberties of S. Edmund's, forwarded it to the abbot for execution. Next market-day the hundred-reeve came to Lakenheath, and shewing the letters of king and sheriff, supported by the testimony of the freemen, forbade the market in the king's name; he was however met with nothing but contempt and abuse. The abbot, who was in London at the time, after consulting with some "wise men" there, wrote to his bailiffs bidding them assemble all the men of S. Edmund's with their horses and arms, overthrow the market by force, and take prisoners as many of the buyers and sellers as they could. In the middle of the night some six hundred well-armed men set out from S. Edmund's for Lakenheath. When they reached it the market was deserted; all the stall-holders had fled. The prior of Ely was at Lakenheath with his bailiffs, having come that same night in expectation of the intended attack; but he "would not come out of his house"; so the bailiffs of S. Edmund's, after vainly demanding pledges from him that he would "stand to right" in the abbey-court, seized the butchers' trestles and the planks which formed the stalls, as well as the cart-horses, sheep and oxen, "yea, and all the beasts of the field," and carried them away to Icklingham. The prior's bailiffs hurried in pursuit, and begged to have their goods on pledge for fifteen days, which was granted. Within the fifteen days came a writ summoning the abbot to answer for this affair at the Exchequer, and to restore the captured animals. "For the bishop of Ely, who was a man of ready and eloquent speech, had complained in his own person to the justiciar and the great men of England, saying that an unheard-of insult had been done to S. Etheldreda in time of peace ; wherefore many were greatly stirred up against the abbot." [1]

The developement of foreign commerce, resulting from the wide-spread relations of the Angevin kings with lands on both sides of the sea which encompassed their island-realm, woke a rivalry no less keen between some of the great trading cities, although they might shew it in less rough and ready fashion than the champions of the mercantile privileges of S. Edmund's.   One interesting illustration has recently come to light, in a writ of Henry II. to the bailiffs of Dublin in favour of the citizens of Chester. Henry, as we know, had granted to the men of Bristol the right of colonizing Dublin and holding it of him and his heirs with the same liberties and privileges as were enjoyed by Bristol itself.   Bristol and Chester had for ages been rivals in the trade with Ireland ; Chester now saw itself in imminent danger of being altogether shut out of that trade, an exclusion which would have meant little less than ruin to the city.   We can hardly doubt that its citizens appealed to the king for a reservation of their commercial privileges in Dublin as against the Bristol merchants.   At any rate, Henry in 1175 or 1176 issued a writ to the bailiffs of Dublin commanding that the burghers of Chester should be free to buy and sell at Dublin as they had been wont to do, and should have the same rights, liberties and free customs there as they had had in his grandfather's days.[2]   Yet more important than the trade of the western seaports with Ireland was that of the eastern coast, not only with the continental dominions of the Angevin house, but with almost the whole of Europe.   Not the least beneficial result of the Angevins' renewal of the old political ties between England and the Empire was the increase of trade which it helped to bring from the merchant-cities of northern Germany and the

---

[1] Joc. Brakelond (Rokewode), pp. 98, 99.

[2] The real meaning of this writ is pointed out by Mr. J. H. Round in the *Academy*, May 29, 1886 (new issue, No. 734, p. 381).   The writ itself is there reprinted from the Eighth Report of the Royal Commission on Historical MSS., where it has been wrongly interpreted, owing to a misreading of the word which stands for Dublin.

Low Countries to the port of London. Nor were the kings themselves blind to the advantage of these commercial relations. Richard on the eve of his return from captivity in 1194 granted to the citizens of Cöln a gildhall in London, "with all their other customs and demands," for an annual payment of two shillings.[1] The hall of the other Teutonic merchants—famous in later days under the name of the Steel-yard—was probably established about the same period ; and early in the following century we find an elaborate and interesting code of regulations for the trade of the Lorrainers, the " men of the Emperor of Germany," the Danes and the Norwegians.[2] The developement of commerce brought with it a corresponding growth of riches, and of the material comforts and refinements of life. Domestic architecture began to improve. Henry Fitz-Aylwine issued at the opening of his mayoralty an " Assize " which has been described as " the earliest English Building Act," and which at any rate shews that the civic authorities were earnestly endeavouring to secure health and comfort in the houses within their jurisdiction, and also to guard against the risk of fire which had ruined so many citizens in times past.[3] Ecclesiastical architecture progressed still more rapidly ; church-building or rebuilding went on all over the country on a scale which proves how great was the advance, both in artistic taste and material wealth, which England had made under the just rule and peaceful administration of her first Angevin king. At the opening of John's reign the citizens of London were contemplating an important architectural work of another kind : they were planning to replace the wooden bridge over the Thames with a bridge of stone. Degenerate representative as he was in more important respects of the " great builders " of Anjou, John had yet inherited a sufficient share of their tastes to feel interested in such an undertaking as this ; and in April 1202 we find him writing to the mayor and citizens of London to recom-

[1] Riley, *Munim. Gildh.*, vol. ii. pt. i. introd. p. xli, from *Placita de quo warranto*, p. 468.

[2] Riley as above, pp. 61, 64, and introd. pp. xxxv-xxxix.

[3] Fitz-Aylwine's Assize is printed by Mr. Stapleton from the *Liber de Antiquis Legibus*, pp. 206-211. It is there dated 1189.

mend them an architect, Isenbert, master of the schools at Saintes, whose skill in the construction of bridges had been lately proved at Saintes and at La Rochelle.[1]   The citizens however seem not to have adopted the king's suggestion ; they found an architect among themselves, in the person of Peter, chaplain or curate of S. Mary Colechurch—the little church beneath whose shadow S. Thomas the martyr was born.   It was Peter who "began the stone bridge at Lon don"; and in a chapel on that bridge his body found its appropriate resting-place when he died in 1205.[2]

There can be little doubt that a large part of the means for this developement of commercial and architectural energy was furnished by the Jews.   The Jewish settlements increased rapidly both in numbers and in importance under Henry II.   In the Pipe Rolls of his first five years we find, in addition to the London Jews who appeared in the thirty-first year of his grandfather, and those of Oxford and Lincoln of whom there are traces in the next reign, Jewries at Norwich, Cambridge, Thetford and Bungay, as well as at an unnamed place in Suffolk, which from other evidence seems to have been Bury S. Edmund's ;[3] and we have already seen that before Henry's death there were important Hebrew colonies at Lynn, Stamford, York, and many other places. At Winchester the Jews were so numerous and so prosperous that a writer in Richard's early years calls it their Jerusalem.[4]   The great increase in their numbers throughout England during Henry's reign is shewn by the fact that in 1177 he found it necessary to grant them permission for the making of a Jewish burial-ground outside the walls of every city in England, instead of sending all their dead to be buried in London, as had been the practice hitherto.[5] Legally, the Jews were still simply chattels of the king.

[1] Rymer, *Fœdera*, vol. i. p. 83.
[2] Ann. Waverl. a. 1205 (Luard, *Ann. Monast.*, vol. ii. pp. 256, 257).
[3] Jews at Norwich, Pipe Roll 2 Hen. II. (Hunter), p. 8 ; Cambridge, *ib.* p. 15 ; Thetford and Bungay, 5 Hen. II. (Pipe Roll Soc.), p. 12.   In 4 Hen. II. (Hunter), p. 127, the sheriff of Suffolk renders an account of twenty silver marks "pro Judæis"; as we find Jews at S. Edmund's at the opening of Richard's reign, it seems probable that they are the persons referred to here.
[4] Ric. Devizes (Stevenson), p. 62.   [5] *Gesta Hen.* (Stubbs), vol. i. p. 182.

Practically, they were masters of the worldly interests of a large number of his Christian subjects, and of a large portion of the wealth of his realm. Without their loans many a great and successful trading venture could never have been risked, many a splendid church could never have been built, nay, many a costly undertaking of the king himself might have been brought to a standstill for lack of funds necessary to its completion. The abbey-church of S. Edmund was rebuilt with money borrowed in great part, at exorbitant interest, from Jewish capitalists. Abbot Hugh, when he died in 1173, left his convent in utter fiscal bondage to two wealthy Jews, Isaac son of Rabbi Joses, and Benedict of Norwich.[1] The sacred vessels and jewels belonging to Lincoln minster were in the same year redeemed by Geoffrey, then bishop-elect, from Aaron, a rich Jew of the city who had had them in pledge for seven years or more.[2] In 1187 Aaron died ; his treasure was seized for the king, and a large part of it sent over sea. The ship which bore it went down between Shoreham and Dieppe, and the sum of the lost treasure was great enough for its loss to be chronicled as a grave misfortune by the treasurer, Bishop Richard Fitz-Nigel ;[3] while two years later the affairs of the dead Jew still made a prominent figure in the royal accounts.[4] His house, as it stands at the head of the " Steep Hill " of Lincoln to this day, is one of the best examples of a mode of domestic architecture to which Christian townsfolk had scarcely yet begun to aspire, but which was already growing common among those of his race : a house built entirely of stone, in place of the wooden or rubble walls and thatched roofs which, even after Fitz-Aylwine's Assize, still formed the majority of dwellings in the capital itself.

It is no wonder that these people, with their untold stores of wealth, their independence of all ordinary jurisdictions, their exemption from all the burthens of civil life,

[1] Joc. Brakelond (Rokewode), pp. 2, 3.
[2] Gir. Cambr. *Vita S. Remig.*, c. 24 (Dimock and Freeman, vol. vii. p. 36)
[3] *Gesta Hen.* (Stubbs), vol. ii. p. 5.
[4] Pipe Roll 1 Ric. I. (Hunter), pp. 8, 59, 219, 226, 229, 246.

their voluntary exclusion from the common brotherhood of Christendom, their strange aspect and their mysterious language, were objects of universal jealousy, suspicion and hatred, which they on their part took but little pains to conciliate or allay. The religious feelings of the whole population of Oxford were outraged by a Jew who publicly mocked at S. Frideswide amid the solemnities of her festival-day, well knowing that neither prior nor bishop, chancellor nor portreeve, dared lift a finger to check or to punish him.[1] Darker stories than this, however, were whispered against his race. They were charged not only with ruining many Englishmen of all classes by their usury, and with openly insulting the Christian sacraments and blaspheming the Christians' Lord, but with buying Christians for money in order to crucify them.[2] A boy, afterwards canonized as S. William, was said to have been thus martyred at Norwich in 1137 ;[3] another, Robert, at S. Edmund's in 1181 ;[4] and a third at Winchester in 1192.[5] Little as we may be inclined to believe such tales, we can scarcely wonder that they found credit at the time, and that the popular hatred of the Jews went on deepening till it broke out in the massacres of 1190. That outbreak compelled the king to interfere in behalf of his "chattels"; but the fines with which he punished it, though they deterred the people from any further attempts to get rid of the Jews by force, could not alter the general feeling. At S. Edmund's Abbot Sampson, immediately after the massacre, sought and obtained a royal writ authorizing him to turn all the remaining Jews out of the town at once and for ever ;[6] and in 1194 Richard, or Hubert Walter in his name, found it needful to make an elaborate ordinance for the regulation of Jewish loans throughout the realm and the security of Jewish bonds. Such loans were to be made only in six or seven appointed places, before two "lawful Christians," two "lawful Jews," two "lawful writers," and two clerks specially named in the

---

[1] *Mirac. S. Fridesw.*, in *Acta SS.*, vol. lvi. p. 576 (October 19).
[2] R. Coggeshall (Stevenson), p. 28.   [3] Eng. Chron. a. 1137.
[4] Joc. Brakelond (Rokewode), p. 12.   [5] Ric. Devizes (Stevenson), p. 60.
[6] Joc. Brakelond (Rokewode), p. 33.

ordinance ; the deed was to be drawn up in the form of an indenture ; one half, sealed with the borrower's seal, was to be given to the Jewish lender ; the other half was to be deposited in a common chest having three locks ; the two Christians were to keep one key, the two Jews another, and the two royal clerks the third ; and the chest was to be sealed with three seals, one being affixed by each of the parties who held the keys. The clerks were to have a roll containing copies of all such deeds ; for every deed three-pence were to be paid, half that sum by the Jew and half by his creditor ; the two scribes got a penny each, and the keeper of the roll the third ; and no transactions whatsoever in connexion with these Hebrew bonds was henceforth to take place save in accordance with these regulations.[1]

It is just possible that this growth of anti-Jewish feeling may have helped in some degree to the growth of a sense of national unity among the other dwellers in the land. All Christians, to whatever race they might belong, whatever tongue they might speak, could not but feel themselves to be one people as against these Oriental intruders. It is at any rate clear that of the foreign elements which had been infused into the population of England during the hundred and forty years which had passed since Duke William landed at Pevensey, the Hebrew element was the only one which had not amalgamated with the native mass. The fusion in blood between Normans and English, which we saw making rapid progress under Henry I., was before the end of his grandson's reign so far complete that the practice of " pre-sentment of Englishry "—that is, the privilege whereby the hundred in which a man was found slain escaped paying the murder-fine to the treasury, if it could prove that the victim was not of Norman blood—had to be given up because the two nationalities had become so intermixed in every class above that of serfs that it could hardly ever be made out to which of them any man really belonged.[2] In this fusion

---

[1] Rog. Howden (Stubbs), vol. iii. pp. 266, 267. These " Capitula de Judæis " form the twenty-fourth chapter of *Forma procedendi in placitis Coronæ Regiæ* (see above, p. 337), printed also in Stubbs, *Select Charters*, pp. 259-263.

[2] *Dial. de Scacc.*, l. i. c. 10 (Stubbs, *Select Charters*, pp. 201, 202).

the English element, as it was far the larger, was also the weightier and the stronger.   In the matter of speech it was fast regaining its supremacy.   Foreign priests and foreign prelates were learning to speak and to preach to the English people in their own tongue ; Norman barons and knights were learning to talk English with their English-speaking followers and dependents ; some of them were learning to talk it with their own wives.[1]   If the pure Teutonic speech of our forefathers had suffered some slight corruption from foreign influences, Walter Map's legend of the well at Marlborough whereof whosoever drank spoke bad French for ever after[2] may hint that the language of the conquerors was becoming somewhat Anglicized in the mouths of some at least of their descendants ; and the temper of these adoptive Englishmen was changing yet more rapidly than their speech.   Of the many individual figures which stand out before us, full of character and life, in the pages of the twelfth-century historians, the one who in all ages, from his own day to ours, has been unanimously singled out as the typical Englishman is the son of Gilbert of Rouen and Rohesia of Caen.

The whole policy of the Angevin kings tended to mould their insular subjects into an united English nation.   Their equal administration completed that wiping-out of local distinctions which had been begun by the wisdom of the Norman kings and helped on by the confusion of the civil war ; their developement of old English methods of judicial and administrative procedure brought the English people again visibly and tangibly to the forefront of affairs.   Even those very qualities and tendencies which were most un-English in the Angevins themselves helped indirectly to a like result.   The almost world-wide range of their political interests gave England once more a place among the nations, and a place far more important than any which she had ever before held.   For, above all, it was England

---

[1] See the story of Helwyse de Morville and her husband—parents of the Hugh de Morville who was one of the murderers of S. Thomas—in Will. Cant. (Robertson, *Becket*, vol. i.), p. 128.

[2] W. Map, *De Nug. Cur.*, dist. v. c. 6 (Wright, pp. 235, 236).

that they represented in the eyes of the continental powers;
it was as "Kings of the English" that they stood before
the world; and it was as Kings of the English that their
successors were to stand there still, when the Angevin
empire had crumbled into dust.   On the eve of that catastrophe the new England found a voice.   The English
tongue once more asserted its right to a place among the
literary tongues of Europe.   The higher English poetry,
which had slumbered ever since the days of Cædmon, suddenly woke again to life among the Worcestershire hills.
The story of the origin of Layamon's *Brut* can never be told
half so well as in the poet's own words.   "A priest there
was in the land, Layamon was he named; he was Leove-
nath's son; may the Lord be gracious to him!   He dwelt
at Ernley, at a noble church by Severn's bank—good it
there seemed to him!—hard by Radstone, where he read
books.   It came into his mind, and into his chief thoughts,
that he would tell the noble deeds of Englishmen—what
they were called, and whence they came, who first owned
English land. . . . Layamon began to journey wide over
this land, and got the noble books that he took for models.
He took the English book that Saint Beda made; another
he took, in Latin, that Saint Albin made, and the fair
Austin, who brought baptism in hither; a third book he
took, and laid there in the midst, that a French clerk made,
Wace was he called, who well could write, and he gave it to
the noble Eleanor who was the high King Henry's queen.
Layamon laid these books before him, and turned the leaves;
he lovingly beheld them; may the Lord be merciful to him!
Pen he took with fingers and wrote on a bookskin, and the
true words set together, and the three books compressed
into one."[1]   We must not blame a dweller on the western
border in the early days of King John if, when setting himself to tell "the noble deeds of Englishmen," he thought it
needful to begin with the fall of Troy after the pattern of
Wace and Wace's original, Geoffrey of Monmouth.   We can
only be thankful to this simple English priest for leaving to
us a purely English poem of more than thirty thousand lines

[1] Layamon (Madden), vol. i. pp. 1-3.

which is indeed beyond all price, not only as a specimen of our language at one of its most interesting stages, but as an abiding witness to the new spirit of patriotism which, ten years and more before the signing of the Great Charter, was growing up in such quiet corners of the land as this little parish of "Ernley" (or Areley Kings) by Severn-side. The subject-matter of Layamon's book might be taken chiefly from his French guide, Wace; but its spirit and its language are both alike thoroughly English. The poet's "chief thought," as he says himself, was to "tell the noble deeds of Englishmen," to Englishmen, in their own English tongue. A man who wrote with such an ambition as this was surely not unworthy of the simple reward which was all that he asked of his readers : "Now prayeth Layamon, for love of Almighty God, every good man that shall read this book and learn this counsel, that he say together these soothfast words for his father's soul, and for his mother's soul, and for his own soul, that it may be the happier thereby. Amen!"[1]

Layamon's *Brut* was written at some time between John's crowning and his return to England, after the loss of Normandy, in 1206.[2] It was a token that, on both sides of the sea, the Angevins' work was all but ended, their mission all but fulfilled. The noblest part of that mission was something of which they themselves can never have been fully conscious; and yet perhaps through that very unconsciousness they had fulfilled it the more thoroughly. "The silent growth and elevation of the English people"— as that people's own historian has taught us—"was the real work of their reigns;"[3] and even from a survey so imperfect as ours we may see that when John came home in 1206 the work was practically done.

---

[1] Layamon (Madden), vol. i. pp. 3, 4.

[2] On the date, etc., of Layamon see Sir F. Madden's preface to his edition of the *Brut*, vol. i. ; and Mr. Morley's *English Writers*, vol. i. pp. 632-635.

[3] Green, *Stray Studies*, p. 217.

INDEX

AARON of Lincoln, ii. 487
Abelard, i. 480
Abingdon, its customs in 1185, ii. 475-477 ; its fair, 481, 482. *See* Faricius
Achard, lord of Châlus, ii. 382, 383
Aclea, battle of, i. 102
Acre taken by the crusaders, ii. 319
Adaland, archbishop of Tours, i. 131, 132
Adalbert, count of Périgord, i. 145
Adam, Master, i. 482, 492, 493
Adam de Bruce, ii. 145
Adam de Port, ii. 162
Adela, first wife of Geoffrey Greygown, i. 121, 135
Adela, countess of Chalon - sur - Saône, second wife of Geoffrey Greygown, i. 121, 134, 135, 199
Adela of France, daughter of Louis VII. and Eleanor, i. 445
Adela, daughter of Louis VII. and Constance, born, i. 468 ; betrothed to Richard, ii. 62 ; offered to John, 314 ; marries the count of Ponthieu, 374
Adela of Blois, daughter of Theobald IV., third wife of Louis VII., i. 468
Adela, daughter of William the Conqueror, wife of Stephen-Henry of Blois, i. 272 ; her children, 273
Adela of Vendôme, daughter of Fulk Nerra and Elizabeth, i. 172
Adela, *see* Hermengard
Adelaide or Blanche, mother of Queen Constance, i. 191, 192
Adelard of Bath, i. 94, 95
Adeliza of Louvain, second wife of Henry I., i. 94 ; married to William of Aubigny, 298 ; receives the Empress Matilda, i. 309
Ademar, count of Angoulême, ii. 316, 381, 398, 399
Ademar, viscount of Limoges, ii. 220, 230, 381, 382
Adrian IV., Pope, i. 476 ; his relations

with the English Church and the *Curia Theobaldi*, 477 ; friendship with John of Salisbury, 485 ; bull for conquest of Ireland, 431 ; ii. 95, 96, 182 ; relations with Henry II., i. 497 ; dies, 498. *See* Nicolas
Ælendis of Amboise, wife of Ingelger, i. 105, 131
Aerschot, *see* Arnold
Agnes of Burgundy, her marriages, i. 174, 197-199 ; kinship with Geoffrey Martel, 136, 175, 199 ; divorced, 212
Agnes of Merania, ii. 395, 401
Agnes of Poitou, daughter of William IV., marries Emperor Henry III., i. 176
"Aids" from towns, i. 25, 29 ; the Sheriff's, ii. 15 ; *pour fille marier*, 125, 126 ; for the king's ransom, 325
Aileach, kings of, *see* Donell, Murtogh
Alan Barbetorte, count of Nantes and duke of Britanny, i. 115
Alan III., duke of Britanny, helps Herbert Wakedog against Avesgaud and Fulk, i. 159, note 4; marriage, 205; death, 206, 211
Alan Fergant, duke of Britanny, his marriages, i. 328, note 4
Alan, count of Nantes, i. 146
Alan of Richmond, i. 318, 319, 321
Albano, *see* Henry
Alberic, bishop of Ostia, legate, i. 299, 300
Alberic, count of Gâtinais, *see* Geoffrey
Albinus or Aubin, S., bishop of Angers, i. 98
Alcuin, i. 181
Aldgate, priory of Holy Trinity at, i. 66
Alençon, i. 208, 209 ; treaty of, 217 ; surrendered to Henry I., 233 ; restored to William Talvas, 236 ; won by Fulk V., *ib. See* Robert, William
Alexander II., Pope, i. 220

Alexander III., Pope, i. 498 ; acknowledged in France and England, 502 ; grants the pall to Thomas, ii. 6 ; meets Henry and Louis at Chouzy, 13 ; holds a council at Tours, 14 ; relation to the Becket quarrel, 29, 50-52 ; condemns Constitutions of Clarendon, 42 ; returns to Rome, 55 ; appoints Thomas legate, 67 ; sends commissioners to mediate between Henry and Thomas, 69, 70 ; authorizes Roger of York to crown young Henry, 71 ; forbids him, 72 ; interdicts the Angevin dominions and excommunicates the murderers of S. Thomas, 79 ; sends envoys to Henry, 80

Alexander, bishop of Lincoln, i. 83, 94, 303, 304

Alfhun, master of S. Bartholomew's hospital, i. 67

Alfonso II., king of Aragon, ii. 133 ; helps Richard in Aquitaine, 230, 231

Alfonso VIII., king of Castille, marries Eleanor, daughter of Henry II., ii. 60 ; submits his quarrel with Navarre to Henry's arbitration, 190

Alfonso Jordan, count of Toulouse, i. 455, 456, 458

Alfred of Beverley, ii. 445, 446

Alice of Maurienne betrothed to John Lackland, ii. 132-134 ; dies, 184

Almeric of Montfort, i. 232, 236, 237, 238, 241

Almeric, viscount of Thouars, ii. 395, 427, 428

Alnwick, ii. 161

Amboise, i. 105, 106 ; house of the Angevin counts at, 151 ; Odo's last attack on, 163. *See* Lisoy, Sulpice

Ambrières, i. 209, 211

Anagni, *see* John

Andegavi, i. 97

Andely, Isle of, ii. 376, 377 ; besieged by Philip, 411, 412 ; John's attempt to relieve it, 413-415 ; taken, 416

Andely, Nouvel or Petit, ii. 377 ; taken by Philip, 416 ; fate of its townsfolk, 417, 418

Andes, i. 97, 130

Andrew of London, i. 363

Angareth, wife of William de Barri, ii. 453

Angers (Juliomagus), i. 98 ; its position as a border-fortress, 101 ; seized by northmen, 103 ; relieved by Charles the Bald, *ib.*, 104 ; its aspect in tenth century, 108 ; palace of the counts, 109, 132-134, 165 ; of the bishops, 133 ; fires at, *ib.*, 152 ; R. Diceto's description of, 134 ; Henry I. of France at, 213 ; betrayed to

Fulk Rechin, 220 ; Urban II. at, 225 ; burghers of, revolt against Fulk V., 234 ; Fulk Nerra's buildings at, 165 ; abbeys of S. Aubin and S. Sergius at, 98 ; our Lady of Charity (Ronceray), 165 ; S. Nicolas, *ib.*, 172, 214, 225, 228 ; Henry II.'s buildings at, ii. 197, 199, 200 ; Henry and his sons at, 224 ; given up to Arthur, 389 ; seized by his friends, 407 ; retaken by John, 428 ; bishops, *see* Alhinus, Dodo, Rainald, Raino, Ulger

Angevin March, the, i. 101 ; its extent, 130

Angevins, *see* Anjou

Angoulême, disputed succession, ii. 220. *See* Ademar, Isabel, Matilda, Vulgrin, William

Anjou, its geographical position and character, i. 97 ; political position, 106, 107 ; its character as a march-land, 107 ; its golden age, 113 ; sources of its history, 126, 127 ; county of, "bipartite," 128, 129, 130 ; its extent, 97, 130 ; dependence on the duchy of France, 130 ; condition at Fulk Rechin's death, 229 ; placed under interdict, 242 ; revolts of the barons, 266-267, 343 ; rebels in (1173), ii. 136 ; condition under Henry II., 194-196 ; John acknowledged in, 388 ; accepts Arthur, 389 ; submits to Philip, 425 ; counts of, their origin, i. 105 ; character, 108 ; palace at Angers, 109, 132-134, 165 ; burial-place, 117, note 3 ; claims upon Nantes, 116, 117 ; upon Maine, i. 124, 140-142 ; the demon-countess, 143 ; house at Amboise, 151 ; rivalry with Blois, 145, 150, 188, 271, 279 ; extinction of the male line, 214 ; decline after Martel's death, 215, 218 ; relations with France, 164 ; ii. 357 ; growth of their power, 187, 188 ; career in Palestine, 239 ; their work for England, 490, 492. *See* Elias, Fulk, Geoffrey, Guy, Henry, Hermengard, Ingelger, Lambert, Matilda, Odo, Robert, Sibyl, William

Annonain, Pont de l', ii. 200, 201

Anselm, S., archbishop of Canterbury, i. 8, 9 ; his struggle with Henry I., 15-18 ; consecrates Malchus to Waterford, ii. 89 ; dies, i. 63 ; proposal to canonize him, ii. 14

Aquitaine, its relations with France, i. 123, 145, 383, 456, 457 ; ii. 202 ; extent and history, i. 454 ; granted to Richard, ii. 62 ; rebels in (1173), 136 ; country and people, 201, 203-205 ; its importance for England, 201 ; relations with Henry II., 203, 205 ; risings in, 58, 109, 220 ; submits, 230 ; proposal to give it to John, 233 ; restored to Richard, 247. *See* Eleanor, Odo, Richard, William

Aquitania, i. 99, 454

Aragon, *see* Alfonso, Ramirez, Petronilla

Arcelles, *see* Saher

Archambald, brother of Sulpice of Amboise, i. 194

Architecture, English, in twelfth century, i. 55

Aremburg of Maine, betrothed to Geoffrey Martel II., i. 226 ; marries Fulk V., 232 ; dies, 245

Argentan, i. 373 ; ii. 79, 80

Aristotle, study of, in the middle ages, ii. 466, 467

Arles, *see* Bertha, Burgundy, Provence, William

Armagh, synod at, ii. 105. *See* Malachi

Arms, Assize of, ii. 177, 178

Arnold, count of Aerschot, i. 362

Arnulf, bishop of Lisieux, i. 500 ; persuades Henry II. to acknowledge Pope Alexander, 501 ; advises Henry to appeal against Thomas, ii. 65 ; rebels, 140

Arques, i. 342 ; ii. 405, 406, 425

Arthur, King, i. 33 ; Henry II.'s correspondence with, ii. 57 note 2, 447 ; invention and translation of, 447, 448 ; romances of, 448, 449

Arthur, son of Geoffrey and Constance of Britanny, born, ii. 245 ; recognized by Richard as his heir, 295 ; in custody of Philip, 370 ; joins Richard, 374 ; acknowledged in Anjou, Touraine and Maine, 389 ; does homage to Philip, 390 ; quarrels with Philip and goes to John, 394 ; flies, 395 ; does homage to John, 397 ; knighted, 404 ; meets the Lusignans at Tours, 405 ; besieges Mirebeau, 406 ; captured, *ib.* ; imprisoned, 407 ; death, 408, 429, 430 ; its consequences, 409

Arundel, i. 10, 309. *See* William

Assize of Arms, ii. 177, 178 ; of Clarendon, 122, 123 ; of the Forest, 177 ; Great, 122 ; Henry Fitz-Aylwine's, 485 ; of Measures, 348 ; of *Mort d'ancester*, 172 ; of Northampton, 172, 173 ; later developements, 338-340

Aubigny, *see* William

Aubrey de Vere, i. 305

Augustinians, *see* Canons

Aulerci Cenomanni, i. 201, 202

Aumale, *see* William

Austin canons, *see* Canons

Austria, *see* Leopold

Autun, *see* Lambert

Auvergne, its feudal relations, ii. 202, 203 ; attacked by Philip, 252 ; Richard gives up his claims upon, 361

Auxerre, Thomas Becket studies at, i. 379

Avesgaud, bishop of Le Mans, i. 159 note 4, 204, 205

Avice of Gloucester betrothed to John Lackland, ii. 184 ; married, 282 ; divorced, 398

Avranches, ii. 81.

Axholm, ii. 152, 155

Azay, conference at, ii. 263

BAGGAMORE, i. 291

"Baille-hache," i. 353, 354

Bailleul, *see* Bernard, Jocelyn

Baldwin II., king of Jerusalem, i. 246

Baldwin III., king of Jerusalem, ii. 239

Baldwin IV., king of Jerusalem, ii. 239, 247

Baldwin, archbishop of Canterbury, takes the cross, ii. 248 ; preaches the crusade in Wales, 249 ; opposes John's marriage, 282 ; dies, 296, 297 ; his proposed college, 437

Baldwin, count of Flanders, i. 235

Baldwin of Clare, i. 318, 320

Baldwin of Redvers, i. 284

Balliol, *see* Bernard, Jocelyn

Ballon, i. 394

Bamborough, i. 288

Bar, i. 167

Barcelona, county of, i. 462. *See* Raymond-Berengar

Barnwell priory, ii. 463

Barri, *see* Gerald, William

Bartholomew, bishop of Exeter, i. 506

Bath, i. 35, 296. *See* Adelard

Bayeux, i. 11, 307. *See* Ralf

Baynard's Castle, i. 44

Beauchamp, *see* Miles

Beaugency, council at, i. 392

Beaulieu abbey (Hants), ii. 400

Beaulieu abbey (Touraine), i. 154, 155, 168

Beaumont, *see* Hermengard

Beauvais, council at, i. 502

Becket, *see* Gilbert, Rohesia, Thomas

Bedford, i. 320.

Bela III., king of Hungary, marries Margaret of France, ii. 235

Bellême, house of, i. 204. *See* Robert

Benedictines contrasted with the Cistercians, i. 73

"Bene-work," i. 57

Berengaria of Navarre, wife of Richard I., ii. 295, 296

Bermondsey, council at, i. 427

Bernard, S., abbot of Clairvaux, i. 70, 72 ;

his influence, 359; relations with Rome, 360, 361 ; with S. Malachi, ii. 94 ; plans for England, i. 364 ; pleads for Gerald of Montreuil, 388 ; recommends John of Salisbury to Abp. Theobald, 483 ; death, 400

Bernard de Balliol, ii. 145, 161

Berry, its feudal relations, ii. 202 ; war in, 245, 251, 252

Bertha of Arles, widow of Odo I. of Blois, marries King Robert, i. 149; separated, *ib.*

Bertha, daughter of Odo of Blois, wife of Alan of Britanny, i. 205 ; of Hugh II. of Maine, 206

Bertha, daughter of Conan III. of Britanny, i. 449

Bertrada of Montfort, marries Fulk Rechin, i. 223, 224 ; elopes with King Philip, 224 ; suspected of contriving her stepson's death, 228 ; her policy, 232

Bertrand de Born, ii. 204, 205 ; stirs up revolt in Aquitaine, 209, 220, 366 ; his *sirvente* for Toulouse, 211, 212; sets the young king against Richard, 222 ; submits, 231 ; enters a monastery, 371

Bertrand, count of Toulouse and Tripoli, i. 455

Beverley, i. 30, 37, 38. *See* Alfred

Béziers, *see* Raymond

Bigod, *see* Hugh

Biota of Maine, i. 217, 218, 254

Bishops, English, their political position, i. 20 ; appeal against Thomas, ii. 67. *See* Church

Blanche of Castille, daughter of Alfonso and Eleanor, ii. 395, 397

Blanche, *see* Adelaide

Blanchelande, i. 223, 257

Bloet, *see* Robert

Blois, counts of, their rivalry with Anjou, i. 145, 150, 188 ; their character, 150. *See* Adela, Bertha, Henry, Odo, Stephen, Theobald, William

Blondel, ii. 324

Bodmin, gild at, ii. 469

"Bogis," Peter, ii. 421, 422

Bohun, *see* Humfrey

Bologna, university of, ii. 460; S. Thomas at, i. 379

Bonmoulins, conference at, ii. 254, 255

Bonneville, i. 307 ; council at, ii. 157

"Boon-work," i. 57

Bordeaux, *see* William

Born, *see* Bertrand

Bosham, *see* Herbert

Boulogne, *see* Matilda, Matthew, Mary, William

Bourbon, *see* Hermengard

Bourges, its feudal relations, ii. 202

Bourgthéroulde, battle of, i. 241

Brabantines, ii. 223

Breakspear, *see* Nicolas

Breffny, ii. 97

Brenneville, battle of, i. 237

Brian Boroimhe, king of. Munster, ii. 85

Brian Fitz-Count, i. 243, 328, 396 ; his "book," 369

Bridgenorth, sieges of, i. 10, 429, 430

Brissarthe, i. 103

Bristol, i. 33, 34, 295, 296 ; its slave-trade, 35, ii. 87 ; Stephen's attempt on, i. 296, 297 ; ill-doings of its garrison, 297 ; Dermot of Leinster at, ii. 98, 99 ; Henry II.'s charters to, 118

Britanny, i. 99 ; its extent under Herispoë, 102 note 1, 130 ; civil wars in, 115 ; Geoffrey Martel's dealings with, 211, 212 ; claimed by Eudo of Porhoët and Conan of Richmond, 449; granted by Henry II. to Conan, 451 ; Henry's designs on, 452, 453; conquered by Henry, ii. 57, 58 ; rebels in (1173), 137; barons of, appeal to Philip against John, 408. *See* Alan, Arthur, Conan, Constance, Eleanor, Geoffrey, Herispoë, Hoel, Juhel, Nomenoë, Odo, Solomon

Broc, *see* Ralf

Bruce, *see* Adam, Robert

Brulon, *see* Geoffrey

Burchard, count of Vendôme, i. 149, 189

Burgundy, kingdom of, granted to Richard I., ii. 331. *See* Hugh, Robert, Rudolf.

Cadoc, ii. 416, 421, 425

Cadwallader, brother of Owen of North Wales, i. 435

Caen, surrendered to Henry I., i. 11 ; to Geoffrey Plantagenet, 307; to Philip, ii. 424 ; hospital, i. 471 ; ii. 198 ; palace, ii. 196, 197. *See* Robert

Cæsarodunum, see Tours

Cahors, i. 464, 466

Calixtus II., Pope, i. 237

Cambridge, ii. 462, 463

Camville, *see* Gerard

Candé, i. 228

Canons, Austin or Augustinian, their origin, i. 64, 65 ; character, 43, 66, 357 ; in England, 66-69. *See* Aldgate, Barnwell, Carlisle, Chiche, Kirkham, Nostell, Oseney, Oxford, Smithfield

Canons, White, i. 357

Canon law, its effects in England, ii. 18

Canterbury, canons of Laon visit, i. 30 ; plot to kill Henry Fitz-Empress at, 403 ; Thomas elected at, ii. 3 ; privilege of the archbishop to crown the king, 62 ; S. Thomas slain at, 79 ;

Henry II.'s penance at, 159 ; Louis VII. at, 216 ; Philip of Flanders at, 235 ; Richard at, 328 ; John crowned at, 400. *See* Anselm, Baldwin, Geoffrey, Hubert, John, Ralf, Richard, Roger, Theobald, Thomas, Walter, William

Capua, *see* Peter

Caputii, ii. 223, 224

Carcassonne, *see* Raymond Trencavel

Carham, i. 286, 287, 292. *See* Wark

Carlisle, i. 36, 37 ; S. Godric at, 76 ; council at, 300 ; Henry Fitz-Empress knighted at, 377 ; meeting of Henry and Malcolm IV. at, 462 ; besieged by William the Lion, ii. 153, 154 ; meeting of William and Henry at, 237 ; earldom of, granted to Henry of Scotland, i. 282 ; claimed by Ralf of Chester, 314 ; see of, 37, 69

Carrick, ii. 109, 111

Carthusians, ii. 435, 436 note 1

Carucage of 1194, ii. 328, 329, 342 ; the Great, 352-354

Carucate, ii. 352

Cashel, metropolis of Munster, ii. 94 ; council at, 115

Castille, *see* Alfonso, Blanche, Constance, Eleanor

Castle Cary, i. 295, 298

Celestine II., Pope, i. 355, 356

Celestine III., Pope, ii. 303, 304, 312, 351

Celle, *see* Peter

Cenomanni (Aulerci), i. 201, 202

Cenomannia, *see* Maine

Châlus, ii. 382, 385

Champagne, *see* Henry, Odo, Stephen, Theobald

Chancellor, the, his office, i. 22, 419, *See* Geoffrey, Matthew, Nigel, Ralf, Robert, Roger, Waldric, William

Charles the Bald, Emperor, i. 99, 102, 103, 105

Charles the Fat, king of West-Frankland and Emperor, i. 104

Charles the Simple, king of West-Frankland, i. 104

Charter of Henry I., i. 8 ; Henry II., 427 ; Stephen, 279, 284

Chartres, *see* Blois

Château - Gaillard, ii. 375 - 380 ; siege, 416-423 ; John's buildings at, 413, 421, 422

Châteaudun, i. 156. *See* Landry

Châteaulandon, *see* Gâtinais

Château-du-Loir, i. 390. *See* Gervase

Châteauneuf-sur-Sarthe, i. 267

Châteauneuf, *see* Tours

Châteauroux, ii. 211, 213, 245, 251

Châtillon, conference at, ii. 253

Chaumont-sur-Loire, i. 272 note 1, 471

Chef-Boutonne, battle of, i. 215, 252, 253

Cherbourg, siege of, i. 340

Chester, i. 36 ; its slave-trade, *ib.*, ii. 87 ; meeting of Henry II. and Malcolm IV. at, i. 438 ; privileges granted to its burghers at Dublin, ii. 484 ; earldom of, its peculiar character, i. 313, 314. *See* Hugh, Ralf

Chiche, priory of S. Osyth at, i. 68, 80

Chichester, *see* Hilary

Chinon won by Fulk Nerra, i. 167 ; Geoffrey the Bearded imprisoned at, 221 ; bequeathed to Geoffrey Plantagenet II., 394, 444 ; councils at, ii. 58, 64⅓ ; Henry II.'s buildings at, 197, 200 ; treasury at, plundered by Richard, 246 ; Henry II. at, 263, 267 ; given up to John, 388, 395 ; taken by Philip, 426

Chouzy, conference at, ii. 13

Christchurch or Twinham, i. 32

Chrodegang of Metz, rule of, i. 65

Chronicle, English, i. 81, 82

Church, English, under Henry I., i. 63 ; the Augustinian revival, 64-69 ; the Cistercian revival, 69-74 ; new sees, 68, 69 ; its national character, 80 ; political position of the bishops, 20 ; condition during the anarchy, 347-360 ; relations with Rome, 378 ; position at accession of Henry II., 474 ; vacant sees (1161), 503 ; Henry's schemes of reform, ii. 17-20 ; question of the "two swords," *ib.* 22, 23 ; quarrel of Henry and Thomas, its effects, 46-50 ; course of the revival after Theobald's death, 432 ; condition in Henry II.'s later years, 433-438. *See* Clergy

Church, Irish, its early glory, ii. 82, 86 ; condition in eleventh and twelfth centuries, 91-93 ; settlement at Synod of Kells, 94 ; submits to Henry II., 115

Circuits, *see* Justices

Cirencester, i. 330, 333

Cistercians or White Monks, their origin, i. 69, 70 ; in England, 71 ; work and influence, 74, 358, 359 ; quarrel with John, ii. 396, 399, 400 ; fall, 434, 435. *See* Citeaux, Clairvaux, Fountains, Newminster, Pontigny, Rievaux, Tintern, Waverley

Citeaux, i. 70

Clairvaux (abbey), i. 70 ; ii. 70, 94

Clairvaux (castle), ii. 222, 224

Clare, *see* Baldwin, Gilbert, Isabel, Richard, Roger, Walter ·

Clarendon, council of, ii. 25-28, 44, 45 ; Constitutions of, 26, 27 ; condemned by the Pope, 42 ; Assize of, 46, 122, 123

Cleobury, i. 429
Clergy, their position under Henry I., i. 63, 64 ; regular and secular, 64, 65 ; attitude in the civil war, 321 ; criminal clerks, ii. 19. *See* Church
Clerkenwell, council at, ii. 241
Clontarf, battle of, ii. 85
Cogan, *see* Miles
Coinage, debasement under Stephen, i. 293 ; new, in 1149, 402 note 1 ; in 1158, 453
Colechurch, *see* Peter
Cöln, gildhall of its citizens in London, ii. 485. *See* Reginald
Colombières, conference at, ii. 265, 266
Commune of Le Mans, i. 222 ; Gloucester, ii. 469 ; London, 309, 310, 344 ; York, 469
Conan the Crooked, count of Rennes and duke of Britanny, i. 121 ; his war with Geoffrey Greygown, 122, 137-139; with Fulk the Black, 146-148
Conan II., duke of Britanny, i. 211, 212, 220
Conan III., duke of Britanny, i. 449
Conan, earl of Richmond, claims Britanny, i. 449 ; duke, 451 ; dies, ii. 80
Conquereux, first battle of, i. 122, 138 ; second, 147, 148
Connaught invaded by Miles Cogan, ii. 184. *See* Roderic, Terence
Conrad III., Emperor, i. 361
Conrad, marquis of Montferrat, ii. 320, 321
Consilt, battle of, i. 436
Constables, *see* Henry, Humfrey
Constance of Arles, wife of Robert I. of France, i. 155 ; her parents, 190, 192 ; her policy, 160, 164
Constance of Britanny, daughter of Conan IV., betrothed to Geoffrey, son of Henry II., ii. 57 ; married, 233 ; marries Ralf of Chester, 369 ; imprisoned, 370 ; joins Arthur in Anjou, 389 ; does homage to Philip, 390 ; marries Guy of Thouars, 395 ; dies, 404, note 4
Constance of Castille, second wife of Louis VII. of France, i. 446, 468
Constance of France, daughter of Louis VI., betrothed to Stephen's son Eustace, i. 384; marries him, 394 ; marries Raymond V. of Toulouse, 458
Constance, heiress of Sicily, ii. 319
Constantine, Donation of, ii. 95
Constitutions of Clarendon, ii. 26, 27 ; condemned by the Pope, 42
Corbeil, *see* William
Cork, its origin, ii. 83. *See* Dermot
Cornwall, *see* Reginald, William
Coroners, their origin, ii. 338, 339

Councils, *see* Argentan, Armagh, Beaugency, Beauvais, Bermondsey, Bonneville, Carlisle, Cashel, Clarendon, Clerkenwell, Chinon, Geddington, Gloucester, Inispatrick, Kells, Lisieux, London, Neufmarché, Northampton, Nottingham, Oxford, Pavia, Pipewell, Poitiers, Rathbreasil, Tours, Wallingford, Westminster, Woodstock, Würzburg, York
Council, the Great, its character, i. 20
Courcy, *see* John, William
Coutances, *see* Walter
Coventry, *see* Hugh
Cowton Moor, i. 289
Cricklade, i. 335
Cross, S., *see* Winchester
Crowmarsh, i. 336, 396
Crown, pleas of the, ii. 337
Crusade, the second, i. 361-363 ; in Spain, proposed by Louis VII. and Henry II., 453, 497 ; the third, ii. 318-321
Curia Regis, see King's Court
Customs, "paternal," i. 16 ; royal, ii. 22, 26, 27; of Newcastle-upon-Tyne, i. 37
Cyprus, ii. 317, 321.

DANEGELD, i. 25 ; abolished, ii. 16, 44
David I., king of Scots, i. 95 ; invades England, 282, 286, 287, 288 ; defeated at Cowton Moor, 289 - 291 ; treaties with Stephen, 282, 300 ; joins the Empress in London, 323 ; escapes from Winchester, 328 ; knights Henry Fitz-Empress, 377 ; dies, 399
David, prince of North-Wales, marries Henry II.'s sister Emma, ii. 181
David, bishop of S. David's, ii. 454
David, brother of William of Scotland, ii. 140, 153; claims on Huntingdon and Northampton, 154
David or Hugh, count of Maine, i. 124, 140
David's, S., bishops of, *see* David, Peter
Defensor of Le Mans, i. 202
Denis, S., *see* Suger
Denmark, *see* Ingeborg
Déols, ii. 211
Dermot Mac - Carthy, king of Cork or South Munster, ii. 114
Dermot Mac-Maelnambo, king of Leinster, ii. 87, 88
Dermot Mac-Murrough, king of Leinster, ii. 97; seeks aid of Henry II., 98 ; returns to Ireland, 100 ; successes in Ossory etc., 102 ; summons Richard of Striguil, 103 ; dies, 106
Dervorgil, wife of Tighernan O'Ruark, ii. 97
Devizes, i. 304, 321, 330

Dialogus de Scaccario, i. 26
Diceto, *see* Ralf
Dinan, *see* Joceas
Dodo, bishop of Angers, i. 109, 133
Dol, ii. 148
Domfront, i. 6, 208, 209
Donatus, bishop of Dublin, ii. 87
Doncaster, earldom of, granted to Henry of Scotland, i. 282
Donell O'Brien, king of Limerick or North Munster, ii. 102, 103, 109, 111, 114
Donell O'Lochlainn, king of Aileach, ii. 90
Donell Kavanagh, ii. 109, 112
Dorchester, *see* Remigius
Dover, i. 295, 299; chief mart of the wool trade, 52 ; Geoffrey of York arrested at, ii. 305, 306. *See* Simon, William
Drausius, S., ii. 65
Dress, English, in twelfth century, i. 56
Dreux, *see* Robert
Drogo of Nantes, son of Alan Barbetorte, i. 115, 116
Dublin, its origin, ii. 83 ; metropolis of Leinster, 94 ; taken by Dermot etc., 105 ; attacked by wikings, 106 ; blockaded by Roderic O'Conor, 109 ; Henry II. at, 114, 115 ; colonized by Henry, 118 ; privileges of the Chester merchants at, 484. *See* Donatus, Godred, Gregory, Laurence, Patrick
Dudley, i. 295, 298
Dulcia of Gévaudan, i. 463
Dunstan, S., lives of, i. 80
Dunster, i. 295
Durham, S. Godric at, i. 77 ; cathedral, 80 ; treaty made at, 300 ; customs of the bishop's estates in 1183, ii. 478-480. *See* Hugh, Ralf, Simeon, William

EADGYTH or Edith, S., i. 33
Eadgyth, *see* Matilda
Eadmer, i. 80, 88
Eadward the Confessor, king of England, his prophecy, i. 1 ; his laws demanded by the citizens of London, 324
Eadwulf, prior of Nostell and confessor to Henry I., i. 68 ; bishop of Carlisle, 69
Ealdhelm, S., i. 84, 86, 90 ; life by Faricius, 81
Earldoms created by Stephen, i. 293
Edith, *see* Eadgyth
Edmund's, S., Henry II. at, i. 430 ; massacre of Jews at, ii. 289 ; its customs, 473, 474 ; merchant-gild, 481 ; dispute with Ely, 482, 483
Eleanor of Aquitaine, daughter of William IX., marries Louis VII. of France, i. 383 ; divorced, 392 ; marries Henry,

393 ; claims on Toulouse, 457, 458 ; attempt to divorce her from Henry, ii. 61 ; turns against him, 129 ; imprisoned, 135 ; Richard gives up Aquitaine to, 235 ; regent for Richard, 273, 282 ; arranges his marriage, 295, 296 ; negotiates at Rome, 303 ; returns to England, 314 ; ravages Anjou, and does homage to Philip, 390 ; goes to Spain, 396 ; retires to Fontevraud, 405 ; besieged in Mirebeau, 406 ; dies, 426
Eleanor, daughter of Henry II., marries Alfonso of Castille, ii. 60, 189
Eleanor of Britanny, daughter of Geoffrey and Constance, ii. 244, 325, 371
Elias, count of Maine, i. 224, 225 ; war with William Rufus, 225, 226 ; Le Mans surrendered to, 227 ; relations with Henry I., 11, 227, 233 ; marriages, 255 ; death, 233
Elias of Anjou, son of Fulk V., i. 343
Elias of Saint-Saëns, i. 235
Elizabeth of Hainaut, first wife of Philip Augustus, ii. 217, 234, note 7
Elizabeth of Vendôme, first wife of Fulk Nerra, 1. 152
Ely, see of, founded, i. 68 ; quarrel with S. Edmund's, ii. 482, 483. *See* Geoffrey, Nigel
Emma, daughter of Geoffrey Plantagenet, ii. 181
Emperors, *see* Charles, Conrad, Frederic, Henry, Otto
Engelram of Trie, i. 467
England under the Angevins, i. 1-3 ; relations with Rome, 15 ; with Normandy, 23, 24 ; invaded by Robert Curthose, 9 ; journey of canons of Laon in, 30-35 ; its peace under Henry I., 48 ; Flemings settle in, 52 ; town life in twelfth century, 54, 55 ; rural life, 56-62 ; revival under Henry I., 64-95 ; religious revival during the anarchy, 356-358 ; effects of the second Crusade, 362 ; rebels in (1173), ii. 138, 139 ; loyal barons in, 144, 145 ; rebel castles in the north, 152 ; royal strongholds, 153 ; condition of rural population under the Angevins, 473-480 ; fusion of races, 489 ; growth of national feeling, 489. *See* Church, Literature, Towns, Trade. *See also* Eadward, Eleanor, Henry, John, Jane, Matilda, Richard, Stephen, William
"English" and "French," i. 24
"English" and "Normans," different meanings of, i. 23, 24
English and Normans, fusion of, i. 24, 48, 49 ; ii. 489, 490

Englishry, presentment of, abolished, ii. 489
Essex, *see* Geoffrey, Henry, William
Este, *see* Hugh
Euclid, Adelard of Bath's version of, ii. 95
Eudo, count of Porhoët, i. 449
Eugene III., Pope, i. 361 ; deposes S. William and consecrates Henry Murdac, 366 ; suspends Henry of Winchester and threatens Stephen, 368 ; makes Abp. Theobald legate, 380 ; forbids the crowning of Eustace, 391 ; dies, 400
Eustace, son of Stephen, king of England, does homage to Louis VI. for Normandy, i. 286 ; knighted, 377 ; goes to York, 380 ; his prospects, 382 ; goes to France, 383 ; betrothed to Constance, 384 ; attacks Normandy, 385 ; receives homage, 391 ; proposal to crown him, *ib.* ; marriage, 394 ; character, 398 ; death, 399
Eustace Fitz-John, i. 72, 288
Eva, daughter of Dermot Mac-Murrough, ii. 104
Evreux ceded to Henry I., i. 11, 62 ; betrayed to Almeric de Montfort, 236 ; fired by Henry I., *ib.*, 237 ; granted to Almeric, 238 ; taken by Philip Augustus, ii. 389 ; ceded to him, 396. *See* Simon
Exchequer, court of, i. 21 ; organization under Bishop Roger, 25-27 ; headquarters, 31 ; Black Book of, ii. 125 ; the Norman Exchequer, 194, 197.
Exeter, i. 32, 284. *See* Bartholomew
Eynesford, *see* William

Falaise besieged by Henry I., i. 11 ; attacked by Geoffrey Plantagenet, 307 ; submits, 338 ; treaties at, ii. 165, 166 ; Arthur imprisoned at, 407 ; submits to Philip, 424
Faricius, abbot of Abingdon, i. 68 note 1, 81
Farringdon, i. 335
Faye, *see* Ralf
Ferm of the shire, i. 25 ; of towns, 29
Ferrers, *see* Robert
Ferté-Bernard, La, conference at, ii. 257
Finchale, i. 77, 78
Fitz-Alan, *see* William
Fitz-Aldhelm, *see* William
Fitz-Aylwine, *see* Henry
Fitz-Count, *see* Brian, Richard
Fitz-David, *see* Miles
Fitz-Duncan, *see* William
Fitz-Gerald, *see* Maurice
Fitz-John, *see* Eustace, William
Fitz-Osbert, *see* William
Fitz-Peter, *see* Geoffrey, Simon
Fitz-Ralf, *see* William

Fitz-Stephen, *see* Robert, William
Fitz-Urse, *see* Reginald
Flambard, *see* Ralf
Flanders granted to William the Clito, i. 243 ; trade with England, 30, 51, 52. *See* Baldwin, Matthew, Philip, Theodoric
Flèche, La, i. 222, 223, 256, 257
Flemings, their settlements in England and Wales, i. 52, 53 ; in England under Stephen, 285 ; plot to kill Henry, 403 ; expelled, 427 ; land in Suffolk, ii. 155 ; at Hartlepool, 162
Fleury, abbey, i. 112
Florence, S., of Saumur, i. 162
Florence of Worcester, i. 82, 88, 89, 90
Foliot, *see* Gilbert
Folkmoot of London, i. 45
Fontevraud, i. 248 ; Henry II. buried at, ii. 270-272 ; Richard buried at, ii. 386 ; Eleanor at, 385, 405
Forest, assizes of, i. 285 ; ii. 171, 177, 356
Fornham, battle at, ii. 150
Foss-Dyke, i. 40
Foss-Way, i. 38
Fougères, *see* Ralf
Fountains abbey, i. 71-73 ; burnt, 366.
France, duchy of, *see* French
France, kingdom of, character of its early history, i. 144 ; condition under Hugh Capet, 145 ; under Louis VI., 230 ; relations with Normandy, 24, 111 ; with Toulouse, 457, 458 ; with Rome, 501, 502 ; union with Aquitaine, 383 ; its developement, ii. 357-361. *See* Adela, Constance, Henry, Hugh, Louis, Margaret, Mary, Odo, Philip, Robert
Frankland, West, northmen in, i. 100. *See* Charles, Lothar, Louis, Odo, Robert, Rudolf
Frederic Barbarossa, Emperor, supports antipope Victor IV., i. 498 ; relations with Henry II., 499 ; ii. 55, 60, 238 ; banishes Henry the Lion, 238, 257 ; takes the cross, 256 ; dies, 318
French, dukes of the, extent of their duchy, i. 103, 105 ; underfiefs, 105 ; claims upon Maine, 124. *See* Hugh, Odo, Robert
" French and English," i. 24
Fréteval, ii. 73, 366
Fritheswith or Frideswide, S., i. 43. *See* Oxford
Fulk the Red, first count of Anjou, i. 106 ; his neighbours, 109 ; political position, 109, 110 ; marriage, 110 ; death, 113 ; chronology of his life, 128, 129, 132
Fulk II. the Good, count of Anjou, i. 113 ; his rule, 113, 115 ; canon of

S. Martin's, 114 ; letter to Louis IV., *ib.* ; marriages, 116 ; claims upon Nantes, *ib.* ; death, 117 ; vision of S. Martin, 118 ; prophecy made to, *ib.* ; its fulfilment, ii. 187, 373

Fulk III., the Black, count of Anjou, his mother, i. 136 ; surnames, 143, note 2 ; character, 144 ; significance of his life, 145, 146, 169 ; war with Conan of Rennes, 146, 147 ; regains Anjou west of Mayenne, 148 ; attacks Blois, 149 ; rivalry with Odo II., 150 ; castle-building, 151 ; seizure of the water-ways, 151-152 ; first marriage, 152 ; first pilgrimage, 153, 192 ; founds Beaulieu abbey, 153-155 ; marries Hildegard, 154 ; second pilgrimage, 156, 192-195 ; his oath, 155 ; contrives the death of Hugh of Beauvais, *ib.* ; sacks Châteaudun, 156 ; alliance with Maine, *ib.* ; victory at Pontlevoy, 157, 158 ; subdues Hugh of Maine, 159 ; imprisons Herbert of Maine, *ib.* ; invested with Saintes, *ib.*, 173 ; fortifies Montboyau, 161 ; takes Saumur, 162 ; besieges Montbazon, 163 ; treaty with Odo, *ib.* ; his policy and its success, 164 ; makes peace between Constance and her son, *ib.* ; joins King Henry's expedition against Sens, *ib.* ; his home, 165 ; buildings at Angers, *ib.* ; third pilgrimage, 166, 195, 196 ; rebellion of his son, 166, 195 ; wins Chinon, 167 ; fourth pilgrimage, 167, 168 ; quarrels with his son, 172, 175 ; death, 168 ; his tomb, *ib.* ; his work, 169, 188

Fulk IV. Rechin, .son of Geoffrey of Gâtinais and Hermengard of Anjou, invested with Saintonge, i. 214 ; his character, 219 ; ntrigues against his brother, *ib.* ; wins Saumur and Angers, 220 ; captures Geoffrey, *ib.* ; does homage for Touraine, 221 ; cedes Gâtinais to France, *ib.* ; his rule, *ib.* ; drives Geoffrey of Mayenne from Le Mans, 222 ; besieges La Flèche, *ib.*, 223, 257 ; receives Robert's homage for Maine, 223 ; his marriages, 224 ; excommunicated, *ib.* ; absolved, 225 ; quarrels with his eldest son, 227, 228 ; dies, 229 ; his reign and its results, *ib.* ; his Angevin history, 127

Fulk V., count of Anjou, i. 229 ; character and policy, 231, 232 ; marries Aremburg, 232 ; quarrel with Henry I. and alliance with France, 233 ; homage to Henry, 234 ; revolt of the burghers against, *ib.* ; joins league against Henry, 235 ; wins Alençon, 236 ; treaty with Henry, *ib.* ; goes to Jerusalem, 238 ; quarrel with Henry, 240 ; offers Maine to Clito, *ib.* ; imprisons the legate's envoys, 242 ; marries Melisenda and becomes king of Jerusalem, 246-248 ; dies, 361

Fulk the Gosling, count of Vendôme, i. 214

GAIMAR, *see* Geoffrey

Galloway, ii. 164, 179, 237

Gandrea, wife of Theobald III. of Blois, i. 255, 256

Gascony, Richard's campaign in, ii. 214 ; revolt in, 316. *See* Guy-Geoffrey, Odo

Gatian, S., bishop of Tours, i. 179

Gâtinais, county of, i. 129 ; ceded to France, 221 ; counts, 249, 250

Gaubert of Mantes, ii. 415

Geddington, council at, ii. 249

Gelduin of Saumur, i. 161, 162

Geoffrey I. Greygown, count of Anjou, i. 118 ; his character, 119 ; joins invasion of Lorraine, 120 ; his marriages, 121, 134-136 ; relations with Britanny, 121, 122, 137-139 ; with Maine, 124, 140-142 ; war with Poitou, 123, 137, 139 ; wins Loudun, 123, 124, 139 ; founds church of our Lady at Loches, 153 ; dies at siege of Marson, 125

Geoffrey II. Martel, son of Fulk the Black, born, i. 154 ; nursed at Loches, *ib.* ; count of Vendôme, 172 ; quarrel with Fulk, *ib.*, 175 ; marries Agnes, 136, 174, 197, 199 ; war with Poitou, 173-175 ; wins Saintonge, 174 ; rebels, 166, 195, 196 ; count of Anjou, 169 ; his character, 170-172 ; invested with Tours, 178 ; besieges it, 184 ; victory at Montlouis, 186 ; treaty with Theobald, 187 ; its significance, 188 ; advocate of see of Le Mans, 205 ; imprisons Bp. Gervase, 206 ; master of Maine, *ib.* ; excommunicated, *ib.* ; revolts, 207 ; wins Alençon and Domfront, 208 ; challenges William and retires, 209 ; war with Aquitaine, 210 ; besieges Ambrières, 211 ; dealings with Nantes, 211, 212 ; marries Grecia, 212 ; blockaded in Saumur, 213 ; joins invasion of Normandy, *ib.*, 214 ; loses Vendôme, 214 ; dies, *ib.* ; break-up of his dominions, 215 ; dispute over them, 218 ; his heirs, 251-252

Geoffrey III. the Bearded, count of Anjou, i. 214 ; victory at Chef-Boutonne, 215, 252, 253 ; receives Robert's homage for Maine, 217 ; wrongs Marmoutier, 220 ; captured by Fulk, *ib.* ; imprisoned at Chinon, 221 ; released and dies, 228

Geoffrey Martel II. of Anjou, son of Fulk Rechin, betrothed to Aremburg of Maine, i. 226 ; joins Henry I., 11; quarrel with Fulk, 227, 228 ; slain, 228

Geoffrey V. Plantagenet, son of Fulk V. and Aremburg, knighted by Henry I., i. 244 ; marriage, *ib.*, 258-260 ; his person and character, 261-265 ; quarrels with his wife, 266 ; with Henry, 269, 270 ; invades Normandy, 281, 306, 307 ; revolts against, 266, 267, 306, 343, 384 ; summoned to England, 330 ; treaty with Theobald, 337 ; conquers Normandy, 338-342 ; recalls his son, 343 ; challenge to Stephen, 369 ; cedes Normandy to his son, *ib.*, 377 ; his siege of Montreuil, 384, 386 ; treatment of Gerald, 387 ; cedes the Vexin to Louis, 388 ; death, 389, 390 ; burial, 390 ; will, 444

Geoffrey of Anjou, second son of Geoffrey and Matilda, born, i. 373 ; seeks to marry Eleanor, 393 ; rebels against Henry, 394, 395, 444, 445 ; count of Nantes, 449 ; dies, *ib.*

Geoffrey I., duke of Britanny, i. 137, 148

Geoffrey, fourth son of Henry II. and Eleanor, born, i. 453 ; acknowledged heir to Britanny, ii. 58 ; duke, 80 ; revolts, 135 ; knighted, 214 ; joins young Henry, 225 ; submits, 232 ; marries Constance, 233 ; dies, 243.

Geoffrey, son of Henry II., bishop-elect of Lincoln, ii., 155 ; takes Kinardferry etc., *ib.* ; chancellor, 245 ; secures castles of Anjou, 256 ; with Henry at Le Mans, 258, 259, 260 ; at La Frênaye, 262 ; goes to Alençon, *ib.* ; rejoins Henry, 263 ; his devotion to Henry, 268 ; appointed archbishop of York, 274, 278, 302 ; early life, 301, 302 ; character, 304 ; consecrated, 305; returns to England, *ib.* ; arrested, *ib.* ; released, 306 ; joins John, 307 ; enthroned, 313 ; quarrel with Hugh of Durham, *ib.*, 316 ; buys sheriffdom of Yorkshire, 330 ; driven from England, 335 ; redeems the Lincoln church-plate, 487

Geoffrey (Alberic), count of Gâtinais, marries Hermengard of Anjou, i. 214, 249, 250

Geoffrey of Brulon, ii. 259

Geoffrey of Chaumont, i. 272, note 1

Geoffrey Fitz-Peter, justiciar, ii. 355, 356 ; earl of Essex, 393

Geoffrey Gaimar, ii. 446

Geoffrey of Lusignan, ii. 59 note 1, 136, 250, 405

Geoffrey of Mandeville, i. 334, 335

Geoffrey de Mandeville, earl of Essex, ii. 124

Geoffrey of Mayenne, i. 211 ; holds Le Mans for Walter of Mantes, 218 ; submits to William, *ib.* ; revolts, 221, 222, 224

Geoffrey of Monmouth, ii. 445, 448

Geoffrey of Rancogne, ii. 214, 250, 367

Geoffrey Ridel, archdeacon of Canterbury, ii. 30, 77 ; vice-chancellor, 142 ; bishop of Ely, 176 ; dies, 277

Geoffrey Talbot, i. 294, 296

Gerald de Barri ("Giraldus Cambrensis"), ii. 452-460

Gerald of Montreuil-Bellay, i. 384, 385, 386, 388

Geraldines, the, ii. 108, 183

Gerard de Camville, ii. 280, 298, 299, 300, 329

Gerard la Pucelle, ii. 449

Gerberga, wife of Fulk the Good, i. 116, note 1

Germany, English trade with, under the Angevins, ii. 484, 485

Gersendis of Maine, i. 221, 254-256

Gervase of Château-du-Loir, bishop of Le Mans, i. 205 ; imprisoned by Geoffrey Martel, 206 ; released, *ib.* ; archbishop of Reims, 207

Gesta Consulum Andegavensium, its authorship and character, i. 126, 127

Gévaudan, *see* Dulcia

Gilbert of Sempringham, S., i. 359, 360

Gilbert Becket, i. 50

Gilbert Foliot, abbot of Gloucester, i. 369, 370, 493 ; bishop of Hereford, 371, 495 ; his earlier history, 492, 493 ; career as abbot, 494, 495 ; relations with Abp. Theobald and with Henry II., 495, 496 ; with Roger of Pont-l'Evêque, 478, 479 ; character, 496, 497 ; remarks on Thomas's election, ii. 3, 6 ; translated to London, 13, 14 ; relations with Thomas, 13, 31, 49 ; at council of Northampton, 35, 36, 37, 39 ; his attitude in the Becket quarrel, 47-49 ; his share in the bishops' appeal, 67 ; excommunicated, 70 ; denies the primate's jurisdiction, *ib.* ; absolved, 72 ; dies, 277

Gilbert, bishop of Limerick, ii. 92 ; legate in Ireland, *ib.*, 93

Gilbert de Clare, earl of Pembroke, i. 377, 395, 396 ; ii. 99

Gilds, i. 29 ; under Henry II. and Richard, ii. 469, 470 ; leather-sellers', i. 30 ; merchant, i. 29, 36, 40, 43 ; ii. 481 ; weavers', i. 30, 52 ; ii. 481

Gildhall, i. 129 ; of German merchants, ii. 485

Gilles, St., *see* Raymond
Giraldus Cambrensis, *see* Gerald
Gisors, i. 231, 234, 343 ; meeting of Henry I. and Pope Calixtus at, 237, 238; of Louis VII. and Henry II. at, ii. 148, 165 ; claimed by Philip, 232, 236
Glanville, *see* Hervey, Ralf
Glastonbury, invention of Arthur at, ii. 447, 448
Gleeman, the, i. 90
Gloucester, i. 35, 36 ; abbey and city, 493, 494 ; council at, ii. 170 ; commune at, 469. *See* Avice, Gilbert, Miles, Philip, Robert, William
Godfrey de Lucy, bishop of Winchester, ii. 277, 288
Godfrey, abbot of Malmesbury, i. 84, 85
Godred, king of Dublin, ii. 88
Godric, S., i. 74-79
"Goliath, Bishop," ii. 452
Gouleton, ii. 396, 402
Gournay, ii. 403. *See* Hugh
Graçay, ii. 213, 361
Grandmesnil, *see* Ivo, Petronilla
Grandmont, ii. 58, 226 ; order of, 435
Gratian, his work on canon law, i. 378
Grecia of Montreuil, second wife of Geoffrey Martel, i. 212
Gregory, archbishop of Dublin, ii. 94
Gregory, bishop of Tours, i. 181
Gué-St.-Rémy, ii. 244
Guerech, bishop and count of Nantes, i. 121, 122, 146
Guimund, prior of S. Frideswide's, Oxford, i. 43
"Guirribecs," i. 306
Guy of Anjou (son of Fulk the Red), bishop of Soissons, i. 112, 113
Guy of Anjou, son of Fulk the Good, i. 119
Guy of Crema, *see* Paschal
Guy, viscount of Limoges, ii. 407
Guy of Lusignan, ii. 59 note 1, 136 ; king of Jerusalem, 247 ; Cyprus, 317, 321 ; ally of Richard, 318, 320
Guy of Thouars, ii. 395, 424
Guy-Geoffrey, count of Gascony, i. 176, 212. *See* William VII. of Aquitaine

HACKINGTON, college at, ii. 437
Hainaut, *see* Elizabeth
Hameline, earl of Warren, son of Geoffrey Plantagenet, ii. 40, 144
Hamo de Massey, ii. 139
Hans-house, i. 29 ; at York, 36
Harding or Stephen, founder of Citeaux, i. 69, 70
Harptree, i. 295, 298
Hascuif Thorgils' son, ii. 105, 106
Hautefort, ii. 204, 231

Haye, La, *see* Richard
Henry I., son of William the Conqueror, his early life, i. 4-6 ; character, 6, 7 ; election and coronation, 7 ; charter, 8 ; marriage, 1, 8, 9 ; treaty with Robert, 9 ; proceedings against traitors, 10 ; Norman campaigns, 11 ; Tinchebray, 12, 13 ; policy, 13-15, 19 ; struggle with Anselm, 15-18 ; character of his reign, 19 ; his work, 19, 20 ; love of "foreigners," 23 ; his ministers, *ib.* ; called "the Lion of Justice," 26 ; charter to York, 30, 36 ; to Norwich, 41 ; London, 45, 46 ; palace at Woodstock, 44, 94 ; court at Oxford, 44 ; his "good peace," 30 note 1, 48, 95 ; settles Flemings in Pembroke, 52 ; dealings with the Church, 63 ; results, 64 ; founds see of Ely, 68 ; Carlisle, 69 ; revival of literature under, 80-95 ; relations with Maine, 227; with France, 230, 231; wars with France and Anjou, 233, 235 ; treaties with Fulk, 234, 236 ; victory at Brenneville, 237 ; meets Calixtus at Gisors, *ib.*, 238 ; treaty with Louis, 238 ; wreck of his hopes, 239, 240 ; quarrel with Fulk, 240 ; quells revolt in Normandy, 241 ; alliance with Henry V., *ib.* ; proclaims Matilda his heiress, 243 ; last years, 268-270 ; death, 271 ; possible successors, 274-275 ; state of England after his death, 279 ; burial, 282 ; his court, 413
Henry II. Fitz-Empress born, i. 268 ; Eadward's prophecy fulfilled in, 1 ; Witan swear fealty to, 269 ; his early life, 372-374 ; tutors, 375, 376 ; goes to England, 334 ; returns to Anjou, 343 ; duke of Normandy, 369, 377 ; goes to England, 377 ; knighted, *ib.* ; returns, 378 ; besieges Torigni, 386, 405 ; does homage to Louis, 388; marries Eleanor, 393 ; ignores Louis's jurisdiction, 394 ; war with Louis and Geoffrey, 395 ; lands in England, 396 ; besieges Malmesbury, 397 ; colloquy at Wallingford, *ib.* ; treaty with Stephen, 400, 401 ; receives homage, 402 ; plot to kill him, 403 ; returns to Gaul, *ib.* ; effects of his visit to England, *ib.* ; resumes Norman demesnes, 404 ; peace with Louis, 405; comes to England, *ib.* ; crowned, *ib.* ; his work, 407 ; person and character, 408-411, 414-417; court, 411-413 ; first ministers, 417, 418 ; relations with Becket, 420, 423-427 ; charter, 427 ; settlement of the country, *ib.* ; of the succession, 429 ; subdues William of Aumale, 428 ; and Hugh of Mortemer, 429 ; holds court at S. Edmund's,

430; goes to Anjou, 431; scheme for conquering Ireland, *ib.*, ii. 95; effects of his first two years' work in England, i. 431-434; returns, 434; demands Northumberland etc., 435; receives Malcolm's homage, 438; wears his crown at Wigford, *ib.*, 439; at Worcester, 439; his position compared with Cnut's, 2, 440, 441; relations with France, 441, 442; does homage, 443; subdues Geoffrey, 444, 445; proposes for Margaret as wife for his son, 446; seneschal of France, 450; grants Britanny to Conan and obtains Nantes, 451; designs on Britanny, 452, 453; claims Toulouse, 458; great scutage, 459-461; his allies, 462, 463; knights Malcolm, 464; takes Cahors and threatens Toulouse, *ib.*; withdraws, 465; treaty, 467; quarrel with Thomas, 469; drives Louis from Chaumont, 471; principle of his reforms, 474; projects of crusade, 453, 497; attitude towards the religious revival, 497; relations with Adrian IV., *ib.*; with Germany, 499, 502; acknowledges Alexander III. as Pope, 502; appoints Thomas archbishop, ii. 1; meets Alexander and Louis, 13; goes to England, *ib.*; receives homage of Welsh princes at Woodstock, 14; quarrel with Thomas, 15, 16; plans of reform in criminal legislature, 17-20; propounds his grandfather's customs at Westminster, 22; meets Thomas at Northampton, 23; at Oxford, 24; publishes constitutions of Clarendon, 26; meets Thomas at Woodstock, 31, 32; council of Northampton, 32-40; sends envoys to the Pope, 41; confiscates the primate's estates and banishes his friends, 42; effects of the quarrel, 46-49; goes to Normandy, 54; receives envoys from the Emperor, 55, 60; plans for his children, 57, 60; conquers Britanny, 57, 58; correspondence with Arthur, 57 note 2, 447; meets Raymond, 58; attempt to divorce him from Eleanor, 61; does homage at Montmirail, *ib.*, 62; holds council at Chinon, 64; appeals to Rome, 65; drives Thomas from Pontigny, 68; meets him at Montmirail, 69; meets Louis and Thomas at Montmartre, 71; at Fréteval, 73; meets Thomas at Tours and Chaumont, 74; goes to Rocamadour, *ib.*; rash words at Bures, 78; absolved, 81; promises help to Dermot, 99; forbids the war in Ireland, 108; summons Richard of Striguil to Wales, 112; goes to Ireland, 80, 113; his fleet, 112; Irish princes submit to, 114; settlement of Ireland, 117; of Dublin, 118; goes to Normandy, 119; relations with the barons, 120, 121, 126, 128; legal and administrative reforms, 122-127; inquest on Norman demesnes, 128; alliance with Maurienne, 131; receives homage of Toulouse, 133; quarrel with young Henry, 134, 135; revolt against, 141; visits England, 143; his adherents, 144-146; takes Dol, 148; meets Louis, *ib.*; subdues rebels in Touraine, 151; regains Saintes, 157; returns to England, 158; pilgrimage to Canterbury, 159; receives news of William's capture, 160; takes Huntingdon and subdues Hugh Bigod, 163; relieves Rouen, 164; subdues Poitou, 165; reconciled with his sons, *ib.*; treaty with William the Lion, 166; treatment of the rebels, 167; end of the struggle, 166, 168; his position after it, 169; administrative work in England, 170-178; his forest visitations, 171; receives homage for Scotland, 178; dealings with Wales, i. 435-437; ii. 179-181, 237, 453, 455; treaty with Roderic O'Conor, ii. 182; appoints John king of Ireland, 184; character of his empire, 185-187; continental policy, 188-191; arbitrates between Castille and Navarre, 190; administration in Normandy, 192-194; buildings, 196, 197; religious foundations, 197 and note 4; hospitals, 198, 199; *Levée*, 200; bridges, *ib.*; relations with Aquitaine, 203, 205; quarrel with Louis, 212; treaty, 213; takes Châteauroux, *ib.*; buys La Marche, 214; house of Blois seek his help, 217; makes peace in France, *ib.*, 219; tries to make peace among his sons, 224; summons a conference at Mirebeau, 225; besieges Limoges, *ib.*; arrests rebel leaders of 1173, 226; forgives young Henry, 227; Aquitaine submits to, 230; interview with Bertrand de Born, 231; homage to Philip, 232; proposes to transfer Aquitaine to John, 233, 242; makes John governor of Ireland, 234; mediates between France and Flanders, 235; receives submission of Galloway, 237; receives the patriarch Heraclius, 240; meets Philip, 244; marches into Berry, 245; truce, 246; reinstates Richard in Aquitaine, 247; meets Philip, 248; takes the cross, 249; musters his forces in Normandy, 252; meets Philip, 253; conference at Bon-

moulins, 254; goes into Aquitaine, 256;
meets Richard, *ib.*; goes to Le Mans,
257; conference at La Ferté, *ib.*;
flies, 259-262; returns to Anjou, 262;
goes to Chinon and Azay, 263; submits to Philip at Colombières, 265, 266;
learns John's treason, 267; last days,
268; death, 269; burial, 270, 272;
points out Arthur's tomb, 447; grants
trading privileges to Chester, 484;
grants burial-grounds to the Jews, 486.
Henry, second son of Henry II. and
Eleanor, born, i. 429, 445; betrothal,
446, 448; does homage for Normandy,
468; marriage, 470; intrusted to
Thomas for education, 471, 472; recog-
nised heir to the crown, 472, 473; receives homage of Malcolm IV., ii. 15;
withdrawn from Thomas, 23; homage
at Montmirail, 62; receives Geoffrey's
homage for Britanny, *ib.*; officiates as
seneschal and does homage to Philip,
ib.; crowned, 72; crowned again, 81;
rebels, 129, 130; flies to France, 134;
threatens to invade England, 158, 162;
reconciled, 165; receives homage of
William the Lion, 178; joins Richard
in Aquitaine, 209, 210; besieges Châteauroux, 211; at crowning of Philip
Augustus, 216, 218, 219; character,
221; quarrel with Richard, 222; enters
Aquitaine, 223; confesses his league
with the Poitevins, 224; holds Limoges
against his father, 225; driven thence,
226; plunders Grandmont, *ib.*; and
Rocamadour, 227; death, *ib.*, 228;
burial, 230, 232
Henry III., Emperor, i. 176
Henry V., Emperor, i. 241, 242
Henry VI., Emperor, his claims on Sicily,
ii. 319; demands for Richard's ransom,
324, 325; negotiates with Philip and
John, 327; grants Burgundian kingdom
to Richard, 331; conquers Sicily, 371,
372; stirs up Richard against France,
372; dies, *ib.*
Henry I., king of France, joins Odo II.
against Fulk Nerra, i. 163; tries to
drive Odo from Sens, 164; revolt
against, 177, 178; grants Tours to
Geoffrey Martel, 178; relations with
Normandy and Anjou, 207, 210; visits
Angers, 213; invades Normandy, *ib.*;
defeated at Varaville, *ib.*, 214; dies,
214
Henry of Blois, bishop of Winchester, his
early life, i. 347; supports Stephen,
277, 279; legate, 305; summons
Stephen before a council at Winchester,
305; advice at siege of Arundel, 309;

escorts Matilda to Bristol, 310;
receives her at Winchester, 321; holds
council there, 322; again declares for
Stephen, 324, 325; his fortress of
Wolvesey, 325; besieged, 326; fires
the city, *ib.*; holds council at Westminster and again proclaims Stephen,
329, 330; his Church policy, 348;
character, 349; position as legate, *ib.*,
350; elected to Canterbury, 350; rivalry
with Theobald, 351; loses the legation,
356; goes to Rome, *ib.*; founds S.
Cross, 357; suspended, 368; appeals,
381; absolved, *ib.*; consecrates S.
Thomas, ii. 5; at council of Northampton, 35, 36, 37, 41; dies, 80.
Henry the Liberal, count of Champagne,
joins invasion of Normandy, i. 394;
betrothed to Mary of France, 445
Henry II., count of Champagne, king of
Jerusalem, ii. 321
Henry the Lion, duke of Saxony, betrothed
to Matilda, daughter of Henry II., ii.
55; married, 59, 60; exiled 238, 257;
regains his lands, 319
Henry, son of David king of Scots, made
earl of Carlisle and Huntingdon, i.
282; Northumberland promised to,
286; at battle of the Standard, 290,
291; earl of Northumberland, 300; at
siege of Ludlow, 301, 302; dies, 399
Henry of Albano, legate, ii. 256, 257
Henry of Essex, constable, i. 434; drops
standard at Consilt, 436, 437; present
in war of Toulouse, 466; defeated in
ordeal of battle, ii. 61
Henry Fitz-Aylwine, mayor of London, ii.
472; his assize, 485
Henry of Huntingdon, i. 82, 83, 94
Henry Murdac, abbot of Fountains, i.
365; opposes S. William, *ib.*; archbishop of York, 366; his troubles in
Yorkshire, 367, 380; reconciled to the
king and enthroned, 381; goes to Rome,
ib.; opposes election of Hugh of Puiset
to Durham, 399, 400; death, 400
Henry of Pisa, cardinal, ii. 2
Heraclius, patriarch of Jerusalem, ii. 240
Herbert I. Wake-dog, count of Maine,
saves Fulk at Pontlevoy, i. 157, 158;
his surname, 159; imprisoned by Fulk,
ib.; quarrels with Bp. Avesgaud, *ib.*
note 4, 204; death, 204; daughters,
254, 255
Herbert II., count of Maine, i. 216
Herbert Bacco usurps the county of Maine,
i. 204; quarrels with Bishop Gervase,
205; expelled, *ib.*
Herbert Lozinga, bishop of Thetford, re-
moves his see to Norwich, i. 41

Herbert, bishop of Salisbury, withstands Hubert Walter, ii. 350

Herbert of Bosham, ii. 9, 10, 38, 40, 75; verdict on the Becket quarrel, 47

Hereford, i. 36; castle seized by Geoffrey Talbot, 294; yields to Stephen, 295. *See* Gilbert, Miles, Robert, Roger

Herispoë, king of Britanny, i. 130, 203

Hermengard of Anjou, daughter of Geoffrey Greygown and wife of Conan of Rennes, i. 121, 135

Hermengard (Adela) of Anjou, daughter of Fulk Nerra, wife of Geoffrey of Gâtinais, i. 214, 249

Hermengard of Anjou, daughter of Fulk Rechin, marries Alan Fergant, duke of Britanny, i. 328 note 4

Hermengard of Beaumont, wife of William the Lion, ii. 237

Hermengard of Bourbon, second wife of Fulk Rechin, i. 224

Hervey of Glanville, i. 362

Hervey of Lions, i. 321

Hervey of Mountmorris, ii. 101, 112

Hicmar, legate, i. 364

Higra, the, i. 34

Hilary, bishop of Chichester, ii. 24, 39

Hildegard, wife of Fulk III. of Anjou, i. 154, 165, 168

Historia Comitum Andegavensium, its authorship and character, i. 126, 127

History, English, under Henry I., i. 81-83, 87-91; decay during the anarchy, ii. 438; new school of, under Henry II., 439-445; romantic school, 445, 449

Hoel, duke of Britanny, i. 222

Hoel I., count of Nantes, i. 117, 121

Hoel II., count of Nantes, i. 212

Hoel of Rennes, count of Nantes, i. 449

Holy Land, *see* Jerusalem

Hommet, *see* Richard

Hospitaliers, i. 357

Hospitals founded in Stephen's reign, i. 357; by Henry II., ii. 198, 199

Houses, English, in twelfth century, i. 54, 55

Howden, *see* Roger

Hrolf the Ganger, i. 111, 124, 203

Hubert Walter, dean of York, ii. 278; bishop of Salisbury, *ib.*, 333; elected to Canterbury, 326; justiciar, *ib.*; suppresses revolt, 327; early life, 332, 333; rivals, 334-336; legate, 336; his policy, *ib.*; administration, 337-341, 348, 352-354; fires Bow church and hangs William Fitz-Osbert, 347; defeated in council at Oxford, 349, 350; expedition to Wales, 351; resigns the justiciarship, *ib.*, 354, 355; negotiates with Philip, 374; regent for John, 390, 391; crowns him, 392; chancellor, *ib.*; persuades John to dismiss the host, 427; dies, 428; his proposed college, 437

Hubert de Burgh, ii. 400, 407, 408, 426

Hugh, S., bishop of Lincoln, excommunicates the De Clères, ii. 306; withstands Hubert Walter, 349; buries Richard, 386; dies, 399

Hugh of Nonant, bishop of Chester or Coventry, ii. 280, 293, 306, 310, 329; his scheme of "new foundation," 436

Hugh of Puiset, treasurer of York, excommunicated, i. 367; absolved, 382; bishop of Durham, 399, 400; rebels, ii. 140, 141; makes a truce with the Scots, 151; fortifies Northallerton, 152; calls in the Flemings, 162; submits, 163; takes the cross, 248; justiciar, 279; earl of Northumberland, 280; character and antecedents, 283-285; quarrels with the chancellor, 288, 291, 292; relations with York, 303, 304; quarrel with Geoffrey, 313, 316; mission to France, 316; besieges Tickhill, 323, 327, 328; resigns Northumberland, 330; tries to regain it, 335; dies, 336; his *Boldon Buke*, 478-480

Hugh, duke of Burgundy, i. 103, 104

Hugh the Great, duke of the French, i. 112, 123, 124, 204

Hugh Capet, duke of the French, i. 120, 124, 141, 142; king, 125

Hugh I. count of Maine, i. 124; subdued by Fulk the Black, 159; dies, 156

Hugh II. count of Maine, set aside by Herbert Bacco, i. 204; restored, 205; marriage and death, 206

Hugh of Este, count of Maine, i. 221, 224

Hugh the Poor, earl of Bedford, i. 320

Hugh Bigod, i. 278; revolts against Stephen, 284; earl of Norfolk, 430; revolts against Henry, ii. 139; takes Norwich, 155; submits, 163; his punishment, 167

Hugh, earl of Chester, rebels against Henry II., ii. 138; taken prisoner, 148; restored, 167

Hugh Bardulf, ii. 283, 330, 335

Hugh of Beauvais, seneschal of France, i. 155

Hugh of Gournay, ii. 146, 403

Hugh de Lacy, ii. 113, 116; governor in Ireland, 117; with Henry in Normandy, 145, 147; viceroy again, 185; slain, 242, 243

Hugh IX., the Brown, of Lusignan, ii. 398

Hugh X. of Lusignan, ii. 398, 405

Hugh of Ste.-Maure, ii. 129, 136

Hugh of Mortemer, i. 429, 430
Hugh de Morville, ii. 78
Hugh of Sillé, ii. 137
Huitdeniers, *see* Osbern
Humbert, count of Maurienne, ii. 132, 133, 134
Humfrey de Bohun, constable, ii. 113, 145, 149
Hungary, *see* Bela
Huntingdon, siege of, ii. 154, 156 ; surrenders, 163 ; earldom of, i. 282, ii. 154 ; weavers at, i. 30, 52. *See* Henry, Simon
Hyde abbey, i. 31

ILCHESTER, *see* Richard
Ingebiorg of Denmark, second wife of Philip Augustus, ii. 395
Ingelger, son of Tortulf, i. 105, 114, 128-131, 182
Ingelger, son of Fulk the Red, i. 112
Inispatrick, synod at, ii. 94
Innocent II., Pope, i. 299, 351, 355 ; ii. 93
Innocent III., Pope, ii. 351
Inquest, *see* Jury
Investitures, i, 15-18
Ireland, English trade with, i. 32, 35, ii. 87 ; northmen in, ii. 82-86 ; civil wars in, 89-91 ; Henry II.'s proposal to conquer, 95, 431 ; plans of Eugene III. and S. Bernard for, 95 ; bull for its conquest, i. 431, 486, ii. 96 ; Henry II. in, ii. 113-118 ; condition in his later years, 181-185 ; John made governor of, 234 ; John in, 242 ; Gerald's treatises on, 457, 458. *See* Brian, Dermot, Donell, Malachi, Murtogh, Niall, Roderic, Terence. *See also* Church
Isaac, king of Cyprus, ii. 317, 319
Isabel of Angoulême, ii. 398 ; married to John, 399
Isabel de Clare, wife of William the Marshal, ii. 274
Isabel de Warren, ii. 29
Issoudun, ii. 361. *See* Ralf
Ivo of Grandmesnil, i. 10

JANE, third daughter of Henry II., betrothed to William II. of Sicily, ii. 60 ; marries him, 189, 190 ; marries Raymond VI. of Toulouse, 371 ; dies, 397
Jane of Montferrat, wife of William the Clito, i. 243
Jerusalem, kingdom of, condition under the Angevin kings, ii. 239 ; taken by Saladin, 247. *See* Baldwin, Fulk, Guy, Henry, Melisenda, Sibyl
Jews in England, i. 27, 46, 53 ; under

Henry II., ii. 486 ; burial - grounds granted to, *ib.* ; massacres of, 289, 290 ; relations with the Christians, 487, 488 ; ordinance for their bonds, 488, 489
Joceas of Dinan, i. 301
Jocelyn, bishop of Salisbury, ii. 37, 67, 76
Jocelyn de Balliol, ii. 66
John "Lackland," son of Henry II. and Eleanor, born, ii. 130; betrothed to Alice of Maurienne, 132-134 ; to Avice of Gloucester, 184 ; appointed king of Ireland, *ib.* ; proposal to give him Aquitaine, 233 ; knighted and sent to Ireland, 234 ; his misconduct in Ireland, 242 ; recalled, *ib.* ; proposal to crown him, *ib.*, 244 ; his treason discovered, 267 ; reconciled to Richard, 274 ; treats with Rees, 280 ; his lands in England, 282 ; marries Avice, *ib.* ; his power in England, 293 ; quarrels with the chancellor, 297-301 ; calls up the barons against him, 307 ; enters London, 309 ; appointed regent, 310 ; alliance with Philip, 314, 323 ; its terms, 363 ; acknowledged heir by the English barons, 314 ; negotiates with the chancellor, 315 ; struggle with the justiciars, 323 ; truce, 324 ; charged with treason, 329 ; reconciled to Richard, 334 ; helps him against Philip, 369 ; acknowledged in Anjou, 388 ; invested as duke of Normandy, *ib.*, 389 ; burns Le Mans, 390 ; goes to England, 391 ; crowned, 391-393 ; administrative arrangements, 393 ; quarrel with Philip, 394 ; treaty, 395, 397 ; visits England, 396 ; receives Arthur's homage, 397 ; Raymond's, *ib.* ; does homage to Philip, *ib.* ; divorces Avice, 398 ; marries Isabel, 398, 399 ; crowned with her, 399 ; meets the Scot king at Lincoln, *ib.* ; founds Beaulieu abbey, 400 ; crowned at Canterbury, *ib.* ; summons the barons to Portsmouth, *ib.* ; goes to Paris, 401 ; seizes Driencourt, *ib.* ; charges the Poitevin barons with treason, *ib.*, 402 ; cited to the French king's court, 402 ; condemned to forfeiture, 403 ; sends troops into Britanny, 404 ; relieves Mirebeau and captures Arthur, 406 ; destroys Tours, 407 ; quarrels with Otto, *ib.* ; cited by Philip for murder, 408 ; condemned, *ib.* ; his apathy, 410 ; plan for relief of Les Andelys, 413, 414 ; letter to garrison of Château-Gaillard, 419 ; goes to England, *ib.*, 420 ; sends ambassadors to Philip, 424 ; summons the host and dismisses it, 427 ; sails to La Rochelle, 428 ; takes Angers, *ib.* ; flies

back to England, *ib.*; comment on Hubert Walter's death, 428, 429; charter to London, 471, 472
John of Anagni, legate, ii. 257, 258
John of Canterbury, i, 354; treasurer of York, 477; ii. 19; bishop of Poitiers, ii. 30, 209
John de Courcy, ii. 184, 242
John of La Flèche, i. 222
John of Marmoutier, i. 126, 127
John the Marshal, ii. 32, 33, 260
John Oldman, ii. 157
John of Oxford excommunicated, ii. 66; negotiations at Rome, 68; escorts Thomas to England, 75, 77; bishop of Norwich, 176
John Paparo, cardinal, legate to Ireland, i. 380; ii. 94
John of Salisbury, his studies and early life, i. 480-483; enters Abp. Theobald's household, 483; becomes his secretary, 484; character, 484, 485; relations with Adrian IV., 485, 486; with Theobald, 486, 504; *Polycraticus*, 486-191; *Metalogicus*, 504; exiled, ii. 30; brings bull "Laudabiliter," 96
John Scotus, i. 86, 87
John, count of Vendôme, ii. 137, 151
John the Wode, ii. 106
John, S., knights of, *see* Hospitaliers
Jouin-de-Marne, S., battle of, i. 174
Judges, *see* Justices
Judicaël, bishop and count of Nantes, i. 148
Juhel Berenger, count of Rennes, i. 116
Julian, S., of Le Mans, i. 202
Juliomagus, *see* Angers
Jury, the grand, ii. 338
Jury-inquest, ii. 122, 123, 353, 354
Justices itinerant under Henry I., i. 26; under Henry II., 433, 434; ii. 124, 125, 173-177; commission of 1194, 337; circuit of 1198, 356
Justiciar, the, his office, i. 21. *See* Hubert, Hugh, Ralf, Richard, Robert, Roger, Walter, William

KAVANAGH, *see* Donell
Kells, synod at, ii. 94
Ketel of S. Edmund's, ii. 472
Kinardferry, ii. 152, 155
King's Court, the, i. 20, 21; its judicial work, 25; Henry II.'s changes in, ii. 174, 175
Kinsellagh, ii. 100
Kirkham priory, i. 67

LACY, *see* Hugh, Roger
L'Aigle, *see* Richer

Lakenheath, dispute about market at, ii. 482, 483
Lambert, count of the Angevin march, i. 101, 130
Lambert, count of Autun, i. 121, 134, 135
Lambeth, college at, ii. 437
Landry of Châteaudun, i. 156, 193, 194
Lanfranc, archbishop of Canterbury, consecrates Patrick to Dublin, ii. 89
Langley, *see* Nicolas
Laon, canons of, their journey in England, i. 30-35
Laurence, archbishop of Dublin, ii. 105, 108, 110
Law, canon, introduced into England, i. 378; Roman civil, 379; study of, in the schools, ii. 466
Layamon, ii. 491, 492
Leather-sellers' gild at Oxford, i. 30
Legates in England, i. 350. *See* Alberic, Gilbert, Henry, Hicmar, John, Malachi, Peter, Theobald, Thomas, William
Leia, *see* Peter
Leicester, siege of, ii. 146, 147. *See* Robert, Petronilla
Leinster, *see* Dermot
Leopold, duke of Austria, ii. 319, 371
Lespec, *see* Walter
Levée, the, on the Loire, ii. 200
Liber Niger Scaccarii, ii. 125
Liber Niger, *see* Peterborough
Lichfield, i. 40
Lidford, gild at, ii. 469
Lidorius, S., bishop of Tours, i. 179
Limerick, ii. 83. *See* Donell, Gilbert
Limoges besieged by Henry II., ii. 225; plundered by the young king, 226; surrenders, 230. *See* Ademar, Guy
Lincoln, i. 38-40; weavers at, 30, 52; merchant gild, 40; castle seized by Ralf of Chester, 315; besieged by Stephen, *ib.*; battle of, 316-320, 344-346; sacked by Earl Robert, 320; castle again seized by Ralf, 334; given up to Stephen, 336; Stephen at, 337; Henry II. at, 438; castle besieged by William of Longchamp, ii. 299; John at, 399; minster-library, 464, 465; Richard's charter to, 470. *See* Aaron, Alexander, Geoffrey, Hugh, Remigius, Robert, William
Lions, *see* Hervey
Lisbon won by English crusaders, i. 363
Lisieux, council at, i. 392. *See* Arnulf.
Lisoy of Bazogers, commandant of Amboise and Loches, i. 157, 184, 185; advice to Geoffrey Martel, 185; captures Theobald, 186
Literature, revival of, under Henry I., i.

80-95 ; under the Angevins, ii. 439-460, 491-492

Loches, i. 110, 153 ; treaty of, 187 ; pledged to Philip, ii. 364 ; taken by Richard, 366 ; taken by Philip, 426. *See* Lisoy, Thomas

Lodden, conferences at the, ii. 307, 308

Lombard, *see* Peter

London, its growing importance, i. 31 ; walls and castles, 44 ; cathedral, folkmoot, portreeve, sheriffs, 45 ; fires, *ib.*, 55 ; weavers, 30, 52, ii. 481 ; constitution under William I., i. 45 ; under Henry I., *ib.*, 46 ; Jews in, 46 ; suburbs, *ib.*, 47 ; schools, 47 ; character of its citizens, 47, 48 ; Normans in, 48, 49 ; trade, 49 ; claim of its citizens to elect the king, 277 ; loyal to Stephen, 313 ; submits to the Empress, 323 ; expels her, 324 ; citizens at siege of Winchester, 326 ; hospitals in, 357 ; councils at, 381, 390, 429 ; ii. 314 ; tumults in (1173), ii. 156-157 ; meeting of barons at, 309, 310, 311 ; the commune, 309, 310, 344 ; rising under William Fitz-Osbert, 345-347 ; gilds in, 469 ; constitution under Henry II., Richard and John, 471, 472 ; foreign commerce, 485 ; gildhall of German merchants, *ib.* ; stone bridge, *ib.*, 486. *See* Andrew, Gilbert, Henry, Richard, Serlo, Thomas, Westminster

Longchamp, *see* William

Lorraine, i. 120

Lothar, king of West-Frankland, i. 119, 120, 122

Lothar, *see* Innocent III.

Lotharingia, i. 120

Loudun, i. 123, 124, 139, 394, 444

Louis the Gentle, Emperor, partition of his realms, i. 98, 99

Louis From-beyond-sea, King of West Frankland, i. 112, 113 ; Fulk's letter to, 114 ; dies, 119

Louis the Lazy (*Fainéant*), King of West Frankland, i. 123 ; marriage, 191 ; death, 125

Louis VI., King of France, his policy, i. 230 ; supports William Clito, 235 ; defeated at Brenneville, 237 ; treaty with Henry, 238 ; marches against the Emperor, 241 ; grants Flanders to Clito, 243

Louis VII., King of France, his quarrel with Blois and alliance with Anjou, i. 342 ; helps Geoffrey to conquer Normandy, *ib.* ; grants him its investiture, 343 ; takes the cross, 361 ; marries Eleanor, 383 ; strife with Blois, 384 ; attacks Normandy, 385 ; dealings with

Geoffrey and Eustace, 386, 387 ; grants Normandy etc. to Henry, 388, 389 ; divorces Eleanor, 392 ; cites Henry to his court, 393 ; war in Normandy, 395 ; receives Henry's homage, 443 ; marries Constance, 446 ; makes Henry seneschal, 450 ; proposed crusade in Spain, 453, 497 ; claims on Toulouse, 457 ; throws himself into Toulouse, 464 ; attacks Normandy, 466 ; treaty, 467 ; marries Adela, 468 ; alliance with Blois, 469, 471 ; driven from Chaumont, 471 ; acknowledges Alexander III. as Pope, 502 ; meets Alexander and Henry at Chouzy, ii. 13 ; threatens war in Auvergne, 31 ; welcomes Thomas, 42 ; his view of the Becket quarrel, 53, 54 ; receives homage of the two Henrys and grants Aquitaine to Richard, 62 ; meets Henry at Montmartre, 71 ; Fréteval, 73 ; supports young Henry's revolt, 135, 136 ; attacks Normandy, 143 ; burns Verneuil, 147 ; meets Henry II. at Gisors, 148 ; besieges Rouen, 164 ; truce, 165 ; renewed quarrel, 212 ; treaty, 213 ; pilgrimage to Canterbury, 216 ; dies, 219

Louis, son of Philip Augustus, ii. 395, 397

Lucius II., Pope, i. 356, 360

Lucy, *see* Richard

Ludlow, i. 301

Lupicar, ii. 413

Lusignan, *see* Geoffrey, Guy, Hugh

MABEL of Glamorgan, wife of Robert, earl of Gloucester, i. 294, 328

MacCarthy, *see* Dermot

MacMurrough, *see* Dermot, Eva, Murtogh

Madoc Ap-Meredith, prince of Powys, i. 436, 437

Maidulf, founder of Malmesbury, i. 83

Maine (Cenomannia), duchy of, i. 203 ; county, 106, 107 ; its defiance of the house of France, 109 ; claims of Normandy and France upon, 124, 203, 204 ; granted to Geoffrey Greygown, 124, 140-142 ; subject to Geoffrey Martel, 206 ; relations with Normandy and Anjou, 216, 217, 222, 223 ; conquered by William, 218 ; revolts, 221, 222 ; revolts against Robert, 223, 224 ; condition under Elias, 224, 225 ; won back by William Rufus, 3, 226 ; Henry I. overlord of, 227, 233, 234 ; united with Anjou, 233 ; settled on William and Matilda, 236, 238 ; on Sibyl and Clito, 240 ; pedigree of the counts, 253-256 ; rebels in (1173), ii.

137. *See* Aremburg, Biota, David, Elias, Gersendis, Herbert, Hugh, Margaret, Paula, Roland

Maine, river, *see* Mayenne

Malachi, S., ii. 93, 94

Malachi II., king of Ireland, ii. 85

Malchus, bishop of Waterford, ii. 89

Malcolm IV., king of Scots, his claims on Northumberland etc., i. 435; submits to Henry II., 438; at war of Toulouse, 462; homage to young Henry, ii. 14, 15

Malmesbury abbey, i. 83-87; castle surrendered to Stephen, 304; taken by Henry, 397. *See* Ealdhelm, Godfrey, Maidulf, Turold, Warin, William

Maminot, *see* Walkelyn

Mandeville, *see* Geoffrey, William

Manorbeer, ii. 452

Mans, Le, (*Vindinum*), its early history, i. 201-203; cathedral, 202, 238; bishop, people and count, 202, 204; advocacy of the see granted to Geoffrey Martel, 205; taken by William, 218; "commune" of, 222; surrendered to Elias, 227; marriage of Geoffrey and Matilda at, 244; Henry Fitz-Empress born at, 268; Geoffrey buried at, 390; the young king buried at, ii. 230; Henry II. at, 257, 258; taken by Philip, 259, 263; submits to Arthur, 389; burnt by John, 390; given up to John, 394; hospital, 198. *See* Ayesgaud, Gervase, Julian, Sainfred

Mantes, *see* Gaubert, Walter

Map, *see* Walter

March, Spanish, *see* Barcelona.

Marche, La, bought by Henry II., ii. 214

Margaret of France, daughter of Louis VII. and Constance, i. 446; betrothed to young Henry, 448; intrusted to Henry II., 451; Vexin settled upon her, 467; married, 470; crowned, ii. 81; quarrels over her dowry, 232, 236; marries Bela of Hungary, 235

Margaret of Maine, i. 216, 254

Marmion, *see* Robert

Marmoutier, abbey of, i. 181.

Marshal, *see* John, William

Marson, i. 125

Martel, ii. 227

Martin, S., bishop of Tours, his life, i. 179-181; appearance to Fulk the Good, 118; "reversion," 128, 131, 182; "subvention," 182, 187; abbey, *see* Tours.

Martin-le-Beau, S., i. 187

Mary of Boulogne, daughter of Stephen and Matilda, i. 469

Mary of France, daughter of Louis VII. and Eleanor, i. 445

Massey, *see* Hamo

Matilda (Eadgyth) of Scotland, first wife of Henry I., i. 9, 17, 93, 94; called "good queen Maude," 66

Matilda, daughter of Henry I. of England, widow of Emperor Henry V., i. 242; acknowledged as Henry's heiress, 243, 268, 269, 274; marries Geoffrey, 243, 244, 258-260; leaves him, 266; goes to England, 268; returns, *ib.*; quarrels with Henry, 270; qualifications for the throne, 274, 275; enters Normandy, 276; lands at Arundel, 309; goes to Bristol and Gloucester, 310; negotiates with the legate, 321; in London, 323, 324; besieges the legate at Winchester, 325, 326; blockaded by the queen, 326; escapes, 327, 328; goes to Oxford, 329; sends for Geoffrey, 330; besieged at Oxford, 332; escapes, 333; returns to Gaul, 344; trial of her claims at Rome, 370; later years, 442, 443; death, ii. 61

Matilda of Boulogne marries Stephen, i. 273; crowned, 283; blockades Dover, 299; mediates between Stephen and David, 300; drives the Empress from London, 324; wins over the legate, *ib.*; besieges Winchester, 326; negotiates for Stephen's release, 328; founds S. Katharine's Hospital, 357; tries to reconcile Stephen and Theobald, 369; dies, 399

Matilda, eldest daughter of Henry II. and Eleanor, born, i. 445; betrothed to Henry the Lion, ii. 55; married, 59-60, 189; aid for her marriage, 125; death, ii. 257 note 2

Matilda of Anjou, daughter of Fulk V., betrothed to William the Ætheling, i. 234; married, 236; quarrel over her dowry, 240; nun at Fontevraud, 248

Matilda of Angoulême, wife of Hugh IX. of Lusignan, ii. 398

Matilda of Saxony, daughter of Henry the Lion, her suitors, ii. 237; marriage, 274

Matilda of Ramsbury, i. 304

Matthew, son of Theodoric count of Flanders, marries Mary of Boulogne, i. 469; dies, ii. 147

Matthew, tutor to Henry Fitz-Empress, i. 375; chancellor, 376

Maude, "Good Queen," i. 66. *See* Matilda

Mauléon, *see* Savaric

Maurice, son of Geoffrey Greygown, i. 134, 135; regent of Anjou, 153, 156, 194

Maurice Fitz-Gerald, ii. 100, 102

Maurice de Prendergast, ii. 102, 110, 111
Maurienne, ii. 131, 132. *See* Alice, Humbert
Mayenne or Maine, river, i. 97
Mayenne, *see* Geoffrey
Measures, Assize of, ii. 348
Meiler Fitz-Henry, ii. 101
Melgueil, i. 463
Melisenda, queen of Jerusalem, i. 246, 361
Melun, i. 149, 189, 190
Merania, *see* Agnes
Mercadier, ii. 383, 390
Merlin's prophecy, its fulfilment, ii. 429
Merton priory, i. 51, 67
Messina, Richard at, ii. 294-296 ; treaty of, 368, 369
Metalogicus, i. 504
Metz, *see* Chrodegang
Metz (in Gâtinais?), i. 168
Meulan, *see* Robert, Waleran
Middle Kingdom, i. 99, 120
Middlesex, sheriffs of, i. 46
Miles Beauchamp, i. 320
Miles Cogan, ii. 105, 106, 184
Miles Fitz-David, ii. 101
Miles of Gloucester defies Stephen, i. 295 ; joins the Empress at Oxford, 324 ; earl of Hereford, 327 ; slain, 334
Mirebeau, castle built by Fulk Nerra, i. 139, 151 ; siege of, by Geoffrey Plantagenet, 267 ; bequeathed to Geoffrey Plantagenet II., 394, 444 ; Eleanor besieged in, ii. 406 ; Arthur captured at, *ib.*
Mohun, *see* William
Molêmes, abbey of, i. 69, 70
Monmouth, *see* Geoffrey
Montbazon, i. 151, 163
Montboyau, i. 161, 163
Montcontour or St. Jouin - de - Marne, battle of, i. 174
Montferrat, *see* Conrad, Jane, William
Montfichet's Castle, i. 44
Montfort, *see* Almeric, Bertrada, Robert, Simon
Montlouis, battle of, i. 186
Montmartre, conference at, ii. 71
Montmirail, conference at, ii. 61, 62, 69 ; razed, 365
Montpellier, *see* William
Montrésor, i. 151.
Montreuil-Bellay, siege of, i. 384-387. *See* Gerald, Grecia
Montrichard, i. 151
Mont-St.-Michel, siege of, i. 5. *See* Robert
Moorfields, i. 47
Mort d'ancester, ii. 172
Mortain, *see* John, Stephen, William

Mortemer, *see* Hugh, Roger
Morville, *see* Hugh, Richard
Mountmorris, *see* Hervey
Mowbray, *see* Robert, Roger
Munster conquered by the Geraldines, ii. 183. *See* Brian, Donell, Murtogh, Terence
Murdac, *see* Henry
Murtogh Mac-Murrough, ii. 109, 111
Murtogh O'Brien, king of Munster, ii. 89, 90
Murtogh O'Lochlainn, king of Aileach, ii. 90, 97, 98

Nantes, i. 101 ; ceded to the Bretons, 102 ; Angevin claims on, 116, 117 ; attacked by Normans, 117 ; counts and bishops, 121, 122 ; seized by Conan, 146 ; won by Fulk, 148 ; Geoffrey Martel's dealings with, 212 ; union with Rennes, 449 ; again independent, *ib.* ; seized by Conan IV. and claimed by Henry II., 450 ; surrendered to Henry, 451 ; significance of its acquisition, 452, 453 ; Henry and Geoffrey at, ii. 58. *See* Alan, Drogo, Geoffrey, Guerech, Hoel, Judicaël
Nest, daughter of Rees Ap-Tewdor, ii. 100, 453
Neubourg, i. 282, 470.
Neufmarché, council at, i. 502
Newcastle-upon-Tyne, i. 37
Newark, i. 304
Niall of the Nine Hostages, ii. 84
Nicolas Breakspear or of Langley, i. 475, 476, 481. *See* Adrian.
Nigel, bishop of Ely and treasurer, i. 302 ; defends Devizes, 304 ; chancellor, 418 ; treasurer again, *ib.*
Nomenoë, king of Britanny, i. 101
Nonancourt, treaty at, ii. 213
Nonant, *see* Hugh
Norfolk, *see* Hugh Bigod
Normandy, duchy of, i. 111 ; confusion under Robert Curthose, 11 ; campaigns of Henry I. in, 11-13 ; relations with England, 13, 23, 24 ; with France, 24 ; invaded by Henry of France, 210, 213 ; claimed by Matilda, 276 ; invaded by Geoffrey, 281, 306-308 ; offered to Theobald of Blois, 282, 337 ; Stephen in, 286 ; granted to his son, *ib.* ; conquered by Geoffrey, 338-342 ; ceded to Henry Fitz-Empress, 369, 377 ; attacked by Louis VII. and Eustace, 385, 386, 394 ; inquest on ducal demesnes, ii. 128 ; rebels in (1173), 138, 139 ; attacked by Louis etc., 143 ; loyal barons in (1173), 146 ; Henry's administration in, 192-194 ; laid

under interdict, 315, 380 ; submits to Philip, 424, 425; dukes of, their claims upon Maine, i. 124, 203, 216. *See* Geoffrey, Henry, Hrolf, John, Richard, Robert, William

Normans destroy Fleury, i. 112 ; attack Nantes, 117 ; fusion of Normans and English, 24, 48, 49 ; ii. 489, 490

"Normans" and "English," different meanings of, i. 23, 24

Northallerton, i. 289

Northampton, Ralf of Chester seized at, i. 336 ; Henry II. at, ii. 23, 143; priory of S. Andrew at, 37 ; meeting of justiciars and barons at, 391 ; Assize of, 172, 173 ; councils at, i. 136; ii. 32-40, 172, 427. *See* David, Simon

Northmen, their work in Frankland and in England, i. 100; enter the Loire, 101 ; sack Nantes, *ib.* ; attack Toulouse, Paris, Bordeaux, 102 ; defeated at Aclea, *ib.* ; sack Tours, *ib.* ; seize Angers, 103 ; driven out, 104 ; besiege Paris, *ib.* ; defeated by Rudolf, 115 ; attacks on Tours, 181, 182. *See* Ostmen

Northumberland, Scottish claims upon, i. 286

Norwich, i. 40, 41; sacked, ii. 155, 156 ; massacre of Jews at, 289 ; castle, i. 284, 430. *See* Herbert, John

Nostell priory, i. 68

Nottingham, i. 320 ; council at, ii. 329

O'BRIENS, their rivalry with the O'Neills, ii. 86. *See* Donell, Murtogh, Terence

O'Conor, *see* Roderic, Terence

Octavian, cardinal, *see* Victor IV.

Odelin de Umfraville, ii. 145, 153, 160

Odo, count of Paris, duke of the French and king of West-Frankland, i. 104

Odo, count of Anjou, i. 109, 133

Odo I., count of Blois, Chartres and Tours, i. 145

Odo II., count of Blois etc., seizes Melun, i. 149, 189 ; character, 150 ; defeated at Pontlevoy, 157, 158 ; count of Champagne, 160 ; besieges Montboyau, 161 ; Saumur, 163 ; attacks Amboise, *ib.* ; seizes Sens, 164 ; aims at the Empire, 166 ; death, 167

Odo, count of Gascony and duke of Aquitaine, i. 174, 175

Odo, son of Robert II. of France, i. 177, 178

Odo of Britanny, i. 211, 212

Oilly, *see* Robert

O'Lochlainn, *see* Donell, Murtogh

O'Neills, their rivalry with the O'Briens, ii. 86

Orderic, i. 24

Orkneys, *see* Ralf

Orléans, viscounts of, i. 249, 250

O'Ruark, *see* Tighernan

Osbern Huitdeniers, i. 353

Oseney priory, i. 43

Ossory, ii. 102

Ostia, *see* Alberic

Ostmen, their settlements in Ireland, ii. 82-84 ; relations with England, 83, 86, 87 ; struggle with Malachi and Brian, 85 ; ecclesiastical relations, 87-89 ; share in Irish politics, 89, 90

Otto I., Emperor, i. 119

Otto II., Emperor, i. 119, 120

Otto of Saxony, son of Henry the Lion, his proposed marriage, ii. 341 ; chosen Emperor, 372, 373 ; quarrel with John, 407

Otto, cardinal, ii. 69

Oundle, i. 60

Owen, prince of North Wales, i. 435, 436, 437; ii. 179

Oxford, i. 41-44 ; Robert Pulein at, 43 ; Henry I. at, 44 ; bishops seized at, 303, 304; Matilda at, 322, 331-333; military advantages, 331 ; taken by Stephen, 332 ; Vacarius at, 379 ; Richard I. born at, 445 ; Henry and Thomas meet at, ii. 24; Gerald de Barri at, 460 ; councils at, i. 283, 402, ii. 349-350, 427 ; castle, i. 41, 331-334 ; gilds, 30, 43, 52 ; S. Frideswide's priory, 42 ; Port-meadow, 43 ; schools, *ib.* ; ii. 462. *See* John

PAGANEL, *see* Ralf

Pageham, ii. 32

Palestine, *see* Jerusalem

Paparo, *see* John

Paris attacked by northmen, i. 102, 104 ; capital of the duchy of France, 105 ; university of, ii. 461. *See* Odo

Paschal III., antipope, ii. 55

Patrick, bishop of Dublin, ii. 88, 89

Patrick, earl of Salisbury, governor of Aquitaine, ii. 58, 59

Paula of Maine, i. 222, 254

Pavia, council at, i. 498, 499. *See* William

Peace, edict for preservation of, ii. 339, 340 ; conservators of, their origin, 340

Pembroke, Flemings in, i. 52. *See* Gilbert, Richard, William

Pencarn, ii. 179

Périgueux, ii. 223

Périgord, *see* Adalbert

Peter, duke of Aquitaine, *see* William VI.

Peter " Bogis," ii. 421, 422

Peter of Capua, cardinal-legate, ii. 375, 395

Peter of Celle, i. 482, 483
Peter of Colechurch, ii. 486
Peter de Leia, bishop of S. David's, ii. 455, 456
Peter Lombard, ii. 461, 467
Peter of Saintes, tutor to Henry Fitz-Empress, i. 375
Peterborough, "Black Book" of, i. 58 ; chronicle, 81
Petronilla, queen of Aragon, wife of Raymond - Berengar IV. of Barcelona, i. 463
Petronilla, wife of Tertullus, i. 128
Petronilla of Grandmesnil, countess of Leicester, ii. 138, 150
Pevensey, i. 430
Peverel, *see* William
Philip I., king of France, i. 220, 221, 224
Philip Augustus, son of· Louis VII. of France, born, ii. 56 ; receives young Henry's homage, 62 ; crowned, 216 ; quarrels with Blois, 217 ; marries Elizabeth, *ib.* ; crowned again, 218 ; succeeds Louis, 219 ; demands Margaret's dowry, 232, 236 ; quarrel with Flanders, 234 ; plots with Geoffrey, 243 ; claims wardship of Eleanor of Britanny, *ib.* ; of Arthur, 245 ; attacks Berry, *ib.* ; truce, 246 ; takes the cross, 249 ; takes Châteauroux, 251 ; attacks Auvergne, 252 ; negotiates with Richard, 253, 254 ; receives his homage, 255 ; takes Le Mans, 259 ; Tours, 264 ; treaty with Richard, 275 ; policy in Palestine, 320 ; returns to France, 313 ; *ib.*, demands the Vexin etc., *ib.*, 314 ; alliance with John, 314, 323, 363 ; attacks Normandy, 363, 364 ; routed at Fréteval, 366, 367 ; secures Arthur, 370 ; war with Flanders, 374 ; truce with Richard, 375 ; takes Evreux, 389 ; receives homage of Arthur, 390 ; of Eleanor, *ib.* ; razes Ballon, 394 ; divorces Ingeborg, 395 ; treaty with John, 395-397 ; takes Ingeborg back, 401 ; cites John to his court, 402, 408; conquers eastern Normandy, 403 ; besieges Arques, 405, 406 ; burns Tours, 407 ; takes Saumur and enters Poitou, 410 ; successes in Normandy, *ib.* ; takes Isle of Andely, 411-416 ; Petit-Andely, 416 ; Radepont, *ib.* ; Château-Gaillard, 416-423 ; Normandy submits to, 424-425 ; conquers Poitou, 426 ; takes Loches and Chinon, *ib.* ; marches against John, 428
Philip, count of Flanders, joins young Henry, ii. 141 ; threatens to invade England, 155, 158 ; his policy in France, 216 ; quarrels with France,

234, 235 ; pilgrimage to Canterbury, 235
Philip de Broi, ii. 21
Philip Gay, i. 297
Philip of Gloucester, i. 335, 336
Philip de Thaun, i. 94
Pierre-Pécoulée, treaty of, i. 234
Pipe Rolls, i. 26, 431-432
Pipewell, council at, ii. 277
Pisa, *see* Henry
Poitiers stormed by Adalbert of Périgord, i. 145 ; Henry and Eleanor married at, 393 ; council at, 458 ; Richard enthroned at, ii. 130 ; taken by Philip, 426. *See* John
Poitou granted to Hugh the Great, i. 123 ; barons of, appeal to Philip against John, ii. 402 ; conquered by Philip, 426. *See* Aquitaine
Polycraticus, i. 486-491
Pontaudemer, siege of, i. 241
Pontigny, abbey of, i. 70 ; S. Thomas at, ii. 42, 54
Pont-l'Evêque, *see* Roger
Pontlevoy, battle of, i. 157, 158
Popes, *see* Adrian, Alexander, Calixtus, Celestine, Eugene, Innocent, Lucius, Paschal, Urban
Porhoët, *see* Eudo
Port, *see* Adam
Portmannimot of Oxford, i. 43
Port-meadow at Oxford, i. 43
Port-reeve, i. 29 ; of London, 45. *See* Gilbert Becket
Portsmouth, ii. 400, 427
Premonstratensians, i. 357, 358
Prendergast, *see* Maurice
Provence, i. 454, 463. *See* William
Provins, i. 482
Pucelle, *see* Gerard
Puiset, *see* Hugh
Pulein, *see* Robert
Pullus, *see* Robert

Quévilly, i. 471 ; ii. 198

Radepont, ii. 403, 416
Rahere, founder of S. Bartholomew's hospital, i. 67
Rainald, bishop of Angers, i. 193
Raino, bishop of Angers, i. 131, 132
Ralf, bishop of the Orkneys, i. 289, 355
Ralf, bishop of Rochester, made archbishop of Canterbury, i. 68
Ralf, earl of Chester, his marriage, i. 314; claims Carlisle, *ib.* ; seizes Lincoln castle, 315 ; brings Robert to relieve it, 316 ; at battle of Lincoln, 317, 320; again seizes the castle, 334 ; joins Stephen, 336 ; imprisoned, *ib.* ; gives

up Lincoln, *ib.* ; revolts again, 377, 395 ; dies, 399
Ralf, earl of Chester, second husband of Constance of Britanny, ii. 369, 370
Ralf of Bayeux, i. 241
Ralf de Broc, ii. 39, 76, 79, 149
Ralf de Diceto, dean of S. Paul's, ii. 439 ; his Angevin History, i. 127
Ralf of Faye, ii. 129
Ralf Flambard, justiciar, i. 8, 9, 21, 32, 432 ; bishop of Durham, 80
Ralf of Fougères, ii. 137, 147, 148, 258
Ralf de Glanville, ii. 145, 160 ; justiciar, 177 ; takes the cross, 248 ; resigns and dies, 279
Ralf of Issoudun, ii. 401, 405
Ralf Paganel, i. 295, 298
Ralf of Varneville, chancellor to Henry II., ii. 142, 297
Ralf of Vermandois, i. 307
Ramirez the Monk, king of Aragon, i. 463
Ramsbury, *see* Matilda
Rancogne, *see* Geoffrey
Rathbreasil, synod of, ii. 93
Raymond-Berengar III., count of Barcelona, i. 463
Raymond Berengar IV., count of Barcelona, i. 463, 466
Raymond of St. Gilles, count of Toulouse, i. 454, 455
Raymond V., count of Toulouse, his marriage, i. 458 ; war with Henry II., 464-467 ; meets Henry at Grandmont, ii. 58 ; does him homage, 133 ; struggle with Aragon, 211 ; quarrel with Richard, 244, 250, 251 ; death, 371
Raymond VI., count of Toulouse, marriage, ii. 371 ; homage to John, 397
Raymond Trencavel, viscount of Béziers and Carcassonne, i. 462, 464, 466
Raymond the Fat, ii. 104, 108, 183
Reading, i. 282, 322 ; ii. 61, 240, 308
Redvers, *see* Baldwin
Rees Ap-Griffith, prince of South Wales, his dealings with Henry II., ii. 164, 179-181, 237 ; with John and Richard, 280 ; death, 351
Reginald, earl of Cornwall, i. 391 ; ii. 144, 146
Reginald, chancellor to Frederic Barbarossa, and archbishop of Cöln, ii. 55
Reginald Fitz-Urse, ii. 78
Reims, councils at, i. 206, 237, 367, 368. *See* Gervase, William
Remigius, bishop of Dorchester, moves his see to Lincoln, i. 39
Rennes united with Nantes, i. 449. *See* Conan, Hoel, Juhel
Richard, third son of Henry II. and Eleanor, born, i. 445 ; first betrothal,

463 ; invested with Aquitaine and betrothed to Adela, ii. 62 ; enthroned at Poitiers, 130 ; revolts, 135 ; submits, 165 ; his character, 206-208 ; fights the barons in Aquitaine, 209, 210, 214, 215, 220, 223 ; refuses homage to his brother, 224 ; takes Hautefort, 231 ; refuses to give up Aquitaine, 233 ; war with Geoffrey and John, *ib.* ; reconciled, 234 ; gives up Aquitaine to Eleanor, 235 ; wars with Toulouse, 244, 250, 251 ; negotiates a truce, 246 ; seizes the Angevin treasure, *ib.* ; reinstated in Aquitaine, 247 ; takes the cross, 248 ; tries to regain Châteauroux, 252 ; negotiates with Philip, 253, 254 ; meets Henry and Philip at Bonmoulins, 254 ; homage to Philip, 255 ; encounter with William the Marshal, 261 ; scene with Henry at Colombières, 266 ; comes to Fontevraud, 271 ; reconciled with the Marshal, 272 ; recognized as Henry's successor, 273 ; duke of Normandy, 274 ; treaty with Philip, 275 ; goes to England, *ib.* ; crowned, 276 ; fills vacant sees, 277, 278 ; his policy, 278 ; appoints justiciars, 279, 283 ; sells sheriffdoms etc., 280 ; dealings with Wales, *ib.* ; with Scotland, 281 ; with John, 281-282 ; goes to Normandy, 287 ; holds council there, 288 ; possible successors, 295 ; treaty with Tancred, *ib.* ; marriage, 296 ; names William of Monreale for the primacy, 297 ; sends Walter of Rouen to England, 297, 298 ; his voyage, 317 ; conquers Cyprus, *ib.* ; alliance with Guy of Lusignan, 318, 320 ; reaches Acre, 319 ; quarrel with Leopold of Austria, *ib.* ; relations with other crusaders, 319-321 ; truce with Saladin, 321 ; homeward voyage, 322 ; wrecked and captured, *ib.* ; given up to the Emperor, 324 ; his ransom, 325, 326 ; negotiates with Philip and John, 327 ; returns to England, 328 ; imposes taxes, *ib.*, 329 ; negotiates with Scotland, 330 ; crowned at Winchester, *ib.*, 331 ; king of Burgundy, 331 ; leaves England, *ib.* ; forgives John, 334 ; gives license for tournaments, 342 ; annuls his charters, 343, 356 ; sends the abbot of Caen to England, 343 ; quarrel with S. Hugh, 350 ; edict against the clergy, 355 ; cessions to Philip, 361 ; difficulties in Gaul, 361, 362 ; treaty with Philip, 364 ; goes to Normandy, 365 ; to Tours, 365, 366 ; regains Loches, 366 ; routs Philip at Fréteval, *ib.*, 367 ; claims wardship of Arthur, 370 ; alli-

ance with Toulouse, 371 ; with Henry VI., 372 ; called to elect an emperor, *ib.* ; league against Philip, 374 ; truce, 375 ; builds Château-Gaillard, 375-380 ; quarrel with Abp. Walter, 380, 381 ; lays siege to Châlus, 382 ; wounded, 384 ; dies, 385, 386 ; burial, 386, 387 ; his encouragement of municipal life, 470 ; grant to merchants of Cöln, 485

Richard, archbishop of Canterbury, ii. 170, 434

Richard I., bishop of London, i. 45

Richard II., bishop of London, i. 502, 503

Richard Fitz-Nigel, treasurer and bishop of London, ii. 277 ; his *Gesta Henrici*, 439

Richard of Ilchester, ii. 66 ; bishop of Winchester, 158, 176 ; work in the Exchequer, 193, 194 ; seneschal of Normandy, 193 ; death, 277

Richard de Clare, earl of Pembroke or Striguil, ii. 99, 100 ; goes to Ireland, 103 ; takes Waterford, 104 ; marriage, *ib.* ; blockaded in Dublin, 109, 110 ; summoned by Henry, 112 ; does homage for Leinster, 113 ; in Normandy with Henry, 145, 182; governor of Ireland, 182; death, 183

Richard le Breton, ii. 78

Richard Fitz-Count, son of Robert of Gloucester, i. 386, 405 ; ii. 146

Richard Fitz-Godoberd, ii. 100

Richard of La Haye, i. 340, 341

Richard of Hommet, constable of Normandy, ii. 146

Richard de Lucy, justiciar, his character, i. 417 ; his share in election of Thomas, ii. 1-3 ; excommunicated, 66 ; takes Leicester, 146 ; marches against the Scots, 149 ; besieges Huntingdon, 154, 156 ; protests against the forest visitation, 171 ; retires to a monastery, 176

Richard de Morville, ii. 139, 161

Richenda de Clères, sister of William of Longchamp, ii. 305

Richer de l'Aigle, i. 51, 395

Richmond, *see* Alan

Ridel, *see* Geoffrey

Rievaux abbey, i. 71

Robert I., king of France, i. 149, 164

Robert the Brave, count of Anjou, i. 102 ; duke of the French, 103

Robert the Magnificent, or the Devil, duke of Normandy, i. 166

Robert, son of William the Conqueror, betrothed to Margaret of Maine, i. 216; homage to Geoffrey the Bearded, 217 ; to Fulk Rechin, 223 ; seeks Fulk's help

in Maine, *ib.*; sells the Cotentin to Henry, 4; wars with his brothers, 5, 6 ; pledges Normandy to Rufus, 3; crusade, *ib.* ; invades England, 9 ; war with Henry, 11 ; taken prisoner, 13 ; dies, 271

Robert Bloet, chancellor, justiciar and bishop of Lincoln, i. 22

Robert II., bishop of Lincoln, ii. 24

Robert I., bishop of Hereford, i. 370, 495

Robert of Melun, i. 481 ; bishop of Hereford, ii. 24

Robert of Bellême, count of Alençon etc., i. 6; banished, 10 ; sues for peace, 11; flies at Tinchebray, 13 ; captures Elias, 225; imprisoned, 233

Robert, count of Burgundy, i. 178

Robert, count of Dreux, i. 394

Robert, earl of Ferrers, ii. 139, 163

Robert, earl of Gloucester, son of Henry I., friend of William of Malmesbury, i. 92, 94 ; escorts Matilda over sea, 243 ; at Henry's death, 270 ; dispute for precedence with Stephen, 274 ; joins Stephen, 283 ; defies him, 294 ; comes to England, 309 ; marches to Lincoln, 316, 317 ; receives Stephen's surrender, 320 ; made prisoner, 327 ; exchanged, 329 ; goes to fetch Geoffrey, 330 ; returns, 332; besieges Wareham, *ib.* ; takes Portland and Lulworth, 333 ; meets his sister at Wallingford, 334 ; routs Stephen at Wilton, *ib.* ; builds a castle at Farringdon, 335 ; helps Geoffrey in Normandy, 338, 339 ; dies, 343, 344

Robert I., earl of Leicester and count of Meulan, i. 16, 54, 56

Robert II., earl of Leicester, joins Henry, i. 400 ; justiciar, 417 ; at council of Northampton, ii. 39 ; refuses the kiss of peace to Reginald of Cöln, 55, 56 ; dies, 61

Robert III., earl of Leicester, rebels, ii. 138, 142 ; goes to England, 148 ; made prisoner, 150 ; restored, 167 ; repulses Philip from Normandy, 363

Robert II., count of Meulan, ii. 138

Robert de Barri, ii. 101

Robert de Bruce, ii. 145

Robert, abbot of Caen, ii. 343, 344

Robert Fitz-Stephen, ii. 100 ; goes to Ireland, 101 ; blockaded in Carrick, 109 ; made prisoner, 111 ; released, 113

Robert of Marmion, i. 335

Robert de Montfort defeats Henry of Essex in ordeal, ii. 60 ; rebels, 138

Robert of Mowbray, ii. 155

Robert I. of Oilly, i. 41, 42, 331

Robert II. of Oilly founds Oseney priory,

i. 43 ; gives up Oxford to the Empress, 322 ; death, 332

Robert Pulein, i. 43, 44

Robert Pullus, i. 483

Robert of Sablé, i. 343

Robert of Selby, chancellor of Sicily, i. 365

Robert of Sillé, ii. 137

Robert de Stuteville, ii. 145, 153, 160

Robert of Torigny or *de Monte*, ii. 194

Robert of Turnham, seneschal of Anjou, ii. 388, 389 ; of Poitou, 426 ; prisoner, 427

Rocamadour, ii. 74, 226, 227

Rochelle, La, ii. 428

Roches, *see* William

Rochester, *see* Ralf, Walter

Roderic O'Conor, king of Connaught, ii. 97 ; of Ireland, 98; treaty with Dermot, 102 ; gathers a host against him, 104 ; blockades Dublin, 109, 110 ; routed, 110, 111 ; promises tribute to Henry II., 116 ; treaty, 182

Roger, king of Sicily, i. 365

Roger of Pont-l'Evêque, i. 354, 368 ; archbishop of York, 477 ; earlier career, 478, 479 ; accepts the royal customs, ii. 24 ; dispute with S. Thomas, 30 ; crowns young Henry, 72 ; appeals to the king, 78 ; dies, 285

Roger, chaplain to Henry I., chancellor, bishop of Salisbury and justiciar, i. 22; his administration, 25, 26 ; called the " Sword of Righteousness," 26 ; his Church policy, 63 ; joins Stephen, 278; his family, 302 ; relations with Stephen and with the Empress, *ib.*, 303 ; seized at Oxford, 303, 304 ; death, 310

Roger, earl of Clare, ii. 12, 16, 180

Roger, earl of Hereford, i. 429

Roger of Howden, i. 82 ; ii. 439

Roger de Lacy, ii. 400, 401 ; at Château-Gaillard, 411, 417, 418, 423

Roger of Montrésor, i. 151

Roger de Mortemer, ii. 299

Roger de Mowbray, ii. 139, 152, 160, 162, 163

Roger " the Poor," chancellor, i. 302, 303

Rohesia, wife of Gilbert Becket, i. 50, 352

Roland, count of Maine, i. 203

Roland of Siena, cardinal, *see* Alexander III.

Rome, relations of William and Lanfranc with, i. 15 ; trial of Stephen's and Matilda's claims at, 370 ; schism at, 498

Ronceray, i. 165 note 3, 166 ; ii. 200

Roscilla of Loches, wife of Fulk the Red, i. 110

Rotrou, archbishop of Rouen, ii. 72, 81

Rouen surrenders to Geoffrey Plantagenet, i. 341, 342 ; besieged by Louis VII., ii. 164 ; palace, 196 ; young Henry buried at, 232 ; Richard's heart buried at, 387 ; Arthur imprisoned at, 407 ; submits to Philip, 425. *See* Rotrou, Walter

Rouergue, i. 454

Roumare, *see* William

Roxburgh, i. 287

Rudolf of Burgundy, king of West-Frankland, i. 111, 115

Rufus, S., priory of, i. 476

SAHER de Arcelles, i. 363

Sainfred, bishop of Le Mans, i. 204

Saintes granted to Fulk Nerra, i. 159, 173; taken by William VII. of Aquitaine, 215 ; regained and lost again, 216. *See* Peter

Saintonge ceded to Geoffrey Martel, i. 174 ; granted to Fulk Rechin, 214 ; war of, 215, 216, 252, 253

Saint-Saëns, *see* Elias

Saints, Old-English, revived veneration for, i. 33, 80

Saladin tithe, ii. 249

Salisbury, i. 32-33. *See* Herbert, Hubert, Jocelyn, John, Patrick, William

Saltwood, ii. 79

Sancho VI., king of Navarre, submits to Henry II.'s arbitration, ii. 190

Sancho VII., king of Navarre, suppresses revolt in Gascony and attacks Toulouse, ii. 316 ; helps Richard, 366, 367

Saumur, i. 161 ; taken by Fulk Nerra, 162 ; blockaded by William of Poitou, 213 ; betrayed to Fulk Rechin, 220 ; burnt, *ib.*; Henry II. at, ii. 256; taken by Philip, 410 ; abbey of S. Florence, i. 162, 163. *See* Gelduin

Savaric of Mauléon, ii. 405, 426

Saxony, *see* Henry, Matilda, Otto

Scarborough, i. 428

Schools, Augustinian, i. 43 ; at Oxford, *ib.*, ii. 462 ; London, i. 47 ; Malmesbury, 84, 85. *See* Universities

Scotland, its relations with Henry I., i. 96. *See* David, Henry, Matilda, William

Scutage, i. 432, 433 ; the Great, 459-461; of 1195, ii. 343 ; 1196, 348

Sees, removal of, i. 40

Selby, *see* Robert

Sempringham, order of, i. 359, 360; helps S. Thomas, ii. 41

Seneschal of France, office of, i. 450

Sens, i. 164 ; ii. 42, 68

Serfdom in twelfth century, i. 61, 62

Serlo the Mercer, mayor of London, ii. 472

Severn, valley of, i. 35
Sherborne castle, i. 304
" Sheriff's Aid," ii. 15
Sheriffs of London, i. 45; ii. 471; Middlesex, i. 46; inquest on (1170), ii. 126, 127
Shrewsbury, i. 295, 298, 299
Sibyl, queen of Jerusalem, ii. 247, 320
Sibyl of Anjou, daughter of Fulk V., i. 240, 241
Sicily conquered by Henry VI., ii. 371, 372. *See* Constance, Jane, Roger, Tancred, William
Sillé, *see* Hugh, Robert
Simeon of Durham, i. 81, 82
Simon, count of Montfort, i. 467
Simon de Montfort, count of Evreux, ii. 138
Simon, earl of Northampton, ii. 144; claim to Huntingdon, 154
Simon of Dover, i. 363
Simon Fitz-Peter, ii. 21
Sleaford, i. 304
Smithfield, i. 47; S. Bartholomew's priory and hospital, 67
Soissons, ii. 42, 65. *See* Guy, William
Solomon, king of Britanny, i. 103
Spain, proposed crusade in, ii. 453, 497
Standard, battle of the, i. 289-291
Stephen Harding, S., i. 69, 70
Stephen of Blois, son of Stephen-Henry and Adela, i. 235, 236; his " Lombard grandmother," 256; brought up by Henry I., 273; count of Mortain, *ib.*; marriage, *ib.*; relations with Henry, 274; oath to Matilda, *ib.*; goes to England, 276; gains the treasury, 277; crowned, 279; first charter, *ib.*; character, 280, 281; treaty with Scotland, 282; early successes, 283; second charter, 284; revolt against him, *ib.*; holds forest assize, 285; goes to Normandy, 286; invades Scotland, 287; relations with the barons, 292, 293; with Earl Robert, 294; revolt in the west, 295-299; grants Northumberland to Henry of Scotland, 300; besieges Ludlow, 301, 302; takes Leeds, 302; seizes Roger of Salisbury and his nephew, 303, 304; summoned before a council at Winchester, 305; penance, 306; truce with Geoffrey, 307; besieges Arundel, 309; sends Matilda to Bristol, 310; keeps Whitsuntide in the Tower, 311; besieges Lincoln castle, 315; exploits at battle of Lincoln, 319, 320; prisoner, 320; exchanged, 329; takes Wareham and Cirencester, 330; Oxford, 332; besieges the castle, 332, 333; routed at Wilton, 334; takes Farringdon, 335; builds

Crowmarsh, 336; imprisons Ralf of Chester, *ib.*; wears his crown at Lincoln, 337; banishes Abp. Theobald, 368; trial of his claims at Rome, 370; reconciled to Theobald, 371; knights Eustace, 377; drives Vacarius from Oxford, 379; refuses a safe-conduct to John Paparo, 380; proposes to crown Eustace, 381, 390; imprisons the bishops, 391; meets Henry, 397; treaty, 400; last days, 403; death, 404
Stephen I., count of Champagne, i. 160
Stephen II., count of Champagne, i. 177; rebels, 177, 178; defeated, 178, 186; dies, 271
Stephen-Henry, count of Blois, Chartres and Champagne, receives Fulk Rechin's homage, i. 221; his parents, 255, 256; marriage, 271, 272; crusade and death, 272
Stephen of Turnham, seneschal of Anjou, ii. 273, 279
Stockbridge, i. 327
Striguil, *see* Richard, William
Strongbow, ii. 99 note 7
Stuteville, *see* Robert, William
Suger, abbot of S. Denis, his views on " Frenchmen and Englishmen," i. 24; policy, 387, 388; opposes divorce of Louis VII., 392; death, *ib.*, 399
Sulpice of Amboise, i. 156, 157, 194
Synods, *see* Councils

Taillebourg, ii. 215
Talbot, *see* Geoffrey
Tallage of 1174, ii. 173; 1194, 337, 342
Talvas, *see* William
Tancarville, *see* William
Tancred, king of Sicily, ii. 295
Tara, ii. 84
Taxation, i. 25, 26, 27; of towns, 29; " Sheriff's Aid," ii. 15; aid *pour fille marier*, 125, 126; Saladin tithe, 249; tax on moveables, 325; taxes in 1194, 328, 329, 337, 342; 1195, 343; 1198, 352; in London, 344, 345
Templars, i. 357
Terence O'Brien, king of Munster, ii. 89
Terence O'Conor, king of Connaught, ii. 90, 91
Tertullus, i. 127, 128
Theobald, abbot of Bec, archbishop of Canterbury, i. 300, 351; joins the Empress, 321; his policy, 351, 352, 378; household, 352, 354, 379, 477; legate, 356, 380; "swimming-voyage" to Reims, 368; banished, *ib.*; consecrates Gilbert Foliot, 371; returns, *ib.*; holds a council, 381; imprisoned, 391; escapes, *ib.*; relations with Henry II.,

418 ; consecrates Roger of York, 479 ; last days, 503-504 ; death, 506

Theobald I. the Trickster, count of Blois, Chartres and Tours, i. 106, 115, 116

Theobald III., count of Blois, Chartres and Tours, i. 177 ; rebels, 177, 178 ; marches to relieve Tours, 184, 185 ; prisoner, 186 ; cedes Tours to Geoffrey Martel, 187 ; his marriages, 255, 256 ; seizes Champagne, 271

Theobald IV. the Great, count of Blois, Chartres and Champagne, i. 273 ; character, 275, 276 ; alliance with Henry I., 231 ; wars with Louis VI., *ib.*, 235 ; invited to Normandy, 282, 337; treaties with Geoffrey, *ib.* ; with Stephen, 286 ; opposes Louis VII.'s attempt on Toulouse, 457 ; quarrel with Louis, 384 ; death, 392, 399

Theobald V., count of Blois etc., seeks to marry Eleanor, i. 392 ; betrothed to Adela, 445 ; ally of Henry II., 466

Theobald Walter, ii. 293, 343

Theodoric, count of Flanders, i. 342

Thierceville, i. 354

Thomas of London, son of Gilbert Becket, his boyhood, i. 50, 51; studies in Paris, 352 ; clerk to Osbern Huitdeniers, 353 ; enters Theobald's household, 353, 354 ; goes with him to Rome, 356 ; to Reims, 368 ; studies at Bologna and Auxerre, 379 ; opposes crowning of Eustace, 391; chancellor, 418 ; archdeacon of Canterbury, 420, 479, 480 ; his person, 421; life as chancellor, 421-425 ; relations with Henry, 423, 425-427 ; embassy to France, 446-448 ; exploits in war of Toulouse, 465, 466 ; combat with Engelram of Trie, 467 ; opposes marriage of Mary of Boulogne, 469 ; takes charge of young Henry and procures his recognition as heir, 471-473 ; relations with Roger of Pont-l'Evêque, 478 ; with John of Salisbury, 485 ; character as chancellor and as primate, 504, 505 ; archbishop of Canterbury, ii. 1-3 ; consecrated, 4-5 ; institutes Trinity-Sunday, 5 ; receives his pall and resigns the chancellorship. 6 ; life as archbishop, 7-10; his *eruditi*, 8 ; plans of Church reform, 11; reclaims alienated lands, 11, 12 ; dispute with Roger of Clare, 12, 16 ; with William of Eynesford, 17; resigns archdeaconry, 13 ; relations with Gilbert Foliot, *ib.*, 31 ; at council of Tours, 14 ; resists Henry at Woodstock, 15, 16 ; refuses the "customs," 22, 23 ; young Henry taken from him, 23 ; meets Henry at Northampton, *ib.* ; consecrates Robert

of Melun, 24 ; accepts the customs, *ib.* ; swears to them at Clarendon, 25 ; rejects the constitutions of Clarendon, 28 ; forbids marriage of William of Anjou, 29 ; dispute with Roger of York, 30; attempts flight, 31 ; meets Henry at Woodstock, 31, 32 ; dispute with John the marshal, 32, 33, 34; at council of Northampton, 33-40 ; flight, 41 ; goes to Soissons and Sens, 42 ; effects of the quarrel in England, 46-49; resigns his ring to the Pope, 52 ; goes to Pontigny, 42, 54 ; life there, 63 ; writes to Henry, 63, 64; pilgrimage to Soissons, 65 ; excommunications at Vézelay, 66 ; legate, 67 ; goes to Sens, 68; meets Henry at Montmirail, 69 ; excommunications at Clairvaux, 70 ; meets Henry at Montmartre, 71 ; proclaims interdict, 71 ; forbids crowning of young Henry, 72 ; meets Henry at Fréteval, 73 ; Tours and Chaumont, 74 ; his estates restored, 74 ; returns to England, 77 ; excommunicates the De Brocs, 78 ; slain, 79 ; canonized, 431 ; results of his life and death, 431-433 ; lives of, 439

Thomas Pactius, prior of Loches, i. 126, 127, 153, note 3

Thorgils, ii. 82

Thouars, *see* Almeric, Guy

Thurstan, archbishop of York, his charter to Beverley, i. 30, 38 ; protects Fountains, 71 ; makes truce with the Scots, 286 ; organizes defence of Yorkshire, 288, 289 ; dies, 354

Tiberias, battle of, ii. 247

Tickhill, ii. 282, 291, 299, 323, 328

Tighernan O'Ruark, chief of Breffny, ii. 97, 109, 111, 114

Tinchebray, battle of, i. 12, 13, 227

Tintern abbey, i. 71

Tithe, the Saladin, ii. 249

Torigni, 386, 405. *See* Robert

Tortulf the Forester (Torquatius), i. 105, 127, 128

Totnes, gild at, ii. 469

Toucques, i. 307

Toulouse, relations with France, i. 457, 458 ; war of Henry II. against, 464-466 ; its results, 468 ; attacked by Sancho of Navarre and the seneschal of Gascony, ii. 316 ; counts, i. 454-456. *See* Alfonso, Bertrand, Raymond, William

Touraine, i. 107 ; ceded to Geoffrey Martel, 187, 188

Tournaments authorized by Richard I., ii. 342

Tours (*Cæsarodunum*) sacked by northmen, i. 102 ; early history, 178-183 ; granted to Geoffrey Martel, 178 ; siege, 184 ; ceded by Theobald, 187 ; council at, ii. 14 ; taken by Philip, 264 ; Richard at, 365, 366 ; meeting of Arthur and the Lusignans at, 405 ; burnt by Philip, 407 ; destroyed by John, *ib.* ; S. Martin's abbey, i. 102, 113, 114, 181-183 ; its banner, 186 ; Châteauneuf, 183, ii. 264, 366. *See* Adaland, Gatian, Gregory, Lidorius, Martin, Odo, Theobald

Towns, English, their origin and character, i. 27-29 ; taxation, 25, 29 ; *firma burgi*, 29 ; condition under Henry I., 30-54 ; fusion of races in, 48, 49 ; progress under the Angevins, ii. 468-472

Tracy, *see* William

Trade, English, with Flanders, i. 30, 52 ; with Ireland, 32, 34, 35, ii. 87 ; of Winchester, i. 32 ; Bristol, 34, 35, ii. 87 ; Chester, i. 36 ; ii. 87 ; Lincoln, i. 39, 40 ; Norwich, 40 ; London, 49 ; under the Angevins, ii. 481-485

Treasurers, *see* Nigel, Richard

Trencavel, *see* Raymond

Trent, river, i. 40, 344, 345

Trèves (near Saumur), i. 162

Trie, *see* Engelram

Trinity Sunday instituted, ii. 5

Trussebut, *see* William

Tuam, metropolis of Connaught, ii. 94

Tunbridge, ii. 12, 16

Turlogh, *see* Terence

Turnham, *see* Robert, Stephen

Turold, abbot of Malmesbury, i. 84

Turones or *Turoni*, i. 179

Twinham or Christchurch, i. 32

ULGER, bishop of Angers, i. 370

Ulster invaded by John de Courcy, ii. 184

Umfraville, *see* Odelin

Universities, ii. 460-468. *See* Bologna, Cambridge, Oxford, Paris

Urban II., Pope, i. 225

Urban III., Pope, ii. 242, 247

Ursus or Ours, S., i. 110

VACARIUS, i. 379

Varaville, i. 213

Varneville, *see* Ralf

Vegetius Renatus, his book *De Re Militari*, i. 386

Vendôme, abbey of Holy Trinity at, i. 172. *See* Adela, Burchard, Elizabeth, Fulk, Geoffrey, John

Verdun, treaty of, i. 98

Vere, *see* Aubrey

Vermandois, ii. 360. *See* Ralf

Verneuil, ii. 364, 365, 425

Vexin, the French, granted to William Clito, i. 243

Vexin, the Norman, ceded to Louis VII., i. 388 ; settled on Margaret, 467, 471 ; seized by Henry II., 470

Vézelay, S. Thomas at, ii. 66

Victor IV., antipope, i. 498, 499 ; ii.f55

Vienna, Richard I. captured at, ii. 322

Villeins in twelfth century, i. 57-62

Vulgrin, count of Angoulême, invades Poitou, ii. 209 ; submits to Richard, 210, 215 ; dies, 220

WACE, ii. 446

Walbrook, i. 46

Waldric or Gualdric, chancellor of England and bishop of Laon, i. 22, 30

Waleran, count of Meulan, rebels, i. 241 ; raises siege of Carham, 287 ; escorts the Empress to Bristol, 310 ; submits to Geoffrey, 337, 338

Wales, Flemish settlers in, i. 52 ; Henry I.'s dealings with, 96 ; condition in twelfth century, ii. 99 ; Henry II.'s wars in, i. 435-437 ; ii. 179-181, 237 ; crusade preached in, ii. 249 ; Gerald's books on, 458. *See* Cadwallader, David, Madoc, Nest, Owen, Rees

Walkelyn Maminot, i. 295, 299

Wallingford, the Empress at, i. 334 ; blockaded by Stephen, 396 ; relieved by Henry, 397 ; treaty of, 400 ; council at, 429 ; granted to John, ii. 282 ; taken from him, 323, 328

Walter of Coutances, archbishop of Rouen, ii. 297 ; sent to England, 298, 300 ; supports John against W. Longchamp, 308, 309 ; justiciar, 311, 312 ; hostage for Richard's ransom, 326 ; quarrel with Richard, 380, 381 ; invests John as duke, 389

Walter, archdeacon of Canterbury, i. 478 ; bishop of Rochester, *ib.*, 506 ; ii. 4

Walter, count of Mantes, i. 217, 218

Walter de Clare, i. 71

Walter Lespec founds Kirkham priory, i. 67 ; Rievaux, 71 ; at battle of the Standard, 289 ; death, 399

Walter Map, ii. 449-452

Walter, *see* Hubert

Wareham, i. 295, 299, 330, 332, 333

Warin, abbot of Malmesbury, i. 84

Wark, ii. 153. *See* Carham

Warren, *see* Isabel, Hameline, William

Waterford, its origin, ii. 83 ; taken by Richard of Striguil, 104 ; Henry II. at, 113 ; bull "Laudabiliter" published at, 182. *See* Malchus

Waverley abbey, i. 71

Weavers, gilds of, i. 30, 52 ; ii. 481

"Week-work," i. 57

Weobly, i. 296

Westminster, i. 46 ; coronations at, i. 279, 405 ; ii. 72, 276, 391, 399 ; councils at, i. 300, 329, 330 ; ii. 3, 22, 23, 190

Wexford, ii. 102, 109, 111, 117

Wherwell, i. 327

White Ship wrecked, i. 239

Wigford, i. 439

Wigmore, i. 429

William, S., archbishop of York, i. 354, 355, 364-367, 478

William the Conqueror, king of England and duke of Normandy, his ecclesiastical customs, i. 16 ; charter to London, 45 ; shelters Bp. Gervase of Le Mans, 206 ; helps King Henry against Geoffrey Martel, 207 ; besieges Domfront, 208, 209 ; regains Alençon and fortifies Ambrières, 209 ; challenges Geoffrey, 211 ; treaty with Herbert of Maine, 216 ; conquers Maine, 218 ; Maine revolts against, 221, 222 ; treaty with Anjou, 223 ; death, *ib.*

William II. Rufus, king of England, regains Maine, i. 3 ; restores Carlisle, 36 ; his palace at Westminster, 46 ; war with Elias, 225, 226 ; death, 3, 226

William the Lion, king of Scots, does homage to young Henry, ii. 72 ; joins his rebellion, 140 ; invades England, 149, 153, 154 ; his border castles, 152 ; prisoner, 161, 162 ; does homage for his crown, 166, 178 ; marriage, 237 ; negotiations with Richard, 281, 330, 341 ; with John, 391, 393 ; homage to John, 399

William II. the Good, king of Sicily, betrothed to Jane, daughter of Henry II., ii. 60 ; marriage, 189 ; death, 318

William the Ætheling, son of Henry I., betrothed to Matilda of Anjou, i. 234 ; receives homage, *ib.*; marriage, 236 ; drowned, 239

William, eldest son of Henry II. and Eleanor, i. 429, 431

William of Corbeil, prior of Chiche, archbishop of Canterbury, i. 68 ; joins Stephen, 278 ; crowns him, 279 ; dies, 299, 300

William, archbishop of Bordeaux, ii. 140

William I. Shockhead (*Tête-d'Etoupe*), count of Poitou and duke of Aquitaine, i. 123

William II. Fierabras, duke of Aquitaine, i. 123, 139, 173

William IV. the Great, duke of Aquitaine, i. 159, 173

William V. the Fat, duke of Aquitaine, i. 173, 174

William VI. (Peter) the Bold, duke of

Aquitaine, i. 176 ; relations with Geoffrey Martel, 210-213 ; death, 213

William VII. (Guy-Geoffrey), duke of Aquitaine, i. 215 ; war with Anjou, *ib.*, 252, 253 ; regains Saintonge, 216

William VIII., duke of Aquitaine, offers his duchy in pledge to William Rufus, i. 3 ; imprisons Fulk of Anjou, 229 ; marriage, 455

William IX., duke of Aquitaine, bequeaths his daughter to Louis VII. of France, i. 383 ; claims on Toulouse, 455

William Longsword, duke of Normandy, i. 111

William of Longchamp, bishop of Ely and chancellor, ii. 277, 279 ; character and antecedents, 285-287 ; justiciar, 288 ; proceedings at York, 290 ; quarrel with Hugh of Durham, 291 ; legate, *ib.* ; his difficulties, 292, 293 ; his rule, 294 ; quarrels with John, 298-301 ; struggle with Geoffrey of York, 305, 306 ; with John etc., 307-311 ; his fall, 311, 312 ; appeals to the Pope and excommunicates his enemies, 312 ; negotiates with Eleanor and John, 315 ; goes to England for Richard's ransom, 325 ; makes truce with Philip, 367 ; mission to Germany, 372 ; death, 373, note 4

William, dean of York, i. 355 ; bishop of Durham, *ib.*; death, 399

William Giffard, chancellor, i. 22 ; bishop of Winchester, 71

William I., count of Arles or Provence, i. 190, 191

William, count of Angoulême, ii. 136

William IV. count of Toulouse, i. 455

William of Aubigny, earl of Arundel, i. 298 ; ii. 144, 145, 149

William of Aumale, earl of York, i. 289

William of Blois, chancellor of Lincoln, ii. 456, 461

William, earl of Gloucester, ii. 144, 163, 184

William de Mandeville, earl of Essex, ii. 144 ; supports Henry II., 145, 260 ; justiciar, 279 ; death, 282

William the Marshal rebels against Henry II., ii. 139 ; relations with the young king, 228 ; early history, 260 ; encounter with Richard, 261 ; arranges Henry's funeral, 269, 270 ; meeting with Richard, 272 ; marriage, 274 ; co-justiciar, 279 ; regent for John, 390, 391 ; earl of Striguil, 393 ; sent to Normandy, 400, 401 ; goes to relieve Les Andelys, 413 ; ambassador to Philip, 424 ; persuades John to dismiss the host, 427

William, marquis of Montferrat, ii. 60

William of Mortain, earl of Cornwall, i. 11, 13
William of Roumare, i. 314 ; earl of Lincoln, 315
William, earl of Salisbury, ii. 144
William Longsword, earl of Salisbury, son of Henry II., ii. 428
William, earl of Warren and count of Mortain and Boulogne (son of Stephen), i. 430, 469
William of Anjou, third son of Geoffrey and Matilda, born, i. 374 ; proposal to conquer Ireland for him, 431 ; death, ii. 29
William de Barri, ii. 453
William the Clito, son of Robert of Normandy, i. 235, 238 ; betrothed to Sibyl of Anjou, 240 ; marriage annulled, 241 ; excommunicated, 242 ; Flanders granted to, 243 ; marriage, *ib.* ; death, 266
William de Courcy, seneschal of Normandy, ii. 146, 193
William of Dover, i. 335
William of Eynesford, ii. 17
William Fitz-Alan, i. 295, 298
William Fitz-Aldhelm, seneschal to Henry II., ii. 113, 116 ; governor of Ireland, 183
William Fitz-Duncan, i. 287
William Fitz-John, i. 295
William Fitz-Ralf, seneschal of Normandy, ii. 194, 260
William Fitz-Osbert or Long-beard, ii. 345-347
William Fitz-Stephen, ii. 38
William of Malmesbury, i. 83-93 ; his account of the Angevins, 196
William of Mohun, i. 295
William " the Monk," i. 342
William, lord of Montpellier, i. 462, 466
William of Newburgh, ii. 441-445
William Peverel, i. 295, 299, 320, 428
William of Pavia, cardinal, ii. 69
William des Roches, ii. 394, 407, 426
William of Soissons, i. 481
William de Stuteville, ii. 160, 393
William Talvas, lord of Alençon, i. 236, 270, 281

William of Tancarville, chamberlain of Normandy, ii. 142
William de Tracy, ii. 78
William Trussebut, i. 307
William de Vesci, ii. 145, 160
William of Ypres, i. 285, 294 ; at battle of Lincoln, 318, 319 ; helps the queen in Kent, 324 ; at siege of Winchester, 326 ; captures Earl Robert, 327 ; tries to reconcile Stephen and Abp. Theobald, 369
Wilton, i. 33 ; battle at, 334
Winchester, i. 31 ; treaty of, 9 ; fair, 32 ; Stephen received at, 277 ; Matilda received at, 321 ; palace, 325 ; siege, 326 ; Matilda's escape from, 327, 328 ; councils at, 305, 322, 402 ; hospital of S. Cross, 357 ; coronations at, ii. 81, 330 ; meetings of John and W. of Longchamp at, 298, 299, 300. *See* Henry, Richard, William
Windsor, ii. 182, 314, 323, 328
Witham, river, i. 38, 40
Wolvesey-house, i. 325
Woodstock, Henry I. at, i. 44, 94 ; Henry II. and Thomas at, ii. 31, 32 ; Welsh princes at, 14, 179 ; council at, 14-16, 43, 44
Wool-trade, Flemish and English, i. 30, 52
Worcester, i. 35 ; its historical school, 81, 82 ; Henry II. at, 439
Würzburg, council at, ii. 56

YORK, i. 36 ; Henry I.'s charter to, *ib.* ; S. Mary's abbey, 71 ; dispute for the primacy, 354, 355, 364-366 ; tumults at, 380 ; Henry Murdac enthroned at, 381 ; end of the schism, 382 ; Henry II. and William the Lion at, ii. 178 ; massacre of Jews at, 289, 290 ; council at, 340 ; commune at, 469. *See* Geoffrey, Henry, Hubert, Hugh, John, Roger, Thurstan, William
Yorkshire, its condition under Henry I., i. 36, 38

END OF VOL. II.